The State Nobility

The State Nobility

Elite Schools in the Field of Power

PIERRE BOURDIEU

with the collaboration of
Monique de Saint Martin

Translated by Lauretta C. Clough

Stanford University Press
Stanford, California

Stanford University Press
Stanford, California
© 1989 Les Éditions de Minuit
English translation © 1996 Polity Press
Foreword © Loïc J. D. Wacquant
Originally published 1989 in France as
  *La Noblesse d'état: grandes écoles et esprit
  de corps* by Les Éditions de Minuit
Originating publisher of English edition:
  Polity Press, Cambridge, in association with
  Blackwell Publishers Ltd.
First published in the U.S.A. by
  Stanford University Press, 1996
Printed in Great Britain
Cloth ISBN 978-0-8047-1778-6
Paper ISBN 978-0-8047-3346-5
Published with the assistance of the
  French Ministry of Culture
This book is printed on acid-free paper.

Original printing 1996
Last figure below indicates year of this printing:
19 18 17 16 15 14 13 12 11 10

Contents

Foreword

Loïc J. D. Wacquant

Of the manifold works by Pierre Bourdieu, *The State Nobility* is perhaps the most formidable and the most paradoxical, and no doubt for these very reasons likely to disconcert, if not confound, many of its foreign readers. First, it is at once doggedly Francocentric in empirical substance and scope, yet irrepressibly universalizing in analytical intent and reach. Second, and this is one of the hallmarks of Bourdieu's sociological style, *The State Nobility* is resolutely empirical, data–laden to the point of saturation, yet animated by a forceful theoretical project that places it at the epicenter of debates over power, culture, and reason at century's end.

Even more so than *Distinction*, which it builds upon and extends in a number of directions,[1] this study of the logic of social domination in advanced society, and of the mechanisms whereby it disguises and perpetuates itself, is anchored deep in the specificities of the French system of class, culture, and education in the two decades following the upheaval of May 68. At the same time, as in every good ethnological report according to Marcel Mauss, "what may appear as futile detail is in fact a condensation of principles"[2] that Bourdieu contends are equally operative in other countries and epochs.

I

The first such principle is the vexing yet obdurate relationship of collision and collusion, autonomy and complicity, distance and dependence, between *material and symbolic power*. As Weber noted well, in every structure of domination, those "privileged through existing political, social, and economic orders" are never content to wield their power unvarnished and to impose their prerogatives naked. Rather, they "wish to see their positions transformed from purely factual power relations into a cosmos of acquired rights, and to know that they are thus sanctified."[3] In feudal society, the Church was the institution entrusted with transmuting the lord's might, founded as it was upon control of weaponry, land, and riches, into divine right; ecclesiastical authority was deployed to justify and thereby solidify the rule of the new warrior class. In the complex societies spawned by late capitalism, Bourdieu maintains, the school has taken over this work of sanctification of social divisions. So that *not one but two species of capital* now give access to positions of power, define the structure of social space, and govern the life chances and trajectories of groups and individuals: economic capital and cultural capital.

Credentials help define the contemporary social order, in the medieval sense of *ordo*, a set of gradations at once temporal and spiritual, mundane and celestial, which establish incommensurable degrees of worth among women and men, not only by sorting and allocating them across the different slots that make up the social structure, but also, and more importantly, by presenting the resulting inequalities between them as ineluctable necessities born of the talent, effort, and desire of individuals. This is because cultural capital, though mainly accumulated and handed down in the family, appears to inhere in the person of its bearers. The fact that it "manages to combine the prestige of innate property with the merits of acquisition"[4] makes it uniquely suited to legitimizing the continued inheritance of social privileges in societies smitten with the democratic ideal.

Here Bourdieu's object is the *operation of social alchemy* whereby a social hierarchy dis-simulates itself, to those it dignifies no less than to those it excludes, as a scale of human excellence, how a historically arbitrary social order rooted in the materiality of economic and political power transmutes itself into what displays every outward appearance of an aristocracy of intelligence. Under this angle, the granting of an elite degree is not so much a "rite of passage" à la Van Gennep as a *rite of institution*:[5] it does not demarcate a before and an after so much as it differentiates – and elevates – those destined to occupy eminent social positions from those over whom they will lord. It evokes reverence for and consecrates them, in the strongest sense of the term, that is, it makes them sacred (anyone who has attended a commencement ceremony at a major British or American university cannot but be struck by their archaic religious feel that would have delighted Robertson Smith). As the etymology of the word "credentials," *credentialis*, giving authority (derived in turn from *credere*, to believe), testifies, the bestowal of a diploma is the climactic moment in a long cycle of production of collective faith in the legitimacy of a new form of class rule.

II

Indeed, much as the "generalization of the ceremony of dubbing" was, according to Marc Bloch, "the symptom of a profound transformation of the notion of knighthood" in the Middle Ages,[6] Bourdieu argues that the generalization of educational titles as prerequisite for ascent to the apex of private corporations and public bureaucracies signals the consolidation of a *new mode of domination* and a corresponding transformation in the system of strategies whereby the ruling class maintains and masks itself, at the cost of swift and continual self-metamorphosis.

In feudal society, the relation between the temporal and spiritual poles of power took the form of a relatively simple, dualistic yet complementary, opposition between warriors and priests, military and hierocratic authority, wielders of swords and wielders of words. With the constitution of the formally rational state and the concurrent ascendancy of the "second capital" (the two, Bourdieu hypothesizes, are correlative historical inventions), this antagonistic couple is replaced by an immensely complex web of criss-crossing linkages among the multiplicity of *fields* in which the various forms of social power now effective circulate and concentrate. The chain of inter-dependencies that sews them together into this peculiar ensemble Bourdieu calls *field of power* (a notion introduced in the early 1970s but elaborated for the first time here both theoretically and empirically) extends from the economic field, at one end, to the field of cultural production, at the other.[7] Industrialist and artist in the nineteenth century, manager and intellectual in the twentieth are, in the case of France, the personifications of the dominant and the dominated poles of the field of power respectively. Between them, and in symmetric and inverse order according to the relative preponderancy they accord to economic or cultural capital, are arrayed the fields of politics, higher civil service, the professions, and the university.

As species of capital diversify and autonomous fields multiply – two propositions which, for Bourdieu, are equivalent conceptual translations of the same epochal trend since capital and field mutually define and specify each other – and as the more transparent "mechanical solidarity" between weakly differentiated and interchangeable powers gives way to the more intricate "organic solidarity" between highly distinct and disparate powers, tensions mount and clashes threaten to break out. For the fact that varie-gated forms of capital now enter into the formula of domination implies that different principles of social primacy and legitimacy must be reckoned with and reconciled. The field of power is precisely this arena where holders of the various kinds of capital compete over which of them will prevail. At stake in these struggles amongst the dominant (oft mistaken for confronta-tions between ruling and subordinate classes) is the relative value and potency of rival kinds of capital, as set in particular by the going "exchange rate" between economic and cultural currencies.

This is where the *system* of elite establishments of higher education enters the picture. In societies characterized by the copresence and contest of diverse forms of power that all rely increasingly upon conversion into cre-dentials as a means for self-perpetuation, this system not only guarantees preferential and speedy access to positions of command to the sons of those lineages who already monopolize them (full membership in the nobility, whether based on blood or diplomas, is essentially a male affair). Its high degree of autonomy and internal differentiation according to the same antinomy between money and culture that organizes the field of power at large enables it also to defuse intranecine conflicts by recognizing and rewarding diverse claims to scholastic, and thence social, excellence.

"Intellectual schools" such as École Normale Supérieure, the seedbed of France's high intelligentsia (Bourdieu is one in a long string of distinguished alumni), draw and honor mainly those students who are most strongly attracted to them in the first place because their dispositions are living embodiments of the kind of capital these schools demand and valorize, viz. children originating from the cultured fractions of the bourgeoisie to which they promptly return. Establishments geared to grooming captains of industry and state, such as École des Hautes Études Commerciales and École Polytechnique, on the other hand, are primarily the preserve of students issued from, and destined for, the economically rich fractions of the French haute bourgeoisie. Situated at midpoint between the two poles of the space of French elite schools, the École Nationale d'Administration, from which cabinet members and high civil servants hail, mingles the two kinds of competencies, cultural and economic, and recruits students whose family patrimony typically cumulates rare credentials and old wealth.

By providing separate pathways of transmission of privilege and by recognizing competing, even antagonistic, claims to preeminence within its own order, the field of elite schools insulates and placates the various categories of inheritors of power and ensures, better than any other device, the *pax dominorum* indispensable to the sharing of the spoils of hegemony. Hence it is not this or that establishment but the field (that is, the space of objective relations) they compose that contributes *qua field* to the reproduction of the evolving matrix of patterned differences and distances constitutive of the social order. The immediate, concrete, object of *The State Nobility* is the structure and functioning of the uppermost tier of France's system of higher education and its linkages to this country's bourgeoisie and top corporations. Its deeper, theoretic, aim is to elaborate, in the very movement whereby it displays empirically one of its historical instantiations, a model of the *social division of the labor of domination* that obtains in advanced societies where a diversity of forms of power coexist and vie for supremacy.

III

Its extreme centralization and high social selectivity, rooted in longstanding ties between class cleavages, state building, republicanism, and education and in the bifurcation between university and grandes écoles, the eagerness with which it sanctifies worldly (that is, bourgeois) cultural baggage and the corresponding brutality with which it devalues its own products as "*scolaires*," all make France's system of higher learning a propitious terrain upon which to expose the surreptitious correlation of academic with social classification and the Janus-faced nexus of connivance-through-conflict between the two poles of the field of power. The specificity of these empirical materials, however, should not detract from the wider applicability of the analytic framework employed to process them. Properly construed, *The State Nobility* offers a systematic research program on any national field of power, provided that the American (British, Japanese, Brazilian, etc.) reader carries out the *work of transposition* necessary to generate, by way of homological reasoning, an organized set of hypotheses for comparative inquiry in her own country.[8]

Bourdieu holds that the chiasmatic organization of the contemporary ruling class, expressive of a historical state of the division of labor between material (economic) and symbolic (cultural) capital,[9] and its projection onto the field of elite schools that both disengages and entwines the two, is characteristic of all advanced societies. But this subterranean structure of opposition takes on phenomenally diverse forms in different countries, depending on a number of intersecting factors, including the historical trajectory of (upper) class formation, state structures, and the shape of the system of education in the society and time under consideration. Similarly, Bourdieu proposes that the rise of the "new capital" translates everywhere into a shift in modes of reproduction, from *direct* reproduction, where power is transmitted essentially within the family via economic property, to *school-mediated* reproduction, where the bequeathal of privilege is simultaneously effectuated and transfigured by the intercession of educational institutions. But, again, all ruling classes resort to both modes conjointly (Bourdieu takes pain to stress that the growing *relative* weight of cultural capital in no way effaces the ability of economic capital to propagate itself autonomically) and their partial preference for one or the other will depend on the full system of instruments of reproduction at their disposal and on the current balance of power between the various fractions tied to this or that mode of transmittance.

It follows that it would be a mistake – Alfred North Whitehead called it the "fallacy of misplaced concreteness"[10] – to look for one-to-one correspondences across national boundaries between the institutions entrusted with perpetuating the network of power positions in different societies (for instance, to seek an exact American or British counterpart to the École Nationale d' Administration, for which there is none). Rather, one must, applying the relational mode of thinking encapsulated by the notion of field, set out in each particular case to uncover *empirically* the specific *configurations* assumed by the complexus of oppositions that structure social space, the system of education, and the field of power, as well as their interconnections.

To illustrate summarily, the structure of the space of elite education turns, in the French instance, on a sharp horizontal dualism between grandes écoles (select graduate schools based on a numerus clausus, special preparatory classes, and national competitive entrance examinations, with direct pathways to high-profile jobs) and university (mass institutions open to all those who complete their secondary cursus and only loosely connected to the occupational world) and, within the field of grandes écoles itself, between, along one axis, major and minor schools and, along the other, establishments oriented toward intellectual values and establishments grooming for economic-political positions. In the decentralized American system of education, these dualities are refracted into a whole series of nested oppositions, vertical as well as horizontal: between private and public sectors (starting at the level of secondary schooling), between community colleges and four-year universities, and between the great mass of tertiary educational institutions and a handful of elite establishments (anchored by the Ivy League) that arrogate the lion's share of command posts in private and public affairs alike.[11] Due to the deep-rooted historic preponderancy of economic over cultural capital, the opposition between the two poles of power, and between the corresponding fractions of the American dominant class, does not materialize itself in the form of rival tracks or schools. It is projected instead *within* each (elite) university in the adversative and tensionful relations between the graduate division of arts and sciences, on the one side, and professional schools (especially law, medicine, and business) on the other, as well as in the antipodean relations these entertain with the powers-that-be and in the contrasted images of knowledge they appeal to (research versus service, critique versus expertise, creativity versus utility, etc.).

Yet, for all the differences in their respective systemic location and circuitry, the tightly integrated network of Ivy League universities and private boarding schools functions as a close, if partial, analogue to the French device of grandes écoles and their associated *classes préparatoires*. Since the "mere assertion that elite schools exist, especially socially elite schools, goes against the American grain,"[12] it is perhaps not superfluous to recall briefly just how exclusive – and exclusionary – the latter are. Suffice it to note that virtually all graduates of the top US boarding schools (who comprise 1 percent of American high school enrollment) enter college, compared to 76 percent of students from Catholic and other private schools, and 45 percent of all public school seniors. These super-privileged students, nine in ten of whom are children of professionals and business managers (two-thirds of their fathers and one-third of their mothers attended graduate or professional school) are also much more likely to land on the most prized campuses, even controlling for scholastic aptitude scores: in 1982, nearly half of graduating "preppies" applied to Ivy League schools and 42 percent of those applicants were admitted, as against 26 percent of all candidates nationwide (though the latter are drawn from the country's top 4 percent of students), thanks to close organizational ties and active recruiting funnels between boarding schools and high status private colleges.[13]

In 1984, a mere 13 elite boarding schools were found to have educated 10 percent of the board members of large US companies and nearly one-fifth of directors of two major firms, as compounding exclusive college degrees with upper-class pedigree multiplies the probability of joining the "inner circle" of corporate power. Among senior managers, possession of prestigious educational credentials interacts with high class origins to decide who will become chief executive, serve on the boards of outside firms, and enter the leadership of major business associations. And just as in France diplomas sanctioning "generalized bureaucratic culture" tend to supersede certificates of technical proficiency, in the United States a top law degree or a bachelor's degree from a select private college gives a manager a greater chance of reaching the vertex of responsibility in the corporate world than a master's degree from a high-ranking MBA program.[14]

Graduates of elite boarding schools and universities coming from well-to-do families listed in the *Social Register* are also massively overrepresented in the upper reaches of the American state (including the cabinet, the judiciary, and government advisory boards), political personnel, high-priced law firms, the national media, philanthropic organizations, and the arts.[15] And those who emerge out of the prep crucible to become "powerbrokers" in Boston, Washington, and Los Angeles feel no less entitled to their positions and prerogatives than their counterparts from the rue Saint-Guillaume in Paris.

IV

Distinguishing the (specific) empirical findings from the (general) theoretical model contained in *The State Nobility* suggests an agenda for a comparative, *genetic and structural sociology of national fields of power* that would, for each society, catalog efficient forms of capital, specify the social and historical determinants of their degrees of differentiation, distance, and antagonism, and evaluate the part played by the system of elite schools (or functionally equivalent institutions) in regulating the relations they entertain.

Such an inquiry would no doubt confirm that the greater opacity of the school-mediated mode of reproduction, and thus its improved capacity to dissimulate the perpetuation of power, comes at a real price. First, it becomes more and more costly to be an inheritor: elite schools everywhere typically subject their students to stringent work regimens, austere lifestyles, and practices of intellectual and social mortification that entail significant personal sacrifice. Second, the stochastic logic which now governs the transmission of privilege is such that, while he enjoys every possible advantage from the start, not every son of chief executive, surgeon, or scientist is assured of attaining a comparably eminent social position at the finish of the race.[16] The *specific contradiction* of the school-mediated mode of reproduction resides precisely in the disjunction it creates between the collective interest of the class that the field of elite schools safeguards and the interest of those of its individual members it must inevitably forfeit to do so.

Bourdieu submits that the (limited) downward mobility of a contingent of upper-class youths and the transversal, "deviant trajectories" that take a number of them from one pole of the field of power to the other – as when offspring from the cultured fractions of the bourgeoisie accede to posts of corporate or political responsibility – are powerful sources of change within the field of power as well as major tributaries to the "new social movements" that have flourished in the age of universal academic competition. At any rate, not all heirs are, under this regime, both capable and desirous of shouldering the burdens of succession.

This means that, to realize itself fully, a generative sociology of the manifold logics of power cannot limit itself to drawing an objectivist topology of distributions of capital. It must encompass within itself this "special psychology" that Durkheim called for but never delivered.[17] It must, that is, give a full account of the social genesis and implementation of the categories of thought and action through which the participants in the various social worlds under investigation come to perceive and actualize (or not) the potentialities they harbor. For Bourdieu, such dissection of the practical cognition of individuals is indispensable because social strategies are never determined unilaterally by the objective constraints of the structure any more than they are by the subjective intentions of the agent. Rather, practice is engendered in the *mutual solicitation of position and disposition*, in the now-harmonious, now-discordant encounter between "social structures and mental structures," history "objectified" as fields and history "embodied" in the form of this socially patterned matrix of preferences and propensities that constitute habitus.[18]

This is why *The State Nobility* opens with an analysis of the practical taxonomies and activities through which teachers and students jointly produce the everyday reality of French elite schools as a meaningful *Lebenswelt*. In part I (chapter 2: "Misrecognition and Symbolic Violence"), Bourdieu takes us inside the mind of the philosophy professor of the École Normale Supérieure so that we may learn how to think, feel, and judge like one and hence grasp from within, as it were, the obviousness of the umbilical – yet continually denied – relation between academic excellence and class distinction. And in part II ("The Ordination"), he reconstructs with painstaking precision and pathos the quasi-magical operations of segregation and aggregation whereby the scholastic nobility is unified in body cum soul and infused with the utmost certitude of the justness of its social mission. The thorough (re)making of the self involved in the fabrication of the habitus of the dominant reveals how power insinuates itself by shaping minds and moulding desire from within, no less than through the "dull compulsion" of material conditions from without.

Far from resolving itself in the mechanical interplay of homological structures (and of second-order correspondences between homologies operating at different levels of the field of power and its constituent subfields), Bourdieu is able to show that domination arises in and through that *particular relation of im-mediate and infraconscious "fit" between structure and agent* that obtains whenever individuals construct the social world through principles of *vision* that, having emerged from that world, are patterned after its objective *divisions*. Thus he can affirm at one and the same time, and without contradiction, that social agents are fully determined and fully determinative (thereby dissolving the scholastic alternative between structure and agency).

Paraphrasing Marx's famous formula, one might say that, for Bourdieu, men and women make their own history but they do not make it through categories of their own choosing. And we may also say without succumbing to idealism that social order is, at bottom, a *gnoseological order*, provided that we concurrently recognize that the cognitive schemata through which we know, interpret, and actively assemble our world are themselves social constructs that transcribe within individual bodies the constraints and facilitations of their originative milieu.

V

One might be puzzled by the fact that official state structures, policies, and personnel – the stock-in-trade of conventional sociologies of the state – hardly turn up in the present book. This deliberate absence is meant to dramatize one of Bourdieu's key arguments: that the state is not necessarily where we look for it (that is, where it silently instructs us to cast our gaze and net), or, more accurately, that its efficacy and effects may be strongest precisely where and when we neither expect nor suspect them.[19]

For Bourdieu, the differentia of the state as an organization born of and geared toward the concentration of power(s) does not lie where materialist theories from Max Weber to Norbert Elias to Charles Tilly typically place it. We remain overly wedded to the (eighteenth-century) view of the state as "revenue collector and recruiting sergeant" when we see in it that agency which successfully monopolizes legitimate physical violence and neglect to notice alongside that it also, and more decisively, monopolizes legitimate *symbolic* violence.[20] The state, Pierre Bourdieu intimates, is first and foremost the "central bank of symbolic credit" which endorses all acts of *nomination* whereby social divisions and dignities are assigned and proclaimed, that is, promulgated as universally valid within the purview of a given territory and population. And the academic title is the paradigmatic manifestation of this "state magic" whereby social identities and destinies are manufactured under cover of being recorded, social and technical competency fused, and exorbitant privileges transmuted into rightful dues.

The violence of the state, then, is not exercised solely (or even mainly) upon the subaltern, the mad, the sick, and the criminal. *It bears upon us all,* in a myriad minute and invisible ways, every time we perceive and construct the social world through categories instilled in us via our education. The state is not only "out there," in the form of bureaucracies, authorities, and ceremonies. It is also "in here," ineffaceably engraved within us, lodged in the intimacy of our being in the shared manners in which we feel, think, and judge. Not the army, the asylum, the hospital, and the jail, but the school is the state's most potent conduit and servant.

Durkheim was in the right when, as the good Kantian that he was, he described the state as a "social brain" whose "essential function is to think," a "special organ entrusted with elaborating definite representations valid for the collectivity."[21] Except that these representations, Bourdieu insists, are those of a class-divided society, not a unified and harmonious social organism, and their acceptance is the product of stealthy imposition, not spontaneous consentaneity. Unlike totemic myths, the "scholastic forms of classification" that provide the basis for the logical integration of advanced nation-states are class ideologies that serve particular interests in the very movement whereby they portray them as universal. The instruments of knowledge and construction of social reality diffused and inculcated by the school are also, and inescapably, instruments of symbolic domination. And thus it is that the credential-based nobility owes the fidelity we grant it, in the twofold sense of submission and belief, to the fact that the "frameworks of interpretations" that the state forges and forces upon us through the school are, to borrow another expression of Kenneth Burke's, so many "acceptance frames"[22] that make us gently bow under a yoke we do not even feel.

VI

In offering, first, an anatomy of the production of the new capital and, second, an analysis of the social effects of its circulation in the various fields that partake in the travail of domination, *The State Nobility* reveals Bourdieu's sociology "of education" for what it truly is, and has been from its inception: a generative anthropology of *powers* focused on the special contribution that symbolic forms bring to their operation, conversion, and naturalization. Much as the founding triumvirate of classical sociology was preoccupied with religion as the opium, moral glue, and theodicy of nascent capitalist modernity, Bourdieu's abiding interest in the school stems from the role he assigns it as guarantor of the contemporary social order via the state magic that consecrates social divisions by inscribing them simultaneously in the objectivity of material distributions and in the subjectivity of cognitive classifications.

Weber's warning that "patents of education will create a privileged 'caste'" has proved prescient: the technocrats who head today's capitalist firms and government offices have at their disposal a panoply of powers and titles – of property, education, and ancestry – without historical precedent. They need not choose between birth and merit, ascription and achievement, inheritance and effort, the aura of tradition and the efficiency of modernity, because they can embrace them all. And yet, Bourdieu's sober diagnosis of the advent of the state nobility does not condemn us to cynicism and passivity, or to the fake radicalism of the rhetoric of the "politics of culture." For the relative autonomy that symbolic power must of necessity enjoy to fulfill its legitimizing function always entails the possibility of its diversion in the service of aims other than reproduction. This is especially true when the "chain of legitimation" grows ever more extended and intricate, and when domination is wielded in the name of reason, universality, and the common weal.

Reason, Bourdieu argues in pushing historicist rationalism to its limit, is neither a Nietzschean illusionist's trick fueled by the "will to power," nor an anthropological invariant rooted in the immanent structure of human communication as with Habermas, but a potent if frail *historical invention* born of the multiplication of those social microcosms, such as the fields of science, art, law, and politics, in which universal values may be realized, albeit imperfectly.[23] That an ever greater number of protagonists in the game of domination find it necessary to concoct rational justifications for their actions increases the chance that they will, paradoxically, foster in spite of themselves the forward march of reason.

To play with universality is to play with fire. And the collective role of intellectuals as bearers of the "corporatism of the universal" is to compel temporal powers to live up to, and enforce upon each other, the very norms of reason they invoke, however hypocritically. This puts science – and social science in particular – at the epicenter of the struggles of our age. For the more science is summoned by the dominant on behalf of their rule, the more vital it is for the dominated to avail themselves of its results and instruments. Such is the political meaning and purpose of *The State Nobility*: to contribute to this rational knowledge of domination which, *non obstante* the jaded jeremiads of postmodernist prophets, remains our best weapon against the rationalization of domination.

Berkeley, February 1995

Notes to Foreword

1 Pierre Bourdieu, *Distinction: A Social Critique of the Judgement of Taste*, trans. Richard Nice (1979; Cambridge: Harvard University Press; London: Routledge and Kegan Paul, 1984).

2 Marcel Mauss, *Manuel d'ethnographie* (1947; 3rd edn, Paris: Bibliothèque Payot, 1989), p. 7.

3 Max Weber, *From Max Weber: Essays in Sociology*, ed. Hans Gerth and C. Wright Mills (Oxford: Oxford University Press, 1946).

4 Pierre Bourdieu, "Forms of Capital," in John G. Richardson (ed.), *Handbook of Theory and Research for the Sociology of Education* (New York: Greenwood Press, 1986), p. 245. This article is a condensation of Bourdieu's generalized theory of capital, including the latter's basic forms, their respective properties and mechanisms of conversion, and the specificities of cultural capital.

5 Pierre Bourdieu, "Rites of Institution," in *Language and Symbolic Power*, trans. Peter Collier (1982; Cambridge: Polity Press; Cambridge: Harvard University Press, 1990), pp. 117–27.

6 Marc Bloch, *La société féodale* (1930; Paris: Albin Michel, 1968), p. 437.

7 Pierre Bourdieu, "Champ du pouvoir, champ intellectuel et habitus de classe," *Scolies* 1 (1971), pp. 7–26; the more general concept of field (*champ*) is discussed synthetically in "Some Properties of Fields," in *Sociology in Question*, trans. Richard Nice (1980; London and Newbury Park: Sage, 1993); for elaborations and exemplary illustrations, see *The Field of Cultural Production*, trans. Peter Collier (Cambridge: Polity Press; New York: Columbia University Press, 1993).

8 For a germane discussion of the seducements of ideographic reduction with regard to Bourdieu's analysis of the French university field, see Loïc J. D. Wacquant, "Sociology as Socio-Analysis: Tales of 'Homo Academicus'," *Sociological Forum* 5 (Winter 1990), pp. 677–89.

9 The historical constitution of the opposition between "money" and "art" in nineteenth-century France is retraced in Pierre Bourdieu, *The Rules of Art: Genesis and Structure of the Literary Field* (1992; Cambridge: Polity Press, 1996).

10 Alfred North Whitehead, *Science and the Modern World* (1925; New York: New American Library, 1948), p. 52.

11 On these cleavages, see, respectively, Ira Katznelson and Margaret Weir, *Schooling for All: Race, Class, and the Decline of the Democratic Ideal* (New York: Basic Books, 1987), esp. pp. 208–21; Barbara Falsey and Barbara Heyns, "The College Channel: Private and Public Schools Reconsidered," *Sociology of Education* 57 (Apr. 1984), pp. 111–22; Peter W. Cookson Jr and Caroline Hodges Persell, *Preparing for Power: America's Elite Boarding Schools* (New York: Basic Books, 1985); Steven Brint and Jerome Karabel, *The Diverted Dream: Community Colleges and the Promise of Educational Opportunity in America, 1950–1985* (New York and Oxford: Oxford University Press, 1989); William Kingston Powell and Lionel S. Lewis (eds), *High Status Track: Studies of Elite Schools and Stratification* (Albany: State University of New York Press, 1990).

12   Cookson and Persell, *Preparing for Power*, p. 15. The figures that follow are also excerpted from this excellent study, ch. 3.

13   Caroline Hodges Persell and Peter W. Cookson Jr, "Chartering and Bartering: Elite Education and Social Reproduction," *Social Problems* 33 (Dec. 1985), pp. 114–29.

14   Michael Useem and Jerome Karabel, "Educational Pathways to Top Corporate Management," *American Sociological Review* 51 (Apr. 1986), pp. 184–200.

15   Michael Useem, *The Inner Circle: Large Corporations and the Rise of Business Political Activity in the US and UK* (New York: Oxford University Press, 1984); Cookson and Persell, *Preparing for Power*, pp. 198–202; Michael Schwartz (ed.), *The Structure of Power in America: The Corporate Elite as Ruling Class* (New York: Holmes and Meier, 1987); George E. Marcus, *Lives in Trust: The Fortunes of Dynastic Families in Late Twentieth-Century America* (Boulder: Westview Press, 1991); G. William Domhoff, *The Power Elite and the State* (New York and Berlin: Aldine, 1993); Steven B. Levine, "The Rise of American Boarding Schools and the Development of a National Upper Class," *Social Problems* 28 (Apr. 1980), pp. 63–94; and, for a historical perspective, E. Digby Baltzell, *Philadelphia Gentlemen: The Making of a National Upper Class* (1958; New Brunswick: Transaction Press, 1989). It should further be noted that bona fide membership in the American field of power via elite education continues to be restricted to the white caste (cf. Richard L. Zweigenhaft and G. William Domhoff, *Blacks in the White Establishment? A Study of Race and Class in America* (New Haven: Yale University Press, 1991).

16   Cookson and Persell stress that the "fit between boarding school attendance and admission to elite circles" is anything but perfect (*Preparing for Power*, pp. 204ff.) and indicate that children from the American ruling class are increasingly unwilling to endure the self-denial, isolation, psychic pain, and severe all-around life asceticism that bequeathal of power henceforth requires. Not a few of them abandon prep school (or are expelled), try to commit suicide, or simply opt to pursue other, less censorious avocations.

17   "We hold that sociology has not completely achieved its task so long as it has not penetrated into the innermost mind [*le for intérieur*] of the individual in order to relate the institutions it seeks to explain to their psychological conditions" (Émile Durkheim, "Sociologie religieuse et théorie de la connaissance," *Revue de Métaphysique et de Morale* 17 (1909), p. 755).

18   For a fuller discussion of the two-way relationship between habitus and field, see Pierre Bourdieu and Loïc J. D. Wacquant, *An Invitation to Reflexive Sociology* (Chicago: The University of Chicago Press; Cambridge: Polity Press, 1992), pp. 12–19 and 97–140.

19   In this, Bourdieu agrees with the late Philip Abrams, who pointed out (in "Notes on the Difficulty of Studying the State," *Journal of Historical Sociology* 1:1 (1988), pp. 58–89) that one of the main obstacles to the sociology of the state resides in the special ability it has to secrete its own power.

20   Pierre Bourdieu, "Rethinking the State: On the Genesis and Structure of the Bureaucratic Field," *Sociological Theory* 12: 1 (Mar. 1994), pp. 1–19. Indeed, one might argue that the state must have captured a great deal of symbolic power if it is ever to establish the legitimacy of its use of force.

21 Émile Durkheim, "Définition de l'État," in *Leçons de sociologie* (Paris: Presses Universitaires de France, 1950), pp. 89 and 87.

22 Kenneth Burke, *Attitudes Towards History* (1937; Berkeley: University of California Press, 1984).

23 Pierre Bourdieu, "The Scholastic Point of View," *Cultural Anthropology* 5 (Nov. 1990), pp. 380–91; and *Raisons pratiques. Sur la théorie de l'action* (Paris: Seuil, 1994), "Un acte désintéressé est-il possible?," esp. pp. 161–7. For two stimulating interpretations of Bourdieu's proposed "third way" between modernist rationalism and postmodern relativism, see Craig Calhoun, "Habitus, Field, and Capital: Historical Specificity in the Theory of Practice," in his *Critical Social Theory: Culture, History, and the Challenge of Difference* (Oxford: Blackwell, 1995), pp. 132–61; and Paul Raymond Harrison, "Bourdieu and the Possibility of a Postmodern Sociology," *Thesis Eleven* 35 (1993), pp. 36–50.

Translator's Note

As a satisfying understanding of this text rests on some knowledge of the French educational system and the organization of the French state, those readers unfamiliar with either will no doubt want to avail themselves of descriptive material as a complement to their reading. To help further I have provided an extra appendix containing a glossary and a simplified chart of the current educational system.

This book is and is not about men, and its pronouns do and do not include women. I have tried to minimize the masculine effect, using feminine pronouns at times (but not "his or her" etc.), altering singular human subjects to the plural "they" when it seemed to make only a superficial difference, using "children" rather than "sons" in many instances when daughters may be included, and choosing plural pronouns in cases of indefinites such as "someone," "a person," etc.

It should be noted that the French *professeur* can be used for both secondary school teachers and professors in higher education, with *instituteur* designating primary school teachers. When *professeur* is being used to mean all or any non-primary rank of educator, I have used the general term *teacher*, and it should thus be understood to include those in higher education. The word *cadre* deserves special note as well, as it designates a category of professional that can be variably but not exactly rendered by a few terms in English (manager, executive, corporate professional, professional staff). Readers will want to adopt a broad sense of categorization when encountering these terms.

To avoid misreadings of culturally nonequivalent terms designating social classes, phrases such as "lower and middle ranges of the social scale" have been used in place of "lower class" or "middle class," etc.

The epigraph to the book has been kept in French, but there is a gloss at the beginning of the notes on p. 394.

I have been fortunate to be able to call on the following generous individuals for information and discussion: Ann Bone, Pierre Bourdieu, Richard Brown, Judith Clough, Nathalie Debrauwere, Manuel Diaz, Joy Esterlitz, Bernard Fronsacq, Madeleine Cottonet Hage, Claude Holmes, Pierre Mounier, Daniel Schubert, Laurence Schumann, Joe O. Smith, Pierre Verdaguer, Loïc

Wacquant, and especially Joseph Brami, whose gift of time, a critical eye, and an encouraging spirit was invaluable. Others in the departments of French and Italian, history, and philosophy at the University of Maryland and the French Embassy of Washington also gave of their time and expertise. I am particularly indebted to the women who took care of the children, especially Judith Clough.

A beaux deniers comptants, des enfants anoblis
Du collège, en un saut, volent aux fleurs de lis.
Là sifflant, chantant, pensant à leurs maîtresses,
Cuirasseés d'ignorance et fiers de leurs richesses,
Ces Catons de vingt ans vont à tort, à travers,
Décider sans appel des intérêts divers.

Le Pot aux roses découvert,
ou le Parlement dévoilé, 1789

PROLOGUE

Social Structures and Mental Structures

In keeping with the usual view, the goal of sociology is to uncover the most deeply buried structures of the different social worlds that make up the social universe, as well as the "mechanisms" that tend to ensure their reproduction or transformation. Merging with psychology, though with a kind of psychology undoubtedly quite different from the most widely accepted image of this science, such an exploration of objective structures is at one and the same time an exploration of the cognitive structures that agents bring to bear in their practical knowledge of the social worlds thus structured. Indeed there exists a correspondence between social structures and mental structures, between the objective divisions of the social world – especially the division into dominant and dominated in the different fields – and the principles of vision and division that agents apply to them.

Although these two approaches, which we might characterize as "structuralist" and "constructivist," are from a theoretical standpoint inseparable, the demands of research mean that precedence has to be given either to exploring objective structures (as in the third part of the present work), or, on the other hand, to analyzing the cognitive structures that agents invest in the actions and representations through which they construct social reality and negotiate the very conditions under which their communicative exchanges take place (as in the first part[1]). But the analysis of structures and "mechanisms" acquires its full explanatory power and descriptive truth only because it includes the results of the analysis of schemata of perception, appreciation, and actions that agents – students as well as teachers – make use of in their judgments and practices.

If the educational institution resembles something like an immense cognitive machine which continually redistributes students submitted to its examination according to their previous positions in the system of distributions, its classificatory action is in reality only the outcome of thousands of actions and effects produced by agents who themselves act like so many independent, yet objectively orchestrated, cognitive machines. Conversely, the analysis of the acts of construction performed by agents, in their representations as much as in their practices, can only become fully meaningful if it also sets itself the task of grasping the social genesis of the cognitive structures that agents implement in them. In so doing, and despite the fact that it also aims to grasp the a priori social forms of subjective experience, this analysis distinguishes itself from all the types of analysis of essence that the ethnomethodologists are bringing back into vogue under more or less revamped guises. While it is no doubt true that agents construct social reality and enter into struggles and transactions aimed at imposing their vision, they always do so with points of view, interests, and principles of vision determined by the position they occupy in the very world they intend to transform or preserve. The fundamental structures of the socially constituted preference systems that form the generating and unifying principle of making choices, whether with regard to educational institutions, disciplines, sports, culture, or political opinions, can be linked by an intelligible relation to objective divisions of social space – such as those that obtain, in the case of students from the grandes écoles,[2] in matters of economic or cultural capital, between the two poles of the field of power.

Anthropology is not a social physics, but neither can it be reduced to a phenomenology or a semiology. The use of statistics enables it to bring to light processes such as those that lead to the differential elimination of students from different backgrounds, processes that exhibit such regularity in their complexity that one might be tempted to use mechanistic metaphors to describe them. In fact, what is at stake in the social world is not inert and interchangeable particles of matter, but agents who, being both discernible and endowed with the ability to discern, perform the innumerable operations of ordination through which the social order is continuously reproduced and transformed. But neither are they beings who are fully conscious of what they are doing. The discernment at the basis of both classificatory acts and their products – that is, of practices, discourses, or works that are different and thus discernible and classifiable – is not the intellectual act of a consciousness explicitly positing its ends in a deliberate choice among a set of possible alternatives constituted as such by a project. Rather, it is the practical operation of habitus, that is, generative schemata of classifications and classifiable practices that function in practice without acceding to explicit representation and that are the product of the embodiment, in the form of dispositions, of a differential position in social space – defined precisely, as Strawson would have it, by the reciprocal externality of positions. Given that habitus is genetically (as well as structurally) linked to a position, it always tends to express, through schemata that are its embodied form, both the space of the different or opposed positions constitutive of social space (for example, top/bottom) and a practical stance toward this space (something like "I'm at the top or the bottom and I'd better stay here"). Its tendency to perpetuate itself according to its internal determination, its *conatus*, by asserting its autonomy in relation to the situation (rather than submitting itself to the external determination of the environment, as matter does), is a tendency to perpetuate an identity that is difference. Habitus is thus at the basis of strategies of reproduction that tend to maintain separations, distances, and relations of order(ing), hence concurring in practice (although not consciously or deliberately) in reproducing the entire system of differences constitutive of the social order.

The double reading that social reality calls for thus implies a double break with unilateral approaches whose shortcomings are never as manifest as when it comes to analyzing forms of power, such as those of the educational system, that are only wielded with the active complicity of those who impose or submit to them.[3] We cannot understand the symbolic violence of what were once hastily designated as the "ideological state apparatuses" unless we analyze in detail the relationship between the objective characteristics of the organizations that exercise it and the socially constituted dispositions of the agents upon whom it is exercised. The miracle of symbolic efficacy evaporates when we realize that this truly magical action of influence or – the word is not too strong – *possession* succeeds only insofar as the one who submits to it contributes to its efficacy; and that it does not constrain her unless she is predisposed by prior experience to *recognize* it. This only truly happens when the categories of perception and action that she puts into practice in the individual acts through which the "will" and the power of the institution are accomplished, whether this be a teacher's grading of an assignment or a student's preference for a given educational institution or discipline, are in direct conformity with the objective structures of the organization because they are the product of the embodiment of these structures.

Throughout this book we will encounter many of these possessed individuals who perform the institution's every wish because they are the institution made man (or woman), and who, whether dominated or dominant, can submit to it or fully exercise its necessity only because they have incorporated it, they are of one body with it, they give body to it. Faced with these different forms of possession, science has a twofold and seemingly contradictory task. Against the initial tendency to take all the passions whose manifestations it observes for granted because they are in the order of things, science must assert their arbitrary, unjustifiable, and, if you will, pathological character. This sometimes requires it to use a distancing rhetoric, often mistaken for the mere critical mood of ordinary polemics, in order to break the doxic adhesion to ordinary evidence.[4] But it must also account for the passions, founded upon *illusio*, the investment in the game, that are engendered in the relationship between a habitus and the field to which it is adjusted; it must restore to these passions their *raison d'être*, their necessity, and thus tear them away from the guilt and absurdity to which they are doomed when they are treated as the choices of a relinquished freedom, alienating itself in its voluntary submission to the fascination of power. Social science thus discards the simplistic alternative between, on the one hand, the "centralist" vision, which sees "ideological apparatuses," invested with a sovereign power of symbolic coercion, as the mechanism behind all alienated actions and representations; and, on the other hand, the vision we might call "spontaneist", which, in a simple reversal of the former, inscribes in each dominated individual the principle of an unnecessary submission to the constraints, the injunctions, or the seductions of power – a submission sometimes described in the language of "voluntary servitude" ("power comes from below").

If it is fitting to recall that the dominated always contribute to their own domination, it is at once necessary to recall that the dispositions that incline them toward this complicity are themselves the effect, embodied, of domination. As are those dispositions, by the way, that mean that, in the words of Marx, "the dominant are dominated by their domination." Symbolic violence is that particular form of constraint that can only be implemented with the active complicity – which does not mean that it is conscious and voluntary – of those who submit to it and are determined only insofar as they deprive themselves of the possibility of a freedom founded on the awakening of consciousness.[5] This tacitly accepted constraint is necessarily implemented whenever objective structures encounter the mental structures that are in agreement with them. It is on the basis of the originary complicity between cognitive structures and the objective structures of which they are the product that the absolute and immediate submission which characterizes the doxic experience of the native world is established. In this predictable world, everything can be taken for granted because the immanent tendencies of the established order continuously appear in advance of the expectations spontaneously inclined to anticipate them.

We shall see that this analysis also applies to agents engaged in the university field, almost inevitably including those who, in writing about power – if not about "voluntary servitude" – spontaneously think of themselves as exceptions to their own analyses. They unknowingly contribute to exercising the symbolic domination that is exercised upon them, that is, upon their unconscious, insofar, and only insofar, as their mental structures objectively conform to the social structures of the microcosm in which their specific interests are formed and invested – in and through this very conformity. Given the homologous relationship that binds them to the structures of social space, the hierarchies organizing academic space, such as those among disciplines, tracks [*sections*],[6] and establishments, are the active mediation through which the hierarchies inscribed in the objectivity of social structures become effective, particularly when these hierarchies function in an embodied state in the form of (formally neutral) principles of hierarchization of academic producers and products. As long as the principles orienting practices remain unconscious, the interactions of ordinary existence are, as Marx put it, "relations between men mediated by things." Between the judge and the judged, in the form of the unconscious of the "subject" of the judgment, there intervenes the structure of the distribution of economic and cultural capital and the principles of perception and appreciation that are its transformed form.

Thus the sociology of education is a chapter, and not a minor one at that, in the sociology of knowledge and the sociology of power, not to mention the sociology of philosophies of power. Far from being the kind of applied, and hence inferior, science (only suitable for educationalists) that has ordinarily been the view of it, the sociology of education lies at the foundation of a general anthropology of power and legitimacy. It leads us, in fact, to an understanding of the "mechanisms" responsible for the reproduction of social structures and for the reproduction of the mental structures that, because they are genetically and structurally linked to these objective structures, favor the misrecognition of their truth and thus the recognition of their legitimacy. Given that, as established elsewhere,[7] the structure of social space as observed in advanced societies is the product of two fundamental principles of differentiation – economic capital and cultural capital – the educational institution, which plays a critical role in the reproduction of the distribution of cultural capital and thus in the reproduction of the structure of social space, has become a central stake in the struggle for the monopoly on dominant positions.

It was necessary to bury the myth of the "school as liberating force," guarantor of the triumph of "achievement" over "ascription," of what is conquered over what is received, of works over birth, of merit and talent over heredity and nepotism, in order to perceive the educational institution in the true light of its social uses, that is, as one of the foundations of domination and of the legitimation of domination. This break was all the more difficult to achieve, and to insist on, because those it most actively involves, that is, cultural producers, are the primary victims – as well as the primary beneficiaries – of the legitimating illusion. For evidence, one need only note the anxious eagerness with which all those who have an interest in this lack of consciousness greet those projects aimed at the restoration of Culture whose sole virtue is that they comfort those privileged with cultural capital, whose narcissism has been wounded by the revelation of the common social foundations of their distinctive delights.

But the suffering that scientific unveiling sometimes causes, in spite of its undoubtedly liberating nature, is also a result of the fact that one of the specific properties of cultural capital is that it exists in an embodied state in the form of schemata of perception and action, principles of vision and division, and mental structures. As shown in the violence of the reactions triggered by the great symbolic revolutions, whether religious, political, or artistic, of which scientific analysis represents one particularly radical variant, the objectivation of implicit schemata of thought and action undoubtedly constitutes an attack – difficult to justify – against the very structures of consciousness, and a violence against the foundations of the enchanted experience of the world that Husserl called the "natural attitude".[8] Nothing resembles a religious war more than "academic squabbles" or debates on cultural matters. If it can seem easier to reform social security than spelling conventions or literary history curricula, this is because, in defending even the most arbitrary aspect of a cultural arbitrary, the holders of cultural capital – and undoubtedly more than any others the holders of petty portfolios, who are a bit like the "poor white trash" of culture – are defending not only their assets but also something like their mental integrity.

It is against this fanaticism, rooted in a fetishistic blindness, that social science spontaneously works when, obeying here as elsewhere its call to denaturalize and defatalize, it unveils the historical foundations and social determinants of principles of hierarchization and evaluation that owe their symbolic efficacy, especially evident in the way academic verdicts take on the weight of destiny, to the fact that they assert themselves and are experienced as absolute, universal, and eternal.

PART I

Academic Forms of Classification

For the judgments and arguments of magic to be valid, they must have a principle that eludes examination. People argue about the presence of manna here and there, but not about its existence. These principles, without which the judgments and arguments are not believed possible, are what philosophy calls categories. Constantly present in language, without necessarily being explicit, they exist rather in the form of guiding practices of consciousness, which are themselves unconscious.

Marcel Mauss, "Introduction à l'analyse de quelques phénomènes religieux," 1906

1

Dualistic Thinking and the Conciliation of Opposites

There is probably no object that could provide a clearer picture of the social structures and mental structures that govern academic verdicts than the system of statistical relations characteristic of a given population of academic *prizewinners*. The prizewinners of the Concours Général,[1] for example, are the quintessential figure of an academic "elite" that, like a projective test, reveals the classificatory schemata that have produced it. The most apparently ineffable principles of the unformulated and unformulable definition of academic excellence are never more likely to give themselves away or betray themselves than in the more or less institutionalized procedures of selection, which are in reality so many operations of *cooptation* oriented by a practical sense of elective affinities.

The research on which the present analyses are based was conducted via a mail survey of prizewinners of the 1966, 1967, and 1968 Concours Général. The response rate was exceptionally high (81 percent, 79 percent, and 71 percent, respectively), giving a good indication of their ethical dispositions (especially if we note that the third mailing was done soon after May of 1968). The population of respondents presents no significant deviation with respect to the criteria for which it is possible to control. For example, we count 33 percent women in the sample, compared to 32.5 percent in the total pool of prizewinners, 23 percent science students in both cases, and 35.5 percent students from Parisian high schools among the prizewinners in the sample, compared to 39 percent overall. Repeating the study over a period of 20 years (from 1966 to 1986) has enabled us to establish that the structure of the population analyzed according to the principal variables has remained perfectly constant over time, except for a slight *upward trend* in social origins within the distribution, a trend no doubt linked to the increase in scholastic competition (cf. appendices 1 and 2, pp. 54–9).

These data are all *dated*. Does this mean, as is usually implied, that they are obsolete or *out*dated? It is true that the state of the educational system as it was when the classification systems analyzed here were fully in use has faded into the past. The events of 1968, student criticism, the dissemination of sociological studies (here we have a perfect opportunity to remind the sociologist that she constantly encounters sociology in her object of study), the transformations in the teaching profession, and especially the upsetting of the hierarchy among academic disciplines (French and especially philosophy finding themselves dethroned, to the benefit of mathematics) – all of this has meant that professorial taxonomies can probably no longer function today with the triumphal innocence that makes a number of the documents cited in this work seem like antediluvian fossils. This said, while philosophy, for example, has lost its statute of somewhat heroic marginality to fall into a marginality that is very difficult to perceive as elective, in certain areas of the intellectual field it is nevertheless still identified with the sovereign (if not exclusive) form of thought, and it still persists in imposing its great classificatory alternatives through the effect of the hysteresis of habitus, continuously reinforced by the nostalgia of cultural journalists. One could likewise show that the teaching of French has succeeded in salvaging its "vocation" as the worship of sacred texts, at the cost of an *aggiornamento* facilitated by the false theoretical breaks of semiology and of various forms of discourse analysis.

But this is not the most important point. Without going so far as to treat the concrete, contextualized, dated object as a simple opportunity, or pretext, the sociologist is not interested in this object in its contingent or, if you will, *historical* aspects (in the naive sense of the word). She does not aim to tell a story, but rather to analyze a state or an event in the social world – this might be the training of future higher civil servants of the Rue Saint-Guillaume[2] today or the education of parliamentarians in Dijon in the eighteenth century – in order to derive principles of understanding or explanation that will be applicable to other historical objects. This kind of theoretical induction aims to derive, from a historical case treated as "a particular case of the possible" (Bachelard), a set of principles or hypotheses likely to become increasingly general with each subsequent application. Thus the analyses presented here invite us to examine, for example, the system of classification and the indices that today's mathematics teachers rely on to apprehend social properties in academic performances as well as, if not better than, their colleagues in French did 20 years ago, and, as it were, to *naturalize* these results.

Sociological analysis of academic forms of classification such as they may be observed in a given situation (and only then – this said in opposition to amateurs of the so-called philosophical disquisitions that are flourishing anew at the very heart of the social sciences) makes it possible to formulate the questions that any research project can and must ask about profoundly different agents and situations (this said in opposition to the hyperempiricist illusion of utter submission to data). How do the categories of perception and forms of expression used by mathematics teachers in 1988 to label differences that no one would deny exist (no more in this case than in the case of papers in French or philosophy) enable them to suppress or repress the social dimension of both recorded and expected performances and to dismiss any questioning of the causes, both those causes that are beyond their control, and are thus independent of them, and those that are entirely dependent upon them, such as their perception of the norm and their propensity to assess performances in a dehistoricized and dehistoricizing language that is nevertheless laden with social connotations and assumptions, and therefore tailor-made for converting them into essences.

In the present case, as in the rest of the work, we were obliged to forgo presenting our results in proportion to the effort their production had required and to resign ourselves to an often painful compromise between two conflicting demands. On the one hand, we were faced with the demands of empirical proof, for which we would need to lay out all the procedures and products of our research in minute and exhaustive detail (specifically, this would mean producing and analyzing several hundred statistical tables and examining and interpreting countless texts – excerpts from interviews and written works as well as historical documents). On the other hand, we were aware of the need for a coherent and understandable presentation of the subject-matter, which would lead us to reduce the apparatus of proof to what was strictly necessary and to ask the reader – who can always consult intermediate publications where all the necessary supporting materials are presented in greater detail – to trust us.

THE DISCIPLINING OF MINDS

Ranking by "order of excellence" is so closely associated with the notion of a *concours* [competitive examination] that it completely overshadows ranking by discipline. Academic subjects assumed to require talent and gifts and associated with the possession of considerable inherited cultural capital (such as philosophy, French, and, in its place, mathematics) contrast with those that are seen to require primarily work and study (such as geography and the natural sciences, with history and modern or ancient languages occupying an intermediate position) (cf. tables 1 and 2). The major differences between the two types have to do with indices of the modality of their relationship to what it means to be educated. On the one side lie disciplines that discourage willingness and academic zeal, as much through the nebulous and imprecise nature of the tasks they involve as through the vagueness and uncertainty of the signs of success or failure they offer, disciplines that require often undefinable previous knowledge ("you have to have read a lot"). On the other lie disciplines that involve research that suits the taste for work "well done" and that appears "safe" and "profitable" because one knows where to direct one's efforts and results are easily measured.

Table 1 Characteristics of Concours Général prizewinners by discipline (percent)

	Phil. (n = 21)	French (n = 12)	Latin Greek (n = 30)	Hist. Geog. (n = 41)	Lang. (n = 52)	Math. (n = 31)	Physics (n = 17)	Nat. Sci. (n = 15)	Other (n = 40)
Sex									
Boys	61.9	66.7	63.3	87.8	26.9	100	100	86.7	57.5
Girls	38.1	33.3	36.7	12.2	73.1	–	–	13.3	42.5
Father's diploma									
NR (no reply)	4.7	8.3	6.7	9.7	21.1	12.9	11.7	13.3	15.0
None	4.7	–	–	4.8	5.7	–	–	–	2.5
CEP	23.8	25.0	13.3	17.1	3.8	3.2	11.7	33.3	17.5
BEPC	14.3	–	13.3	12.2	7.7	6.4	5.9	20.0	7.5
Baccalauréat	4.7	8.3	30.0	17.1	9.6	12.9	5.9	6.7	17.5
Tech. school	–	–	–	2.4	–	9.7	5.9	6.7	5.0
Licence	33.3	41.7	23.3	21.9	46.1	35.5	17.6	20.0	30.0
Agrégation	14.3	16.7	13.3	14.6	5.7	19.3	41.2	–	5.0
Age in *première-terminale*									
NR	–	16.5	–	–	–	–	–	6.5	5.0
<15–16	–	–	–	–	–	6.4	–	–	–
15–16	4.7	33.3	26.7	7.3	7.7	29.0	5.9	–	2.5
16–17	38.1	8.3	40.0	43.9	42.3	41.9	52.9	6.7	25.0
17–18	42.8	41.7	30.0	41.4	30.7	16.1	41.2	66.7	30.0
18–19	14.3	–	3.3	7.3	19.2	6.4	–	20.0	37.5
Opinion of work									
NR	19.0	8.3	3.3	4.9	5.8	6.4	5.9	–	50.0
Fair	4.7	25.0	–	2.4	13.5	12.9	5.9	–	7.5
Good	66.7	50.0	66.7	70.7	61.5	45.2	47.0	60.0	22.5
Very good	4.7	16.7	23.3	22.0	15.4	32.2	35.3	40.0	15.0
Excellent	4.7	0	6.7	0	3.8	3.2	5.9	–	5.0
Prizes obtained this year									
NR	23.8	–	3.3	2.4	11.5	12.9	–	6.7	15.0
None	–	8.3	–	4.9	5.8	3.2	5.9	13.3	50.0
One	9.5	33.3	3.3	7.3	11.5	3.2	5.8	26.7	12.5
Several	38.1	41.7	30.0	39.0	38.5	32.3	29.4	20.0	12.5
Prix d'excellence	28.6	16.7	63.3	46.3	32.7	48.4	58.8	33.3	10.0
Are you the best student?									
NR	14.3	8.3	–	–	5.7	6.4	17.6	6.7	2.5
Don't know	–	16.7	6.7	2.4	–	6.4	–	–	2.5
No	42.8	50.0	33.3	46.3	55.8	48.4	11.8	53.3	80.0
Yes	42.8	25.0	60.0	51.2	38.5	38.7	70.6	40.0	15.0
Success due to									
NR	–	8.3	3.3	–	–	6.4	–	–	5.0
Talent	28.6	50.0	40.0	31.7	50.0	29.0	47.0	6.6	45.0
Work	19.0	–	3.3	2.4	3.8	9.7	5.9	13.3	2.5
Luck	4.8	8.3	–	4.9	3.8	3.2	–	–	–
Method	19.0	25.0	40.0	43.9	21.1	29.0	29.4	46.7	25.0
Teacher	19.0	8.3	3.3	12.2	13.5	16.1	11.8	26.7	22.5
Other	9.5	–	10.0	4.9	7.7	6.4	5.9	6.6	–
Former prizewinners mentioned and/or known									
NR	52.4	50.0	50.0	58.5	59.6	51.6	47.0	40.0	55.0
None	14.3	16.7	10.0	12.2	15.4	12.9	11.7	40.0	22.5
1 or more	33.3	33.3	40.0	29.2	25.0	35.5	41.2	20.0	22.5
Kind of student you are									
NR	52.4	41.6	46.7	53.7	51.9	54.8	41.2	40.0	60.0
Ease	19.0	16.7	16.7	22.0	21.1	16.1	23.5	33.3	25.0
Rigor	9.5	16.7	26.7	19.5	7.7	16.1	29.4	–	–
Tenacity	14.3	8.3	3.3	2.4	15.4	9.7	5.9	26.7	12.5
Brilliance	4.8	16.7	6.7	2.4	3.8	3.2	–	–	2.5

Table 2 Characteristics of Concours Général prizewinners by discipline (percent)

	Phil. (n = 21)	French (n = 12)	Latin Greek (n = 30)	Hist. Geog. (n = 41)	Lang. (n = 52)	Math. (n = 31)	Physics (n = 17)	Nat. Sci. (n = 15)	Other (n = 40)
Professions in order of interest									
NR	–	–	10.0	4.9	7.7	9.7	5.9	–	7.5
Lawyer	–	–	3.3	2.4	1.9	3.2	–	–	2.5
Diplomat	4.7	25.0	3.3	48.8	9.6	–	5.9	26.7	7.5
Engineer	–	–	–	–	5.7	12.9	11.7	13.3	–
Teacher/research	71.4	41.7	63.3	31.7	32.7	67.7	76.5	53.3	42.5
Artist	23.8	33.3	20.0	12.2	42.3	6.4	–	6.6	40.0
Interest in geography									
NR	4.7	–	3.3	–	3.8	3.2	–	6.7	–
None, little	28.6	41.7	26.7	–	25.0	45.2	29.4	13.3	42.5
Fair	33.3	33.3	40.0	12.2	44.2	35.5	41.2	60.0	32.5
Great, strong	33.3	25.0	30.0	87.8	26.9	16.1	29.4	20.0	25.0
Ideal teacher									
NR	–	–	3.3	–	–	3.2	–	–	2.5
Brilliant	9.5	25.0	3.3	14.6	9.6	12.9	11.8	6.7	7.5
Conscientious	9.5	–	6.7	19.5	3.8	12.9	–	40.0	5.0
Pedagogue	33.3	16.7	46.7	48.8	63.5	58.1	58.8	33.3	55.0
Erudite	4.8	–	10.0	4.8	3.8	–	17.6	6.7	10.0
Creative	42.9	50.0	16.7	12.2	15.4	12.9	11.8	6.7	15.0
Other	–	8.3	13.3	–	3.8	–	–	6.7	5.0
Go to movies									
NR	4.7	–	–	–	1.9	6.4	–	6.7	7.5
Never	9.5	–	10.0	4.9	3.8	6.4	–	13.3	–
1/week	23.8	50.0	10.0	9.7	25.0	16.1	17.6	26.7	25.0
1/month	47.6	25.0	43.3	51.2	38.5	32.3	52.9	33.3	37.5
Irregular	14.3	25.0	36.7	34.1	30.8	38.7	29.4	20.0	30.0
Political leanings									
NR	19.0	16.7	23.3	14.6	17.3	19.4	5.9	20.0	15.0
Don't know	–	8.3	–	4.9	13.5	3.2	5.9	6.7	7.5
Far left	19.0	8.3	3.3	9.7	7.7	6.4	17.6	13.3	10.0
Left	33.3	50.0	30.0	22.0	28.8	32.3	47.1	13.3	25.0
Center	23.8	–	20.0	26.8	17.3	12.9	17.6	40.0	27.5
Right	4.7	8.3	6.7	7.3	13.5	9.7	–	6.7	10.0
Far right	–	–	3.3	7.3	1.9	6.4	–	–	2.5
Other	–	8.3	13.3	7.3	–	9.7	5.9	–	2.5
Grande école you would like to attend									
NR	61.9	58.3	56.7	70.7	69.2	58.1	52.9	46.7	80.0
None	23.8	8.3	–	–	5.7	–	–	13.3	20.0
ENS	14.3	33.3	40.0	19.5	15.4	16.1	29.4	6.7	–
Polytech.	–	–	3.3	–	3.8	12.9	17.6	6.7	–
ENA	–	–	–	4.9	1.9	3.2	–	6.7	–
Sc. Po.	–	–	–	4.9	3.8	3.2	–	–	–
Other	–	–	–	–	–	6.4	–	20.0	–
How are you at math?									
NR	4.7	–	3.3	4.9	–	6.4	–	–	2.5
Very poor	14.3	25.0	–	12.2	15.4	–	–	–	7.5
Poor	28.6	25.0	6.7	12.2	21.1	–	–	33.3	27.5
Fair	33.3	33.3	46.7	48.8	42.3	3.2	–	53.3	42.5
Strong	14.3	16.7	33.3	17.1	21.1	35.5	47.1	13.3	17.5
Very strong	4.7	–	10.0	4.9	–	54.8	52.9	–	2.5

The prizewinners in Latin and Greek, a very large proportion of whom have received the *prix d'excellence*[3] (63.5 percent, compared to 28.5 percent in philosophy and 16.5 percent in French), are characterized by a set of systematic traits. They more often consider themselves the best students in their class than the other humanities prizewinners (60 percent, compared to 43 percent for philosophy students and 25 percent for the prizewinners in French) and they are the most likely among the humanities prizewinners to consider themselves good in mathematics (43.5 percent compared to 19 percent); they never rate themselves as very poor. They are more inclined to judge their work as very good or excellent (26.5 percent compared to 18 percent), and tend to use the same adjectives to describe the kind of student they are and the kind of student they would like to be, signs of a *certitudo sui* commensurate with their academic consecration. Almost all of them expect to go to the École Normale Supérieure (92.5 percent, excluding non-responses). They are more inclined than the others to rank as highest the occupations of teacher or researcher (63.5 percent, compared to 41.5 percent of the French prizewinners, 35 percent of the geography prizewinners, 33 percent of the prizewinners in languages, and 29 percent of the history prizewinners). It is again among these prizewinners that one finds the highest rate of students who are able to name former prizewinners (80 percent, as opposed to 33.5 percent of the prizewinners in the natural sciences) and intend to join the Association of Concours Général Prizewinners.

The antagonism between the positions – succinctly captured in the canonical antithesis of the verdicts "brilliant" and "earnest" [*sérieux*], or in the opposition between the literature agrégation[4] and the grammar agrégation – is most striking when we compare the prizewinners in French (a large proportion of whom are women) from the dominant regions of social space to the prizewinners in ancient languages from the middle positions. The latter, often from small families, have been "pushed" by their families (they learned to read before going to school; they heard about the Concours Genéral very early on, etc.) and an extremely high proportion of them (75 percent) have demonstrated the virtues of docility and consistency that the *prix d'excellence* seems to sanction. Strongly beholden to academic values (they justify joining the Association of Concours Général Prizewinners by invoking the need to "defend the humanities" and take as their responsibility the professorial theme of "declining standards"), they are headed for the most part for the preparatory classes[5] and rank the occupations of teaching and research in first place. At the opposite end of the spectrum, half of the French prizewinners from the dominant pole of social space (who are always very precocious) have skipped a grade in the course of their studies. All require that a teacher be above all creative or brilliant, name talent as the principal factor in success, show more openly than the others their disdain for geography, and maintain the most independent relationship to academic culture.[6]

"Talent subjects", which offer the most profitable investment to inherited cultural capital – that is, to so-called "independent" (as opposed to "academic") culture and to the familiar rapport with culture that can only be acquired through the diffuse teachings of familial education – recruit at a higher social level than those subjects that give students from the dominated regions of social space the occasion to exhibit just those ethical dispositions whose compensatory function is liable to be more fully realized here than in other areas.

It is among the prizewinners in French and mathematics that disdain for geography is most often demonstrated (45 percent of the prizewinners in mathematics and 41.5 percent of the prizewinners in French stating that they have little or no taste for geography, as compared, for example, to 25 percent of the prizewinners in languages and only 13.5 percent of the prizewinners in the natural sciences). The prizewinners in French are also the most inclined to invoke "talent" to account for their success (while those in history, geography, and the natural sciences are more likely to attribute their success to methodical and regular work). Finally, the prizewinners in French and philosophy most often define the ideal teacher as "creative", while those in history, geography, and the natural sciences characterize the ideal teacher as "earnest".[7] More significant still is the fact that the prizewinners in the most noble humanities, French and philosophy, distinguish themselves from the others through the extent and diversity of their reading and their knowledge in subjects not directly taught, such as painting and music (they mention rarely-named painters and musicians more often than the others).

Unlike those who, owing their entire education to their schooling, have "classical", "bookish", or "scholastic" knowledge, preferences, and practices (all of which are directly subordinate to the educational system, even when not directly produced by its exercises), the prizewinners in French and philosophy demonstrate in every way that they have a margin of freedom and security that is broad enough to enable them to maintain a relationship of educated dilettantism and eclectic familiarity with culture (understood in a more "independent" and less "academic" sense), a relationship that may be spread or transferred to domains not yet recognized and consecrated by the school. They are thus the most likely to go to the movies (50 percent of the prizewinners in French and 24 percent of the prizewinners in philosophy do so at least once a week, compared to 17.5 percent of the prizewinners in geography and 10 percent of the Latin/Greek winners),[8] and above all, have the strongest propensity to adopt a "cultured" stance in these "independent" subjects (such as film and jazz).

A few opinions on jazz clearly illustrate this contrast: (1) "very rich and appealing type of artistic expression" (French, son of chemical engineer); "There is sometimes in jazz what you might call an affective language" (philosophy, son of journalist); "Jazz is an original artistic endeavor, stemming from the original fusion of black religious folklore and European folklore. The 'black' input gave it a strong and irresistible rhythm . . . you 'feel' everything the musician puts into his art. Also, a jazz tune is not fixed or static, but rather admits of variation and new and original interpretations, unlike the other musical genres, which are 'imprisoned' in their score" (mathematics, son of engineer). (2) "The rhythm is modern and seems to express all the aspirations in the world, especially when it is played by blacks" (natural sciences, son of merchant); "There is a certain 'black' sadness about the jazz of the New Orleans blues era" (natural sciences, daughter of mechanic).

We can see a further sign of this inclination to adopt the posture of an apprentice intellectual in the fact that the winners in French and philosophy show a strong tendency to reverse or muddle the direct relationship between social origins and political opinions, a relationship that remains clearly discernible in the other disciplines. They often profess opinions on the left or far left (58.5 percent and 52.5 percent, respectively), even more often than the geography prizewinners (24 percent), a large number of whom place themselves in the center (35 percent), while the prizewinners in ancient languages, although somewhat less socially privileged, place themselves somewhat more often on the right (10 percent and 25 percent). We may note, first, that this propensity becomes increasingly obvious (at least in the humanities) the higher the individual's scholastic achievement (12.5 percent of those who received the *prix* place themselves on the far left, compared to only 7.5 percent of those who received *accessits*); second, that the total number of moderates (left, center, right) and abstentions, which reaches 70 percent in geography, 60 percent in the natural sciences, and 56.5 percent in the classics, falls to 33 percent in French; and finally, that the prizewinners from superior social positions describe themselves as being on the left more often in French and philosophy than in the other disciplines; as a result we may assume that this political choice reveals their adherence to the representations and values that are the most widespread among intellectuals, or, more precisely, the sense that they have the right and in fact the need to conform to a certain image of the intellectual by adopting positions on subjects that, according to the current social definition, are considered a must for any true intellectual.

The prizewinners in philosophy demonstrate that they are more inclined than all the others (including the winners in French) to adopt the posture of an intellectual, in their practices as much as in their statements. Nearly all read one or several "intellectual" journals (*Les Temps Modernes, Critique, Tel Quel, Cahiers Pour l'Analyse*); they have no trouble identifying the school of thought that best expresses their views (in contrast to the prizewinners in Latin/Greek, most of whom do not answer, or the prizewinners in French, who show some hesitation in defining themselves) and they sometimes add reservations and nuances to their answer, as if to highlight more clearly the originality of their thought: "The important thing is not what best conveys my thoughts, but rather what is necessary. Marxism, informed by Hegel's fine exegeses, has a lot to teach us" (son of commercial manager). Almost all have grand intellectual plans, expecting to devote their careers to literature ("It isn't the story of a voyage, it's the voyage itself" – son of higher civil servant) as writers, poets, or novelists ("I feel deeply that I must write' – son of commercial manager), or to philosophy ("It's the absolute discipline" – son of commercial manager; "Philosophy encompasses all the other subjects" – son of composer). In a similar vein, when invited to indicate what the ideal future would be for them, the prizewinners in philosophy frequently answer in general "visionary" terms: "Revolution, the end of exploitation" (son of head of postal distribution center); "a classless society" (son of commercial manager); "a future without war, an open society" (son of executive). They thus contrast very markedly with the prizewinners in the natural sciences, who express more direct concerns, often connected to their own futures and, more specifically, to their future occupations: "For me, to be a doctor" (son of merchant). "It would be to be able to practice the trade of my choice and to raise a family" (son of tradesman). When they do not limit themselves to their own personal affairs, the prizewinners in the least noble disciplines act as defenders of meritocratic ideology: "The end of inequality founded on money, birth, and race, to be replaced by a hierarchy founded on the establishment of a peaceful society in which all needs would be met and where time would be devoted above all to art and culture" (geography, son of postal supervisor).

Thus all the traits by which the French educational system recognizes the elite of its elite, and which define the way to excel *par excellence*, are concentrated in these successful ideal types – the prizewinners in French and, to a lesser degree, philosophy.[9] This should come as no surprise; there is perfect agreement here between the values expressly professed by the entire tradition of the humanities and the values revealed in the practices and statements of the people who have succeeded in them. More telling than a long analysis of the relationship of the literate to literary culture, a quick examination of the two prizewinning essays from 1969 (which, through a kind of objective chance, discuss "creation" and "reading") reveals the profound affinity between the tradition of training in the humanities thoroughly permeated with a humanistic, personalist, and spiritualist ideology, and the pedagogical tradition that associates the academic devaluation of everything that has anything to do with school with the cult of so-called "personal" expression.[10] It is in fact a charismatic representation of the act of writing, described as "creation" and "mystery", and of the deciphering of a written text, seen as a "creative" reading involving the spiritual identification of the "I" of the reader with the "I" of the author, that is at the basis of the subjectivist praise of the arbitrary of sensations and feelings, a pretext for the complacent egoism of self-centered effusions, romantic mysticism, and existential pathos.[11]

Analyzing the systematic differences that oppose students in "talent" disciplines to students in "work" subjects thus reveals very clearly the system of oppositions between antagonistic and complementary properties or qualities that structures judgments. One can thus draw up a *table of the categories* that, deeply inscribed as they are in the minds of teachers and (good) students, are applied to all academic and academically thinkable reality (this reality itself, moreover, being organized according to the same principles) – in other words, to persons, teachers or students, as well as to their output (courses, research, ideas, discourses): brilliant/dull; effortless/laborious; distinguished/vulgar; cultured/scholastic; inspired/banal; original/common; lively/flat; fine/crude; noteworthy/insignificant; quick/slow; nimble/heavy; elegant/awkward, etc.

Among the many possible sources of illustration, we shall use examining committee reports from the agrégation and the entrance examination to the École Normale for their value as quasi-legal official declarations. "In short, whether it be a matter of the soundness of the information (. . .), the accuracy of the terms, or the feeling of true *elegance*, the explications de texte as a whole (. . .) left us with a disquieting impression of ignorance, confusion, and *vulgarity* (literature agrégation, men, 1959). "The committee is prepared to forgive many *awkward* phrases and even the isolated misinterpretation, but it will always be merciless when faced with stupid *pretention, pedantry*, and *vulgarity*" (entrance examination, École Normale Supérieure d'Ulm, French explications de texte, 1966). "We could thus move beyond the *humble* and *morose effort* of a *laborious* reading, attaining the *fluidity* of a translation marked by both *elegance* and exactitude" (ibid.). "One would hope that this simplicity [of subject-matter] would allow a few to demonstrate their facility *brilliantly*" (grammar agrégation, men, 1962). Of all the opposing categories with which academic judgment is armed, the strongest is probably the one between erudition (always suspected of bearing the mark of a laborious effort of acquisition) and talent (with the concomitant notion of wide-ranging knowledge and sophistication [*culture générale*]), an opposition that underlies the discredit of those disciplines assumed to require only memory, the most disdained of all skills. "What we noticed was the lack of *culture générale* (. . .) more useful to the candidates than the *erudite* works they get lost in" (literature agrégation, men, 1959). "Not *everyone* is *given talent*" (ibid.). "About ten papers revealed genuine *talent*" (ibid.). "The subject that allowed for *talent*" (literature agrégation, men, 1962). "This text allows us to rank the *talented* with greater assurance" (ibid.). "We might almost say: better that they know even *less*, but that they know it *better*" (ibid.). "It is, moreover, on the qualities of *taste* and *judgment* and not *just flatly* on *memory* that we should like to distinguish among the candidates" (literature agrégation, men, 1959). "Without, of course, being able to disregard the effort of *memorization*, indeed necessary in philology, the fact remains that it is the *global understanding* acquired through reflection that gives linguistic facts their meaning and, finally, their pedagogical and human importance" (grammar agrégation, women, 1959).

The language used by the humanities prizewinners to explain why their work was singled out is a perfect illustration of the correspondence that obtains between objective positions in the hierarchy of disciplines and self-image, an image inseparable from the representation of the qualities socially associated with the different disciplines.

On the one hand: "Might it be the style?" (French, son of professor of medicine); "Originality, rigor, sensitivity" (French, son of chemical engineer); "I think my work was singled out thanks to a certain original quality [*personnalité*]" (French, son of journalist); "original [*personnel*], not too academic, clear" (philosophy, son of blue-collar worker). On the other hand: "Maybe because of the maps, which were quite thorough, and greater knowledge about the Massif Central and the Vosges than about the other mountainous regions" (geography, son of clerical worker). "Clarity of outline" (geography, son of postal inspector). "Clarity, charts, references" (natural sciences, son of drawing teacher). "Restraint, clarity" (natural sciences, son of blue-collar worker). "Quality and number of charts, rigor of outline" (natural sciences, son of commercial manager). The ancient languages seem to occupy an intermediate position. The prizewinners in mathematics and physics most often mention clarity, rigor, accuracy, and precision, but comments about style are not completely absent: "writing, rigor, and construction of argument" (mathematics, son of naval training teacher). "I think my work was set apart by its clarity and the rather quick solutions to the questions I treated" (mathematics, son of *hypokhâgne*[12] teacher). "The brief and elegant nature of my solutions" (mathematics, son of physician).

Given that the same taxonomies that serve both to classify academic disciplines and to determine the personal qualities they require also organize the perception and appreciation that "disciplined" students (who will have to choose among them) have of their own qualities, it is not surprising that academic verdicts should have the power to determine one's "vocation" and that statistical analysis should uncover just as rigorous a connection between the properties socially conferred on the different disciplines and the dispositions of those who excel in them (or teach them).[13] Disciplines choose their students as much as students choose their disciplines, imposing upon them categories of perception of subjects and careers as well as of their own skills (hence the sense they may have of the affinity between the different classes of disciplines or ways of practicing them – theoretical or empirical, for example – and their own academically constructed and consecrated abilities). The belief that one has been predestined, a conviction produced or reinforced by academic verdicts (often expressed in the language of "gifts") and largely determinative of "vocations" is one of the means by which the *predictions* of the institution are realized.

THE PRIVILEGE OF EASE

Differences among disciplines both cover up and recover social differences. The canonical disciplines, such as French or classics and mathematics or physics, socially designated as the most important and most noble, consecrate students who come most often from well-positioned families with abundant cultural capital, correspondingly more of whom have followed the royal path of lycées and classical tracks from the *sixième* to the *terminale* and skipped grades in the course of their secondary schooling, and who are better informed about possible vocations and careers. This should come as no surprise if the academic hierarchy of disciplines coincides with the hierarchy established according to the average age of the prizewinners, a hierarchy extending in the sciences from mathematics to physics and the natural sciences and in the humanities from French or classics to history and geography or modern languages.

One of the clearest attestations of the privilege that is granted to charismatic values, leading the educational institution to disregard strictly scholastic learning, is the cult of precocity, valued as an indicator of "gifts."

The idea of *precocity* is a social construct simply defined by the relationship between the age at which a practice is achieved and the age considered "normal" for its achievement or, more precisely, the modal age at which it is achieved in the population of reference – in other words, for academic precocity, the modal age of the individuals who have reached a determined level of studies. We immediately see that, just as the idea of sexual precocity assumes reference to more or less firmly established divisions of age categories, the idea of academic precocity assumes the existence of a *cursus* distributed among school classes, indicating so many age-dependent stages (*gradus*) in the progressive acquisition of knowledge. As Philippe Ariès has shown, such a structure developed only at the beginning of the sixteenth century. The undifferentiated pedagogy of the Middle Ages did not assume a structural relationship between abilities and age.[14] As the structure of the *cursus* became increasingly defined and set, and particularly from the seventeenth century on, precocious careers became more rare, and it was only then that they began to appear as an index of superiority and a promise of social success.

Through the near miraculous speed of her learning, the precocious student (the extreme example of which is "the child prodigy" or, as we would say today, "the exceptionally gifted child") demonstrates the extent of the natural gifts that enable her to avoid the slow work ordinary individuals must perform in order to learn. In fact, *precocity* is but one of the many academic retranslations of cultural privilege. We thus note that the percentage of prizewinners whose father and mother have a diploma beyond the baccalauréat goes from 38 percent and 3 percent (respectively) among those who are 18 or older in the *première*, or 19 or older in the *terminale*, to 39 percent and 21 percent for 17–18 year olds, 52 percent and 31 percent for 16–17 year olds, and 69.5 percent and 37 percent for 15–16 year olds (social origins following a similar pattern). This should come as no surprise if what we call precocity, and what is in reality a manifestation of cultural heritage, is closely related to all indicators of success.

The idea of "gifts" is so closely associated with that of precocity that being young tends to constitute a guarantee of talent in and of itself. So, for example, agrégation examining committees will identify a *concours* as "brilliant" according to the proportion of "young talent" among the newcomers. "We have seen several of these young recruits distinguish themselves this year. Of 27 candidates accepted, we count 14 who have never taught, and 8 of these are ranked among the top ten (. . .). Their success does not lead us to forget the *merits* of the practicing teachers who, placed in less favorable working conditions, put forth a *valiant effort* and triumphed over difficulty (. . .). But to those who succeeded so well *in their first concours*, we are grateful not only for their having *enlivened* the oral with their *spirit* and their desire to persuade, but also for their having provided us with precious testimony" (grammar agrégation, men, 1963). "In the oral, the youngest candidates turn out to be the best, *livelier* in the interview, more *alert, sharper.* Throughout the examination, *grace* has been substituted for *inelegance*" (entrance examination to École Normale Supérieure d'Ulm, philosophy oral, 1965). The precocious student, darling of the examining committee, receives special treatment, her lacunae and mistakes (interpreted as "youthful transgressions") sometimes even taken as partial proof of her talent. "They are younger than in past years. Might we not think that many have erred through lack of maturity and experience, and that their faults will be quickly corrected (. . .)? Beneath their *awkwardness,* beneath their *naivety,* we at times find *talents* and personal qualities that are in fact so many *promises* of things to come" (literature agrégation, women, 1965).

In fact, precocity is but one of the indices of the mode of cultural acquisition favored by the educational institution – but a particularly reliable one. If the systems of manners set apart by academic taxonomies (whatever their degree of refinement) always refer back to social differences, this is because the way education is acquired lives on in what is acquired in the form of a certain way of using the acquisition. The *modality* of the relationship an individual maintains with the school, with the education it transmits, and with the language it uses and requires depends on the distance between her family milieu and the academic world and on her generic chances for survival in the system – or, in other words, on the probability of her acceding to a determined academic position that is objectively attached to her group of origin. Thus, when, in the indefinable nuances that define "ease" or "natural" talent, we think we recognize behavior or ways of speaking considered authentically "cultured" because they bear no mark of the effort and no trace of the work that go into their acquisition, we are really referring to *a particular mode of acquisition*: what we call ease is the privilege of those who, having imperceptibly acquired their culture through a gradual familiarization in the bosom of the family, have academic culture as their native culture and can maintain a familiar rapport with it that implies the unconsciousness of its acquisition.

Support provided by the family takes on different forms in different milieus: the amount of explicit support (advice, explanations, etc.) perceived as such increases as social level increases (rising from 10 per cent in the lower classes to 25 per cent in the middle categories and 36 per cent in the upper categories), although it appears to decrease with a student's increased success (38 per cent of the *accessit* winners say they have had help compared to 27 per cent of the *prix* winners). It is nevertheless a fact that support is only the *visible* part of the "gifts" of all kinds that children receive from their families. If we recall, for example, that the percentage of prizewinners who made their first visit to a museum during their childhood (before age 11) with their family increases with social origin – and this constitutes only one among many indicators of the indirect and diffuse encouragement given by the family – we see that upper-class children receive both diffuse and explicit support while middle-class children (particularly the sons of clerical workers and primary school teachers) receive mostly direct support, lower-class children, with few exceptions, being unable to count on receiving either of these two forms of aid, with their direct academic returns.

By making outward behavior [*la manière*], that is, a person's relationship to culture and to language (obviously associated with very real differences in both content and form), the central point of application of professorial judgment, the traditional taxonomy unconsciously implemented by teachers in the form of an inherited corpus of stereotypical epithets and ritual phrases (predestined to structure the inseparably technical and aesthetic or ethical bases of academic "valuation") functions as a *relay/screen* that both establishes and obscures the relationship between students' social origins and their grades. Vested with the self-evidence institutions acquire when they are perceived by minds structured according to the very structures that have organized them, the academic taxonomy, through the traditional vocabulary that conveys it, exercises its powers of social discrimination beyond the reach of pedagogical or political vigilance.[15] This is how teachers, under the illusion of neutrality, can profess academic judgments that, as their choice of metaphors and adjectives demonstrate, barely mask social prejudices.[16] For example, with the constellation of epithets used to express the idea of "earnestness" [*le sérieux*] the academic taxonomy designates the generating and unifying principle of the practices characteristic of students from the middle positions, students who must find in their own willingness to work the resources necessary to compensate for the handicaps related to their lack of cultural capital. In claiming qualities of tenacity more often than the others,[17] the prizewinners from the petty bourgeoisie reveal, with a lucidity that is merely a sign of their subordination to academic verdicts, the objective truth of their academic practice, which is necessarily marked, in its laborious and strained modality, by the continuous and sustained effort they have had to put forth in order to remain in the system (or, as we say, to "hang in there").

In addition to all the previously mentioned characteristics, we should point out that the prizewinners from the middle positions are the most likely (relatively) to belong to a cultural group (at the rate of 29.5 percent, compared to 14 percent for the upper categories) – a tendency that is particularly strong for children of clerical workers and primary school teachers – and to associations in general, for that matter. We can see another (albeit no doubt much more ambiguous) sign of their tendency to concentrate all their efforts on academic activities in the fact that they participate in sports less often than the others (with 39 percent nonparticipants), a rate similar to that of the children of blue-collar workers (at 46 percent), and in contrast to that of children from privileged families (24.5 percent). Most importantly, the middle-class prizewinners have had a normal school career more often than the others (no skipped or repeated grades), and have received the *prix d'excellence* somewhat more often that the others, a distinction which, in contrast to signs of approval such as honors [*mention*] on the baccalauréat, rewards their hard work and probably also their docility with regard to teachers, their teaching, and the disciplines they impose. Upwards of 40 per cent of them have received the *prix d'excellence* within the year, compared to 38 per cent of the students from upper positions. The pattern is similar among the children of primary teachers (60 percent) and secondary teachers/professors (35 percent) (this difference being insufficiently explained by the fact that the children of the latter most often graduate from Paris lycées in which the selection criteria and competition are the stiffest). In the preparatory classes for the science and humanities grandes écoles, the students from the middle regions are also the most likely (along with the lower-class students) to have obtained the *prix d'ex-cellence* and the least likely to have received honors on the baccalauréat.

Everything seems to indicate that the longer the period of time over which the control of knowledge, abilities, and ethical dispositions (always taken into account in academic judgment) extends, the more likely it is that the students from the dominated regions will be in a position to gain appreciation for their perseverance, tenacity, and docility. Students from the upper positions, on the other hand, more easily impose their positive qualities on the occasion of final exams, especially orals (which, under their current definition, require more charismatic prowess and a clearer exhibition of brilliance than written exams). The contrast between *discontinuous* and *continuous* efforts and especially between *quick* and *slow* work, which recall the antithesis between the precocious student and the late bloomer, thus arbitrarily become part of the evaluation of knowledge and abilities (they will become the primary criteria of selection in the preparatory classes, where speed of comprehension and execution are one of the conditions for survival).

ACADEMICA MEDIOCRITAS

Teachers' pedagogical practices, particularly those involving selection, betray the tension within the educational institution between academic and worldly values and petty bourgeois and bourgeois dispositions. While fully recognizing only that relationship to culture that is acquired wholly outside the school, the educational institution cannot completely devalue an academic relationship to culture without denying its own method of inculcation. While reserving its favors for those students who owe it the least with respect to what matters most, the educational institution cannot completely deny those who owe it everything and who breathe forth a willingness and a docility that it cannot disdainfully ignore.

And, in fact, the school tends to treat a poor relationship to culture with indulgence when this relationship appears to be the price paid for a good relationship to the school. Agrégation examining committees, who condemn "casual attitudes" and "cavalier self-confidence" with the utmost vigor (as a sign of disrespect for both knowledge and the examining committee), demand that aspiring teachers profess adherence to the institution and the values it protects at least through the energy of their bearing and the enthusiasm of their discourse. They continually make appeals for *"personal involvement"* and *"conviction"*, which contrast with both "guilty insouciance" and "clever cautiousness." "She even had the courage to involve herself personally, with intelligence and restraint" (literature agrégation, women, 1965). They demand that style and elocution be "lively," and they rejoice over the young candidates' "freshness," even if it be a bit *"naive"*. They point out that "tact, cleverness even, and that minimum of *enthusiasm* by which the *grammatical pensum* becomes a true pleasure for the mind are also necessary for the preparation of a good lecture" (grammar agrégation, women, 1959). "Examiners too often get the impression that an *academic* love of *language play* and verbal complexity ends up dulling their understanding of the questions, as well as the capacity for critical writing and lucidity" (entrance examination, École Normale Supérieure d'Ulm, philosophy oral, 1965). They criticize the "candidates who are *skeptical* in literary matters, used to *acrobatics exercises* and manipulations of the *sic* and *non*" (literature agrégation, men, 1959), without for all that condemning the use of a "genuine rhetoric which, within reason, shuns neither *warmth* nor humor" (grammar agrégation, women, 1959).

Thus, the ambivalent relationship the school maintains with petty bourgeois and bourgeois dispositions (never perceived in their social foundations) overlaps, as if it were *superimposed* upon it, with the ambivalent relationship it maintains with the academic mode of production of academic manners. It goes without saying that the intentions or the wishes of the institution, which the personification evident in collective terms like "the school" allows us to identify, are only accomplished through special intermediary agents (or more accurately, through the mediation of their dispositions) who serve as it were to "reactivate" the immanent tendencies of their position. This is why, in this particular case, teachers from petty bourgeois backgrounds (particularly the sons of subaltern teachers) are especially predisposed to occupy the paradoxical, if not contradictory, position that the educational system sets up for them. Inclined to see themselves as different on the one hand from the proletaroids and the consecrated independent intelligentsia, and on the other hand from the occupants of the dominant positions in the field of power, and consequently finding themselves compelled to define themselves with reference to radically opposed stances in matters of education, these teachers are spontaneously inclined to adopt "middle of the road" stances that are perfectly suited to a bureaucracy of cultural conservation responsible for arbitrating between the audacities of the intellectual avant-garde and the conservative inertia of the bourgeoisie.

Like the contradictions between scorn for the slavish dispositions of the simple intellectual worker and moral reprobation for worldly success, the tensions between the cult of "brilliance," correlative to the academic devaluation of "academic" qualities, and the necessary recognition of genuine academic virtues are resolved in the glorification of the happy medium and of the moderation that defines that ensemble of average (or priestly, by contrast with prophetic) qualities we might call *academica mediocritas*. Thus, just as the tame eclecticism of the "well-rounded good student" contrasts with the good but "dull" student's "laborious" fervor for work and the dilettante's pretentious nonchalance, so the measured balance of academic good form (consisting of discreet elegance and restrained enthusiasm), which assumes both knowledge and a detached attitude toward it, contrasts with the suspect cleverness of vacuous virtuosity and the uncontrolled audacities of creative ambition no less than with the pedantic platitudes of didacticism or the uninspired stuffiness of pure erudition.

Agrégation reports, which repeatedly remind candidates to avoid excess of any kind, may explicitly recognize distinct realizations of the two forms of excellence. "The two best papers show that there is no one obligatory recipe. Completely wrapped up in itself, the first one stands out from the rest through a kind of constant *appropriateness* of tone, through its extraordinary faithfulness to its diapason, as if, present from the very start, this very evenness made the work *shine*; the other one, while rather poorly written, *laborious, methodical,* and *dense,* succeeds, paragraph by paragraph, and as if through a great struggle, in getting to the very heart of the question in a rational progression worthy of every praise. In consecrating both *ease* and *effort,* the examining committee wishes to make all candidates understand that the finest *gifts* are spoiled through inaction and that *work* always ends up by producing a *talent*" (classics agrégation, men, 1967). But what they are praising is nothing more than the measured combination of toned-down variants of the two opposing forms of intellectual virtue. "*Two equally reprehensible attitudes* must be avoided at all costs: admiration on command and systematic disparagement" (classics agrégation, women, 1962). "*Between stark prose and verbosity* there is a supple, clean, *subtle way* to move gradually toward the essential conclusions" (ibid.). "Once you have read the text intelligently, *without at the same time taking yourself for a first-class wordsmith* and without *stumbling* or making errors in liaison (. . .)" (grammar agrégation, men, 1963). "We found fewer *pretentious* and *uselessly abstract* expressions . . ., fewer *stylish* words. (. . .) But this praiseworthy effort toward *simplicity* and *clarity* should not lead to the abandonment of written style and a subsequent *descent* into relaxed, or *vulgar,* conversational style" (literature agrégation, women, 1965); "We would like to remind future candidates that the French explication (. . .) is an *intelligent combination* of the necessarily literal explications and literary explications (. . .); it requires skillfully managed choices" (grammar agrégation, men, 1957); "Relaxed elocution, which *avoids* improprieties such as *emphasis* or *overly ambitious* generalities. Just as in the classroom, *simple* vocabulary (. . .) and, if possible, *elegant* discourse are essential qualities here' (literature agrégation, men, 1965). "What is *shocking* and ridiculous is his *arrogant* and *superior* tone, as if he were *giving a lecture* to the great writers; not merely the absence of respect, but also a sort of disdainful pity. We learned that Hugo immodestly 'parades' his rhetoric" (literature agrégation, men, 1962).

The qualities that positively define academic "good form" flow naturally from this search for the conciliation of opposites. It is just this dual combination of "judgment" and "taste," of "restraint" [*mesure*] and "subtlety" [*finesse*], that gives rise to the thoughts, nuances, and distinctions obsessively referred to as "sound and subtle" [*justes et fines*] and pushes aside "errors of tone and taste," "immodesty," and "vulgarity."

"In these sensitive cases, (. . .) *the only criterion is taste*, the only possible attitude one of vigilant sympathy" (classics agrégation, women, 1962). "To comment with *clearheadedness* and *tact*" (grammar agrégation, women, 1959). "One must *capture a certain appropriate tone*" (literature agrégation, men, 1962). "We usually ended up waiting in vain to find those qualities we have the right to demand of future teachers – or of practicing teachers, for that matter: a certain *alacrity*, *talent* for getting others to listen to and appreciate a translation, the *taste* to render not only its constructions but also its *subtleties*" (grammar agrégation, women, 1959). "This text requires that its reader (. . .) combine elementary grammatical knowledge with the qualities of *reflection* and *subtlety*" (literature agrégation, men, 1962). "A French explication has the privilege of revealing qualities of *subtlety*, intellectual *agility*, and the *gift of discernment*" (entrance examination to Ulm, French explication, 1965).

The contradictions experienced by teachers in their relationship with the truth of their practice, which undoubtedly become more and more acute the higher they rise in the professional hierarchy, can be seen most clearly in the self-deceptive games they are forced to play when, in their role as graders, they expect an essay designed for judging future teachers to be more than or anything other than a scholastic exercise. "It was really according to more humble, if not more *humiliating* criteria that we had to judge the papers" (literature agrégation, men, 1959). They can praise "creative" dispositions ("originality," "invention," etc.) and "personal" qualities to the detriment of knowledge and technical mastery (downgraded to the level of "academic recipes" or "textbook knowledge") without giving up the practice of penalizing the merest deviation from scholastic observances. But what should one do when out from under the charismatic image of an "ordeal by talent" there appears the pedestrian reality of a recruitment examination for secondary school teachers? "Perhaps the solution would be not to forget for a minute that people are taking an exam (which is obviously impossible), but to keep in mind that the texts it includes weren't written to become examination topics: they were appeals men were making to other men" (grammar agrégation, men, 1962). When he brings the truth of the examination too sharply to mind, the good student who is nothing more than a good student and who promises to be nothing more than a good teacher breaks the spell; he reduces to its truth an occupation that undoubtedly demands more than any other that it be experienced as distinct from the others. How else could all these exhortations to "appearances" be understood if everything, including fiction, were not more important than destroying this fiction? The simulated creativity and feigned sincerity of a long-prepared improvisation is guaranteed to meet with an approval that is necessarily refused to those

who, through their publicized didacticism or admitted borrowings, are suspected of either not knowing how to or not wanting to "play the game." "It
is unacceptable for a candidate to substitute an interpretation borrowed
from a critic, (. . .) modestly declaring 'I couldn't say it any better,' for what
we expect from him – the original development of his topic" (literature
agrégation, men, 1962).

But the objective truth of what "scholastic" implies is never so clearly noticeable
as in the stereotypical denunciations of scholastic routine. "Some candidates seem to
think that an essay can't be good unless it's divided into three parts" (literature agrégation, men, 1959). "They [the candidates] merely apply old-time recipes, transmitted by a scholastic tradition in which automatic devices that people expect will save
you from having to think have been internalized for generations" (ibid.). "It seems
as if every text included in the test is immediately invested with solemnity" (ibid.).
"We hope the candidates can persuade themselves that a work included in the syllabus does not consequently cease to be a human work" (literature agrégation, men,
1962). And, if the candidate is so often reproached for "lecturing," when he is in fact
there for that very purpose, this is undoubtedly because he is usurping before his
time a privilege of the magisterium, and also because he is too conspicuously calling
attention to the truth of the exercise.
   One would have no difficulty showing that the same contradictions are found,
even more obviously in fact, in the representation that the student forms of his
work, his teachers, and his own attitudes. Thus, the aspiration to a narrower more
"scholastic" frame of learning alternates with the ideal and prestigious image of
noble independent work, free of control and discipline. The expectation that a
teacher [*maître*] be prestigious, "brilliant," "not too bookish," lit with a "sacred
fire," "energetic," and able to "make others love what he is presenting and to establish communication with his audience" (according to comments noted, among others, in interviews with students from Lille) coexists, often within a single individual,
with a taste for the "useful," "well done," "well organized," "easy to follow," and
"well documented" "lecture." While the two types of expectations carry altogether
variable weights according to the categories and, more particularly, the social origins
of the students, as well as discipline (as we saw in the case of the Concours Général
prizewinners), charismatic values nonetheless always predominate to such a degree
that all "scholastic" demands appear shameful and guilty.

But, paradoxically, through the medium of the cult of the "master"
[*maîtrise*], to which philosophy teachers have conformed more than any
other category of teacher, the educational institution succeeds in obtaining a
devotion and selflessness that no institutional regulations could guarantee.
It is the institution in fact that provides both the constraints, curricula,
schedules, and texts, and the freedom (whose various forms are themselves
institutionalized) to play with institutional rules (not in order to break
them, but to transcend them, leaving them untouched). The most typically
charismatic feats, which are almost always based on the more or less ostentatious renunciation of the most visible protections of the institution,

supreme resort of the affirmation of the excellence of the individual, including verbal acrobatics, hermetic allusions, disconcerting references, or unfathomably obscure passages – as well as the technical formulae that serve as support or substitute, such as concealing sources or using prepared jokes – owe their symbolic efficacy to the conditions of authority that the institution sets up for them. By authorizing those who aspire to the status of "master" to divert the authority of the office to their personal advantage, the institution assures itself of the most certain way to get the public servant [*fonctionnaire*] to put all his resources and enthusiasm toward fulfilling his office [*fonction*], while at the same time tending to redirect onto the contents of the communication the prestige (itself diverted) that the "irreplaceable" way of communicating these contents provides the interchangeable author.

Here we must quote a few passages from an ideal-typical work that reveals both the truth of the professorial function, through disclaimers ("it is true . . . but"), and the truth of the experience of this office, which, encouraged by the traditional definition of the mission of public servants, is part of the complete definition of any accomplished professorial practice. "*It is true* that the master encounters his disciple according to the norms and institutions of public education, at least in the most general case. *But*, as long as these technical modalities predominate, the relationship *remains* one of teaching, and teachers who honorably play out their role as civil servants, *are not, strictly speaking, masters.* Mastery *ordinarily presupposes* certain material and technical conditions, *but* it uses them more than it serves them. Educational establishments, cycles [stages of secondary school], and curricula furnish *pretexts* and opportunities for *encounters.* These conditions are not necessary, however, for the relationship between master and disciple can be established independently. Nor are they sufficient, for teaching can exist without mastery." "You don't become a master by rectorial nomination or ministerial decree the day you pass your exams for the certificate of pedagogical aptitude, the *licence*, or the agrégation. *A nominative decree can designate someone as a teacher or a professor*; it is powerless to consecrate a *master*, just as, moreover, no decree can suspend or revoke this standing. (. . .) Once again, most teachers are not masters. They teach their classes and give their lectures like good public servants. They redistribute the knowledge they've accumulated, but they have never stopped to think that beyond the truths they are professing, there lies a greater truth. (. . .) Of the teacher, we ask only knowledge; of the master, we demand a further competence that assumes both going beyond knowledge and relativizing it." "The reality of schedules, curricula, and textbooks, carefully prescribed by ministerial technocrats, is only a kind of optical allusion. *It is true that* the rituals of the work schedule usually manage to tax their executants as well as the mass of ordinary citizens. But of course work schedules are necessary; without them academic society (. . .) would very quickly succumb to material and moral decay. *But* work schedules are only a *pretext*; their true function is to bring about the furtive chance *encounter* and the *dialogue* between master and disciple, in other words, each person's confrontation with himself."[18]

Thus the homology observed between, on the one hand, the objective structures of the institution (such as the distribution of knowledge, authors, and, correlatively, teachers and students among objectively hierarchized "disciplines," or "subjects") and, on the other hand, the mental structures evident in their classified output or in the discourse accompanying acts of classification warrants us to conclude that it is through the structures of the educational institution as much as through direct teaching that the schemata that structure perception, appreciation, thought, and action are inculcated and imposed.

The harmony between the properties objectively linked to the different positions in the objective structures and the social and academic properties of the corresponding students and teachers is grounded in the seemingly inextricable dialectic that obtains between the mental structures and the objective structures of the institution (such as the hierarchy among tracks, establishments, and disciplines). While we should bear in mind, in opposition to a certain mechanistic view of action, that social agents construct social reality, both individually and collectively, we must take care not to forget, as interactionists and ethnomethodologists are wont to do, that they have not constructed the categories that they implement in this construction. The subjective structures of the unconscious that carries out the acts of construction, of which academic evaluations are but one example among many, are the product of a long, slow, unconscious process of the incorporation of objective structures. It is thus the objective structures of the educational institution (such as the hierarchy among disciplines) and, through the homology that binds them, the structures of social space that, at least negatively, orient acts aiming at preserving or transforming these structures. The problem does not lie where some locate it – those who, according to the fashion of the day, announce in the media the death or the resurrection of the "subject." It is simply a matter of granting to individual *agents* who are not necessarily the subject of their thoughts and actions the share that effectively falls to them in the preservation or transformation of structures, and at one and the same time, of returning to them the responsibility they unknowingly assume when, in letting themselves be guided by unconsciouses we may justifiably call *alienated*, since they are but internalized externality, they agree to make themselves the apparent subject of actions that have the structure as their subject.

2

Misrecognition and Symbolic Violence

The hypotheses we have formulated concerning the categories tacitly imple-mented in professorial judgments in order to account for the academic and social characteristics of a population of prizewinners (distinguished chiefly by discipline) may appear to challenge the positivist view of scientific rigor. How indeed can we empirically validate an approach aimed at substituting for an examination of facts, an examination of the examination that pro-duced these facts, in other words, research that sees its object as the practi-cal agenda agents have used in producing the apparent object of research, an agenda that is also present, in a practical sense, in the mind of the researcher (and the reader)? In fact, just such a direct and systematic verification of what we had to assume in order to account for the facts established in our study of Concours Général prizewinners has been made possible through the discovery and analysis of very ordinary material that, because it was *methodically constructed*, has turned out to be an exceptional document:[1] a set of 154 individual reports in which a philosophy teacher in a women's *khâgne* in Paris kept a record of her students' written and oral grades (5–6 per student), along with descriptive comments, over a period of four years during the 1960s. Accompanying the students' grades are their dates of birth, the secondary schools they attended, and their parents' occupations and places of residence.

This material makes it possible to examine the relationship between the different adjectives used in the *evaluation* of student papers – adjectives, we can assume, that form a system of differences giving each its distinctive value and that structure professorial judgment as much as they express it – and, on the one hand, the numerical grades assessed and, on the other hand, the social origins of the students being evaluated in these two ways (adjec-tives and grades). Most importantly, analyzing this type of overview of the acts of jurisprudence performed by an ordinary teacher along with the sup-porting remarks used as justification should enable us to grasp the *academic forms of classification* that, like the "primitive forms of classification" dis-cussed by Émile Durkheim and Marcel Mauss, are the product of the incor-poration of social structures, specifically those which organize the

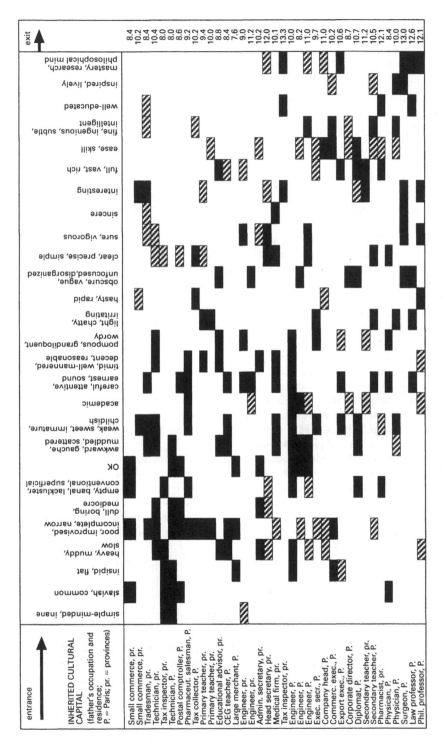

Figure 1 The categories of professorial understanding

educational ˙institution, especially through divisions into disciplines and tracks, and that are themselves homologously related to the structures of social space.

Rather than appealing to more refined statistical techniques, we have chosen to use a very simple procedure (borrowed from Jacques Bertin)[2] to lead this exploration into the cognitive structures that organize professorial judgment, a procedure that has the advantage of presenting the data analyzed in a material format that gives the *model* a directly visible form capable of accounting for them.

Our first step was to set up as many columns as there were adjectives, giving one line to each student according to social class and marking a black square whenever one of the adjectives appeared in her report and a hatched square whenever the adjective was qualified (for example, "fluent but uneven elocution"; "applies herself, but slavish"; "incomplete but accurate and well constructed"; "diffuse and lackluster form, but more or less organized"). Each line of figure 1 thus represents the range of judgments the teacher was likely to make of a particular student. Next, we divided the adjectives into 27 classes according to similarity of meaning and co-occurrence. Then we "diagonalized" the data (by successive transposition of lines or columns), establishing the closest thing possible to a linear distribution in the relationship between the hierarchy of adjectives and the hierarchy of social origins (shown in the distribution of the black squares on the diagonal). Finding that the adjectives arranged themselves roughly from the most pejorative to the most positive and that the hierarchy by social origin was very similar to the one we could have set up a priori using family cultural capital as our sole criterion, we distributed the students from one of the years under study according to the volume of their inherited cultural capital – or, more accurately, according to their distance from the educational system and the culture it represents – using, for lack of more precise criteria, parental occupation and place of residence (Paris or the provinces). We thus go from the students from the middle positions (children of farmers, blue-collar workers, or minor clerical workers are rarely represented at this level of the *cursus*) to the students from the dominant positions, and within these two positions, from the areas relatively poorest in cultural capital (industry and management), to the richest (university professors), with the professions occupying an intermediate position. Finally, we included the *average grade* received by each student throughout the year on the right-hand side of the diagram.

A COGNITIVE MACHINE

We immediately see that the most positive comments appear with increasing frequency as social origins rise, and that the same goes for the grades (with a few exceptions). Coming from Paris appears to be an additional advantage; if we compare students of equivalent social standing, those from the capital always receive a slightly higher rate of exceptional adjectives, even though at this level of the *cursus* and in a *khâgne* reserved for the academic elite, the non-Parisian students have been very highly selected. Students from the middle regions of social space (who make up more than half of the group whose grades range from 7.5 to 10, and who are completely absent from the small group whose grades average above 12)[3] are the privileged target of negative assessments – in fact, of the most negative among them, such as "simple-minded," "slavish," or "common." One only has to group the adjectives most often applied to these students to see emerge the bourgeois view of the petty bourgeois as a lesser bourgeois: "poor," "narrow-minded," "mediocre," "OK," "awkward," "clumsy," "muddled," etc. Even the virtues they are esteemed to possess are themselves negative ones: "book-ish," "painstaking," "careful," "earnest," "methodical," "timid," "well-behaved," "decent," "reasonable." When they do happen to be judged to possess the more exceptional qualities, such as clarity, strength of mind, skill, subtlety, intelligence, or breadth of knowledge, the comment is almost always qualified (see table 3, evaluation 1b, for a perfect example). Students from the business bourgeoisie completely escape the most damaging opin-ions, and the negative comments that do befall them are often qualified. They receive the most exceptional adjectives, but here again, the comments are often qualified. As for students from intellectual quarters, they almost never suffer either the most negative assessments, even euphemized, or the petty bourgeois virtues, and are often judged to possess the most valued qualities.

In fact, the classification method we have adopted actually tends to mini-mize the differences. The great dispersal in the distribution of the adjectives that occupy a median position in the taxonomy is not entirely due to the particular effect of this position, or even to the effect of grouping different adjectives into sets, as similar as they may be. Rather, it is undoubtedly essentially due to the fact that the same adjective can appear in different combinations with a resultant change in meaning. This is especially true in the case of adjectives such as "sound" [*solide*], which, accompanied by "painstaking" [*soigneux*] and "careful" [*attentif*] may merely be a euphemistic way of expressing the merits of infallible petty bourgeois medi-ocrity (that the "*but no better*" of "correct but no better"[4] so admirably captures) while, combined with "intelligent" or "subtle," it expresses the perfect synthesis of scholastic virtues.

We also note that for equal or equivalent grades, the comments become more severe and more harshly and less euphemistically expressed as the social origins of the students descend. (For a concrete picture of this ten-dency, see table 3 summarizing the judgments made of students of different social origins who received similar grades, reading across a single line, for example, 1b, 2b, or 3b). We can see that the *reasons adduced for a judgment* seem more closely linked to social origin than the grade that expresses it. This is no doubt because the teacher's written comments more directly

Table 3 Synopsis of several evaluations

	1	2	3
a between 8 and 10	Father technician Paris foolish, mediocre, allusive, badly written, small points with no follow-up summary OK but slavish completely insipid a few good points (borrowed?) but minor and vague	Father engineer, Mother secretary Paris area muddled. Philosophical detritus floating on the surface, looks good but no deep thought, purely scholastic work disorganized, lively, fluent but uneven elocution disorganized, many gaps in knowledge, worse than no knowledge a few ideas but poorly connected adequate work better	Father physician Paris some understanding but uses philosophical concepts for their stylistic color; high-flown wordiness. Otherwise, some knowledge and organization slavish summary some understanding and clarity of expression, but no direct analysis some good elements but not well connected, heteroclitic quotes
b between 10 and 12	Father woodworker Mother post office clerk Provinces not stupid but a bit childish, incomplete and awkward but interesting, proof of some knowledge understanding a bit off; solid but incomplete sincere, earnest, somewhat timid; good use of German same remarks; awkward but sincere, earnest, good examples	Father assistant manager, export company Paris rich, long, pretty accurate, albeit a bit wordy earnest, deliberate, confused, stumbles over difficulties somewhat organized but vague flat presentation, overall approach to subject well constructed, horrible handwriting, cross-outs pretty good; well intentioned, but doesn't define subject clearly weak and a little silly with some accurate points too many misunderstood terms	Father physics/chemistry teacher Mother natural science teacher Paris area precise, very careful, clear but a bit narrow a few stupid mistakes but some good points precise and irritating; some conviction, some sophistry fine, pretty well written, not always very accurate
c 12 and above		Father administrative executive Mother primary teacher Provinces good, proof of solid background, well thought out, pretty well written, sometimes takes risks and goes beyond what she knows pretty good interesting, shows mastery	Father surgeon Paris interesting but disorganized very solid and well argued; conclusion a bit too mystical but sincerely philosophical very original, well constructed, but poorly written vigorous, pretty well written interesting but obscure, not well expressed

We have given here full sets of written comments from the reports for several students, together with their average grades. The number of remarks reported for each student varies because the teacher sometimes assigned a grade without making any comments.

betray the picture she has formed of her students based on her knowledge of their *bodily hexis*, gained from other sources, and on her evaluation of it, based on criteria far removed from those that are explicitly recognized in the technical definition of the required performance.

In contrast to the situation in which professorial judgment is applied to an anonymous paper, here we have a situation in which evaluations depend on direct and prolonged familiarity with the very "person" of the student, in other words, on an entire set of diffuse indices, never explicitly recognized, laid out, or systematized, that are provided by school assignments and exercises as well as the physical appearance of their authors. Handwriting, explicitly mentioned when strikingly "ugly" or "childish," is perceived and judged according to a practical taxonomy that is far from socially neutral, and is structured around oppositions such as "distinguished" and "childish" or "coarse." Physical appearance, while only rarely mentioned, is also perceived according to a socially marked grid; both excessive negligence and meticulous care are censured. Style and "breadth of knowledge" are explicitly taken into account, but to varying degrees and undoubtedly according to varying criteria depending on the discipline (philosophy or French, for example).

Everything seems to indicate that specific knowledge – in the present case, this would mean familiarity with philosophical writers, mastery of the technical vocabulary of philosophy, the ability to set up a problem and develop a rigorous argument, etc. – determines how written work is graded to a lesser degree than is normally thought. Aside from a few adjectives that can be used to refer specifically to properties of school work ("incomplete," "hasty," "muddled," "scattered," "methodical," "obscure," "vague," "unfocused," "disorganized," "clear," "precise," "simple"), almost all of the adjectives in our study pick out *personal qualities*, as if the teacher were acting on the authority of academic fiction in judging (rather like a literary critic or art critic) not a student's ability to conform to rigorously defined technical requirements, but rather her overall disposition to conform to an in fact undefinable ideal: a unique combination of clarity, strength of mind, and rigor, of sincerity, ease, and skill, of finesse, subtlety, and ingenuity. The very vagueness of the comments that, just like adjectives used in praising a work of art, are really *interjections* conveying hardly any information (except on one's state of mind) suffices to show that the qualities they designate would remain imperceptible and undistinguishable to anyone who did not already possess, through experience, the classification systems that are inscribed in ordinary language.

Judgments meant to apply to a whole person clearly take into account not only strict physical appearance, which is always socially marked, but also clothing, accessories, make-up, and especially manners and behavior, which are perceived according to socially constituted taxonomies and thus read as signs of the quality and the value of the person.[5] If, as we note in obituaries of École Normale graduates, discourse intended to evoke deceased persons devotes so much space to a description of their physical appearance, this is because physical descriptions function not only as memory triggers, but also as the tangible *analogon* of a person, and this from the first moment of encounter, which provides the opportunity for a kind of "original intuition," often summed up in the evocation of a bodily *hexis* and an accent: "Everything about him gave you the feeling that he only had a body because you have to have one, even if you don't quite know what to do with it. His long neck supported a head that was both pleasant and strange, and that was almost always tilted to one side or the other. He had that fair complexion characteristic of tender children who are perhaps too pampered by fearful women past their prime, huge eyes of an uncertain and vaguely marine blue, a nose that was, if not exactly *à la Condé*, at least very seventeenth century, and a magnificently developed, yet not disproportionate forehead" (obituary of Robert Francillon, *Annuaire ENS*, 1974, p. 46). If the overall intuition expressed in this portrait captures just as effectively the intellectual and moral qualities of the person, this is because bodily *hexis* provides spontaneous physiognomy with the entire system of indices through which class origin is *recognized-misrecognized*: "very distinguished," "a poet," "originality partially obscured by a timid communicative style," "easily offended sensitive spirit." Likewise, the list of properties attributed to another alumnus ("strong work," "varied and prolific scientific activity," "robust, ready to work, cheerful, and good") is merely a long paraphrase of the spare comments through which his *hexis* is captured: "cast-iron strength in an athletic body," a "hearty fellow" (obituary of Louis Réau, *Annuaire ENS*, 1962, p. 29).

If we were to confine our attention to the two outside columns of figure 1, that is, social origin and grades, as we must ordinarily do in order to establish a correlation between social origin and academic achievement, we might merely see this diagram as the schema of a simple machine that, receiving products hierarchized according to an implicit social classification, reproduces products hierarchized according to an explicit academic classification that is in reality quite similar to the initial classification. In fact, this would be to miss the specific workings of this strange cognitive machine that performs a whole series of operations of cognition and evaluation objectively tending to establish a close correspondence between the entry classification and the exit classification without ever *officially being aware of or recognizing* strictly social principles or criteria. The teacher who judges one or another of her students to possess the most typical petty bourgeois attributes would be shocked if she were ever to be accused of basing her verdicts on class distinctions, even implicit ones. In fact, the official taxonomy, objectivated into a system of adjectives, fulfills a dual and contradictory function. It is both a relay and a screen between the entry classification, which is not explicitly taken into account in grading,[6] and the exit classification. Functioning within a logic of denial, this taxonomy permits the realization of a social classification in guises that allow it to be accomplished invisibly.

The taxonomy that expresses and structures academic perception practically is a neutralized and misrecognizable, in other words, euphemized, form of the dominant taxonomy. It is structured according to the hierarchy of qualities commonly attributed to members of the dominated classes (the "*classes populaires*") (servility, vulgarity, awkwardness, slowness, poverty, etc.), to occupants of the middle ("petty bourgeois") positions (small-mindedness, narrow-mindedness, mediocrity, uprightness, earnestness, etc.), and to the dominant groups (sincerity, breadth, wealth, ease, skill, finesse, ingenuity, subtlety, intelligence, culture, etc.). The academic taxonomy, a system of principles of vision and division implemented at a practical level, rests on an implicit definition of excellence that, by granting superiority to the qualities socially conferred upon those who are socially dominant, consecrates both their way of being and their state.

It is in fact by means of this classification system that academic forms of classification establish the correspondence between social properties and academic positions, which are themselves hierarchized by level, establishment, discipline, and track, and in the case of teachers, by rank and the location of the establishment where they teach. This collocation of agents into hierarchized academic positions constitutes in turn one of the primary mechanisms of the transformation of inherited capital into academic capital. But this mechanism can only function if the homology remains hidden and if the pairs of adjectives that in practice express and structure perception are the most socially neutral oppositions in the dominant taxonomy ("brilliant" "dull," "light" "heavy," etc.) or euphemized forms of these oppositions: "heavy" [*lourd*] giving way to "labored" [*lourdaud*], "solidly constructed" [*charpenté*], or "thoroughly worked" [*appuyé*], "simple" [*simple*] to "artless" [*simplet*], "light" [*léger*] to "an easy read" [*qui se lit bien*], all ostensibly pejorative forms, in fact attenuated by the gruff, paternalistic benevolence they are proof of.

The manifest harshness of some of the comments, which would be excluded from ordinary usage – where "slavish," for example becomes "humble" (as in "of humble origins") or "modest" ("modest beginnings") should not deceive us. Neither the academic fiction that maintains that the judgments are meted out to as yet perfectible adolescents, who are thus deserving of rougher and more sincere treatment (cf. "sweet but . . ." [*gentil*], "immature," "childish"), nor the *punishment* situation that authorizes the infliction of symbolic punishment (like the physical punishment found in other places and times), nor the tradition of harsh discipline that all "elite schools" maintain suffices to account for the complacency and freedom in symbolic aggression that is left to teachers, which appears all the greater the more academically consecrated are their students.

Both written and oral comments provide an opportunity to assert and inculcate the professorial values that, given the near complete dependence and docility of elite students, can be asserted baldly. It is significant that, in his obituary of a *khâgne* teacher, a former student should recall with emotion the perfectly traditional comments – traditional in content as well as form – that the teacher used to write on his students' papers. "Nor has anyone forgotten his expectations. We felt them to be legitimate; we were grateful for the energetic way he imposed them on us (. . .). His method? Exceptional, and perfectly befitting him: he would type up his comments and attach them to the papers he was giving back, thus setting up a real dialogue with us – already at that age! There were forty or more of us, and we would turn in sometimes illegible papers of easily eight long pages. His 'letter' would often run to a half a page or more! He wanted so much to be useful to us, to understand us, and he had such keen perception that we knew his often stinging ruler was wielded out of affection. His tirades, *the full range of which were showered upon us*, were imaginative, often funny, and quite effective: 'doubtful ability – washed out, weak style – you're pouring your arguments out into a waffle iron – a long trip during which one would only notice the telephone poles – a whirlpool in still water – you write like people box: in the fray, you sometimes accidentally hit the mark' . . ." (obituary of Paul Tuffrau, *Annuaire ENS*, 1974, p. 52).

Professorial self-satisfaction would not encounter such student complacency were everyone not communing under the conviction that "brutal frankness" is the only mode of communication befitting the elite. Although no doubt born of the combination of aristocratism and asceticism that defines professorial ethos, the invectives and excommunications that the elite teacher hurls at her elite students in the name of their inadequacy with respect to her idea of the elite, and that in the guise of universality, are in fact only aimed at a few among them (as figure 1 clearly shows), are part of the rituals aimed at inculcating elitist representations.

The extraordinary collective denial that makes the direct apprehension of the social foundations of academic judgments unthinkable (reducing them to ordinary acts of the derealizing ritual of initiation), as much for those who pronounce them as for those upon whom they are pronounced, is not simply the result of the aggregation of a set of individual denials. In fact, collective belief, here as elsewhere, is inscribed in the direct conformity between the objective structures of the divisions of the academic world and the cognitive structure of the principles of vision and division that the agents engaged in this world apply to it. We have come, in fact, to the most obscure principle of action, which lies neither in structures nor in consciousness, but rather in the relation of immediate proximity between objective structures and embodied structures – in habitus. There is action, history, and preservation or transformation of structures only because there are agents. But these agents are only effective and efficient because they are not reduced to what is ordinarily meant by the notion of the individual. As socialized organisms, they are endowed with a set of dispositions that imply both their propensity and their ability to enter into and play the game. What is operative in every teacher or student when they perceive and judge a paper as "dull" or an oral presentation as "OK," or when, seeing themselves as they are seen, they see themselves as destined for Latin or geography, is neither the objective structure of social space nor the subjective consciousness of the positions in this space. It is the relation of ontological correspondence between objective structures and subjective structures, between, on the one hand, the structure of a field organized and divided according to principles of classification – into establishments (facultés and grandes écoles), disciplines, tracks, etc. – that reproduce the principles of the most fundamental social classifications (dominant/dominated, etc.) in a misrecognizable form and, on the other hand, the taxonomy implemented in the practical operations of academic classification. This taxonomy is in fact a *neutralized form* of the dominant taxonomy that, being produced by and for the functioning of a relatively autonomous field, takes the taxonomies of ordinary language to a second degree of neutralization. Thus the academic language that is the principal vehicle for these principles of vision and division is in part responsible for the functioning of mechanisms that can only operate if agents decide to act according to their logic, which presupposes that they offer them their objectives in a misrecognizable form.

It is undoubtedly through the successive classifications that have made them what they are from the point of view of the academic taxonomy that the classified products of the educational system, both students and teachers, have acquired – to differing degrees according to their position in these structures – the practical mastery of principles of classification circumstantially adjusted to the objective classifications enabling them to classify all things (starting with themselves) according to academic taxonomies, and functioning within each of them, in all good faith, like a machine for transforming social classifications into academic classifications, that is, into recognized-misrecognized social classifications. As objective structures that have become mental structures through a learning process that takes place in a universe organized according to these same structures and subject to sanctions formulated in a language also structured according to the same oppositions, academic taxonomies classify according to the very logic of the structures that have produced them, as do the objects to which they are applied. Given that they find never-ending confirmation in a social universe organized according to the same principles, the taxonomies are implemented with the sense of "self-evidence" that characterizes the doxic experience of the social world, and its reverse of the unthought and the unthinkable.

Agents entrusted with acts of classification can fulfill their social function as social classifiers only because it is carried out *in the guise* of acts of academic classification. They only do well what they have to do (objectively) because they think they are doing something other than what they are doing, because they are doing something other than what they think they are doing, and because they believe in what they think they are doing. As fools fooled, they are the primary victims of their own actions. It is because they think they are using a strictly academic or even, more specifically, "philosophical" (or "literary") classification, because they think they are awarding certificates of charismatic qualifications in literature or philosophy ("philosophical mind," etc.), that the system is able to effect a veritable *deviation of the meaning* of their practice, thereby getting them to do what they would not otherwise do for all the money in the world.

It is also because they think they are making strictly academic judgments that the social judgment masked by the euphemisms of their academic language can produce its particular (positive or negative) effect of consecration.

By making those who are being judged think that the judgment is being made of the student or apprentice philosopher within them, of their "person," their "mind," or their "intelligence," and never in any case of their social being or, to put it more bluntly, of a "teacher's kid" or a "shopkeeper's kid," academic judgment acquires a degree of recognition, actually, misrecognition, that the social judgment of which it is the euphemized form would undoubtedly not elicit. The transmutation of social labels into academic labels is not a simple inconsequential writing game, but rather a process of social alchemy that grants words their symbolic efficacy, their power to have a lasting effect on practices. A statement that in its nontransformed form ("you're nothing but a worker's son") or even transformed up one degree ("you're common") would be completely devoid of symbolic efficacy and would even be liable to incite a revolt against the institution and its priests – if such a statement is really even "conceivable," as we might say, coming from a teacher – becomes acceptable and accepted, admitted and internalized in the *unrecognizable form* that the specific censorship of the academic field imposes ("OK," "unimportant work," "insipid style"). The academic taxonomy of the academic qualities that the institution proposes as the set of categories of human excellence comes between each agent and her "vocation." It is this taxonomy that determines orientation toward one or another discipline or track, for example, an orientation predicted in advance by academic verdicts ("I really like geo[graphy]').

The tirelessly renewed academic verdicts that accompany a teacher from her first report card to her final obituary undoubtedly owe much of their symbolic efficacy as insidious injunctions to the euphemization professorial rhetoric performs whenever it comes to making an unfavorable judgment within the bounds of academic protocol or prudence. In book reviews, letters of recommendation, dissertation reports, or the panegyrics showered on candidates on the occasion of operations of cooptation (all of which are discourses intended for peers able to read between the lines and understand unspoken clues), praise can negate itself by straying toward "dominated" or "minimal" qualities (as below: "earnest and hard-working," "intellectual honesty," "unassuming") that call to mind the absence of the complementary class ("brilliant," etc.), or by betraying itself as conventional and forced through agreed-upon signs ("not bad," "promise for the future," "following further work," "a bit too close to her notes"). "I have known Ms X since the beginning of her university career. She has always seemed an extremely earnest and hard-working student. She has given me agrégation papers several times that were not bad at all. This shows promise for the future. I therefore hope that, following further work, she will be able to pass the examination." "Ms X did her master's thesis under my direction in 1970–71. It was a very solid and well-documented piece of work that showed great intellectual honesty, although she based it a bit too closely on her notes rather than taking a step back to get the big picture. The qualities I was able to discern in Ms X lead me to think that despite her first unsatisfactory attempt, she should make a good agrégation candidate. I hope that she will be able to prepare well. Let me add that she is both hard-working and unassuming, which should be taken into account" (recommendation files, September, 1972).

In order to account fully for the power of discourse, we see that it is necessary to connect language to the social conditions of its production and use and to search beyond words, among the mechanisms that produce both words and the people who emit and receive them, for the basis of the power that a certain way of using words allows one to mobilize. The established use of established language is only one of the preconditions for the efficacy of symbolic power, and one that operates only under certain conditions. The power of academic euphemisms is only absolute when it is exercised on agents selected in such a way that the social and academic conditions of their production predispose them to recognize them absolutely.

The effect of symbolic imposition produced by the educational institution is at its most accomplished when the structure of the content that the educational system is charged with transmitting accords with the mental structures of the teachers charged with its transmission and the students to whom the message is addressed. Such is the case, for example, when, in speaking to bourgeois adolescents prepared to recognize themselves in her teachings, a philosophy teacher, investing her entire social unconscious, raises the Platonic distinction between *episteme* and *doxa*, or the Heideggerian discourse on "Everyman" and "idle talk," which, reduced to their simplest terms for the needs of academic communication, come down to the aristocratic affirmation of the distance between a thinker and everything "vulgar" or "commonplace," the secret principle of the professorial philosophy of philosophy and of the enthusiasm that it readily inspires in adolescents.[7] The legitimate disclosure to certain legitimate recipients of a more or less simplified version of a philosophical discourse that presents the dominant view of the social world in an esoteric and highly euphemized form is sure to encounter a recognition that is in fact, if the reader will pardon the expression, only a form of re-misrecognition. The distinguished and the vulgar, the exceptional and the commonplace are in fact perfectly misrecognizable when, after a detour through the heavens of philosophical ideas, they return in the "uncommon" guise of the "authentic" and the "inauthentic," or the *Eigentlichkeit* and the *Uneigentlichkeit*, depending on the degree of initiation of the master and his disciples.[8]

PEER JUDGMENT AND ACADEMIC ETHICS

Those who, at the end of a series of evaluations made according to the categories of professorial understanding, enter the teaching profession continue to be subject to judgments based on the same principle of vision and division. To demonstrate this, we have analyzed the obituaries published in the *Annuaire de l'Association des Anciens Élèves de l'École Normale Supérieure* [ENS alumni association yearbook], following the procedures used in our study of the evaluations made of those aspiring to entry into the school. In the final judgment passed by the group on one of its departed members, these obituaries once again implement the principles of classification that originally determined his membership in the group.[9] We thus observe that a system of classificatory adjectives very similar to the one that emerged in our study of recorded professorial evaluations is still operative in the obituaries, and that this academic taxonomy has continued to be active throughout the career of the deceased as an instrument of social classification. Proof of this is found in the fact that we again note differences in career related to differences in social origin among *normaliens* who have nonetheless been formally and effectively "equalized" through the combined effects of their consecration, their education, and above all, their high degree of selection.

In figure 2, arranged similarly to figure 1, and based on data from obituaries published in the ENS alumni yearbooks for 1962, 1963, 1964, and 1965, we have ordered the 34 alumni whose obituaries mention social origin according to the extent of their original cultural and social capital, at least as far as it could be determined from the available data (primarily, father's occupation, occasionally mother's occupation, parental residence at the time of the birth of the child, and a few more or less specific indications of the family's cultural milieu). As in the case of the preparatory class students, this classification obviously admits to a degree of arbitrariness, particularly in the case of students from the bourgeoisie and the upper ranks of the petty bourgeoisie. The insufficiency of the available data – we do not always know the rank of the officers, even less their education (Saint-Cyr or Polytechnique, for example); we do not always know the exact status of the teachers; we do not know the size of industrial and commercial firms – is not the only problem; any rigorous analysis of social trajectories must rest on a social history of the structure of the field of power and the evolution of the differential positions of the different occupations in this structure. Such a social history, a prerequisite superbly overlooked by all studies of social mobility, is likewise imperative *a fortiori* for the establishment of a linear hierarchy such as the one being attempted here for reasons specific to our analysis. It is furthermore extremely difficult to evaluate the relative weight of the professional and residential status of the family. We are led to believe that at this very high level in the *cursus*, where the qualities associated with the academic image of excellence are most insistently required, the opposition between Parisian and provincial origins (heightened by the opposition between speakers of *langue d'oil* [Northerners] and speakers of *langue d'oc* [Southerners], lastingly inscribed in habitus as *accents*) takes on critical importance.[10]

Having set up 26 classes of descriptions found in our examination of about ten years of the yearbook, we marked a black square (never exceeding ten markings) for the qualities (usually designated by adjectives) that

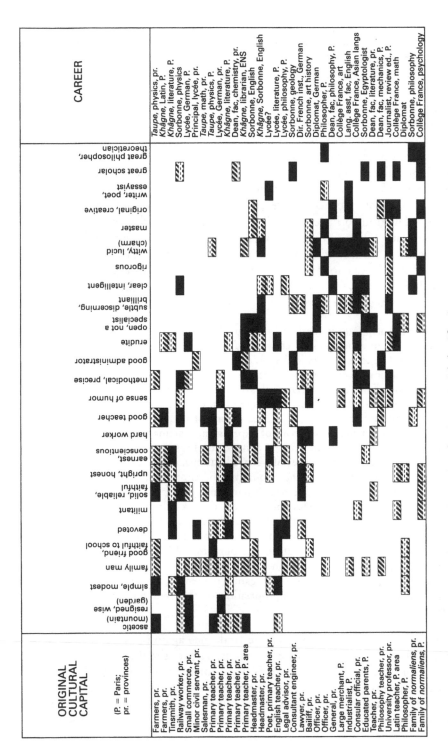

Figure 2 Classificatory machine 2: from academic classification to social classification

seemed to carry the greatest relative weight in each of the obituaries considered (either because, in the longer obituaries, they were mentioned several times, or because, in the shorter ones, their importance was underscored by the force or the emphasis with which they were expressed).[11] The system of adjectives used to characterize the various deceased teachers defines *the space of possible ethics* associated with the position of teacher, a space whose truth would be fully revealed only through comparison with other spaces, associated with other positions in the field of power. We reach the concrete boundaries of this space in noting that the taxonomies that organize it in the guise of universality prove to be completely inadequate in describing the properties of those *normaliens* who leave the university field (diplomats, for example), whose obituaries are entrusted to other proud defectors. Here (with "devotion to his country," or "career dedicated solely to the service of the state") we enter a discourse domain that suggests quite another, antagonistic, if not antinomial, social universe ("no vocation for teaching," "found the old-fashioned framework of a class too limiting," "all his aspirations led him toward wider horizons") – that of the higher civil service and the top business bourgeoisie.

The field of power is the locus of struggles that have as one of their stakes the hierarchy of the principles of ethical evaluation. The first task of a sociology of ethics would be to inventory and analyze the systems of properties that are associated, on a practical or explicit level, with the different positions in the field of power; in preparation for a comparative analysis, we have begun to collect a set of celebratory discourses – eulogies, reception speeches, etc. – in which various groups sing their own praises in singing the praises of one of their members. These discourses are essential moments in the work of expression, systematization, and universalization through which a group tends to convert its ethos into an ethic, transmuting the objectively systematic principles of a shared habitus, nearly universalized within the confines of a group, into an intentionally coherent system of explicit norms with claims to universality. Eulogies offer a particularly propitious opportunity for such an enterprise of ethical production. Indeed, they require that divisive conflicts be suspended and they authorize the praise of the entire group, and first and foremost, of the author of the eulogy himself – as we can clearly see in those prefaces that practice annexation by identification – through the praise of one of its eminent (and, as such, potentially threatening) members, someone who is from that moment on, however, both disqualified from the game, rendered harmless, and made into the object of a struggle over the appropriation of the symbolic capital accumulated around his name.

The statistical correlation that we find once again between the social origins and academic success of *normaliens*, despite the various homogenizing operations they have undergone, is not a function of mechanical causality.[12] It develops progressively and continuously through the innumerable acts of evaluation – and self-evaluation – that implement those instruments of reality construction that are the academic taxonomies. As classified products themselves, teachers never cease to classify each other and themselves according to academic principles of classification. Through the constant acts of self-evaluation by and through which aspirations and self-esteem are defined, teachers' ambitions anticipate and invite the verdicts that the institution will render regarding their ambitions. Seen in this light, obituaries are only apparently deceptive when they praise the modesty of those who have sacrificed a "brilliant career" in a university or in Paris for the "joys of provincial or family life." Because the dialectic between opportunities and hopes is so closely woven, it is fruitless to try to separate the role of objective determinants from that of subjective determination. The provincials did not want to have anything to do with a Paris that did not want to have anything to do with them. The secondary school teachers refused the university as much as it was refused to them. All successful socialization tends to get agents to act as accomplices in their own destiny.

The infinitesimal "choices" through which the trajectory leading to a probable future slowly takes shape in fact constitute so many contributions to the acts of divestiture that, at the cost of a few insincere tricks, will end in *amor fati*, that funereal virtue celebrated in obituaries. The relative independence of the different principles of hierarchization (institution, residence, discipline) produces a scrambling effect that greatly contributes to facilitating the work one must do in order to convert failures into elective rejections and bury vain hopes. The philosophy teacher at a large Parisian lycée has no trouble convincing herself, as long as she writes for intellectual journals, that she has no reason to envy the English teacher at an obscure provincial university. And vice versa. The praise imposed by the rules of the obituary genre thus gives a rather accurate idea of the mourning through which those who saw themselves as "destined for greatness" can always reestablish their self-esteem.

Classes produced by academic taxonomies are united by relations that are never purely logical. In the present case, the hierarchy observed in the universe of professorial virtues (that is, in the universe of ways of realizing academic excellence) closely corresponds to the hierarchy of possible careers (that is, to the hierarchy among educational institutions). Everything happens as if each agent were objectively situated by the position of his properties within this universe of hierarchized qualities that the teaching corps recognizes as its own by recognizing them in the best of its own. At the low end of the scale are the minimal qualities expected of every "educator of youth," the domestic virtues of being a good parent or spouse or the most elementary professorial virtues of devotion to one's students or professional integrity. At the other extreme stand the highest accomplishments, which deny the negative aspects of the more ordinary virtues without ever going so far as to negate their positive principles (a great philosopher is also praised for being a good father or for his dedication to the school).

Thus, in this final test, "departed comrades" find themselves classified as

they were classified throughout their lives, that is, through subtly hierarchized academic qualities that still bear a verifiable, yet invisible relationship
to social origin at this final point in the *cursus*. Upon the least well known,
the lesser provincial teachers, are conferred the elementary qualities of any
good teacher, usually associated with those of a good parent or spouse.
Next come the low-ranking intellectual qualities (earnestness, erudition,
integrity) or the superior qualities applied to inferior activities, such as
translations or critical editions, projects of a somewhat scholastic nature
that the educational institution, as everyone knows, only ever half recognizes. Beyond the minor virtues of the simple servants of culture lie the
eminent qualities of those who know how to demonstrate their excellence
by transgressing the limits of the academic definition of excellence. The final
homage that the group pays to the member who has realized its idea of
excellence, penned by one of his (academic) relations, consists in placing
him in that ethereal beyond of academic classifications for which academic
classifications always provide.

The following obituaries, taken from the 1962 ENS yearbook, will serve as examples of these three broad categories:
Paul Sucher, born in Versailles on January 10, 1886, son of shopkeeper, German
teacher in a provincial high school.
"Following his master's thesis on Hoffman, his numerous translations showed
the ease, the elegance, and the exactitude with which he could transpose a text, while
his long introductions always brought out the fundamental points of often confusing and controversial literary questions.
"(. . .) Sucher could have written an excellent dissertation in a short period of
time, one that would have gained him access to our universities, to the great joy of
his former teachers. I don't think he was held back by any difficulties (which were in
fact not so to him), or by the demands of erudite work, to which he would freely
and ably devote himself anyway. His inner life satisfied him: reading, meditation,
travel, long hikes, backpacking, bike trips, wide horizons conquered in the Alps by
the strength of his legs or his fingers gripping onto rocks, the peaceful home life that
he created in 1926 through his marriage to one of our colleagues in public school
teaching, all this was enough to fulfill and enrich his existence as he wished it"
(pp. 36–7, 38–9, 54–5).

Roger Pons, born in Equeurdreville on August 28, 1905, mother primary school
teacher, grandparents farmers, literature teacher in the *khâgne* of the Lycée Louis-
le-Grand.
"We must seek the explanation for his unique success in his ceaseless self-sacri-
fice. A great humanist, Roger Pons put himself at the service of texts and writers,
taking great pains, whether with Pascal or Diderot, Claudel or Gide, to help them be
understood and appreciated according to their own genius, without taking their
place or searching for faults – and all this in a climate of simplicity and openness. A
scrupulous judge of agrégation examinations and a General Inspector,[13] Roger Pons
remained forever a teacher, one who dedicated his experience and his scholarship to
the service of teaching and teachers. (. . .) Roger Pons wrote a great deal and, in the

least little note as in any well-developed essay, it was always with extreme care and attention to accuracy and the perfection of detail, and always in a lively, clear, moving style. And yet, this fine craftsman who ceaselessly created the useful and the usable for others, who was forever consumed by his occupation, his friends, and his duties, and betrayed in the end by destiny, has given us only samples, preliminaries, sketches of the great ethical and critical masterpiece he had within him. Academic asceticism and Christian humility combined (for virtue can by chance be cruel and destructive) to prevent him from revealing his most important and most original thoughts, which were implicit everywhere, but never freely expressed."

Maurice Merleau-Ponty, born in Rochefort-sur-Mer in 1908, son of artillery officer, member of the entrance examining committee for the École Normale Supérieure, professor of philosophy at the Collège de France.

"I can see him as he was then, with his reserved manner, his extremely attentive way of listening, his fitting responses, which had an aura of the enigmatic in the silences that surrounded them. There was something aristocratic about him, a distance that allowed deep relationships to develop. (. . .) Maurice Merleau-Ponty belonged to the race of great philosophers; in one way, he continued the work of Alain and Bergson, in another he was akin to J.-P. Sartre, and like him, he had been influenced by Husserl and Heidegger."

THE SPACE OF POSSIBLE VIRTUES

It is thus with reference to the structure of the space of possible virtues that lies before every *normalien* entering the teaching profession that the *social value* of the virtues attributed to each of them is defined. The space of possible positions (which, in the sample studied, extends from the modern language teacher in a provincial high school to the philosophy professor at the Collège de France[14]) likewise defines the limits of the space of possible trajectories that, given the initial lack of differentiation, is presented to all members of a particular cohort of *normaliens* and in relation to which the distinctive value of their individual trajectories is objectively defined, serving as the objective foundation of their subjective experience of success or failure. It follows that the virtues and careers indiscriminately praised in obituaries are the object of dual perception and judgment. Apprehended in and of themselves, the lesser virtues of the academic definition of excellence (through their minimal yet fundamental, that is, banal yet primordial, components) receive absolute and unconditional recognition, the absence of these qualities being enough to raise doubts about a person's membership in the group. Yet the truth of academic asceticism, making a virtue out of necessity, and of the thoroughly negative form of academic excellence that comes down to this asceticism can never be entirely forgotten. The simple, modest lives, filled with wisdom and inner sincerity, resignation and dignity, rectitude and devotion, of any of these ordinary teachers who cultivate their garden, go backpacking in the mountains, and care for their children cannot fail to be seen for what they are as soon as they are placed back into the field of possible trajectories.[15] The lesser virtues, as well as the average virtues, by this point more specific and less exclusively moral, such as teaching skills (clarity, methodical style) or the lesser intellectual virtues (erudition, rigor, and exactitude), are none other than mutilated forms of dominant properties and can only yield their full value in association with the dominant properties, these alone being capable of redeeming and saving the remaining vestiges of the labor and mediocre scholarship that the inferior and average virtues entail. Erudition is never worth its full weight unless it is "adorned with elegance" and the scholar is only truly recognized if she is not "trapped within her specialization." Gradually taking over in the obituaries as the superior virtues become more rare, moral virtues alone must be what enables one to accept the limits of the intellectual virtues in a universe that places the highest value on these virtues. Here again, the most cynical truth always cuts through the most enchanted praise; it is indeed significant that people generally associate the virtues of submissiveness, modesty, discretion, refusal of honors, and moral rectitude with the dominated qualities, virtues that enable a person to accept an inferior position without succumbing to the resentment normally associated with frustrated overinvestment. Obscure agents have for their part the entire complicity of a corps that honors the values of humility when, in a complete reversal, they attempt to transform their obscurity into a virtuous choice and thus to cast disrepute or suspicion on the necessarily ill-begotten prestige of overly lustrous glory.[16]

The resignation and wisdom praised by official memorialists find an objective foundation in the relative autonomy that the different teaching domains enjoy within their globally hierarchized field. Each subfield offers a particular form of achievement to the ambition that is implied in belonging to the class of *normaliens* in the form of a trajectory at least subjectively incomparable to any other and the resolutely distinct way of life that goes along with it: an *agrégé* in philosophy in a small provincial high school inspires respect in his less credentialed colleagues through the simplicity of his ways and the perfectly philosophical wisdom of his existence; a *khâgne* or *taupe* teacher bathes in the absolute admiration of successive generations of pretenders to the title of *normalien*, who are naturally led to include him in their worshipful representation of the school; and so forth and so on, at every level.

Here are two among a thousand possible illustrations: "On another day, dressed in work clothes, he was taking a truckload of fertilizer to Saint-André along a winding road. He stopped halfway up for a cigarette, and sat down to relax on a bench with a good view. A family of vacationers from the city came and sat nearby. The father pointed out to his children the beauty of the landscape and the countryside, and recited a verse of the *Georgics* in Latin. Rising, Passeron recited the next verses and then got back into his truck, leaving the vacationers speechless, full of admiration for those Niçois peasants who knew Virgil, and by heart no less!" (obituary of Jacques-Henri Passeron, *Annuaire ENS*, 1974, p. 120). "It was then that he learned that he had been outdistanced by a German who had rushed to publish his results (...). He was profoundly disappointed and quite distraught as a result of this discovery, and despite all the encouragement he received, he asked to return to secondary school teaching (...). At La Flèche as at the École Normale, he lived only for his loved ones, never drawing attention to himself. Although he remained outside public life, he was nevertheless very well known and highly esteemed throughout the city. He just knew how to lend a hand and always did so with the simplest touch (...). He stayed at La Flèche for thirty-five years until his retirement, extremely modest to the end, free of ambition, and never asking for anything for himself" (obituary of Paul Blassel, *Annuaire ENS*, 1962, p. 41).

Thus every *normalien*, to varying degrees, partakes of that universe of possible virtues to which *normaliens* quite naturally apply the adjective *normalien* ("*normalien* humor"). Everything that defines the position of this corps in social space is expressed in that unique combination of intellectual and moral virtues that the "elite" of the teaching corps both claim as their own and require themselves to possess. The dispositions that specifically characterize teachers, in contrast to "bourgeois" (who hold dominant positions) and "artists" (who hold temporally dominated positions in the dominated region of the field of power), follow from the position they occupy at the midpoint in the two hierarchies that structure the field of power – the hierarchy of political and economic power and the hierarchy of intellectual authority and prestige. Too "bourgeois" in the eyes of writers and artists, too "intellectual" in the eyes of the "bourgeoisie," teachers are only able to find compensation for their double half-failure in an aristocratic resignation or in the satisfactions associated with the domestic life favored by their living conditions, by the dispositions linked to their social trajectory, and by their correlative marriage strategies. Through their domestic virtues, through the aristocratic asceticism that forms the basis of their lifestyle and offers them a last chance for self-esteem when all other principles of legitimation have disappeared, as well as through their faithfulness to the world and its glories, witnessed by the spirit of "public service" and "devotion" (often consecrated by decorations) that leads them to careers in public administration, teachers have more in common with higher public servants than with the intellectuals and artists whose religious worship they perform.

One of the most notable properties of the teaching corps is its high rate of endogamy. Research done in 1964 on the matrimonial strategies of six classes of humanities *normaliens* (1948–1953; 155 respondents, or 83 percent of the total) shows that 85 percent were married, 59 percent of these were married to a teacher, 58 percent of those who married teachers married an *agrégée*, and 49 percent of those who married an *agrégée* married a *sévrienne*[17] (as for the rest, their wives either held positions in the intellectual (6 percent) or liberal professions (4 percent) or mid-level management (2 percent), or were not in the workforce at the time of the survey (28 percent)). We cannot overestimate the degree to which this type of matrimonial strategy contributes to the hermetic nature of the teacher's overprotected universe. A comparison of academics with artists brings to light the first group's more "bourgeois", more "ordered" ways. Looking at a sample of professors and artists or writers featured in *Who's Who in France* (1969–70 edition), we see that a very low percentage of the academics are single (0.9 percent), a rate much lower at least than that of the writers and artists featured in *Who's Who* (who, although probably not representative of the most "independent" portion of the category, include 16.6 percent singles); we also find a very low rate of divorce (0.9 percent compared to 10.7 percent) and a much higher average number of children (2.39 compared to 1.56). Finally, a high percentage of decorations among the academics points to their high degree of integration into the social order (65.1 percent have the Légion d'Honneur, compared to 39.2 percent of the writers).

The dual truth of this corps, which could not itself achieve the merits that it recognizes and celebrates in writers and artists without sacrificing the ones that correspond to its true function, can be read in the highly ambiguous comment once made by the head of the University of Lille about the novelist Jules Romains, then a young high school philosophy teacher: "an educated and original thinker, perhaps a bit distracted by his literary ambitions, which are, all the same, quite justified."[18] The only ones who have any chance of overcoming the contradiction inherent in the very definition of their role, reproduced by the social characteristics of the corps, are those who achieve the proclaimed ideal of intellectual excellence outside the university field (or, at the very least, in the "free domains" within it, such as the Collège de France). Thus, more so even than in the dual intellectual and temporal renunciation imposed upon the lower echelons of the teaching corps by their subordinate position in a temporally dominated universe, it is in the temporal semiconsecration of the intermediate echelons of this body that the truth of professorial asceticism and disdain for honors (a symbolic reversal of their dispossession) is revealed or betrayed. Either, along with those who achieve the intellectual ideal within the limits of the university, these teachers accede to a form of intellectual glory that remains inferior from the point of view of the very criteria they recognize, or, along with those who seize and adapt to the forms of power available in this universe of powerlessness (deans, presidents, etc.) – and these are often the very same people – they recognize the twofold ambition inscribed in this double half-success.

Professorial schemata of perception and appreciation also function as generative schemata that structure their entire practice, particularly the production of that particular category of cultural products consisting of strictly academic works: courses, textbooks, and doctoral dissertations. The dispositions constitutive of *academica mediocritas*, that cult of the virtues of moderation and poise in things intellectual that implies the rejection of all forms of excess, even in matters of invention and originality, are no doubt inscribed in the intermediate position (of double negation) that the academic occupies between the artist and the bourgeois. We indeed find the equivalent, in the realm of the intellectual virtues, of the contradictions observed in the realm of the moral virtues. So, for example, the contradiction between requiring originality and requiring knowledge and eclecticism, in the tradition of the Summa Theologica, is inscribed in the very objectives of an enterprise of cultural production that, given that it is subordinate to the demands of reproduction, is always part simple reproduction. The role of pure reproduction becomes increasingly weak, and, most importantly, better disguised, as we move from the inferior forms, courses and textbooks, to the superior forms, such as doctoral dissertations and written syntheses (often based on lecture courses), encountering those exemplary instruments of the power of academic canonization – encyclopedias, dictionaries, etc. – along the way.

Our obituary analysis finds no secondary school teachers who have produced written works (with the exception of one person, who has translations to his credit). The production of *khâgne* and *taupe* teachers consists nearly exclusively of textbooks and other various educational works. "These well-developed and clearly written books are accurate summaries that serve as excellent student tools" (obituary of Guillaume Rumeau, *taupe* physics teacher, *Annuaire ENS*, 1962). As for the output of the higher civil servants of the Ministry of Education – general inspectors and university heads – we could borrow the very language used to characterize the work of Dean Hardy: "But Hardy's grand project, from the moment he arrived in Dakar, was to provide the textbooks and other written materials necessary for setting up the various curricula. Hardy provided the example, opened doors, started book series. He published educational books that range from textbooks and didactic treatises to provisional syntheses" (*Annuaire ENS*, 1965, p. 38). Most of the university professors have produced dissertations and works of synthesis ("A true feat of brilliant synthesis supported by vast and unassuming scholarship," obituary of Aurélien Digeon, *Annuaire ENS*, 1963, p. 58); only exceptionally do we find novels or "original" essays, written with "wit," "subtlety," "charm," or "lucidity." It is only in connection with professors at the Collège de France that we find the words "work" [*oeuvre*] or "great work" used in the sense intended by intellectuals.

The schemata of perception and appreciation unearthed in our sociological analysis of the obituaries also enter into academic readings of Epicurus and Spinoza, Racine and Flaubert, Hegel and Marx. The works whose preservation and consecration are entrusted to the educational system are thus continually reproduced at the cost of a distortion that is all the greater the further removed are the schemata that engendered the works from those applied to them by their *qualified interpreters*, convinced that they can do no greater thing than to read them through "spectacles tinted with their whole outlook," as Weber would say, and to recreate them thereby in their own image. These generic dispositions are in fact specified by the position occupied by each reader in the academic field. How, for example, could we not see what the most common reading of classical texts (O, Epicurean garden!) may owe to the properties of provincial gardeners, and what the ordinary or extraordinary interpretation of Heidegger may owe to that aristocratic asceticism that runs along forest paths or mountain roads, fleeing from weak and common crowds or their concrete *analogon*, the forever renewed (poor) students who must ceaselessly be torn away from "mundane" concerns and "trivial" curiosities?

The same system of classificatory schemata thus functions continuously throughout the academic *cursus* – that strange racecourse in which everyone classifies and everyone is classified, and where the best classified become the best classifiers of those who will next enter the race. This holds from the Concours Général to the École Normale entrance examination and the agrégation, from the agrégation to the doctorate, from the doctorate to the Sorbonne, and from the Sorbonne to the Institut de France,[19] the end of a race in which the best classified of any *concours* have *de facto* control over all operations of classification by controlling access to the classification authority of the next level down, which in turn controls the following one, and so forth. The external regulation that is imposed through this hierarchy of authority – the academic concerned about improving her rank being obliged to appear respectful of the current classifications, in what she produces as much as in her academic practice – only reinforces the effects of the spontaneously adjusted and consistent dispositions that were selected and inculcated through all the previous operations of classification. For the "true" academic, the judgment of the university is the last judgment.

We thus see how the educational institution, with no explicit instructions and, most of the time, even contrary to the intentions both of the agents who assign it its objectives and of most of those who are supposed to realize them, is able to function like an immense cognitive machine, operating classifications that, although apparently completely neutral, reproduce pre-existing social classifications. Yet we should not be misled by the metaphor of the machine, however useful it may be in highlighting the overall workings of the institution, which are normally hidden from view. The very model of a classification machine proposed above in the diagrams illustrating the logic of the transformation of social classifications into academic classifications and academic classifications into social classifications places instruments (the classes of adjectives) and acts (the evaluations) of cognition at the very center of the mechanism. The cognitive function fulfilled by the educational institution through its capacity to know and recognize the most socially endowed as academically talented is achieved through innumerable cognitive acts that, although performed under the illusion of singularity and the conviction of neutrality, are objectively orchestrated and objectively subordinated to the imperatives of the reproduction of social structures because they implement at the level of practice categories of perception and appreciation that are the transformed product of the incorporation of these structures.

We are as far removed – need it be said? – from the so-called "structuralist" view that, conferring a sort of self-sufficient dynamic upon the "dominant ideology" and the "state ideological apparatuses," sees agents as being off on vacation and hence offside in the game in and through which structures are reproduced or transformed, as we are from the so-called "individualist" view that reintroduces agents into the picture, but agents who are reduced to the pure and interchangeable intentions of calculators without a history. What is being missed in both cases is the true logic of practices that are defined in the relationship between habitus (socially structured biological individualities) and objective structures inherited from history, an exemplary realization of which can be seen in the daily acts of classification performed by teachers. To account for this logic, we must apply to magisterial judgments the relational or structuralist mode of thought used by ethnologists in reference to kinship terminology and plant, animal, and disease classifications, without at the same time accepting the philosophy of action most often invested in the study of these exotic *curiosa*. It is clear that the taxonomies implemented in academic evaluation or artistic judgment are able to wield their structuring power only because they are themselves structured. But, while it is true that we cannot understand the meaning or function of a classificatory opposition or a pair of adjectives outside the system into which they have been placed, this does not mean that they are justiciable to a strictly internal analysis that would remove them from their practical conditions of use. We must accept, without the least contradiction, both that practices always include acts of reality construction that engage complex cognitive structures, and that this cognitive activity bears no relation to a self-conscious intellectual operation. Practical knowledge implements generative schemata that organize perception and structure practice through reference to practical functions. As products of the practice of successive generations, these schemata, acquired in and through practice and implemented at a practical level, without ever acceding to explicit representation, function like operators of transformations, operators through which the objective structures of which they are the product acquire an effective existence and concretely tend to be reproduced or transformed.

Appendix 1

The Social Origins of Concours Général Prizewinners (1966–1986)

Our survey, which was repeated at regular intervals, and for the most part according to identical procedures (although from 1968 on, we only have abbreviated questionnaires), reveals that the structure of the distribution of prizewinners according to social origin, whether measured according to father's or mother's occupation, has remained largely stable. Contrary to received wisdom about "democratization," we even observe a slight increase (also noted at the level of the "elite" channels) in the proportion of the social categories that were already the most highly represented in the initial years of the study. The prizewinners whose fathers are teachers represent 24 percent of the total in 1986, compared to 15 percent in 1966, and those whose fathers are executives represent 40.5 percent in 1986, compared to 27 percent in 1966 (an analogous tendency is seen for the mothers: the prizewinners whose mothers are teachers represent 29 percent of the total in 1986, compared to 12 percent in 1966).

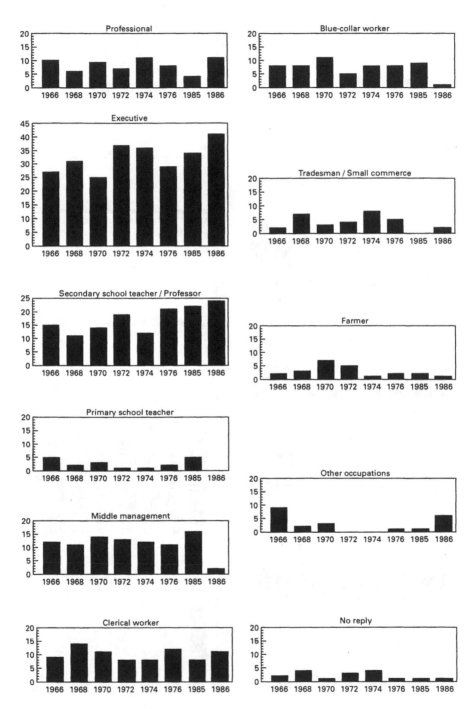

Social origins of prizewinners according to father's occupation

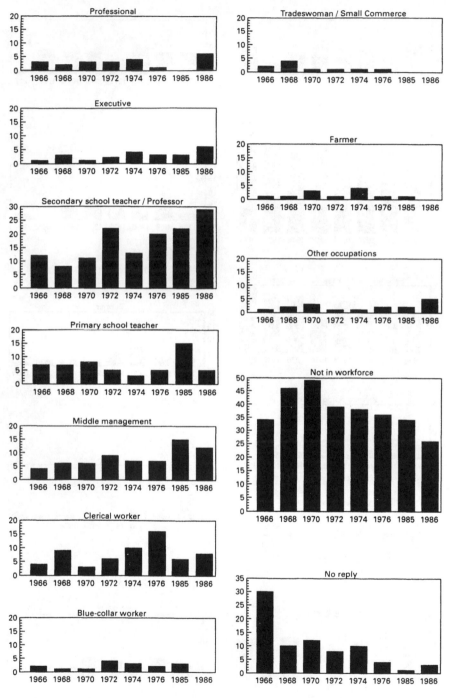

Social origins of prizewinners according to mother's occupation

Appendix 2

Election and Overselection

Our analysis of the social and academic characteristics of Concours Général prizewinners reveals that the selection of this population obeys the general law governing procedures of selection and elimination, that is, that the social composition of any academic category will directly depend on the rigor of the selection that has produced it. An academic population will grant a proportionally greater place to the most privileged the higher its level in the *cursus* or, at any given level, the higher the position it occupies in the academic hierarchy of establishments, disciplines, and tracks. Thus, a systematic set of social advantages distinguishes the population of prizewinners from that of the *terminale* classes from which it has been handpicked through a two-part selection process, the first selection being made by the secondary schools as they designate their best students for the *concours*, and the second by the examining committee as it selects among its candidates. The prizewinners are younger (50 percent were under 17 in the *première* class or under 18 in the *terminale* class, compared to 32 percent for all students in the same classes);[1] they more often come from lycées in the Paris area (at 35.5 percent, compared to 20 percent for all lycée students) and are more often enrolled in a lycée in the *sixième*[2] (at 80.5 percent, compared to 27 percent of all students enrolled in the *sixième* in 1962–3, that is, at the time when the prizewinners were in this class); they also belong to more privileged milieus, both in social status (61 percent belong to the well-to-do classes, compared to only 17 percent of all students in the *seconde* classes, or 31.5 percent of the total pool of students) and cultural capital (the fathers of 47 percent have post-baccalauréat degrees, compared to 3 percent of the total workforce; the mothers of 23.5 percent have post-baccalauréat degrees, compared to 1.1 percent of the total workforce). The proportion of prizewinners originating in the upper classes (61 percent) is distinctly higher than that of university students and, in contrast, very close to that of students in the preparatory classes (62.5 percent for *khâgnes* and 57.5 percent for *taupes*) and the grandes écoles.[3]

We know that secondary school (or university) students originating in a given category have fewer and fewer of the demographic, social, and academic characteristics of that category taken as a whole (and conversely, more of the characteristics that are *exceptional* for that category) the less likely that category is to be represented (precisely because it has a greater degree and/or a greater number of the characteristics that determine academic elimination). This is increasingly the case at higher levels of the *cursus* and, at any given level, when the students occupy a higher rank in the academic hierarchy of establishments, disciplines, and tracks. Although gaps in general statistics prevent a systematic comparison of the social and academic characteristics of Concours Général prizewinners from different social classes with the characteristics of the corresponding social categories of *terminale* classes as a whole, we do have an entire set of indices that, owing to their convergence, warrant the conclusion that, in this case yet again, the law is verified. Thus sons and daughters of blue-collar workers, who constitute 5 and 9 percent of the prizewinners respectively, come from families that seem to be set apart as a group by their relatively high level of education.[4] Only 8.5 percent of the fathers of prizewinners from the blue-collar sector do not have some kind of diploma and 19 percent have the BEPC,[5] while the corresponding numbers in the workforce overall are 58 percent and 2 percent. The blue-collar prizewinners show the lowest rate of repetition of grades (5 percent, compared to 19 percent of all candidates) and, from the very beginning of their schooling, have skipped grades at a relatively high rate (23 percent, a rate more or less equivalent to that of the average of all the candidates, at 24 percent), a privilege normally granted only to students from the upper classes.[6] Likewise, in addition to coming from relatively small families (1.8 children on average, compared to 3.33 for farmers in general and 2.85 for all prizewinners), sons of farmers often enter a lycée in the *sixième* (46 per cent, compared to 16.5 percent and 11 percent for all farmers and farmworkers) and are often attending a Parisian lycée at the time of the Concours (23 percent).[7]

All of the sons of mid-level managers and primary school teachers enter the lycée in the *sixième*. They hear of the Concours Général very early (before the *troisième* in 36.5 percent and 40 percent of the cases, respectively, compared to 27.5 percent for all prizewinners) and attend lycées that have had prizewinners in previous years at the same rate as the sons of executives or professionals (65 percent and 61 percent, respectively).

We observe likewise that the girls, who have a markedly lower chance of figuring among the prizewinners (as they constitute only 32.5 percent of nominations to the Concours even though they make up 48 percent of *terminale* classes), are endowed with more favorable characteristics than the boys: 67 percent come from the upper classes, compared to 58 percent of the boys; for 79.5 percent, their father has a diploma beyond the BEPC, compared to 66 percent for the boys; their mothers have received a postsecondary diploma as often as the mothers of the boys, but they are more likely to have the BEPC and the baccalauréat (40 percent, compared to 25.5 percent), and to be primary or secondary school teachers (26 percent, compared to 9 percent); finally, the girls come from large families in which postsecondary education is more frequent (the average number of people in their family who have gone on to higher education is 2.9 percent, compared to 2.5 percent for the boys). In addition, they have for the most part had a more rapid school career than the boys: 26 percent have skipped a grade after the *sixième*, compared to 19.5 percent of the boys; only 21 percent have stayed back, compared to 27 percent of the boys. For our comparison to be perfectly rigorous, however, it should take into account the fact that the girls, who in the humanities are younger than the boys (69 percent are under 17 in the *première* and under 18 in the *terminale*, compared to 29.5 percent of the boys), experience their greatest success in languages (where they represent 73 percent of the prizewinners), disciplines that are low in the academic hierarchy, as well as the fact that, with the exception of the natural sciences (where they represent 13.5 percent of the prizewinners), girls are completely shut out of the scientific disciplines. It follows that all the empirical relations concerning the population of prizewinners as a whole tend to underestimate the compensatory advantages from which girls must benefit in order to accede to the same rank as boys.

In a similar vein, we also see that success in mathematics or physics, which is less frequent (there are half as many prizewinners in these subjects as in the humanities) and indeed accessible only by students in *mathématiques élémentaires* [advanced mathematics level] (only 21.5 percent of *terminale* students, and therefore relatively overselected) – in contrast to students in philosophy and especially the applied sciences (38.5 percent and 31.5 percent of *terminale* students, respectively), who are often led to these studies by a negative vocation – assumes the possession of greater capital than success in the humanities. Exclusively male, markedly younger (77.5 percent of the mathematics prizewinners were under 17 in the *première*, or under 18 in the *terminale*, compared to 50 percent of the prizewinners in French), and more likely to have been educated in one of the greater prizewinner-producing schools (80.5 percent of the mathematics prizewinners and 82.5 percent of the physics prizewinners graduate from high schools that have produced prizewinners in preceding years, compared to 50 percent of the prizewinners in French or philosophy), the prizewinners in mathematics and physics come from families with social and cultural advantages (73 percent are from the upper classes, compared to 66.5 percent and 57 percent of the prizewinners in French and philosophy; 65 percent of their fathers have a post-baccalauréat degree, compared to 58.5 percent and 47.5 percent for the prizewinners in philosophy and French).[8]

Once again one merely has to apply the general rule in order to see that the younger the prizewinners are (that is, the less time it has taken them to reach a given level of success), the greater number of category-exceptional characteristics they display (for those from disadvantaged categories, this means displaying a greater degree of compensatory advantages).[9]

Thus, as we approach the younger age levels, we see an increase in the proportion of prizewinners from relatively small families with social and educational advantages – as can be seen from the variation in the indices of level of parents' education, or again, from the variation in the number of teachers among the fathers or from the age at which the students make their first visit to a museum. The most precocious are privileged not only socially, but also academically; proportionally more of them have followed the noblest route from the *sixième* on, attending a lycée in the Paris area, and they are the best informed about school-related matters. This precocity, which, as we have seen, emerges very early – two-thirds of the prizewinners could read and count prior to primary school – and never wanes throughout their schooling, will find its consecration in the grandes écoles, which are able to ensure lasting precocity to those who have made it that far by immediately placing them on a *social trajectory* that will lead them in every case either more quickly to the same point, or, if they prefer, farther and higher in the same amount of time.

Appendix 3

Prominent Themes from Two Prizewinning Essays

The two essays (E1 and E2) analyzed here were published in the literary supplement to *Le Monde*, June 21, 1969. The subject was the following: " 'Because literary creation can only reach its full accomplishment in reading, because the artist must entrust the completion of what he has begun to another, because it is through the consciousness of the reader alone that the artist can perceive himself as essential to his work, any literary work is an appeal. (. . .) The writer appeals to the freedom of the reader to collaborate in the production of his work. (. . .) The work of art has value because it is an appeal,' wrote J.-P. Sartre in 1948. And in 1953 the literary critic G. Picon provided a sort of echo to Sartre in stating, 'Every work calls for a value judgment, and we feel frustrated by the critic who does not respond to this appeal.' Does your personal experience as a reader accord with the statements made by this writer and this critic on the subject of the relationship between a literary work and its readership?"

CREATION

"There is something like a phenomenon of *'spontaneous creation'*" (E1). "It is 'another self' that writes the work" (E1); "The work leads one's hand" (E1).

MYSTERY

"The *mystery* of the artistic gift" (E1); "Magical power [of words]" (E1); "The *mystery* of its beauty" (E1); "The *mystery* of reading" (E1).

SPIRITUAL IDENTIFICATION

"*I am* beside the blue waters, *I* meet this gaze" (E1); "This work that we *ourselves have created*" (E2); "*I* encounter *myself*" (E2); "*I* am writing" (E2); "Finding myself amazingly *me*" (E1). "The work becomes *my own creation*" (E2); "The role of the reader cannot be reduced to one of *passivity*" (E1) "I can participate in the literary *creation*" (E2); "The character I mean to *create*" (E2).

SPIRITUALISTIC SUBJECTIVISM

"So many *different interpretations* of one character, one gesture, one sentence!" (E1); "And *for each reader*, the novel's characters and sentiments will take on a particular *meaning*" (E1); ". . . moves me" (E1). "*Can one judge . . .?*" (E2); ". . . is *for me*" (E2); ". . . remains *for me*" (E2); "The literary work opens up *echoes in me* of *impressions and sensations"* (E2); "So that we may interpret them in *our own fashion, according to our own sensitivity"* (E1); "We can understand a literary work, explicate it, and most importantly, *feel it"* (E2). The subjectivism of partialities naturally goes along with a rejection of all approaches that might appear "reductive": "It is always dangerous to apply criteria to a work as you would an *industrial product"* (E2); "Does a literary work come down to a single character?" (E2); "A literary work represents *much more than all that"* (E2).

For those who would doubt the validity of this analysis and of the representative nature of the documents upon which it is based, we will simply quote passages from reports from the literature and grammar agrégation and the École Normale Supérieure entrance *concours* that "define" the principles of the interpretation of literary texts, hoping to show in this way that there is a striking similarity in the explicit precepts of the teaching of "explication de texte" and the language used in the essays of students who have been well trained in "creative" reading. So, for example, on the theme of "sensitivity" alone: "Two essays showed evidence of a *refined literary sense"* (literature agrégation, men, 1959). "Here we find a surprising lack of literary *sensitivity"* (literature agrégation, men, 1962). "It was absolutely necessary to demonstrate *musical and poetic sensitivity"*; "*Sensitivity* is imperative – a *fresh* sensitivity, perhaps a bit *naive*, that *refuses to seek the secret* of a poem in the deep corners of a wise saying the origins of which are unclear, besides . . ., a sensitivity that reacts to the *moving intimism* of the 'kind-hearted servant girl' [reference to Flaubert, Tr.] with *simplicity*, a *sensitivity* refined by the memory of *love"*; "We immediately pick out important terms, *original* strains, dense passages that *pulsate* with an *inner life* or with a deeply *felt* albeit perhaps latent intent"; "The *freshness of mind* of an initial contact may have an advantage over cumbersome knowledge . . . Why gracelessly mention Nerval's madness when one is treated to a tender and amusing passage from *Sylvie*?" (entrance *concours* to the École Normale Supérieure, Ulm, French explication de texte, 1966). "Once the hemistich has been put back into its context, let us allow it to *resonate within us . . . Poetic exorcism* has not destroyed *anguish*, and we *feel* the final line of the poem in *our flesh and in our soul, like an open wound"* (grammar agrégation, women, 1959). "When the candidate comes to these *magical lines . . .* We would like to advise the candidates to stop and *dream* a while about the subject . . ." (literature agrégation, men, 1959).

EGOTISM

"It is in this *self-reading*, this *outpouring* of our *personality*, that the novel becomes complete" (E1).

ROMANTIC MYSTICISM

"So I *escape"* (E2); "*This dream* is for me full of . . ." (E2); "The fugitive sensations that make up *the imaginary and supernatural* qualities of my daily existence" (E2); "The *enchanted* domain" (E2); "*Mysterious* shadow" (E2); "*Magical* power of [of words] (E1); "This work that we ourselves have created in transferring *our dreams and imaginings* into it" (E2); "*Strange and sometimes fantastic*" (E2); "The work is a reality that at times *defies the laws of logic*" (E2).

EXISTENTIAL PATHOS

"All the dreams that ceaselessly *torment me and tear me apart*" (E2); "*Tireless quest*" (E2); "The *desperately useless* railroad . . ." (E2); "A man's *cry of anguish*" (E2); "*Heartbreak*" (E2); "*Uncertainty*" (E2).

Appendix 4

A Sketch of Four Prizewinners

Sketch of four prizewinners in different disciplines

	Accessit *French*	Accessit *Translation*	Accessit *Geography*	Accessit *Natural sciences*
Occupation and residence of father	Head of the Paris office of the American Stock Exchange	Electrical engineer, Lille	Salesman, Autun	Deli tradesman, Chartres
Reasons for success	Originality of novel chosen. Style, perhaps?	Accurate translation	. . . my work was about average, no more. I probably didn't put enough soul into it, not being sufficiently fond of geography, and I have to admit that there were a lot of things I didn't know . . . Given these circumstances, my work must only have stood out through its tone, treating the subject from above, never getting bogged down in minor details (and with good reason!), a smooth read, no facts or figures interrupting its flow	Restraint. Clarity
Preparation for *concours*	None. Heavy reading but independent of Concours Général	Nothing in Latin	No. I do do reading beyond the syllabus, but only rarely in geography. I usually stick to history and French	Yes. Natural science texts

Desired occupation(s) and reasons for choice	Writer, judge in juvenile court, painter: independence and relative solitude	Teacher, journalist, diplomat: they allow you numerous and varied relationships with society	Bit of a silly confession: I would have liked to write. Seeing that I couldn't base my life on this most vain hope, I decided to prepare for a career in Water and Forestry Management so that I could be close to the nature that I so love. This profession unfortunately being closed to me by its very scientific nature, only teaching is left open. I therefore expect I'll be a history teacher, in a preparatory class or at a university, if possible	Researcher, teacher of natural sciences, vet (possible): I like anatomy, the study of animals
Favorite writers	Garcia Lorca, Baudelaire, Rimbaud, Lautréamont, St John Perse, Pascal, Montaigne, Cendrars, Breton, Durrell, Kafka, Queneau, Mallarmé, Claudel, Shakespeare, the Bible, Dostoevsky, Gogol, Bosquet, Apollinaire, Michaux, Vian	Camus, Hemingway, Flaubert	Once again the question is tricky. It's obvious that each writer has a contribution to make. But you are asking me to choose (...): Rousseau, then Vigny, and in another line of thought, Valéry and Gide	NR

Table continued overleaf

Sketch of four prizewinners in different disciplines – *continued*

	Accessit *French*	Accessit *Translation*	Accessit *Geography*	Accessit *Natural sciences*
Favorite painters	Goya, Bosch, Van Gogh, Chagall, Modigliani, Picasso (drawings), Vieira da Silva, Dubuffet, Matta, Tapies	Delacroix, Rembrandt, Renoir	The list is long, and not surprisingly includes painters from different schools, there is good in all: Cézanne, Van Gogh, Manet, Monet, Degas, Gauguin, Braque, Toulouse-Lautrec, Daumier, Pissaro, Renoir, for French; El Greco, Goya, Velasquez for Spanish; Titian, Veronese, Correggio, da Vinci for Italian, and for the Flemish, the Brueghels, Rembrandt, and Rubens	Picasso, Van Goht (*sic*)
Attend concerts	5 or 6 times. Bayreuth (3 evenings in a row)	Never	I haven't gone to any concerts	Once this year
Visit museums	Every Saturday, special exhibits and the Louvre, Orangerie, etc. Once to the Musée de l'Homme	Fine Arts, Lille. Van Gogh exhibition	I've never been able to visit an important museum or see a major exhibit. Everything happens in Paris or the big cities. It's not very interesting to say that I've been to the Autun Museum and every other museum in the area, generally quite poor. I've been to a few minor painting exhibits, but never to a big show	Museum of Modern Art, Palais de la Découverte [science]. Museum of Natural History

Attend cinema	Between once a week and once a month	Once a trimester	We have one showing per week at school, the films are generally what you might call duds	Once a trimester
Read newspapers and magazines	Regularly: *Art in America, L'Express, Réalités, Le Figaro Littéraire, Candide, L'Oeil, Iris, Tintin, Spirou, Mad, Le Canard Enchaîné.* Sometimes: *Match, Elle*	*Paris Match, L'Express.* Sometimes: *Le Monde, Historia*	Of course I read magazines and newspapers, such as *Le Monde, Janus, Miroir de l'Histoire, Historia, Paris-Match, Les Nouvelles Littéraires* (…). I have looked through others on occasion (*Transmondia, La Revue Universitaire*)	Regularly: *Le Monde.* Sometimes: *Science et Vie, Chasseur Français*
Closest school of thought	Existentialism	I'm waiting to take philosophy to decide	I think it's somewhat premature when one is not yet sufficiently informed or mature, and when the discovery of philosophy still awaits, to place oneself within a school of thought	Romanticism
Last vacation	Greece, with school friends. Went to Peloponnesus, the Greek islands, stop in Turkey	With German friends. Germany: birthplace of Schiller, Jaxthausen, Ludwigsburg, Stuttgart, Tübingen	I usually spend my vacations alone, which is how I like it, although I do stay with my family at X … There we have the magnificent forest of X …, a true Rousseauistic retreat	NR

Table continued overleaf

Sketch of four prizewinners in different disciplines – *continued*

	Accessit French	Accessit Translation	Accessit Geography	Accessit Natural sciences
Foreign countries visited	Switzerland (1952–1966). England (64, 65, 66). Greece (67). Austria (65). Italy (67). Spain, Sardinia, Belgium	West Germany (1961–1967). East Germany (65). Austria, Switzerland (1964)	I've not yet had the pleasure of visiting a foreign country, despite my great desire to do so. I make up for it by trying to get to know France better	Belgium (65)
Most important contemporary poets	Alain Bosquet, St John Perse, P. Emmanuel, H. Michaux	Apollinaire, Claudel, Prévert	NR	Brassens
Most important playwrights	Ionesco, Beckett, Pinter, Obaldia, Cocteau	Giradoux, Anouilh, T. Williams	NR	NR
Cultural activities: plays attended this school year	*Le retour. Les girafes. Un jour j'ai rencontré la vérité. Becket. L'été. L'idiot. La cuisine. Cripure. Le roi Lear. Les chaises. Oh! Les beaux jours. Le roi se meurt. La prochaine fois je vous le chanterai. Témoignage irrecevable. Se trouver*	*Marie Stuart*	I've already said that this lycée doesn't make cultural activities available, so you shouldn't be surprised by my poor knowledge in these different areas. I have managed to see three plays this year: *Phèdre, Huis-clos,* and *Cinna.* Also, because I live in the country, far from any important cultural center, it's hard for me to make up for this lack even on vacation	*L'agression. Le Revizor*

Artwork	Outside lycée, yes: painting and drawing	No	I'm satisfied with my solitude and with nature, but can this be considered an avocation? Well, let's say photography, then	No
Opinion on jazz	Yes [I like it]. I don't know very much about it, but it's as beautiful as classical music and it has perhaps even more life in it	Yes [I like it]. No [I can't say why]	I can't give a meaningful judgment on jazz, since I'm not very familiar with it; let's just say that it is the rare piece that moves me, and few draw me in	No [I don't like it]
Sports	Riding, tennis, classical dance, skiing, swimming in sports clubs	Swimming	I have to put up with the sport imposed on me by my school. And I do mean "put up with," too, since I have little taste for it, or ability either, for that matter. It's true that it's partly because I'm forced into it that I reject it	Soccer, basketball at the École Normale d'Instituteurs
Radio	Sometimes. France-Musique and France-Culture. My favorite programs: "The Violin and Violinists" [preconcert talk]	Often: Europe no. 1. France-Inter. Sometimes: France-Culture	Of course I listen to the radio, especially programs on France-Culture and France-Musique, the only enriching ones there are. Barring this, I fall back on France-Inter (...) I wish we were more often treated to theater or literary discussions; even so, these stations are excellent cultural instruments	Often. RTL. Europe no. 1. France-Inter. BBC. Favorite programs: variety shows, game shows

Part II

The Ordination

"If God gives someone an office, he also gives him the necessary brains" is an old joke that no one would take very seriously these days.

Hegel's Philosophy of Right

1

The Production of a Nobility

The common representation of pedagogic action, which reduces it to its technical function, is so powerfully asserted that it is difficult to cast doubt on it in the very cases where the facts most strongly argue against it. This applies, for example, in cases where the skills most clearly of use in a given professional position are acquired solely on the job, while the greater part of the skills one actually possesses, or that are officially guaranteed by one's title[1] (such as mastery of classical Greek or descriptive geometry), are never used. And what can be said in response to our observation that the higher the social return of the titles supposedly guaranteeing technical skills, the less are these school-acquired skills used in professional practice, or in any case, the shorter is the period of time over which they are used, the best indicator of the social success of a *polytechnicien* undoubtedly being the more or less precocious age at which he escapes from the purely technical duties required of an engineer or a researcher to accede to a position of authority? But the most troubling case along these lines involves institutions like English public schools, Sciences-po, and the ENA, whose recruitment procedures are so obviously designed to guarantee them students already endowed, through their background, with the dispositions they require that we have to wonder whether, as the Romans used to say, they aren't merely "teaching fish to swim."

At the risk of seeming to be overdoing it, and of giving cautious minds the opportunity for restrained and moderated appraisals, we must "turn the tables" and, contrary to the dominant representation that is only interested in the technical consequences of pedagogic action, ask whether any pedagogic action meant to prepare students to hold dominant positions is not in part – even in its most specifically technical dimension – an act of consecration, a *rite of institution* aimed at producing a separate, sacred group; whether, in other words, the technical function of elite schools does not effectively disguise their social function as agents of ritual exclusion, or give a seemingly rational justification to the ceremonies of consecration through which societies claiming to be rational produce their nobility.[2]

To answer these questions, we have chosen an object that raises them through its very existence – the preparatory classes for the grandes écoles – an object that is contextualized and dated and thus suitable for empirical observation and analysis, but which must be treated as a particular case of the entire universe of "elite schools," institutions entrusted with the education and consecration of those who are called to enter the field of power – in which most of them have their origins. We can thus immerse ourselves in the particular features of a particular institution in order to grasp, in the most complete and concrete way possible, both the invariant and the variable aspects of its effects and of the mechanisms through which it produces them.

But it would also be necessary – and this would be the task of a genuine enterprise of comparative history – to explore the universe of all the possible forms of "elite schools," of which the schools studied herein represent only one particular case. Having brought to light the logic behind the initiation rites (based on retreat and ascesis) that characterize elite schools as a whole, for example, we could then proceed to systematically examine cross-cultural variations in the form and nature of the prescribed rites, which can be based on virtually any activity in producing distinction (classical languages, cricket, soccer, martial arts, etc.). It would furthermore be necessary to seek the principle behind these variations in the particular aspects of the structure of the field of power that characterize the different national traditions and to try to link the cult of team sports in English public schools during the Victorian era, for instance, not only, as people ordinarily do, to the anti-intellectualism that is a further result of the same causes (a phenomenon observed in other aristocracies as well, such as in Japan), but also, more directly, to the dispositions of an imperial elite founded on the military values of loyalty and submission to the interests of the group. More specifically, it would be necessary to ask if the essence of the entirely practical work of the legitimation of power and, more broadly, of sociodicy (the justification of society), which dominants always and everywhere demand of the educational institutions to which they entrust their heirs, does not vary, in its definition, according to the form of power or type of capital that makes domination in the field of power possible at any given time.

The research on preparatory class students was conducted in 1968 with Yvette Delsaut and Monique de Saint Martin. The survey questionnaire was distributed in March of that year in the *khâgne* classes of the Lycées Condorcet, Fénelon, Louis-le-Grand, and Molière in Paris, Kérichen in Brest, Blaise-Pascal in Clermont-Ferrand, Faidherbe in Lille, du Parc in Lyons, and Pierre-de-Fermat in Toulouse (with 330 responses) and in the A, Á, and B [various math and science divisions] *taupe* classes of the Lycées Honoré-de-Balzac, Condorcet, Louis-le-Grand, and Saint-Louis in Paris, Pasteur in Neuilly-sur-Seine, Blaise-Pascal in Clermont-Ferrand, Faidherbe in Lille, du Parc in Lyons, Pierre-de-Fermat in Toulouse, and at the Ecole Saint-Geneviève in Versailles (with 881 responses). We chose to construct the sample so that it would be representative of the population of "integrable" students. This meant that rather than weighting the individual preparatory classes according to the ratio of their students to the total number of preparatory class students, we weighted them according to the proportion of their students who got into a top grande école out of the total number of students admitted to these schools. Thus the Parisian *khâgne* students, who make up 60.5 percent of the acceptances to ENS Ulm and ENS Sèvres (humanities) in 1967, represent 58.5 percent of the students in the sample (but only 52 percent of students enrolled in *khâgne* classes in 1967–8); and the top Paris lycées, Louis-le-Grand, Henri-IV, and Fénelon, which provide 49.5 percent of the acceptances to Ulm and Sèvres (humanities) in 1967, represent 48 percent of the sample (but only 31 percent of all *khâgne* students). Likewise, the *taupe* students from Louis-le-Grand, Saint-Louis, and the École Sainte-Geneviève in Versailles, who in 1967 made up 43 percent of the acceptances to the École Normale Supérieure Ulm (sciences), 39 percent of the acceptances to Polytechnique, and 36 percent of the acceptances to Centrale, represent 37 percent of the students surveyed (but only 20 percent of the students enrolled in 1967–8 in first-year scientific preparatory classes). Similarly, the top provincial high schools, especially the Lycée du Parc in Lyons, were given a greater weight in the sample than would have been the case had we simply calculated the proportion of their students among all preparatory class students.

For the sake of comparison, we also used the results of two previous studies, one on a sample of 6,000 science students, and the other on a sample of 2,300 humanities students. In February and March of 1968 we initiated a series of interviews (40 in all) with preparatory class and university students, along with a study based on in-depth interviews conducted in Paris and the provinces (160) with 20 *khâgne* and 20 *taupe* teachers, as well as 40 mathematics and physics and 40 French, Latin, and Greek professors from science and humanities facultés. Finally, we consulted varied informants (headmasters of top lycées, former *khâgne* and *taupe* teachers and students, etc.) and written sources (in-house newsletters, magazines, commemorative works, novels, etc.) for everything to do with the most ritualized aspect of preparatory class life (slang, rites of passage, etc.) while making every effort to record all the accounts of the intimate, indeed secret, experience of the effects produced by this process of consecration and belief production.

As genuine total institutions descended from the Jesuit college and the Napoleonic university, the preparatory classes for the grandes écoles assemble adolescents with many similar social and academic properties and isolate them in a separate space. This selective confinement produces a very homogeneous group whose homogeneity is further increased through the mutual socialization brought about by continued, prolonged contact (see tables 4 through 7). In so limiting the social area of possible associations, confinement contributes to limiting the chances of unsuitable alliances (in the broad sense). Its influence is a lasting one, moreover, for through the affective ties that bind particularly tightly during adolescence, it predetermines subsequent acts of cooptation.

Table 4 *Taupe* students 1967–1968 (percent)

	All (n = 881)	Louis-le-Grand (n = 146)	Saint-Louis (n = 96)	Sainte-Genev. (n = 88)	Other Paris[1] (n = 133)	Lyon (n = 83)	Other provinces[2] (n = 335)
Social characteristics							
Father's occupation							
Farmworker, farmer	3.5	1.5	2.0	–	–	6.0	7.0
Blue-collar worker	4.5	2.5	2.0	2.0	3.0	5.0	6.5
Clerical worker	5.0	2.5	5.0	2.0	2.0	6.0	7.0
Tradesman	3.0	1.5	5.0	–	2.0	5.0	4.0
Small commerce	5.0	5.5	4.0	8.0	3.5	2.0	4.5
Mid-level manager	14.0	12.5	20.0	5.0	20.5	11.0	13.5
Primary school teacher	4.5	1.5	3.0	–	–	6.0	8.5
Farm owner	1.5	–	1.0	3.5	–	–	2.0
Industrialist, large merchant, exec.	26.0	35.5	24.0	35.5	31.0	31.0	19.0
Engineer	14.0	16.5	10.5	21.0	22.0	11.0	9.5
Professions	8.0	7.0	9.5	18.5	7.0	5.0	6.0
Teacher/professor	8.5	7.0	11.5	1.0	5.5	8.5	12.0
NR and misc.	3.0	6.5	2.0	3.5	3.5	3.5	0.5
Mother's occupation							
None	52.0	49.5	49.0	50.0	56.5	53.0	52.0
Blue-collar worker, farmworker	2.5	1.5	2.0	–	–	5.0	4.0
Tradeswoman, small commerce	2.5	2.5	1.0	4.5	1.0	1.0	3.0
Clerical, mid-level manager	9.0	12.5	12.5	3.5	10.0	8.5	8.0
Primary school teacher	9.5	1.5	10.5	2.5	4.5	13.5	15.5
Executive, professions	3.5	8.0	1.0	5.5	4.5	1.0	2.0
Teacher/professor	4.5	5.5	8.5	3.5	3.0	5.0	4.5
NR	16.5	19.0	15.5	30.5	20.5	13.0	11.0
Paternal grandfather's occupation							
None	1.0	–	2.0	–	0.5	–	1.5
Farmworker, farmer	10.5	7.0	7.5	3.5	4.5	11.0	16.5
Blue-collar worker	9.0	7.0	11.5	4.5	5.5	8.5	13.0
Tradesman, small commerce	17.0	18.0	19.0	12.5	10.0	23.0	19.0
Clerical worker	5.0	5.5	4.0	1.0	4.5	7.0	5.5
Mid-level manager	7.0	13.5	3.0	5.5	7.5	6.0	5.5
Primary school teacher	2.5	4.0	–	1.0	2.0	2.5	2.5
Exec., teach./prof., professions	21.5	18.0	19.5	38.0	30.0	24.0	16.0
NR	26.5	27.0	33.5	34.0	35.5	18.0	20.5
Father's education							
None	1.5	2.5	2.0	1.0	3.0	–	1.0
CEP-CAP	12.0	15.0	10.5	1.0	6.5	19.5	14.5
BEPC-BEI	8.0	4.0	13.5	3.5	6.0	12.0	8.5
BS-bac	15.5	18.0	19.0	3.5	10.0	14.5	19.5
Trade school, higher educ. uncompleted	8.5	7.0	4.0	7.0	10.0	9.5	10.0
Licence, second-ranked école	22.0	29.0	20.0	43.0	27.0	20.5	13.0
Agrégation, grande école	13.5	15.0	13.5	18.5	19.5	12.0	9.5
NR	19.0	9.5	17.5	22.5	18.0	12.0	24.0
Mother's education							
None	2.0	2.5	2.0	–	1.5	1.0	3.0
CEP-CAP	10.5	12.5	9.5	1.0	4.0	14.5	15.0
BEPC-BEI	11.5	11.0	18.0	3.5	16.0	12.0	10.0
BS-bac	24.0	31.5	16.5	27.5	20.5	27.5	22.0
Trade school, higher educ. uncompleted	3.0	5.5	2.0	2.0	2.0	5.0	2.0
Licence, second-ranked école	11.5	12.5	10.5	19.5	11.0	11.0	8.0
Agrégation, grande école	1.0	1.0	1.0	1.0	2.0	–	1.0
NR	38.0	23.5	40.5	45.5	43.0	29.0	39.0

Table 4 – *continued*

	All (n = 881)	Louis-le-Grand (n = 146)	Saint-Louis (n = 96)	Sainte-Genev. (n = 88)	Other Paris[1] (n = 133)	Lyon (n = 83)	Other provinces[2] (n = 335)
Parents' place of residence when child entered *sixième*							
Outside country	2.0	1.5	4.0	5.5	–	2.5	1.0
<10,000 inhabitants	20.0	8.0	13.5	23.0	3.0	29.0	31.0
10,000–100,000 inhabitants	22.5	18.0	12.5	12.5	1.5	29.0	37.5
>100,000 inhabitants	21.0	9.5	17.0	35.0	6.0	32.0	25.5
Greater Paris area	31.5	59.0	51.0	23.0	87.0	5.0	1.0
NR	3.0	4.0	2.0	1.0	2.5	2.5	4.0
Family size							
Only child	12.5	13.5	10.5	4.5	12.0	8.5	16.0
2 children	31.5	31.5	28.5	16.0	35.5	33.5	34.5
3 children	24.0	23.0	25.0	21.5	26.5	23.0	24.0
4 children	15.0	18.0	16.5	21.5	12.0	19.5	10.5
5 children	7.5	7.0	14.0	12.5	6.5	7.0	8.0
6 or more children	9.0	7.0	14.5	21.5	7.5	8.5	6.0
NR	0.5	–	1.0	2.5	–	–	1.0
Average number children	3.05	3.0	3.3	4.0	2.9	3.1	2.8
Advised to do *hypotaupe* by[3]							
Teacher	56.5	55.0	59.5	59.0	46.5	62.5	58.5
Relative	43.5	45.0	33.5	60.0	46.0	52.0	38.0
Someone else	13.0	5.5	10.5	14.5	8.5	12.0	18.5
No one	10.0	11.0	8.5	7.0	11.5	6.0	10.5
NR	5.5	5.5	7.5	4.5	9.0	5.0	4.5

[1] Other Paris lycées: Balzac, Condorcet, Pasteur (in Neuilly-sur-Seine).
[2] Other provincial lycées: Clermont-Ferrand, Lille, Toulouse.
[3] *Hypotaupe* is the first preparatory year. The total exceeds 100 because of possible multiple answers.

By comparison with the universities, the preparatory classes and the grandes écoles are regarded as more satisfactory by the upper business bourgeoisie, long wary of public education and anxious to keep its children away from the "dangers" and "temptations" of student life and the corrupting influence of an intellectual milieu. The École Saint-Geneviève, for example, a Jesuit school that prepares its students for the top scientific *concours*, undoubtedly represents the realized ideal of an ascetic education that even the Catholic bourgeoisie itself finds increasingly difficult to reconcile with a way of life and models of authority that have been profoundly transformed. By ensuring a complete overlap between life disciplines and academic disciplines and between place of residence and place of work, this institution integrates the preparation for the *concours* into a more complete education, simultaneously "human and spiritual," "unifying everything students must learn in school into one kind of work" (*Servir*, alumni newsletter of the École Saint-Geneviève, no. 82, April 1969, pp. 57, 87, 108). Indeed, any institution that organizes cultural activities, community service activities (reading for the blind, tutoring North Africans, organizing activities in youth centers), or conferences that bear witness to a political, social, or religious commitment, and takes on the spiritual guidance and well-being of souls through its corps of chaplains and alumni, any institution, in short, that strives to provide each of its students with all the possible means of "blossoming" bears a "total assumption of responsibility" (pp. 100–2). Saint-Geneviève serves as a good example of the outside limit of this type of institution. In addition, it has the virtue of reminding us in passing, contrary to the view that the

Table 5 *Taupe* students 1967–1968 (percent)

	All	Louis-le-Gd	Saint-Louis	Sainte-Genev.	Other Paris	Lyon	Other provinces
Academic characteristics							
Age							
17	3.0	2.5	3.0	6.0	5.5	3.5	1.0
18	34.5	42.5	28.0	46.5	29.0	29.0	34.0
19	39.5	34.5	41.5	35.0	40.0	44.5	40.0
20	18.5	14.0	20.0	10.0	21.0	23.0	21.5
21 and over	3.5	4.0	6.5	2.5	4.0	–	3.5
NR	1.0	2.5	1.0	–	0.5	–	0.5
School and track in *sixième*							
CEG	7.5	9.5	6.0	–	4.0	13.5	9.5
Modern lycée or collège	15.5	22.0	25.0	–	16.5	8.5	15.5
Classical lycée or collège	57.5	55.0	49.0	43.0	67.5	60.0	60.5
Modern private school	2.5	1.5	2.0	3.5	3.0	–	3.0
Classical private school	13.0	8.0	8.5	46.5	3.0	17.0	10.0
NR	4.0	4.0	9.5	7.0	6.0	1.0	1.5
Grades repeated in secondary school							
2	3.0	–	1.0	5.5	4.0	–	5.0
1	12.5	16.5	16.5	17.0	19.5	7.0	7.0
None	83.0	83.5	82.5	75.0	75.0	92.0	86.0
NR	1.5	–	–	2.5	1.5	1.0	2.0
Concours Général							
Not entered	57.5	46.5	54.0	☼	55.0	47.0	67.0
No prize	29.0	40.5	28.0		31.0	48.0	18.5
Prix or *accessit*	2.0	6.5	3.0		1.5	–	0.5
NR	11.5	6.5	14.5		12.5	5.0	14.0
Prix d'excellence							
None	36.0	37.0	37.5	20.5	54.0	25.5	35.0
1–2	28.0	29.0	31.5	29.5	28.5	27.5	27.0
3–4	14.5	11.0	12.5	21.5	9.0	23.0	14.5
5–6	9.0	9.5	8.5	14.0	4.0	11.0	9.0
7 or more	9.5	12.5	6.0	7.0	1.5	13.0	11.5
NR or number not given	3.0	1.0	4.0	8.0	3.0	–	3.0
Mention on baccalauréat							
Average	27.5	15.0	25.0	24.0	42.0	11.0	32.5
Good	34.5	34.5	37.5	41.0	37.0	25.0	34.0
Very good	26.5	34.5	25.0	22.5	13.5	47.0	25.0
Excellent	10.0	15.0	9.5	8.0	6.0	17.0	7.5
NR	1.5	1.0	3.0	4.5	1.5	–	1.0
Boarder/Day student							
Always boarder	46.5	45.0	45.0	7.0	88.5	47.0	41.5
Boarder and day student	6.5	18.0	4.0	8.0	1.5	2.5	4.5
Always day student	43.5	34.0	41.0	85.0	4.5	49.5	51.0
NR	3.5	3.0	10.0	–	5.5	1.0	3.0
Year in *taupe*							
First	65.0	75.5	60.5	71.5	61.0	56.5	64.5
Second	34.0	24.5	37.5	27.5	38.0	42.5	35.0
Third	0.5	–	2.0	–	–	–	0.5
NR	0.5	–	–	1.0	1.0	1.0	–
Cultural life and political opinions**							
Cite as highest in prestige							
Ulm	64.0	72.5	62.5	65.0	47.5	73.5	65.0
Polytechnique	33.5	26.0	33.5	35.0	46.0	26.5	32.5
NR	2.5	1.5	4.0	–	6.5	–	2.5

Table 5 – *continued*

	All	Louis-le-Gd	Saint-Louis	Sainte-Genev.	Other Paris	Lyon	Other provinces
Regular reading of weeklies							
None	49.0	52.0	51.0	34.0	47.5	38.5	54.5
At least one	47.5	46.5	41.5	65.0	43.5	59.0	43.5
L'Express	15.5	7.0	10.5	36.5	13.5	18.0	15.0
Le Nouvel Observateur	10.0	13.5	9.5	17.0	8.5	15.5	6.0
Le Canard Enchaîné	3.0	1.5	2.0	1.0	6.0	1.0	4.0
NR	3.5	1.5	7.5	1.0	9.0	2.5	2.0
Student union							
Against	18.0	9.5	26.0	25.0	10.5	24.0	19.5
No opinion	31.5	34.5	25.0	34.0	31.0	40.0	29.5
For	15.0	15.0	14.5	7.0	17.5	14.5	16.0
Member	7.0	15.0	4.5	7.0	4.5	–	6.5
Militant	2.5	5.5	2.0	–	2.0	3.5	2.0
NR	26.0	20.5	28.0	27.0	34.5	18.0	26.5
Political views							
Far left, left	32.5	42.5	33.5	10.0	37.0	36.0	31.0
Center left, center, center right	31.5	35.5	25.0	46.5	23.5	36.0	30.0
Right, far right	15.0	8.0	14.5	21.5	17.0	12.0	15.5
Other	5.5	2.5	5.0	6.0	4.5	5.0	8.0
NR	15.5	11.0	22.0	16.0	18.0	11.0	15.5
Sports practiced							
None	41.5	42.5	45.0	20.5	43.5	46.0	44.0
Tennis and/or riding	14.5	12.5	13.5	24.0	19.5	6.0	13.0
Other	42.0	42.5	39.5	54.5	32.5	48.0	42.0
NR	2.0	2.5	2.0	1.0	4.5	–	1.0

* Not counted (Concours Général for Catholic schools).
** Response rates are highest for questions regarding students' academic characteristics or opinions (such as the hierarchy among schools) and decrease for questions regarding unions or political opinions.

spatial and affective separation linked to the retreat and confinement imposed by establishment schools (English public schools, for instance) represents a break with the family, that this separation does not exclude social continuity. The real break instituted by these "second families," with which bourgeois families draw up a contract of unconditional delegation of authority, is not with the family, but with the excluded, common, ordinary students and, *a fortiori*, with nonstudents.

But most importantly, when the process of social rupture and segregation that takes a set of carefully selected chosen people and forms them into a separate group is known and recognized as a legitimate form of election, it gives rise in and of itself to symbolic capital that increases with the degree of restriction and exclusivity of the group so established. The *monopoly*, when recognized, is converted into a *nobility*. This is confirmed and strengthened by the fact that each of the members of the group of the chosen people, in addition to sharing in the symbolic capital collectively held and concentrated in their *title*, also shares, in a logic that is truly one of *magical shareholding*, in the symbolic capital that each member of the group holds as an individual. Thus an extraordinary *concentration of symbolic capital* is effected.

Table 6 *Khâgne* students 1967–1968 (percent)

	All (n = 330)	Louis-le-Grand (n = 110)	Fénelon (n = 48)	Other Paris[1] (n = 35)	Lyon (n = 42)	Lille (n = 49)	Other provinces[2] (n = 46)
Social characteristics							
Sex							
Boys	65.5	100.0	–	51.5	100.0	59.0	39.0
Girls	34.5	–	100.0	48.5	–	41.0	61.0
Father's occupation							
Farmworker, farmer	2.5	1.0	4.0	–	2.5	4.0	6.5
Blue-collar worker	3.5	–	–	3.0	2.5	12.0	6.5
Clerical worker	4.0	–	–	–	9.5	10.0	6.5
Tradesman, small commerce	3.0	2.0	–	6.0	4.5	2.0	6.5
Mid-level manager	13.5	11.0	19.0	11.5	12.0	14.5	15.5
Primary school teacher	5.5	7.5	2.0	3.0	4.5	8.0	6.5
Farm owner	2.0	1.5	4.0	–	2.5	–	–
Industrialist, large merchant, exec.	33.0	38.0	41.5	40.0	28.5	26.5	19.5
Engineer	5.0	8.0	4.0	5.5	2.5	4.0	2.0
Professions	10.5	12.0	12.5	14.5	4.5	6.0	13.0
Teacher/professor	14.5	18.0	8.5	11.5	26.0	10.5	8.5
NR and misc.	3.0	1.0	4.0	5.5	–	2.0	8.5
Mother's occupation							
None	45.5	41.0	33.5	48.5	57.0	55.0	46.0
Blue-collar worker, farmworker	2.0	2.0	–	–	–	6.0	4.5
Tradeswoman, small commerce	3.5	2.0	–	3.0	12.0	4.0	4.5
Clerical, mid-level manager, primary school teacher	19.0	14.5	25.0	17.0	19.0	22.5	19.0
Executive, professions	6.5	12.0	12.5	8.5	–	–	–
Teacher/professor	16.0	20.5	21.0	8.5	12.0	8.0	15.0
NR	7.5	8.0	8.0	14.0	–	4.0	11.0
Paternal grandfather's occupation							
None	0.5	–	–	3.0	–	–	–
Farmworker, farmer	12.5	12.0	12.5	8.5	19.0	10.0	15.0
Blue-collar worker	10.0	14.5	–	–	7.0	16.5	13.0
Tradesman, small commerce	16.0	16.5	12.5	14.0	14.5	26.5	11.0
Clerical worker, mid-level manager, primary school teacher	17.0	18.0	16.5	8.5	16.5	16.5	21.5
Exec., teach./prof., professions	26.0	23.5	46.0	43.0	26.5	12.0	11.0
NR	18.0	15.5	12.5	23.0	16.5	18.5	28.5
Father's education							
None	0.5	–	–	–	–	2.0	–
CEP-CAP	11.0	10.0	8.5	8.5	2.5	16.5	19.5
BEPC-BEI	6.5	2.0	8.5	3.0	5.0	12.0	15.0
BS-bac	17.5	17.5	12.5	8.5	19.0	20.5	26.0
Trade school, higher educ. uncompleted	8.5	7.0	12.5	5.5	14.5	8.0	6.5
Licence, second-ranked école	26.0	34.5	29.5	37.0	16.5	16.5	13.0
Agrégation, grande école	15.0	19.0	16.5	11.5	23.5	8.0	4.5
NR	15.0	10.0	12.5	25.5	19.0	16.5	15.5
Mother's education							
None	3.5	5.5	–	5.5	2.5	4.0	–
CEP-CAP	8.5	5.5	8.5	8.5	2.5	16.5	13.0
BEPC-BEI	11.0	9.0	12.5	5.5	14.5	10.0	15.0
BS-bac	24.0	22.5	25.0	20.0	28.5	35.0	15.0
Trade school, higher education uncompleted	4.0	5.5	4.0	3.0	–	4.0	4.5

Table 6 – *continued*

	All (n = 330)	Louis-le-Grand (n = 110)	Fénelon (n = 48)	Other Paris[1] (n = 35)	Lyon (n = 42)	Lille (n = 49)	Other provinces[2] (n = 46)
Licence, second-ranked école	20.5	19.0	33.5	26.0	26.0	8.0	13.0
Agrégation, grande école	4.5	9.0	8.5	–	–	–	2.5
NR	24.0	23.5	8.5	31.5	26.0	22.5	37.0
Parents' place of residence when child entered sixième							
Outside country	2.5	2.5	–	–	–	–	11.0
<10,000 inhabitants	14.0	8.0	8.5	3.0	28.5	22.5	19.5
10,000–100,000 inhabitants	28.5	23.0	21.0	14.0	31.0	53.0	32.5
>100,000 inhabitants	19.5	14.5	12.5	3.0	35.5	22.5	32.5
Greater Paris area	34.5	52.0	54.0	80.0	2.5	2.0	2.0
NR	1.0	–	4.0	–	2.5	–	2.0
Family size							
Only child	17.0	13.5	17.0	20.0	9.5	18.5	28.5
2 children	30.5	33.5	41.5	25.5	35.5	22.5	17.5
3 children	23.5	30.0	12.5	25.5	21.5	22.5	22.0
4 children	11.5	7.5	12.5	14.5	19.0	8.0	15.0
5 children	8.0	4.5	8.5	3.0	12.0	16.5	8.5
6 or more children	7.5	7.5	4.0	11.5	–	12.0	8.5
NR	2.0	3.5	4.0	–	2.5	–	–
Average number children	2.9	2.8	2.7	3.0	2.9	3.2	2.9
Advised to do hypokhâgne *by*[3]							
Teacher	67.5	65.5	66.5	65.5	64.5	83.5	61.0
Relative	42.5	41.0	54.0	45.5	50.0	28.5	39.0
Someone else	16.5	21.0	25.0	5.5	16.5	4.0	15.0
No one	6.5	6.5	8.5	5.5	2.5	4.0	13.0
NR	1.5	2.0	–	3.0	2.5	–	2.0

[1] Other Paris lycées: Condorcet, Molière.
[2] Other provincial lycées: Brest, Clermont-Ferrand, Toulouse.
[3] *Hypokhâgne* is the first preparatory year. The total exceeds 100 because of possible multiple answers.

Each of the young people brought together becomes rich by proxy in all the current symbolic capital (nominations to the Concours Général, honors on the baccalauréat, prestigious family names, etc.) as well as all the potential symbolic capital (exceptional jobs, famous works, etc.) brought in by each of his classmates as well as the entire society of alumni.

All of these actions, as well as many others that we will need to analyze in more depth because they more fully escape ordinary perception, are means by which the preparatory classes tend to impose upon and inculcate in all those placed in their care (and not merely the ones who will be crowned by success in a given *concours*) a genuine common culture, in the anthropological sense of the term.

Occasionally, the most ritualized aspects of this culture (in the ethnological sense of the term) are codified, as with the *Notions* of the English public schools, a 38-page publication containing rules, traditions, songs, and expressions to be learned by heart (J. Wakeford, *The Cloistered Elite* (London: Macmillan, 1969), p. 56), or the "code X" (see *La Jaune et la Rouge*,[3] no. 31 (June 1978), pp. 39–40), and the Honor Code of the cadets at West Point, which express in a burlesque style the unwritten

Table 7 *Khâgne* students 1967–1968 (percent)

	All	Louis-le-Grand	Fénelon	Other Paris	Lyon	Lille	Other provinces
Academic characteristics							
Age							
17	2.0	–	8.5	–	2.5	–	4.5
18	32.5	26.5	50.0	28.5	26.0	26.5	43.5
19	39.0	36.5	33.5	48.5	43.0	49.0	30.5
20	18.0	22.5	4.0	20.0	26.0	18.5	13.0
21 and over	5.5	9.0	4.0	–	2.5	4.0	6.5
NR	3.0	5.5	–	3.0	–	2.0	2.0
School and track in *sixième*							
CEG	0.5	–	–	3.0	–	–	2.0
Modern lycée or collège	2.5	–	4.0	–	5.0	6.0	2.0
Classical lycée or collège	80.5	85.5	83.5	71.5	74.0	79.5	80.5
Modern private school	–	–	–	–	–	–	–
Classical private school	14.5	13.5	12.5	17.0	19.0	14.5	13.0
NR	2.0	1.0	–	8.5	2.0	–	2.0
Grades repeated in secondary school							
2	2.0	2.0	–	5.5	2.5	2.0	–
1	9.0	3.5	–	23.0	12.0	12.0	13.0
None	88.5	94.5	100	68.5	85.5	86.0	87.0
NR	0.5	–	–	3.0	–	–	–
Concours Général							
Not entered	42.0	29.5	21.0	48.5	37.0	57.0	61.5
No prize	47.5	59.0	66.5	51.5	46.0	34.0	25.5
Prix or *accessit*	5.0	8.0	8.5	–	8.5	2.0	2.5
NR	5.5	3.5	4.0	–	8.5	7.0	10.5
Prix d'excellence							
None	22.5	16.5	25.0	43.0	28.5	24.5	13.0
1–2	25.0	30.0	4.0	34.0	19.0	32.5	24.0
3–4	16.5	21.0	12.5	6.0	9.5	20.5	19.5
5–6	12.5	12.0	21.0	6.0	19.0	8.0	11.0
7 or more	17.5	13.5	37.5	3.0	19.0	10.5	21.5
NR or number not given	6.0	7.0	–	8.0	5.0	4.0	11.0
Mention on baccalauréat							
Average	14.5	14.5	8.5	31.5	9.5	12.0	13.0
Good	40.5	26.5	37.5	45.5	52.5	51.0	52.0
Very good	33.5	43.5	41.5	14.5	28.5	31.0	24.0
Excellent	10.0	15.5	12.5	3.0	7.0	6.0	6.5
NR	1.5	–	–	5.5	2.5	–	4.5
Boarder/Day student							
Always boarder	62.5	53.5	79.0	88.5	47.5	57.0	65.5
Boarder and day student	7.5	12.5	8.5	–	9.5	4.0	2.0
Always day student	26.0	28.5	12.5	3.0	40.5	37.0	26.0
NR	4.0	5.5	–	8.5	2.5	2.0	6.5
Year in *khâgne*							
First	65.0	52.0	79.0	57.0	66.5	75.5	74.0
Second	26.5	34.5	21.0	34.5	21.5	18.5	19.5
Third	8.0	13.5	–	8.5	12.0	6.0	2.0
NR	0.5	–	–	–	–	–	4.5
Cultural life and political opinions							
Cite as highest in prestige							
Ulm	59.0	60.0	50.0	45.5	74.0	43.0	78.5
ENA	31.0	24.5	50.0	48.5	21.5	36.5	15.0
NR or other	10.0	15.5	–	6.0	4.5	20.5	6.5

Table 7 – *continued*

	All	Louis-le-Grand	Fénelon	Other Paris	Lyon	Lille	Other provinces
Regular reading of weeklies							
None	69.5	72.0	87.5	57.0	66.5	71.5	54.5
At least one	25.0	22.5	12.5	31.5	26.5	18.5	43.5
L'Express	2.5	3.0	–	–	2.5	6.0	4.5
Le Nouvel Observateur	9.5	9.0	8.0	11.5	9.5	10.0	8.5
Le Canard Enchaîné	4.5	2.0	4.0	5.5	7.0	–	13.0
NR	5.5	5.5	–	11.5	7.0	10.0	2.0
Student union							
Against	18.0	16.5	8.5	25.5	21.5	10.0	30.5
No opinion	24.5	26.5	25.0	23.0	21.5	26.5	21.5
For	18.0	10.0	41.5	14.5	24.0	16.5	11.0
Member	12.5	17.0	8.5	8.5	7.0	22.5	2.0
Militant	5.5	11.0	4.0	3.0	2.0	6.0	–
NR	21.5	19.0	12.5	25.5	24.0	18.5	35.0
Political views							
Far left	16.0	21.5	21.0	14.5	14.5	6.0	11.0
Left	32.0	30.0	42.0	25.5	26.0	45.0	21.5
Center left, center, center right	17.5	15.5	29.0	14.5	12.0	10.5	26.0
Right, far right	12.0	12.0	4.0	20.0	16.5	6.0	15.5
Other	6.5	12.0	4.0	–	9.5	4.0	2.0
NR	16.0	9.0	–	25.5	21.5	28.5	24.0
Sports practiced							
None	56.0	65.5	62.5	45.5	50.0	36.5	58.5
Tennis and/or riding	11.0	7.5	12.5	14.5	5.0	14.5	19.5
Other	29.0	23.5	16.5	34.5	42.5	43.0	22.0
NR	4.0	3.5	8.5	5.5	2.5	6.0	–

rules governing student conduct, or still further, the "tradition booklets" of the Gadz'arts schools (applied engineering schools). Hazing, which is merely the most obvious and most superficial aspect of the vast rite of institution performed in the preparatory classes and in the grandes écoles themselves, is one of the occasions for inculcating these traditions.

More than sharing a culture, in the traditional sense of the term (in other words, a body of legitimate knowledge and know-how), here as elsewhere it is the imponderables of manners and deportment, the typical expressions of school slang (condensed from crystallized values), the shared turns of phrase, the particular kinds of jokes, and the characteristic ways of moving, speaking, laughing, and interacting with others, and especially with like-minded individuals, that create and forever sustain the immediate complicity among schoolmates (which goes much deeper than a simple solidarity founded on shared interests) and hence all the effects attributed to the "freemasonry" of the grandes écoles.

The blessed experience of social harmony ensured by the accord between schoolmates' habitus and the reassuring rigor of the discipline of their work and their lives undoubtedly greatly enhance the nostalgia that, for the most integrated among the alumni, is often attached to the memory of their years spent at a grande école or in a preparatory class. "Why this enchantment?

Why does the X [Polytechnique] graduate take such pleasure in seeing the thrilling film of his life at school pass before his eyes? Is it because he is recapturing his youth and believes himself transported back in time? Being 20 again even for an hour would be miracle enough. But that's not it. What delights him is not just recalling his youth, it's above all recalling a particularly happy moment in his life, one he has remembered perfectly."[4] We better understand what is known as the *strength of tradition* when we see that it can dictate a perception of the present structured according to the categories put forward by graduates' retrospective representations. As with this *khâgne* student who experiences the present as a future fond memory: "[The *khâgne*] is a rather exceptional milieu. We'll have great memories of the contacts it has given us. People who have been in a *khâgne* feel united by a common something that they remember fondly and that has been crucial in the development of their way of thinking" (Louis-le-Grand, 19-year-old). This affective enchantment, born of the ability to love and admire oneself in one's like-minded neighbors, is one of the foundations, along with the *logical conformity* linked to the homogeneity of mental structures, of what is known as *esprit de corps*. This feeling of group solidarity in fact lies in the community of schemata of perception, appreciation, thought, and action that grounds the reflex complicity of well-orchestrated unconsciouses.[5]

FORCING GROUND AND INTENSIVE CULTIVATION

What distinguishes the preparatory classes from all other institutions of higher learning is above all the system of institutional means – encouragements, constraints, and controls – that together reduce the entire existence of people still referred to as "pupils" [*élèves*] (as opposed to "students" [*étudiants*]) to an uninterrupted succession of intensive academic activities whose timing and rhythm are rigorously regulated and controlled. What is important, from the point of view of outcome, is less what is explicitly taught than what is tacitly taught through the conditions under which the teaching takes place; the main aspect of what gets transmitted is not found in the overt content (syllabuses, courses, etc.), but in the very organization of the pedagogic action.

Many authors impute the effects produced by "elite schools" to the confinement associated with boarding and tend to turn this visible characteristic into the condition *sine qua non* of their ability to function as total institutions. In fact, while the discipline of the communal cloistered life of the boarding school represents the most visible aspect of an education that tends to center a student's entire existence around exclusively academic concerns, we should take care not to attribute what is in fact a consequence of rigorously structured intensive work to the effects of boarding. Thus our survey suggests that in the case of *khâgnes* and *taupes* the status of boarder is not associated with any significant systematic difference in practices.

This is evidence that the strictly organizational effect is much stronger than the effect of the confinement resulting from boarding. All else being equal, the difference between boarders and day students is far less pronounced with regard to quantity of schoolwork completed or use of free time than the difference between preparatory class and university students. So, for example, day students, who hand in as much work as boarders, work more often on Sundays and go less often to the movies. We find no significant difference in other uses of free time, whether it be reading periodicals (except that day students more regularly read dailies, while boarders more regularly read weeklies) or cultural activities (except that *taupe* boarders go somewhat more often to the theater, while day students more often go to concerts).[6]

Like any traditional education, the preparatory class education is largely accomplished through a set of organizational conditions and practices that we cannot, strictly speaking, call pedagogic since they are not actually deliberately laid out as such in an explicit project.[7] The transmission and inculcation of knowledge and techniques, which is the visible, and official, aspect of the pedagogic enterprise, is carried out in a social situation in which nonthetic theses and practical petitions of principle are tacitly inscribed. Thus, an entire definition of education and intellectual work is imposed on students through the very organization of their schoolwork, particularly through the subordination of learning to the imperatives of urgency.

Everything happens as if the institution's agency consisted above all in creating a situation of extreme urgency conceived as a sort of initiatory trial in which newcomers must demonstrate that they are capable, on the model of their predecessors or teachers, of finding the means and resources necessary for confronting the critical situations in which the relentless laws of the selection of the best adapted are carried out.[8] As in the Jesuit schools where "twice as much time was spent drilling as lecturing,"[9] the fundamental action of the institution consists in creating the necessary conditions for an intensive use of time and in making sustained, rapid, indeed even rushed work the necessary precondition for *survival* and for adapting to the requirements of the institution.[10]

Although there is no common scale against which to measure the relative amount of work produced by students in science or humanities facultés and in preparatory classes, given the significant differences in their content, form, and spirit, statements made by students and teachers in both categories of institution suggest that productivity is incomparably higher in the preparatory classes than in the universities.[11]

Taupe students complete two to three times as many mathematics and physics problem sets (between about 20 and 25 in each subject) as university mathematics and physics students each year, not counting several French and foreign language assignments. In addition, while nearly all *taupe* students complete just about all the assignments they are given, most of the university students only do one or two out of three, and over a much shorter time period (November to April).[12] The most characteristic effect of the highly structured environment of the preparatory classes is that they manage to get maximum productivity out of nearly every student: three-quarters (73 percent) of *taupe* students, for example, regularly give themselves extra work (for a fifth of these, this amounts to at least five additional hours of work per week), a kind of self-discipline virtually unknown among university science students (only 6 percent of whom say they often – and 43.5 percent occasionally – do work beyond what their teachers assign them). The same divergence distinguishes the humanities preparatory classes from the humanities facultés. The extreme homogeneity in the practices of *khâgne* students, who, at the Lycée Louis-le-Grand, for example, over the course of a school year, write ten or 12 papers and do between 30 and 35 translation exercises, not counting the writing and translation they do for "practice *concours*," contrasts with the very great diversity in the academic practices of university students in the same discipline, who rarely come even close to the productivity of the *khâgne* students.

The high productivity of the preparatory classes presupposes a set of institutional conditions. Teachers openly impose a wide variety of forms of discipline and grading and they use means of encouragement meant to intensify the competition among schoolmates. So, for example, attendance being mandatory, teachers directly and unhesitatingly fulfill their disciplinary function by acting as attendance takers. With only the rare exception, immediately denounced by the students themselves, moreover, they assign a large volume of outside written work, which they require to be handed in on time and which they correct according to the most scholastic norms of the scholastic tradition.

"They all hand in the homework. It would be really something if they didn't! They wouldn't dare come back! When they have to miss study hall, they let me know. They do their work at home and hand it in the following Monday" (*khâgne* Latin/Greek teacher). Asked whether students are given specific instructions on the form of their written work: "Yes (smiling). I require an extra space between paragraphs. They have to hand in a detailed outline along with their papers. Five spelling errors gets them a zero. I mean I don't even finish correcting – when I get to five errors, I stop reading, I give them a zero, and I put down my pen" (*khâgne* Latin/literature teacher). "They have to do at least two rough drafts. Margins are very important. I always require a wide margin for my written corrections, which are, alas, often abundant. Their translations into Greek must be very clearly written. Every poorly formed letter counts as an error, just as it does in the *concours*" (*khâgne* Latin/Greek teacher). Most assignments are followed by the public awarding of grades, usually in descending numerical order. Some of the teachers who have given up these practices continue to post the trimester ranking, while others merely write the class average next to the grade they give each paper. While preparatory class teachers seem to be using the most obvious techniques of stimulation by emulation (such as publicly announcing the results of the "practice *concours*" along with their comments, or reading out grades from lowest to highest, etc.) with decreasing frequency, they rarely completely deny themselves the most effective of all the traditional techniques of getting students to work hard – either implicit or explicit mention of the *concours*. "I constantly refer to the *concours*. I try to show them that it's not a joke. I tell them whether they're up to competing. I tell them what goes on technically" (*khâgne* history teacher). "Yes, I often mention it. Unfortunately, it's a point of reference: 'you'd be below average here on the *concours*; don't forget, only three more months.' A shiver goes up their spines. They're not panic-stricken or anything, but there's a major defect in these otherwise admirable prep students and that's their obsession with the *concours*, especially for the fourth-year students [who are repeating, Tr.]. It's a kind of constant obsession for them" (*khâgne* French/Latin teacher).

By turning a student's entire life into a competition placed under the sign of urgency – a "race against the clock" – preparatory classes, like sports in other traditions, create a simulated equivalent of the real struggles of ordinary life within the universe of the school, of the *skholè*, that is, of leisure, of freeness, of finality without end. And, without needing to explicitly state underlying principles, they thus also inculcate the deep-seated dispositions that, because they do not have to be asserted and professed as values, do not have to reveal their hidden and sometimes inadmissible side: these being the propensity and the capacity to make an intensive use of time, which without doubt give one a considerable advantage in academic competition (particularly in *concours*) and also, later, in the struggles of professional life, but which also go hand in hand with an instrumental, pragmatic, and indeed, narrowly calculating relationship to education and intellectual work; and ambition and the taste for intellectual prowess, academic equivalents of the "will to win" exalted elsewhere in sports, which lead the most highly consecrated students to stretch themselves, but which, as in sports, do not always lead to fair play, and ready them more for the game of "every man for himself" than for teamwork and cooperation.

The logic of urgency at the basis of all these dispositions being one of action, it is not surprising that, contrary to what is thought, it undoubtedly prepares students better for the demands of working life than for research and intellectual pursuits. This is why, for example, in ordinary *khâgne* life, all activities that are neither directly profitable ("useful for the *concours*") nor easily assignable at a certain time (such as a general reading list) are sacrificed in favor of expressly required graded work, such as translations or the memorization of course material. Likewise, the need to be able to give an immediate answer to any possible question at all costs requires the use of the recipes and ruses of the art of dissertation, which save a student the trouble of doing in-depth research, while at the same time masking what he does not know and enabling him to hold forth *ad infinitum* by recycling the most timeworn and predictable "*topos.*"[13] It also necessitates the use of anthologies and textbooks, those products of scholastic routine that are designed to provide the means for satisfying scholastic demands at the lowest cost. More generally, it encourages students to use subterfuges and ploys, precocious mastery of which predisposes them neither to intellectual rigor nor to honesty, and to practice study habits that are more akin to a practitioner's "tricks of the trade" than to the methods and techniques of a researcher.[14]

Thus everything combines to make these "elite schools" genuine executive training grounds.[15] The subordination of learning to the pressure of urgency and the strict, continuous nature of the work are tailor-made for inculcating that simultaneously docile and confident relationship to culture that predisposes students more to wield power than to perform research, which is in fact what is meant by the term *"culture générale."*[16] The art of being able to mobilize instantly all available resources and to get the most out of them, taken to its highest form by certain prestigious *concours*, such as the ENA exam, and the statutory confidence that goes hand in hand with this mastery are undoubtedly among the primary "leadership qualities" that are sanctioned and consecrated by all grandes écoles and which indeed predispose students more to the pragmatic, disciplined calculations of decision-making than to the daring and originality of scientific or artistic research.

At their core, the virtues attributed to grande école students are always among those commonly expected of a *man of action*. "The *concours*, and particularly the oral section, favors candidates who can keep their *cool*. And a *pleasant appearance* never hurts. Of course, appearance and the ability to keep one's cool are fundamental qualities of *professional life*. Likewise, the special effort necessary here is not unlike what every individual must periodically exert throughout his career (. . .). The candidate who falls apart on a question that he in fact knows the answer to is often the one who can't handle the critical moments in life" (*Les conditions de développement, de recrutement, de fonctionnement et de localisation des grandes écoles en France*, Report to the Prime Minister, Sept. 26, 1963, Research and Monographs 45 (Paris: La Documentation Française, 1964), p. 41). Another semi-official text reminds us that "in addition to theoretical and technical knowledge," *taupes* also give their students "discipline, *rapid and rigorous* work habits that are *highly valued* by both the public service and national and private firms." For the benefit of the detractors of this training, it mentions the "efficiency of the work habits" *taupes* inculcate and "the taste for hard work they develop" ("Rapport sur l'enseignement supérieur et les grandes écoles," submitted by the Couture Committee, *La Jaune et al Rouge* (July 1967), pp. 16–17).

"Culture générale" is also that confident relationship to specialized, particular, parcelized knowledge and its bearers that is afforded by the sense of having (had) access to the one true foundation, to *science*, matrix of all specific *techniques*, which are left to mere agents of *execution*. This undoubtedly explains the apparent wastefulness which leads to the requirement that

countless useless facts be learned, and at the same time to a much longer period of schooling than would be necessary to gain the skills strictly necessary for a particular job. This contradiction between technical and social demands, between the competence required by the technical description of a job and the competence socially required by the demands of legitimation, is at the core of the relationship that dominants, especially heads of firms (primarily at the nonstate pole of the economic field), maintain with the diploma as a selection criterion for their managerial staff. This contradiction overlaps with and reinforces the contradiction that the holders of economic capital, as dominants in the field of power, encounter in their relationship both to the dominated in this field (intellectuals, artists, and even teachers) and to the culture they produce or reproduce. Led to range themselves on the side of intelligence, thought, disinterestedness, refinement, culture, etc. when they think of themselves in relation to the "common people" (whether practically, in the everyday choices of lifestyle, or explicitly, in their justifying discourses), they are located at – or returned to – the side of power, action, virility, pragmatism, and efficiency when they think of themselves in relation to intellectuals or artists, and especially in relation to the strictly intellectual definition of intelligence as having a critical mind, being distanced from power, or simply as erudition, *scholarship*, or research.[17] This twofold contradiction is at the basis of the profound ambivalence in corporate management's relationship to the educational system. Insofar as it expects an institution for the training of the "elite" to introduce its students to intellectual matters without turning them into intellectuals, to educate them without warping them [*former sans déformer*], to condition them without "contaminating" them,[18] as has oft been said and written, especially after 1968, or, as was said in former times, without "corrupting the youth," these employers are logically led to show an indisputable preference for the preparatory classes and the grandes écoles (especially the science sections) that, although not created for this purpose, seem tailor-made to respond to the profoundly contradictory aspect of their expectations.

General knowledge and specialized knowledge, general education and technical education, but also conception and execution, theory and empiricism, synthesis ("synthesizing notes," "synthesizing report") and analysis – what is at stake in these antitheses is the most obvious, the most contested, and the most threatened social boundary, the very one that integration into a grande école consecrates, and that establishes a sacramental break between *polytechniciens* and technicians (in the broadest sense of the two words), people we like to call "specialists of the general" and specialists proper, the so-called upper-level and mid-level managers [*cadres*]. Thus, despite everything that differentiates them, the "young men" at the École Polytechnique or the École Nationale d'Administration (whose "artificial and apparent precocity" predisposes them to take up the duties of a "*cadre* for the nation" very early on, with a strong sense of superiority and every appearance of legitimacy, while they await their more lucrative jobs in the private sector) have more in common than it may seem (once you discount a certain conformity in nonconformity) with the "young masters" of the École Normale Supérieure, who are trained, as Durkheim again says, to "produce work prematurely and without genuine thoughtfulness" and led, by their overconfidence in books or their own genius, to a state of intellectual self-sufficiency, like big naive schoolboys who have seen it all, so sure of themselves that they smile knowingly at anything that does not bear the inimitable stamp of the school and, perhaps in a provincial high school or a magisterial chair, or in some "obscure" textbook or "brilliant" essay, profess inherited certitudes.

SYMBOLIC CONFINEMENT

In fact, the state of urgency and anxiety created by the constant competition in the anxious wait for the final trial produces a *symbolic confinement* more effectively even than boarding. No doubt because it is difficult for *khâgne* and *taupe* students to imagine learning strategies that would be more profitable than the ones prescribed by a tradition born of an unconditional subordination to the need for academic efficiency, and because the statutory confidence that the entire logic of the institution tends to inculcate in them prevents them from detecting the mutilation that is the counterweight of their chosenness, they gradually learn to identify what "interests" them with what is "useful for the *concours*" and, at the same time, to ignore what they do not know and to be satisfied with what they do know.

One index of the self-contained nature of this universe can be seen in the fact that school slang (which, as a sign of one's membership or exclusion, also contributes to containment) refers solely to school life. Within École Normale slang, there are references to places at the school, to school food, to hazing, and secondarily, to religion, to the army, and finally and above all to *hierarchies within the school*. At the École Polytechnique, the vocabulary surrounding the internal school hierarchy is more extensive than the vocabulary referring to academic hierarchy, which is understandable when we recall that many practices, beginning with the rites of passage that, until 1968, were much more intense there than at the École Normale, tended to substitute the hierarchy of *seniority* within the institution for the hierarchy of academic rank. Compared to the lexicon of the École Normale, the *polytechnicien* lexicon naturally has a greater proportion of military slang, and an even greater proportion of terms referring to social life and school functions.[19]

When asked whether preparatory classes should teach material not directly related to the *concours*, 66 percent of *khâgne* students and 62 percent of *taupe* students either answer in the negative or abstain. This massive adhesion to the definition of education implied in the syllabus and the structure of their work is again expressed in the fact that *taupe* students, 85 percent of whom claim to be unable to keep up with current research in mathematics and physics, nevertheless believe that the content of their education is superior to a university education (at 56.5 percent). In any case, their heavy workload would prohibit *khâgne* and *taupe* students from adding classes at the university, an institution often presented to them in a most unfavorable light, especially since 1968. Only 1 percent of *taupe* students and 10 percent of *khâgne* students attend classes at the university (in Paris). This split has the effect of encouraging the rejection of the unknown, or at least, a satisfied withdrawal into the elementary social unit. "The *taupe* is a cell with boundaries that are rarely crossed. It is very rare that a *taupe* student would go to another *taupe* to do an assignment. Rightly or wrongly, *taupe* students think their own courses are the best" (*taupe* mathematics teacher).

Given that this enterprise of hothouse cultivation is carried out on adolescents who have been selected and who have selected themselves according to their attitude toward the school, in other words, according to their *docility*, at least as much as their academic ability, and who, shut up for three or four years in a protected universe with no material cares, know very little about the world other than what they have learned from books, it is bound to produce *forced* and somewhat immature minds that, more or less as Sartre writes about some of his reading at age 20, understand everything luminously and yet understand absolutely nothing.[20] And we cannot help thinking once again of the Jesuit education as described by Durkheim. "The Jesuits' education was extraordinarily intensive and crammed. One feels that an immense effort is being made in order almost violently to drive the mind to a kind of apparent and artificial precociousness. Hence, this plethora of written assignments, forcing the pupils incessantly to *stretch* their active resources, to produce work prematurely and without genuine thoughtfulness. The general tempo of university teaching was less hurried, less urgent, less vertiginous."[21]

In fact, there is no point on which the contrast between the preparatory classes and the university is more striking. Thus, while 62 percent of *taupe* students characterize a good *taupe* student by his ability to work fast and only 15 percent by his ability to do in-depth work, 69.5 percent of second-year university mathematics and physics students consider the ability to do in-depth work the most important characteristic of a good student (compared to 18 percent for speed of work). Similarly, 23.5 percent of second-year mathematics and physics students, compared to only 11 percent of *taupe* students, attribute the ability to be inventive to a good university student (rather than the ability to apply acquired knowledge).

But the confinement would no doubt not be complete if the teachers entrusted with the structuring of student life were not themselves completely confined within the magical prison of which they are ostensibly the guards. And in fact, given that they are almost entirely recruited from among graduates of this very institution, *khâgne* and *taupe* teachers are spontaneously inclined to transmit and to sanction its values – usually without being aware of it – and above all the recognition of the value of the institution, from which their own value is often wholly derived. As a type of *coach*, it is by contributing to the creation of favorable conditions for intensive training, rather than through direct and explicit teaching, that they inculcate in their students, in addition to a certain type of culture and relationship to culture, the practical mastery of a certain number of techniques that make it possible for them to meet the challenge of academic urgency.[22]

Recruited from among the elite of secondary school teachers, often asked to sit on the examining committees of the top *concours* recruiting this level of teacher (agrégation, CAPES,[23] etc.), and almost always led to finish up their exemplary careers in the role of secondary school general inspectors, preparatory class teachers are completely devoted to their jobs, which they take to be to structure, indeed to "continually frame" their students' activities. Unlike university educators, who are divided, to differing degrees, between teaching and research, between the university field and the intellectual or scientific field, preparatory class teachers almost never undertake research projects (sometimes going so far as to consider any time devoted to other activities as time "stolen" from their students); if they have not published textbooks, they have in many cases at least intended to do so.

According to a survey of 3,500 secondary teachers conducted in 1972 by the Center for European Sociology (under the direction of Jean-Michel Chapoulie and Dominique Merllié), preparatory class teachers exhibit all the characteristics that define the perfect product of the school system. As former good students, they have received the most sought-after and most exceptional signs of consecration at an earlier age than most. The majority (78 percent, compared to 58 percent of certified [CAPES] and 32 percent of uncertified teachers) have earned at least one high grade on the baccalauréat and thus were selected for the Concours Général much more often than the others (48.5 percent, compared to 34 percent of *agrégés*, 12.5 percent of certified teachers, and 5.5 percent of uncertified teachers). Almost all of them have spent at least a year in a preparatory class (86 percent, compared to 61 percent, 34 percent, and 20 percent). Some 66 percent have competed in the *concours* of one of the Écoles Normales Supérieures (compared to 43.5 percent, 16.5 percent, and 4 percent of the others) and have earned the agrégation earlier than the other teachers with this title (before 24 years of age for 30.5 percent of them, compared to 20 percent of the other *agrégés*). Finally, 25.5 percent graduated from Ulm or Sèvres, compared to 10.5 percent of secondary school *agrégés* and 0.5 percent of certified teachers; 19.5 percent graduated from Fontenay or Saint-Cloud, compared to 9 percent of the *agrégés* and 2 percent of the CAPES teachers. Women who teach in a preparatory class, who are more highly selected than the men, exhibit the highest degree of these characteristics. From the point of view of social origin, preparatory class teachers fall somewhere between secondary school teachers – they come from families who are better off, especially culturally – and higher education teachers; less often from the dominant categories, their origins are more frequently in the middle classes and the dominated regions of the field of power. Most (84 percent) state that they are not involved in research. As teachers first and foremost, 39.5 percent have intended at one time or another to develop a textbook and 44 percent have sat on an examining committee (agrégation, CAPES, or grande école entrance exam). Only exceptionally do they intend to move into higher education. When asked what they will be doing in ten years, the vast majority (85 percent) answer that they will still be teaching in a preparatory class (only 10.5 percent are thinking of higher education, compared to 18.5 percent of teachers with the agrégation).[24]

These masters of the elite devote themselves completely to fulfilling a pedagogic task from which they expect everything in return. Their pedagogic action resembles that of a *coach* who passes on the structure of an exercise and the framework of learning over knowledge itself. The lectures they give are primarily aimed at supplying material that will be specifically useful for the *concours*. They give assignments, correct papers, supply model answers, and check their students' progress through written and oral examinations, issuing up to 30 or even 50 grades per student by the end of the year (usually strictly recorded).[25] Personally interested in the success of each of their students, or at least the best ones, and performing all the tasks implied in the complete definition of the professorial role (unlike university educators, especially tenured professors), they tend, like Jesuit school prefects and monitors, to develop a total patrimonial-style relationship with their students, one that extends to every dimension of their lives.[26]

The relationships between preparatory class teachers and students are at one and the same time more intense, more undifferentiated, and more all-encompassing than student–teacher relationships in the universities, as can be seen, for example, from the terms of address students use for their teachers in particular *khâgnes*. "Sometimes the fourth-year students will come up to me and say, 'Master [*maître*], may I miss your class?'; I say of course they can. Yes (smiling), all *khâgne* teachers are called master, and only they, at least at Henri-IV. This goes back at least as far as Alain.[27] It's not that we wanted to put ourselves in the same camp as scholars, but it's a term that sets us apart from secondary school teachers. You see, we enjoy a certain familiar relationship with our students; we have them for three years in a row. It's a very highly selected milieu, already an elite; there are no discipline problems. It's really the last bastion of Greek education! (laughing) I also teach at the Sorbonne, ancient history. The students disappear, we never get to know them" (*khâgne* history teacher). "When they've been absent, they make their excuses, calling you 'master' (. . .). The students call you 'master' especially when they have something to apologize for" (*khâgne* Latin teacher).

The teachers, especially the ones who teach major subjects, and particularly philosophy, like to envision their job as that of a wise old master, or even a spiritual advisor, authorized to intervene in every question directly or indirectly touching on a student's work life: their reading, homework, studying, sleep, nutrition, outings, etc. "About four or five years ago, our students took their cue from university students and wanted to abolish *taupes*. I told them, 'That's childishness; you're the privileged ones. You're letting yourselves be led along by people who don't give a damn about you.' Today all that's over. They no longer call for the end of *taupes*. They can see the mess the universities are in. They know it's not a matter of unfairness, that we're acting in their best interests. They feel supported, led; they have a spiritual father, or rather, spiritual fathers" (*taupe* mathematics teacher).

Placed at the center of the reproduction mechanisms of the system of which they are the most perfect products, preparatory class teachers do not need to expressly seek to adjust their teaching to the demands of a *concours* in which they have never stopped competing. The continuity between the *khâgne* or *taupe* student that they were and the teacher they have become is so complete that they merely need to be fully what they are in order to offer up perfectly "prepared" students to examiners who, as products of the same conditions of production, have only to let themselves be who they are "to be in the spirit of the *concours*." "I'm on the examining committee for the history agrégation. In correcting my students, I feel I'm getting into the spirit of the *concours*. The *concours* graders are my schoolmates, besides. Their questions could be my own" (*khâgne* history teacher). The proper functioning and harmonious perpetuation of the institution depend almost entirely on the homogeneity of habitus that it produces. With this automatic concordance of habitus, both at a particular moment and across time, in other words, regardless of age differences, there is immediate, intuitive, and practical harmony in a euphoria of shared certainties, independently of any explicit codification in the form of contracts, rules, or bureaucratic control.

This perfect harmony between agents who are interchangeable in their role as instruments tuned to the same institutional necessities is innocently expressed in the following remark made by a *khâgne* teacher: "I recommend general texts to them, such as the Lévêque, who is one of my friends." In treating one of his colleagues in the space of a single sentence first as a thing, a common scholastic textbook ("*the* Lévêque"), then, at the cost of a sudden "change of space," in the sense of Gilles Fauconnier,[28] as an individual endowed with a proper name capable of being characterized (with the relative clause: "who is one of my friends") as his pedagogic alter ego, this teacher reveals his own reality as the institution made man. Another states, "I have a very hard time distinguishing what I owe the *khâgne* I attended from what I owe the one I was assigned to teach in, rather early by the way – I was 27. It's really all a jumble in my mind. What I do know is that for someone like me, it's very simple. As silly as it may sound, I don't know of any other job, not a single one, that would suit me better" (*khâgne* literature teacher).[29]

Class lectures, especially in French and philosophy, are structured as model answers for possible homework assignments, which are themselves modeled after actual *concours* questions. Charged with preparing their students to answer scholastic questions, *khâgne* teachers are led to structure their lectures in advance according to the structure that the students will have to reconstruct in forming answers to these questions. Most *taupe* teachers get their assignments directly from collections of problems and questions from past *concours* – although they may "alter them somewhat" to break up the routine. Their role is not to challenge their students, but to put together "montages," to program minds to fit the curriculum. It follows that the subjects passed down by scholastic tradition are not merely topics that serve as a pretext for the variations of a scholarly tradition; they act as genuine *categories of thought* that define the universe of the thinkable by imposing the clearly circumscribed set of questions likely to be actually asked. They are categories that, when imposed upon an entire social universe, produce the illusion of a finite, enclosed, perfect world.[30]

In a *taupe* or *khâgne*, courses are usually designed to be a kind of oral textbook offering prepared material in a handy condensed form for scholastic use ("lecture questions," for example). As one *taupe* teacher put it, "I try my best to give lectures in which knowledge is already extremely well digested, as well as a large number of assignments that are also predigested." For his part, a history teacher admits excusing the fourth-year students from his lectures when they have heard them two years previously in scarcely altered form. The attempt to maximize the quantity of information transmitted and assimilated in a limited amount of time necessitates a dogmatic method of inculcation in which only professorial "predigestion" can make up for the lack of assimilative work (costly in time) permitted by less bluntly directive methods. The teachers can count on the consenting approval of the students, who are all too concerned about not wasting time to interrupt a lecture with questions or objections.[31] Only 9.5 percent of *taupe* students and 12 percent of *khâgne* students say they have spoken in class often, which may seem surprising given that in university discussion sessions, where conditions are more or less equivalent, students speak much more frequently (38 percent in second-year mathematics and physics). "I give two-hour lectures, very magisterial in style. They [the students] sometimes interrupt, but they know that there's a minimum amount of information we have to get through. They realize that they save time by just listening. They have a lot of work to do; you don't come to a *khâgne* as a dilettante, to dabble. The courses are compulsory magisterial lectures; it's like in law school, if you will. They're really lecture courses, with all the imperfections this implies" (*khâgne* history teacher).

The lecture course, intended primarily to transmit the greatest amount of useful information in the least amount of time, most often obeys the most traditional rules of scholastic exposition, with a clear outline that, as Thomas Aquinas, master of the three-point presentation, would have it, must *reveal itself* in the discourse, via signs of hierarchized subdivisions (I, II, III, 1, 2, 3, a, b, c), among others, as well as introductions, transitions, and conclusions consistent with the canons of rhetoric. This authoritarian and dogmatic pedagogy, the arbitrary nature of which only rarely becomes apparent to the students because it is functionally linked to the *concours* and its most specific demands, explicitly acts to *reduce the amount of reading and research* an individual must do, rather than to stimulate either activity.

"I never give out a bibliography – there would be no point. They have to be able to speak on any topic without really knowing anything. I bring them predigested knowledge" (*khâgne* English teacher). "I had them get a few essential texts for their libraries. (. . .) Don't you think the student who has studied a good little elementary grammar book knows plenty enough for the *concours*, and even the agrégation? When there are difficult questions, they let me know (. . .). I write out answers and I know they get them copied" (*khâgne* Latin/Greek teacher).

But the paradox of such a thoroughly routinized education is that it can provide teachers with all the institutionalized resources of a *charisma of office*. Indeed, teachers are spoiled for choice when they turn to the typically academic tradition of "academic anti-academism"[32] for the proven games and tricks of the theatricalization of pedagogic action in order to give the most strictly scholastic acts (such as preparing lectures or handing back papers) the appearance of an inspired quest or a literary ceremony, and thereby strengthen belief in the cult of culture and its servants. These coaches are also professionals in academic enthusiasm, able to get fired up on demand in discussing the canonical topics that their oratory makes seem novel. These games played with the objective definition of the job are perfectly designed to foster, in teachers and students, both overinvestment and the subtly maintained bad faith that grounds faith in the institution and in the future it promises. It is no accident that philosophy teachers, who undoubtedly have greater difficulty than others in reconciling the truth of their job with their representation of it (a representation encouraged by the traditional definition of their function), have become masters at these games of faith and bad faith. Just as the church that preaches the evangelical anathema against the Pharisees may feel excluded from ritualism because it ritualizes the denunciation of ritualism, there is no school philosophy that cannot give itself and others the illusion of being free from the routines of school philosophy by invoking the patronage of one or another of those anti-institutional philosophies that the philosophical institution canonizes. But, as can be seen, for example, in the extensive use philosophy teachers have always made of the Socratic model and, more generally, their use of all the facile denunciations of professorial routinization (such as the use of textbooks), it is still the educational institution that assures for its agents the well-spring of their charisma by providing them with the conditions and the instruments of the ritualized denunciation of scholastic ritual.

A DUALIST ORGANIZATION

The most well-hidden effect of the existence of noble channels is without doubt related to the very duality of pedagogic organization – public schools and grammar schools in Great Britain, grandes écoles and universities in France. It is the *relationship of systematic opposition* between the two categories of institution that gives rise to the originality of each, and to the (positive or negative) *distinction* and the symbolic value that each bestows on its products. The division between preparatory class students and university students overlaps with and strengthens the opposition between two styles of work, indeed, between two systems of dispositions and two visions of the world, an opposition that is continuously reinforced by the sanctions of a universe that is predisposed to recognize its manifestations.

Education in humanities or science facultés owes its most important characteristics to the inferior and dominated position that these institutions hold in the field of institutions of higher education and to the difference between the aims they proclaim – those insisted on by the highest level of their faculty – in other words, research and the teaching of research, and their objective functions, producing teachers and mid-level managers for public and private enterprise.

Sixty-five percent of men and 74 percent of women with a master of arts degree (excluding the social sciences) and 37 percent of men and 72 percent of women with a master of science degree who graduated from a university in 1969–70 and were working in 1973–4 were primary or secondary school teachers. In contrast, only 5 percent of men and 1 percent of women with a master of arts degree and a job were working in research or higher education, the corresponding proportions in the sciences being 14 percent and 10 percent, respectively. While it makes sense that almost everyone with the CAPES or the agrégation, in both the humanities or the sciences, should be teaching in secondary schools, it is more surprising that people with a third-cycle humanities Ph.D.[33] should also be more likely to go into primary or secondary teaching than research or higher education (for the men, 52 percent as opposed to 23 percent; for the women, 43 percent as opposed to 14 percent).[34]

The most relevant characteristics of the pedagogic action of the universities and the methods of imposition and inculcation they have at their disposal all have at their foundation the absence of the institutional conditions of intense and sustained pedagogic work systematically observed in the preparatory classes. Here again, the characteristics of particular pedagogic practices can be deduced, as it were, from the organizational conditions in which they are implemented and the dispositions of the sector of the student population where they are used. Thus nothing could be more radically different from the organization of the preparatory classes, where, as we have seen, nearly all pedagogic tasks are concentrated in the hands of two or three teachers, responsible for giving classes, assigning homework, correcting papers, and administering oral and written examinations, than the atomization of the professorial function observed today in science facultés – and also, although to a lesser degree, in humanities facultés.

In Paris, mathematics and physics university students had seven or eight levels of teachers at the time of our survey. Professors gave the lectures; lecturers organized the exercises and activities in the discussion sessions and labs; papers and problem sets, the content of which was determined by the different lecturers in turn, were often corrected by graduate students or grandes écoles students; the oral exams were given by lecturers or *"colleurs"*,[34,35] for the most part, grande école or university students nearing the end of their studies. It was thus unusual for a teacher to see the same group of students for more than four hours per week or to have more than ten grades per student at the end of the year.[36]

While the preparatory class teacher demonstrates a strong identification with the professorial function, university professors generally keep their distance from the most obviously "scholastic" disciplines and demands.[37] They often relegate pedagogic activities to second place. Even the ones most devoted to their role as teachers feel compelled to at least appear to be doing research. Through many details of their pedagogic practice, they manifest their refusal to allow themselves to be reduced to the minimal definition of their role. This is why, even in science facultés, where attendance in discussion groups is mandatory, most teachers refuse to check attendance or lateness (especially in Paris). The same aversion to "scholastic" or "primary school" procedures leads them to refuse to use any blunt or crude techniques of incitement or control. Most assistant professors and lecturers give their students great freedom in choosing both the due date and the frequency of graded assignments. "The department says it's mandatory. I've told my students up front that I'm not going to count attendance. I refuse to go by the rules (. . .). At any rate, I'm not for making things mandatory. I mean, if a teacher isn't interesting in himself, you're not going to make him interesting by making his classes required (. . .). I would never say anything to a kid who comes in late" (assistant professor of physics).

They are of one mind in avoiding making the public awarding of grades appear too formal or grandiose, deliberately depriving themselves thereby of one of the most effective techniques of the *khâgne* or *taupe* teacher. If they mention the final exam, it is more to reassure their students, giving them advice and offering technical tricks. As a free encounter between two free intellectual projects, the pedagogic relationship should not take the form of a brute imposition of subjects and skills; learning must take its own course ("the students must find what suits them"), the quality of the assimilation being more important than the quantity of facts assimilated.

It is interesting to note that university teachers, a great many of whom have attended a preparatory class, seem to take the opposite tack from common preparatory class practice in all matters of classroom management – giving out grades, mentioning the final exam, overseeing student work, etc. "It is necessary at any rate to avoid making negative remarks to a student in front of the class, for, we might say, psychological reasons. Given the principle I've adopted, I tend to make only flattering comments" (lecturer in Latin). "I have a thoroughly empirical method for handing back papers: I give out the first few in descending order, then I mix up the rest. I think waiting to have your name called out last, when compositions are being handed back, is really humiliating. Getting a poor grade feels bad enough . . . I hand them back without comment (. . .). In the model correction, I very often may quote from a particularly good or bad translation, but I never mention the students' names" (lecturer in French). "Of course I bring up the final from time to time. But it's never to scare them! My own tendency would probably be quite the opposite – to lessen some of the drama surrounding the whole thing. No, I don't terrorize them about the exam. I try to guide them toward pure philology" (lecturer in Greek philology). "I don't think giving lots of homework makes any sense. Doing one assignment carefully is better than whipping through three" (assistant professor of Latin).

Among lecturers and assistant professors of mathematics and physics, fewer than a third report having given one or more tests since the beginning of the school year, and several indicate that they have not yet given a single grade. "Written tests are all well and good in secondary school, but totally out of place at the university level" (lecturer in engineering). Many lecturers encourage students to be on their guard against anything that might seem dictated or mandatory, as well as survey textbooks and all forms of "routinized" knowledge. "I would even prefer that they not automatically and systematically take down everything I write on the board, that they not recopy everything" (assistant professor of mathematics). "The students must above all not use outdated books; I point out a few recent dissertations for them to look at, a few books . . ." (assistant professor of mathematics).

The systematic differences that contrast the two antagonistic forms of pedagogic action can be explained in part by differences in the circumstances of their use and in part by the different positions occupied by preparatory class and university teachers in the structure of educational institutions, which means that they are predisposed to develop different relationships to their occupation. University professors, obliged to take into account a social definition of their office that tends to exclude the tasks involved in providing a framework for their students' work, deeming such tasks unworthy of higher education, and put in the position of competing for a changing, irregular, and large student population that is often not much inclined to discipline itself for work and is always poorly prepared for it, have no other choice but to reject every practice that might make them seem like secondary school teachers lost in the corridors of higher education, alienate the population over which they already have such little hold, and also, in most cases, give them an added workload out of proportion to the time they have available for either elective or required research. The "liberalism" or "laxness" in their teaching thus constitutes a response adapted to their objective situation. In addition, in a faculty that is hierarchized, unlike preparatory class teachers, and in which tenured professors have the power to determine the division of labor either by making specific assignments or by the mere fact that they can exempt themselves from activities most clearly recognized as "pedagogic" (and therefore devalued as subordinate), the rejection of "anything secondary schoolish," as Renan used to say, always includes an implicit reference to the structure of the university hierarchy.[38] The liberties that lecturers and assistant professors grant their students also appear to be so many liberties taken with the most demanding

definition of their job or, what amounts to the same thing, so many concessions to necessity. And this *new job description* is all the more imperatively
imposed upon them because, given the increasing student population and
the added faculty positions that have resulted, they are less and less prepared to perform the job as it was defined in a previous state of the system,
that is, at a time when lecturers barely outnumbered tenured professors and
thus both expected to and were prepared to succeed them.[39] The desire to
establish less distant relationships with students and to exhibit understanding that often approaches a tacit or open complicity is also, for the least
consecrated among the subordinate teachers (doomed to a permanent rupture – and a double game – between teaching and research), a way of
demanding and obtaining a form of understanding or indulgence in return
and also, more simply, of lessening their often overwhelming workloads,
especially in the most crowded disciplines taking in students with extremely
diverse skills and work capabilities.[40]

Such a pedagogic organization tends, more or less by omission, to get students to use strategies homologous to those of their teachers. Many of their
practices partially follow from the fact that they do not think of themselves
as students, because the objective circumstances in which they are placed do
not give them the means to do so. Denied the sustained assistance of the
institution and forced to envision learning as an individual enterprise, students are usually condemned to shift back and forth between an academic
activity whose means and ends are not very certain and a dilettantism that is
expressed in particular in their rejection of scholastic disciplinary measures
and grades or their enchanted adherence to an exalted image of the intellectual vocation, a double negation of the objective truth of learning and the
occupation to which it objectively leads.

It thus suffices to look at the series of traits that characterize the two
types of educational institutions as a whole to catch a glimpse of the effects
these institutions produce in and through their very opposition. The organization able to produce a greater academic output through its methods of
incitement to work, its continuous framing of student activity, and its
checking of assimilation is matched to the students who are most socially
and academically advantaged (nearly exclusively male). In contrast, the student body of the organization that is less able to obtain a high academic
return (with respect to the goals objectively stated by the two types of institutions) is both very disparate in age, academic capital, and intellectual
interests and less well-off academically and socially, and therefore particularly susceptible to the wasted effort that naturally follows from an absence
of institutional encouragement, constraint, and checking.

It is not enough to say that the effect of the dualist structure of higher
education is to strengthen initial disparities, with the best education from
the point of view of the dominant norms going to the most socially and academically well endowed. In fact, there is no better proof that the functions

of the educational institution cannot be reduced to the purely technical function of producing and reproducing technical skills than this kind of chiasmatic structure in which the most scientifically rarefied education and educators go to the least highly selected students, while the students who appear to be the best prepared for research are submitted to the most scholastic education, which is the least open to research, but at the same time the most perfectly suited, through its strict organization and its entirely devoted body of teachers, to fulfil the social functions of the reproduction of the social structure.[41] These strange facts can only be explained if we realize that the social stakes and consequences of the division into hierarchized channels do not all lie in the intellectual and scientific domain, and that the logic of the division of intellectual and scientific labor is constantly blurred by the logic of the division of the labor of domination.

2

A Rite of Institution

The existence of two separate channels, which, like the sacred and the profane, are mutually determined by the very relationship of exclusion that
unites them, in itself reminds us that "elite schools" always fulfill a function
of *consecration*, and that the technical operations of the educational process
they accomplish are at one and the same time, and inseparably, moments of
a *rite of institution*: selection is also "election," exams are also "trials,"
training is also "ascesis," isolation is also initiatory retreat, and technical
skills are also charismatic qualifications. In other words, the process of
transformation accomplished at "elite schools," through the magical operations of *separation* and *aggregation* analogous to those produced by rites of
passage as described by Arnold van Gennep, tends to produce a *consecrated*
elite, that is, an elite that is not only distinct and separate, but also recognized by others and by itself as worthy of being so. The action performed
on the novice, modifying his own idea of himself and his function, as well as
on the others, transforming their idea of him, changes this "ordinary being"
into "something he formerly was not." He has "purified and sanctified
himself by the very act of detaching himself from the base and trivial matters that debased his nature."[1]

In selecting the students it designates as the most gifted, that is, the most
positively disposed toward it (the most *docile*, in the true sense of the term),
and the most generously endowed with the properties it recognizes, the elite
school reinforces these predispositions through the consecration that it
bestows simply by separating its students from the rest. This invisible action
is effected through the statutory assignation (*"noblesse oblige"*) that results
from attaching students to a place and a status that are socially distinguished
from the commonplace, which we might think of as a type of *marking* that
creates a magical boundary between insiders and outsiders, often sanctioned
by an actual enclosure.[2] As is shown in exemplary fashion by the logic of
examinations that introduce an absolute break between those who pass and
those who flunk, or, more dramatically, in the case of *concours*, between the
student with the lowest passing grade and the student with the highest failing grade, academic sanctions fulfill a social function *par excellence*. This

social function consists in producing special, separate, sacred beings merely by getting everyone to be aware of and to recognize the boundary separating them from the commonplace, by making the consecrating distinction public, widely known, and guaranteed by the *consensus omnium*, and by creating thereby the conversion of belief that leads the chosen people to (re)cognize themselves as different. The *concours* is a way of imposing a form of *numerus clausus*, an act of cloture that introduces the discontinuity of a *social boundary* between the last person chosen and the first rejected. As Simmel observed, this boundary can lend social relations a rigidity they do not have so long as the points of encounter between might and right are not precisely and explicitly defined. The operation of division that distinguishes two separate populations – for life – from within the continuum of academic performances (people often mention differences of as little as a quarter of a point) is an act of consecration or, if you will, *ordination* that, as in Marc Bloch's account of dubbing, *institutes* an order, in other words, a legitimate, magically produced, and juridically guaranteed division of the social world.[3] Like military nobility, academic nobility comprises a set of individuals of superior essence. The hierarchy of classes juridically instituted through academic verdicts is substituted once and for all for the hierarchy of classified individuals whose performances, as realizations of different essences, are *socially incomparable*, even when they are "technically" interchangeable (as in the case of persons holding the title "acting x" or powerful behind-the-scenes players).

CONSECRATING THOSE WHO CONSECRATE THEMSELVES

But we must take a moment to pause before this mysterious process, only seemingly self-evident because it is so familiar that we normally pay it only distracted attention, and try to truly understand the principles underlying the *magical efficacy* of institutional *dubbing*. In fact, the process leading to the production of a nobility (in the broadest sense of the term) is simply founded in the relationship between, on the one hand, agents who are socially designated as distinct (nobleman in relation to commoner, oldest in relation to youngest, boy in relation to girl, etc.) and thus (socially) predisposed to accept their destiny as exceptions, and on the other hand, a collective conversion effort that is necessary if those who know and feel that they are "destined for greatness" (academic tradition would say "gifted") are to realize their destiny, their essence.

Owen Lattimore has said that the Great Wall of China was built as much to keep the Chinese in as to keep their neighbors out.[4] This is perhaps the case with all caste boundaries, especially the one that "elite schools" attempt to permanently establish. Academic consecration has to get the "elite" boundary (the one separating the managerial bourgeoisie from the task-oriented petty bourgeoisie, etc.) recognized by those it excludes no less than by those it includes, and the latter, in order to maintain their status, must not only accept the necessary constraints and sacrifices but also, as Wilkinson notes, experience their privilege as a duty, a public service.[5]

We clearly see that election – the election accomplished by *concours*, for instance – results in making the excellence of the chosen people known and in getting it recognized, in publicizing it at large, and in giving it the social force of a collective representation. It is less obvious but no less true that election also and especially consists in getting the chosen people to recognize their own individual dignity. The magic of the assignment of distinctive names or titles only works if those they distinguish accept the exceptional obligations they imply. As shown by statistics on the academic and social characteristics of preparatory class students – and even more clearly by those on grande école students, who have undergone a further process of training and selection – the die is essentially cast in advance. The operation of training and transformation succeeds as well as it does only because it is performed on individuals who have already been trained in a manner consistent with the expectations of the training establishment and because its principal function is to strengthen the investment in the institution that has led the novices to turn toward the institution.[6]

Preparatory class students are the product of a long series of acts of consecration that are in fact so many acts of separation and aggregation.[7] Each of these successive acts – good grades, *prix d' excellence*, nominations to the Concours Général, honors on the baccalauréat, etc. – is both cause and effect of the predisposition to recognize academic goals and values, this predisposition itself being both cause and effect of academic success, which in turn strengthens the predisposition to recognition, all this in an unending process of circular reinforcement (negative sanctions, in contrast, underlie a circular process leading to failure and renunciation).

This *dialectic of consecration and recognition*, at the end of which the elite school chooses those who have chosen it because it has chosen them, is one of the mechanisms that enables it, through the consecration that it bestows, to attract individuals who most closely conform to its explicit and implicit demands and who are the least likely to alter it. While the school can take advantage of its relative autonomy in order to establish hierarchies whose crowning glory is the university career and to redirect for its own gain a few of the adolescents from milieus the least likely to recognize its verdicts, it only fully succeeds when it preaches to the converted: teachers' children and those students who are like oblates, being devoted from a very early age to a school they cannot criticize since they owe it everything and expect everything from it in return, the "miracle children" from the dominated regions of the social world.[8]

There is no doubt that it is in looking at these uncommon destinies, which serve as justification for the myth of the "school as liberating force," that we can best perceive the long process of segregation that leads to the final consecration. Indeed, it appears at the very level of statistical analysis that, while preparatory class students from the dominated regions of social space are distinguished from the rest of their group of origin by their greater academic success, they are also set apart from it, from the very beginning, by secondary advantages that may help to explain their election.

As was seen earlier in relation to Concours Général prizewinners, the survivors within a category defined according to social origin, sex, or age exhibit fewer of the social characteristics of that category taken as a whole and, conversely, more of the characteristics that are *rare* for that category the less likely it is that their category will be represented at this point in the selection process (precisely because it exhibits a higher degree or a greater number of the characteristics that lead to elimination). At the level considered here, for example, working-class students, who make up 4.5 percent of *taupes* and 3.5 percent of *khâgnes*, come from families who seem to be set apart from other working families by their relatively high level of education and social standing. Among working-class *taupe* students, 48 percent have a grandfather from the middle classes, while only 18 percent of all workers are of middle-class origin. Upwards of 33 percent and 25 percent of the working-class mothers of *taupe* and *khâgne* students have at least the BEPC.[9] Working-class students are also distinguished from their classmates by their particularly impressive previous achievement. Some 97 percent of *taupe* students and 91 percent of *khâgne* students from the working class have never repeated a grade in secondary school, compared to 83 percent and 88.5 percent of all preparatory class students. Similarly, 66.5 percent and 81 percent have earned the *prix d' excellence* at least twice, compared to 48 percent and 64.5 percent of all students. Sons of farmworkers and small farmers are similarly set apart from the rest of their original social category. They are more likely to be enrolled in a lycée in the *sixième* (52 percent in *taupes*, 62.5 percent in *khâgnes*, compared to 28.5 percent in science facultés, and only 16.5 percent and 11 percent among all children of farmers and farmworkers) and have almost never been held back (89 percent and 100 percent).

This same logic also explains why female *khâgne* students, who are more highly selected (as they make up about 1 in 200 of all women in post-secondary humanities, while male *khâgne* students make up approximately 1 in 100 of the corresponding population), are distinguished from the men by an entire series of compensatory academic advantages. They are more likely to be enrolled in a lycée in the *sixième* (84.5 percent, compared to 79 percent of the men) and more often owe their presence in a *khâgne* to their very high rate of success (94 percent have never repeated a grade, compared to 86.5 percent of the men; 45 percent have had at least four *prix d' excellence*, compared to 32 percent of the men). In addition, 26.5 percent have mothers with at least the licence, compared to 24 percent of the men. The mothers of 27.5 percent are primary or secondary school teachers, compared to 23.5 percent for the men. At Fénelon, where the overselection of women is particularly striking (and where the rate of acceptances to Sèvres is the highest), the students (who are very young) have never been held back, have very often been invited to compete in the Concours Général, and, with an equivalent number of honor grades on the baccalauréat, come from smaller families than the men; most importantly, their mothers, a high proportion of whom have a diploma equivalent to or beyond the licence, frequently work outside the home.

Contrary to the illusion that a less authoritarian relationship between teachers and students gives more "democratic" results (here, as elsewhere, laissez-faire tends to make the better-off better off), there can be no doubt that the explicitly scholastic organization of the pedagogic action encountered in the preparatory classes tends to ensure the oblates of a compensatory advantage likely to enable them to reduce their handicap and to gain an occasional advantage in the closed field set up by the institution. The recognition, no doubt completely relative, that this academic world grants to the values and virtues advantageous to students from the dominated regions of social space, and the consecration – all the more miraculous because it is so rare – that it can thus bestow upon them create a fascinated adherence to the institution in return. The sense of miraculousness that accompanies election is in proportion to its improbability.[10] This is one of the effects that make the so-called ultimate consecration (even though there is always something that lies beyond, as the logic of never-ending competition requires) succeed so perfectly in producing both membership in the group of the chosen and, inextricably, separation from those kept out, thus, in the present case, from the group of origin.

Crossing the boundary separating the "masses" from the "elite," and the breaks, indeed, the denials, that this act implies, are simply the last in a long series of infinitesimal breaks, the culmination of innumerable differential deviations that in the end constitute the great shifts in social trajectories.[11] Those whom the school distinguishes and consecrates, as far back as we might go, have already been separated or, as we say, *cut off* from their peers. Often "pushed" by a father who has frequently made a break himself, one undoubtedly all the more noticeable the weaker it was and the less it physically removed him from the group he left (we might think of foremen, technicians, minor engineers or clerical workers, all of whom have to live in direct contact with their group of origin), these students have from the outset been set apart by the slight gaps that are at the source of a cumulative process of distancing: knowing how to read before going to school, skipping grades, receiving exemptions, scholarships, top prizes, *prix d' excellence*, nominations to the Concours Général, honors on the baccalauréat, and so on.[12] Each act of academic consecration only deepens the initial rupture by establishing it both in reality and in consciousness – in reality, through symbolic acts that have wholly real social consequences, like the naming of spaces (high school versus junior high) or time periods (school vacation, for example) that are too profoundly separate not to be separating, if only through the ambivalent respect shown to the lycée student or the admiration professed for the "good student"; in consciousness, through the naively elitist pride that consecration inculcates, and that assuages the secret guilt of the transplant [*transfuge*] and gets the parvenu to forget his *double isolation*, without ever being able to completely erase their nostalgia for reintegration into their community of origin, also perceived as a refuge from the rejections placed in the way of the emancipated by the adoptive universe.

It is no accident that crossing the line that marks entrance into a grande école is, as for Nizan, the occasion of a return to the father, principle of the originary *clinamen*.[13] Indeed, it comes down to either accepting oneself as a transplant, child of a transplant, but at the precise moment when, from a series of small shifts, the break instituted by the father gives rise to a break with the father, who is never completely separated, or murdering the father twice over, denying the part of him that remains working class as well as the part that has become petty bourgeois – support and betrayal, solidarity and scorn, etc. The result is no less painful in the borderline cases where the initial break was made *in the face of* parental indifference or even hostility. In this case, the transplant can neither desire nor therefore fully achieve a success that he cannot share with his "loved ones."

In fact, for individuals as for groups, the relationship to the past is a function of the present, or more precisely, of the future promised to the individual or collective past. The fluctuations that can be seen in this relationship, both across individuals and within a single individual at different times in his life, undoubtedly follow from the fact that this category of social trajectory requires a dual relationship to the trajectory and hence a dual, variable, and contradictory view of history and the meaning of history. In their practical evaluation of their social standing, which is one of the unconscious bases for positions adopted toward the world, optimistic or pessimistic, progressive or regressive, those who have crossed over may look at the class of probable trajectories for their group of origin and see their present position as an instance of progress inseparable from world progress, from the "liberating" school, from "democratic" society, etc. But they may also refer to the class of probable trajectories for the academically defined class of chosen people to which they now belong ("*normaliens*," "*agrégés*," "professors," etc.) and see their own trajectory as the product of a negative deviation from the modal trajectory, sometimes imputed to the effects of social origin, and thus as a sign of failure. Furthermore, one's relationship to one's trajectory always implies a relationship to the starting point of the path. This is why transplants never say so much about themselves, that is to say, about the state of their trajectory and their relationship both to the past and to the future it governs, as when they mention anything to do with their origins ("common people," "region," etc.). Whether talking about rugby or Occitan, working on the land or life in a workers' compound, their childhood school or their first boarding experience, they are usually merely revealing their relationship to the object, that is to say, the false proximity of their forced return, making itself felt by their (always partially elective) failure to fully assimilate into the bourgeoisie, or their distance from aestheticism (in the case of the so-called regional novelists, for example), indeed, from ethnography, which enables them to pay the price of integration by giving away the game.[14] Nevertheless, teaching, along with certain political activities (neither of which excludes the other), undoubtedly appears to be the most acceptable of possible social functions, for all the aforementioned reasons, and also because, given its position in the field of power, its occupants have the status of dominated among dominants, as well as because it provides the opportunity for cultural proselytizing to recent converts who are anxious to cancel out their privilege by exposing it.

Thus academic acts of consecration are only so effective because they are nearly always performed on converts. Like the dubbing of a knight or the ordination of a priest, the official bestowal of a title (which may give rise to a formal ceremony, such as the commencement proceedings at English and American universities) formally marks the end of a long preparatory initiation. Through an official act, it ratifies the conversion achieved at the end of the gradual transformation brought about in and through the anticipation of the consecration.[15] And the wonder of satisfied love is the most undeniable expression of the success of an educational enterprise that is never so miraculous, in a sense, as when it manages to take what is actually the most likely destiny and turn it into the anticipation of a miracle, that is, in the case of the inheritors, who must accept being inherited by their inheritance (which only appears to go without saying).

We could quote any number of accounts of the extraordinarily joyful outbursts which greet consecration: "Rabosson was drunk, staggering with joy (. . .). A *normalien*! Finally, he was a *normalien*!"[16] As the same causes will produce the same effects, we should not be surprised to find most of the characteristics observed in the case of the top French *concours* in any description of the dispositions required and strengthened by the multiple *concours* of the mandarin system – for example, complete adherence to tradition (which might mean going as far as rebellion in order to enforce its respect), recourse to tricks and ruses necessitated by the scramble for success at all costs, and especially, perhaps, all the signs of a total and absolute self-investment, such as working oneself to death or committing suicide following failure, and, as is the case below, marveling at one's election.[17]

What agony it was thirty years ago
At Peking, waiting for the lists to appear!
I met someone who told me I had passed;
I was bowled over by this thunderclap of joy and surprise,
I thought it was a mistake, thought it was only a dream;
I was in a sorry state of doubt and dread.
Yet it was true; that staunch master Tench . . .
Had written that my name was to figure on the list,
Had rescued me out of my dark abyss. . . .

Parents, however much they love a child,
Have not the power to place him among the chosen few.
Only the examiner can bring the youth to notice,
And out of darkness carry them up to Heaven.[18]

ASCESIS AND CONVERSION

Yet, while it was necessary to bring to light everything that the efficacy of academic acts of consecration assumes on the part of those upon whom they are performed – to which we would need to add those who perform them as well as the entire social universe in which they are performed, in short, the entire *universe of belief* that Marcel Mauss saw to be the basis of magical efficacy – we should not for all that lose sight of the efficacy of the operations that are intentionally designed to determine the conversion process.[19]

Far from being simply the last relic, within a rationalized system of education, of techniques used to awaken a novice's charismatic qualifications and put them to the test, as Weber would have it,[20] hazing, which, as Durkheim notes, aims to "shape individuals for their new existence and assimilate them into their new environment,"[21] is merely the most visibly ritualized aspect of a vast consecration ritual. The ordinary *cursus* of "elite schools" exhibits all the characteristics of a charismatic initiation process that aims to instill the recognition of a *social competence* (while still inculcating elements of a technical competence), including retreat from the habitual environment, a break with all family ties (both of these through more or less strict boarding practices), entry into an educational community, the transformation of an entire way of life, ascesis, physical and mental exercise intended to awaken aptitude for rebirth, and repeated testing of the degree of charismatic qualification attained, all of these being so many trials leading gradually to the formal reception of the "approved" into the circle of the chosen and granting access to the "consecrated life."[22]

By immediately dispossessing individuals of the value they believe themselves to have (this might be the academic value at which they are led to appraise themselves as docile disciples of the institution that has consecrated them), the educational institution puts itself in the position of being able to restore the value it initially took away from them by means of the *title* that establishes them as licensed members of the group. By making an individual's value depend on the institution, it dictates an unconditional adherence to the institution that is thereby confirmed in its monopoly on the giving of value. For example, the physical or symbolic pranks constitutive of hazing that aim above all to force newcomers to publicly repudiate their ambitions or pretensions[23] in the end fulfill the same function as the no less ritualized strategies that teachers traditionally resort to when, for example, on the pretext of reminding their students of the requirements of the *concours*, they destroy the overall grading system (by giving lower than average grades to the best students in the class and negative grades to the weakest, for example) or hurl invectives at their entire audience as if to glorify the object of all their ambitions by lamenting the distance that still stands between this object and the least unworthy of the claimants.

The logic of *constant competition* and the unending trial it implies also obviously plays a major role in achieving the conversion that claimants to the title must undergo in order to identify completely with the social identity it consecrates. Competition compels individuals selected by and for competition and enclosed in the closed world of competitors to invest themselves completely in the competition. This academic form of struggle for one's life, which tends to turn each student into the adversary of all the others, assumes and gives rise to enormous investments in what is taught and how, in tests, teachers, and competitors, in short, to complete adherence to the game and all the values that, being produced by the game, seem to found and justify it.

In addition, if all schools destined to reproduce an elite commonly impose ascetic practices, starting with the exercises necessary for an education [*culture*] that is both formal and divorced from real life, this is undoubtedly because, as Durkheim points out, asceticism "is an integral part of every human culture" and because those who intend to ensure themselves a monopoly on the sacred and on human excellence must go through this "necessary school, where men form and temper themselves, and acquire the qualities of disinterestedness and endurance"[24] likely to further their control over nature, that is to say (although these are no longer Durkheim's words), over those who cannot control their nature. The phrase "I am master over myself and over the universe" is an ethical profession of faith in which a dominant individual justifies his domination in his own mind by referring to his natural capacity to dominate his nature. Becoming educated is in this sense a rite of mourning; the old (in this case, young) man, with his passions, his desires, in a word, his nature, must die.[25]

It is only if we bear in mind this deep and unconscious desire for cultural ascesis (in the broadest sense of "cultural") and for all the trials that, as public proof of one's self-control, stand as proof of one's right to control others, that we can understand why, in an apparent paradox, "elite schools" in all times and all places should subject those who are destined to wield power to such rough treatment.[26] We find, in fact, that despite all statements to the contrary, these institutions always attach a great deal of importance to subjects and activities that are formal, gratuitous, and not very gratifying because they have been reduced to mere intellectual and physical discipline: dead languages, for example, treated as pretexts for purely formal grammar exercises rather than as instruments that could afford access to works and civilizations (classical Latin in Europe, classical Chinese in Japan, etc.); all the ancient, venerable, sacred, and perfectly useless texts, totally foreign to the present, that in widely differing historical contexts have been the basis for enormous educational investments and have marked the boundary between laymen and clerics (Latin authors in the Renaissance, for example) as well as between the common, familial, feminine, maternal world and the learned world of men;[27] or today's modern mathematics that, despite its apparent efficacy, is no less derealizing and gratuitous than the former gymnastics of the classics.[28] While nearly any activity (archery, cricket, rugby, Latin, music, mathematics, watercolors, Homeric poetry, etc.) can function as a basis for pedagogic ascesis, as historical comparison clearly demonstrates, this is because what is taught is above all a pretext for formal exercises that function as negative rites, in the Durkheimian sense, and hence as instruments of a magical break between real men, who have the capacity to engage in these pure activities, that is, in activities that have been purified of all profane, pragmatic, and profitable purpose, and common ordinary men. The sublime are doomed to sublimation. It is likewise because the material taught is less important in and of itself than what is taught above and beyond this material through the ordeal required for its acquisition. "We are often told that they taught us nothing at Eton. It may be so, but I think they taught it very well."[29] The arguments used to justify one or another subject in the curriculum, which scarcely vary from Latin to cricket, bring to light the true function of the ascetic exercises constitutive of an elite education. In contrast to any kind of purposeful or potentially useful activity, they find their justification in their very doing, or, if you will, in the fact that in and of themselves they provide virtually no satisfaction, unless this be the satisfaction gained from utter obedience to rules.[30] But perhaps such voluntarism is a "well-founded illusion": given the practical indeterminacy of the goals of pedagogic action – excellence being by definition beyond definition – and of the means of achieving them, and thus of their effective return, much of the efficacy of pedagogic techniques no doubt lies in the collective belief in their efficacy. People who have spent their youth learning Greek or playing rugby, believing in the educational efficacy of these practices because everyone around them believed in them, have been objectively and subjectively transformed by this belief.[31]

NOBLESSE OBLIGE

The social boundaries drawn by *concours* examining committees would undoubtedly not command such widespread belief if they did not have some basis in fact; which does not mean that they do not owe a portion of their reality to the fact that they are grounded in belief. Those wishing to prove that the division established by *concours* is justified (by comparing, for example, the careers or works of *khâgne* students according to whether they did or did not become *normaliens*) should thus take care not to forget that the establishment of a more or less arbitrary break has altogether real consequences which cannot be isolated by analysis – not only because it inscribes that difference into reality by getting the greatest possible number of people to recognize it and by predisposing those who believe it to be real to recognize it in reality, but also and above all because it embeds itself in the beliefs of those it separates and as a result dictates behavior likely to justify their distinction in their own minds as well as in the minds of others.[32] We are thinking here of nobility as described by Norbert Elias. One is born noble, but one becomes noble. One must be noble to act noble, but one would cease to be noble if one did not act nobly. In other words, social magic has very real effects. Assigning someone to a group of superior essence (noblemen as opposed to commoners, men as opposed to women, educated as opposed to uneducated, etc.) causes that person to undergo a subjective transformation that contributes to bringing about a real transformation likely to bring him closer to the assigned definition. Thus the inevitable practices imposed upon preparatory class and grande école students by their sense of difference tend to objectively reinforce their difference. It is undoubtedly through their efforts to dress themselves in the trappings of nobility and intellectual grandeur, especially in the presence of their peers, that they acquire not only the assured manners and style that are among the surest signs of nobility, but also the high opinion of themselves that will lead them, both in their lives and in their work, toward the most lofty ambitions and the most prestigious enterprises.[33]

Nothing better demonstrates this preoccupation with raising oneself to the level of one's high opinion of oneself than the somewhat scholastic industriousness that the most ambitious École Normale students (especially those who have been led by their exceptional consecration to the most prestigious disciplines, such as philosophy) manifest in adopting the heroic postures or the character roles of the intellectual nobility or, if you will, "in learning the tough job of being great":[34] "Each dorm member must become his own myth, assuming the character that everyone expects him to be, one that is larger, bigger than life. This is why everyone knows perfectly well that every night at eleven o'clock one student will get out of bed and announce in a hollow voice that he hates himself; that another will as ever hurl out the same stupid, charming insult; that a third will let out the same delightfully awkward statement every time visitors come by. Don't bother asking them not to: they are driven by an inner fate, and the group would see any change in behavior as a kind of betrayal; it would consider itself royally deprived – deprived of the ever-renewed laughter that rings out each time – it would feel as if there were a hole in its ranks.[35] These practices, so rigorously stereotyped and ritualized that *normaliens* of any era could probably attach proper names to each of the characters evoked, are both more than and other than the expression of an individual attempt to act as a foil (which, moreover, constitutes a very good investment, if we keep in mind that postsecondary cooptation is frequently founded on direct or reported adolescent memories and affections). The "fate" that makes every *normalien* feel bound to participate in this enterprise of collective mystification, as much for himself as for his peers, whose self-image he would wound if he were to fail to offer them the *normalien* image they are expecting, originates in the distance between the probable future and the future promised by the institution, a distance that must be made up for at all costs.[36]

The institution of an academic nobility, a group designated by collective belief for the brightest futures, has the effect of defining "bright futures" (symbolized by the highest, yet most unlikely trajectories) according to the standards of the modal futures, in other words, the most frequent and hence the most ordinary or standard futures. The academic act of consecration unites individuals who in fact constitute a *statistical class*, and hence, by definition, include diversity, into one *juridical class* (designated and constituted by its *title*). It thus leads the chosen people *as a whole* to expect to be crowned by accomplishments that will only be achieved by a small fraction of the class. It also succeeds in getting all the members of the class, most of whom are destined for trajectories very different from the royal paths it seems to guarantee, to make investments (in every sense of the word) that, because they are at the level that would support the highest trajectories, will never receive their full return except for a very small fraction of the students, who are themselves destined to serve as security for future extorted investments. "Reading through two pages of the alumni review and doing some elementary calculations of probability is enough to convince anyone that you have a greater chance of finding an *archicube* [graduate of École Normale, Tr.] at any lycée whatsoever than you do in an embassy, at an *NRF* cocktail party,[37] at the Polytechnique dance, or in any other place where great minds are supposed to meet. How many Cotards for every Ponte, how many Farigoules for every Jules Romains, how many Sorianos for every François-Poncet?"[38] But statistics are powerless against the system-wide conspiracy that tends to guide aspirations toward the most desirable and most unlikely trajectories and, by removing the genuine experience of the real distribution of careers, gets those it destines for the most likely and most ordinary trajectories, such as that of a secondary school teacher, to make investments that could only be justified by the extraordinary trajectories, embodied in prestigious names, such as that of a philosopher or a writer, or, in another field, an ambassador, a higher civil servant, or the President of the Republic. "I thought I was thinking about my career, but I wasn't really thinking about teaching. Since I only ever liked a couple of my own teachers, I didn't hold the profession in very high regard. What led to it, though – ENS – that did have a lot of prestige. I was thinking of the exceptions, the guys who'd escaped into politics, journalism, and even literature. Since I didn't know any *normaliens* personally, knowledge that would have given me middling results anyway, I could only think about the famous and consequently heartening cases."[39]

It is within the system of trajectories actually offered to members of a class produced by academic classification (a concrete picture of which is provided by the careers of a given year's graduates taken as a kind of practical standard) that the objective and subjective value of each particular trajectory is defined and, consequently, that the level of divestiture necessary to "cut your losses," as they say (that is, in other words, to counterbalance overinvestment), is determined. In fact, alumni disillusionment is never as complete or as painful as the difference between anticipated and materialized futures might lead one to expect. The strictly juridical effect of a title is never entirely nullified and, just as a bankrupt nobleman is still noble, the *normalien* or *Polytechnicien* continues all his life to profit materially and symbolically from the statutory difference that separates him from the common people. In addition, the mere fact of belonging to a group that is generically offered the possibility of greatness (symbolized by all its famous alumni) entitles one to a share (at once subjective and objective) in this success or, more precisely, in the symbolic capital guaranteed to the group as a whole by all the exceptional properties accumulated by all of its members, and particularly by the most prestigious among them.[40] The weakest member of the class both perceives himself and is perceived by others as being separated by a sort of mystical barrier from all those with whom he has everything in common but this share.

While it is true that one's investment in a group is generally proportional to the severity of the ordeals one has braved and the sacrifices one has made in order to become a member,[41] the extent of this investment and the way one manages one's divestiture undoubtedly vary according to social origin. So, for example, an unpublished study of art teachers finds that those who aim from the start and over the longest period of time to make their career as a painter (most of whom have bourgeois backgrounds and attended Beaux-Arts) contrast very sharply and very systematically, both in their practices and in their aesthetic and political opinions, with those who head for teaching early on (mostly from the petty bourgeoisie or the upper fringes of the working class). The same contrast would no doubt surface among "philosophers": any given trajectory is undoubtedly harder to tolerate the further it veers from the trajectory dreamed of, this latter often being linked to a charismatic vision of philosophy and the "philosopher." This discordance between aspirations and opportunities, and thus the resentment stemming from a painful divestiture, are undoubtedly less likely in disciplines that offer less diverse career paths, disciplines that are consequently much less attractive to upper-class students, such as geography and geology.

The fact remains that, faced with the problem of investment and divestiture that every educational institution has to resolve in one way or another, the École Normale Supérieure is in a unique position, especially during times when *normaliens* are distanced from secular forms of power. Threatened with the dismal possibility of perceiving themselves sooner or later as "bourgeois family idiots," *normaliens* must convince themselves

that they have chosen to give up trying to collect dividends in secular territory on the frenzied investments the educational institution got out of them.
Moreover, it is all the easier for them to succeed in this the more abundantly
they have been rewarded with the symbolic dividends that can only be procured through the (never assured) success of the intellectual enterprise.

3

The Ambiguities of Competence

One cannot get an accurate picture of the educational institution without completely transforming the image it manages to project of itself through the logic of its operation or, more precisely, through the symbolic violence it commits insofar as it is able to impose the misrecognition of its true logic upon all those who participate in it.[1] Where we are used to seeing a rational educational enterprise, sanctioning the acquisition of multiple specialized competences[2] through certificates of technical qualification, we must also read between the lines to see an authority of consecration that, through the reproduction of the technical competences required by the technical division of labor, plays an ever-increasing role in the reproduction of social competences, that is to say, legally recognized capacities for exercising power, which are absolutely essential if the social division of labor is to endure. No one can deny that the school plays a crucial role in the distribution of knowledge and know-how, although a less important one than is ordinarily thought, but it is equally clear that it also contributes, and increasingly so, to the distribution of power and privilege and to the legitimation of this distribution. It is currently the school that has the responsibility for performing the magical action of consecration (often entrusted to religious authorities in other domains) that consists in effecting a series of more or less arbitrary breaks in the social continuum and in legitimating these breaks through symbolic acts that sanction and ratify them, establishing them as consistent with the nature of things and the hierarchy of beings by making them official through public, formal declarations in ceremonies modeled on the sacred, or through discourses of which social "theories" such as the division into castes or orders are perfect examples. Only the ordinary definition of religion, which is much too narrow, prevents us from seeing that the school is in fact a religious authority, in the Durkheimian sense. In establishing a boundary that separates those chosen by the great academic trials from the common people, the school institutes an "elite" vested by very fact of its segregation, with all the properties normally granted to sacred beings.[3] We can thus describe the process of separation leading to the consecration through which the school produces the state nobility –

endowed with a universally recognized title (within the limits of the reach of the state in question) entitling its members to a determined category of positions of power, as well as to recognition and respect – as a rite of passage, in the sense of Arnold van Gennep, or better yet, as a rite of institution.[4]

Seen in this new light, the educational institution appears to play a crucial role in the permanent redistribution of power and privileges, and in two distinct yet complementary ways. On the one hand, it distributes students among academic classes that are (statistically) matched to their social class of origin by imposing principles of division that are both objectivated into structures and embodied into dispositions. On the other hand, it gets students to contribute to its enormous task of aggregation and segregation by implementing in their choices among tracks, subjects, and disciplines, just as teachers do in evaluating their work, academic taxonomies that, as simple disavowed social taxonomies, have slowly been inscribed in their unconscious through their prolonged experience with magisterial verdicts and divisions of the educational institution established according to these principles. The educational institution thus makes a critical contribution to the state's monopoly on legitimate symbolic violence, particularly through its power to *nominate*. Granting an academic title is in fact a legitimate juridical act of categorization, through which the undoubtedly most determinant *attribute of one's social identity* is conferred (along with the occupation that this attribute largely determines). Given that this social identity is always – must we say it again – social difference, distinction (positive or negative), it is indissociable from the differentiation of groups separated by magical boundaries. The most exemplary manifestation of this power of nomination is the *certificate* (for particular studies, aptitudes, etc.), an attestation of competence conferred by a competent authority (that is, an authority socially mandated to guarantee and authenticate the technical and social competence of the title holder), credit credentials founded on the collective belief in the authority that awards them.

Academic judgments, through their "Oedipal effect," are nowadays undoubtedly one of the crucial factors in the construction of personal identity. Children, especially the least well endowed, have no recourse, no authority to which to appeal in response to these verdicts (which are usually absolute and blunt, whether in praise or in condemnation, and nearly always repeated and reinforced by their peer group and especially by their family) – except child psychologists and psychiatrists. Social magic manages to transform agents in a real way by getting everyone[5] – hence the interested parties themselves, who cannot but be affected by the consequences of this proclamation – to be aware of and to recognize an expectation or, better still, a prediction about their identity that, invested as it is with the prophetic authority of the group, becomes their destiny. "Become who you are." The certificate, which assigns an essence, produces what it certifies as much as it ratifies it. In a reversal of cause and effect characteristic of social alche-my, the educational institution confers, not just a certificate of technical competence giving one the right to a particular job, but a pass to a job in which the major portion of the necessary technical competence is often acquired on the job. The magic of the academic title rests on a power held and exploited by all groups, the power to act upon bodies through the sym-bolic efficacy of signs. Whether dignifying or dubious distinctions, public criticism or praise, the solemn verdicts of socially recognized authorities, as predictions vested with the authority of officialdom, tend to produce what they predict, both benedictions and maledictions being equally fatal.

Thus the academic process of consecration is one of those rites of institu-tion that constitute the consecrated group, all men in most rites of passage, all those possessed of a title in the academic rite, as holders of a *legitimate monopoly on a social virtue* or *competence*, in the juridical sense of the term, that is to say, a legally recognized capacity to wield a form of power that is effective because it is legitimate (such as giving orders). This can be *virtus*, "*man's excellence*" (*vir*), virility, a point of honor, an essentially masculine property, in the case of a rite like circumcision;[6] or, in the case of the great scholastic trials, *competence*, a capacity that is inseparably technical and social, if only because it includes typically masculine and bourgeois virtues, such as the "*character*," "*manliness*," "*leadership*," and "*public spirit*" of the great elite universities dominated by WASPs. Among all the indices showing how independent social dignity is of technical skills, the most obvious are without a doubt the opportunity to claim material compensa-tion (significantly called *honoraria*) and symbolic profits adjusted not to one's achievements but to one's title and to the *status* it guarantees, and especially the fact that the academic title acts not only as a pass but also as a *lifelong* guarantee of *competence*. While technical competence is always in danger of decline, through loss or obsolescence, dignity, as the canonists used to say, does not die, or at least only dies with its possessor. It does not age; it is protected, like royal dignity, from the vicissitudes and failures of human intelligence and memory (*imbecillitas*). We can recognize social magic from the fact that it almost always intervenes, as it does here, to tran-scend anthropological limits.

But, while it was absolutely necessary to stress the magical dimension of the title, as opposed to the technical dimension that conceals it, we obvious-ly do not want to lock ourselves into the alternative of the *technocratic faith* in the exclusively technical foundation of social competence or the *radical nominalism* that would credit the educational institution with the power to arbitrarily create dignities. In fact, the technocratic illusion is partially justi-fied, and of the effect of misrecognition at the basis of the magical efficacy of titles, and of the symbolic violence of all acts of nomination, is only possible because titles *also* certify the acquisition of technical skills (along with the properties we might call stylistic or symbolic). Titled individuals are legitimate titulars of exceptional positions, but to a certain extent they also possess uncommon technical competences, which provide a foundation for their monopoly.[7] And we also note that the market value of a title, however fully it may depend on the power of symbolic imposition, is always partially determined by the scarcity of the concomitant technical skill in the market.

Having said this, we cannot establish once and for all and for all cases how much of each of the forms of academically guaranteed competence is strictly technical *skill* and how much strictly social *dignity*. First of all because there is no definition of technical competence in and of itself, and each social universe, by virtue of its historical traditions and its cultural arbitrary, determines the technical competences that can be required of its dominants insofar as these competences are of a nature to found their domination; dominants always tend to impose the skills they have mastered as necessary and legitimate and to include in their definition of excellence the practices at which they excel. Secondly because corps founded on the monopoly of a title manage to get everyone to believe that their academically guaranteed cultural attributes are necessary for fulfilling the technical requirements of their position and that their monopoly on privileges rests on a monopoly on skills; they indeed have the means to disclaim *de facto* and *de jure* all the purely technical aspects of technical competence that, by neutralizing the effect of their title, could call this competence into question and so put the entire process of consecration and even the existence of the corps in danger. Finally and above all because what is ascribed to skill and to dignity, to doing and to being, to the technical and the symbolic, varies greatly according to the hierarchical position of titles and the jobs to which they give access. So, for example, in official taxonomies agents are increasingly defined in terms only of *what they do*, by the technically defined skills or tasks that fall under their title or job, the further one descends in the hierarchy, and conversely, by *what they are* as one moves up, as if (relatively) fewer technical guarantees were required as dignity increases. The *Dictionnaire des métiers* [occupational dictionary] lists on one particular page the *côneur*, lengthily described as "a skilled worker responsible for hammering bells out on a cone so as to smooth out imperfections" and the Conseiller d'État, simply and tautologically defined as a "member of the Conseil d'État."

The academic title is both a weapon and a stake in the symbolic struggles in which what is at stake is social standing. The higher the academic title, the more likely it is to function as a title of nobility, a dignity, freeing its holder from ever having to prove himself or practically demonstrate his skill, and the greater advantage it gives in *classification struggles*, in which what is principally at stake is the choice of granting priority either to the symbolic or to the technical dimension of titles and jobs, or the reverse. Of course, in the symbolic struggles of everyday life, it is to an agent's advantage to see his own title treated as the guarantee of a dignity and, on the other hand, to treat others' titles as guarantees of a skill. This is why the economically powerful, when they act as purchasers of a workforce, naturally tend to favor technical skills and to treat the symbolic dimension of a title as an obstacle to the free play of competition and market forces.[8] They thus become the perfect expression of the logic of the economic field that, given its exclusive attention to production and productivity, officially at least, tends to measure the value of (subordinate) workers solely in terms of their technical skills.

Except when they benefit from it, these employers are hostile to the strictly symbolic effect that the academic title is able to exercise given that it guarantees a *de jure* competence, endowed as such with three major properties: first, it may or may not correspond to a *de facto* competence (particularly because, as we have seen, the timelessness of the title may mask the obsolescence of the skill); secondly, it may claim to be recognized in every market: in contrast to the title *"maison,"*[9] which ties one to a particular job, the academic title universalizes competence (in the manner of a common currency), and hence the employee, who is thus promoted to the status of "free worker"; thirdly, it may not be adapted to job-internal changes brought on by technological changes and competition. In other words, the autonomy ensured to economic agents and their social competence with respect to the laws of the job market by universal and relatively timeless academic titles may also benefit the dominated, particularly in their dealings with employers. Their offer of work and their social identity, rather than being reduced to their (technically adjudged) ability to perform a job at a particular point in time, are durably guaranteed by a title that may imply a right to a determined class of jobs.[10]

This is a further source of the ambivalence in the relationship maintained by the heads of the largest companies with the educational institution, especially when they themselves have obtained the attestations of competence that are daily becoming increasingly necessary for wielding economic power. More and more likely to be graduates of the grandes écoles (no doubt the least "academic"), they cannot openly contest the legitimacy of the titles upon which their power is founded when these same titles limit its exercise with respect to their subordinates. In their desire to dissociate the logic of the technical reproduction of a qualified workforce from the logic of the social reproduction of the distribution of power (of which the guarantees given to the dominated are an undesirable counterpart), they dream of a tripartite system of education: the grandes écoles – especially those most amenable to their interests (HEC, ENA, and Centrale) – for reproducing the masters of the economy and higher public service; technical schools, more or less directly under their control, for reproducing a qualified workforce (with, as a last resort, the possibility of educational institutions connected to or forming part of businesses – "in-house programs"); and the university, whose sole purpose is to reproduce the university and research. More generally, the contradictions in the discourse of the dominants on the subject of education are a result of their wanting to have the profits provided by the educational institution in contributing to social and technical reproduction without having to reckon with their downside, whether this be the guarantees titles give the dominated or the strictly technical inefficiencies of the educational system, such as the structural delay in the production of producers, partly due to the school's tendency to structure itself primarily according to the demands of its own reproduction, but also attributable to the fact that, whenever it comes to dominants, it gives precedence to the demands of social reproduction over those of technical reproduction.[11]

It is largely through the crucial role it plays in individual and collective transactions between employers (who wish to secure the skills ensured by a title at the lowest cost) and employees (who intend to assert the rights inscribed in their diplomas) that the educational system directly contributes to the reproduction of social classifications. We cannot truly understand how the school, in issuing individuals juridically guaranteed academic identities that (more or less strictly) give them the right to certain social positions, can intervene in a very real way in the symbolic and practical construction of social reality unless we move beyond the academic opposition between the analysis of structures – with all its easily articulated discourses on "the articulation of economic and academic authority" – and the analysis of strategies, in order to examine in particular the games and double games afforded by the ambiguity in the simultaneously technical and social definition of titles and jobs.

If we truly want to get back to "the things themselves," according to the Husserlian slogan taken up by the ethnomethodologists, we must focus on strategies, but always in reference to the structural conditions under which they develop, that is, to the relations of power that govern the innumerable confrontations (which are all different but all equally necessary given the relative status of the agents concerned) between title-holders and job-holders. Through the academic title, the educational institution is ever-present in the conflicts, negotiations, individual contracts, and collective conventions that arise between employers and employees regarding all the stakes that separate them: job descriptions, that is, the duties employees must carry out and those they may refuse; the qualifications necessary for employment, that is, the properties – particularly academic titles – that candidates must bring with them to the job; remuneration, both absolute and relative, nominal and real; and finally, job titles, which are part of symbolic remuneration – both positive, in the case of prestigious positions, and negative, in the case of dishonorable, shameful, or lowly occupations, often used as insults and referred to officially by euphemisms.

In these confrontations, what job candidates have to offer may be entirely reduced to the skills implied by their employment history or, on the other hand, to their title, which may have nothing to say about their ability to perform a particular job (such as *agrégé* or Conseiller d'État), with many agents, to be expected especially in the middle regions of social space, possessing properties that are partially attributable to their job and partially attributable to their title. The more the description of a title and the description of a job, and hence the relationship between the two, are imprecise and uncertain, sketchily or poorly codified, and variously subject to interpretation (as with the new occupations, for example, jobs in representation, communication, social work, etc.), the greater room there is for bluffing and the greater the opportunities are for the holders of social capital and symbolic capital (noble name, "honor," etc.) to earn a high return on their academic capital.

In fact, conflicts and negotiations, even the most strictly individual among them, do not take place in a social vacuum, and nothing would be less fruitful, in this case as elsewhere, than undertaking an analysis (however subtle) of the discourses produced in interactional dialogue without taking into account the structural constraints weighing on the exchange, and particularly everything that previous individual or collective struggles have left behind, as so much sediment, in social structures and mental structures. The struggle is institutionalized in instances of collective negotiation and in *collective conventions*, which establish a juridically guaranteed state of the relations of power between employers and employees in matters of classification. Taxonomies codified like salary tables are the product at a given time of both previous classification struggles and the work of *homologation* that aims to establish a common discourse (*homologein*) on the material or technical and symbolic or nominal dimensions of a position. But they are at one and the same time instruments and stakes in the strategies that aim either to preserve or to transform them. Symbolic satisfaction can thus be granted or accepted as compensation for the renunciation of material satisfaction, either positive (such as a raise) or negative (such as a decrease in the level of difficulty of required duties). An agent or group of agents can be given a job without receiving all the material and symbolic profits that titular holders enjoy. They can be given all the material advantages with the exception of the title (as in "acting X"), or, on the other hand, they can be paid in words, receiving a more acceptable designation ("janitor" becoming "custodian") or a more prestigious occupational title, without the corresponding material advantages (a "technical assistant" who becomes an "engineer" with no corresponding increase in salary, for example). Those with academic credentials can counter these strategies by attempting to create *fait accompli* situations: they may attempt to exploit the norms governing the relationship between academic and occupational titles by seizing an occupational title in an attempt to gain the corresponding remuneration or duties, or, on the other hand, by taking over certain functions in an attempt to appropriate the corresponding title.

In short, the permanent existence of a gap – the extent of which varies according to period of time and sector – between the symbolic and the technical, the nominal and the real, opens up infinite possibilities for strategies aiming to bring the nominal in line with the real or the real in line with the nominal.[12] As products fixed at a given point in the struggle and the negotiation among groups, occupational titles and job titles, like academic titles, are both weapons and stakes in the struggle and the negotiation. Semantic negotiation being one of the means of expressing or producing social distance, one group can change its name in order either to keep its distance from or to move closer to another. And bureaucratic taxonomies, the paradigm for which is undoubtedly INSEE's code of socioprofessional categories,[13] are the product of an *act of recording* that, as an official, authenticated, and authenticating transcription, sanctions and ratifies classifications that were not produced scientifically, but rather negotiated *practically* in the material and symbolic struggles and compromises between employers and employees.[14] Taxonomies produced by bureaucratic recording, an act of a positivist nature that transforms the object of knowledge into an instrument of knowledge, become meaningful only if we examine them for traces of the conflicts and negotiations that have produced them, conflicts and negotiations in which academic titles have played a crucial role as the principal constituents of the establishment of the official and legitimate experience of the social world.[15]

The terminology of occupational titles, like kinship terms in other societies, belongs to the order of official categories that, in societies endowed with an educational institution, owe the most essential aspects of their logic and their authority to the educational system. If this terminology is able to integrate the most diverse professional positions into a system of explicit, homogeneous categories, this is undoubtedly because the educational system, by means of the academic title, provides it with the *universal standard* that, increasingly as the diploma gained ground as a universally required pass within the overall job market, placed all occupations, even the least rationalized and those most entirely left to the traditional method of transfer, into the strictly hierarchized universe of academic classifications.

Appendix

Accounts of Life in Preparatory Classes and Grandes Écoles

Readers with no direct experience of the institutions we are describing, or whose only knowledge of them comes from graduates' hagiographic representations, as well as those readers who do have direct knowledge and who may be hurt by our objectivation, may well think that we have exaggerated, emphasizing certain indisputable characteristics of *"normalien"* and *"polytechnicien"* life to the point of caricature. We have thus decided to include the following exemplary texts on crucial aspects of the experiences analyzed.

CONFINEMENT

"An absolutely insane workload, liable to traumatize a developing mind; prohibits any participation in outside life since it's impossible to keep up with what's going on or, even more importantly, to take an interest in anything whatsoever"; "It's not an education. It's a totally mind-numbing experience the only purpose of which is to get the diploma. I only hope I haven't entirely lost my youthfulness here, or my zest for life . . ." When asked what school of thought (religious, philosophical, political, economic) they feel closest to, the *taupe* students at Sainte-Geneviève who speak in this way can only repeat, obsessively, that they don't have time to "think about anything other than math or physics"; "None. I have other things to do besides getting into all that"; "We don't have time to think about such important problems"; "I don't have time to think about anything but the *concours.*"

And their statements are corroborated by their teachers' observations: "If we do some internal statistics, we see that for material reasons, it's true, they don't have a lot of time. And the few minutes of free time they do have, well, they want to use it for relaxing. So what do they do to relax? They read. And what books do they relax with? You can probably guess. They'll start first with *Spirou*, which obviously doesn't take much effort; they're in the universe of elementary psychology. Plus, *Spirou*, *Tintin*, and other comic books like that don't require any imagination or creative effort, whereas good reading means creating the text you're reading, remaking it, in a way, going halfway. So they choose books like these comics: *Tintin*, *Spirou*, etc., that don't require this creative effort. A second type of book they'll willingly read, and this is much more serious, as there's a presumption going around that's hard to combat, and that's that reading detective novels, the second type of relaxation, is reading for scientists. These books depict a conventional universe that's pretty abstract and that really doesn't give them anything too different from the habitual exercises they're used to. Consequently, they throw themselves into detective novels, and they drown in them. And really, what are they going to get out of it, what's going to stay with them? Absolutely nothing, you have to admit. Besides, they've forgotten them a few hours after they put them down" (*Servir*, Sainte-Geneviève alumni newsletter, 58 (Apr. 1963), pp. 59–60).

AN ENCHANTED EXPERIENCE

"Rue des Postes! [former location of Sainte-Geneviève, Tr.] It's one of my fondest early memories. I came in from the provinces, proud as could be to have my bac, and I trembled at the mere thought of seeing Paris, of living in Paris, of being up on Sainte-Geneviève hill between the École Polytechnique and the École Normale Supérieure, a few feet away from the famous Sorbonne and the École des Mines, knowing that for a few century-long years, I would do nothing but math. It was all beyond my wildest dreams. From that day on, I was completely taken by the superior way the school was run; by the marvelous discipline that prevailed, which was both strict and maternal; by the knowledge, devotion, and kindness of our teachers; by the obvious sainthood of some of them; by the cultivation of the vast majority of my new classmates. I can never think back without fondness on Father Du Lac, our rector, or Father Bellanger, our dean of studies, or Father Bernière, my first-year math teacher, or the Fathers d'Esclaibes and Saussié, my second-year math teachers; or on the pleasure I felt in witnessing an elegant proof or a clear, intelligent exposition of a hitherto undreamt of property of numbers, cones, or quadrilaterals; or on our Wednesday walks during which we would chat with our friends as we explored the capital, reading the history of France as it appeared on walls, in the sand of public garden paths, or on the cobblestones of ancient streets. When we walked down Sainte-Geneviève hill, whether toward or away from the school, we would remove our hats in one sweeping unanimous gesture on passing the gates of the École Polytechnique. For us, these were the gates of a temple, the threshold of an oratory reserved for the elite of the human race, the facade of which we would have liked to have seen engraved in gold not the idiotic and false trinomial 'Liberty, Equality, Brotherhood,' but Plato's mysterious words: 'God is the eternal geometer.' (. . .)

"After Sainte-Geneviève, I went on to the École Polytechnique where I spent two years in a state of intoxication. I was intoxicated by our outings in uniform, swords swinging at our sides, hat cocked slightly to one side, [. . .], with all of Paris watching us transfixed; intoxicated by my first contact with high-level analysis; and by the slow walk through the garden of delight whose flowers were differential equations, elliptical functions, integrals between imaginary limits, physics, the laws of chemistry, the unveiled splendors of astronomy; intoxicated by those *polytechnicien* friendships, which get their start in the study hall or in the long breaks when students would walk as one in a circle around the courtyard, which take shape in outings off campus, and which are cemented for life; friendships a thousand times deeper and more meaningful than any you make later because they are so youthful, spontaneous, close, generous, disinterested, and fraternal, because you speak the same language, you are moved as one by the slightest attack, the slightest blast, the least emotion. Yes, I was very happy at the École Polytechnique, and I defy any X to have been prouder than I to be one. But still, this *polytechnicien* enthusiasm has not managed to erase the happy memory of my years on Rue des Postes; and now, nearly half a century later, the two are like a double exposure in my mind, each image as deep and clear as the other" (Pierre Termier, Mines inspector general, member of the Academy of Sciences, *Servir* 37 (Apr. 1931), pp. 11–14).

"I owe my good fortune in being accepted at the Lycée Louis-le-Grand to a Sorbonne professor, Monsieur Ernout, I believe it was. (. . .) It was a Haven of

Grace for me: I found teachers who would take me under their wing and classmates who would round out the education provided by the teachers. But first, I found the kind of material security barracks can give, for during the years 1928 to 1931, Louis-le-Grand still maintained something of a Napoleonic discipline, symbolized by drum rolls. (. . .) What I remember most vividly are my teachers' voices. And those of my classmates.

"My *masters* were named Bayet, François, Bernès, Bolavon, Canat, Cayrou, Ponchont, Travers, Roubaud, Huby. I may be butchering their names, but what does that matter when, with the clarity of the memories of youth, I remember their voices, their gestures, their odd ticks, their clothing, and most especially their lectures. And their interest in and concern for the few 'exotic' ones among us: Pham Duy Khiem, from Vietnam; Louis Achille, Aimé Césaire, and August Boucolon, from the West Indies. What first drew my attention to the teachers was this interest, the kindness they showed their students of color, their rejection of *racial discrimination*, which, through their acts, gradually turned into a kind of unspoken protection, though they never fell into favoritism. This, for me, was the first feature of *French genius*.

"My teachers' lectures essentially gave me a sense of *method*. (. . .) When I think back today on those critical years, I find that my teachers gave me something else I didn't notice at first, and that is *a sense of Man*. That's a third feature of French genius. It's clear when you look at literature. More than the Latin writer, whose *ratio* was efficiency in service to the glory of Rome, more than the Greek writer, whose *logos* was truth for the harmony of the *Polis*, the French writer remains a *moralist*, even a poet like Baudelaire. If he challenges morality, he is challenging the official morality in the name of a future morality, which will have the *person* as both subject and object. (. . .)

"I have said that what one learns from one's classmates rounds out what one gets from the teachers. Of course, this complementary education is not carried out *ex cathedra*. It came about for me through contact with my classmates: in our open discussions and friendly conversations, in the courtyard, in the study hall. (. . .) My best friends today are still my old *khâgne* buddies. They first opened their hearts and shared their concerns. They were my introduction to contemporary France, its art, its literature, its politics. Why not say it – Georges Pompidou had a profound influence on me in this regard. He's the one who converted me to socialism, who got me to love Barrès, Proust, Gide, Baudelaire, and Rimbaud, who gave me a taste for the theater and museums. And Paris too. I remember our long walks in the warm rain and the grey-blue fog. I remember the sun in the streets in spring and fall, the soft golden light on the patina of stones and faces.

"If I became interested in men and ideas, if I became a writer and an art lover, if I am still a friend of France, I owe it all essentially to my classmates at Louis-le-Grand.

"It shouldn't be surprising that in my golden years I think back fondly on my time at Louis-le-Grand, on my teachers and classmates, through whom I was able to bring out the best in myself: a sense of humanity that enables me to put honors in their rightful place. For in the end, what counts is friendship, *love* – these are what give Art its true expression, and its value" (Léopold Sédar Senghor, "Lycée Louis-le-Grand, haut lieu de la culture française," in *Quatrième centenaire du lycée Louis-le-Grand, 1563–1963, études, souvenirs, documents* (Paris: Lycée Louis-le-Grand, 1963).

THE ETERNAL RETURN

"And it's true that I have often spoken in this dear old place, and I thank you, Headmaster, for having surely thought that this would bring me back my youth. I have spoken here since 1911, as a student, a teacher, and a general inspector, and at pretty regular intervals, every 15 years or so, so that I may be allowed to think I'm not getting old, but merely experiencing an eternal return. (. . .)

"But I spoke in January of 1911 with much more confidence than I do today. I was young. (...) After many battles, I was a student in the *khâgne* at Louis-le-Grand. It was the culmination of all my dreams. I had heard that it was here better than anywhere else in France that they taught the practice of that famous logos, that means to falsehood and truth, that art of convincing others that creates as many sophists as wise people, and that here at the end of my life I see more and more as a rather frightening power, perhaps the foundation of all the order, but also of all the disorder, in the world. There were about 50 of us young boys working with this power to become masters. I could never begin to say how much I owe these classmates. For a *khâgne* is first and foremost a group of students. (. . .) We had the best teachers, Lafont, Darcy, Belot, and one that I would like to mention with particular gratitude, Henri Durand, because he interpreted La Fontaine wonderfully, and because in listening to him I sensed for the first time what a French teacher could be, a sorcerer conjuring magic from the shadows, an artist, mediator of all artists, the one who maintains and transmits the thought and the language of his country in all their grandeur and beauty.

"Thirty years later, in the very same room, in the same magisterial chair even, I had my turn at interpreting La Fontaine as well as many other writers, and I tried to do so as well as master Henri Durand had done. I had not left the *khâgne*. *I've been a khâgne student all my life*. I see that I will never be able to talk about my profession with the detached politeness that befits this kind of ceremony. You'll have to excuse me. I imagine there are many teachers here. I'm sure they understand me, even if I seem to be giving my specialty, French, a particular importance. We all believe strongly in what we do. Teaching children their language is teaching them the use of what will become a sort of universal key for them, and that is surely the most important thing anyone could do. But to have the good fortune to teach it in a *khâgne* full of young people who love it and who are brought together expressly to recognize all its secrets, its tricks, and its power – and this from facts, from the most worthy texts – and to seek truth and beauty together, to be filled with ideas, to sort out the interplay of the forces of thought and the forms of language, no, really, I can't tell you what an immense pleasure you can get from this profession, and what a wondrous exchange a class becomes" (J. Guéhenno, Speech, in *Quatrième centenaire du lycée Louis-le-Grand, 1563–1963, études, souvenirs, documents* (Paris: Lycée Louis-le-Grand, 1963), pp. 8–9; emphasis added).

PART III

The Field of the Grandes Écoles and its Transformations

In the last analysis this compelling struggle for ever-threatened power and prestige was the dominant factor that condemned all those involved to enact these burdensome ceremonies. No single person within the figuration was able to initiate a reform of the tradition. Every slightest attempt to reform, to change the precarious structure of tensions, inevitably entailed an upheaval, a reduction or even abolition of the rights of certain individuals and families. To jeopardize such privileges was, to the ruling class of this society, a kind of taboo. The attempt would be opposed by broad sections of the privileged who feared, perhaps not without justification, that the whole system of rule that gave them privilege would be threatened or would collapse if the slightest detail of the traditional order were altered. So everything remained as it was.

Norbert Elias, *The Court Society*

1

A State of the Structure

We can no longer count the articles and books written on the subject of the grandes écoles: they include both overt and covert celebratory discourses, which are one of the clearest signs of the effects of the consecration bestowed by being gathered into the elite, satirical tracts, which often betray ambivalence, and scientifically inspired studies, which may share some of the characteristics of one of the aforementioned categories in a more or less disguised form and which, even when written from a historical perspective, are only rarely free of apologetic or polemical intent.[1] A person's interest in a given institution, even when an attempt is made to sublimate it in science, remains deeply rooted in their socially established relationship to this institution. The authors of these studies, nearly always alumni of the schools in question, are often bound to their object by psychological ties that for the most part vary in intensity and kind (positive or negative) according to the degree to which their social value still depends on their initial group membership. (We were in fact able to establish in a previous study that agents generally appear to be all the more wedded to a title or an academically guaranteed skill, knowledge of Latin, for example, the more completely their social value depends on this title or this property, and when they have no other more exceptional characteristics – a Nobel Prize winner may be quite indifferent to his belonging in a group.)

What stands out is that, without exception, all of these works relate to just a single grande école, taken in an isolated state, independently of the objective relations linking it to the other grandes écoles and, more generally, to the other institutions of higher education – even though the current and potential status of the school within the hierarchy of establishments is almost always the real object and even the principle of the discourse, usually normative, that is brought to bear on it.[2] But, in the social sciences, nothing is more critical than the initial carving out of one's object. And the inseparably constructivist and realistic epistemology that is essential to any science requires that the choice of investigative techniques and analytical methods be subordinated to a concern for constructing the object studied in a manner consistent with its articulations (which inevitably implies a form of circular logic since the data produced to validate a proposed model are a product of the data construction implied in that model). We can in fact posit, without going into a lengthy epistemological discussion of the "foundation of induction," that the historicist rationalism produced by a sociological analysis of the genesis and functioning of the scientific field as a field of socially and scientifically regulated struggles enables us to avoid the alternative that is forever recycled, in scarcely revamped guise, by reflection on science. To posit that scientific reason is a product of history and that it becomes increasingly authoritative with the growth of the relative autonomy of the field with respect to external determination and as the scientific world more completely asserts its specific laws of operation, particularly with regard to discussions, criticism, etc., is to reject both the "logicist" absolutism that, with Carnap, Popper, or Reichenbach, seeks to provide the scientific method with a priori "logical foundations" and the "historicist" or "psychologist" relativism that, in Quine's version, for example, holds that the failure of the attempt to reduce mathematics to logic leaves no other choice but to "naturalize epistemology" by assigning it to psychology.[3]

In the present case, it is both our prior knowledge of the general laws of the functioning of fields (social microcosms characteristic of differentiated societies) and empirical attention to the field effects that can be detected within the universe of establishments of higher education (grandes écoles or petites écoles,[4] universities, preparatory classes, etc.) that have led us to treat this universe as a field and to give ourselves the means to construct the network of the *objective relations* among establishments that, like heavenly bodies belonging to the same gravitational field, produce effects upon one another from afar. The existence of field effects – for instance, the transformations undergone by the École Normale and the École Polytechnique following the creation of the ENA – is one of the chief indicators of the fact that a set of agents and institutions functions as a field, as well as one of the reliable instruments for empirically determining the limits of this field, which are simply the point at which these effects are no longer found. For example, the absence of such effects leads us to doubt that organizations within a particular city, administrative region, or (in the United States) state, constitute a field. On the other hand, it is clear that universities as a whole, at least in the United States, form a field whose structure dictates to each of its member institutions the strategies befitting its position, as is shown by all studies that consider at least a few different positions in academic space (the work of Jérôme Karabel comes to mind, for example).

This methodological stance led us to gather all the relevant properties, that is, all those subject to significant and signifying variation per establishment, for all the students (or a representative fraction thereof) at all the relevant institutions, that is, all the institutions that were absolutely essential to reveal the system of objective relations existing among them.[5]

THE MODEL

Whether we apprehend the field of establishments of higher education on the scale of an entire set of institutions characterized, for the purposes of comparison, by a single indicator, their students' social origins (84 institutions), or on the scale of a structured sample of schools of differing status, characterized by a systematic set of relevant criteria (21 schools), we find that it is differentiated, in its first dimension, according to a cumulative index of social and academic prestige, running from the most prestigious grandes écoles – Ulm, Polytechnique, ENA – which are avenues to the highest social positions, down to the minor institutions (often in the provinces), which lead to positions as mid-level managers (for a list of the schools, see table 8). In a second dimension, based on the amount of academic capital required and on the degree of autonomy of the criteria and the stakes of the competition in properly academic terms, the field stretches out between an academically dominant but economically and socially dominated scientific and intellectual pole, featuring Ulm-sciences and Ulm-humanities, and an academically dominated but socially and economically dominant administrative and economic pole, featuring the ENA and HEC.

Table 8 List of schools (acronym/abbreviation, full name, location at time of survey, founding date)

Agro or INA Institut National Agronomique, National Agronomy Institute, Paris, 1876.

Archi Toulouse École d'Architecture de Toulouse, School of Architecture of Toulouse, which became Unité Pédagogique d'Architecture in 1968, Toulouse, 1904.

Arts Déco École Nationale Supérieure des Arts Décoratifs, National Advanced School of Decorative Arts, Paris, 1795.

Arts et Industries Textiles École Nationale des Arts et Industries Textiles, National School of Textile Arts and Industries, Roubaix, 1948.

Beaux-Arts École Nationale Supérieure des Beaux-Arts, National Advanced School of Fine Arts, Paris, 1795.

Bibliothécaires École Nationale Supérieure de Bibliothécaires, National Advanced School of Library Sciences, Paris, 1963.

Breguet École Supérieure d'Ingénieurs d'Électrotechnique et d'Électronique, ESIEE, Advanced School of Electrical Engineering, Paris, 1904.

Centrale (unless further specified) École Centrale des Arts et Manufactures, Central School of Arts and Manufacturing, Paris, 1829.

Centrale Lyon École Centrale Lyonnaise, Central School of Lyons, Lyons, 1857.

Chartes École Nationale des Chartes, National School of Palaeography and Librarianship, Paris, 1821.

Chimie Industrielle École Supérieure de Chimie Industrielle de Lyon, Advanced School of Industrial Chemistry of Lyons, Lyons, 1883.

Douanes École Nationale des Douanes, National Customs School, Neuilly-sur-Seine, 1946.

Continued on next page

Table 8 – *continued*

ECAM École Catholique d'Arts et Métiers, Catholic School of Engineering, Lyons, 1900.

École de l'Air Air Force Academy, Salon-de-Provence, 1933.

École Spéciale d'Architecture Advanced Architecture School, Paris, 1865.

Électronique Grenoble École Nationale Supérieure d'Électronique et de Radioélectricité, National Advanced School of Electronics and Radio/TV Electronics, Grenoble, 1957.

ENA École Nationale d'Administration, National School of Public Administration, ENA first *concours* (limited to students), ENA second *concours* (limited to civil servants), Paris, 1945.

ENS École(s) Normale(s) Supérieure(s) d'Ulm, de Sèvres, de Fontenay, de Saint-Cloud, and ENSET. Advanced Normal Schools. If ENS is written in the singular, with no further detail, it refers to the Ulm school.

ENSA École(s) Nationale(s) Supérieure(s) Agronomique(s), National Advanced Schools of Agronomy, Montpellier, 1872; Nancy, 1901; Rennes, 1830; Toulouse, 1947.

ENSAE École Nationale de la Statistique et de l'Administration Économique, National School of Statistics and Economic Administration, ENSAE first division (training INSEE administrators and statisticians); ENSAE second division (training assistants for the above), Paris, 1960.

ENSAM École Nationale Supérieure d'Arts et Métiers, National Advanced School of Engineering, Lille, 1881.

ENSET École Normale Supérieure de l'Enseignement Technique, Advanced Technical Normal School, Cachan, 1912.

ENSI École Nationale Supérieure de Chimie de Lille, National Advanced School of Chemistry, Lille, 1894.

ENSIAA École Nationale Supérieure des Industries Agricoles et Alimentaires, National Advanced School of Agriculture, Massy, 1893.

ESCAE or ESC École(s) Supérieure(s) de Commerce et d'Administration des Entreprises, Advanced Business and Management Schools, numbering 17 at the time of our data collection. The oldest are in Le Havre, 1871; Lyons, 1871; Rouen, 1871; the most recently established are in Amiens, 1962; Nice, 1962.

ESSEC École Supérieure des Sciences Économiques et Commerciales, Advanced School of Business and Economics, Paris, 1913.

Fontenay École Normale Supérieure de Fontenay-aux-Roses, Advanced Normal School of Fontenay-aux-Roses, arts and sciences, Fontenay-aux-Roses, 1887.

Grignon École Nationale Supérieure Agronomique, National Advanced School of Agronomy, Grognon-Thiverval, 1826.

HEC École des Hautes Études Commerciales, Advanced Business School, Jouy-en-Josas, 1881.

HECJF École de Haut Enseignement Commercial pour les Jeunes Filles, Advanced Business School for Women, Paris, 1916.

Horticulture École Nationale Supérieure d'Horticulture, National Advanced School of Horticulture, Versailles, 1873.

ICAM Institut Catholique d'Arts et Métiers, Catholic Institute of Engineering, Lille, 1898.

IEJ Institut d'Études Judiciaires, Institute of Judicial Studies, Paris, 1961.

IEP (unless further specified) Institut d'Études Politiques de Paris, Sciences-po, Political Science Institute, Paris, 1872.

IEP Bordeaux Institut d'Études Politiques de Bordeaux, Political Science Institute of Bordeaux, Bordeaux, 1948.

Table 8 – *continued*

IEP Grenoble Institut d'Études Politiques de Grenoble, Political Science Institute of Grenoble, Grenoble, 1948.

Institut Industriel du Nord de la France Industrial Institute of the North of France, Lille, 1854.

Institute Polytechnique de Grenoble Polytechnical Institute of Grenoble, Grenoble, 1901.

Internat Internat de Médecine de Paris, Resident Medical School of Paris.

IUT Institut(s) Universitaire(s) de Technologie, University Technology Institutes, Paris and the provinces, 1965.

Magistrature École Nationale de la Magistrature, National Magistrature School, Bordeaux, 1958.

Mécanique (et Électricité) École Spéciale de Mécanique et d'Électricité, National Advanced School of Mechanics and Electricity, Sudria, Paris, 1905.

Mines (unless further specified) École Nationale Supérieure des Mines de Paris, National Advanced Mining School of Paris (engineering students of the Corps des Mines in Paris principally recruited from among Polytechnique students and students who pass a *concours* at the end of the preparatory classes), Paris, 1783.

Mines Nancy École Nationale Supérieure de la Métallurgie et de l'Industrie des Mines de Nancy, National Advanced School of Metallurgy and Mining of Nancy, Nancy, 1919.

Mines Saint-Étienne École Nationale Supérieure des Mines de Saint-Étienne, National Advanced Mining School of Saint-Étienne, Saint-Étienne, 1816.

Navale École Navale, EN, Naval Academy, Lanvéoc-Poulmic, 1830.

Notariat École(s) de Notariat, Notary Schools, Paris (1896) and the provinces.

Physique-chimie École Supérieure de Physique et de Chimie Industrielles, EPCI, Advanced School of Industrial Physics and Chemistry, Paris, 1882.

Polytechnique École Polytechnique, Polytechnical School, Paris, 1794.

Polytechnique Féminine École Polytechnique Féminine, Polytechnical School for Women, Paris, 1925.

Ponts École Nationale Supérieure des Ponts et Chaussées, ENPC, National Advanced School of Bridges and Roads, Paris, 1747.

PTT École Nationale Supérieure des PTT, National Advanced PTT School (*postes, télégraphes, téléphones*), Paris, 1888.

Saint-Cloud École Normale Supérieure de Saint-Cloud, Advanced Normal School of Saint-Cloud, arts and sciences, Saint-Cloud, 1882.

Saint-Cyr École Spéciale Militaire (Saint-Cyr), ESMIA, Advanced Military School, Coëtquidan, 1802.

Sciences-po See IEP.

Sèvres École Normale Supérieure de Jeunes Filles, Advanced Normal School for Women, arts and sciences, Paris, 1881.

Supelec École Supérieure d'Électricité, ESE, Advanced Electricity School, Paris, 1894.

Tannerie École Française de Tannerie, French Tannery School, Lyons, 1899.

Télécom École Nationale Supérieure des Télécommunications, ENST, National Advanced School of Telecommunications, Paris, 1878.

Ulm École Nationale Supérieure de la rue d'Ulm, ENS, Advanced Normal School on Rue Ulm, arts and sciences, Paris, 1794.

Veto École Nationale Vétérinaire, National Veterinary School, Maisons-Alfort, 1765.

X See Polytechnique.

The principal social effect of the field of institutions of higher education and the subfield of the grandes écoles is based on a *double structural homology*: the homology between the fundamental opposition in the field of establishments of higher education, separating the grandes écoles from the petites écoles and the universities, and the opposition (which the previous opposition helps to institute within social space as a whole by establishing a distinct and definitive social boundary between the *grande porte* and the *petite porte*[6] at one of the most strategic points of this space) between the upper and the petty bourgeoisie, between top-level executives, vested with their definitive status from adolescence on, and so-called mid-level managers, who have often "risen in the ranks," and who must pay for their ascension in time even in the best of cases; and the homology between the fundamental opposition within the field of the grandes écoles, which sets "intellectual" schools apart from establishment schools, and the opposition within the field of power between the intellectual or artistic pole and the pole of economic or political power. In both cases, the principal effects of the functioning of the two academic universes are a consequence of their functioning as *structures*, as systems of academic differences, giving rise, within their own logic, to systems of social differences. (Tables 9–12 give detailed statistics on the characteristics of the students in the schools.)

In language that is simpler, being closer to ordinary intuition, but also less adequate, we might say – based on the fact, for example, that we are more likely to find sons of primary or secondary school teachers and professors at the École Normale Supérieure, sons of higher civil servants at the ENA, and sons of top commercial and industrial executives at HEC – that students generally tend to choose the institution (and later, the corresponding positions in the field of power) that requires and inculcates the (aesthetic, ethical, and political) dispositions that are most similar to those inculcated by their family and to those required and reinforced by the positions in the field of power into which this institution feeds. But described in this way, that is, in terms very much like the usual representation, this finding runs the risk of sending us back to the naive philosophy that governs "theories" of "social mobility," viewed as *inheritance from father to son* (it is significant, for example, that the author of a book that performs such a regression should have chosen for his title the common saying "like father, like son," which sums up this common philosophy).[7] In fact, the concept of a mode of reproduction as a system of structural mechanisms that tend to guarantee the reproduction of social structures – both the structure of social space as a whole and the structure of individual sectors of this space, such as the field of power – stands in opposition to the usual view of hereditary transfer as a direct or indirect transfer of forms of power or privileges from one individual or group to another, and particularly from father to son.[8] This is why, refusing to be satisfied with merely recording the processes of "social mobility" that occur within the population of grandes écoles students

Table 9 Father's occupation (percent)

	Farmworker	Farm owner	Laborer, semiskilled	Skilled, foreman	Clerical	Tradesman	Small commerce	Mid-level manager	Technician	Primary teacher	Secondary teacher	Professor	Intellectual prof.	Engineer	Private sector exec.	Public sector exec.	Military officer	Professions	Large merchant	CEO industry	NR
Ulm	2.1	0.5	1.6	4.1	4.1	3.1	1.6	10.9	2.6	3.6	10.4	7.2	2.6	8.8	8.8	12.4	2.1	8.8	2.6	2.1	–
Sèvres	1.3	0.6	0.7	2.0	5.2	2.0	2.0	5.9	2.6	7.8	13.7	9.1	2.6	8.5	7.8	11.1	2.0	7.8	2.0	3.9	1.3
St Cloud	5.6	0.7	9.4	5.6	12.1	5.6	5.6	10.3	3.7	9.4	11.2	0.9	–	2.8	5.6	3.7	1.9	1.9	1.9	1.9	0.9
Fontenay	5.9	0.6	5.9	3.7	8.1	9.6	2.2	8.8	7.4	13.2	11.8	2.9	0.7	4.4	1.5	8.1	0.7	2.9	–	1.5	–
Polytec.	1.7	0.6	1.2	2.7	3.8	1.2	1.9	9.0	1.2	5.2	8.1	3.5	0.8	14.2	16.2	7.9	2.3	10.6	2.5	5.2	0.2
Mines P	5.2	–	1.5	3.8	2.3	1.5	1.5	9.0	3.8	6.0	1.5	–	3.0	10.5	16.5	11.3	2.3	8.3	3.0	6.0	3.0
Mines N	1.8	1.2	–	6.6	2.4	1.8	3.0	9.0	3.6	9.6	5.4	1.8	0.6	11.4	12.6	9.6	3.0	8.4	4.8	2.4	0.6
Mines SE	3.1	–	3.1	4.7	3.1	–	3.1	7.8	3.1	4.7	1.6	–	–	15.6	20.3	14.1	4.7	6.2	3.1	1.6	0.6
Ponts	3.2	2.4	3.2	4.7	5.6	4.8	4.8	6.4	2.4	4.0	10.4	1.6	–	10.4	12.8	13.6	4.0	4.8	1.6	3.5	0.8
Supelec	5.4	0.7	0.9	4.7	7.5	2.6	4.7	10.1	5.1	3.5	4.7	0.2	1.9	10.1	12.0	5.9	3.4	6.1	3.7	3.9	2.6
Central	3.9	0.9	1.6	3.6	5.0	3.4	4.1	10.9	2.0	4.8	5.2	0.5	0.7	10.4	13.8	9.7	3.4	9.3	2.3	3.9	0.7
Télécom	6.4	1.1	3.2	4.8	5.9	1.1	5.4	9.7	3.2	6.4	3.2	2.1	2.1	13.4	7.5	5.9	1.6	5.4	5.4	1.6	4.3
Ph-Ch.	3.2	–	2.1	4.3	4.3	2.1	3.2	19.3	2.1	2.1	1.4	2.1	1.1	14.1	18.3	8.6	2.1	4.3	2.1	3.2	–
Breguet	3.4	1.0	1.0	6.8	3.9	2.9	7.3	12.2	2.4	1.9	1.4	0.5	1.0	16.1	17.1	4.9	2.4	5.8	4.9	1.9	1.0
Mécaniq	–	–	1.1	4.4	1.1	4.4	3.3	7.8	3.3	2.2	2.2	–	2.2	15.5	22.2	5.5	2.2	8.9	4.4	7.8	1.1
ENSAM L	0.3	2.8	15.8	–	12.0	6.0	5.3	19.0	–	6.7	3.5	–	–	15.1	12.3	–	–	–	–	–	1.1
Agro	8.3	7.2	–	0.7	2.2	1.8	2.2	9.1	2.5	4.7	5.4	1.5	1.4	11.2	14.9	11.6	2.5	6.2	1.4	4.3	0.7
Grignon	18.4	9.2	3.1	3.1	3.1	–	1.5	3.1	–	6.1	1.5	1.5	–	13.8	13.8	12.3	1.5	7.7	–	–	–
ENSIAA	8.5	7.0	4.2	4.2	2.8	4.2	2.8	5.6	4.2	4.2	2.8	2.8	–	9.9	14.1	8.4	1.4	4.2	–	5.6	2.8
Hortic	16.7	16.7	6.5	–	7.4	3.7	7.4	16.7	–	7.4	3.7	3.7	–	12.9	5.6	–	–	1.8	–	–	–
Montpl	15.5	11.1	2.2	4.4	4.4	2.2	2.2	6.7	8.9	6.7	6.7	–	–	6.7	4.4	6.7	–	8.9	–	–	2.2
Rennes	8.0	14.0	–	–	–	2.0	4.0	10.0	4.0	6.0	2.0	–	4.0	8.0	24.0	4.0	–	4.0	4.0	–	2.0
PTT	6.3	–	18.8	–	12.5	12.5	25.0	3.1	–	3.1	3.1	–	–	3.1	12.5	–	–	–	–	–	–
ENSAE1	2.3	2.3	2.3	–	4.6	3.1	5.7	9.4	11.5	8.1	6.9	–	–	9.2	34.4	–	–	8.1	–	4.5	–
ENSAE2	10.9	–	7.8	6.2	10.9	3.1	4.7	7.5	1.5	–	4.7	3.1	1.6	6.2	7.8	14.1	1.6	1.6	–	4.7	1.6
IEP	1.7	1.5	0.7	0.7	1.3	1.1	3.6	8.2	1.5	1.4	2.6	1.7	1.6	6.0	19.6	14.4	3.2	14.8	5.6	8.8	0.9
IEP PS	1.7	1.2	0.3	0.5	1.0	1.3	3.5	8.2	1.3	1.7	2.7	1.5	2.3	5.3	18.7	16.0	3.0	17.0	4.2	7.8	0.7
IEP Bx	1.8	4.7	6.5	–	5.4	3.0	10.1	14.3	–	3.6	4.7	–	–	3.6	27.4	–	–	13.1	–	–	1.2
ENA 1	1.0	2.0	–	–	4.0	2.0	3.0	11.1	–	1.0	4.7	5.1	3.0	8.1	35.4	–	4.0	14.1	1.0	4.0	1.0
ENA 2	11.1	2.8	11.1	2.8	8.3	2.8	2.8	11.1	5.5	–	5.1	5.5	–	2.8	19.4	–	2.8	2.8	2.8	5.6	2.0
HEC	1.1	0.7	–	0.7	2.8	1.4	4.1	7.3	1.2	1.6	2.1	0.7	1.2	6.6	24.4	11.6	4.8	8.9	9.8	7.7	0.9

Table 10 Father's diploma and mother's occupation (percent)

	Father's diploma								Mother's occupation									
	None	CEP, CAP	BEPC, BEI	BS, bac	Petite école	Licence	Agrég.	NR	None	Farming	Blue-collar worker	Clerical	Tradeswoman, small commerce	Mid-level manager	Primary teacher	Exec., professions	Other	NR
Ulm	2.1	14.0	8.3	12.9	6.2	31.1	19.2	6.2	58.5	1.0	0.5	6.2	3.1	3.6	11.4	14.5	–	1.0
Sèvres	1.3	9.8	4.6	20.2	8.5	28.7	21.6	5.2	49.0	0.6	0.6	5.2	1.3	2.6	20.9	19.6	–	–
St Cloud	2.8	41.1	13.1	20.5	3.7	9.3	4.7	4.7	60.7	0.9	5.6	2.8	4.7	0.9	19.6	3.7	–	0.9
Fontenay	5.1	30.9	8.8	22.8	6.6	9.5	10.3	5.9	41.2	5.1	2.9	8.8	2.9	5.1	25.0	8.8	–	–
Polytechnique	3.1	12.1	7.1	14.4	9.1	27.0	22.1	5.0	65.7	0.6	0.4	5.6	1.9	4.2	9.0	11.7	–	0.8
Mines Paris	2.3	15.0	12.0	18.0	6.8	21.8	15.8	8.3	62.4	1.5	2.2	3.0	3.0	5.2	12.0	7.5	–	3.0
Mines Nancy	3.6	12.6	9.6	18.1	17.5	15.6	15.0	7.8	66.3	0.6	–	5.4	3.0	0.6	13.8	8.4	0.6	1.2
Mines St Ét.	4.6	12.3	6.1	16.9	13.8	26.1	9.2	10.8	69.2	–	–	4.6	3.1	1.5	10.8	9.2	–	1.5
Ponts&Chauss.	6.4	24.0	12.0	14.4	11.2	13.6	13.6	4.8	60.8	2.4	0.8	9.6	4.8	5.6	8.0	1.6	4.8	1.6
Supelec	3.3	17.1	12.7	13.1	12.7	19.9	5.6	15.5	56.6	0.9	1.6	6.3	3.0	5.4	7.5	1.9	3.0	13.6
Centrale	4.5	17.0	8.4	15.2	7.5	26.5	11.5	9.3	63.9	0.7	0.9	6.1	2.9	3.4	11.3	6.8	–	3.8
Télécom	8.1	17.7	9.7	12.9	8.1	18.8	10.7	14.0	50.5	1.6	2.7	3.7	2.7	2.7	7.5	3.7	5.4	19.3
Physique-Ch.	2.1	18.3	6.4	15.0	19.3	16.1	14.0	8.6	82.8	–	1.1	7.5	2.1	2.1	–	1.1	2.1	1.1
Breguet	4.4	21.9	10.7	8.3	18.0	20.5	4.9	11.2	54.1	1.4	1.4	12.2	8.3	6.8	3.4	1.0	1.0	10.2
Mécanique	4.4	14.4	11.1	6.7	20.0	26.7	6.7	10.0	56.7	–	2.2	10.0	5.5	2.2	5.5	2.2	3.3	12.2
ENSAM Lille	3.9	22.9	16.9	13.7	2.8	17.2	1.4	21.1	65.1	0.7	1.4	8.1	7.7	2.4	8.8	3.5	–	2.1
Agro	12.7	12.0	6.2	14.1	7.2	34.4	9.4	4.0	69.9	5.1	–	5.8	1.4	2.5	8.0	6.9	–	0.3
Grignon	26.1	7.7	6.1	12.3	4.6	27.7	15.4	–	72.3	6.1	1.5	–	3.1	3.1	7.7	1.5	–	4.6
ENSIAA Massy	22.5	11.3	8.4	12.7	8.4	25.3	8.4	2.8	60.5	2.8	2.8	7.0	4.2	2.8	8.4	8.4	–	2.8
Horticulture	16.7	25.9	3.7	18.5	9.3	16.7	7.4	1.8	50.0	12.9	–	11.1	1.8	1.8	11.1	3.7	–	7.4
Montpellier	22.2	20.0	13.3	11.1	6.7	17.8	4.4	4.4	68.9	8.9	2.2	6.7	8.0	–	8.9	2.2	–	2.2
Rennes	20.0	4.0	12.0	22.0	12.0	20.0	6.0	4.0	64.0	10.0	2.0	2.0	8.0	2.0	6.0	4.0	–	2.0
PTT	15.6	43.7	12.5	18.7	–	9.4	–	–	68.7	–	3.1	12.5	6.2	–	6.2	–	–	3.1
ENSAE 1D	5.7	6.9	4.6	17.2	17.2	26.4	19.5	2.3	63.2	1.1	–	2.3	1.1	6.9	11.5	10.3	1.1	2.3
ENSAE 2D	18.7	21.9	7.8	9.4	9.4	14.1	9.4	9.4	68.7	3.1	–	10.9	1.5	7.8	4.7	3.1	–	–
IEP overall	4.1	8.9	5.1	12.3	10.5	40.7	13.8	4.6	71.7	0.2	0.5	4.0	3.1	3.4	3.1	9.8	0.2	4.0
IEP Publ. Serv.	3.5	7.8	4.5	13.4	11.3	38.9	16.0	4.5	70.6	0.3	2.4	3.5	3.2	3.8	3.0	11.7	0.2	3.7
IEP Bordeaux	3.0	15.5	5.9	19.6	6.5	32.1	4.7	12.5	73.8	1.2	2.0	5.4	2.4	4.2	4.7	4.7	0.6	0.6
ENA 1	2.0	9.1	10.1	12.1	7.1	38.4	18.2	3.0	61.6	–	2.0	5.0	2.0	–	3.0	21.2	–	5.0
ENA 2	19.4	36.2	8.3	5.5	8.3	19.4	2.8	–	52.8	5.5	2.8	5.5	8.3	11.1	5.5	5.5	–	2.8
HEC	3.9	10.2	4.8	14.1	8.6	36.8	14.1	7.5	67.7	0.7	0.2	5.3	3.4	4.4	5.2	10.2	–	2.8

Table 11 Residence (percent)

	Place of residence at start of sixième								Parental residence at time of survey			
	Abroad	*<2,500 inhabitants*	*2,500–10,000*	*10,000–50,000*	*50,000–100,000*	*>100,000*	*Paris + Paris area*	*NR*	*Abroad*	*Provinces*	*Paris*	*NR*
Ulm	2.1	8.8	3.6	13.5	5.7	31.6	33.1	1.5	2.6	59.6	37.3	0.5
Sèvres	2.0	7.8	3.3	14.4	5.2	33.3	33.3	0.6	0.6	56.8	41.8	0.6
St Cloud	0.9	32.7	5.6	14.9	2.8	24.3	18.7	–	0.9	79.4	19.6	–
Fontenay	0.7	20.6	11.7	15.4	3.7	16.2	28.7	2.9	2.2	63.2	33.8	0.7
Polytechnique	0.6	11.0	5.6	11.4	4.6	26.2	39.1	1.5	4.6	55.3	38.9	1.1
Mines Paris	4.5	14.3	6.0	15.8	1.5	15.0	38.3	4.5	2.2	54.9	40.6	2.2
Mines Nancy	2.4	16.3	8.4	13.8	3.6	24.1	30.1	1.2	3.0	57.8	38.5	0.6
Mines St Etienne	9.2	13.8	10.8	13.8	–	30.8	21.5	–	1.5	64.6	33.8	–
Ponts	12.8	8.8	2.4	8.0	2.4	26.4	37.6	1.6	9.6	50.4	39.2	0.8
Supelec	5.4	11.0	8.4	13.8	3.5	20.9	35.4	1.4	4.7	55.9	38.2	1.2
Centrale	2.0	12.5	4.7	15.0	3.6	24.7	37.4	–	1.1	58.0	39.7	1.1
Télécom	19.9	5.9	6.4	14.5	2.7	21.5	27.4	1.6	19.3	50.5	29.0	1.1
Physique-Ch.	3.2	3.2	4.3	15.0	4.3	9.7	58.0	2.1	2.1	34.4	63.4	–
Breguet	1.9	6.3	6.3	9.7	1.9	9.3	63.9	0.5	1.0	29.3	69.7	–
Mécanique	2.2	7.8	3.3	12.2	6.7	15.5	48.9	3.3	2.2	37.8	60.0	–
ENSAM Lille	1.7	10.2	7.7	16.2	2.1	12.3	48.2	1.4	1.0	48.6	49.6	0.7
Agro	5.8	24.6	4.0	8.7	4.7	18.5	33.0	0.7	0.7	59.4	39.5	0.3
Grignon	1.5	36.9	3.1	6.1	7.7	15.4	23.1	6.1	–	70.8	24.6	4.6
ENSIAA Massy	–	25.3	2.8	16.9	4.2	22.5	25.3	2.8	–	70.4	28.2	1.4
Horticulture	–	42.6	–	3.7	7.4	24.1	20.4	1.8	–	75.9	22.2	1.8
Montpellier	2.2	28.9	13.3	11.1	6.7	15.5	20.0	2.2	2.2	75.5	22.2	–
Rennes	–	22.0	10.0	10.0	6.0	20.0	32.0	–	–	76.0	24.0	–
PTT	21.9	15.6	6.2	3.1	9.4	31.2	12.5	–	–	84.3	15.6	–
ENSAE 1D	3.4	13.8	5.7	14.9	2.3	24.1	34.5	1.1	1.1	47.1	49.4	2.3
ENSAE 2D	3.1	20.3	15.6	14.0	7.8	9.4	29.7	–	–	65.6	32.8	1.5
IEP overall	6.0	6.4	4.7	11.3	4.3	16.8	48.0	2.3	5.4	37.1	56.4	1.1
IEP Publ. Serv.	3.5	8.5	4.2	11.3	4.3	16.8	49.1	2.2	3.0	38.2	58.2	0.5
IEP Bordeaux	4.2	20.8	7.1	20.2	12.5	28.6	2.4	4.2	5.3	94.0	0.6	–
ENA 1	1.0	2.0	3.0	13.1	4.0	12.1	56.6	8.1	2.0	38.4	59.6	–
ENA 2	–	13.9	11.1	25.0	–	19.4	22.2	8.3	–	77.8	22.2	–
HEC	3.6	4.4	5.0	8.4	2.0	24.3	52.1	0.2	1.2	43.2	54.8	0.7

– which would ensure that we appeared completely neutral and altogether in line with the objectivity of simple bureaucratic record-keeping – we must endeavor to apprehend the field of the grandes écoles as such, a field whose functioning as a structure contributes to the reproduction of the structure of social space and the structure of the field of power.

In channeling toward each educational institution the students richest in the dispositions that the institution is supposed to inculcate, a high proportion of whom have been brought up in families located in the very region of the field of power fed by the institution, academic mechanisms tend in effect to perpetuate the differences constitutive of social space and, in the particular case of the grandes écoles, the differences according to the structure of inherited capital between students who are themselves originally

Table 12   Academic background (percent)

	Type of establishment in sixième				Section in première							
	CEG	*Collège, lycée*	*Private*	*NR*	*Tech.*	*M & M'*	*Class.*	*B*	*C*	*A*	*A'*	*NR*
Ulm	4.7	79.8	15.5	–	1.5	12.9	1.0	3.1	32.1	19.7	28.5	1.0
Sèvres	1.3	87.6	9.1	2.0	–	9.8	0.6	3.3	41.8	20.9	22.9	0.6
St Cloud	39.2	50.5	7.5	2.8	0.9	65.4	–	11.2	12.1	4.7	5.6	–
Fontenay	28.7	64.7	5.1	1.5	–	55.1	–	16.2	17.6	4.4	4.4	2.2
Polytechnique	5.0	79.9	14.8	0.2	2.5	16.6	0.2	–	58.0	0.8	21.2	0.8
Mines Paris	6.0	76.7	15.0	2.2	0.7	13.5	0.7	–	58.6	1.5	22.5	2.2
Mines Nancy	7.2	79.5	12.6	0.6	4.8	22.3	1.2	–	54.2	–	15.0	2.4
Mines St Et.	10.8	63.1	26.1	–	7.7	18.4	3.1	–	50.8	–	20.0	–
Ponts&Chauss.	4.8	84.8	5.6	4.8	8.0	28.8	9.6	–	38.4	–	12.0	3.2
Supelec	10.5	64.5	12.2	12.7	6.8	30.7	7.3	0.5	37.3	0.5	9.4	7.5
Centrale	9.1	77.5	13.1	0.2	4.3	22.9	–	0.9	55.1	0.4	15.6	0.7
Télécom	13.4	63.4	5.9	17.2	5.4	32.9	3.8	0.5	30.3	0.5	10.8	15.7
Physique-Ch.	4.3	66.7	12.9	16.1	3.2	27.9	6.4	1.1	45.1	–	8.6	7.5
Breguet	20.0	60.0	12.7	7.3	17.1	46.8	8.3	0.5	22.4	–	1.9	2.9
Mécanique	5.5	66.7	14.4	13.3	21.1	35.5	8.9	–	28.9	–	1.1	3.3
ENSAM Lille	35.9	58.4	4.6	1.1	75.0	9.8	–	–	11.6	0.3	2.4	0.7
Agro	6.2	76.8	15.6	1.4	2.5	29.7	0.7	1.4	54.3	0.7	9.0	1.4
Grignon	9.2	78.4	12.3	–	1.5	35.4	–	1.5	52.3	1.5	6.1	1.5
ENSIAA Massy	15.5	66.2	15.5	2.8	7.0	36.6	1.4	1.4	45.1	1.4	7.0	–
Horticulture	16.7	62.9	16.7	3.7	12.9	50.0	1.8	1.8	18.5	1.8	9.2	3.7
Montpellier	24.4	64.4	11.1	–	8.9	44.4	4.4	2.2	37.8	2.2	–	–
Rennes	14.0	72.0	10.0	4.0	4.0	44.0	2.0	2.0	36.0	–	12.0	–
PTT	12.5	56.2	28.1	3.1	18.7	40.6	–	–	31.2	6.2	3.1	–
ENSAE 1D	8.0	73.5	17.2	1.1	2.3	19.5	1.1	3.4	54.0	1.1	17.2	1.1
ENSAE 2D	14.0	65.6	20.3	–	9.4	59.4	–	1.5	25.0	1.5	–	3.1
IEP overall	2.2	63.9	31.3	2.6	1.1	17.6	1.9	25.6	28.3	13.8	9.7	1.8
IEP Publ. Serv.	0.7	66.4	31.9	1.0	0.2	13.2	1.5	24.0	30.2	16.5	13.8	0.5
IEP Bordeaux	5.3	66.1	28.0	0.6	4.2	27.4	4.7	31.5	13.1	13.1	3.5	2.4
ENA 1	2.0	68.7	29.3	–	–	9.1	2.0	17.2	26.2	22.2	22.2	1.0
ENA 2	11.1	66.7	22.2	–	5.5	33.3	8.3	19.4	8.3	11.1	5.5	8.3
HEC	2.1	76.8	20.9	0.2	0.7	20.9	1.1	2.3	61.1	0.7	13.0	0.2

Key: Tech. = technical; M & M' = modern (not Latin); Class. = general classical; B = Latin, languages; C = Latin, mathematics; A = Latin, Greek; A' = Latin, Greek, mathematics.

from the different regions of social space and the field of power. To speak of "academic mechanisms," as we have just done, is simply a shorthand way of reminding the reader that all individual actions leading to the channeling, selection, and distribution of students among the different "boxes" that the educational system offers them are carried out "under structural constraints" and consequently take on an inevitability that cannot be reduced to the result of a statistical aggregation of individual "choices."[9] Indeed, choices, whether those made by teachers as they channel and select their students or those made by students as they channel and select themselves according to the logic of the "vocation," are governed by the structure of the establishments, disciplines, or tracks in relation to which agents must define themselves by implementing principles of vision and division homologous to these objective divisions of the academic order.[10] In other words, the observed distribution of students among the different schools according to social origin and academic capital is the outcome of countless "choices" founded on the relationship between the structured habitus of the "selectors" and the "selected" and the structure of the field of educational institutions, whose most powerful and best hidden effects are achieved through the homology linking it to the fundamental structures of social space, and particularly those of the field of power.

It is not easy to encompass in just a few sentences the universe of the operations of successful cooptation that give rise to the statistical correspondence between positions in the space of institutions and the dispositions of their occupants. We will simply remind the reader that the matching of the relevant properties is carried out through the application of categories of perception and appreciation that, like the pairs of adjectives in which they are expressed, are primarily the product of the internalization of objective structures of the academic order, which are thus transformed into academic forms of classification. "Sympathy" grounded in the affinity of habitus essentially rests on infinitesimal indices through which the fundamental principles of habitus are revealed, in other words, on ways of acting, speaking, etc., that express the modality of a person's relationship to the corps being reproduced, or, in the final analysis, their belief in and adherence to the ultimate values in which the corps recognizes itself. But we would be sorely mistaken if we were to reduce the process of cooptation to explicit operations of selection. The chosen also play a role in successful cooptation in choosing their choosers by offering themselves up for the choosing, while others spontaneously exclude themselves from a competition that would exclude most of them anyway. Agents (statistically) tend to recognize only those authorities that are likely to recognize them, among other reasons because their way of presenting themselves, and the mere fact that they come forward, show that they recognize them.

Thus, through countless practical operations of subjective and objective selection, at the conclusion of which adolescents originating in different sectors of the field of power find themselves channeled into different educational institutions in such a way that in each of these institutions we find the greatest possible number of individuals from the same sector of the field of power, and, consequently, the greatest possible number of individuals endowed with systems of dispositions that are internally similar and as different as possible from those of the students in another institution, the educational system acts as an objectivated *classification algorithm*. It distributes the individuals offered up to it into classes that are as internally homogeneous and as externally heterogeneous as possible with respect to a number of fundamental criteria. Inasmuch as it tends to establish the greatest possible distance between highly homogeneous classes, it contributes to reproducing and legitimating the ensemble of distances that, at any given time, constitute social structure.

These, then, are the principal effects that institutions of higher learning help to produce. They institute two significant breaks within the student population: the first, between petite école and grande école students; and the second, within the latter group, chosen people who together have been instituted as an "elite" whose excellence is socially guaranteed, between students of the different grandes écoles. And all this by producing, and more importantly, by consecrating, both *social identities* that are at once in competition and complementary and, in the same move, *corps* (the "grands corps"[11]) that, despite the competition that sets them against each other within the field of power, are united by a genuine organic solidarity.

GRANDE PORTE AND *PETITE PORTE*:
TWO MODES OF ENTRY

The field of institutions of higher education tends to establish distinct, rigid, and definitive discontinuities among competitors whose officially evaluated and classified abilities are actually in continuous distribution. As rites of institution that fulfill a function for our societies very similar to that of the rites of nomination through which sexual and genealogical identities are assigned (baptism, circumcision, etc.), the acts of official nomination through which the educational system grants exclusive titles (at the conclusion of a veritable course of initiation – retreat, trials, etc.) delimit and arrange an order among groups that, founded as they are on the dualist logic of inclusion and exclusion, gather their members together to partake of a kind of socially instituted *essence* – that is, social identity as difference, both produced and designated by the name assigned (*"normalien"*, *"polytechnicien,"* etc.). The consecration ensured by assimilation into the different schools tends to rescue the chosen ones from the uncertainties and risks of biographical history by giving the starting point of the ensuing trajectory the power, if not to determine its entire subsequent evolution, at least to delimit a class of probable trajectories for each of the academically defined orders, that is, a set of careers whose path at any given moment is only approximately determined with respect to the starting point.[12] The academic title, an act of nomination guaranteed by the state, in this case assigns a social destiny to those it distinguishes; the efficacy of this socially guaranteed official prediction rests in part in the effect of auto-verification that it produces on its beneficiaries.

In an attempt to uncover the principles of differentiation active in the field of establishments of higher education, we initiated two complementary studies, early on, the first on all institutions of higher learning characterized by one specific indicator, and the second on a more limited number of grandes écoles characterized by a set of data on the social and academic properties of their students. For the first study, we selected 84 institutions characterized by the only comparable data available for all of them – their students' original social class (which we know to be closely associated with many other relevant indicators), with parents' place of residence and sex serving as illustrative variables.

In choosing to work on this scale, we had to resign ourselves to accepting the limitations related to the comparative lack of truly comparable indicators for all the relevant properties: student academic status and achievement (type of secondary school attended, baccalauréat subject, age at which the baccalauréat was taken, honors on same, nominations to the Concours Général); student social status (parents' and grandparents' occupation, geographical origin); academic status of the institution (level of faculty, credentials required for acceptance, length and type of preparation required, length of program, etc.); social status of the institution (founding date, prestige, local or national recruitment, the latter with the aid of a national *concours*, general or specialized education, social value of the diploma, private – religious or otherwise – or public support). It would have been particularly useful to have found a single index of academic success for all 84 institutions since that is the only way we would have been able to distinguish the socially and academically superior institutions such as the Paris École des Mines or the École Polytechnique from socially superior but rather more academically inferior institutions such as the École de Mécanique et d'Électricité, the Écoles Supérieures de Commerce et d'Administration des Entreprises, etc. But Ministry of Education statistics, which include father's occupation, parents' place of residence (by *département*), students' sex, a yearly breakdown of students, and the lycée at which students prepared for entry into schools that recruit through *concours*, give no data on secondary schools attended or baccalauréat results.

The data on which this first analysis is based were obtained through close examination of statistics provided by the Service Centrale des Statistiques et de la Conjoncture of the Ministry of Education (documents housed in the National Archives in the series F 17 *bis*). We examined available statistics on more than 200 establishments of higher education for the period 1963 to 1971 before determining which institutions could be included in our study. For several crucial institutions, such as the Internat de Médecine and the Paris Institut d'Études Judiciaires, we made up for the absence of reliable archival data by receiving permission from the individual schools to consult their files.

What we wanted in fact was to have at least one institution for each of the *relevant positions* within the different regions of the field of institutions of higher education that correspond to the different regions of the field of power, these being art and architecture, teaching and research, the higher civil service, the magistrature, medicine, heads of industrial firms (and managers or engineers), heads of commercial firms, and the military. Of the 84 institutions used, ten are represented by two points (one a principal variable, the other a supplementary variable), corresponding to the two available data sources (our own study and the government sources), which were interesting to compare because they turned out to be equally insufficient, but for different reasons (variable quality of information, variable degree of representativeness of the sample). In fact, as the charts show, in most cases, the two points are very close together. We also used as supplementary variables those schools for which the data furnished either by our direct research or government statistics did not seem sufficiently reliable (high rate of nonresponses to the question of father's occupation, two categories differentiated in our analysis not differentiated in their documents). This turned out to be the case, for example, for the École de l'Air and the École Navale, the ENSET, the Conservatoire de Musique, the École des Douanes, the École de la Magistrature, and the Institut d'Études Judiciaires.[13]

The first factor, which represents 31.4 percent of the total inertia,[14] clearly shows (cf. figures 3 and 4) the opposition between the *grande porte*, with the top grandes écoles (École Nationale d'Administration, École des Hautes Études Commerciales, École Normale Supérieure d'Ulm, École Polytechnique, etc.) boasting a very high percentage of students from the dominant class (60 percent or more at ENA, Sciences-po, and HEC), and the *petite porte*, represented by humanities and science facultés, Instituts Universitaires de Technologie,[15] petites écoles, engineering schools, PTT schools [Postes, Télégraphes, Téléphones], etc., which have only a relatively small proportion of upper-class students (35 percent or fewer in humanities and science facultés, Instituts Universitaires de Technologie, and engineering schools).[16] On the right-hand side, we find all the establishments of national rank, which are the most prestigious and also the most comprehensive, since they prepare students for the most noble careers in industry, business, higher civil service, and research, and because they facilitate future transfers from one sector to another (*"pantouflage"*). On the left-hand side, we find the establishments that prepare students for executant positions, jobs as technicians, mid-level managers, secondary school teachers, or, at best, narrowly specialized "minor engineers," jobs that rarely permit changes of career or transitions from one sector or job to another. As we descend in the hierarchy, the establishments become *increasingly specialized*. So, for example, we move from the École Polytechnique or the Écoles des Mines to Supelec, the École des Télécommunications, or the École Centrale de Lyon (at the center of the diagram), to the Institut Polytechnique de Grenoble, the ENSI de Chimie de Lille (left of center), and finally to the École de Tannerie de Lyon or the École Nationale Supérieure des Arts et Industries Textiles de Roubaix (on the far left).[17]

Thus, as we can see from the fact that the structure of the distribution of the points corresponding to the occupations of the families of the students in the different establishments is very similar to the structure of the distribution of these occupations in social space, the hierarchy of institutions based on the social status of their students corresponds quite closely to the general social hierarchy – which tends to reveal the limits of the specific effect of a selection like that of the educational institution, which claims nonetheless to be based on autonomous criteria free of social determination. This being said, because indices of academic success are not included in our study, the hierarchy corresponds more closely to the *market value* of the titles than to their purely academic value (measured by the relative "difficulty" of a particular *concours*). This is why institutions like Sciences-po and HEC occupy higher positions than Ulm and Polytechnique, which are nevertheless higher

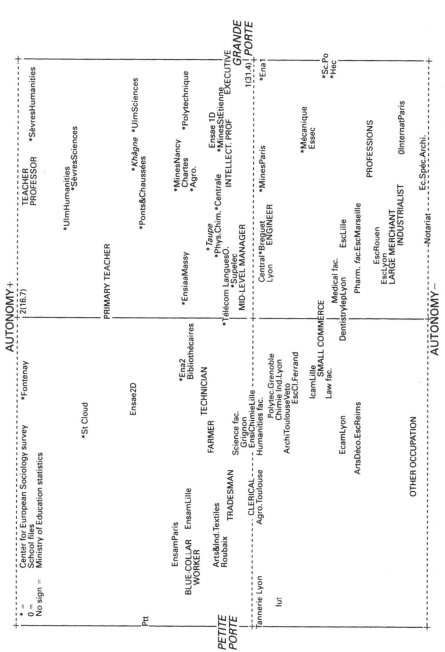

Figure 3 The space of establishments of higher education (principal variables)

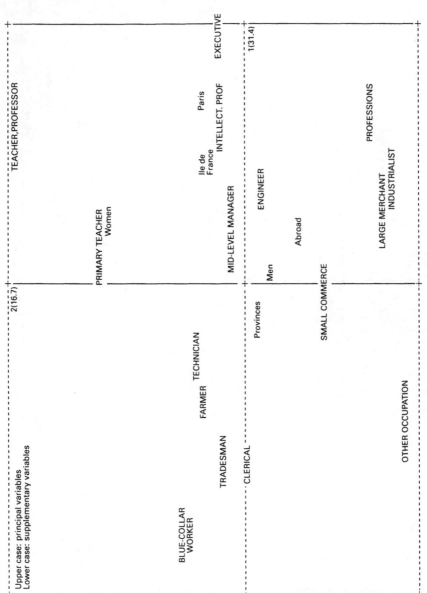

Figure 4 Social characteristics of students (principal and supplementary variables)

up in the specifically academic hierarchy; for the same reason, "sanctuary schools" whose academic selectivity and autonomy are low (Breguet, Mécanique et Electricité) turn out to be closer to the schools ranked highest by purely academic criteria, such as Ulm and Sèvres.

This cardinal opposition is found within each of the subspaces of the university field that correspond to the broad sectors of the field of power. For schools of education and research, the opposition lies between, on one side, Ulm and Sèvres, and, on the other, the ENSET (the most specialized and technical normal school), with Fontenay and Saint-Cloud falling in between, although closer to the ENSET.[18] In the sector of schools of public administration, the opposition lies between the ENA, the Paris IEP, and the ENSAE, and the schools that prepare for entry into the least prestigious ministries and corps (Douanes, PTT) or provincial schools (such as the IEP in Bordeaux or Grenoble), both of these being institutions with a high proportion of provincial students from the wage-earning portion of the middle classes. Within this same sector, we find an even more significant opposition between the two paths of access to a single grande école, in other words, between those who enter young by way of the *concours* limited to students (ENA 1, students who have been successful in the first *concours*; ENSAE 1, first division) and those who have come by way of the internal promotion limited to civil servants (ENA 2, civil servants who have been successful in the second *concours*; ENSAE 2, second division).[19] In the subspace of schools of business and management, the two most prestigious schools, HEC and ESSEC, are opposed to the various ESCAE (Écoles Supérieures de Commerce et d'Administration des Entreprises). Within the universe of engineering schools, the top grandes écoles – École Polytechnique, Écoles des Mines, Écoles des Ponts et Chaussées, etc. – which prepare students for the highest careers, are opposed to the most technical and to the most provincial schools, which most directly prepare their students for narrowly defined sectors and occupations, often those in decline, or devalued (Arts et Industries Textiles de Roubaix, Tannerie de Lyon, and to a lesser extent, Écoles des Arts et Métiers and Écoles de Chimie Industrielle).[20] We also find an opposition between the École Navale, founded in 1830 for the training of naval officers, and the École de l'Air, founded in 1937 and situated closer to the pole occupied by the establishments that are the most technical, the most specialized, the most directly oriented toward professional life and vocational training, and at the same time the most open to students from the working and middle classes.[21]

Before going into the social significance of this most important opposition in more depth, we must examine the form it takes in the second analysis, where we study a more limited number of educational institutions, but use a wider range of data in their characterization (13 specific points). These data were collected through direct survey and chiefly concern scholastic achievement.

Effectively, we had at our disposal, for each of the 21 grandes écoles selected, a set of indicators of student academic capital (school attended in *sixième* and *première*, *première* track, baccalauréat results) and the cultural and social capital of their families (occupation of father, mother, and both grandfathers, father's and mother's level of education, number of siblings, number of family members having done post-secondary work, parents' place of residence at the beginning of the *sixième*). We were thus able to keep together the two main principles of differentiation within educational institutions: scholastic achievement and social origins.

The surveys (which were analyzed in collaboration with Monique de Saint Martin) were administered between 1965–6 and 1968–9 at a group of establishments from which we chose 15 schools (or preparatory classes) as principal variables corresponding to the principal regions of the field of power: teaching and research (the Écoles Normales Supérieures d'Ulm, Sèvres, Saint-Cloud, and Fontenay), higher civil service (École Nationale d'Administration, first and second *concours*, Institut d'Études Politiques de Paris), heads of industrial firms, managers, and engineers (Polytechnique, École Centrale, Écoles Nationales des Mines de Paris, Nancy, and Saint-Étienne, Institute National Agronomique, École Nationale Supérieure des Industries Agricoles et Alimentaires), heads of commercial and management firms (École des Hautes Études Commerciales), and agricultural firms (Agro). (We were unable to conduct our research in military or art schools.) In order to keep engineering schools as a whole from carrying too much weight in our analysis, we counted six of them as illustrative variables (Ponts et Chaussées, Supelec, Télécom, École de Physique et Chimie de Paris, Breguet, École de Mécanique et d'Électricité).

As in the preceding analysis, the first factor (which here represents 34.3 percent of the total inertia) opposes the schools with the highest proportion of students from the bourgeoisie (the Paris Institut d'Études Politiques, HEC, and the external *concours* of the ENA) to the schools with relatively more modest social recruitment (Saint-Cloud, Fontenay, and the internal *concours* of the ENA), with most engineering schools occupying an intermediate position, near the center, but nevertheless closer to the dominant pole in the case of the most prestigious schools (Polytechnique and Mines de Paris) (cf. figure 5). At one end of the space, we generally find the children of members of the professions or heads of commercial firms, who were often living in Paris at the beginning of the *sixième*, whose paternal and maternal grandparents were already executives or members of the professions, and whose mothers are also executives, members of the professions, or teachers (these students often have a large number of siblings). At the opposite pole, we find the children of semiskilled workers, clerical workers, or tradesmen, who were living in small towns when they entered the *sixième*, whose paternal and maternal grandfathers were blue-collar workers or farmers and whose mothers are blue-collar workers (and who usually have few or no siblings). The first factor also enables us to distinguish the different schools according to their students' inherited cultural capital. The establishments with a relatively high number of students whose fathers have a

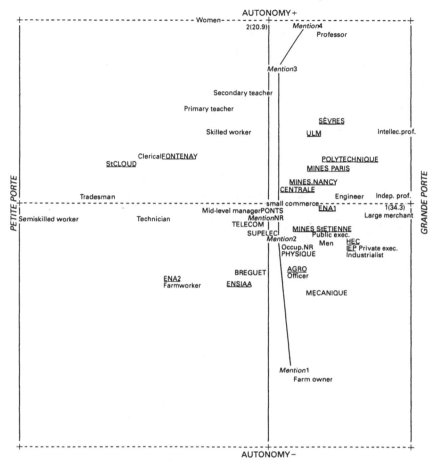

Figure 5 The space of the schools (n = 21)

diploma requiring at least three years of post-secondary study, or even the agrégation or a grande école diploma, whose mothers also hold such a diploma, and at least five of whose relatives (brothers, sisters, uncles, aunts, cousins) have some post-secondary education, are opposed to institutions with a significant proportion of students whose fathers and mothers have only the primary school certificate and who are the first in their family to have gone beyond high school.

These differences in the social and cultural make-up of the family are retranslated throughout the *cursus* into academic differences. The students from the Parisian bourgeoisie who are endowed with a large amount of cultural capital and who go to the IEP, HEC, and the ENA have quite often gone to private school and were in the most highly regarded academic tracks in the *première* (which combine the sciences and the humanities). The students from the middle or working classes, sometimes rather poorly endowed with cultural capital, who go to Saint-Cloud and Fontenay, were more likely to have attended collèges d'enseignement général (CEG) and to have gone through modern tracks (no Latin) or less respected classical tracks (such as Section B, limited to the humanities).

Thus it is precisely because the field of institutions of higher education fulfills its classificatory function by channeling students into institutions that are themselves classified that the principal effect of its operation can only be grasped on the scale of the entire field. The opposition between the *grande porte* and the *petite porte*, the fundamental principle of division in this universe, is inscribed both in the objective space of the educational institutions (or, if you will, in the very structure of the social division of the labor of social reproduction) and in representations of school work, the act of learning, and intellectual activity itself. The barrier that separates the *polytechnicien*, specialist of the general, from the simple *technicien*, doomed to application and execution, and the executive from the mid-level manager, is a genuine cultural boundary, analogous, in this order, to the one that, until the 1960s, separated people who had completed secondary school – and studied Latin – from all those known as "primaries," defined negatively, by what they lacked (as are students who leave school at 14 or have a secondary school background in "modern" subjects).

Symbolic consecration has very real effects, among other reasons because those it differentiates are already differentiated and because, as we have seen, the distinctive practices it imposes upon them, particularly in getting enormous investments out of its chosen people (in line with the logic of "noblesse oblige"), constantly reinforce these differences. Through a process very similar to the one that produces social differentiation between the sexes, the educational institution tends to produce embodied, and hence naturalized, social differences by building on preexisting social differences, which it reinforces by enabling them, through official recognition, to become fully realized and lastingly inscribed in objectively measurable dispositions, constantly asserted in the objectivity of practices. Credited from the very start, and for life, with a superior essence, the cultural nobility is destined to follow swift careers toward dominant positions and so-called positions of authority, which, because they are never defined (or only apparently defined) solely by their technical dimension, call for "a broad outlook," well-roundedness, a global view of things, cultivation, wide-ranging opinions, the ability to synthesize, in short, all the inseparably intellectual and moral properties that occupants of the dominant positions in the different fields attribute to themselves in agreeing to require them of the newcomers at those moments when cooptation is put into operation.

As for the commoners, they are directly drafted for the positions that lack a symbolic surplus value, positions to which they are assigned by the narrowly specialized and strictly technical nature of their competence.

Condemned to go on proving themselves forever, they must pay for their slow and destined-to-be-limited ascension in time and *achievement*. Before them stands a barrier as insurmountable – even though they have so often taken over the *de facto* role of the mere "acting" person in charge – as the one that separates an infinite series of nines following a decimal point from unity. They are thus doomed to exemplify properties that are often simply the lowly underside of a dominant property, whose very absence they evoke, properties such as earnestness, painstaking care, rigor, and efficiency.

Thus the organization of the field of institutions of higher education according to the opposition between the *grande porte* and the *petite porte* helps to reproduce, both in reality and in people's minds, one of the primary oppositions of the social order, the one separating executives from mid-level managers, agents of conception (orders, plans, programs, instructions, memos) from agents of execution, which, at a higher level of division, corresponds to the fundamental opposition between nonmanual and manual workers, theory and practice. By recording, in the guise of (academically consecrated) differences of "aptitude" or "intelligence," differences that have been socially fashioned within the family or the school itself and that, transmuted in this way, tend to be perceived as natural differences ("gifts"), this organization helps to produce and legitimate one of the most tangible and most likely-to-be-contested boundaries of the entire social order.

The logic operative here is no different in principle from the one that governed orders of the *ancien régime*. Through juridically guaranteed symbolic sanctions, it tends to establish differences of essence, analogous to those established by nobility of birth, in other words, definitively assigned differences that are (relatively) independent of achievement. In the particular case of the division between those who conceive and those who execute or manage execution, it tends, very concretely, to hinder or block the dialectic of pretension and distinction by assigning a definitive, insurmountable limit to the pretensions of those who are destined to occupy the intermediate positions in social space and perform jobs as intermediaries between the occupants of the dominant positions and the occupants of the dominated positions.

This is abundantly clear in the domain of education, where it is particularly difficult to ensure that the symbolic break established by rites of institution is unequivocally recognized and to get it acknowledged with neither second thoughts nor mental reservations. In addition to the fact that it is always difficult in these matters to measure and to mark out definitive differences between "levels" of achievement, the difficulty becomes all the greater when it comes to separating future teachers – primary and secondary school teachers, for example – since one can always quarrel not only over the very content of the knowledge necessary for teaching, but also over whether priority should be given to knowledge or to its method of transmission. And the opposition our study finds between students at the different Écoles Normales Supérieures (Ulm and Sèvres, on the one hand, Saint-Cloud and Fontenay on the other), which, in contrast to most of the hierarchies observed among the scientific grandes écoles, is primarily determined by the more or less ambitious dispositions that lead either toward the risks of the most prestigious *concours* or the security of the second order *concours*,[22] lies in the long series of bureaucratic and pedagogic devices that institute an absolute break, a difference of order, between two levels of teaching (primary and secondary school, for example) or two diplomas (the brevet supérieur [in former system, earned after the troisième, Tr.] and the baccalauréat), which means that the first in the lower hierarchy is forever incomparably lower than the last in the upper hierarchy.[23]

THE SPACE OF THE GRANDES ÉCOLES:
A CHIASMATIC STRUCTURE

The various institutions of higher education are distributed in the second dimension as revealed by the two correspondence analyses (more clearly by the second, which includes detailed indicators of inherited capital and academic success) according to two clearly related principles: on the one hand, the degree of their autonomy, in other words, the degree to which they assert strictly academic selection criteria (both technical and ethical), which thus differ from the criteria that hold sway in the markets most directly controlled by those with economic power; on the other hand, the amount of their students' academic capital and the structure of the capital their students have inherited from their families. More precisely, the institutions located at the dominant pole in the first dimension, collectively known as the grandes écoles, which constitute a fairly clearly defined subfield, are arranged (when treated separately, as in our third analysis) according to these two principles of division, that is, according to a structure homologous to the structure of the field of power.

In the first analysis, which treats establishments of higher education as a whole, the second factor (which represents 16.7 percent of the total inertia) chiefly opposes schools of management, public administration, architecture, and art (in other words, a set of often *private* establishments that set relatively high tuition rates, but require neither superior past academic performance nor an exceedingly long preparation period) to schools of engineering, agronomy, and education and research (in other words, to a set of usually *public* establishments that cost less and receive more highly selected students, academically speaking, following a longer course of preparation). (It shows a homologous opposition between law and medical facultés and science facultés.) On one side, we find establishments that, in their selection criteria, their faculty, and their curricula, as well as in the career prospects they open up, have close ties to industrial and commercial firms. These schools attach a great importance to less directly academic properties, such as particular ways of behaving, carrying oneself, and speaking, or *culture générale*, a concept whose content and contours are poorly defined, leaving ample room for everyday journalistic-style trivia. On the other side, we find establishments that stress strictly academic demands and, because they give considerable weight to the scientific disciplines, or technical or erudite knowledge (École des Chartes), and to more codified and strictly measurable skills, are relatively independent of the demands of the economic system. At the same time, this second factor opposes the categories that depend relatively more heavily on their economic capital for their reproduction (heads of industrial or commercial companies) and those that, because they are able to draw on both economic capital and cultural capital, have always had easy access to higher education (the professions) to those categories that more exclusively depend on academic and cultural capital (professors and primary and secondary school teachers).

In the second analysis, the second factor (representing 20.9 percent of the total inertia) chiefly opposes schools according to their students' academic capital. By far the most important element in this factor is in fact the level of success on the baccalauréat, with a relatively weak indicator being the *première* track (either Á, Latin, Greek, mathematics, on one side, or B, Latin, languages, or general classics, on the other). On one side, we find schools with a large proportion of students who received the most exceptional baccalauréat results ("very good" or "excellent"), these being the Écoles Normales Supérieures d'Ulm, Sèvres, Saint-Cloud, and Fontenay, the École Polytechnique, the École des Mines de Paris, and the École Centrale. On the other side, we find the schools with a large proportion of students with low or average passing grades on the baccalauréat ("average" or "good"), these being the ENA (both first and second *concours*), Agro, the École Normale Supérieure des Industries Agricoles et Alimentaires, the École des Mines de Saint-Étienne, the Institut d'Études Politiques de Paris, and HEC. This opposition based on academic capital is indissociable from an opposition based on inherited cultural capital or, better, on the *structure of the capital held by students' families*. The schools whose student body is primarily made up of children of families with greater cultural capital than economic capital (such as teachers) are opposed to schools with a relatively large proportion of students from families with greater economic capital than cultural capital (such as farm owners or private sector executives).

The schools that prepare their students for teaching or research (the Écoles Normales Supérieures) or include some amount of research training (École des Mines de Paris, Polytechnique), schools whose principles of selection and evaluation are the most autonomous and the most specifically scientific, or at least the most exclusively academic, are opposed to the schools that lead their students to positions of power or to jobs as private or public sector executives or engineers (HEC, IEP, Institut National

Agronomique, ENSIAA, ENA internal *concours*), schools that do not require as high a level of scholastic achievement and that more fully recognize the evaluative criteria in force in the economic and administrative fields. The external *concours* of the ENA occupies a position on this second axis close to the center, although nearer the group of the least academically autonomous schools.

Whereas, in both analyses, the first two factors determine systems of oppositions based on the very same principles – the opposition between the *grande porte* and the *petite porte* for the first factor, the opposition based on academic capital for the second – we note differences between them that can be explained through the differences among the populations chosen for analysis and the data used in their characterization. The variables that directly measure academic capital, which enter into the second analysis, differentiate schools that seemed quite similar when student social status alone was taken into account. So, for example, Ulm, Sèvres, Polytechnique, and the École des Mines de Paris in both cases occupy positions not far from one another, but the Agro and the ENSIAA, which are relatively close to this group of schools in the first analysis, are clearly set apart from them on the second axis in the second analysis. Likewise, the first ENA *concours*, which occupies a position very near that of HEC and Sciences-po in the first analysis, is more clearly separated from these two schools in the second analysis. Within the same logic, institutions like the École Brequet and the École de Mécanique et d'Électricité, whose students are rather high-placed socially and relatively weak in academics – "sanctuary schools," in other words – are distinctly opposed on the second axis to the most academically competitive and socially autonomous schools (particularly the École des Mines de Paris), even though they are very close to them in the first analysis.[24]

Within the realm of the grandes écoles proper, the opposition indicated by the second factor in the two previous analyses moves to the foreground. The space of the institutions that lead to the dominant positions in the different sectors of the field of power is organized here according to a structure entirely homologous to that of the field of power, with the different populations no longer being differentiated in terms of the total amount of their inherited capital, but rather in terms of the amount of their academic capital and the structure of their inherited capital.

In the third analysis,[25] we selected Ulm, Sèvres, Polytechnique, the École des Mines de Paris, Centrale, the ENA (first *concours*), HEC, and Agro, and we treated as supplementary variables several second-ranked schools that correspond to each of the positions represented by the major schools, these being Saint-Cloud, Fontenay, the Écoles des Mines in Nancy and Saint-Étienne, the ENA (second *concours*), the Paris IEP, and the École Nationale Supérieure des Industries Agricoles et Alimentaires (ENSIAA).[26] We used all the data that could help us place each student – and thus, each institution – both in *the space of positions*, using the objective characteristics of the student's social trajectory (parents' occupation and education, grandfathers' occupation, size of family, place of residence), academic trajectory, and academic capital (schools and tracks, baccalauréat results), and in *the space of stances* ["position-takings," Tr.], using data on their involvement in sports and cultural activities (attending theater or concerts, daily or weekly newspapers and magazines read) and their intellectual, religious, and political practices and opinions.

We treated as supplementary variables properties (such as sex[27]) that, through the very large role they would have played in the construction of the first factor, would have obscured the effect of less powerful but equally relevant principles of differentiation, as well as those properties that would have been redundant, considering the variables already represented (such as school attended in the *première* or number of newspapers read daily). Also treated as supplementary variables were data corresponding to questions that we were not able to ask at every school, such as the students' political leanings (excluded from the École Polytechnique questionnaire), or questions that took on different meanings in the different schools, such as attendance at film clubs (which some schools do not have).

In this third analysis, which focuses solely on the universe of the grandes écoles (see figure 6), the first factor, which represents 37.3 percent of the total inertia, shows two parallel oppositions: on one side, Ulm, Sèvres, and Mines de Paris, establishments whose students are richer in cultural capital than economic capital (they are more often sons of teachers and members of the intellectual professions; their father and mother are more often *agrégés* and their grandfathers were often primary school teachers) and are endowed with significant academic capital (they have often gone through the best tracks and have a very high rate of honors on the baccalauréat); on the other, institutions like HEC, Agro, Centrale, and the ENA, whose students are less academically selected and richer in economic capital than cultural capital (sons of farmers, heads of industrial and commercial firms, and private sector executives), with Polytechnique occupying the central point in the factorial plane, at the intersection of the two axes.

Agro's position can essentially be explained by the fact that it is very strongly marked by an entire set of characteristics that distance it from the schools located at the intellectual pole, which include the social status of its student body (the proportion of farmers' sons relatively lacking in cultural capital is highest at Agro and lowest at Ulm), their academic trajectory, their cultural practices, and their intellectual, religious, and political attitudes. The positions occupied by the sons of skilled workers can be explained by recalling that selection is particularly intense at the point of entry into the grandes écoles – the probability of acceptance for sons of farmers, blue-collar workers, and subordinate clerical workers is therefore particularly slim, and the effects of overselection, as observed in the previous studies, consequently become most acute here. The rare grande école students originating in these categories are "wonder children"; the probability of their acceptance indeed becomes so low that it takes on the logic of a miracle or an accident. It follows that these *survivors* have few characteristics in common with their category of origin. For example, workers' sons in the grandes écoles come from the most well-educated and best-qualified portions of the working class and are distinguished in particular by the fact that their mothers frequently belong to the middle classes and are better

Key to diagram 6

Codings for occupational social category and level of education:

Father's, in upper case
Mother's, preceded by *
Paternal grandfather's, preceded by +
Maternal grandfather's, preceded by =

Levels of education on diagram:

No diploma
CEP (includes CAP)
BEPC
Baccalauréat
Petite école (includes higher education not completed)
Licence
Agrégation (includes doctorate, diploma from leading grande école).

Size of family:

Fam1 = 1 child, up to
Fam6 = 6 or more children

Residence at start of *sixième*:

R2.5 = town of fewer than 2,500 inhabitants
R10 = 2,500–10,000
R50 = 10,000–50,000
R>100 = over 100,000
Paris = Paris and Paris area

Institution in *sixième* (coded 6ᵉ):

CEG
Lycée (includes collège)
Private school

Institution in *première* (coded 1ᵉ):

ENI (école normale for primary school teachers)
Collège
Lycée
Private school

Section in *première*:

Technical
M, M' (modern)
Classical
A (Latin, Greek)
B (Latin, languages)
C (Latin, mathematics)
A' (Latin, Greek, mathematics)

Mentions on baccalauréat

Mention1 = no points (see table 21 in appendix 2)
Mention2 = 1–2 points
Mention3 = 3–4 points
Mention4 = 5–8 points

Schools represented as principal variables are underlined
In each case, NR or nr conveys nonresponse.

Figure 6 The field of the grandes écoles: the space of social, cultural and academic properties (n = 15)

educated than their fathers. So, for example, at Polytechnique, among the sons of foremen, the mothers of two are primary school teachers, another is a midwife, and several others do not work outside the home but do have the brevet supérieur.

We indeed recognize a chiasmatic structure here homologous to the one observed in our analyses of the field of power,[28] with capital at the two poles exhibiting opposing structures, the central positions being occupied by categories more or less equally endowed with economic capital and cultural capital, such as sons of higher civil servants.

The worldly and temporal hierarchy that can be established among these schools on the basis of objective indices such as the flow from one school to another or the value granted to the various diplomas in the different markets, particularly in the field of economic power, is almost the exact opposite of the strictly academic and intellectual hierarchy determined on the basis of indices of academic capital such as baccalauréat results or nominations to the Concours Général. Initial salaries appear to increase when we move from Ulm to Polytechnique and HEC, passing ENA along the way, in other words, when we move from the university field to the field of upper-level public administration and the economic field, with social capital playing an ever-greater role as we move away from the university field (where, as we have seen, its role is already not insignificant). Within each of these fields, academic hierarchies nevertheless tend to be maintained, with HEC alumni, for example, earning higher salaries than ESSEC graduates.[29] There are a few exceptions, however (which our model can account for), specifically, those schools that function, at least in part, as sanctuaries. So, for example, the École Centrale, more closely tied to management than Polytechnique – and from its very earliest days – receives students who are less academically endowed but more often come from the milieu of company heads and are consequently in a better position to get the most out of their diploma, particularly through their social capital.[30] Indications are that the gap between the incomes afforded by the different diplomas increases with the age of the graduate, particularly because graduates of less prestigious schools (business schools and others) reach their ceiling at about age 40.[31] Nevertheless, the relationship between a diploma's academic and social value may be upset, in one or another field, given the possibility for sudden changes in its market value, related to market behavior (this has happened, for instance, in the case of ENSAE graduates, who have recently found a large number of job openings in banking).[32]

The structure of positions (and trajectories) corresponds to the structure of stances, particularly in matters of culture, politics, and sports. Near the intellectual pole, we find the highest concentration of those who go to theaters and concerts, associated with very low involvement in sports, and the highest number of readers of intellectual periodicals and left-wing or far left-wing newspapers (*L'Humanité*), associated with a stated affinity for Marxism. Near the temporally dominant pole, we observe lower proportions of those going to concerts and theaters, a greater participation in sports, more readers of *L'Express* and *Le Figaro* [conservative weekly and conservative daily, Tr.] and a greater likelihood of regular or occasional practice of Catholicism. Projecting the supplementary variables confirms this opposition. Closer to the intellectual pole, people more often declare themselves to be on the left or the far left, and we note a higher rate of more or less militant union support, while at the opposite pole we more often encounter indifference to syndicalism and more or less marked right-wing positions.

The second factor, which represents 22.4 percent of the inertia, reveals an opposition that more or less corresponds to the opposition between the technical corps and the administrative corps (shown in previous analyses by the third factor). On one side, we find those who are destined to occupy the dominant positions in the field of *administrative*, political, or sometimes economic power. Frequently originating in the Parisian bourgeoisie (more often sons of private sector executives or members of the professions, grandsons of executives, whose mothers are also executives), they have followed a chiefly *humanities* course in secondary school, and often in fashionable *private* establishments. On the other side, we find those who are headed toward positions as more or less high-class *technical* managers, engineers, or researchers, who, with their primarily *scientific* background, are more often from families on their way up (more often sons of primary school teachers, technicians, and grandsons of blue-collar workers or farmers). The ENA (first *concours*), located on the side of the positive values, contrasts in this respect with the École Centrale, the Institut National Agronomique, and the École des Mines de Paris – just as the Paris IEP and the ENA (second *concours*) are opposed, for the illustrative variables, to the ENSIAA, the Écoles des Mines in Nancy and Saint-Étienne, and the Écoles de Saint-Cloud and Fontenay. It is reading *Le Monde* [center left, Tr.], an indicator of the degree of one's real or anticipated participation in the political world and higher public service, that most clearly separates the two groups, with *L'Express* and *Le Nouvel Observateur* [left; weekly, Tr.] being secondary indicators. This difference in attitude towards politics and the political is also registered by the illustrative variables. Agro, Mines, and Centrale students reveal their distance or their indifference by classifying themselves more often as "center" with no further detail (18 percent, 23 percent, and 27.5 percent, respectively), while ENA students, more of whom also join political parties, show a refined sense of political positioning by classifying themselves to an exceptionally high degree as center-left and center-right (25 percent and 22 percent), as if they were intending to get all the mileage they could out of the limited margin of freedom that their statutory neutrality leaves them, but they do also position themselves on the left (28.5 percent), and, much more rarely, on the far left or on the right. There is no better illustration of this opposition between politico-technocrats and techno-engineers than the following somewhat disenchanted statement made by a spokesman of the latter group: "You can tell the graduates of our schools apart. *Polytechniciens, centraliens, mineurs, agros,* etc. – they all have their own personality, but they share an engineering mentality: they're hard-working, disciplined, objective. They know how to factor the data involved in a problem and to examine every repercussion before proposing a solution. They dispense with literature, which hardly creates its characters with them in mind. They show an equal disregard for politics, and distance themselves from power so they can concentrate on their work. (. . .) They are capable of humor, but they don't take themselves seriously enough to feel bad about the lack of attention that has been paid to them . . . ever since the time of Jules Verne, even though the mechanics' century succeeded the century of the philosophers, and even though the press gives fact after fact about technical and scientific progress, pointing out the upheavals it causes. (. . .) And yet engineers are *rarely seen in public life*. There are none in the cabinet and very few in parliament. If we count a few dozen in the Economic and Social Committee, it is because they represent very diverse specific interests (nationalized or private firms, trade unions . . .), but they don't sit on the committee as engineers."[33]

This opposition, which we will encounter again in nearly identical form in the field of economic power, tends, despite its minor objective importance, to occupy a place of utmost importance in the representations of agents engaged in the competition for corporate power over businesses, because, *from their point of view* and at that particular point in time, it constitutes the most crucial principle of division. This shows, parenthetically, that a sociology of the perception of the social world should determine not only the *social frames of perception*, in other words, the taxonomies used in ordinary experience, their social genesis, and the practical conditions of their implementation (particularly the – usually practical – context of their use), but also the differential power of differentiation that the different principles of classification collectively used to construct the social world – for example, economic or cultural criteria ("class") and ethnic criteria ("race") – effectively wield, in the objectivity of the practices of the different categories of agents, in accordance with the position they occupy in the objective classifications. This sociology must at the same time determine the potential gaps between the constructed classifications of science and the practical classes of everyday perception. Some of the oppositions that play a major role in representations may obscure much more crucial oppositions, either by relegating them to the background – as when the opposition between the scientific and literary grandes écoles, or technical (Polytechnique) and economico-political (ENA and HEC) grandes écoles conceals the opposition between the *grande porte* and the *petite porte* – or by disguising them through a kind of superimposition (for example, by reducing to its simple academic dimension the social opposition at the basis of the academic opposition between the scientific schools and the economico-political schools).

One might thus be led to raise questions about the mechanisms that, like the educational system, a genuine objectivated ideological operator, tend to foster or determine such *collective illusions of perspective* – for example, the mechanism that, in imposing the opposition between humanities and science students as a fundamental one, obscures the fact that science *normaliens* are farther removed from *polytechniciens*, even though they have usually gone through the same course of studies and the same *concours*, than they are from humanities *normaliens*, whose entire academic past separates them. But one should not forget that there is nothing illusory about collective illusion and that the divisions (whether solidly or poorly founded in objectivity) that agents institute for practical reasons are part of the objective reality that science must account for, and contribute in a way to creating this reality. Scientific analysis itself makes its own contribution, although in an opposite sense, for in uncovering the real oppositions that the visible antagonisms of the classification struggle conceal, it tends to weaken the social effects related to misrecognition.

A MATRIX OF PREFERENCES

Correspondence analysis brings to light a structure that – even though it can only be obtained by breaking with incomplete descriptions of artificially isolated units – may seem self-evident to all (though only) those who possess the practical mastery of objective structures that familiarity affords. But this sense of self-evidence may well prevent any questioning of the processes that underlie the observed distributions. How does the distribution of students among the various schools (that is, within the space of differences they constitute) actually come about? And how are students' social characteristics, such as the structure of their inherited capital, actually transmuted into academic properties? How is the relationship we have observed between the space of the positions occupied by agents or institutions and the space of their corresponding stances established? It can clearly be shown that in both cases the distribution of practices (interest in one establishment or another, for example) and views (political preferences, for example) is closely tied to the distribution of the structure of the capital inherited by the different students, or, more precisely, to the relative weight of the economic and cultural portion of their inheritance. But we have still not arrived at a complete and systematic explanation of the observed phenomena. For that we must go back to the real basis of their "choices," in other words, to habitus and to the sociogenesis of this generating principle of practices and representations through which the aforementioned relationship becomes effective.

Economic patrimony and cultural patrimony – the sum of all the resources held by the family group in an objectivated state, in the form of material goods (such as, for example, books, musical instruments, or, nowadays, personal computers) or, in the domain of culture, in an embodied state, in the very person of the members of the family group – tend to impose upon their holders the practical and tacit recognition of their value insofar as they favor the development of dispositions adjusted to the social position they characterize. This they accomplish through the lifestyles they determine, but also by their very existence. We must indeed accept as a fundamental principle of social existence that individuals and groups are inclined to appraise the foundations of their existence and their social value at a superior value and that they more or less consciously strive to institute objective conditions likely to ensure that their properties (everything they have and everything they are) will be the grounds for recognized advantages, or, in more precise terms, that their patrimony will function as capital.

But while it explains that, barring statistically improbable accidents, the inheritance inherits the inheritor, this general principle, which is at the foundation of any process of socialization, cannot account on its own for the observed relationship between an initial position in the field of power (defined by the structure of a person's capital) and an interest, at an equal level of academic achievement, in establishments that are more or less oriented toward economic or intellectual life, or between this same initial position and practices or views in the area of culture, sports, religion, and politics. In fact, the principle that defines the process of socialization in its most general sense can be specified, and, in this case, what structures experience and, through it, dispositions is the *relative weight* of the economic or cultural portion of one's heritage or, more precisely, the *priority* that is objectively given, in the lifestyle associated with a given position, to culture or economics, art or money, or, as people used to say, "spiritual power" or "secular power." It is this fundamental ratio that, when internalized, becomes the generating structure of practical preferences, for example, those that guide choice of discipline, subjects, teachers, and authors, or, on a more general level, the priority given to reading or sports, to *L'Humanité* or to *Le Monde*, etc.[34]

Everything leads us to assume that the greater the increase in the relative amount of cultural capital, the more frequent are the ethical dispositions that favor the intensive use of this capital, particularly in the academic market; and that, in contrast, the closer we get to the pole of economic power, the more frequently the dispositions favorable to academic ascesis are in competition with or supplanted by other dispositions, those corresponding to more comfortable, more leisure-filled lifestyles. We can also assume that the unconditional support of intellectual pursuits that is always tacitly required by the school is subterraneously thwarted by the insidious anti-intellectualism that haunts bourgeois families and is discreetly and subtly reinforced by Catholic tradition. (We know indeed that the dispositions associated with adherence to Catholicism help to turn people away from certain academic careers, both directly, in prompting a sort of a priori suspicion of the scientific view, and indirectly, by guiding them toward private secondary establishments, assumed to be guarantees of better company, and either less inclined to transmit scientific knowledge or less equipped to do so successfully – with a few exceptions, such as Sainte-Geneviève).

Agents located at the two opposing poles of the same field undergo a structuring operation that is organized according to the fundamental opposition in the field. They thereby tend to perceive the social world according to the same principle of division, which is objectivated in a number of *inevitable alternatives*, such as involved or disinterested, gratuitous or useful, temporal or spiritual, political or aesthetic, along with all the other antagonistic pairs that are more or less consciously subsumed under the opposition between the right and the left. But these agents give opposing priority to each of the branches of the alternatives depending on the position they occupy in the structure. This is another remarkable example of the logic behind the fact that fundamental structures of the social order are converted into mental structures shared by agents whom they differentiate or oppose in the reality of social existence, agents who must share them in order to be able to divide up the products of the partition the structures bring about. And we may posit that, in general, the topics structuring ordinary language (such as those brought out by Oswald Ducrot) are grounded in the social structure from which they spring, a structure that, by definition, unites the terms it opposes, at one and the same time establishing agreement on the field of disagreement (the common space of possibilities in terms of which argumentation may be carried out) and the principle of disagreement (the antagonistic preferences that orient confrontation between points of view).

The distribution of students among the different schools is a result of the action of two hierarchized, and partially independent, principles. Academic capital, which is itself closely tied to a person's initial position, particularly through their inherited cultural capital, and which, at the moment of entry into the field, is objectivated in indices of academic consecration such as honors on the baccalauréat and nominations to the Concours Général, determines both chances for access to the grandes écoles and the limits within which choices can be made. With nearly juridical rigor it prohibits those who are bereft of it from gaining access to the preparatory classes, or at least to the most prestigious among them. And it governs chances for success in the various *concours* all the more completely the more completely these *concours* are governed by academic norms.[35] And yet we cannot understand the distribution of students among the various schools or the subsequent use they will make of the titles these schools award unless we assume that, at equal levels of academic capital, students are still separated according to their differential sensibilities toward forms of temporal power or intellectual prestige. This "tropism," which develops through all the infraconscious experiences by means of which children sense, from very early on, the various configurations of the structure of the relationship between the economic and cultural portions of their family's capital, is the second factor that orients vocational choices within the limits of the possibilities opened up by academic capital.

Our survey provides a direct demonstration of this tropism: ENA students are more likely to declare themselves to be in favor of leaving public service for the private sector the closer their family is to the pole of economic power, and although we have only a small number of cases on which to base our claim, we can suggest that in cases where students have succeeded in both *concours*, the choice between Ulm and Polytechnique follows the same pattern, within the limits of the effect of their ranking in the *concours*. Again, the same deep-seated relationship to temporal power means that students are more likely to succumb to the lure of academic consecration – thereby helping to confirm or to reinforce their originary exclusion from the sphere of power – the closer their family is to the dominated regions of the field of power (sons of teachers, professors, or intellectuals, for example) or social space ("wonder children"), and the less symbolically recognized (or more stigmatized) are the ethnic, religious, or sexual categories to which they belong (such as women or homosexuals).[36] This may well be the basis, for example, of the difference between science *normaliens*, closer in origin to the intellectual pole, and *polytechniciens*, who, although not as strongly attracted to the pole of temporal power as ENA students, participate in it to a sufficient degree, through their initial position and its correlative dispositions, to continue to feel strongly drawn by it.

Differential dispositions toward forms of temporal power are at the basis of the relationships that students maintain with the different categories of educational establishments, particularly public or private. Students from the regions of the field of power nearest the intellectual pole tend to recognize themselves in the most autonomous forms (Ulm, in particular) of an educational institution, whose verdicts they will recognize all the more readily because these verdicts sanction not only technical competences, but also the recognition granted to the institution and to its specific values, a recognition that is to a certain degree the basis for the successful acquisition of technical competences, and accompanies their implementation and their manifestation. They grant public schools the right and the duty to produce a "disinterested education," in other words, an education that is gratuitous and often critical, and free both of the proprieties of the "social world" and the technical and economic constraints of the business world. At the opposite pole of the field of power (and increasingly so the more closely people are connected to private enterprise), the school (especially the public school) seems more like a necessary evil, and the constant concern for minimizing the "corrupting" effects it can produce through its autonomy is expressed in recourse to less autonomous institutions, such as private establishments, which are sought after less for the values they profess explicitly (such as religious values) than for everything they exclude practically. The creation of the HEC at the end of the nineteenth century, or of the ENA in 1945, like measures taken today "to bring education in line with business," are so many manifestations of the resistance that economic and administrative power holders, often through their most "enlightened" representatives, have unceasingly put up against the claims of the most autonomous educational institutions (the ENS and the École Polytechnique, in particular) to a monopoly on legitimacy in educational matters, and hence in cultural and social reproduction.

The pressure exerted by the economically powerful in favor of an education subordinate to their technical, and especially their social demands, in other words, to their ethico-political demands, is a structural constant that has never ceased to be operative, both in practices (the creation of schools and official channels, different levels of aid, etc.) and in discourses. So, for example, Edmond Demolins, a disciple of Le Play's who founded the École des Roches, offers an explicit formulation of the principles behind the veiled resistance to the school's insistence on new forms of excellence accessible to petty bourgeois on their way up. To the strictly scholastic abilities and values recognized by the petty bourgeoisie and by teachers (of which Latin translation stands as the symbol) and to the pedagogy of docility, which prohibits self-assertiveness, Demolins opposes an aristocratic school modeled on the English system and designed to inculcate a lifestyle that leaves more room for will, courage, and leadership qualities (just the dispositions fulfilled in sports, so dear to his friend the Baron de Coubertin). He places the doctrine of *self-help*, of private initiative, at the foundation of a private education directly oriented toward private enterprise and its values, favoring "ease" over "erudition," "well-roundedness" [*éducation*] over "specific knowledge" [*instruction*].[37]

As we cannot trace the entire history of the troubled relations between the educational institution and the business world, and particularly the role played by management in the struggle against compulsory schooling,[38] we will simply take from very recent history the example of the work of the National Committee for the Development of the Grandes Écoles, created in 1970 in response to the 1968 movement with the stated aim of "promoting, in all its forms, the development and progress of (both public and private) establishments of higher education that train the managers of the economic world, through proper pluridisciplinary selection and training" and "ensuring a better relationship between the economic world and any and all establishments entrusted with this training, with a view to encouraging the sharing of information and the development of common research and action." Bringing together 94 heads of schools of engineering and "advanced management training" and 235 leaders from the "economic community" who, as shown by the list of the companies granted honorary membership, are recruited from within the sector of the most powerful businesses with the closest ties to the public sector, both through their economic structure and through the characteristics of their heads, very often grandes écoles graduates (Paribas, Compagnie Bancaire, Compagnie Générale d'Électricité, Électricité de France, Péchiney, Rhône-Poulenc, etc.), this body has since its inception carried out both symbolic (a report on "the grandes écoles of tomorrow," booklets, brochures, opinion polls, etc.) and practical (lobbying government officials, public meetings, etc.) acts on behalf of the grandes écoles, which appear as a rampart and a refuge guarding against university disorder. Rather than presenting the full range of management's declarations on the necessity of taking control of the university, which flourish particularly after crises such as those of 1968 or 1987 (sudden reminders of the contradictions in the current mode of reproduction), it is enough for our purposes to point out that during a 1969 conference on the educational system, the number of those in favor of a system more closely tied to demand greatly increases when we move from the "intellectual" pole to the economic pole in the field of power: some 13 percent of members of intellectual professions and only 19.5 percent of secondary school teachers stated that they were very much in favor of an "education that would be more directly oriented toward professional preparation," compared to 40 percent of industrialists and large merchants and 42.5 percent of corporate executives. Members of the professions, engineers, and executives from the public sector held an intermediate position, at 27.5 percent for the first two groups and 34.5 percent for the third (data from L'Association pour L'Expansion de la Recherche Scientifique analyzed at the Center for European Sociology).

If conflicts regarding education take the form of insuperable antinomies regarding ultimate values, this is because what is at stake in these conflicts, through control over instruments of cultural and social reproduction, is the reproduction of the very foundations of domination, of the existence and the value of the dominants, and of the hierarchy of the principles of domination.[39] Thus, if, despite all appearances, we are correct in saying that the École Nationale d'Administration functions as the most prestigious of the sanctuary schools given that, as the least "academic" of the grandes écoles, it enables the children of the top business bourgeoisie and the top public and private bureaucracies to get around the obstacle that their limited scholastic achievement might represent for their continued hold on power, this is conditional on simultaneously bearing in mind that those who wield power over the most academic instruments of reproduction spontaneously tend to make them work to their own advantage by linking the technical demands of the transmission of technical competences to forms of social competence and to values that, if they were to succeed in imposing them, would ensure them a *de facto* monopoly on cultural reproduction and, in the end, on the instruments of domination.

Teachers, through the autonomy of the academic universe, can use the antinomies linked to the fundamental oppositions of the field of power (often condensed in those pairs of terms and authors that are, or were, the "good essay topics") to impose, in all innocence, a point of view that directly reflects the interests associated with the structure of their capital. Thus, we may simply follow Louis Pinto when, having noted the frequency of philosophy essay topics based on the opposition between two concepts in which "a 'low' term is surpassed by a 'high' term," he points out that "the 'high' term is always on the side of knowledge and/or autonomy, while the 'low' term is always on the side of ignorance and/or heteronomy. So, for example, in the current curriculum for *section* A [liberal arts, Tr.] of the pre-baccalauréat year (as in earlier philosophy class curricula), most of the terms can be placed on either one side ('consciousness,' 'culture,' 'judgment,' 'ideas,' 'sense,' 'truth,' 'right,' 'justice,' 'duty,' 'will,' 'the self,' 'freedom') or the other ('the unconscious,' 'desire,' 'passions,' 'illusion,' 'nature,' 'the imagination,' 'irrationality,' 'violence'). These 'concepts' are unequally valued with regard to 'autonomous reflection.' "[40] The unconscious "a priori" that underlies most of the choices offered is simply the particular point of view of the teachers who, within the series of alternatives imposed, are led to systematically privilege the terms with which they are intimately connected, all the while retaining the illusion of neutrality and universality.

Thus, analyzing the processes according to which the dispositions at the basis of *academic placement* are determined helps to explain the seemingly miraculous homology we find between the field of the grandes écoles and the field of power, both point of origin and goal of these placement strategies. Following a statistical logic, the mode of academic reproduction tends to bring about a continuous redistribution of academic titles – and hence positions of power – that differs significantly from what it would be under the hypothesis of a completely random throw-in, without being for all that an identical, mechanical reproduction of the current distribution (every teacher's son is not at the École Normale and the entire student body of the École Normale is not made up of teachers' sons). As we have just seen, two mechanisms combine to minimize the frequency of *crossed trajectories*, which lead from one pole of the field of power to the other, at the price of reconversions and conversions as costly as they are unstable. On the one hand, the selection of students according to academic criteria, or, if you will, according to professorial schemata of perception and appreciation that, even in the most autonomous institutions, are never all and entirely technical and that, even for the most strictly technical, are never indifferent to social characteristics, tends to direct a large proportion of the occupants of the different initial positions in the field of power toward the institutions occupying homologous positions in the field of the grandes écoles, and hence toward positions in the field of power homologous to their initial positions. On the other hand, the selection students themselves operate, by virtue of dispositions closely linked to their original positions, plays a very significant role in either reducing or canceling out the effect of the adjustments that the specific logic of the educational institution was able to impose on the direct exercise of social determinants. It is not unusual for academic consecration, in attracting students from the intellectual pole to the academic world, to discourage a portion of them from turning toward the economic field or from investing their qualifications in this field. And it often happens that the dispositions with regard to power that students from the temporally dominant regions of the field of power owe to their origins lead them to ignore or to reject the lure of things educational (witness the renunciation of intellectual and even academic activities that so often follows entry into a grande école) and to put their academic success in the service of extra-academic values.

The discordances between dispositions and positions that academic classification allows to subsist tend to be corrected after entry into a grande école. Either the "misplaced" individuals eliminate themselves by resigning or by turning to institutions better suited to their expectations, or the criteria excluded from academic selection become fully active at the moment of final selection or upon entry into the workforce, when inherited social capital recovers all its efficacy. These effects are particularly evident in the case of an institution like HEC, caught in the contradiction between the social constraints linked to the demands, either vague or explicit, of both its titled clientele and businesses and the specifically academic constraints associated with its position in the space of the grandes écoles, and particularly to the competition forced upon it by the other business schools, which are of more recent date and less solidly consecrated, and which prompt HEC to maintain, and even to raise, the specifically academic level of its *concours* and its curriculum. We thus note frequent departures from HEC among teachers' sons who find in their education, as well as in the lifestyle of their classmates, a foretaste of a professional future to which they have been led by the logic of academic competition, but which they have not really chosen and for which they show no real promise. A 1965 study shows in fact that professional success is much more closely tied to social origin than to indicators of academic capital such as class rank at graduation (HEC alumni association, results of 1964 survey on professional lives of HEC alumni, 1920 to 1962, confidential document, 24 pp.). The importance of social capital in the social return of an academic title seems to be at its greatest for highly valued schools like HEC and Centrale, or, *a fortiori*, for sanctuary schools like Breguet and Sudria. HEC graduates who secured their jobs through family or business connections or a placement service had a significantly higher annual salary (between 90,000 and 95,000 francs, 1971 data) than those who got their jobs through an HEC-sponsored internship or job announcements (between 65,000 and 75,000 francs) (HEC occupational survey, 1971). So, although it may seem completely paradoxical at first glance, the existence of very active political groups on the far left at HEC around 1968 is not unrelated to the fact that students who lack connections in the business world are able to sense through many diverse signs that the title bestowed by their school is a necessary but not a sufficient condition for the professional success the school promises, which is in reality only accessible to the heirs of an estate made up of goods and connections, that is, to genuine *"fisticis."*[41]

Similarly, a larger proportion of the Polytechnique graduating class of 1966 (cf. table 13) from categories whose capital is more cultural than economic (teachers and professors) are headed toward applied engineering schools or careers nearest the intellectual pole (research, École Nationale de la Statistique et de l'Administration Économique, École des Mines). In contrast, proportionally more sons of industrialists or large merchants enter the Corps des Ponts et Chaussées or resign to enter directly into the private sector (principally owing to their poor class rank).[42] Finally, two students go directly on to the ENA, one from the professions, the other the son of a private sector executive.[43]

Table 13 Choices of corps and careers on graduation from Polytechnique (class of 1966) (percent)

	Research	Mines	ENSAE	Télécommunications	Ponts et chaussées	Génie rural	Météo et instruments de mesure	Navigation aérienne	Armement	ENA	Resignation	Various and NR	Total
Farmworker (n = 14)	14.3	–	–	–	21.4	–	7.1	14.3	21.4	–	21.4	–	100
Clerical (n = 9)	33.4	–	–	11.1	–	–	–	–	22.2	–	11.1	22.2	100
Tradesman, small commerce (n = 13)	–	–	–	7.7	7.7	7.7	–	–	7.7	–	30.7	38.5	100
Mid-level mgr, tech. (n = 34)	14.7	2.9	–	8.8	2.9	–	5.9	–	26.5	–	32.3	5.9	100
Primary teacher (n = 21)	9.5	9.5	14.3	–	14.3	9.5	4.8	–	9.5	–	28.6	–	100
Secondary teacher (n = 23)	34.8	–	4.3	8.7	26.1	4.3	4.3	–	4.3	–	8.7	4.3	100
Higher ed., research (n = 17)	47.1	5.9	–	17.6	–	5.9	5.9	–	–	–	17.6	–	100
Public exec. (n = 23)	8.7	4.3	–	–	17.4	4.3	–	4.3	17.4	–	30.4	13.1	100
Officer (n = 12)	8.3	–	8.3	–	16.7	–	–	8.3	50	–	8.3	–	100
Engineer (n = 38)	21	5.3	5.3	10.5	5.3	2.6	7.9	2.6	13.1	–	21	5.3	100
Professions (n = 32)	18.7	–	6.3	–	3.1	6.3	6.3	6.3	15.6	3.1	28.1	6.3	100
Private exec. (n = 37)	13.5	5.4	5.4	5.4	8.1	2.7	2.7	–	27	2.7	24.3	2.7	100
Industrialist, large merchant (n = 26)	23	–	3.8	7.7	19.2	3.8	–	–	7.7	–	30.8	3.8	100
All	18.7	3	4	6	10.4	3.7	4	2.3	16.7	0.7	24.1	6.4	100

In relying upon preexisting social differences (already partially converted into academic differences) that separate students from the different regions of the field of power in order to assign incoming students, with their active complicity, to the academic destiny that best suits their preference systems, the distribution machinery that divides the ever-renewed flow of the "junior members of the dominant class," as Sartre calls them, among the different establishments produces several important effects. Reducing the extent and the frequency of *crossed trajectories*, which take the son of a banker or an industrial head to the ENS and from there to a position as a teacher or an intellectual, for example, or the son of a teacher to the ENA or HEC and from there to top positions in banking or business, first of all minimizes the costs of reconversion and the inculcation that must take place in order to kill the old man and produce the new man, or, more concretely, in order to produce specific belief, interest in the game and its stakes, the *illusio* that is the precondition for successful entry into the field. But, as we shall see, it also favors the enchanted experience that can only be afforded by dispositions that are perfectly adjusted to a position's most obligatory requirements. In addition, it minimizes the risks of conflict inherent in situations where a gap or a discordance exists between dispositions and position, minimizing as well the threat of subversion raised by those placed in an unstable position. Finally, it sets limits on struggles over succession, by assigning so many closed and separate fields to the ambitions of the pretenders.

POSITIONS, DISPOSITIONS, AND STANCES

Insofar as the principle of differentiation governing the distribution of students within the space of establishments of higher education lies in the dispositions associated with the volume and structure of their inherited capital, it is not surprising that we should find a close correspondence between the structure of the stances they adopt in cultural, religious, and political matters and the structure of their positions. Indeed, ethical, aesthetic, and political "choices" are once again based on the *matrix of preferences* born of the incorporation of the structure of inherited capital. If we choose to ignore the institutional boundaries introduced into what might otherwise be a continuum by the distribution of students among the different schools, we see that the frequency of cultural practices (specifically, theater, concerts, and movies) tends to decrease as we move from the academically dominant and socially dominated pole toward the socially dominant and academically dominated pole, while the frequency of participation in sports displays the opposite tendency, as do all direct and indirect indices of politically conservative dispositions as well. The generating and unifying principle of these sets of individual choices and of their distribution can in the main be found in systems of dispositions that, as products of conditions of existence characterized by a certain practical hierarchy among economic and cultural matters, systematically guide choices toward one or another term of the alternatives that organize a complete vision of the world – temporal or spiritual, worldly or extraworldly, physical or intellectual, etc.[44] So, if, rather than simply recording the apparently self-explanatory facts that familiarity suggests, we should wish to truly understand the priority the École Normale gives to intellectual values, we must first consider the relative proportions of teachers' sons and sons of chief executives among its students (20 percent are sons of teachers and 6 percent sons of *normaliens*; 4.5 percent are sons of industrial and commercial heads). This ratio more or less reproduces at the level of the entire student body the disequilibrium between the cultural capital and the economic capital in the heritage of the modal category, that of teachers (cf. figure 7). But, in addition, we must take into account the fact that these very good students (75 percent of whom have received at least one "very good" on one of the two baccalauréats [the French portion is taken one year before the general exams, Tr.]), who have been consecrated by the educational system from a very early age (most have received *prix d'excellence* throughout their school careers), have also consecrated themselves very early on to the school and its values. At the end of a series of shrewd investments (principally in the area of establishments and tracks) and a continuous line of successes, they have fully achieved the conversion of inherited cultural capital into academic capital, a conversion that is nothing less than automatic.

The difference between the academic value of these students and the economic and social value granted to their titles is undoubtedly at the root of a kind of meritocratic indignation that is perhaps not unrelated to their "anticapitalist" inclinations. Their political choices and choices of union (cf. figure 8) unquestionably lean toward the side on which the day's dominant intellectuals also tend to be found: 60 percent position themselves on the left or the far left, 17 percent declare affinities with Marxism, and 66 percent say they are associated with a union, either simply as militants or as leaders – and the number who claim no religious affiliation is very high (42 percent), while elsewhere (not including the other écoles normales), regular practice of Catholicism is the norm. While *Le Monde* is the most widely read newspaper at the École Normale (61 percent), a rather significant proportion of *normaliens* read *L'Humanité* (12 percent, a rate incomparably higher than at the other schools, where it does not go above 2 percent, with the exception of Saint Cloud) and *Le Nouvel Observateur* (as opposed to *L'Express*, which is more likely to be read at the ENA or at HEC). But most importantly, a particularly high rate of *normaliens* read "intellectual" journals such as *Les Temps Modernes, Esprit, Critique, La Pensée*, and *Cahiers pour l'Analyse* (24 percent read at least one), as well as film and music journals. They go to concerts and film clubs much more often than all the others

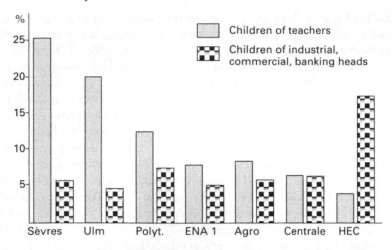

This histogram, representing the proportions of children of teachers and children of industrial, commercial, and banking heads in each school, illustrates the chiasmatic structure of the system of the grandes écoles. It shows, in effect, that the proportion of sons and daughters of teachers and members of the intellectual professions and the proportion of the sons and daughters of industrial and commercial heads in the top grandes écoles vary more or less inversely, the greatest opposition being the one separating HEC from Sèvres and Ulm. While Agro seems farther away from the economic pole than might be expected, this is because the children of industrial and commercial heads are relatively few in number (5.5 percent) and also because a more accurate picture of Agro's position would be obtained if the figures included the children of farm owners, who make up 7.2 percent of the students, compared to at most 2 percent in the other schools. The proportion of children of commercial and industrial heads at Centrale is undoubtedly underestimated in our study; this school is probably somewhat closer to HEC than the chart suggests.

Figure 7 Sons and daughters of teachers and chief executives in the grandes écoles

(except Sèvres women, who are channeled much more directly still toward the artistic and literary arena by the logic of the division of labor between the sexes). Their preferences in theater run toward classical or avant-garde works, and they never attend boulevard plays (in order of frequency, Aristophanes' *The Frogs*, Boris Vian's *The General's Tea Party*, Chekhov's *The Cherry Orchard*, Giraudoux's *The Madwoman of Chaillot*, Albee's *Who's Afraid of Virginia Woolf?*, as well as Brecht's *Master Puntila*, Marguerite Duras's *Whole Days in the Trees*, Cervantes's *Numance*, etc.).

At the opposite end of the space, at HEC, it is the upper Parisian bourgeoisie, very firmly attached to private education, that predominates (52 percent of the families live in Paris or the Paris area at the beginning of the *sixième*; the sons of top industrial or commercial heads make up 17.5 percent and the sons of private sector executives 24.5 percent; most of the

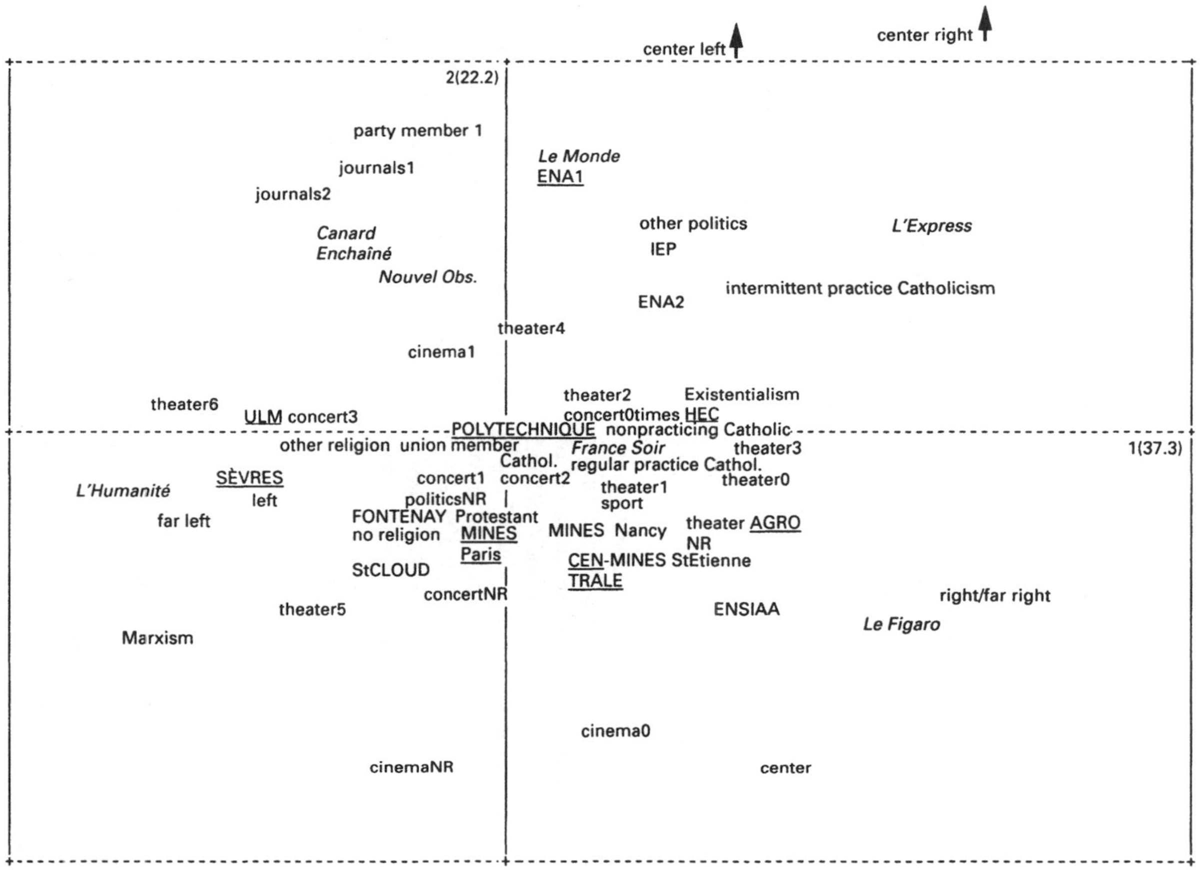

center right

center left

2(22.2)

1(37.3)

party member 1

journals1

Canard Enchaîné

Nouvel Obs.

journals2

Le Monde
ENA1

other politics
IEP

ENA2

L'Express

intermittent practice Catholicism

theater4

cinema1

theater2

Existentialism

concert0times HEC

POLYTECHNIQUE nonpracticing Catholic-

France Soir theater3

Cathol. regular practice Cathol.

theater1 theater0

sport

theater AGRO

MINES Nancy NR

CEN-MINES StÉtienne

TRALE

concert1 concert2

politicsNR

FONTENAY Protestant

no religion MINES

Paris

other religion union member

ULM concert3

left

SÈVRES

far left

StCLOUD

concertNR

theater5

cinema0

cinemaNR

ENSIAA

center

right/far right

Le Figaro

L'Humanité

Marxism

theater6

Figure 8 The space of cultural, religious and political practices and opinions (n = 15)

mothers do not work outside the home). Academic values are far from triumphant (honors on the baccalauréat are rare). The students seem to devote
a very large portion of their time to sports (riding, rugby, fencing, golf, skiing, tennis, sailing, etc.) and various other activities, some of them forms of
professional preparation (two examples being organizing the Boom, the
annual gala event of Jump HEC, "third-ranked equestrian show in France,"
and the Junior Entreprise, HEC Études, which in 1982, according to Loïc
Wacquant, involved primarily the sons of industrial heads, corporate directors, and executives in business and finance[45]). Rather significant diversity is
found in politics, but there is a higher rate of stances on the right than at the
other schools. Similarly, while 61 percent of the students read *Le Monde*,
there are also 10 percent who read *Le Figaro*; few have a taste for intellectual
journals. Cultural practices, particularly visits to the theater and concerts,
are less frequent than at the ENA or Polytechnique.

   Statistics are bound to be abstract and incomplete; what reveals even more clearly
the profound values of HEC (and especially the contradictory intention to reconcile
opposites inherent in the very idea of a "business school") are the interviews and
texts dedicated to the glory of the institution and its activities of self-presentation.
Not wanting either to "push the intellectuals toward the universities" or to "leave
the stadiums to the athletes," HEC officials see the new Jouy-en-Josas campus as a
chance to integrate academic and athletic activities on the model of American universities, "which can pride themselves on lavishing an excellent education on their
students, some of whom are Olympic champions," and which "prove that it must be
possible to develop an intermediate notion of the scholar-athlete." Just as the cus-
tomary opposition between body and mind, sports and culture, is resolved in the
glorification of "the scholar-athlete," the opposition between the business world [*le
monde des affaires*] and the cultural universe, between economics and culture, fades
away to make way for "cultural affairs." "HEC Cultural Affairs, in addition to theater and music presentations, organizes an annual lecture series. Theater directors
and actors, corporate heads, and politicians as diverse as Debré, Defferre, Giscard
d'Estaing, Mendès France or Tixier-Vignancour are invited to take part in these
debates" ("Spécial Jouy-en-Josas. La nouvelle école des HEC," *HEC 65*, brochure
published for the opening of the campus at Jouy-en-Josas in 1964, Feb. 8–9, 1965,
pp. 45–6).

   We could, here again, simply be satisfied with facts that, as people mis-
takenly say, "speak for themselves." In reality, we can only truly understand the oppositions noted between the two extreme poles of the field of
the grandes écoles if we recognize in them the antithesis underlying the
opposing practices and representations of the occupants of the two poles of
the field of power: on the one hand, the values of virility and responsibility
expressed in taking part in sports, often in a group, as well as in organized
activities (principally those arranged by the Student Office) that are almost
explicitly experienced as foretastes of one's entry into economic life; on the
other hand, introverted and extraworldly dispositions revealed in intellectual

activities, at once individual and autonomous, such as reading or going to plays or concerts, as well as in hallucinatory and lyrical political alignments, inspired more by a rejection of the realities of the present world than by a real will to wield power over it.

In both the space of objective positions and the space of stances, the École Polytechnique and the ENA fall midway between the École Normale and HEC, the first closer to the École Normale, the second closer to HEC. Many of the most typical characteristics of students' religious, political, and aesthetic stances are directly linked to the structure of their inherited capital, which is usually more balanced than at the other institutions. At Polytechnique, the modal category (at 14 percent) is that of sons of engineers, an occupation that occupies a central position (leaning more toward the intellectual pole) in the distribution based on capital structure, and there are more sons of teachers (11.5 percent) than sons of industrialists or large merchants (while at the ENA the two categories are about equal).[46] In short, *polytechniciens* – more often from a mid-level wage-earning bourgeoisie and less often from the top Parisian bourgeoisie than ENA students – hold an intermediate position between the latter and *normaliens* (they were more likely to be living in Paris at the start of the *sixième* than *normaliens* and less likely than ENA students).[47] We find similar patterns with regard to politics and cultural practices. When they place themselves within a school of thought, they usually name Catholicism (15 percent), Christian existentialism (9 percent), and Marxism (8 percent), which enables us to situate them politically midway between Ulm and the ENA. While the great majority (84.5 percent) indicate religious preferences, they are less regular in their practice of Catholicism than ENA students. They represent a kind of equilibrium between the ENS and the ENA with regard to cultural practices as well. A large proportion read *Le Monde* (71.5 percent), but we also find a minority who read *Le Figaro* (6.5 per cent), with *L'Humanité* claiming only the rare reader (1 percent). Many regularly read *Le Nouvel Observateur* (27.5 percent), but also *L'Express* (20.5 percent), a lower percentage than at the ENA, but greater than at Ulm. In contrast to *normaliens*, almost all *polytechniciens* are involved in sports, but they are also frequent theater-goers (their favorite plays being classics, such as Molière's *Don Juan*, Montherlant's *La reine morte*, Anouilh's *Becket*, and Chekhov's *The Seagull*); 44.5 percent have been at least four times during the year, compared to 39.5 percent at Ulm and 37.5 percent at the ENA.[48]

At the ENA, the modal category is made up of sons of higher civil servants, private sector executives, and members of the professions – the latter occupying a position in the field of power homologous to the ENA's position in the field of the grandes écoles.[49] Very often Parisian (56.5 percent were living in Paris or the Paris area at the beginning of the *sixième*), more often coming from the nobility (for the years 1964–9, we count 7.5 percent at the ENA, 5.5 percent at HEC, 3 percent at Polytechnique, and 2 percent at Ulm), and rather likely to have gone to private schools (29.5 percent), ENA students have been somewhat average in school, below the level of *normaliens* and *polytechniciens*, but above HEC students.[50] Their attitudes, especially with regard to politics, always place them in the central regions. They *all* read *Le Monde*, a practice that is part of their professional training (as the reading of intellectual journals is for *normaliens*). They almost never identify with Marxism (1 percent), only rarely with socialism (8 percent), and they only exceptionally locate themselves on the far left (5 percent; none read *L'Humanité*). In contrast, 47 percent consider themselves to be center left or center right, a percentage that is much higher than at the other grandes écoles.[51] Finally, they quite often name Christian existentialism (14 percent) or Catholicism as their religion, 39.5 percent stating that they practice it regularly, 21 percent occasionally. They place themselves more or less on a par with *normaliens* in the area of theater-going, but less often go to concerts (56.5 percent have not been at all during the year, compared to only 35 percent of *normaliens*). They are avid newspaper readers, but they leave little room in their reading for intellectual journals (with the exception of *Esprit*) and they turn instead to magazines of popularized economics and politics (*Problèmes Économiques, Projet, Revue Française de Science Politique, Revue de la Défense Nationale*, etc.).

Thus the space of positions finds rather faithful symbolic expression in the space of position-taking. The most striking evidence of this homology is provided by the top names on the lists proposed by students at the different schools when asked to name the five people they would like to see invited to give a talk at their school, which we may read as a test in which each school projects its own image of excellence (see table 14).[52]

Humanities *normaliens*, whose choices are widely scattered (they propose an average of 2.6 different names, compared to 1.7 at the ENA) and who put in a lot of joke suggestions (as do *polytechniciens*, as well), give precedence to intellectuals – philosophers, such as Sartre, Ricoeur, and Foucault, experts in the social sciences, such as Lévi-Strauss, or artists such as Godard and Boulez. While they mention political figures with some frequency (especially the science students), they choose first and foremost the most intellectual among them, such as Mendès France, or great historical figures, de Gaulle or Mao Tse-tung, and only much more rarely mention politicians on the right, Giscard d'Estaing or Debré, for example. École Normale science students are much closer to their counterparts in the humanities than are Polytechnique science students. A good proportion of their suggestions are philosophers, and they sometimes name great thinkers (Grothendieck, Monod, Schwartz, "Bourbaki," Oppenheimer, Heisenberg), which is very rarely the case for *polytechniciens*, from whom they also distinguish themselves in their much more frequent modernist choices in both art and literature (Boulez, Stockhausen, Xenakis, Ionesco).

In keeping with the division of labor between the sexes, which assigns politics to men and aesthetics to women (particularly literature, considered more "feminine" than philosophy), Sèvres women carry the precedence given to the cultural over the

Table 14 Most popular speakers (percentage of students naming specific speakers in their answers)

Ulm (humanities and sciences) (n = 96)		Sèvres (humanities and sciences) (n = 69)		Polytechnique (n = 100)		ENA 1 students (n = 69)		HEC (n = 100)		Centrale (n = 100)	
Sartre	24	Sartre	29	Giscard d'Estaing	34	Mendès France	45	Mendès France	59	Mendès France	24
Mendès France	22	J. Vilar	20.5	Sartre	28	Aron	16	Giscard d'Estaing	58	Giscard d'Estaing	22
De Gaulle	14.5	Godard	16	Dali	22	De Gaulle	16	Sartre	21	Dali	22
Godard	13.5	S. de Beauvoir	13.5	De Gaulle	21	Giscard d'Estaing	16	Debré	15	L. Armand	18
Mitterrand	13.5	Barrault	11.5	Pisani	19	Sartre	11.5	Pompidou	11	Sartre	13
Lévi-Strauss	10.5	Mendès France	11.5	Mendès France	14	Godard	11.5	Godard	9	Fourastié	11
Boulez	9.5	Boulez	10	Mao Tse-tung	9	Dali	8.5	Mitterrand	9	De Gaulle	9
Mao Tse-tung	9.5	Weill-Hallé	10	Mitterrand	7	Debré	8.5	Pisani	8	Mitterrand	9
Ricœur	7.5	Aragon	8.5	Rueff	6	Pisani	8.5	De Gaulle	8	B. Bardot	8
Aragon	5	Lévi-Strauss	8.5	Godard	5	Bloch-Lainé	7	Domenach	7	Malraux	8
Aron	5	Ricœur	7	Waldeck-Rochet	5	Malraux	7	Lecanuet	6	L. Schwartz	7
Debré	5	J. Rostand	7	Kastler	4	Mitterrand	7	Malraux	6	Antoine	6
Fouchet	5	Brassens	6	Picasso	4	Picasso	7	Defferre	6	Kastler	6
Foucault	4	Picasso	6			Pompidou	6	Althusser	5	Pompidou	6
Giscard d'Estaing	4	Saint-John Perse	6			Lévi-Strauss	6	Bloch-Lainé	4	J. Rostand	6
Lecanuet	4					Massé	6	Fidel Castro	4	Aron	5
Queneau	4							E. Faure	4	L. de Broglie	5
J. Vilar	4							Floirat	4	Godard	5
								Kennedy	4	Leprince-Ringuet	5
								J. Vilar	4		

political to its extreme as it were; we find one lone political figure, Mendès France, among the 15 most frequently mentioned speakers. Jean-Paul Sartre holds first place, as at Ulm, but, in contrast to the men, *sévriennes* give ample weight to theater directors and actors (Vilar, Barrault), artists, filmmakers, musicians, men of letters, and well-known women, primarily those known for their feminist work, such as Simone de Beauvoir and Dr Weill-Hallé-Lagroua.

Here again, *polytechniciens* occupy an intermediate position between *normaliens* and ENA students. Like the latter, they most often name political figures, Giscard d'Estaing, an X alumni (named by one respondent in three), being the first choice, followed by de Gaulle, Pisani, Mendès France, Mao Tse-tung, and Mitterrand. But they attach somewhat greater importance to intellectuals, Sartre in particular. While most of the writers, painters, and composers they mention are established, classical even, they do occasionally mention a few avant-garde creators, and a small minority choose Boulez, Beckett, Butor, Robbe-Grillet, Althusser, Pierre Schaeffer, and Xenakis, names that do not appear on the ENA lists. Although they never name Raymond Aron, the favorite contemporary author of ENA students, they choose graduates of their school relatively often, Rueff for them being the equivalent of Bloch-Lainé for ENA students.

ENA students (student *concours*) and especially HEC students are poles apart from the École Normale. The former primarily name political figures, more often on the right than on the left (Mendès France being the most frequently mentioned by far, but also Giscard d'Estaing, de Gaulle, Debré, Pisani, and Pompidou), and, in a much smaller proportion, higher civil servants, embodiments of the technocratic ideal, such as Bloch-Lainé, Pierre Massé, and Paul Delouvrier (and also, but only rarely, one or another private sector head, Rothschild or Peugeot, for example).[53] Among the intellectuals named, Sartre is offset by Aron, whose name was completely absent from the *sévriennes* lists and in tenth place at Ulm. Next to Picasso and Dali, avant-garde artists for the general public, we find Malraux. In each domain, only the greatest names, embodying safe and dominant values, are mentioned, and in contrast to the Écoles Normales lists, the avant-garde (with the exception of Godard) never appears. The full representation that these future higher civil servants have of themselves is condensed in the well-bred eclecticism that characterizes the following perfectly ideal-typical list: "Aron, Michel Debré, Pierre Massé, Pierre Mendès France, Saint-Geours" (son of higher civil servant). And this one, which illustrates the student's concern for avoiding commitment and his desire to situate himself above and beyond political alternatives, in that *neutral place* where the great state bureaucracy is assumed to reside: "Pompidou, Mendès France, Edgar Faure, Seydoux, Giscard D'Estaing" (son of executive). These prudent, eclectic, and miraculously balanced choices, Giscard d'Estaing acting as a counterweight for Mendès France, in line with the principle of equilibrium that also governs essays and their divisions into two parts, perfectly suit the future "great servants of the state" (and of large public and private companies) who, according to the official view of their official role, will have to maintain a steady balance between public interests and corporate loyalties and serve administrations of opposing orientations with the same competent neutrality. The implicit philosophy of culture and politics from which they draw their inspiration, which gives culture a political foundation and political functions, fits in with the one expressed in the lists of authors submitted for student commentary in the *concours*, where we once again find Raymond Aron (who taught for a long time at

Sciences-po), alongside Montesquieu, Valéry, Alain, and Tocqueville, and where Michel Debré and Albert Camus are far and away more prevalent than Sartre and Simone de Beauvoir.

It is indeed politics that provides the principles for the selection and classification of authors, excluding as a result all references to formal properties. So, for example, in 1972 the ENA preparatory course drawn up by the center for professional training and improvement of the Ministry of Economics and Finance classifies twentieth-century writers according to the following categories: "traditionalists" – "Saint-Exupéry, G. Bernanos, H. de Montherlant"; "neomonarchists" and "neofascists" – "C. Maurras, M. Barrès, R. Brasillach"; "politically committed writers" "striving for a new humanism" (S. Weil, "E. Mounier: le personalisme et la revolution du XXe Siècle"). The pantheon of canonical authors ("whose texts are often proposed for candidates' reflection in the major oral exam, or used as the central point of discussion in the interview that follows the student's presentation") and the length of their treatment in the same ENA preparatory textbook are significant: Father Teilhard de Chardin (striving to "fuse these two deep-seated passions (...) human reign and God"), 3 pages; R. Brasillach, 2.5pp.; G. Bernanos, 2.5pp.; P. Valéry, 2pp.; C. Maurras, 2pp.; C. Péguy (a "taste for the people" and "fraternity"), 2pp.; J. Giraudoux, 2pp.; J. Romains, 2pp.; H. de Montherlant ("the great lyricism of sports"), 2pp.; A. Malraux, 2pp.; J.-P. Sartre, 2pp.; A. Camus, 2pp.; Alain, 1.66pp.; A. Maurois, 1.66pp.; F. Mauriac, 1.66pp.; M. Barrès, 1.66pp.; R. Martin du Gard, 1.33pp.; G. Duhamel, 1.33pp.; R. Rolland, 1.33pp.; A. de Saint-Exupéry ("stoicism"), 1p.; A. France, 1p. The list of texts proposed for the candidates' commentary is based on the same principles: "Between 1945 and 1965, the examining committees for the student, special, and civil servant *concours* selected 3,268 texts by 775 authors (...). Some authors are a veritable gold mine for the committees: Montesquieu comes in first (with 108 texts, 15 of which appear in the October 1945 special *concours* alone), immediately followed by Valéry (105 texts), then by Alain (93), Tocqueville (67), Renan (66), Raymond Aron (45), Anatole France (38), Taine (37), Péguy (35), Napoleon I, Jules Michelet, André Siegfried and Simone Weil (34). We should also note that J.-J. Rousseau (45 texts) comes in above Voltaire (32) and that Proudhon (43 texts) crushes Marx (13), Lenin (3), Stalin (3), Trotsky (5), and Mao (1). The following each provide between 20 and 30 texts: Machiavelli, Montaigne, Pascal, La Bruyère, Chateaubriand, Benjamin Constant, Guizot, Balzac, Sainte-Beuve, Gide, Bergson, Léon Blum, Giraudoux, René Grousset, Aldous Huxley, Alfred Sauvy. And between 10 and 20: Gabriel Ardant, Bainville, Barrès, Benda, Bernanos, Curtius, Georges Duhamel, Jacques Ellul, Lucien Febvre, Fénelon, Guglielmo Ferrero, Fustel de Coulanges, Gaxotte, Guéhenno, Victor Hugo, Jaurès (Guesde: 1), Bertrand de Jouvenel, Lamartine, Louis XIV, Maurois, Nietzsche, Pareto, Prévost-Paradol, Rivarol, Robespierre, (Danton: 1), Jules Romains, Jean Rostand, Saint-Exupéry, George Sand, Stendhal, Talleyrand, Thibaudet, Turgot, Vauvenargues, Vidal de la Blache. Camus (19 texts) wins out over Emmanuel Mounier (8), Sartre (6) and Simone de Beauvoir (5); Michel Debré (19 texts) outdistances General de Gaulle (11). (...) If we look at the first and last two texts proposed to the candidates between 1972 and 1982, we note that the choice of authors has barely changed: Jouvenel comes in first, followed by Aron and Camus; General de Gaulle tops M. Debré ... and G. Pompidou, and ties with Tocqueville; Turgot, Robespierre, Napoleon, Guizot, Marx, Nietzsche, Renan,

Taine, Jaurès, Péguy, Lenin, Blum, Alain, Vauvenargues, Valéry, Sauvy, Chateaubriand, Balzac, Michelet, etc. are still represented. But the need to keep things current means that some newcomers do make the list: R. Garaudy, J.-F. Revel, M. Jobert, M.-A. Macciochi, E. Le Roy Ladurie, F. Braudel, P. Ariès, E. Maire, R. Debray, A. Peyrefitte, A. Zinoviev, J.-M. Domenach, A. Touraine, A. Cohen, M. Tournier . . . not counting famous unknowns, as always" (cf. J.-F. Kesler, *L'ENA, la société, L'État*, pp. 93–4).

Like ENA students, HEC students would most like to be visited by politicians: Giscard d'Estaing, Mendès France, Debré, Pompidou, and Mitterrand. They are practically the only ones to suggest top chief executives, focusing on the category of the great corporate founding fathers (Sylvain Floirat, Bleustein-Blanchet, Beghin, Prouvost, Dassault), and they only rarely mention higher civil servants (and then only Bloch-Lainé). In the area of culture and intellectual life, their choices are highly classical and occasionally very much in line with popular culture, particularly in their heteroclitic nature; for example, "Garaudy, Sanguinetti, Malraux, Hitchcock, Tixier-Vignancour" (son of corporate chief executive), or "Mitterrand, Sartre, Debré, Bresson, Father Oraison" (son of director of pathology laboratory).[54]

The same logic can be seen in the hierarchy established by students at the different schools in ranking the following occupations: Inspecteur des Finances, high-ranking officer, doctor in public hospitals, Sorbonne professor, appeals court lawyer, engineer in a large company, chief executive of a large company, a top film director. ENA students rank Inspecteur des Finances first (the more often the higher their social origins), film director second, and public hospital doctor third, while Polytechnique students give first place to Sorbonne professor (ranked sixth at ENA), second place to film director, and third place to public hospital doctor, Inspecteur des Finances falling to fifth place. Centrale students distinguish themselves from *polytechniciens* in giving first place to chief executive, ranked fourth at Polytechnique.

ESPRIT DE CORPS

We hope we have shown convincingly that it is not through a meticulous and spuriously exhaustive exploration of a preconstructed object in its apparent singularity that its specificity can be grasped, as we are led to believe by the idiographic illusion, the ethnographic variant of positivist faith, but rather through a methodical construction of the space in which this object is located and from which it derives its distinctive, differential, and relational properties. It is only by breaking with the arbitrary absolutization produced by ordinary intuition and semilearned description that one is able to see the different schools for what they truly are, miniature closed societies that, like the insular universes so dear to ethnologists, share a single lifestyle, visible not only in coherent and distinctive systems of cultural references and ethical or political values, but also in bodily *hexis*, clothing, ways of speaking, and even sexual habits – all of which has the effect of encouraging, and outwardly legitimating, individual monographs.

Primarily through practices of cooptation entrusted to teachers educated there themselves, each of the schools selects and concentrates homogeneous classes of habitus – or, if you will, it "recognizes its own," in both senses of the word, identifying what distinguishes them and consecrating them in their *distinctive identity*, that of a subclass within the "elite" of the school system's chosen people.[55] This identity, being by definition *difference*, can only survive in its relational existence at the cost of adjusting its substantial reality. There can be no doubt that in relation to the *normaliens* of 20 years ago, on the eve of 1968, fewer *normaliens* today read *L'Humanité* and more play tennis. But it is no less certain that because the principle according to which they are differentiated from *polytechniciens* and ENA students has not been radically transformed, it has found expression in systems of differences that can immediately be understood within the same logic as the past differences of which they are the structural equivalent.

A number of the misunderstandings to which sociological analysis gives rise stem from the fact that people read *relational* thinking *substantially*, to use Cassirer's distinction – for example, raising the disclosure of tennis playing in the middle and lower regions of social space as a counterexample to the description that brought out its distinctive value at a given point in time, in a particular state of the space of participation in sports. The properties attached to agents or groups that are themselves defined relationally have meaning and value only in and through the relations into which they enter. No practice, object, or discourse is ever distinguished or vulgar, noble or common, in and of itself, as distinguished common sense would have it, but only in relation to other objects, practices, or discourses. It follows, then, that, contrary to the *existentialist absolutism* inherent in the legitimate experience of legitimate culture, the notions of nobility, distinction, culture, and human excellence can be linked (within a single cultural tradition and, *a fortiori*, in different social universes) to different, even opposing, properties, practices, and discourses at different points in time, or, at a given moment in time, according to the *relation of distinction* into which these essentially relational entities are practically inscribed. People have not always understood that the very word *distinction* refers to an essentially relational notion that, in its social use, is diverted toward a substantial, essential meaning. For example, the relation of distinction can be expressed (in language as in clothing or any other symbolic manifestation) by an ostentatious show of riches, when one wishes merely to distinguish oneself from poverty (in some cultures, beauty, especially feminine beauty, is associated with being plump). It can also be shown through a more or less ostentatious rejection of ostentation, with all the values of discretion and sobriety that are asserted through modest consumption or language use in contrast to the tendency of the nouveau riche and the parvenu to exploit every form of *conspicuous consumption*. And so forth and so on indefinitely, with every imaginable about-face reversal (this could be shown in the recent evolution of sexual morality). None of this rules out raising – although in less naive terms than those our philosophers of television use to denounce, on television, the harm done by television culture – the question of the limits that some of the objects and discourses originating in the relativist games of the intellectual or artistic field can set on relativist reduction, by very reason of their intrinsic structure and the particular conditions that produce them.

Distributing streams of students into groups as homogenous as possible in terms of the fundamental determinants of their dispositions means that, as we have seen, the cultural insulation so constituted provides all those who share in the modal habitus (the teacher's son at the École Normale, the son of a top business leader at HEC) with the enchanted experience of a *social paradise*, where everyone has every chance of recognizing in everyone else a *like-minded person*, a neighbor so socially similar that he is able to love himself in him. (The nostalgia for a paradise lost so often expressed in alumni memories betrays the fact that their authors have never since been able to find a universe so "perfect," in other words, so perfectly suited to their dispositions.) Continuous and prolonged contact with classmates endowed with similar or related dispositions can only reinforce in each student the dispositions and values shared by all, and hence each student's confidence in his own value. The *certitudo sui*, inseparable from a *certitudo salutis*, strengthened by their sense of wonder at belonging to an exceptional group, is further increased by the effect of consecration. In constituting elite students as a *separate group*, and hence, as a socially recognized social elite, publicly instituted distinction predestines them to practices imposed by their sense of difference that tend to reinforce difference.

Of all social groups, academically based corps established through the assignation of a title and a common identity upon individuals brought together by very strong social similarities, which are thereby recognized and legitimated, are undoubtedly the group most closely related to the family. Indeed, the deep and lasting affective ties of fraternity that inevitably develop among adolescents so thoroughly in tune with one another that everything predisposes them to "get along" give a seemingly natural foundation to the solidarity of the corps (as do familial sentiments for domestics).[56] The aggregative segregation operated by the educational institution is undoubtedly the strongest operator of the *social structuring of affects*, and friendships or love relationships among classmates are one of the surest and most thoroughly dissimulated forms taken by the constitution of that particularly valuable kind of *social capital* – school acquaintances – a lasting basis for solidarities and exchanges of every kind among members of the same age group academically instituted as a "graduating class." Love, like academic "brotherhood" or "sisterhood," is always in part the manifestation of a particular form of "esprit de corps." As social positions embodied in bodily dispositions, habitus contribute to determining whether (biological) bodies [*corps*] come together or stay apart by inscribing between two bodies the attractions and repulsions that correspond to the relationship between the positions of which they are the embodiment. This is how the academic mechanisms of aggregation and segregation, exemplified by the field of the grandes écoles, have today become one of the hidden mediations through which social homogamy is achieved. Better than any debutante party, ball, or other institution aimed at circumscribing the area of approved encounters, the algorithm of academic classification, through the groups of socially homogeneous classmates that it produces, fosters togetherness among like-minded people and, above all, tends to exclude the "undesirable company" that always carries with it the threat of unsuitable marriages, and that is all the more likely in less advanced stages of the academic selection process, that is, as we move further down toward primary school. And we would be justified in thinking that progress in coeducation in the grandes écoles will only strengthen this homogamy.[57]

More profoundly, however, loving oneself in others and in the group as a whole, a condition fostered by the prolonged togetherness of like-minded individuals, is the true foundation of what is known as "esprit de corps" (of which "esprit de *famille*" is one particular case). It is in fact enchanted adherence to the values and to the value of a group that makes this group an integrated corps prepared for every kind of exchange likely to reinforce the integration and solidarity of its members. These members are thus inclined to make available to each individual the resources held by all the others (at least up to a certain point), in line with the saying "all for one and one for all." The thoroughly extraordinary notion of "esprit de corps," which calls to mind the mystical language of the canonists (*corpus corporatum in corpore corporato*), thus refers to the subjective relationship that each member of the corps, as a social body incorporated into a biological body, maintains with the corps to which he is immediately and seemingly miraculously adjusted. This esprit de corps is the precondition for the constitution of cultural capital, that collectively held resource that enables each of the members of an *integrated* group to participate in the capital individually held by all the others.[58]

DEVIANT TRAJECTORIES

It nevertheless happens that the social mechanisms of academic aggregation and segregation that produce corps and esprit de corps misfire. The homology between positions and the dispositions of their occupants is never perfect, and the permanent dialectic between the properties of a school and the properties of its students is one of the major determinants of change in the field of the grandes écoles as well as the field of power, with every significant change in the social composition of a particular student body bringing on a change in both the reality and the representation of the corresponding school, and vice versa. Deviant trajectories, which lead some students to the pole opposite the position to which they were promised and which was promised to them (such as the sons of professors and teachers who wander off into HEC, or the sons of bankers and industrial heads who stray down toward the École Normale), along with the interrupted trajectories of those who have remained within their universe but have not attained their probable future, are undoubtedly one of the most important factors in the transformation of the field of power, as well as the transformation of specific sectors of this field, such as the literary or artistic fields.

The distance between starting position and arrival position, and, more specifically, the extent and direction of the final deviation, directly experienced in a person's subjective distance from the practices and representations of the model (hence "normal" and normative) portion of the new group arrived at, may be what underlies *reactional* stances (particularly in politics) that are thus entirely different from the stances of the individuals of similar background who have found their "natural place" (sociologically speaking). Given that the field of power is a hierarchized space in which direction matters, *crossed trajectories* have different effects according to their direction, but they always lead to unstable, unsteady positions favoring stances that are themselves entirely unstable, shaky, and often doomed to constant shifts or, in time, to reversals.

Thus displacements toward the temporally dominant pole, when they lead to an objectively or subjectively successful integration into the new group, are accompanied by an adjustment to its modal practices and opinions that may approach hyperidentification. When they lead to an objectively or subjectively poor fit, on the other hand, they often foster a reactional counteridentification. Everything happens as though those who either truly are *out of place* in their new universe or feel that way had no other recourse than to exclude that which excludes them and to transform their destiny into a choice, by carrying the critical positions associated with the modal trajectory of their group of origin to the extreme. So, for example, sons of teachers or professors who enter schools where their presence is unlikely, such as the ENA and especially HEC, almost never identify themselves as center right or center left like the majority of their classmates, but rather place themselves on the left or the far left, for the most part, like their "brothers in origin" at ENS, while only a small fraction of them identify with the right (the choice of working-class students, incidentally, who, at HEC for example, where they number only four, place themselves with one lone exception on the right or just to the right of center).[59]

In the case of displacements leading from the temporally dominant pole of the field of power to the intellectual schools, everything suggests that they are felt deep down to be a descent, even when they give the impression of and are experienced as an elective conversion. Indeed, in a kind of one-upmanship that may be the result of overidentification, or of an unconscious rejection of the banality of overly common convictions, the members of the upper bourgeoisie "gone astray" often adopt the most "radical" positions among those available in their adopted universe. Thus, for example, descendants of industrial and commercial heads, who never place themselves on the left or far left at the ENA, and only do so somewhat infrequently at HEC (certainly less than students from the other regions of the field of power, in any event), join up with the left at Sèvres and Ulm (four of five respondents, with four abstentions) and often claim an affinity with Marxism (a choice that, in the other schools, is only made by students at the popular end or middle of the social scale); at Ulm they only rarely choose the right (one in nine), which at HEC is quite a frequent choice for students of the same origins (one in four). Thus students from dominant positions in the field of power who have made a choice that goes against the hierarchy tacitly accepted in their original universe and secretly present in their unconscious, such as *normaliens* from families of corporate heads or higher civil servants, tend to diverge from the modal choices of their group of origin more than those whose choices are consistent with this hierarchy. Another example of this effect is that at the École Normale (proportionally) more sons of engineers and members of the professions, categories that at most of the schools only very rarely consider themselves regular in their religious practice, claim no religious affiliation, but when they do remain faithful to their tradition, more claim to be regular in their practice. We should note that these effects are observed above all in domains where the "norm" defining the legitimate intellectual posture is more clearly established both in the intellectual field, through exemplary figures, journals, etc., and in the universe of the school itself, through established groups (churchgoers, the communist group, etc.), domains such as political opinions, religion, and school of thought; they tend to disappear in areas of practice free of the pressure to conform, such as sports or parlor games.

Thus, in order to give a sociological account of practices and opinions that might appear to be due to chance, or freedom, we must assume that in a certain number of cases – particularly when the stakes include not only a certain position in the social world, with all its correlative interests, but also a certain comfortable or uncomfortable relationship to this position – the principle of a person's practical relationship to their position is in fact based on the objective *gap* between their individual trajectory and the modal trajectory of their group of origin, in other words, between the slope of their actual trajectory and the modal slope of the probable career that remains inscribed in the deepest regions of a person's habitus as a penchant, a propensity, an inclination, a tendency (to persevere, to hope, etc.) generating expectations, whether adjusted or out of touch, satisfied or disappointed. For grandes écoles students, and also more generally, this gap is concretely felt in a sense of being either at home in a group, as a likely member among likely members, or out of place, when the improbability of one's presence is felt as a practical difference (experienced as malaise or antipathy) in relation to the most likely dispositions. The reactional behavior of those who have strayed from the paths of power is one example of this effect. For those born into the universe of power, any deviation from the royal route, which leads back to the point of departure, goes against the socially constituted tendency to persevere in one's social being. It follows that when "heirs" enter into the deviant trajectories that lead them down to an intellectual or artistic life, they have no right to failure, that is, to what in the eyes of others would represent a normal or even ideal success (such as an ordinary teaching career). They are condemned to excess, to extremes, to bold ostentation, which alone can justify their renunciation of temporal certainties. (Symbolic revolutions and religious heresies were often incumbent upon just these agents in the past, as great artistic breaks have been in our time.) Similarly, when they take the route that is socially assigned to them, but only achieve mediocre success, they cannot accept without some resentment a position that others would take to be a crowning achievement. This is how we must view the fact that at scientific petites écoles like Mines in Nancy and Saint-Étienne, or even at Centrale and Agro, a large proportion of the sons of industrial and commercial heads turn toward positions on the right or the far right, while at the same schools, or even at schools of lesser rank, such as Grignon, the École Supérieure des Postes et Télécommunication, the ENSAM, or second-ranked écoles normales, students with backgrounds at the popular end or middle of the social scale adopt positions on the left. This is to say that what might appear to be an individual school phenomenon, linked to the composition of a particular student body or to the direct constraints of collective pressure, can only be understood with reference to the space of the grandes écoles, which, in its relationship to the space of positions of economic or cultural power, both point of departure and endpoint of most trajectories, determines the actual meaning of experiences by determining the meaning socially assigned to the different displacements in social space.

Viewed in this way, the space of the grandes écoles becomes a complex network of objective structures whose structural constraint is imposed upon the strategies used to accomplish the continuous social production and reproduction of a certain structure of domination, that is, of a certain social space, understood as an ensemble of objective differences and distances more or less directly retranslated into subjective distances and more or less completely recognized as legitimate. The analysis itself, having been set up with the intention of grasping as a whole the ensemble of institutions responsible for redistributing the different forms of power and prestige, and for producing and reproducing the ordered relations constitutive of the social order, retrospectively validates the methodological decision that lay behind it. It indeed demonstrates that this ensemble is only able to produce these effects insofar as it itself functions as a space of hierarchized differences, and that it is therefore only possible to understand how it works and what it does by grasping it as a whole, in the complex diversity of the structural and functional oppositions that form it and assign to each individual institution its differential weight and effects.

The field of the grandes écoles *institutes* breaks and objective and subjective distances, which are at the basis of differences in positions and concerns [*écarts* and *égards*]: first between conception and management professionals, who have entered through the *grande porte* of the top *concours*, and executants, technicians who, both in the cultural sphere and the domain of public administration and economics, have gone only to second-ranked schools; secondly, within the caste of the *grands corps*, between different positions associated with functions that are simultaneously complementary and noncomparable. The existence of a number of partially independent principles of hierarchization places a limit on the struggle of every man for himself within the field of power and encourages a form of complementarity in the competition that is the foundation for a genuine *organic solidarity in the division of the labor of domination*. The antagonism between spiritual power holders and temporal power holders, which is the source of the polarization of the field of power, does not rule out a functional solidarity that, as the recent crises in the educational institution have shown, is never so evident as when the very foundation of the hierarchical order is threatened.

But, while this mode of reproduction, in comparison with other, older forms, seems remarkably well-adjusted to the specific demands of a particularly complex structure of domination, founded as it is not on a unique and unilinear hierarchy, but on a hierarchy of partially autonomous hierarchies, the statistical logic of its operation means that it also contains some formidable contradictions. It can only produce its most powerful effects, particularly with regard to legitimation, by requiring often enormous efforts, and constant anguish, of the very ones who have the privilege of being able to hope to benefit from it – without ever completely reducing the tension, which increases concomitantly with its contribution to the redistribution of power, between the hopes that it must plant in all and the satisfactions that it can only grant to a few.

2

A Structural History

How valid are the results of a 1967 study of the field of the grandes écoles 20 years after the fact? And if today's *normaliens* are less likely to read *Le Nouvel Observateur* and more likely to read *Libération* [left, intelligentsia, Tr.] (which did not exist in 1967), or if Maoists have disappeared from HEC while future ENA graduates (moderately) criticize their education,[1] does this mean that such a study is only valid as a historical description of a past age, or even that it no longer holds any interest, based as it is on old data? Those who advance such arguments are admitting that they are only considering the most superficial aspect of scientific work, that is, the description of facts taken at face value, and that they identify the task of sociologists or historians with that of journalists, doomed to writings as ephemeral as their objects. In reality, it is attending to structures, and to the hidden mechanisms that ensure their continuation and their transformation, that makes it possible to move beyond the illusion of contingency we may have as long as we simply direct our attention to whatever arouses our curiosity from one day to the next (the latest reform in the ENA *concours* or the nomination of a new head of the École Normale Supérieure), ignoring functional substitutions and structural equivalents.

But even the most rigorous historians do not always escape this anecdotal view, especially when, failing to apprehend the entire space that is effectively present, through its effects, in the object they carve out of it (such as the whole of the field of power in one or another of its sectors – management, the university, or upper-level administration), they fall into a form of what we might call the paralogism of the missing context. The paradigm of this fallacy is provided by those authors who could see a sign of "democratization" in the fact that the proportion of middle-class students in the humanities facultés was increasing, without noting the structural decline that these institutions were experiencing at the same time. In fact, it is only by bearing in mind all the transformations in the structure of the field of institutions of higher education – and particularly the structure of the subfield of the grandes écoles – that it is possible to interpret adequately facts as apparently simple as the evolution in the numbers of students from different social milieus at a given institution.

We might thus be tempted to determine whether the public served by one or another school has been "democratized," and to compare, for example, the figures given by Robert J. Smith for the École Normale of the Third Republic to our own numbers.[2] But, before concluding anything from the fact that the proportion of working-class students, adjusting the figures according to the conventions proposed by R. J. Smith, has slightly increased (moving, if you will, from nothing to next to nothing), we should examine the evolution of the structural position of the École Normale during the same period. The same critical vigilance should be applied to any comparison of the numbers of *normaliens* holding positions in higher education at different time periods, or even of the differences between the distribution of humanities and science *normaliens* by social origin at different points in time.

STRUCTURAL VARIATIONS AND STRUCTURAL INVARIANTS

The distance in time from our initial study becomes an advantage as soon as we take on the project of trying, at some 20 years' remove, to determine to what degree the structure of the field of establishments of higher education has remained constant and to what degree it has been deformed or transformed. Thus, using statistics on the social status of grandes écoles and university students for the year 1984–5, we can analyze the current structure of the institutions of higher education (universities, grandes écoles, IUTs, etc.) and compare it to the structure established on the basis of our comparable 1966–70 data.

Our analysis relies on a 1984–5 survey administered by the office of statistical surveys and studies of the Ministry of Education on a sample of 84 institutions[3] that mark relevant positions in the different "regions" of the field of power, characterized by the only piece of data available for every school, the distribution of students according to father's occupation. (The ENA did not provide this particular information, but its administration allowed us access to data on the social, geographic, and academic characteristics of the students competing in their different *concours*, those qualifying for the oral section, and those accepted.) Rather than seeking formal comparability by purely and simply reproducing the first study sample (which would have been impossible, in any case, given that some schools, such as the Paris Institut d'Études Politiques, the École de la Magistrature, the Paris Internat de Médecine, the École Centrale, the École des Langues Orientales, and a few Écoles de Notariat, were unable to respond to our survey, or to the particular question we were interested in, or, like HEC, answered too briefly), we sought to ensure real comparability by giving greater weight to business and management schools, the number of which increased considerably over the 20 years. The principal limitation of this analysis, like that of the analysis of the state of the field in the 1960s, is the absence of reliable and comparable indicators of students' previous academic success. It follows that the distribution we obtained corresponds more closely to the market value of the diplomas than to their specifically academic value. Institutions such as the ESSEC, the

ESCAE de Lille, and even the European Business School occupy higher positions in the hierarchy based solely on student social background than Ulm and Polytechnique, which are located at the top of the academic hierarchy.

The overall structure of the distribution of schools in 1984–5 proves to be very similar to what we found for the period prior to 1968. So, for example, as in our previous study, the distribution of the occupations of students' families almost exactly reproduces the distribution of these occupations in social space (cf. figures 9 and 10). The first factor (which represents 31.5 per cent of the total inertia) distinguishes schools according to total amount of inherited capital (with the sons of executives on one side and working-class students on the other), opposing institutions in which students from the dominant class make up the great majority (76 percent at the European Business School, 74.5 percent at the ESSEC, 72 percent at the ENA, first *concours*) to those with a very low percentage of upper-class students (22.5 percent in the IUTs, 27 percent in the humanities facultés, 33 percent at the ENSI de Chimie de Lille). If we find the top academic grandes écoles (such as Ulm and Polytechnique) at the top of this hierarchy, we also find academically undemanding business and management schools, and in greater numbers than in the past. These institutions offer a refuge to students from the dominant regions of the field of power who have been unsuccessful in the entrance *concours* of the top grandes écoles and who have refused to fall back on the universities or second-ranked petites écoles.

In the second dimension of the space, teaching and research training schools, engineering schools, and agronomy schools, which are nearly always public and very academically selective, are opposed, as in the previous time period, to schools of management, business, and public administration (and also, although to a lesser degree, schools of art and architecture). The Écoles Normales Supérieures d'Ulm, Saint-Cloud, and Fontenay and the École des Chartes, on the one hand, and the École Supérieure de Commerce et d'Administration des Entreprises de Lille, the European Business School, the École d'Administration et de Direction des Affaires, on the other, make the greatest absolute contribution to this second factor (representing 19 percent of the inertia), a factor that also opposes sons of primary, secondary, and higher education teachers and sons of industrial and commercial heads (following a logic observed in the earlier period as well – that of the distribution of the structure of inherited capital).[4]

Thus the principal oppositions were maintained from the 1960s to the 1980s in spite of the sudden jolt of 1968, which, far from revolutionizing the structures of the field of institutions of higher education, seems to have encouraged individual and collective reactions tending to reinforce them. We do nevertheless find a set of deformations in the field, which should be interpreted with caution. The schools that were and still are at the highest

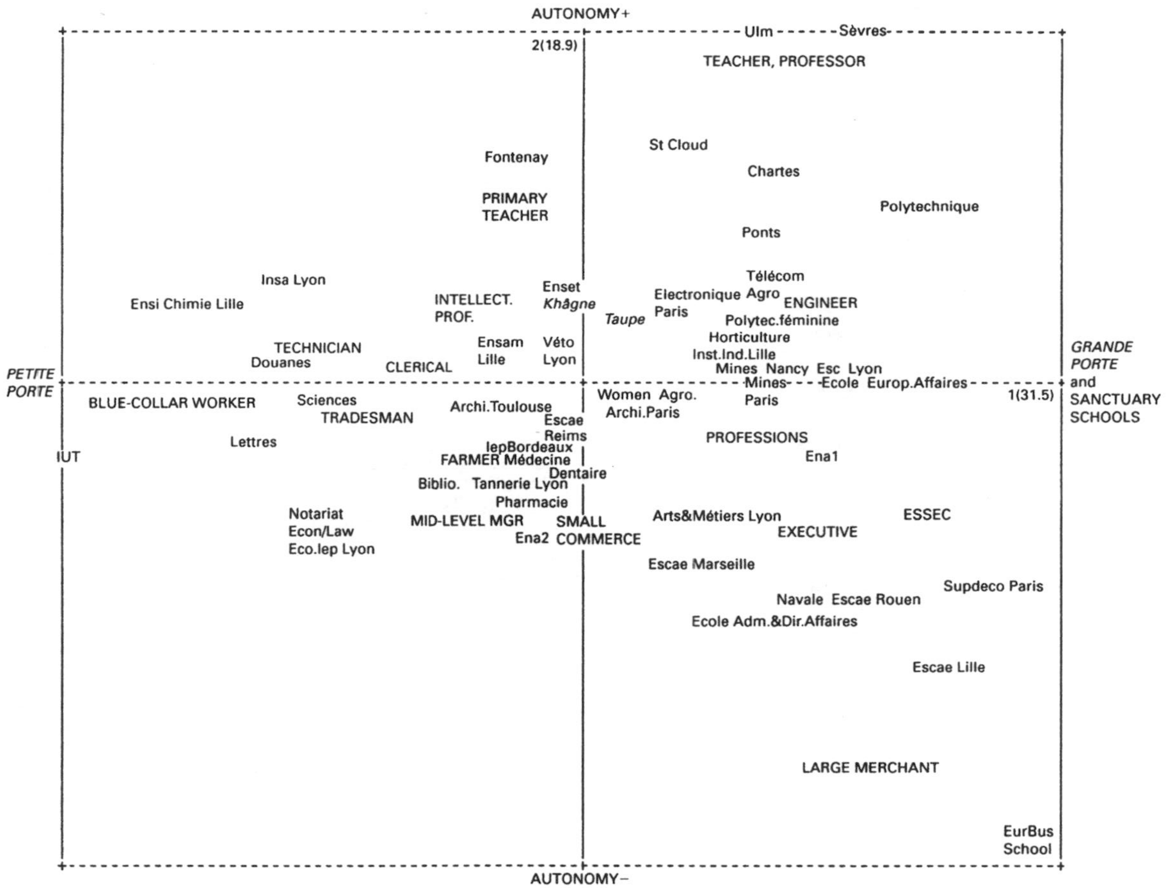

AUTONOMY+

PETITE PORTE

IUT

GRANDE PORTE and SANCTUARY SCHOOLS

----- Ulm ----- Sèvres -----

2(18.9)

TEACHER, PROFESSOR

Polytechnique

St Cloud

Chartes

Télécom
Electronique Agro ENGINEER
Paris   Polytec.féminine
Horticulture
Inst.Ind.Lille
Mines Nancy Esc Lyon
Mines- -École Europ.Affaires ----- 1(31.5)
Ponts

Fontenay

Enset
Khâgne

PRIMARY TEACHER

Véto
Lyon

INTELLECT.
PROF.

Ensam
Lille

Taupe

Women Agro.
Archi.Paris

Paris

Ena1

PROFESSIONS

ESSEC

CLERICAL

Archi.Toulouse
Escae
Reims
IepBordeaux
FARMER Médecine
Dentaire
Biblio. Tannerie Lyon
Pharmacie
MID-LEVEL MGR   SMALL
Ena2 COMMERCE

Arts&Métiers Lyon
EXECUTIVE

Escae Marseille

Supdeco Paris

Navale Escae Rouen

Ecole Adm.&Dir.Affaires

Escae Lille

Insa Lyon

TECHNICIAN
Douanes

Sciences
TRADESMAN

Ensi Chimie Lille

BLUE-COLLAR WORKER

Lettres

Notariat
Econ/Law
Eco.Iep Lyon

LARGE MERCHANT

EurBus
School

AUTONOMY−

Figure 9 The field of institutions of higher education in 1984–1985 (principal variables)

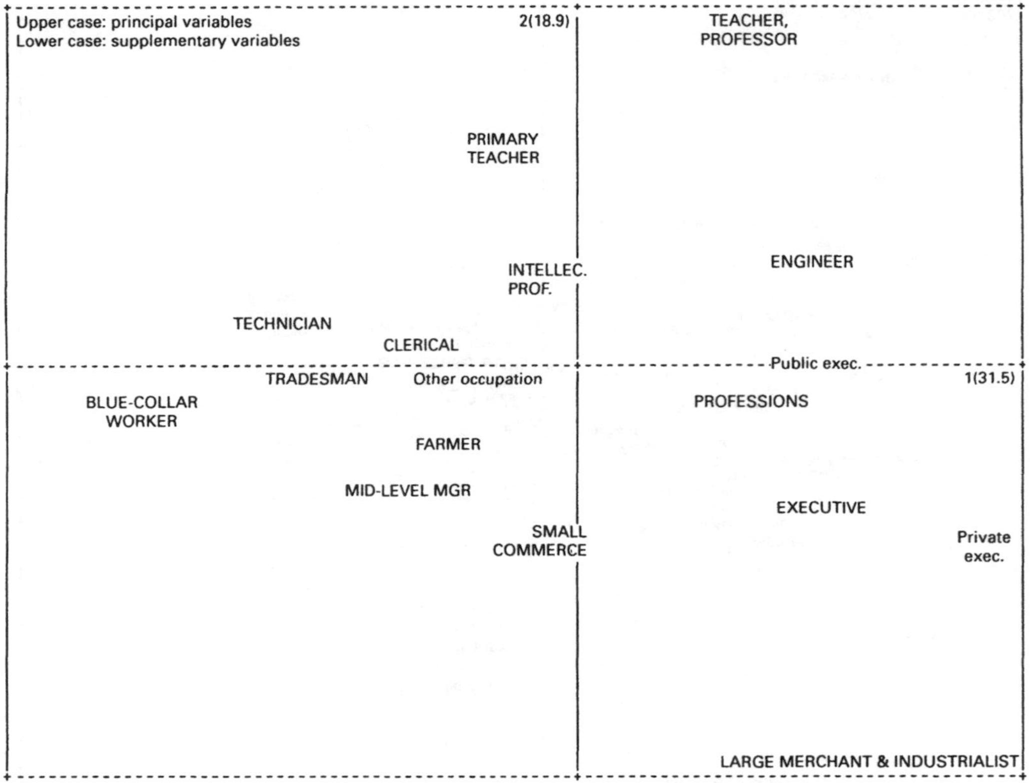

Upper case: principal variables
Lower case: supplementary variables

2(18.9)

1(31.5)

TEACHER,
PROFESSOR

ENGINEER

Public exec.

PROFESSIONS

Private
exec.

EXECUTIVE

INTELLEC.
PROF.

PRIMARY
TEACHER

Other occupation

SMALL
COMMERCE

CLERICAL

FARMER

MID-LEVEL MGR

TECHNICIAN

TRADESMAN

BLUE-COLLAR
WORKER

LARGE MERCHANT & INDUSTRIALIST

Figure 10 Social characteristics of students (principal and supplementary variables)

point in the strictly academic hierarchy have seen a further rise in the percentage of their students from the dominant classes, which has resulted in turn in an increase in the gap separating them from the petites écoles and the universities. This tendency is also found in the institutions that we were unable to include in our analysis, such as Sciences-po, where the proportion of children of clerical workers and minor civil servants has greatly diminished, while the proportion of sons of executives has increased. This decrease, correlative to the rise in competition and the increased selectivity of the institutions, is also a result of the advantage that the most favored students gain from their sense of *placement*, which has become absolutely essential for finding one's way effectively among the establishments and, if need be, getting around the purely academic obstacles to entry. This is particularly clear, for example, in the case of the University of Paris/Dauphine, where the institution of selection, principally through the increase in prestige and attraction that selection introduces in and of itself, and independently of anything even remotely related to the content or methods of the curriculum, was accompanied by a very noticeable rise in the proportion of students from privileged milieus.[5] It is undoubtedly the same logic, related to the increase in academic competition, that explains why the social distance between the ENS d'Ulm and the ENS de Saint-Cloud should have decreased very significantly, as if, under the pressure of the need to avoid relegation to the universities at all costs, the barrier preventing bourgeois offspring from demeaning themselves by choosing a school of inferior reputation, marked by its overtly pedagogical orientation, had been torn down.[6]

Although our method does not really enable us to measure the distances and their transformations, indications are that the gap in terms of inherited capital and the social value of diplomas has widened considerably between the *grande porte* and the *petite porte*, and, more specifically, between establishment schools – the ENA, Sciences-po (not represented here), HEC, the ESSEC – and humanities, sciences, and also law facultés, whose social recruitment falls continuously as the proportion of women increases, or even petites écoles in applied subjects, École Supérieure des P et T, École des Douanes, École de la Magistrature, not to mention the École des Arts et Métiers, the ENSI, and the Instituts Nationaux des Sciences Appliqués, so many schools that used to offer the sons of the petty bourgeoisie the hope of reaching the highest positions in public service. This is principally due to the differential increase in the numbers of students enrolled at the different institutions; the more selective the different schools were at the beginning of the period, the smaller was the increase in their student body (with the university population increasing significantly, while the preparatory classes and the top grandes écoles barely grew at all), and the gap in relative exclusiveness thus widened considerably.

Between 1950 and 1972, the universities, especially the humanities and law facultés, grow very rapidly, particularly between 1959 and 1972. Their numbers increase by a factor of 3.6 overall, with humanities facultés increasing by 4.3, compared to 1.7 for all preparatory classes (see figure 11). Growth is much more marked in the preparatory classes for the "middle-ranked" schools, such as Saint-Cloud and Fontenay, than in the preparatory classes for the top grandes écoles. The number of students in first-year *taupes*, for example, increases by a factor of only 1.3. While we count one new preparatory class student for every four new university students in 1960–1, by 1972–3, we only count one for every nine. Since 1972, university growth has slowed considerably, especially in the science facultés, in part due to the creation in 1966–7 of the Instituts Universitaires de Technologie, which grow very rapidly

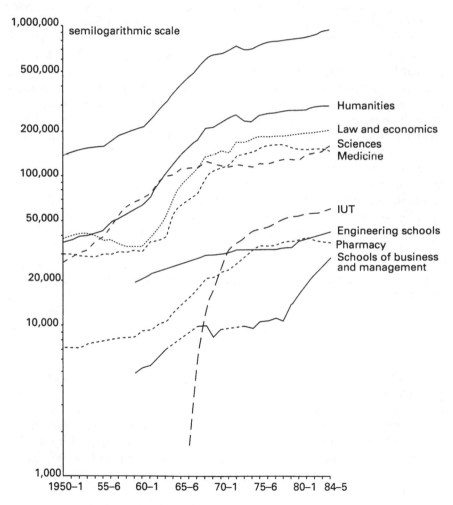

Figure 11 Evolution in numbers of students enrolled in universities and schools of engineering and business, 1950–1984

until 1974–5 (going from 1,644 students to 41,949). The same tendency can be seen starting at the end of secondary school, where the increase in students with the non-technical baccalauréat remains quite moderate (105 in 1978 against 100 in 1972) while the number of technical *bacheliers* increases considerably (163 against 100). The number of students in medicine has been regularly decreasing since 1978–9, and in pharmacy since 1982–3. The population of engineering schools (especially the schools with no specific specialization, such as the Instituts Nationaux des Sciences Appliquées) slowly grows throughout the period, with its pace increasing from 1959–60 to 1967–8 and slowing from 1969–70 to 1979–80, only to increase again in recent years. Business schools, which, as a whole, grow relatively moderately until the end of the 1970s, double in size between 1977–80 and 1984–5, going from 13,000 to 27,000.

Throughout this period, the size of the top Parisian lycées, which provide an increasing proportion of the students accepted to the grandes écoles, remains virtually constant. Between 1964–5 and 1980–1, the number of students entering *khâgne* and *taupe* divisions increases from 880 to 937 at Louis-le-Grand, from 1,027 to 1,110 at Saint-Louis, and from 565 to 692 at Henri IV. Female students, who represent only 4.7 percent of the preparatory class population at the three top lycées in 1964–5 (and who are absent from Louis-le-Grand), stand at 28.2 percent in 1980–1. They are particularly highly represented in the humanities and biology, and they make up 11.6 percent of the students in the M and P (mathematics and physics) divisions at Louis-le-Grand, and 19.4 percent at Saint-Louis (they are somewhat younger than the boys, and probably owe their presence in these groups to a high degree of academic success). The heightened competition that results seems to have led to a *rise in the social recruitment of these establishments*. In 1980–1, the number of students from the dominant categories approaches 70 percent in the M and P classes of the top Parisian lycées, while in our 1967–8 study it stands at between 55 percent and 65 percent. (See also table 15.)

Sources: Ministry of Education, office of computer and statistical studies central division of statistics and surveys, Ministry of Universities, statistical working group, *L'enseignement supérieur en France, Étude statistique et évolution de 1959–1960 à 1977–1978, Études et documents*, 80.2; *Statistiques des enseignements, Tableaux et informations*, section 5–3 beginning in 1967–8, and *Informations statistiques*, nos 19, 23, 27 and 44 for the preceding years; Ministry of Education, office of computer and statistical studies, central division of statistics and surveys, *Liste descriptive des établissements publics d'enseignement de second degré* (gives the numbers of students enrolled in preparatory classes from 1964–5 on by establishment); Ministry of Education, central division of statistics and surveys, *Enquête 13, 1980–81 dans les classes préparatoires*; Ministry of Education, *Repères et références statistiques sur les enseignements et la formation*, 1986 edn (Paris: Imprimerie Nationale, 1986); Ministry of Education, *Notes d'information*; S. Breillot, "Les écoles d'ingénieurs regroupées par niveau principal de recrutement: Evolution sur vingt ans des effectifs," in Ministry of Education, *Education et formations, Études et documents* 1 (Oct.–Dec. 1982), p. 47; Ministry of Education, state secretariat to the universities, central division of statistics and surveys, statistical data on the development of the numbers of students in higher education in France since 1960, *Études et documents* 31 (1975); INSEE, *Annuaire statistique de la France, Résumé rétrospectif* (Paris: INSEE, 1966) (for the population of the universities from 1950–1 to 1963–4) and *Annuaire statistique, 1984*.

Table 15 Breakdown of student bodies of the different institutions of higher education according to father's occupation (percent)

	IUT	Sciences	Humanities	Law, economics	Pharmacy	Medicine	Humanities prep.	Science prep.	Top lycées, humanities	Top lycées, sciences
						Universities			Preparatory classes	
Farmworker	0.7	0.5	0.5	0.5	0.3	0.2	–	0.2	–	–
Farm owner	9.0	6.5	4.6	5.5	6.8	3.5	2.1	3.7	0.9	0.4
Service personnel	1.7	0.8	1.0	1.0	0.5	0.5	1.0	0.6	0.5	0.4
Laborer	1.3	0.8	0.8	0.7	0.3	0.4	0.2	0.3	0.2	–
Semiskilled worker, miner	8.3	3.7	3.5	3.6	1.8	2.1	1.7	2.1	0.6	–
Skilled worker	9.8	5.8	6.2	5.8	3.1	3.1	3.6	3.6	2.8	1.8
Foreman	4.8	2.4	2.2	2.2	1.6	1.6	2.6	2.6	2.4	1.2
Tradesman	4.8	3.0	3.0	2.8	3.2	2.6	2.6	3.3	1.3	2.8
Small commerce	4.4	4.5	4.3	4.6	5.8	4.5	2.7	2.4	2.8	1.3
Clerical	9.8	8.3	8.9	8.9	6.2	6.4	8.8	8.0	4.3	4.8
Technician	6.8	4.8	3.8	3.6	3.3	3.6	} 19.4	18.3	14.4	12.0
Medical, social	0.6	0.6	0.9	0.8	0.8	0.8				
Mid-level admin. mgr	6.8	8.0	7.5	8.6	7.2	7.6				
Prim. teacher, intellect. prof.	2.5	3.6	3.2	2.3	2.9	2.9				
Industrialist, lge merchant	2.0	2.2	2.6	3.2	3.4	3.1	2.7	3.2	2.3	4.8
Administrative exec.	6.7	10.1	10.1	13.7	14.6	16.1	} 41.6	42.1	59.6	62.8
Engineer	4.1	7.2	4.8	4.4	8.6	9.1				
Humanities, sciences prof.	2.4	5.2	5.0	3.0	4.7	5.0				
Professions	2.2	4.9	5.7	7.3	13.1	13.2				
Other	5.5	6.2	7.5	5.5	3.7	4.4	3.5	3.2	1.9	2.5
None	1.8	2.6	2.9	3.3	2.8	3.5	} 7.4	6.4	6.0	5.1
NR	4.1	8.3	10.9	8.7	5.3	5.9				
Total	100	100	100	100	100	100	100	100	100	100

Universities The data given here concern the total number of students enrolled in 1979–80. For the purposes of comparison with the preparatory classes, it would have been preferable to use only first cycle university students [see chart of ed. system, Tr.]. But pharmacy students are not included in first cycle statistical tables (which use less well-defined occupational categories); comparing the breakdown of students by discipline, social origin, and cycle has shown that the breakdown by social origin was not much different for the first cycle than for the university as a whole (except that the proportion of students at the popular end and middle of the social scale is slightly higher in the first cycle, in every discipline; the distance between the universities and the preparatory classes is consequently even more striking than it appears here).

Humanities prep. All second-year preparatory classes for the Écoles Normales Supérieures d'Ulm, Saint-Cloud, Sèvres, and Fontenay, the École des Chartes, and Saint-Cyr (our data do not enable us to distinguish between the different types of humanities preparatory classes).

Science prep. All *mathématiques spéciales* (M, M', P, and P'), *mathématiques spéciales techniques*, *mathématiques spéciales technologiques*, *biologie mathématiques spéciales* classes (not including technical *mathématiques spéciales* classes TA, TB, TB', and TC or the ENSET preparatory classes).

Top lycées, humanities Preparatory classes for the Écoles Normales Supérieures d'Ulm and Sèvres at the Lycées Fénelon, Henri IV, and Louis-le-Grand in Paris (second year).

Top lycées, sciences *Mathématiques spéciales* classes of type M and P at the Lycées Janson, Louis-le-Grand, and Saint-Louis in Paris.

Sources: For the universities, Ministry of Education, office of computer and statistical studies, central division of statistics and surveys, Ministry of Universities, *Statistiques des étudiants inscrits dans les établissements universitaires, 1979–1980*, Document 5061, Feb. 1981; for the preparatory classes, Ministry of Education, central division of statistics and surveys, *Enquête 13, 1980–1981* (unpublished tables).

As and although the social recruitment of the most academically prestigious establishments simultaneously rose in response to the heightened competition, the social distance between the two poles of the field of the grandes écoles continued to increase. The gap has probably never been so wide, both in terms of dispositions and stances, between, on the one hand, the establishment schools, both old and new variants, which enable the offspring of the business bourgeoisie to get around the obstacle of academic demands while still ensuring them a form of consecration (especially the management schools, which have shifted toward the right-hand side of the diagram), and, on the other hand, the highly intellectually prestigious grandes écoles, such as the École Normale and Polytechnique, which are the only schools that can still really compete with the new dominants for administrative and economic power. At each school, the proportion of students from the corresponding positions in the field of power (sons of teachers at the ENS, sons of engineers and executives at Polytechnique, sons of higher civil servants at the ENA, and sons of business and industry heads at HEC) has grown considerably, reinforcing the homogeneity, and the self-enclosed nature, of the different schools.

In order to move beyond this first synoptic treatment of the structural changes that have arisen in the field of institutions of higher education over the past 20 years, we must now attempt to describe and explain the two transformations that have most greatly affected this universe: the rise in the relative importance of the ENA, which, girded by the positions acquired by its alumni in the administrative, political, and economic fields, has appropriated an increasing share of the positions for which grandes écoles students must compete, thereby determining profound transformations in the field as a whole; and the development of an entire set of new institutions, schools of management, marketing, advertising, journalism, communications, etc., which came along just at the right time to serve the innumerable independent, yet objectively orchestrated strategies by means of which the adolescents of the business bourgeoisie and their parents were attempting to circumvent the increased rigor of academic law.

PALACE WARS

The inadequacy of the monographs that treat isolated institutions is never as apparent as when it comes to understanding the changes that have occurred in the grandes écoles most directly responsible for reproducing the field of power, changes that can only be grasped on the basis of the structure of the subfield these schools constitute within the overall universe of institutions of higher education. The competitive struggles underlying these changes are in effect determined by the structure of the relations of power that obtain among the schools at any given moment. The strategies that an institution may implement to ensure or improve its position depend on the overall amount of its specific (inseparably social and academic) capital as well as the structure of this capital, that is, on the relative weight of both its academic capital (measured in terms of the specific value of the competences guaranteed) and its strictly social capital (linked to the current or potential social value of its student body present and past – its alumni).

Only a structural history designed to grasp both the objective relations that obtain among the different institutions by virtue of their relative positions in the social and academic hierarchies and the competitive struggles that oppose them can thus enable us to perceive the logic of invariant and inevitable processes where we usually see nothing but the chronological succession of arbitrary and contingent events. As a result, we cannot help but be struck by the analogies between two histories as apparently different in time and social place as the one that led HEC, starting in 1881, to exercise its hegemony on the subfield of the schools of business and management, and the one that enabled the ENA, starting in 1945, to gradually extend its hold over the field of the grandes écoles.

Brainchild of the Paris Chamber of Commerce and the business world, which were anxious to provide themselves with their own training ground, independent of the university (on the model of Centrale, a private school that already fulfilled this role), the École des Hautes Études Commerciales was long considered a minor school (people spoke of a "sub-Saint-Cyr"), offering students whose origins destined them for social success a means of concealing their academic failure (either on the baccalauréat or in one of the more prestigious higher education *concours*). It has only managed to assert its preeminence over the other business schools, some of which are older, but located in the provinces, by means of an entire set of collective and individual strategies aimed at the accumulation of symbolic capital. These include all the initiatives designed to guarantee the school one or another of the privileges and distinctions enjoyed by the first-ranked schools, such as obligatory military preparation or the Légion d'Honneur and the Croix de Guerre (officially conferred upon the school in 1927, and just what was needed to strengthen its position with regard to Saint-Cyr, its closest rival).[7] They also include such highly distinctive traditional events as the year-end reviews that first appear at the beginning of the century and continue through 1966–7, or public hazing rites, so many activities in which the grandes écoles both recognize themselves and create recognition for themselves. Still further, and especially important, is the famous Boom HEC, a genuine institutional enterprise of commercial self-promotion mobilizing HEC students for nearly a month in a sort of full-scale marketing exercise, the preparation of the party serving as an exercise in professional training. We should also include the sporting events that provide opportunities for encounters with students from the most prestigious schools, both in France (Polytechnique, Centrale) and abroad (the London School of Economics, the universities of Milan, Munich, Amsterdam, Lausanne, and Stockholm, European Business Schools, etc.). Finally and most importantly, we note all the judiciously concerted ventures organized by the alumni association that aim to increase the value of HEC's title in the business market, both practically, through a system of job placement, founded on the rational use of school connections (since 1928, the organization has kept files enabling the rational guidance of students seeking jobs toward the different positions controlled by alumni), and symbolically, through prestigious shows, banquets, charity galas, and anniversary ceremonies where the association shows off its most prestigious members (Albert Lebrun, Paul Reynaud, etc.), and through the publication of a magazine intended for executives and corporate heads. But, alongside all the activities that aim to increase its notoriety in the business world, this institution, located in an unstable position between the university field and the economic field, finds it must make a constant effort, in the other direction, to ensure that it will be granted certificates of legitimacy by a university whose own legitimacy is contested, or defied, by its very existence, and to gain from the powers that be (in other words, from the Ministry of Education, the University Board, or other legitimating authorities, as the case may be) institutionalized advantages in the competition that pits it against the other business schools. Thus, between the two World Wars, HEC steps up its attempts at obtaining the equivalent of the baccalauréat to validate the non-*bacheliers* among its students, and, failing in this, strives to assert its membership in the upper nobility of the grandes écoles by securing the services of renowned teachers.

Nothing is more telling in regard to the objective power relations among the different competing institutions or the efforts aimed at strategically manipulating them than the measures that may be unilaterally adopted by a school, or imposed by a semiofficial arbiter (such as the grandes écoles associations) or the authority of the state, in an attempt to regulate the relative values of the titles conferred by the different schools or the authorized passage from one school to another. According to the logic of all enterprises geared toward the accumulation of symbolic capital, the game consists in setting up distances either by excluding others or excluding oneself. So, for example, in 1914 HEC asserts that it is unique among business schools by instituting its first preparatory classes and advertising throughout France. In response to the reaction of the other schools to what strikes them as an assertion of HEC's pretension to national recruitment, HEC refuses to participate in a common meeting of all business schools, citing its students' more advanced age and superior credentials (the baccalauréat). Immediately after the war, it reasserts its superiority by creating a channel for direct second-year entrance for graduates of other advanced business schools. Next comes the establishment of an examination, followed by a *concours*, and especially the lengthening of its course of studies, which, in this case as elsewhere, is much more a result of competition within the field than of any intrinsic educational need.[8]

Strategies designed to increase symbolic capital by strengthening belief in its increase are always part bluff, but their success depends on the state of the belief they intend to strengthen. HEC's strategies for setting itself apart from the other business schools are the more likely to hit their mark the more inclined are their principal targets (that is, potential students and their families) to *recognize* the particular difference it aims to reaffirm, for example, by choosing HEC when they have passed several *concours*. And the institution's administrators can thus act on the authority of these acts of difference recognition in order to initiate collective action designed to make the difference known and get it recognized, often legally, and to encourage new acts of recognition, in a "snowballing" process – the reverse of which is the panic that arises at the first sign of a crisis in belief, doomed to feed on itself, as it were, to the point of symbolic bankruptcy.

The process that led the École Nationale d'Administration to attempt to dominate the entire field of the grandes écoles, principally to the detriment of the École Normale Supérieure, relegated to reproducing teachers and intellectuals, as well as the École Polytechnique itself, more and more frequently deflected back to purely technical, read subordinate, functions, is similar in many respects to the process that carried HEC to the top of schools of business and management, enabling it to rival the ENA (and Sciences-po) today in the competition for the dominant positions in the economic field. Undoubtedly it is not possible to analyze in detail the curious drift of an institution that – originating out of a stated intention, doubtless sincere, to rationalize and democratize the recruitment of higher public servants by doing away with dynasties founded on nepotism and the insidious heredity of offices – has come to fulfill a function altogether similar to the one that fell to HEC and Centrale at the end of the nineteenth century, that is, providing the bourgeois children socially predestined to occupy dominant positions with the academic guarantee that the most academically legitimate institutions were increasingly refusing them during a period of intensified academic competition. How did the indirect route become the royal route, and how did an institution originally invented by an avant-garde fraction prompted by reformist intentions and mindful of the existence of a new social demand (a "market gap")[9] gradually manage to impose itself as the proper goal of all the strictly temporal ambitions that could up until that time be expressed and fulfilled in other institutions?

In order to apprehend this evolution, we would need to closely analyze the countless individual and collective strategies through which the schools that were able to compete with the newcomer, principally the École Normale Supérieure and the École Polytechnique, saw themselves gradually reduced to the strict definition of their official mission of training teachers and engineers: including the strategies employed by the jilted students of the schools whose hegemony was threatened, principally those sons of higher civil servants, initially directed by academic logic toward the ENS and HEC, who aim to reestablish their position by preparing for the ENA; the misdirected strategies of the administrators of the threatened schools, such as the ENS, who confirm the supposed inferiority of their institution in demanding diploma equivalences unworthy of their former position, only to see them refused [by the government, Tr.]; or, conversely, the judicious symbolic investments of the administrators of the ascendant institution. Here we enter the logic of symbolic capital, where what counts is making others see and believe, notice and recognize – the logic of society marriages, where a rejected proposal irrevocably determines the hierarchy between two groups, or the logic of the salons of which Proust was the self-appointed ethnographer – a domain requiring the same prudence in investments and negotiations as portfolio management. The École Nationale d'Administration has enjoyed a considerable advantage from the very start in the struggles in which symbolic capital is both instrument and stake, struggles that, in this particular case, are aimed at imposing the representation of a hierarchy. What its rivals are only able to offer through a kind of legitimate usurpation, specifically, the promise of positions of power inscribed in the careers of successful alumni (Presidents of the Republic, ministers, ambassadors, or chief executives), is very officially included in the stated curriculum and goals of an institution specially equipped to prepare its students for the highest government jobs. (The very creation of the ENA leads to the demise of the special *concours* that up until then granted access to the grands corps not controlled by Polytechnique, preventing *polytechniciens* from entering the Inspection des Finances directly, without first going to the ENA. Despite the 1954 decree granting two ENA slots to Polytechnique students graduating in the top third of their class, the ENA is thus assured of a veritable monopoly on the top positions in higher public service.) The advantage ENA students gain from the *concentration of symbolic capital* that results from the establishment of a unique name (the acronym ENA), generator of a known and recognized group whose members are bound together through their shared symbolic capital, is coupled (especially during a period of the "technocratic" redefinition of politics) with the practical advantage lent them by their proximity to the political field (which takes on a concrete form in their tenure in the ministerial cabinets of the Fifth Republic) as well as by the solidarities, converted into esprit de corps, among members of the Parisian bourgeoisie traditionally associated with the profits and prestige afforded by mastery of the state.[10]

We can get a rough idea of the variations in the strength of the attraction this dominant institution exerted and the social distances it marked out with respect to its rivals at different periods in its history in the evolution at each of the various institutions of the number of students who, turning aside from the ordinary paths toward which their school leads them, agree to compete in the ENA *concours* and do so successfully (see figure 12). We see in comparing the histograms that the ENA's attraction was exerted upon

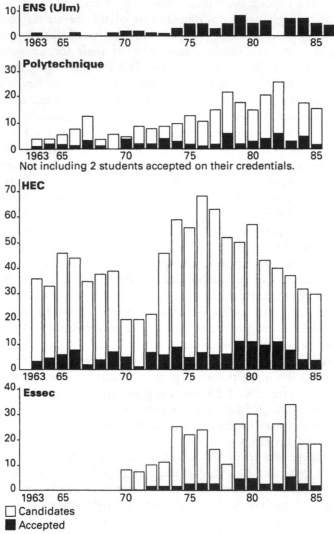

Based on: École Nationale d'Administration, external and internal *concours*, statistics (from 1963 to 1985). These statistics did not enable us to distinguish Ulm *normaliens* from other *normaliens* (or, at the beginning of the period, from *agrégés*). It is only in 1984 that ENA statistics begin to count Ulm *normaliens* separately. We thus used ENA and ENS yearbooks to tally up those ENA students who had gone to Ulm. The diagram thus represents the number of *normaliens* who enter the ENA each year (and not the number of students who pass the *concours* each year). (Depending on when the students do their military service, the time lag between success in the *concours* and entering school may vary.)

Figure 12 Evolution in the number of candidates and students accepted to the ENA, 1963–1985

the different competing institutions all the earlier and all the more strongly the more similar their stated functions (and their students' most frequent dispositions toward power) and the lower their position in the strictly academic hierarchy. Here again, what is statistically and sociologically significant is *the structure of the differences among the different schools*. HEC students compete in the ENA *concours* very early on, and in large numbers, but only a few pass; Polytechnique students, who also compete very early, but in limited numbers (especially considering the size of their school), are only moderately successful; the success rate for École Normale students, who take an interest in the ENA late, but in large numbers, starts out high, but follows a downward slope; finally, ESSEC students, who begin to consider the ENA relatively late, well after HEC students in any case, do rather poorly. This structural reading enables us to more clearly identify the laws governing the relations among the institutions and, more specifically, the transformations in their relative positions in the field (transformations that can be assumed to be themselves related, with a certain time lag, to transformations in the positions of the corresponding graduates in the field of power).[11]

Thus a large number of HEC students compete in the ENA *concours* as early as the 1960s, no doubt because they see in the École Nationale d'Administration a surer and more efficient means of access to the positions of power they had expected from their own school. Our 1967 survey indicates this preference clearly: asked to classify nine grandes écoles (Polytechnique, Ulm-humanities and Ulm-sciences, ESSEC, Sciences-po, Centrale, HEC, the ENA and Harvard Business School), on the one hand for prestige and on the other hand for interest of education and professional promise, HEC students ranked their own school only fifth for its education and professional training (after the ENA, Polytechnique, Harvard Business School and Ulm – with the École Centrale, the ESSEC, and Sciences-po falling in behind HEC), and sixth for prestige (Polytechnique and the ENA captured the first two slots under this criterion), and they were all the more inclined to this relative depreciation of their school the higher their social origins. The tendency to turn toward the ENA was boosted by the creation in 1972 of two distinct *concours* tracks, one in the law, the other in economics. The subsequent fall in the number of candidates is due to three factors: the policy of the new HEC administration, which since 1983 has explicitly discouraged flight to other institutions (principally by favoring the decline of the "industrial economics" option, traditionally chosen by future ENA candidates), the increase in the symbolic capital the school acquires through the success of its alumni in the economic field, where they compete with *polytechniciens* and ENA alumni, often emerging victorious, and the transformation in student attitudes toward business, which is doubtless not unrelated to the change in the dominant mood on the subject since 1981.

Indications are that while the attraction exerted by the dominant institution on the other institutions is likely to become stronger the wider the gap in symbolic capital (in the images of the institutions, that is), it nonetheless ceases to exert any pull beyond a certain threshold, as the difference in attitudes between HEC and ESSEC students shows. The status of the latter institution has to rise considerably – to the point of causing HEC concern – for aspiration to the ENA to develop and become overt.[12] The continuous and growing interest *polytechniciens* show in the ENA up to the early 1980s (discounting a dip around 1968), which is legally recognized as it were by the decree granting them two ENA slots, is one among many indices of the fact that the École Polytechnique remains oriented much more toward power than toward science – even though, undoubtedly through an inverse effect of the competition from the ENA that blocks a number of careers, we see a continuous increase in interest in research.[13] In fact, because they were the most directly threatened, *polytechniciens* were the first to react against the advances of the ENA. Starting in 1962, with the X alumni association commission on "the choice of careers upon graduation from Polytechnique" and especially in 1967,[14] with the commission on "Higher Education and the Grandes Écoles" (chaired by Pierre Couture, as was the preceding one), followed by the Lhermitte Commission in 1968, the leaders organize their defense and draw up their sales pitch.[15] Louis Armand, Mines engineer general and president of Polytechnique's board, but also member of the board of the ENA, where he has been a lecturer since 1947, brings the debate out into the open in two *Figaro* articles (April 10–11, 1967) in which, while apparently defending technicians against technocrats, he demands that *polytechniciens* be given the right to hold technocratic positions. And the rapporteur for a project for the creation of a corps of Armement engineers betrays the concern gnawing at the corps of *polytechniciens* in stating before the National Assembly on November 15, 1967 that one of the amendments he had proposed had been suggested to him "by a number of senior military engineers, including *polytechnicien* alumni, who were alarmed by the invasion of young ENA students into every domain of the administration, including the most technical."[16] We can see that in this case, *the defense of the corps* is not abandoned to the whims of individual initiatives; rather, it mobilizes a large fraction of the corps under the leadership of members specifically chosen for the task and equipped with specific tools of action. One of the primary functions of this collective effort is to provide a codified set of tried and tested arguments, establishing the form and the formulae of a professional ideology based on a small number of themes and key words, such as those that supposedly capture the inimitable *polytechnicien* virtues: a mind for synthesis, concern for the public good, the ability to work with others, a taste for responsibility, the ability to get things done, leadership, and solid training in the sciences.[17]

All of these attempts at symbolic promotion are marked by nearly obsessive reference to the new dominant institution. For example, people may deplore the discomfort of the "young engineer" who, fully aware that he has "been selected according to very stringent criteria and that he has succeeded in a course of studies that counts among the longest and most rigorous (. . .), may *feel excluded, a priori, and groundlessly*, from jobs that allow close participation in the study of policy and the preparation of the crucial decisions that determine the fate of the nation."[18] They may also express the opinion that in order to handle complex administrative and industrial phenomena, "a legal and administrative education, even if it is *tinted with qualitative economics* (an obvious allusion to ENA training) will no longer be enough for higher civil servants."[19] Or still further, that the École Polytechnique produces "a particular kind of engineer, neither a 'technician,' that is, someone who specializes in a technique but does not accede to positions of policy-making and decision-making, nor a 'technocrat' *who sometimes arbitrarily appropriates these positions*, but a 'technologue' " (this neologism condenses *the twofold difference* that distinguishes the *polytechnicien* both from the mere technicians of the minor science schools, such as Centrale and Arts et Métiers, and from ENA students).[20] Or finally, while somewhat self-assuredly denouncing the monopoly held by particular schools on particular corps thus converted into "fiefs," people may bemoan the absence of "civil servants with advanced training in the sciences in organisms such as the [economic] planning council, ministerial cabinets, ministry directorates, etc., "and assert that" nothing precludes an engineer from heading an administrative region or performing diplomatic functions."[21] Finally, in a crowning gesture, they may propose the creation of an "Institute for Advanced Studies in Public Affairs," naturally limited to *polytechniciens* and ENA students.[22]

In addition to these demands, people propose curriculum improvements and reorganization intended to better arm *polytechniciens* in the competition with ENA students. "One undeniable weakness in young Xs is their difficulty in expressing their thoughts, in organizing and communicating their ideas. It is clear that Polytechnique doesn't prepare them as well as other programs – ENA or the humanities – for manipulating language. Something needs to be done."[23] Similarly, the Couture report demands that their general education be systematically redesigned "to include more economics, management techniques, and computer science, as well as a solid introduction to psychosociology and its applications (techniques of expression and communication, group dynamics, etc.)."[24] Finally, a number of pedagogic innovations, such as the institution of economics courses at Polytechnique[25] or management courses at the École des Mines, and later at Polytechnique, are obvious counters to ENA competition.[26]

In these struggles, where what is at stake is the redefinition of the division of labor of domination, the strategies of the ENA are bounded by the system-wide distribution of academic and social advantages among the schools. While the ENA triumphs in the temporal domain and, if we measure success by the number and quality of positions held, in the economic field and higher public service, it remains dominated in the strictly academic hierarchies. The symbolic strategies through which it attempts to gain recognition, especially from its rivals, are weakened by the fact that it enjoys less of the legitimacy conferred by academic consecration, taken as a guarantee of merit and competence. Proof of this can be found in the results of a survey of the opinions of grandes écoles graduates (table 16), which show that ENA graduates tend to relegate Polytechnique graduates to technical positions and HEC graduates to commercial or marketing positions as well as positions in finance, while a good proportion reserve high-level management positions for themselves (although at a lower rate than Polytechnique and especially HEC alumni, their direct rivals for these positions).[27] The

Table 16   In your opinion, which grande école best prepares its students . . .

X		ENA		HEC		ESC-Rouen		Mines Nancy	
For business and marketing jobs									
HEC	62	HEC	65	HEC	64	HEC	29	HEC	52
Essec	9	Essec	10	Essec	2	ESCP	9	Essec	12
Insead	3	ESCP	4	ESCP	1	Essec	8	ESCP	3
others/		others/		others/		others/		others/	
don't know	26	don't know	21	don't know	33	don't know	54	don't know	33
total	100	total	100	total	100	total	100	total	100
For technical and engineering jobs									
Centrale	33	X	31	Centrale	36	Centrale	22	Centrale	36
Arts et M.	22	Centrale	27	X	16	X	10	Mines Paris	12
X	8	Arts et M.	14	Arts et M.	9	Arts et M.	6	Arts et M.	10
others/		others/		others/		others/		others/	
don't know	37	don't know	28	don't know	39	don't know	62	don't know	42
total	100	total	100	total	100	total	100	total	100
For jobs in finance									
HEC	35	HEC	42	HEC	68	HEC	42	HEC	37
X	7	ENA	12	ENA	3	ESC-Rouen	6	IEP	3
IEP	6	IEP	5	Essec	2	ESCP	5	Insead	2
others/		others/		others/		others/		others/	
don't know	52	don't know	41	don't know	27	don't know	47	don't know	58
total	100	total	100	total	100	total	100	total	100
For jobs in personnel management									
IEP	4	ENA	6	HEC	12	HEC	8	IEP	4
HEC	3	HEC	6	IEP	11	ESC-Rouen	2	Mines Nancy	3
Essec	1	IEP	6	Essec	10	Essec	2	Essec	3
others/		others/		others/		others/		others/	
don't know	92	don't know	82	don't know	67	don't know	88	don't know	90
total	100	total	100	total	100	total	100	total	100
For high-level management positions									
X	33	ENA	29	HEC	57	HEC	39	X	17
HEC	13	HEC	17	X	10	ESC-Rouen	6	HEC	8
Insead	7	X	8	other gr. éc.	3	X	6	Insead	8
ENA	2	Insead	1	ENA	2	Essec	6	Mines Paris	7
Essec	1	other grande		Essec	1	ESCP	4	ENA	4
ESCP	1	école	1	Mines Paris	1	ENA	2	Mines Nancy	3
others/		others/		others/		others/		others/	
don't know	43	don't know	44	don't know	26	don't know	37	don't know	53
total	100	total	100	total	100	total	100	total	100

Sources: Heidrick and Struggles International/IPSOS, Paris, Sept. 1987, and *Expansion,* 11–24 Sept. 1987.

entire logic of symbolic struggles is captured in these crossed imputations in which each of the rivals tends to claim for itself a set of coveted properties (here, the right to occupy high-level management positions; elsewhere, the title of writer or great writer, philosopher or great philosopher, etc.) to an extent that the others would not concede, while it assigns the rejected properties to the others more than they assign them to themselves (here, for example, positions in personnel, rejected by everyone). The structure of the distribution of the reflexive judgments through which the alumni of the three top establishment schools, the ENA, HEC, and Polytechnique, attribute management positions to one another and through which each school reveals an index of its socially recognized pretensions (what is attributed to it, especially by its rivals) and of the gap between these socially recognized pretensions and its declared pretensions (what it attributes to itself) shows that the ENA, which grants itself high-level management positions much more often than the others grant them to it, is opposed to both Polytechnique and HEC, whose pretensions are much more modest and at any rate much closer to what their rivals attribute to them. The word "pretension," which comes up again and again in judgments on the ENA and its products, expresses the sense of usurpation provoked in its rivals and undoubtedly many others in view of its increasingly broad hold on positions of power, which it enjoys without being able to match the École Normale or Polytechnique in providing the academic guarantees that have become one of the surest instruments of legitimation.[28] For various converging reasons, not least the composition of its examining committee,[29] the nature of its examinations, and the social characteristics of its chosen people, the effect of legitimation produced by academic consecration is less powerful here than at the École Normale or Polytechnique, and the awareness of a gap between academic "merits" and social rewards, which often leads to a generalized questioning of all justifications based on "competence," increases the sense of arbitrariness that is inevitably produced in any case by very precocious accession to positions of power.

For their part, *normaliens*, differing from HEC students in the two factors that help to determine interest in the ENA, did not really enter the race until very late (in the early 1970s), undoubtedly due to a sort of collective disenchantment with their probable future. This sudden disillusionment seems attributable at least as much to a deep transformation in dispositions and hopes, correlative with the rise in student social status, as to the objective transformation of the positions to which students had effectively been promised. More than 12 candidates per year are recorded between 1976 and 1984 (24 in 1978 and 1979), while preceding years saw only the rare candidate who was often attempting to make up for failure elsewhere.[30] Indeed, although nominally identical teaching positions actually have very little in common before and after World War II, having been significantly transformed and, undoubtedly, globally devalued by the surge in the number of students and the corresponding increase in the teaching corps,[31] the reversal of the proportion of *normaliens* teaching in secondary schools (including preparatory classes) and higher education does point to a marked upward shift overall that it would be a mistake to describe as purely nominal. In any case, there are no grounds for concluding that there is a significant and lasting restriction on their chances for access to positions in higher education and research (even if students entering ENS between 1970 and 1980 undoubtedly suffer some delay in their careers as a result of the intensive recruitment of the 1960s) or an increase in the number of *normaliens* who are sent back to teach in high schools and junior highs (even if the relegation of some positions lends a particularly dramatic character to some career debuts, likely at any rate to dash people's spirits).

We are thus compelled to look at changes in image in order to explain the gap between what really occurs at the École Normale and what people say about it – above all at the École Normale. In effect, the uneasiness experienced by a portion of the students, which is continuously orchestrated and heightened by both teachers and administrators, on the pretext of encouraging the students to realistically adjust their aspirations to available job openings, undoubtedly results from the destruction of the harmony that existed between dispositions and positions from the Third Republic until the 1960s, a harmony that ensured an accommodation between the aspirations of the oblates of the "liberating school"[32] (principally sons of primary and secondary school teachers) and the careers that the École Normale Supérieure made available to them, glorified by all the republican imagery. It is this harmony that was destroyed when, with the heightening of competition, overall student social status rose (to the point where the modal *normalien* undoubtedly ceased to be the son of a provincial primary school teacher, but became rather the son of a Parisian higher education teacher). The *normaliens* of the 1980s, when they do not find in the ENA a means of reestablishing their ambitions, are led to experience as a downward turn what would in any event have been an undreamt-of ascension for most of those who came before them – with their disappointment also being attributable to the fact that they are starting out in their careers just after a period of extraordinary expansion in the opportunities for acceding to positions in higher education.

The ENS de Saint-Cloud and the ENS de Fontenay have probably experienced the greatest rise in social recruitment. In 1960–1, students from the lower and middle parts of the social scale make up 65 percent of the student body at Saint-Cloud-humanities, 62 percent at Saint-Cloud-sciences, 60 percent at Fontenay-humanities, and 62 percent at Fontenay-sciences. In 1969–70, they make up only 43 percent, 44 percent, 34.5 percent, and 34 percent, respectively. The fall is particularly noticeable at Saint-Cloud among sons of blue-collar workers and primary school teachers, at Fontenay-sciences among working-class students, and at Fontenay-humanities among children of tradesmen, clerical workers, and primary school teachers. In contrast, the children of executives and engineers see a sharp rise in their numbers at Saint-Cloud and Fontenay (recently, children of members of the professions, nearly absent in the past, have appeared at Saint-Cloud, where they make up 11 percent of the student body in 1985–6). And the same thing holds for the children of secondary and higher education teachers, especially in the sciences. On the whole, within the fractions heavily endowed with cultural capital, we are witnessing a shift from the middle classes toward the upper classes – without a corresponding rise in student academic capital. The proportion of Saint-Cloud students who received a "very good" or "excellent" on the baccalauréat is the same in 1969 as in 1960–1.[33]

The disharmony between dispositions and position, experienced as uneasiness, is undoubtedly worsened by the breakdown of the privileged relationship that once united the oblates of public education with the "republic of teachers." Under the Fifth Republic, the École Normale ceases to be the state's eldest daughter, and the same ethical and political complicity that bound it to the state under the Third Republic henceforth obtains between the technocratic state and the new "elite" – by and large Parisian, bourgeois, and ENA-trained. Increasingly distanced from power, its undertakings, and its philosophy, *normaliens* thus find themselves back in their pre-Third Republic position, one that often leads them to experience their relegation to a socially and economically devalued teaching or research job as a downclassing.

The symbolic devaluation that resulted from the numerical growth in the teaching profession, especially in the lower echelons, and the correlative loss of exceptional status, was accompanied by a fall in the economic status of academics, a consequence of a slowdown in the professorial career, which takes only a small fraction to the top of the professional hierarchy. As Georges Bonet and Jean-Michel de Forges have shown, most full professors see their careers blocked at a level of pay barely above that of assistant professors – rather than reaching the second level after three or four years and receiving regular standardized raises thereafter, as in the past. Given that professors do not receive any of the extra benefits members of the higher civil service regularly enjoy (bonuses, expense accounts, tax exemptions, etc.), their "buying power, at an equal level of seniority and total public income, is between 1.5 and 4 times lower than that of other civil servants of equal standardized rank" (that is, "1.5 times as compared to the *administrateur civil* who contents himself with his bonuses, and 4 times as compared to a Conseiller d'État who supplements his 'principal' job with five secondary public activities."[34]) As a consequence of this devaluation, a number of professors, especially in law facultés, where the devaluation is felt particularly acutely (no doubt because the specific rewards associated with investment in research are less likely in law facultés than in humanities and science facultés), are led to secure supplementary income by providing expert opinions, consulting, or arbitration, indeed, through the ordinary activities of the professions (this is obviously much more the case for professors of private law than professors of Roman or public law). Humanities and science professors expect the same advantages from supplemental teaching activities, especially abroad, and principally in the United States, or from journalism and publishing – which undoubtedly goes a long way toward accounting for the penetration of the American model into French intellectual life, as well as the growing influence journalist-intellectuals exert on the university field through their power in journalism and publishing. We see in passing how economic changes come to affect the specific structures of the intellectual field and how deterioration in the economic and social foundations of university autonomy, together with a transformation of ethical dispositions associated with a change in modal personnel, can contribute to transforming the intellectual lifestyle.

Within this logic, direct confrontation with the ENA, even though it may involve only a small minority of École Normale students, has a strategic importance. It is undoubtedly one of the sources of the "decline" rhetoric that feeds on itself in a process of circular reinforcement characteristic of *self-fulfilling prophesies*, and thus helps to produce the catastrophes that it predicts (and all the more infallibly because it is often used by school administrators who actually reinforce it in attempting to exorcise it). Unlike bluffing, which, provided it remains within the limits of what is socially plausible, may enable an institution to gradually bring what others grant it up to the level of what it grants itself (just as it does an individual agent), prophesies of doom favor *defeatist behavior* in which everyone tends to act according to the most pessimistic estimations of their opportunities, thereby effectively reinforcing the pessimism of everyone else's estimations and giving credit to belief in decline, which, in a game such as this one, in which everything (or almost everything) is a matter of belief, self-confidence, self-assurance, and self-certainty, is already a form of decline.

The indices relied on in the general perception of the state of a particular institution and its position relative to the others are subject to contradictory and generally unreliable or fallacious interpretations – this applies, for example, to the number of candidates participating in a given *concours*, which we know to vary more or less according to the number of places available, but which takes on a great importance in the minds of school administrators by way of the professorial myth of "level." Consequently, the confrontation between *normaliens* and the ENA *concours* is already an admission of recognition (no one would dream of evaluating the chances of ENA students on the École Normale *concours*, or of drawing conclusions from the fact that a good portion of future ENA students went to Sciences-po after failing in a *khâgne* or in the École Normale *concours*). It takes on the value of an absolute measure of relative values, although it is neither more nor less revealing than a confrontation between soccer or tennis teams (which, inasmuch as sports practices are closely linked to social and geographical origins, can be very instructive). In fact, on the occasion of these academic trials themselves, conscious and unconscious representations of the relative values of the different institutions play a significant role in the evaluation of student performances. The fall in the success rate of *normaliens* competing in the ENA *concours* should thus be read as an indicator of a progressive increase in the self-assurance of the members of the temporally dominant institution. Everything in fact occurs as if ENA administrators – once the time had passed when, still dominated by academic values, they could seek to academically ennoble their institution by taking in *normaliens* (obeying a logic that leads to the arrangement of prestigious marriages in other universes, a logic that may suit the interests of the institution without being the product of any explicit calculation) – bolstered as they were by proofs of recognition in the form of repeated attempts by *normaliens* at the ENA *concours* (not to mention their failures) and by equivalency demands made by École Normale officials, felt more and more free to assert their values and their criteria, even in educational matters. The social distances created by the misguided strategies of a number of ENS students and administrators themselves were officially sanctioned in the elimination (decreed in 1986) of the equivalences granted to ENA's rivals (Polytechnique since 1948 and Ulm since 1984)[35] and in the "objective" sanctions of the *concours*.[36]

The acceptance rate was initially extremely high, as if the ENA, still symbolically dominated (this was the period in which ENA students from the École Normale would always mention their initial affiliation with pride), were prepared to greet *normaliens* with open arms, and, if you will, to take them as they were. The top *concours* winner in 1973 was a classics major who went into the *concours* with no special preparation, while, as time goes on, the students accepted, some of whom are science majors, come to have at least some background in social and political science. The acceptance rate tended subsequently to decrease, while remaining at about 50 percent until after 1982. The fall in the number of candidates in recent years is not entirely due to the transformation of institutional dispositions;[37] it is rather a sign of the erosion of the idealized reputation of the ENA-educated Inspecteur des Finances that managed to seduce *normaliens* and lead them along for a while (or at least those among them whose origins placed them closest to the promised positions); *normaliens* are henceforth more likely to perceive their chances of success, and especially the reality of available careers, more realistically, as the resignations of *agrégés* accepted to the ENA can attest.

Recognizing here again the power of representations, we are less inclined to denounce as naive the statements of those who speak in moral terms in analyzing the evolution of the ENS. To quote a philosophy teacher at a Parisian *khâgne*, "the myth of the École Normale is no longer what it once was, principally because of the ENA. Today, morally bankrupt but brilliant and ambitious bastards choose the ENA. The École Normale has become somewhat old-fashioned. It's still tied to the Third Republic, while the

ENA belongs to the Fourth and Fifth." This opinion rightly links morals to what is often termed *morale*. Collective confidence in the professional destiny offered by the École Normale and in the ability of its chosen people to live up to it took root, among the *normaliens* of the Belle-Epoque (or most of them at least), in the form of a moral code (in the sense of an ethos associated with a particular social experience) that inclined them to accept the most unpleasant aspects of their promised future without question, while still harboring a naive, wonderstruck hope for the most glorifying, and most unlikely, aspects of it, such as future scientific or intellectual greatness. Collective morale and morals are in a highly interdependent relationship; the ethical dispositions that created the devoted or resigned servants of education and science were bound up with the collective support and censure that were the inevitable obverse of an elevated idea of the profession and those who practice it. What causes people to complain about "the decline" of the École Normale, especially within the institution itself, is undoubtedly the decay of this morale and these morals that was determined by the coincidence of two converging factors: on the one hand, the increase, especially since the 1970s, in the proportion of students from privileged families who, as victims of a hysteresis, undoubtedly expected something from the École Normale other than what it could give, in other words, what anyone would expect from a genuine establishment school;[38] on the other hand, the weakening of the autonomy of the university field with respect to the journalistic and political fields, which was accompanied by a decline in what might be called the intellectual values to the benefit of the values of secular success, whether in terms of positions of power in the bureaucratic or political field or so-called "media" glory and the material and symbolic profits afforded by frequent visits to press rooms and television studios.

The symbolic weakening of the École Normale and the decline of the intellectual values of "disinterestedness" and "freeness" go hand in hand. The rivalry between the École Normale and the ENA is one (no doubt truly fundamental) aspect of the struggle over both the definition of the dominant figure of a cultural producer and the establishment of a new way of living the intellectual life. The unification of the field of the grandes écoles around the ENA, and the correlative destruction of the bipolar structure that, in endowing "intellectuals" with their own separate powers of reproduction, forms the basis of two independent and incommensurable hierarchies, would undoubtedly sooner or later sound the death knell for the independent intellectual, of which Jean-Paul Sartre was probably the most perfect incarnation. And the strange enterprise of symbolic promotion through which Raymond Aron, beacon author for Sciences-po and the ENA, found himself raised to the rank of legitimate adversary of Jean-Paul Sartre, with the help of an imperceptible slipping of the intellectual field toward a conservative disenchantment, is itself merely a sign of the pretension of the technocrats who, exercising a temporal power in the name of an academic guarantee, consider it increasingly within their right to exercise intellectual authority in the name of their temporal power. In this they can count on the complicity of a number of intellectuals whose subordinate position in the strictly academic hierarchies predisposes them to act as accessories to the lowering of these hierarchies. Sartre and Aron, whose confrontation was orchestrated to accompany the political conversions and reconversions of the 1970s and 1980s (described as the "revenge" of Aron on Sartre, of de Tocqueville on Marx, of political realism on intellectual utopianism, etc.), were thus made into champions of the two camps set against each other in the intellectual field, in the name of two opposing representations of culture and politics, and into emblematic figures of the two cultures (in the ethnological sense of the term) that are developed to the fullest in the closed and homogeneous universes of the Rue d'Ulm [ENS] and the Rue Saint-Guillaume [ENA].

For want of a detailed proof, elements of which may be found in our analysis of transformations in the university field, published elsewhere,[39] we will simply quote, for its exemplary value, a brief passage from an article written by a former ENA director, previously head of Saint-Gobain, about a book in which an ideal-typical ENA product proposes a version of the vulgate produced and reproduced at Sciences-po and the ENA[40] (and a strikingly perverse version at that, since it contrives to use arguments traditionally associated with the left in support of the most traditional theses of the right, referring to the fate of "the excluded" [referring to unsuccessful candidates, Tr.], for example, in order to justify doing away with the status of civil servant, particularly for teachers): "We thought the intellectuals had gone home and that France had had enough of all those lessons in lucidity and virtue from the pen of masters of thought out of touch with corporations and the business world. Might Alain Minc's latest book, *La machine égalitaire*, be ushering in a springtime for philosophers? Certainly not in the sense of those oldtimers Sartre and Foucault, but much more in the sense of our eighteenth-century writers, who were on top of what was going on in politics and the salons, curious about everything, omnipresent, familiar with and critical of those in power, extremely skeptical, but nonetheless in all ways defenders of the right."[41] As we can see, this attack goes straight for the jugular undoubtedly because the *hubris* of the new mandarins is sure to find support, within the intellectual field itself, from all those who have made a specialty over the last ten years or so, in dailies and weeklies, of predicting the end of all the great intellectual adventures of the day, and who work toward producing and imposing a definition of the intellectual more in tune with their own capacities, and better adjusted to the expectations of the technocracy.[42] And the triumphant attitude that occasionally leads the new mandarins to lose all touch with reality to the point of claiming the scepter of the philosopher-king can undoubtedly be explained in part by the fact that their conception of the left, and of philosophers, takes shape in a universe where choosing positions on the left, traditionally granted to philosophers, as incarnations of the old-style intellectual, seems rather closely related to lesser "intellectual" success.[43]

Thus, just as the struggles among establishment schools are a dimension of the struggles within the field of business and higher public service, the confrontation between the École Normale and the ENA is a fundamental dimension of the struggles within the field of cultural production through which those who hold economic and political power (who are these days increasingly vested with the appearance of intellectual legitimacy), with the support of intermediary intellectuals and in the name of the need for economic realism and vague reference to the American model of the government-involved expert (usually identified with the economist), aim to impose a new, and more docile, if not more useful, figure of the cultural producer.

ROUNDABOUT ROUTES AND SANCTUARY SCHOOLS

The recent history of the various institutions of higher education, especially the unequal growth in their student bodies, the transformation in the social composition of their students, and all the corresponding effects of these changes, cannot be thoroughly understood unless one grasps the structure of the objective relations that link them. The gap between the preparatory classes, which have accomplished a *de facto* selection, and the universities, especially the science and humanities facultés, located at the low end of the hierarchy of institutions of higher education and hence destined to receive the largest, and least highly selected, portion of a constantly growing flux of students (especially after 1959), has widened both quantitatively and qualitatively, with the result that the dual nature of the channels has never been so pronounced. The cumulative effects of the growth in the educated population, the change in the social composition of this population, and the transformations in the academic (and social) characteristics of the teachers charged with molding it have given rise to transformations in institutional organization that tend to distance the universities from the model of the preparatory classes even further. The fact that nearly all of the students from the dominant categories, and an increasing number of those with origins in the middle of the social scale, have access to higher education has meant that the universities have included students who lack both cultural capital and the tacitly required dispositions. These students, with a low level of identification with the system and its values, and not very susceptible to the effect of academic sanctions, and hence somewhat unlikely to enter into the dialectic of consecration and recognition that attracts the individuals who are the most apt to reproduce the educational system as it is, nevertheless adopt the aspirations inscribed in the traditional definition of their position and feel the discordance between statutory ambitions and success (or the social value of the titles that consecrate success) with a disappointment that is all the greater the higher their social origins and the higher the aspirations they are thus inclined to harbor. The resulting latent anomie or full-fledged crisis are worsened by the fact that the increase in the number of students has lead to a weakening (at least qualitatively) in the institution's ability to manage them all, despite the accelerated growth it induced in the population of teachers, especially at subordinate levels (particularly between 1965 and 1975).

The heightened competition led to the extension of the organizational model of the preparatory classes down into lower and lower levels, that is, at least down to the *secondes* C [science] of all the top lycées. The infiltration of the logic of constant competition into earlier and earlier stages of schooling tends to impose a unitary principle of hierarchization and a more and more perfectly unified system of criteria throughout the whole of secondary education. The titles corresponding to the various tracks and majors no longer guarantee relatively incommensurable abilities, as was the case in more segmented states of the academic market, and instead become *ranks* in a unilinear hierarchy (whose highest point is *section* C leading to the scientific grandes écoles). The nearly perfect unification of the market in which academic value is defined means that at every level the different titles end up serving as little more than passes allowing a move to the next level. The most prestigious, least common, and most sought-after titles, whatever the nature of the skills they guarantee or the import of the studies they sanction, are those that allow their holders to remain in the channel that will take them highest and farthest – with the hierarchy of schools and tracks, both in the final year of the lycée and the preparatory classes, being measured according to the chances they afford for entry into the grandes écoles. Chances of getting into these schools can be compromised as early as the *seconde*, and they are at stake at every subsequent crossroad – choice of establishment and track in the final lycée year, choice of *taupe* establishment and track, etc. Consequently, one of the primary preconditions for success is thereafter a sense of *placement* [also *investment*, Tr.], which is essential for steering through this judiciously hierarchized universe, for recognizing the different hierarchies (the hierarchy among schools and tracks, for example), and for accurately evaluating real chances for admission into the various channels at a given level of past achievement.

The ambivalence of the relation that binds the dominants to an educational system capable of asserting its own principles of vision and division, and, within the limits of its jurisdiction, of submitting the "heirs" handed over to its judgment to its specific criteria of evaluation, could only rise as the steady increase in the objectivated cultural capital and technical knowledge required of corporate professionals and chief executives was playing its part in considerably lessening the social acceptance of the solution that consisted in making the dominant lifestyle (at times supported and accepted by the school, as was the case in nineteenth-century English public schools, with their cult of sports and virile values) into the principle of cooptation – and as the increased access to secondary education resulting from the generalization of the academic mode of academic reproduction was entailing an unprecedented increase in academic competition, which meant that adolescents from those regions of the field of power that were (relatively) the least well endowed with cultural capital were faced with an ever more serious threat. All of which was occurring, as it happened, at a time when the combined effect of factors analyzed elsewhere meant that academic titles were becoming ever more essential for the reproduction of social positions, even in the sectors of social space apparently the most closely tied to economic capital alone.[44]

One of the clearest signs of the increase in academic competition is the barriers, both spoken and unspoken, that were raised at the point of entry into many institutions, even second-ranking ones. So, for example, preparation for HEC, which, prior to these changes, almost never went beyond one year, tends to extend increasingly often to two years. Beginning with the class entering in 1988, the plan is to require two years of preparatory work. The ESCAE, which until 1967 laid down no requirements for their applicants, have introduced a selection procedure based on diplomas, and require one year of preparation. The University of Paris IX/Dauphine, which primarily trains students in economics and management, introduced new demands in 1979 (an average grade of at least 12 on the C and D baccalauréats [math/physical science; natural science], 13 on the others). Similarly, since 1987, Sciences-po candidates may take the entrance examination only twice, the first time in their baccalauréat year, the second no more than one year later. Candidates for direct acceptance into the second year are subject to more rigorous selection criteria as well. We have likewise noted an increase in the training necessary for entering the notary profession, which probably results from competition in the other legal professions (such as legal advisors and lawyers). Whereas training used to be entirely practical (after a six-year internship, the candidate went before an examination committee composed of notaries and a registrar), since the 1973 decree, applicants must first obtain either a master's degree in law, followed by a certificate of "aptitude for notarial duties" from a regional professional training center (for those who choose the professional route of the three-year internship), or an advanced degree (DESS) in notarial law (for those who choose the university route).

Students from the business bourgeoisie who see themselves shut out of the top academic institutions, as well as the institutions that were traditionally more hospitable to their dispositions, such as Centrale, HEC, and even Sciences-po, must, in order to get around the academic obstacle, choose the least autonomous and least academically controlled sectors of academic space, in other words, that is, the sanctuary schools whose numbers have grown considerably over the past 20 years, especially in the area of management (where the pressure of demand was simultaneously exerting its influence).[45]

The creation of a large number of schools of management within the universities (Institut d'Administration des Entreprises (IAE), master's degree, doctorate) and the restructuring and diversification of existing schools were accompanied by a marked increase in the number of diplomas awarded, which, according to the estimates of Bertrand Girod de l'Ain, went from about 1,300 in 1950 to 7,500 in 1976 for "advanced management training." The number of students completing short-term training in business or management (programs for senior technicians, Instituts Universitaires de Technologie, private schools) grew even more rapidly, increasing from about 2,000 to 17,000 in 1976, only to slow down in recent years, especially among the grandes écoles and second-tier schools, the oldest and most prestigious of which are no longer increasing the size of their graduating classes. Finally, the number of applicants to the various kinds of training programs – preparatory classes, *écoles*, universities specializing in management (such as Paris/Dauphine), master's degrees in management, etc. – has increased considerably since the 1950s, while the network of preparatory classes has expanded with the creation of numerous private programs.[46]

Thus a school of management such as the Institut Européen d'Administration des Affaires (INSEAD, founded in 1958), which is only open to graduate students who have (for the most part) already held jobs, provides a second chance, as it were, to students who have not received from the academic world the recognition they had been anticipating (a large proportion of whom are from the business bourgeoisie). Only ten of the 54 students interviewed by Jane Marceau say that the school they attended before coming to the INSEAD was the one they had hoped for. Those who went to the Institut Industriel du Nord de la France would have preferred Centrale; those who came from the École des Mines de Nancy would have liked to have been accepted at the École de Mines de Paris; the graduates of the École Supérieure de Commerce de Paris would have chosen HEC, and so on.[47] There is no doubt that a school such as this one, endowed with all the external trappings of modernity – starting with the international character of its faculty and its student body – is perfectly designed to provide an honorable substitute for the more prestigious diplomas. And we can be sure that, in time, and with the social capital brought in by the students themselves, it will see its origins forgotten.

In fact, the success of these management schools appears to be the result of the convergence of two independent processes, each stemming from a specific need: on the one hand, the development of a new educative demand, related to the need for bourgeois children shut out of the most selective and prestigious courses of study to find roundabout routes that would lead them to ever more necessary academic titles, necessary even in private firms, provides the new schools with an abundant clientele; on the other hand, the increase, particularly between 1968 and 1975, in the supply of jobs for technicians, engineers, and commercial managers, corresponding to transformations in the economic field, such as the growth in international trade,[48] guarantees the output of these schools continuously increasing job prospects. Similar convergences between independent causal series, which, when observed retrospectively, seem like a kind of miraculous accident, generally constitute one of the primary preconditions for the success of innovations introduced into a relatively autonomous field – undoubtedly because, in guaranteeing an abundance of resources from without, the conjuncture enables students to find the means for surviving selection in the (necessarily unequal) competition that is imposed upon them by their rivals already well-established in the field.

Census data does not permit very precise analysis of the evolution from 1954 to 1982 of the various categories of corporate professionals [*cadres*] according to function (production, administration, management, directorate, etc.). Fluctuations in titles, the use of new terms, and the introduction of new questions (in 1982) make comparison very difficult. So, for example, due to the addition of a single question on the function of *cadres* and supervisors on the individual census form in 1982, the number of "*cadres supérieurs,* no further detail" and "administrative *cadres supérieures*" is halved between 1975 and 1982, while the number of "commercial *cadres supérieurs*" soars.[49]

Several indices suggest that the greatest increase in the population of corporate professionals holding commercial, technico-commercial, and management positions occurs between 1968 and 1975, that is, a short time into the period during which many schools of business and management are either created or restructured. Thus the figures show 20,000 computer specialists and 14,000 organization and management specialists in 1975, but only 8,000 total in 1968 (which corresponds to a particularly rapid annual growth rate of 24 percent). The number of technico-commercial engineers also grows markedly between 1968 and 1975 (9 percent).[50] A number of intermediary technico-commercial occupations (such as buyers, which go from 9,000 to 16,000 between 1968 and 1975) develop very rapidly during this same period. With the job restructuring that follows the consolidation of businesses, small shopkeepers are in large measure replaced on the one hand by unskilled employees (cashiers, salespeople), and on the other hand by *cadres*.[51] According to the APEC [Association pour l'Emploi des Cadres] "modern distribution is a great creator of white-collar positions." Between 1975 and 1982, "the appearance and development of hypermarkets, minimarkets, and mail-order companies increased the workforce by 3.5 percent."[52] Self-taught employees are gradually replaced by graduates of business schools, particularly ESCAE, in jobs as salespeople and sales representatives. In the service sector, new positions appear (franchisees, for example).[53]

The movement that led a large percentage of young people from the bourgeoisie to take up professions in business should without a doubt be imputed more to the logic of individual strategies, arising in the relationship between inherited dispositions and the possibilities opened up by past achievement, than to the exhortations, cautions, and warnings of the "enlightened milieus." Indeed, up until 1975, the various government committees and commissions (particularly the planning council on the skill levels of the workforce) make no mention of a possible lack of managers, while they do stress the deficit in engineers.[54] One of the principal advantages enjoyed by bourgeois adolescents could well be their ability to move rapidly into the newly opened courses of study, which are often initially both easier and more profitable. Their network of social, familial, and academic connections gives them access to the information they need to shore up their practical intuition of the *value* of the different institutions, channels, and diplomas, information that is absolutely essential for discovering the channels that are at once new and promising, the placements that are risky and productive, *in time.*

This sense of placement, an intuition about the structure and the dynamics of a field that enables agents to anticipate its future, is particularly essential when, with the diversification of the space of possibilities, a number of objective factors tend to favor errors in perception, starting with the increased number of competing institutions (IUT, petites écoles, new master's degrees formerly AES [Administration Economique et Sociale]), through the imperceptible transformation of the best-established hierarchies and the *scrambling* of these hierarchies instigated by the administrators of the new institutions and perpetuated by their current and former students, predisposed to glorify the image of the institution they come from. And this intuition is probably never more useful than in difficult situations, when it enables one to overcome a series of failures at the cost of a more or less risky reconversion.

Thus most of the students interviewed at the European Business School had first heard of their school from friends or family acquaintances. One of them, the son of a dental surgeon, following his graduation from a series of private schools and a prematurely interrupted stint in medical school (he "couldn't take the atmosphere" of the university), and after failing several times to get into lycée preparatory classes, managed to get into a private preparatory class at Sainte-Barbe, where he negotiated his acceptance directly with the head, calling him twice on the telephone. Having been rejected by several business schools (he "was 'had' by the ESSEC *concours*" and was rejected by every ESCAE), he passed the *concours* of the European Business School, which he knew of because he had friends who went there, and because one of his teachers at Sainte-Barbe had spoken of it saying that it was "not bad at all".[55] Another, the son of a commercial manager and an interpreter, chose the European Business School over the Institut Européen des Affaires, which "seemed stimulating enough, but unfortunately not very rigorous," and the École des Cadres, which "takes in Daddy's boys" and "doesn't seem that great."

The categories of perception that agents apply to the social world are the product of a prior state of this world. When structures are modified, even slightly, the structural hysteresis of the categories of perception and appreciation gives rise to diverse forms of allodoxia. Classificatory schemata originating in the common perception of a former state of the educational system, such as the distinction between humanities and science students or between the grandes écoles and the universities, lead to representations of present reality that do not account for new realities (for example, all the channels created at the intersection of the sets delineated by the categories of the past). Indications are that this structural delay is all the greater when the agents are further removed (either through their position in the academic universe or through their family's position in social space) from the appropriate information that becomes particularly crucial in periods of rapid change. The utter confusion caused by the resulting *disorientation* often leads the least well-off to simply give up. Many of those who drop out speak of a kind of state of *indifference* to which they found themselves reduced, for want of principles of discrimination, in a bewildering universe where nothing is clear, nothing is certain. Lacking the minimum hold on the future that the very intention to take hold of it assumes, they let themselves fall into various forms of *strategies of despair*. As in a game of chance, they may attempt to minimize their risks by trying somewhat haphazardly to cover all the bases – for example, by applying to several schools at the same time, and in widely different disciplines. Hence multiple applications become ever more frequent (the same student may, for example, apply to scientific, commercial, and veterinary preparatory classes). The unequal distribution of pertinent information is undoubtedly one of the factors at this crucial point in an academic career (the move into higher education having replaced entry into the *sixième* as the critical moment of choice) that doom students with the multiple handicaps related to geographical and social distance to compulsory choices that are often a form of deferred elimination. The confusion they experience in this bewildering universe of multiplied channels compels them to submit to the advice of professional or volunteer guidance counselors who for the most part only reinforce their (socially constituted) inclination to choose the paths they see as the safest, in other words, that is, the shortest, most scholastic paths.

The competition between the new schools of management and the other institutions of higher education, and the competition among the management schools themselves, within their specific subfield, is played out in the favorable conditions created by the conjunction of two independent processes, an increased supply of management positions and an increase in the social demand for substitute training and diplomas. Like the overall field of the grandes écoles, the subfield of schools of management is the product of a process of growth that, while it is not guided by any internal or external finality, creates a reality vested with a form of coherence and necessity. At the conclusion of a long series of independent additions, the institutions of unequal seniority that make up this subfield are affected, in their very being, by the objective relations that have dominated their creation and continue to govern their functioning. The oldest bear the signs of the transformations they have undergone over time, in response to the various changes occurring in their environment, starting with the challenges raised by the new competing institutions. The most recently founded are also marked, from their very inception, by reference to the older institutions they must confront in order to exist, and it is not unusual for the new schools, prompted by their fundamentally heteronomous intention to *rival*, to contradictorily combine a desire for assimilation that can go as far as plagiarism with a desire for distinction that is all the more ostentatious as the real differences are but slight.

The École Spéciale de Commerce de Paris, which under Napoleon III became the École Supérieure de Commerce de Paris, was created on the initiative of the Paris

Chamber of Commerce in 1820, more than a century after the founding of the first engineering school. It was not until 1870 that two new institutions were created, the École Supérieure de Commerce de Rouen and the École Supérieure de Commerce du Havre, followed by other provincial schools. The École des Hautes Études Commerciales de Paris (HEC) was created in 1881, again at the behest of the Paris Chamber of Commerce, on the model of the École Centrale, a private grande école with close ties to the business world and a well-established reputation. There was talk for a while, as if to symbolize the desire for assimilation that inspired the very invention of this new institution (the first director is a Centrale graduate), of calling it the "École Centrale de Commerce."[56] The École Supérieure des Sciences Economiques et Commerciales (ESSEC) de Paris was founded in 1913. In 1940, there were 21 business schools.

The creation of schools of business, management, and public administration picked up again from the mid-1950s especially, and increased throughout the 1960s. According to the national yearbook of business schools and management training programs, 23 schools were created between 1950 and 1959, 28 between 1960 and 1969, and 31 between 1970 and 1979; the movement continued after 1980 (with 14 new schools founded between 1980 and 1983).[57] During the 1950s, it consisted primarily of institutes of business administration, set up within the universities (12 between 1954 and 1958). The 1960s witnessed the provincial development of the network of advanced schools of business and business administration (ESCAE), and especially private petites écoles, entered after the baccalauréat. A few schools that take only graduates also appear: the INSEAD in 1956, and the ISA in 1969. Since 1968, the Fondation Nationale pour l'Enseignement de la Gestion des Entreprises [National Foundation for Business Management Education], created by the Conseil National du Patronat Français [national employers' union, Tr.], the Association of Chambers of Commerce, and the Ministry of Industry, has coordinated management education, which is spread over a large number of institutions. In the 1970s and 1980s the network of ESCAEs continued to expand, with new schools opening in Paris and the provinces.

Over the past 30 years, the top grandes écoles, which are also the oldest, have instituted significant changes, seeking out new modern spacious campuses (HEC at Jouy-en-Josas, the ESSEC at Cergy-Pontoise, the ESC at Ecully in Lyons) and diversifying their activities in response to competition from the other schools of business and management, and especially in response to the competition coming from the engineering schools that have introduced management programs into their curriculum. The history of the ESSEC is particularly significant in this regard. Pitted against HEC and the chambers of commerce from its very inception, it immediately had to accept that it would have to play the card of innovation and modernity at the level of both structure and teaching methods. More generally, given that each of the different schools has to contend with multiple competitors with multiple and only slightly differentiated goals, they are compelled to compete in every domain, including teaching methods and means (as would be shown, for example, in the history of the introduction of the case history as a teaching method), and to fulfill many poorly defined functions (training technicians and mid-level and upper-level managers, offering managerial continuing education programs, engaging in research, etc.).[58]

The subfield of the schools of management, globally located in the academically second- and third-ranked regions of the field of institutions of higher education, is characterized by a heavy dependence on demand (usually converted into an elective submission to the demands of the economy) that increases as we descend in the hierarchy of establishments. The petites écoles tend to operate like small businesses, which take pride in rejecting the logic of the educational system in order to introduce, within the educational institution itself, the demands and values of the future users of their products.

All of these schools are and wish to be as little inclined toward the academic as possible – without making it possible to distinguish how much of this is a function of choice, how much necessity, and how much necessity made choice. Their directors are often endowed with relatively poor academic capital and see themselves as "training designers"[59] rather than teachers. We note that one became a psychotherapist in a provincial city; another is a graduate of a similar type of management school (which he attended after failing at both the science faculté and the medical faculté), who, in order to "settle a score with the university," then prepared a DEA [between master's and doctorate, Tr.]. At the Institute de Préparation à l'Administration et à la Gestion (IPAG), "you don't find any pure teachers who are involved in research and are completely cut off from the working world." The "teacher coordinators" themselves are at the school "one, two, two and a half days tops; the rest of the time they're out in the business world." The students, most of whom are sons of chief executives, managers and engineers,[60] spend as much time working in a firm as studying at school.

Because they receive no government support (or no longer do so), and because the state does not recognize their diploma, schools such as the European Business School, the Institut Supérieur de Gestion, and the IPAG depend on training fees paid by businesses and tuition paid by their students' families (16,700 francs at the European Business School in 1983, 16,150 francs at the IPAG, and 21,000 francs at the Institut Supérieur de Gestion). They are thus forced to operate like corporations and undertake promotional activities as well as "campaigns" for collecting the training fees. A former IPAG director describes his role as more that of a corporate head than that of the head of a school: "I didn't feel like a teacher (. . .), at least in the devalued sense in which people see teachers, that is, as somewhat irresponsible people (. . .) whose salaries drop, whereas I, perhaps more than others, was familiar with the problem of bills coming due at the end of the month, in other words, with the fact that I had 25 collaborators with me, plus I don't know how many students behind them, and that I knew that I had to protect the resources of an institution that lacked outside support. I felt as though I was in charge of a small or mid-sized business whose field of operation happened to be education."

The entire public relations policy of the academic chief executive aims both to impress or seduce parents, on whom he also depends when it comes to the placement of students (the European Business School used to organize parental dinners in select locations: the Conciergerie, the Bois de Vincennes, etc.), and, most importantly, to make allies or, better yet, symbolic stockholders out of them. Its success is primarily a function of the social and academic capital of its founding members, and their ability to mobilize the social capital of the parents of its students (rather than that of its graduates, as is the case for more prestigious institutions), who are thus invited to collectively accomplish the symbolic promotion of the school, and hence, of their own progeny. So, for example, the Institut d'Économie et de Coopération Européenne (IECE), abandoned by the banking world, was able to survive its serious financial crisis thanks to the establishment of a parents association, which included well-known figures from the business world (developers, bankers, etc.) and enabled the school to make a comeback as the European Business School.

The administrations of these highly dependent institutions are obliged to make a virtue of necessity and to deliberately recognize the demands and values of their clients – students, parents, and businesses. This they do first and foremost in the way they recruit their students, either completely abandoning the selective procedures through which the most prestigious educational institutions secured their special status, or purely and simply reversing the ordinary criteria: "We recruit our candidates somewhat on the model of corporate recruitment. We don't use scholarly *concours* that ask complicated questions; quite the contrary, we're much more interested in their personality, their ability to reason, their future ability to succeed in a school such as ours. We work with a graphologist. So we ask them for an application letter, which is then studied by a recruitment firm (. . .) that handles the recruitment for many businesses" (director of public relations for one of the schools, who was charged, among other things, with "organizing promotions" to publicize the school).

Schools of management compete in coming up with imaginative new ways of evaluating their candidates, whether by openly taking into account their ways of behaving, of asserting themselves, indeed of posing, or imposing themselves (which the more legitimate institutions pretend to ignore or to subordinate to specific knowledge), or even (in an attempt to convert their students' weaknesses into virtues and their own shortcomings into advantages) by striving to overturn the table of academic values and to lay the groundwork for a new educational legitimacy. The schools on the lowest rungs of the academic ladder, such as the European Business School, or even lower still, the IPAG or the École des Cadres, most of whose students have previously failed either the entrance *concours* for the more sought-after schools (HEC, ESSEC, ESCAE) or in other career paths (medicine, law, economics, sciences, etc.), all resort to forms of tests and exercises intended to valorize a sense of connections, the art of conversation, and style in self-presentation. So, for example, in addition to an individual oral examination of a general nature – a conventional test on the model of the oral of the most prestigious grandes écoles, such as the ENA – the European Business School includes in the oral portion of its *concours* a "videotaped press review," the object of which is "to assess the candidate's ease in expressing himself in front of a camera and to evaluate his skill in doing a press synthesis based on documents provided him on the spot."[61] The École Supérieure de

Commerce et d'Administration des Entreprises de Grenoble developed an "unusual and difficult" examination during which the candidate is interviewed by a member of the admissions committee, a corporate executive. The interview instructions describe a procedure in which the interviewer must "answer the candidate in the most simple, succinct, and accurate way possible in order to fully bring out his thought processes, the relevance of his questions, and his adaptability."[62] In the open-ended conversation that follows, the interviewer should continue to ask questions on "general aspects of the candidate's personal development, his main interests, his past experiences, and his future plans." Finally, in a true reversal of the techniques used in other institutions, which reveals the fictive nature of this examination, the interviewer is also asked to "avoid making the candidate feel uncomfortable and to refrain from asking trick questions, unanswerable questions, or questions that either contain partial answers or are too personal." In another case, the desire to avoid all academic reference is asserted openly: the stated objectives of the entrance *concours* for the IPAG are to "assess abilities" and "judge personality," not to "evaluate previous learning."[63]

In fact, recourse either to revamped variants of old methods of evaluation or to ostentatiously new methods is only one dimension (the most obvious) of an overall strategy designed to enable both the candidates and the institution that accepts them to conceal (from themselves) the academic failure that is at the basis of their candidacy, or even to convert this failure into capital, thereby ensuring a *rehabilitation* that will pave the way for their *reinstatement*. "If you get in, your slate will be wiped clean. Your police record will be locked away, and you'll be able to have a normal school career if you want, and if you put your mind to it. We're interested in you as a person. Your past grades. . . really, who cares?" These were the words with which the director of one of these schools greeted a young man who had come in for information. The image of the police record was no exaggeration. And it would be no exaggeration to use the term "academic record," for one of the most crucial powers of an educational institution is undeniably its ability to consecrate or, on the other hand, to relegate, degrade, or symbolically abase. Economic power holders, who sometimes fall victim to this magical effect, can counter it with the pedagogic action of institutions whose primary function is undoubtedly to erase not only one's academic past but also the social and psychological stigma inflicted by the educational system. In order to exorcise the influence exerted by academic verdicts, these paradoxical educational institutions must encourage and foster anti-academic dispositions in students who are already more than half converted, all the while guaranteeing them the more or less deceptive forms of prestige offered by fallacious academic titles.

It is thus understandable that, in the extreme cases, schools that are mandated to destroy a particular academic effect seem to deny that they are themselves schools, not only in their specific organization, but also in their pedagogic activity. The École des Hautes Études Commerciales du Nord provides an ideal-typical illustration of this self-destructive educational project when it asks its incoming students in 1985 to spend three days creating a fictitious wine distribution company, buying and selling wine, employing personnel, obtaining bank loans. "The doors of the teachers' offices sport new name plates. Here on the right we have the bank. Next door is the Ministry of the Interior, farther along we have the data-processing department and the advertising office."[64] However, the logic that leads the schools that are the least endowed with strictly academic capital to glorify "*savoir-être*" over *savoir-faire* and knowledge [*savoirs*], and personal development over the rigor of academic disciplines, to play the hand of openness to life and to business, of a break with "scholasticism" and academic canons and yokes (such as formal, that is, exclusive, examinations, codified exercises, etc.) – as has always been the case with HEC, whose position with respect to the humanities and science grandes écoles is homologous to the position the petites écoles occupy with respect to it – is counterbalanced by their desire for integration into the university field, which requires a move toward the accumulation of academic capital, even if this be at the cost of an ostentatious exhibition of external signs of educational avant-gardism: for example, displaying treasures of modernist invention, in both equipment (language laboratories, computer resources, audiovisual aids) and teaching techniques, which are seen as more interactive, more modern, and more international (internships in Japan and the United States being one of the symbols of an institution's innovative capacity).

As concerned as they may be to conform to the demands of the economic world and to imitate corporate logic, the less prestigious petites écoles cannot completely escape academic logic. They are only able to activate (however slightly) the specific legitimation granted by the educational institution (primarily through diplomas) provided they enjoy a minimum of autonomy with respect to the demands of the business world, as well as the demands of the parents who recognize them in advance. It follows that all the schools founded in the 1960s and 1970s, each according to its own modality and rhythm, go through the same stages of a single process: lengthening their program, instituting an entrance *concours*, campaigning for government support, requesting official recognition of their diploma, etc.

If one of these schools, established in 1967, waited 12 years to apply for government recognition, according to its general secretary, this is because "P.G. (the director) was never interested in recognition. Why? Because our curricula have really and truly evolved according to the job market, according to what's really happening (. . .). So we really adapted to the needs of the business world. And we continue to adapt. I think that the day we're recognized, on the other hand, our curriculum will be frozen, it will be dictated to us." In fact, because it is impossible to ignore the symbolic consecration and economic insurance that a recognized diploma represents, they did request recognition in 1979, for "financial reasons" and because "some companies (. . .), often the nationalized ones, have their categories of recognized schools, with varying levels and echelons."

As the new schools become increasingly distanced from the lower region of the field, and as they progressively free themselves from complete dependence on their clientele, they must reconcile two contradictory objectives: asserting their originality (that is, in other words, their difference with respect to the most academically consecrated institutions) by overturning the table of values in an attempt to transform deprivation into rejection and destiny into choice, or, more radically, by means of heretical breaks with academic norms, always instituted in the name of the "realities" of economic life (or, in other sectors of the academic field, in the name of "life," plain and simple), and likely to put them in danger of being forever excluded from academic legitimacy; and, in an opposite move, staking their claim to legitimacy by adopting at least the outward signs of academic dignity (established teachers, recognized academic titles, research laboratories, etc.), but thereby accepting their overt relegation to inferior positions in the legitimate academic universe. As heretical institutions gain recognition, the oscillations that carry them alternately either toward academic institutions or toward the economic world tend to become increasingly uneven. The ambivalence that led the École des Hautes Études Commerciales to oppose its curriculum to that of the university, all the while upholding university requirements so as to ensure its prestige and attract a strong group of students, is resolved, in spite of it all, with the publication in the 1970s of the ministerial decrees stipulating the conditions for equivalency between the HEC diploma and university diplomas.

The principle of the oscillation between the academic pole and the economic pole, between autonomy and heteronomy, between recognition and the rejection of the outside world and its academic values lies in the relationship between the academic field and the economic field and, more generally, the social world as a whole. Dominated institutions within the academic field are only able to assert their existence with respect to established institutions by countering them with the demands of "life," which academic logic brackets;[65] but they are only able to obtain academic recognition provided they bow to the specific demands of the field in selecting their students and organizing their operations, especially in the area of pedagogy, a strategy which they are all the more likely to adopt the more highly endowed they are with the specific resources that are the precondition for its success (socially recognized teachers and students, etc.).

These analyses suggest that the observed increase in academic competition, by reinforcing the contradiction between purely academic demands and the dominants' social demand for reproduction, gave rise to an entire set of reactional transformations in the field of institutions of higher education, and particularly in the subfield of the grandes écoles. These transformations are paradoxically expressed in a sort of *structural decline* in the most autonomous institutions and, at the same time, in everyone they attract through their consecration. The minor educational enterprises that sprang up in the sector of the academic market closest to the economic world provide a final recourse for the offspring of the great business dynasties and higher public service who were unable to find a place in the more prestigious refuges traditionally provided by the traditional institutions most open to bourgeois dispositions, such as Sciences-po, the ENA, and HEC. The success of most of these schools would probably not have been so complete if it had not coincided with the profound changes that were taking place in the economic field (such as the increase in financial and commercial jobs as opposed to technical jobs, which can be detected in the very significant increase, between 1952 and 1972, in the proportion of HEC and Sciences-po graduates among the top business leaders, and in the fall in the proportion of *polytechniciens* in these ranks). Given that the field of establishments of higher education is in an interdependent relationship with the field of power, any increase in the number or value of a certain category of dominant positions is accompanied by an increase in the value of the educational institutions that provide access to these positions, and conversely, any increase in the social and academic value granted to the products of a particular educational institution is accompanied by an increase in the value granted to the corresponding "corps" and to its ability to stake its claims within the field of power, with the same relationship obtaining in cases of decline, but in reverse.

Thus, it is understandable that the structure and the functioning of the field of institutions of higher education should give the analyst (and perhaps readers of the analysis as well) the sense of nearly miraculous inevitability that one gets from the "internal finality" of certain biological systems or certain works of art. But this kind of amazement, which undoubtedly helps to foster an accurate understanding, does not mean that the principle of the logic of social mechanisms and their effects, whether beneficial or harmful, should be sought in mysterious, subjectless functions, as a functionalism for better or worse would have it, and even less that this logic, which transcends individual intentions, should be imputed to individual or (with conspiracy theories) collective will. Just like the extraordinary logical necessity that the ethnologist discovers in the symbolic organization of the interior of a house or the structure of a kinship network, the logical necessity the sociologist perceives in the structure and operation of a field as subtly constructed as that of the grandes écoles, and particularly in the effects, liable to give the impression of a preestablished harmony, that are produced by means of the homology between the space of the institutions charged with reproduction and the space of the positions to be reproduced, is the product of a historical process of progressive and collective creation that follows neither a plan nor an obscure immanent Reason, without for all that being a product of pure chance. Similar to old houses whose charm is a result of the countless changes made to them over time by their successive occupants, who, in their alterations, are compelled to conform to the constraints bequeathed by the choices of the former occupants, social mechanisms of the type analyzed here are the product of countless individual choices, but choices that are always limited by constraints. The constraint of the embodied structures that ceaselessly orient a person's perception and appreciation of a situation, and the constraint of the objectivated structures to which any positively approved innovation has necessarily had to bow (even if only in choosing to fill a void, a gap) in order to establish itself, and to which it has constantly had to defer since its inception, because the field into which it has been introduced operates a veritable social selection according either to its own logic or to the interests of those who dominate it: it is structure, acting as a barrier to entry, that determines which innovations will succeed, that is, which innovations will be inscribed into objectivity in the guise of institutions capable of producing a lasting effect within the structure. The nearly miraculous logic of the classification performed by the educational institution can be understood if it is realized, on the one hand, that the selection operated by the field at each moment in its history, according to its own logic, retains the properties that are "functional" from the point of view of its own perpetuation as well as the perpetuation of those who dominate it; and, on the other hand, that the innovations that have the greatest chances of being positively approved and ratified are those that are based on the practical mastery of the structure and dynamics of the field, which enables individual actions to anticipate its immanent necessities. As a practical mastery of or knack for the game, which in the main depends on immediate agreement between embodied structures (categories of perception and appreciation) and objective structures, habitus is never as practically in control of its field of action as when it is fully inhabited by the field of forces because its structures are the product of it.

Thus the distribution of establishments solely according to the social composition of their student body (in other words, according to the amount and the structure of the capital held by their students' families), discounting academic achievement, reveals a striking pattern. The fact that this distribution is very similar to the distribution in social space of the professional positions that are either the point of origin or the destination of the students in the various schools demonstrates that the educational system, while it may appear to effect a thorough, random mixing likely to prevent any correspondence between the starting positions and arrival positions of its students, in fact tends to perpetuate the space of the differences that separate them before they enter the system (at least statistically). This system undoubtedly does bring about a minor adjustment by providing a passageway to the top grandes écoles for a small fraction of those who do not start out in the positions to which these schools give access, and by eliminating a fraction of those who are statutorily destined for these institutions. But these adjustments, dictated by strictly academic criteria, are themselves adjusted, in fact canceled out, on the one hand through the logic of the "vocation" that leads the "wonder children" (particularly sensitive to the attraction of the positions offered by the school to which they owe their election) to accept being turned away from the positions of power made available by their academic promotion, and on the other hand through the countless compensatory strategies that students from the families richest in economic capital continually produce, both within the educational system itself (with its sanctuary schools) and beyond, so as to reestablish the positions threatened by the effects of the autonomy, entirely relative, of academic verdicts. It is thus understandable that the increase in academic competition should paradoxically have given an extraordinary boost to the institutions that provide the means for escaping the effects of academic verdicts.

The increase in the number of graduates of higher education, which tends to lead to the exclusion of both nongraduates and the self-taught, especially at the management level, and to a decline in older forms of promotion, the universalization of the recognition granted to the academic title, the unification of the job market, at least in this domain, and the heightening of the competition among title holders are so many concomitant processes that provided their own counterweight: the diversification of the academic market and, owing to the objective collusion of the demands of the top bourgeoisie relatively lacking in cultural capital and the demands of the purveyors of rather unusual academic services, the appearance of a nebula of academic institutions more directly geared to the demands of the corporate world and able to compete with the traditional educational institutions in their monopoly. These "nonscholastic" schools, institutions with a low level of autonomy, often created, financed, or controlled by corporations, became weapons in the struggle between the middle categories of technicians, whose entire value in the job market is tied to the academic title, and the economic leaders to whom these schools provide not only suitable sanctuaries, if necessary, for their academically impoverished heirs, but also a place for the production of producers made to their specifications, or, if you will, made to order, that is, endowed with a minimum of technical training, without being for all that protected against "dequalification" or "disqualification," in the manner of the patented products of the educational system, by the "rigidity" of a juridically guaranteed title.

Appendix 1

A Discourse of Celebration

The more famous a school is, the more it is celebrated, and the more books and articles it attracts. In the latter part of the nineteenth century, the École Normale Supérieure and the École Polytechnique, each already a century old, inspired a large number of works, usually penned by high-ranking school staff (directors or librarians), who rely on the hagiographic mode in their historiographies (for the École Normale, Paul Dupuy, Fustel de Coulanges, Désiré Nisard, among others; for the École Polytechnique, G. Claris, A. de Lapparent, G. Pinet, etc.).[1]

Works on these two schools abound in the first half of the twentieth century. In the case of the École Normale, they are usually novels (Giraudoux, Jules Romains, etc.) or reminiscences of one or another famous graduate (Charles Andler, Lucien Herr, Péguy, Jules Tannery . . .), most of them referring to the period from 1880 to 1900. There are fewer well-known novels set at the École Polytechnique, but a great many hagiographic works treat the school and its founders, such as Monge and other savants, and we find many books and articles on the teaching of this or that discipline, as well as studies of Polytechnique slang.[2]

After 1945, we still find a few hagiographic works on Ulm and Polytechnique,[3] but the texts already bear traces of irony. There are few if any novels, and an increasing number of scientific studies, most of them produced by American researchers. Since the 1960s, and especially since the 1970s, it is clearly the ENA that has attracted the most attention and interest; the number of books (essays or works of scientific aspiration), articles, and studies on the ENA increases considerably. In contrast, few if any works are published on the lesser-known schools, such as HEC, Mines, or *a fortiori*, Fontenay or Saint-Cloud. The École Centrale falls somewhere in between, with a fair number of works in the nineteenth century, but relatively few in the twentieth.

The scientific works generally tend to focus on the well-known schools and are only rarely free of apologetic complaisance. Ties between authors and the schools they are writing about have been proven in the great majority of cases, the exceptions almost always being in the case of foreign researchers. We shall use the ENA as a particularly telling example. J. Mandrin, author of the first work on the ENA, which caused quite a stir and greatly contributed to the school's renown, was the pseudonym of two ENA graduates, Jean-Pierre Chevènement, class of 1965, and Didier Motchane, class of 1956. Nearly all of the works on the ENA in the late 1970s and early 1980s are written by alumni, most of whom are also teachers or high-ranking staff at either the ENA or Sciences-po. Jean-Luc Bodiguel is a *directeur de séminaire* at the Institut d'Études Politiques; José Freches, class of 1978, published his book in the series entitled L'Énathèque [play on *bibliothèque*, library, Tr.]; its preface was written by Pierre Desprairies, class of 1984: Jean-François Kesler, class of 1959, is currently its assistant director, responsible for research and continuing education; he was a member of the ENA reform committee in 1981–2. Marie-Christine Kessler, researcher at the CNRS [National Center for Scientific Research], is the wife of ENA graduate Philippe Kessler; the preface of her book is by Michel Debré, ENA's founder; Guy Thuillier, class of 1961, currently teaches at the IEP. Odon Vallet, class of 1973, is a *maître de conférences* at the IEP. Michel Schifres, editor-in-chief of the *Journal du Dimanche*, is the exception: his book, written in the style of an admiring reporter, is proof of the fame of an institution that, like Polytechnique and its two-cornered hats in former times, can make the front page of popular newspapers and family weeklies.[4]

Appendix 2

On Method

The principle on which the population under study was to be constructed slowly took shape as our research progressed. A research project, especially one of this magnitude with so many social obstacles to overcome, inevitably includes some contingency and chance. Yet, while it is true, as Georges Canguilhem has said, that empirical scientists are akin to pirates, taking advantage of opportunities as they arise, they are nonetheless distinct in that, in setting their course, they obey principles that are less than a method (a route that one retraces after the fact) and more than a simple theoretical intuition. In the present case, this regulating principle of scientific practice was condensed into the notion of a field, understood as a space, that is, an ensemble of positions in a relationship of mutual exclusion. Constructing the space of establishments thus meant constructing the system of the criteria that could account for the set of meaningful and significant differences that objectively separate these establishments or, if you will, enable the set of relevant differences among these institutions to arise. Having established this principle, it was a matter of gathering together all the establishments that were essential for revealing as completely and precisely as possible the system of relevant oppositions (which are not necessarily those that first come to mind, such as the opposition between humanities and science schools, for example, so powerful in people's representations): first, the opposition based on gender, through the introduction of Sèvres and Fontenay; second, the multiform opposition between the schools leading to research or the university and the schools that provide access to positions of economic and bureaucratic power, themselves differentiated according to various secondary principles; and lastly and most importantly, the opposition between the "grandes" and the "petites" écoles.

It is not easy to describe after the fact a project that lasted more than three years, and in which, according to one's tastes, one can find either the constant intervention of chance or the ever-present signs of methodic intent. This would require a description of everything that goes into actual scientific research, particularly the long series of initiatives that must be improvised, often quite hurriedly, in order to take advantage of a given situation, or everything that has to be done without too much attention to theoretical considerations, while still holding to the conviction that there is no decision, however small, that does not make an equally crucial contribution to the scientific construction of the object. This goes for the composition of the research team (whose structure in terms of sex, age, social origin, and professional standing may have critical effects), the training of the coders, the manner in which the populations under study are determined, the way the corpus of documents is delineated, and, of course, the choice of methods of data collection (observation and/or questionnaire, object and form of the questions asked, etc.) and codification. For anyone not intending to conceal the arbitrary aspects that are inevitably part of all these operations, the only choice is to come armed with epistemological vigilance and sociological lucidity in order to make a scientific virtue of social necessity by adapting choices that are always more or less imposed by social logic to the demands of scientific logic.

The starting point of our entire project was the initiative of a group of *normaliens* from the cartel of the Écoles Normales Supérieures representing each of the schools in the Union Nationale des Étudiants de France (UNEF), who, following the publication of *The Inheritors*,[1] came of their own accord to offer to do a study of their schools, with our collaboration. It immediately seemed necessary to study at least the set of schools that, through their structural weight, play a critical role in the structuring of the universe; which, in addition to the École Normale Supérieure (Ulm), would mean the École Polytechnique, the École Nationale d'Administration (ENA), the École des Hautes Études Commerciales (HEC), and the Institut National Agronomique (INA or Agro). In order to be able to measure the effects of the major principles of differentiation, especially the opposition between the "grandes" and the "petites" écoles, we were led to extend our research beyond the five institutions traditionally recognized as constituting the universe of the grandes écoles. In addition to our research at Ulm and Sèvres (March–April 1966), we also studied Saint-Cloud and Fontenay (in April–May 1966).[2] In addition to our work on the ENA (1967), we also studied, that same year, the École Nationale Supérieure des PTT, the ENSAE (École Nationale de la Statistique et de l'Administration Économique), and the Instituts d'Études Politiques (excluded by the current taxonomy from the universe of the grandes écoles), and we paid particular attention to analyzing the differences between students entering the ENA in the first and second *concours* (students or public servants) and between students in the first and second division of the ENSAE. Finally, and most importantly, in addition to our study of Polytechnique (April 1967), we also studied second-tier and third-tier engineering schools. Since the subfield of scientific schools is very large (numbering 138 schools at that time) and very diverse, varying according to several factors that may partially overlap (academics, social status, public or private administration, location in Paris or the provinces, etc.), we found it necessary to extend the study to include many categories of engineering schools: schools of high social status but average academics, such as Centrale (in 1967) or the École Supérieure d'Électricite (Superlec), schools of high social status and weak academics, such as Breguet (École Supérieure d'Électronique) or the École Spéciale de Mécanique et d'Électricite (in 1969), schools of low social status and average academics, such as the École Nationale Supérieure des Arts et Métiers de Lille (in 1967),[3] and various schools holding pertinent positions in this subspace, such as the École des Ponts et Chaussées, the École Supérieure de Physique et de Chimie, and the École Supérieure des Télécommunications (September–October 1969). Because the École Nationale Supérieure des Mines de Paris had rather high social and academic status, the 1967 study of the École des Mines de Nancy and the École des Mines de Saint-Étienne was designed to enable us to analyze the opposition between location in Paris and the provinces and to see to what degree it conceals a social opposition. Having studied HEC (May–June 1967), we would have liked to have studied the ESSEC, which falls immediately behind HEC in the commonly accepted hierarchy, as well as an advanced business school in the provinces (for example Le Havre or Rouen), but we came up against various administrative and practical obstacles. Because the subfield of schools of business management underwent profound transformations during the very time when our research was being carried out, we conducted an individual study aimed at determining the principal characteristics of these schools (founding date, admission criteria, social and academic characteristics of their student body, curricula, etc.). It was also impossible, for various reasons, to do a direct survey at the military schools (Navale, École de l'Air, Saint-Cyr) or the École des Beaux-Arts, but, in the latter case, we were able to use the results of a study carried out subsequently on the model of our work and with our collaboration.

Using schools of agronomy as an example, we can describe the logic according to which we attempted, within the limits of what was possible and as opportunity permitted, to determine the relevant positions of a sector of the field. The survey was conducted, in May, June, and October of 1966, at the Institut National Agronomique (Agro) in Paris and at the École Nationale Supérieure Agronomique de Grignon in Thiverval-Grignon in the Paris area. At the Agro, where, in contrast to Ulm, we counted a low proportion of student union members, those in charge of the student council[4] distributed the questionnaires among the students, while at Grignon the questionnaire was administered to the entire student body in an auditorium. In order to account for the oppositions between the agronomy schools in Paris and the provinces, as well as those between the schools directly under the jurisdiction of the Ministry of Agriculture and those directly under the jurisdiction of the Ministry of Education and closer to the university, we also conducted the survey at two provincial schools under the aegis of the Ministry of Agriculture, the École Nationale Supérieure Agronomique de Montpellier and the École Nationale Supérieure Agronomique de Rennes, as well as at two schools belonging to the Ministry of Education, the École Nationale Supériure Agronomique de Nancy and the École Nationale Supérieure Agronomique de Toulouse. Finally, we conducted the survey at two sample schools that were less strictly centered on "agronomy" and more specialized: the École Nationale Supérieure d'Horticulture de Versailles (students majoring in horticultural engineering, with the exception of those majoring in landscaping) and the École Nationale Supérieure des Industries Agricoles et Alimentaires de Massy (ENSIAA).[5] It would also have been necessary to be able to study the École Nationale du Génie Rural des Eaux et des Forêts, which trains the engineers of the rural corps, in order to permit comparison with other schools that prepare for the grands corps (ENA, Mines, Ponts), as well as a national advanced school of agronomy for women, in order to analyze the form the opposition between men and women takes on in agronomy schools. These gaps were subsequently partially filled through secondary analysis of data provided by the Ministry of Education.

It was not our objective in any case to produce statistical data on grandes écoles students as a group, or even on the students of any particular category of school (agronomy or engineering, for example). When it is a matter of grasping the *structure* of a field, as in this work, the ordinary procedures of random sampling are completely inadequate, since, through the very operation of random choice, there is every possibility that certain crucial elements in the objective structure will be missed, and the aim is to produce an *accurate picture* of it, that is, a *structurally homologous representation* (the problem becomes even more acute in the literary field, where certain positions may be represented by a very small number of individuals, sometimes only one).[6] Having defined representativity thus, we may take the structural sample we have studied to be representative of the objective structure of the field of the grandes écoles, even though, from the very point of view of the methodological course adopted, certain gaps (such as the military schools) either had to be left or were filled only through recourse either to secondary sources or to the files of the institutions in question (such as the Internat de Médecine, the École de la Magistrature, and the Institut d'Études Judiciaires, for example).

QUESTIONNAIRES AND DIRECT OBSERVATION

Given that we were primarily interested in collecting data that would enable us to differentiate the institutions under study according to the pertinent principles of division, we had to privilege questions on the questionnaire that were designed to provide *objective indicators of the position* occupied by the various agents in the space of the grandes écoles and, through them, by the institution to which they belong, over questions that would enable us to situate them in one or another sub-field (for example, the universe of the scientific grandes écoles) or, *a fortiori*, in a particular institution (for example, the École Normale Supérieure). This method-ological choice required us to continuously fight against the temptation to increase the number of idiographic questions, likely to indulge homegrown curiosity, to the prejudice of questions common to all, and to resist the pressure naturally exerted in this direction by the staff of the schools as well as the members of our research team responsible for administering the study in a single or several institutions.[7]

The survey was initially planned as a training operation that could be adminis-tered according to the procedures adopted for the ENS, with the participation of members of the institution under study, and, in line with our desire to remain inde-pendent from bureaucratic demands, with no special financing.[8] Consequently, the survey was administered at the various schools with the collaboration of young researchers who might be graduates of the school in question and who, in certain cases, enjoyed a privileged relationship to it: Christian Baudelot, Noëlle Bisseret, and Antonio Linares, at several engineering schools, Polytechnique, École Centrale, Écoles des Mines de Paris, Nancy, and Saint-Étienne, École Nationale Supérieure des Arts et Métiers de Lille; Jacqueline Boutonnat at the École Nationale de la Statistique et de l'Administration Économique; Patrick Champagne at several other engineering schools, École Supérieure de Physique et de Chimie Industrielle (EPCI), École Spéciale de Mécanique et d'Électricité (ESME), École Nationale Supérieure des Télécommunications (ENST), École Supérieure d'Ingénieurs d'Électrotechnique et d'Électronique (ESIEE, Breguet), École Supérieure d'Électricité (ESE, Supelec), École Nationale des Ponts et Chaussées; Claude Grignon and Pascale Maldidier at the various schools of agronomy named above; Victor Karady and Henri Le More at HEC; Jean-François Kesler at the ENA; Dominique Schnapper at the Paris and Grenoble Instituts d'Études Politiques and the École des PTT; Pierre Birnbaum at the IEP de Bordeaux; and Philippe Fritsch at the École des Mines de Nancy.[9]

The decision to devote most of the questionnaire to questions common to all institutions, with questions specific to a particular establishment either confined to a separate sheet or left to direct observation, proved in the end to be a sound one.[10] The decision to subordinate all technical choices (starting with the choice of ques-tions and the codes and methods of analysis used) to the need for *comparability* appeared, upon analysis, to be the precondition for bringing to light the most speci-fic characteristics, while certain concessions made to our concern for taking particu-larisms into account ended up precluding comparisons that might lead to genuine particularities. A simple collection of monographs, especially if it were intended to be comparative, would already have represented considerable progress over scientifically based studies that, given their failure to systematically include comparison, are really no different from studies done for apologetic or practical purposes by alumni associations and clubs. Adherence to the preconstructed object, in other words, to the object enclosed in the decisive isolation of exclusive self-interest, reveals time and time again the survival of a privileged relationship, either direct or inverted, to a particular school, an adherence that may be hidden both in the false distances of objectivism and in the shattering inversions of an initial relationship of enchantment. As for the questions that the students at each school asked themselves, they generally had to do with group-internal differences, ignoring the extraordinary resemblances that these very differences conceal; and, for example, a number of the problems that the humanities *normaliens* were concerned about (the existence of a relationship between social origin and choice of discipline, for instance, or between discipline and political opinions) could not really be resolved in a study involving a relatively limited population.

The price paid for the generality associated with our comparative intent was the danger of creating a false picture of reality, given that formally identical questions can elicit different interpretations in different contexts – without anyone's being aware of it. To get around this problem, it was necessary to complement the statistical survey with more probing ethnographic-style surveys conducted at each school according to very precise guidelines for observation and interviewing, established according to our knowledge of the school's position in the structure and the specific institutions into which this position is retranslated. Thus at each school we conducted numerous wide-ranging interviews (both individual and collective) with high-ranking staff, teachers (for example, the various "agrégation coaches" and research seminar directors of the Rue d'Ulm), and students, primarily on the subject of the view that one group or another might have of the field of the grandes écoles and of the synchronic and diachronic position of their school within this space. We also gathered all the real indices of the effects that this position and its future development might exercise on practices (such as the *normaliens'* tendency to prepare for the ENA *concours* or the *polytechniciens'* attempts at increasing the value of their titles in the markets where competition from the ENA was beginning to threaten them). Finally, we increased our analyses of practices characteristic of each school (such as clubs at HEC, the oral at the ENA, or, at various schools, rites of institution, alumni associations, rituals, and publications, especially obituaries, etc.).[11]

In addition, we sought to gather the historical data necessary for constructing a genuine *structural history* of the space of the grandes écoles. The monographs that trace the history of a single school indeed either fail to capture the effects of the change in the overall structure of the field of the grandes écoles, or risk recording them unknowingly in the guise of, for example, signs of disarray or decline.[12] We need only think of the considerable effects produced in the field as a whole by the creation of HEC in the late nineteenth century, and of the ENA immediately after the war. Given that the structural history of institutions of higher education is inseparable from a structural history of the field of power as a whole, we were faced with a formidable task.[13] There did exist partial works on the Inspection des Finances, the Cour des Comptes [two of the top nontechnical *grands corps de l'État*, Tr.], etc., often written by former corps members, which shed no light on what was most important from the point of view of our problematics, in other words, the relationship between the structure of the field of power and the structure of institutions of higher learning. These studies hold to the naive theory whereby the grandes écoles produce the grands corps, and give no thought to the preexisting social differences these schools consecrate.

In thus giving ourselves the opportunity to determine both the synchronic and diachronic position of each institution in the overall space, we have armed ourselves with an instrument so powerful that the specific and at times laboriously collected data on each of the institutions and the practices and opinions of their occupants often seem either redundant or anecdotal.[14]

THE ORGANIZATION OF THE SURVEYS AND THE SAMPLE OF RESPONDENTS

But social facts are more easily yielded when one agrees to take them as they come: dominant institutions (the church, management, the grandes écoles) present a preconstructed image of themselves, not only through the *representations* they spontaneously offer (particularly through their celebratory discourses), but also through the "data" they provide, at times quite readily. As much as any monument, *documents*, and particularly those considered worthy of being saved and passed on to posterity, are the objectivated product of the strategies of self-presentation that institutions, like agents, implement, unknowingly and even unintentionally, and that the threat of objectivation, embodied in the sociologist, often brings into explicit consciousness.

Is it necessary to mention the good or bad procedures sociologists must implement in order to achieve their work of objectivation and to overcome the resistance put up by their object, resistance that naturally increases in strength the more the sociologists diverge from the point of view that the agents or the institutions under consideration want to see adopted? Below are a few very partial indications of the social work of negotiation (which includes a variable share of seduction, dissimulation, blackmail, ruse, etc.) that has to be done to get permission to administer a survey, ask particular questions, and gain access to certain documents, files, in-house studies, etc., especially the ones protected by *confidentiality*. Some of the documents so labeled, which can usually only be obtained by resorting to ruses that one might or might not want to admit to – sociologists have their secrets too – actually contain some of the most valuable information on the institution in question, which protects itself from objectivation by protecting documents "from the eye of the outsider" (this was the case, for example, with a study HEC did on the professional future of its graduates, analyzed according to their social origins and *concours* rank). All of which suffices to show that the "objective truth" that science establishes, far from having always and completely escaped agents' awareness, or at least the awareness of all of them, is rather, in more cases than one, censored and repressed. And if sociological objectivation provokes the cry of scandal (while earning itself the reproach of banality), this is because it destroys the belief relationship that binds initiates to their institution. Founded as it is on misrecognition, as denied recognition of objective truth, belief does not take kindly to being unveiled outside the circle of initiates, which is defined precisely by participation in belief, in collective bad faith, in a dual consciousness of realism and denial. In fact, a researcher's strategies and strategems owe their efficacy to the fact that, given the gap between the constructed object and ordinary vision, agents are never completely sure of what they should hide, or even of what they are betraying or concealing. Indeed, useful data are usually outside their control, in the objective relationship between the information they cannot help but reveal (even through their resistances) and information drawn from other sources, principally with regard to other institutions. For this reason, we momentarily considered challenging positivist propriety by including in the correspondence analysis diagram *polytechniciens' estimated* political positions (clearly labeled as such). We are in fact able to *deduce* political stances that we were unable to record empirically (given the administration's refusal to allow any question relating to political preferences or union membership), using our knowledge of the position the École Polytechnique occupies in the space of the institutions of higher education (established, among others, through correspondence analysis). And we can do it with all the more certainty because student attitudes are also open to empirical recording through choices that are equally revealing of political positions, such as their preference for a particular newspaper or school of thought.

The success of our project depended heavily, in any case, on all the public relations work that is essential for ensuring that survey results respond to theoretical demands (people forget, or are unaware, for example, that large-scale official surveys, particularly in the area of consumption, sometimes, and increasingly often, reach such a rate of nonresponses that the samples obtained are not far from being spontaneous samples – of which one should at least analyze the social make-up). The principal difficulty indeed lay in the need to obtain both the authorization of the authorities and the support of the students. And we have reason to believe that the study was treated differently at the different schools depending on whether it was perceived as being run by the students (or a portion of them), imposed by the administration, or imposed by the administration with student support.

Administrators often looked on the survey as an intrusion. In every case it was necessary to explain, convince, reassure; we had to give assurances and offer guarantees. Such preliminary negotiations and discussions affected not only the very possibility of conducting the survey, but also the quality of the data collected. It indeed played a very significant role in determining both the quantity and the quality of the responses (if a survey is not really accepted by a group, it risks being skewed in ways that are often difficult to unravel). In short, the principal merit of this study is probably that it managed to exist, albeit with imperfections stemming from the fact that the variations in the form of the social relations in which it was carried out were translated into the diversity of the conditions under which the questionnaires were administered. For example, by "choosing" the official route (virtually inevitable in a military school) for our Polytechnique survey and by requesting permission from the general in command, we were ensuring ourselves of a very high response rate, but condemning ourselves to the form of survey administration inherent in the school's hierarchical structure. The rather "military" administration questionnaire (the entire student body was assembled at one time in an auditorium) undoubtedly favored more or less subtle forms of passive resistance (while a survey on tastes conducted several years earlier, with students as intermediaries, resulted in something quite similar to one done at Ulm). In general, the more or less indispensable approval of the administration was not enough. Especially since in most cases, student attitudes tended to be defined in opposition to the presumed attitude of the administration. We thus always made every effort to convince the students – or at least a portion of them – that the survey was legitimate, and indeed necessary.

The problem may appear to have been resolved at the écoles normales since the initiative came from the students themselves. But the fact that those involved were a minority of student union leaders introduced a slight distorting factor, undoubtedly attenuated by the fact that the union was run as an association and that nonmembers also participated in the administration of the survey.[15] Although union members are slightly overrepresented among our respondents, observations made by the survey team show that among the students who refused to answer, there are a few members of the SGEN [Syndicat Général de l'Éducation Nationale] and the SNES [Syndicat National de l'Enseignement Secondaire] (especially among fourth-year students, who had the highest rate of non responses) as well as a few UNEF members belonging to a group hostile to the party line of the time.

To get a better idea of how the survey was administered when students were in charge, as well as the effects that this method of data collection may have had on the propensity of different categories of students to respond, let us take a closer look at the case of the various écoles normales. The fact that the initiative came from the students themselves undoubtedly greatly contributed to neutralizing resistance to the study, which was particularly strong in the intellectual grandes écoles. At Ulm, following our instructions, the group in charge did a good amount of urging, reminding, verifying, and list-checking. The rate of nonresponses per class shows that nonresponses are related to the degree of involvement of the student survey team and their ability to inspire confidence; it is very low in the third year in the humanities, the class to which the principal leaders belonged, and in the second year in the sciences, which boasted one union leader who was able to get a 90 percent response rate (as was his equivalent at Sèvres for second-year science students). Judging from a comparison of our results with official Ministry of Education statistics gathered in a study of Ulm files, and from observations made by those administering the survey, it appears that nonresponses are somewhat related to social origin (students from the upper classes responding somewhat less often than students from the lower end or middle of the social scale), place of residence (it seems that some day students were left out, particularly in the sciences), discipline (with students in the classics responding at a somewhat lower rate, and a group of first-year students in the natural sciences not participating at all), and finally, religion and politics (with the practicing Catholics and the conservatives undoubtedly responding at a somewhat lower rate).[16] In fact, hostility toward student unions and hostility to our survey are probably based on the same principle: the rejection of anything that might smack of reducing things to the social. At Sèvres, thanks to the efficiency and competence of the students in charge, the survey was completed successfully and the responses were both very numerous (57 percent at Sèvres-humanities, 73 percent at Sèvres-sciences) and very complete. This is probably due to the fact that the students are less spread out in space and less concerned with external matters than at Ulm, where some day students rarely set foot in the school; and perhaps also because the claim to the intellectual role is less strong (among the science students, it was the fourth-year students, very often day students, who answered relatively less thoroughly; among the humanities students it was the language and history majors). At Saint-Cloud, we obtained a 35 percent response rate for the first three years in the humanities, and 34 percent for the first three years in the sciences. This relatively low rate can no doubt be explained by the fact that the students running the study were less involved (the head of the ENS cartel was at that time an Ulm student, and the fact that the initiative came more from Ulm and Sèvres may have been a negative factor). The distribution and collection of the questionnaires was done by floor, as at Fontenay (and not by year, as at Ulm and Sèvres, probably a better basis for familiarity among students), and the students administering the survey were unable to get it going again using any other system. Nonresponses are related even more strongly here than at Ulm to social origin (upper class students participated less), discipline (language and natural science students have a low response rate), politics, and union involvement (few nonunion members participated). (Indications are that if the overseeing of the study had been as intense at Saint-Cloud as it was at Ulm, the rate of respondents would have been greater, particularly because Saint-Cloud students come from lower classes, relatively, because their intellectual pretensions are more moderate, and because the level of hostility toward the survey was lower as well.) At Fontenay, where the response rate was higher than at Saint-Cloud in the humanities (49 percent), and roughly equal in the sciences (33 percent), the overseeing of the survey was much less overt than at Sèvres, and the students remained relatively indifferent to it, with the exception, it seems, of the first-year students, who had the highest response rate. As at Saint-Cloud, the language and natural science students, as well as the upper-class students, are underrepresented (we are unable to measure the effect of union membership because we have no data on the rate of union membership during that time, especially in the sciences).

Our experience with the École Normale survey enabled us to set up standardized questionnaire collection procedures that were subsequently implemented as rigorously as possible within the limits of the constraints and possibilities offered and imposed by the various other institutions. Whenever possible, we made students party to the study by discussing with them the best ways to distribute and collect the questionnaires (by year, by major, by building, or by floor), the advisability of reminders, and the arguments most likely to convince the hesitant. Aware that the very circumstances in which the survey was being carried out contributed to determining the limits of its subsequent interpretation, and also that they revealed a good deal of information on the object, we wrote very detailed reports on how the survey had been run and on the exchanges that had made it possible. In certain cases, detailed observations were made, particularly with regard to the resistance encountered from both administrators and students. For each school, in addition to the specific data provided by the questionnaires, we collected all other available data (previous surveys, government documents, interviews with administrators and students, etc.), and whenever we could have access to them, we submitted student files to statistical analysis.

As we moved away from the "intellectual" pole of the field of institutions of higher education, resistance to the survey, to sociology, and, more specifically, to analysis of the social factors involved in academic success either diminished or changed character. Once we had obtained permission from the administration, specific objections to the study did not arise, and the major obstacle tended to be indifference. At Polytechnique, as we have seen, the survey was imposed on the students by military authority. We were able to administer the questionnaire to the entire student body on the same day at the same time and under the same conditions, under the supervision of members of the research team, with the only drawback being that we were not allowed to ask questions about political opinions (which later created great difficulties for our analysis). Elsewhere, with slight variation, depending on the degree of student participation or administration involvement, the survey took on the form it had taken either at Ulm or at Polytechnique.[17]

The engineering schools had the highest survey response rate: 53 percent at Centrale (and 64 percent for the first two years), 74 percent at Mines de Nancy, 78 percent at Mines de Paris (for engineering students), 86 percent at Polytechnique, 93 percent at the ENSAM de Lille, etc. The survey was almost always administered to the student body during an assembly with the approval of the administration, which more or less required participation. In most cases, this would be preceded by meetings with the students in which the objectives of the survey were presented and debated. In the engineering schools where the survey was conducted at the beginning of the school year 1969–70, the questionnaires were usually given out by the administration along with initial registration material. At the agronomy schools, where school officials were sometimes favorably disposed toward the study but never involved in an authoritarian way (either at the École Nationale Supérieure Agronomique de Grignon and the ENSA de Montpellier, where the questionnaire was passed out to students assembled together in an auditorium – by researchers at Grignon, by student presidents at the ENSA – or at the ENSA de Nancy and the ENSA de Rennes, where the questionnaire was distributed by students and student presidents), the response rate was closely linked to the method of organization of the study and to the cooperation and support of the students in charge.

At HEC, the questionnaire was given out to students in their rooms, with an accompanying explanatory letter and a return envelope. The students who participated in the preparation and running of the study made numerous reminders and pleas, which enabled us to get a relatively high rate of return (68 percent). But a conflict that arose between the administration and the student association at the time of the survey contributed to creating a relatively tense atmosphere, while a small group of Marxist students were openly hostile to the study. At the Institut d'Études Politiques de Paris, the questionnaires were given out by professors. The response rate was highest (63 percent) among the students in public service; it was lowest for students in international relations (42 percent). If we take into account the fact that a considerable number of students (about 30 percent) drop out over the course of a year, we can estimate that the response rate was actually appreciably higher (on the order of 80 percent for the public service students and 65 percent for international relations). The students who did the preparatory year at the IEP participated in the survey at a greater rate than those who were admitted directly into the second year, just as students who took other courses while they were studying at the IEP were slightly overrepresented in relation to those who were only registered at the IEP. Thus a total of 6,249 questionnaires were tallied – not counting the foreign students, whose answers were not included in the statistical analysis, except for the international relations department of the Institut d'Études Politiques.

Why not just use the numbers provided by official sources, one might ask, especially Ministry of Education surveys, which are genuinely synchronic, homogeneous studies run by a central body? In fact, in addition to the fact that they only provide a very limited amount of information, they include rates of nonresponses that are hardly lower. So, for example, in 1967–8, the rate of nonresponses to the question on father's occupation was 20.9 percent at the École Nationale des Douanes and 20.5 percent at the École d'Architecture de Bordeaux; 12.4 percent of *polytechniciens* were classified in the category "other," as were 23.6 percent of students at the École de Physique et Chimie de Paris. In addition, ministry data sometimes appear to be less than completely reliable. So, for example, it seems highly unlikely that the 1967–8 student body of a provincial school of management (which we cannot name here) would be made up of 32.6 percent sons of members of the professions, when there is a maximum of 10 percent of this category in the other schools of business and management, or that another provincial political science school could attain a relatively high rate of students from families in the "intellectual professions" (9.5 percent) when the analogous institutions claim no more than 2 percent.[18] We could go on and on. In addition, the method of presentation of the government studies is probably largely responsible for the insufficient nature of the classifications and groupings made by the schools. A great many of the questionnaires from the survey conducted by the Ministry of Education in 1984–5 were unusable; in other cases, the schools had to be used as supplementary variables. Indeed, a number of establishments did not distinguish between public sector managers and teachers or science professionals, or between engineers and corporate technical managers and administrative and commercial managers. And they also combined primary school teachers, mid-level health and social work professionals, and mid-level public sector managers; in several schools, small, mid-sized, and large merchants were grouped together, probably because students failed to provide enough detail. Generally, the method of collection used and the absence of regulations or clear directions (they did not want to "weigh down the study") mean that the data collected are neither very accurate nor very reliable, especially where social origins are concerned, and also that we have to make do with very rough statistical categories.

In contrast, our questionnaire, through joint questions on the occupation and educational level of the father, the mother, and both grandfathers (paternal and maternal), enabled us to see in what ways the father's occupation, as rigorously as it may be defined, may be insufficient for characterizing social position. In addition, by giving our subjects examples of *detailed occupational descriptions* in order to avoid meaningless or vague statements ("public service" or "father deceased"; "farmer")[19], and in asking them to characterize their father's position both at the time of the study and at the time of their birth, we encouraged them to provide more detailed information than they would on the official forms they ritually fill out at the beginning of the year (which do not guarantee anonymity). This degree of precision in our data collection enabled us to verify what we had already observed in our research on management, the episcopate, and high-level public servants: formally identical classes in the occupational categories of the INSEE conceal very significant differences. So, for example, the members of the professions whose children go to Beaux-Arts tend to be architects; at Polytechnique, they tend to be physicians, and the rare architects whose sons do go to Polytechnique differ in other secondary characteristics from those who send their children to Beaux-Arts or the ENA; at Ulm and Sèvres, especially in the sciences, they are also physicians, and very often pharmacists. Similarly, in the case of mid-level government employees, at Polytechnique they tend to be accountants, while at Ulm they tend to be drafters or chief town clerks, in the registrar's office. It is the sum of these minor secondary differences that then enables us to account for differences with regard to schools, disciplines, careers, and political choices that might at first have escaped us. For example, the fact that at Polytechnique, and especially at Centrale and HEC, families tend to be more connected to the private sector than at Ulm, where they are more tied to the public sector, seems to be at the basis of a whole set of differences in ethical, aesthetic, and political choices.

We should also set out all the reasons, derived from an analysis of our survey results and their comparison to data from research in progress, that persuaded us to overcome our doubts and uncertainties and decide to publish this work. There is probably no better measure of the power of censorship wielded by the scientific field than the genuine positivist *crisis* into which we were thrown, for many years, by an obsessive awareness of the gaps (the schools we had not been able to study), imperfections (the schools where the response rate was low), and weaknesses (particularly those resulting from uncontrollable variations in the formulation of the questions or the time period during which the survey was conducted) in our study. Paradoxically, this awareness only increased with our increased knowledge of the object; in fact, the logic behind the theoretical construct that began to take shape from the very first results of our analysis caused us in a sense to double the stakes, and hence the risks, by prompting us to study the structure of the field of power, incurring the same difficulties, in order to relate it to the structure of the field of academic institutions that help ensure its reproduction.[20]

Given that the data collection stretched from March 1966 for the Écoles Normales Supérieures to October 1969 for the last engineering schools (Ponts, Supelec, Breguet, etc.), the information gathered, so far as it depends on a specific moment or period of time, may no longer be strictly comparable.[21] So, for example, when we asked students how often they had gone to the movies, to concerts, or to the theater since the beginning of the school year in October, as at the ENSs, Agro, and HEC, or since the month of September at the École Polytechnique and the École des Mines, we did not imagine that, because of the length of time required for the survey, which we had obviously underestimated, the period of reference could differ from one school to another (for example, at the Agro, the survey was administered later in the year than at the ENS). It follows that studying variations in cultural practices according to occupational category of the father, age, etc., is possible within schools, but that interschool comparisons are not a simple matter. By neutralizing variations in the length of time measured that are linked to variations in the date of the survey, however, we can establish indisputable tendencies. It is clear, for example, that Sèvres students go to the theater more often than Ulm students, who in turn go more often than Agro students. But it is not easy to neutralize the possible variations in what is playing in the theaters (such as the appearance in a given year of a highly popular play, for example). Similarly, it is difficult to compare involvement in sports. Unfortunate variation in the formulation of the questions, particularly with regard to the circumstances and the frequency of participation has meant that we have no reliable indication of the latter. Nevertheless, analyzing variations in activity within the school is entirely legitimate and quite instructive. So, for example, at Polytechnique, working-class students are more often involved in collective sports, while the others more often take up fencing, which is an important indication of the way in which both groups will later be able to cash in on their capital as *polytechniciens*. In any case, we know that sports are not distributed by chance among the schools and that the social hierarchy of sports corresponds to the social hierarchy of schools. So, for example, at Polytechnique, where sports play an important role, cross-country, track, and fencing are the top sports; at HEC, it would be rowing or golf; at Sciences-po, where squash has developed rapidly over the last few years, and where there is a strong rugby team, a student may be a golf champion. In any case, here as elsewhere, we stood by the rule of not trying to get more precision in our coding than was warranted by the data collected.

Our very keen sense of our instrument's imperfections ended up by making us forget that the deficiencies in the collected material were nearly always the price we had to pay for our initial intention to grasp the entire field of institutions of higher education. Of all the projects undertaken, with the energy desperation provides, over nearly 20 years of silence and hesitant, partial publications,[22] the most typical was an attempt to develop a mathematical program to rectify the sample, which, in order to correct the data, whose inaccuracy we could measure quite accurately, often relied upon bureaucratic data whose imprecision was impossible to state precisely . . .[23] Assisted in this by critical studies on government statistics[24] and also, paradoxically, by the publication of one monograph or another providing valuable data and corroboration for our structural analysis, we were in the end able to overcome our positivist anxiety, which was being fed by knowledge of the object only to constantly uncover new imperfections in the instrument of knowledge, and which was prompting us to forever conduct new surveys and research on controls, pressing forward with no other result than to prevent publication.

Appendix 3

Data Tables

Table 17 Paternal grandfather's occupation (percent)

	Ulm	Sèvres	St Cloud	Fontenay	Polytech.	Mines Paris	Mines Nancy	Mines St Et.	Centrale	Agro	ENSIAA	ENA1	ENA2	IEP	HEC
None	1.0	0.6	–	0.7	1.0	0.7	0.6	1.5	3.6	1.1	–	5.0	–	0.7	3.2
Farmer	12.9	14.4	20.5	25.0	13.5	16.5	9.0	12.3	12.0	22.4	22.5	13.1	19.4	11.0	6.8
Blue-collar worker	10.3	7.8	19.6	12.5	8.1	7.5	12.0	7.7	8.4	8.0	11.3	3.0	13.9	5.0	3.6
Clerical	6.2	11.7	14.0	16.9	9.6	7.5	9.0	9.2	6.8	5.4	7.0	5.0	8.3	3.8	5.2
Tradesman, small commerce	17.6	15.0	14.9	16.9	15.6	12.0	21.7	10.8	17.9	13.4	5.6	8.2	13.9	18.0	17.1
Mid-level manager	4.7	5.9	3.7	5.9	3.1	6.0	4.2	7.7	6.6	5.1	7.0	5.0	5.5	6.7	9.8
Primary teacher	5.7	4.6	5.6	1.5	3.1	–	3.0	1.5	2.9	3.6	2.8	3.0	5.5	1.8	1.2
Exec., professions	30.0	28.7	5.6	10.3	31.0	28.6	23.5	24.6	24.0	28.2	25.3	40.4	19.4	44.1	42.5
Other	–	–	–	–	0.2	–	–	–	–	1.1	–	–	2.8	0.7	0.8
NR	11.4	11.1	15.9	10.3	14.8	21.0	16.8	24.6	17.7	11.6	18.3	17.2	11.1	8.2	9.6
Total	100	100	100	100	100	100	100	100	100	100	100	100	100	100	100
Number	193	153	107	136	519	133	166	65	441	276	71	99	36	599	560

Table 18a Maternal grandfather's occupation (percent)

	Ulm	Sèvres	St Cloud	Fontenay	Polytech.	Mines Paris	Mines Nancy	Mines St Et.	Centrale	Agro	ENSIAA	ENA1	ENA2	IEP	HEC
None	–	–	–	0.7	2.3	1.5	1.8	–	3.8	1.1	–	2.0	2.8	1.7	2.8
Farmer	7.8	9.8	23.3	18.4	10.4	14.3	10.2	20.0	12.5	20.3	14.1	8.1	11.1	8.7	8.9
Blue-collar worker	12.9	7.2	18.7	11.0	8.1	5.2	4.2	6.1	7.5	6.5	15.5	5.0	13.9	4.5	3.9
Clerical	8.8	10.4	9.3	12.5	9.4	6.8	8.4	9.2	10.2	6.9	9.8	5.0	16.7	4.5	5.3
Tradesman, small commerce	17.6	15.0	20.5	25.7	13.5	15.0	15.1	13.8	16.3	11.9	12.7	13.1	25.0	14.7	15.7
Mid-level manager	5.2	5.2	2.8	6.6	6.0	6.8	6.6	4.6	5.4	2.9	2.8	6.0	5.5	7.0	7.5
Primary teacher	3.6	9.1	3.7	7.3	3.3	–	4.8	3.1	1.8	1.4	5.6	2.0	–	1.8	1.1
Exec., professions	30.6	34.0	6.5	8.8	32.2	28.6	25.3	26.1	23.3	35.1	18.3	40.4	11.1	46.7	42.3
Other	0.5	0.6	–	–	0.6	–	–	–	–	0.7	–	–	–	0.7	–
NR	12.9	8.5	14.9	8.8	14.2	21.8	23.5	16.9	19.0	13.0	21.1	18.2	13.9	9.7	12.3

Table 18b Size of family (percent)

	Ulm	Sèvres	St Cloud	Fontenay	Polytech.	Mines Paris	Mines Nancy	Mines St Et.	Centrale	Agro	ENSIAA	ENA1	ENA2	IEP	HEC
1 child	16.0	12.4	12.1	19.8	10.2	12.8	10.2	13.8	9.7	11.6	9.8	12.1	11.1	11.0	11.9
2 children	24.9	33.3	30.8	23.5	29.3	29.3	30.1	29.2	26.7	17.4	19.7	23.2	33.3	23.4	25.2
3 children	21.7	25.5	23.3	24.2	24.3	21.8	26.5	13.8	23.8	20.3	26.7	26.3	22.2	24.5	25.7
4 children	17.1	8.5	17.7	16.9	15.8	17.3	12.0	12.3	14.7	17.7	18.3	16.2	11.1	16.8	18.0
5 children	9.3	9.8	3.7	6.6	10.2	8.3	10.8	16.9	11.8	10.5	14.1	11.1	13.9	12.5	7.7
6 or more	10.9	9.8	10.3	8.1	9.8	8.3	10.2	13.8	12.7	22.1	11.3	11.1	8.3	9.0	11.1
NR	–	0.6	1.9	0.7	0.4	2.2	–	–	0.4	0.3	–	–	–	2.7	0.3

Table 19 Number of family members with some higher education (grandparents, uncles, aunts, cousins, but excluding parents and siblings)

	Ulm	Sèvres	St Cloud	Fontenay	Polytech.	Mines Paris	Mines Nancy	Mines St Et.	Centrale	Agro	ENSIAA	ENA1	ENA2	IEP	HEC
None	26.4	20.2	60.7	43.4	20.6	26.3	18.7	20.0	26.5	22.1	39.4	17.2	52.8	15.7	16.1
1	17.6	18.3	14.0	22.8	13.1	13.5	17.5	16.9	14.5	9.8	12.7	13.1	8.3	10.2	10.5
2	6.7	12.4	7.5	7.3	11.9	6.8	13.2	13.8	11.1	11.9	11.3	4.0	11.1	9.8	8.7
3	8.8	5.9	3.7	7.3	9.2	9.8	6.6	4.6	9.7	8.7	4.2	15.1	8.3	8.0	10.9
4	9.3	9.1	1.9	8.1	7.7	3.7	9.6	1.5	4.5	7.2	5.6	8.1	2.8	6.7	9.1
5–8	18.6	20.9	7.5	6.6	18.7	14.3	17.5	16.9	14.7	19.9	15.5	23.2	11.1	19.0	23.7
9–11	3.6	5.2	2.8	2.2	6.0	3.7	5.4	4.6	4.7	6.9	2.8	9.1	–	9.2	7.7
12–15	3.1	3.3	0.9	0.7	5.4	4.5	4.8	9.2	4.1	4.3	4.2	3.0	–	6.3	5.9
16 or more	5.2	3.3	0.9	–	6.2	13.5	5.4	6.1	6.1	8.3	2.8	6.0	5.5	9.0	6.1
NR	0.5	1.3	–	1.5	1.1	3.7	1.2	6.1	3.8	0.7	1.4	1.0	–	6.0	1.2

Table 20a Schools attended in *première* (percent)

	Ulm	Sèvres	St Cloud	Fontenay	Polytech.	Mines Paris	Mines Nancy	Mines St Et.	Centrale	Agro	ENSIAA	ENA1	ENA2	IEP	HEC
ENI	1.0	–	44.8	32.3	0.2	–	0.6	–	0.2	–	1.4	–	5.5	0.2	–
Collège	5.2	4.6	3.7	11.0	3.3	9.8	12.0	9.2	12.9	18.5	18.3	4.0	16.7	3.5	6.2
Private	10.9	6.5	7.5	2.9	11.7	12.8	13.8	26.1	11.5	13.4	14.1	28.3	19.4	28.7	19.8
Lycée	82.9	86.9	43.9	53.7	84.4	75.2	72.9	64.6	74.4	66.7	64.8	67.7	55.5	66.3	73.6
NR	–	1.9	–	–	0.4	2.2	0.6	–	0.9	1.4	1.4	–	2.8	1.3	0.3

ENI = École Normale for primary teachers; Collège = public.

Table 20b Grades repeated (percent)

	Ulm	Sèvres	St Cloud	Fontenay	Polytech.	Mines Paris	Mines Nancy	Mines St Et.	Centrale	Agro	ENSIAA	ENA1	ENA2	IEP	HEC
2, incl. *terminale*	.	.	.	.	0.2	–	0.6	1.5	0.4	1.4	1.4	–	2.8	–	4.1
2, not *terminale*	.	.	.	.	–	–	–	3.1	–	0.3	2.8	1.0	2.8	–	1.1
Terminale	.	.	.	.	0.2	1.5	2.4	4.6	2.5	10.1	28.2	9.1	16.7	–	10.2
Another grade	.	.	.	.	5.0	3.0	7.8	9.2	6.6	19.9	15.5	7.1	13.9	–	11.9
None	.	.	.	.	93.6	84.9	88.5	80.0	90.5	66.7	49.3	64.6	50.0	–	71.8
NR	.	.	.	.	0.9	10.5	0.6	1.5	–	1.4	2.8	18.2	13.9	100.0	0.9

Question not asked at Écoles Normales Supérieures.

Table 21 *Mention* on baccalauréat (percent)

	Ulm	Sèvres	St Cloud	Fontenay	Polytech.	Mines Paris	Mines Nancy	Mines St Et.	Centrale	Agro	ENSIAA	ENA1	ENA2	IEP	HEC
0 point	5.7	5.2	13.1	8.8	3.8	5.3	16.9	26.1	4.5	45.3	50.7	12.1	16.7	44.4	39.1
1 point	5.2	10.4	18.7	15.4	11.9	12.0	21.1	27.7	17.3	29.3	33.8	27.3	41.7	26.0	27.8
2 points	14.5	20.3	21.5	29.4	24.5	15.8	24.1	29.2	16.5	13.0	12.7	26.3	22.2	15.4	19.3
3 points	23.8	26.1	21.5	21.3	22.5	17.3	22.3	7.7	18.8	7.2	2.8	17.2	5.5	8.0	8.0
4 points	26.4	24.2	15.9	18.4	20.2	29.3	12.0	6.2	9.8	3.3	–	15.1	–	4.0	3.6
5 points	11.9	9.1	4.7	4.4	9.6	10.5	1.2	1.5	6.8	0.4	–	–	2.8	0.8	0.9
6 points	11.4	3.9	4.7	–	6.0	5.3	–	1.5	1.5	0.4	–	1.0	–	0.3	0.4
7 points	–	–	–	–	–	0.7	0.6	–	–	–	–	–	–	–	–
8 points	1.0	–	–	–	0.4	0.7	–	–	–	–	–	–	–	–	0.2
NR	–	0.7	–	2.2	1.0	3.0	1.8	–	24.8	1.1	–	1.0	11.1	1.0	0.7

At Centrale, only second-year students were counted.

Points calculated as follows: *mention* of good = 1; very good = 2; excellent = 3. At the time of the study, students took two baccalauréat examinations; some might take the mathematics baccalauréat and then the philosophy baccalauréat.

Table 22a Concert attendance over a measured period (percent)

	Ulm	Sèvres	St Cloud	Fontenay	Polytech.	Mines Paris	Mines Nancy	Mines St Et.	Centrale	Agro	ENSIAA	ENA1	ENA2	IEP	HEC
Not at all	35.2	34.6	53.3	40.4	55.9	47.4	53.6	66.1	57.6	45.6	52.1	56.6	88.9	47.7	46.4
1 visit	18.6	20.9	9.3	13.2	13.1	21.8	24.1	13.8	15.9	18.1	11.3	16.1	2.8	12.7	23.4
2 visits	9.3	9.1	8.4	13.2	10.4	11.3	9.6	7.7	7.7	8.0	11.3	7.1	5.5	7.3	13.2
3 or more	26.9	24.8	15.9	22.1	16.8	17.3	10.2	9.2	18.1	12.3	11.3	16.1	–	13.0	14.5
NR	9.8	10.5	13.1	11.0	3.8	2.2	2.4	3.1	0.7	15.9	14.1	4.0	2.8	19.2	2.5

Table 22b Theater attendance over a measured period (percent)

	Ulm	Sèvres	St Cloud	Fontenay	Polytech.	Mines Paris	Mines Nancy	Mines St Et.	Centrale	Agro	ENSIAA	ENA1	ENA2	IEP	HEC
Not at all	17.6	5.9	18.7	7.3	17.1	12.8	28.9	29.2	27.7	18.1	9.8	17.2	30.5	16.5	23.2
1 visit	11.4	11.1	15.9	9.5	11.9	12.0	21.1	16.9	17.9	15.6	14.1	13.1	22.2	16.0	16.8
2 visits	17.6	10.4	18.7	9.5	13.1	15.8	11.4	12.3	15.9	17.4	14.1	16.1	19.4	15.2	17.3
3 visits	8.8	5.2	12.1	15.4	11.4	9.0	9.6	7.7	9.5	17.0	21.1	10.1	8.3	14.7	11.1
4 visits	10.9	9.8	11.2	14.0	9.2	9.0	3.6	6.1	8.8	8.3	5.6	14.1	2.8	8.8	12.7
5 visits	9.3	10.4	6.5	11.7	9.8	9.0	2.4	9.2	6.8	4.3	5.6	3.0	5.5	7.3	4.6
6 or more	19.2	41.2	13.1	29.4	25.6	27.8	16.3	9.2	5.4	8.0	22.5	20.2	8.3	12.8	8.4
NR	5.2	5.9	3.7	2.9	1.7	4.5	6.6	9.2	7.9	11.2	7.0	6.0	2.8	8.5	5.9

Table 23a Involvement in sports (percent)

	Ulm	Sèvres	St Cloud	Fontenay	Polytech.	Mines Paris	Mines Nancy	Mines St Et.	Centrale	Agro	ENSIAA	ENA1	ENA2	IEP	HEC
No	40.9	35.9	40.2	43.4	12.5	24.8	20.5	20.0	10.0	14.5	11.3	19.2	19.4	28.0	19.1
Yes	54.4	59.5	57.0	51.5	86.9	73.7	78.9	80.0	89.3	82.6	87.3	79.8	77.8	65.9	80.7
NR	4.7	4.6	2.8	5.1	0.6	1.5	0.6	–	0.7	2.9	1.4	1.0	2.8	6.0	0.2

Table 23b Daily newspapers read regularly (percent)

	Ulm	Sèvres	St Cloud	Fontenay	Polytech.	Mines Paris	Mines Nancy	Mines St Et.	Centrale	Agro	ENSIAA	ENA1	ENA2	IEP	HEC
L'Humanité	11.9	1.3	20.5	5.1	0.9	–	1.8	4.6	0.4	3.2	1.4	–	–	1.7	0.2
Le Monde	61.1	33.3	52.3	41.2	71.7	44.3	43.4	38.4	30.1	46.0	26.7	100.0	100.0	90.0	60.9
France-Soir	8.3	1.9	0.9	2.2	4.6	3.0	19.3	18.4	7.2	6.2	7.0	5.0	–	4.7	3.9
Le Figaro	5.7	1.3	0.9	–	6.5	16.5	13.2	13.8	20.8	19.6	28.2	11.1	2.8	15.0	10.0
NR	3.6	5.9	3.7	1.5	1.1	0.7	0.6	–	1.1	6.5	8.4	–	–	0.7	0.3

Percentage of students who state that they regularly read each of these newspapers, so that total may be less than or more than 100%.

Table 24a Weeklies read regularly (percent)

	Ulm	Sèvres	St Cloud	Fontenay	Polytech.	Mines Paris	Mines Nancy	Mines St Et.	Centrale	Agro	ENSIAA	ENA1	ENA2	IEP	HEC
L'Express	7.2	4.6	2.8	5.1	20.6	12.8	19.3	13.8	16.3	22.1	8.4	31.3	30.5	28.5	24.6
Nouvel Observateur	26.9	20.3	26.2	17.6	27.5	18.8	24.7	21.5	16.8	11.6	9.8	30.3	13.9	28.5	22.8
Canard Enchaîné	5.7	5.9	12.1	8.8	5.4	5.2	7.2	3.1	5.0	2.5	5.6	9.1	8.3	5.5	3.0
NR	4.1	5.9	3.7	1.5	1.2	0.7	0.6	–	0.9	5.8	7.0	–	–	0.8	0.3

Percentage of students who state that they regularly read each of these weeklies.

Table 24b Reading of "cultural" journals (percent)

	Ulm	Sèvres	St Cloud	Fontenay	Polytech.	Mines Paris	Mines Nancy	Mines St Et.	Centrale	Agro	ENSIAA	ENA1	ENA2	IEP	HEC
None	70.5	74.5	71.9	75.7	94.8	85.7	94.6	98.5	94.5	90.6	90.1	75.7	83.3	91.1	89.6
1 journal	12.9	11.1	9.3	13.2	3.3	5.2	3.6	–	3.2	3.2	2.8	13.1	11.1	5.8	5.7
2 or more	10.9	7.8	14.9	9.5	0.9	7.5	1.2	1.5	1.3	0.3	–	11.1	5.5	2.0	4.1
NR	5.7	6.5	3.7	1.5	0.9	1.5	0.6	0.9	0.9	5.8	7.0	–	–	1.0	0.5

"Cultural" journals were listed as: L'Arc, Bizarre, Critique, Diogène, Esprit, Études, Europe, Les Lettres Nouvelles, La Nef, La Nouvelle Critique, La NRF, La Pensée, Preuves, Recherches Internationales, La Table Ronde, Tel Quel, Les Temps Modernes.

Table 25a Political scale (percent)

	Ulm	Sèvres	St Cloud	Fontenay	Polytech.	Mines Paris	Mines Nancy	Mines St Et.	Centrale	Agro	ENSIAA	ENA1	ENA2	IEP	HEC
Far left	14.0	11.7	26.2	11.7	*	10.5	11.4	6.1	7.5	3.3	5.6	5.0	2.8	5.5	5.5
Left	45.6	51.6	49.5	54.4	*	33.8	29.5	29.2	30.6	26.8	14.1	28.3	36.1	28.0	28.6
Center left	6.7	7.8	4.7	5.9	*	10.5	12.0	10.8	6.1	6.9	5.6	25.2	41.7	7.3	11.1
Center	10.9	9.8	2.8	8.1	*	18.0	16.9	18.4	27.6	23.2	18.3	4.0	5.5	20.2	20.0
Center right	2.1	2.0	–	–	*	3.0	4.8	3.1	4.1	7.2	5.6	22.2	2.8	5.7	6.4
Right	4.1	3.9	1.9	1.5	*	9.8	14.5	15.4	15.2	14.5	26.8	5.0	2.8	18.9	21.6
Other	2.1	–	–	2.2	*	1.5	0.6	1.5	1.4	2.5	1.4	3.0	–	2.3	–
NR	14.5	13.1	14.9	16.2	*	12.8	10.2	15.4	7.5	15.6	22.5	7.1	8.3	12.0	6.8

* Question could not be put at the École Polytechnique.

Table 25b Religious faith (percent)

	Ulm	Sèvres	St Cloud	Fontenay	Polytech.	Mines Paris	Mines Nancy	Mines St Et.	Centrale	Agro	ENSIAA	ENA1	ENA2	IEP	HEC
None	42.0	37.9	52.3	42.6	10.2	24.0	28.3	23.1	24.0	15.2	16.9	15.1	33.3	3.2	20.4
Jewish	1.0	1.3	–	–	3.8	2.3	4.2	3.1	1.6	0.4	–	–	–	4.5	3.7
Protestant	4.7	3.9	–	2.9	3.8	4.5	3.0	1.5	3.6	4.0	5.6	4.0	2.8	3.0	3.2
Nonpracticing Catholic	8.8	9.1	11.2	12.5	25.2	8.3	15.7	13.8	12.9	9.4	12.7	12.1	13.9	27.0	16.9
Intermittently practicing Catholic	5.7	10.4	7.5	11.0	16.2	15.0	14.5	15.4	16.3	14.1	18.3	21.2	22.2	20.9	22.3
Regularly practicing Catholic	29.5	31.4	22.4	27.2	35.2	33.1	28.9	40.0	36.3	51.1	29.6	39.4	22.2	36.2	31.4
Other, NR	8.3	5.9	6.5	3.7	5.4	12.8	5.4	3.1	5.2	5.8	16.9	8.1	5.5	5.2	2.0

Table 26 Level of union involvement (percent)

	Ulm	Sèvres	St Cloud	Fontenay	Polytech.	Mines Paris	Mines Nancy	Mines St Et.	Centrale	Agro	ENSIAA	ENA1	ENA2	IEP	HEC
Against	5.2	5.2	1.9	1.5	*	9.0	9.0	16.9	0.2	8.0	8.5	**	**	11.2	18.9
Indifferent	11.9	11.1	6.5	11.8	*	30.8	26.5	23.1	–	25.3	19.7	**	**	20.9	32.0
Sympathizer	0.5	–	–	–	*	4.5	1.2	4.6	0.2	1.1	1.4	**	**	0.2	33.6
Member	47.7	45.7	50.5	36.7	*	25.5	21.7	7.7	13.6	30.4	19.7	19.2	47.2	25.7	8.2
Militant	7.8	7.2	17.7	10.3	*	6.0	3.0	3.1	4.7	7.6	5.6	6.1	11.1	7.2	2.3
Leader	10.3	7.8	10.3	5.9	*	7.5	5.4	4.6	3.2	2.5	2.8	9.1	2.8	2.5	3.4
No – no details	11.4	17.6	7.5	24.3	*	15.8	30.7	38.5	73.9	20.3	35.2	61.6	30.5	26.9	0.5
Yes – no details	2.6	0.7	1.9	6.6	*	0.7	–	–	0.7	1.1	–	–	–	1.7	–
NR	2.6	4.6	3.7	2.9	*	–	2.4	1.5	3.4	3.6	7.0	4.0	5.5	3.8	1.1

* No union at the École Polytechnique.
** At the ENA, the question was worded thus: "Did you belong to a union (or several) before coming to the ENA? If so which one(s) and for how long? Were you – a leader – a militant – member only?"

Table 27 School of thought (percent)

	Ulm	Sèvres	St Cloud	Fontenay	Polytech.	Mines Paris	Mines Nancy	Mines St Et.	Centrale	Agro	ENSIAA	ENA1	ENA2	IEP	HEC
Marxism	17.1	13.7	28.0	15.4	7.9	9.0	6.6	1.5	3.8	3.6	5.6	1.0	–	5.3	3.7
Existentialism	4.1	3.9	1.9	4.4	9.2	6.8	9.0	–	4.1	4.3	–	4.0	–	2.5	10.3
Christian existentialism	7.2	6.5	5.6	8.1	10.8	9.0	7.2	9.2	7.5	12.7	2.8	14.1	5.5	8.7	12.3
Catholicism	10.3	10.4	14.0	15.4	15.2	11.3	6.6	6.1	6.1	19.9	21.1	12.1	8.3	13.2	3.9
Socialism	2.6	0.6	1.9	3.8	3.8	4.5	3.0	1.5	4.1	1.1	1.4	8.1	13.9	7.0	5.9
Rationalism	3.6	3.3	2.8	5.9	7.1	3.7	10.8	–	4.7	1.4	1.4	3.0	11.1	3.0	5.7
Humanism	3.1	4.6	0.9	2.2	3.5	1.5	5.4	–	1.3	3.2	2.8	–	–	2.0	2.5
Technocracy	–	–	–	–	1.3	–	2.4	–	1.3	1.1	–	4.0	2.8	2.7	3.7
Unclear	8.3	4.6	1.9	2.9	10.6	5.2	6.6	13.8	6.3	6.9	14.1	14.1	11.1	21.9	15.9
None/NR	43.5	52.3	43.0	44.8	30.4	48.9	42.2	67.7	60.5	45.6	50.7	39.4	47.2	33.7	35.9

Appendix 4

Blindness

When it comes to analyzing the social effects of the educational system, it is not enough to prove something a hundred times over, because those who are offended by truth can always appeal the verdicts of science in the court of orthodox opinion, which will always rule in their favor. The strictly scientific art of convincing does not have the power to open the eyes of those who will not see. People who are affected by scientific disclosure in their most deeply held convictions, in the vital principle of their existence and their social worth, the culture that possesses them, the school that has made them, and the job that occupies them, can always cling to the shared facts of common sense to denounce as ideology, through a reversal that would be unthinkable, at least today, in any other science, scientific conquests that, here as elsewhere, are the product of the destruction of commonsense beliefs.

I will mention one significant case of such blindness here. In his book on the ENA, from which he "graduated," as they say, only to return as assistant director, Jean-François Kesler starts out by conceding, in as pure an understatement as you could ever find, that "the success rate of candidates from the higher occupational categories is *somewhat higher* than that of candidates originating in the lower categories." He then goes on to state, in perfect contradiction with what he has just written and, as we shall see, with the five pages of statistical tables he provides for his reader, that, on the basis of his study of "individual dossiers," the results of which he does not provide, he is able to conclude that "between 1945 and 1965, there was no correlation between social origins and 'first day exercises', [first day of *concours*, Tr.] or between social origins and 'technical' tests." Carried away by his feeling of triumph, he throws himself into ambitious reflections on education in general: "Contrary to currently fashionable theories, education is not produced by and for the bourgeoisie; it is a common good accessible to all. Students from privileged milieus are always far from being cultured (or from writing correctly at all times)."[1] The rhetoric is that of political polemic, denouncing the unnameable without naming it ("currently fashionable theories"), reducing the theses criticized to the absurd vacuity of the slogan ("by and for the bourgeoisie"), discrediting and disqualifying by reference to shared values ("fashionable"), so many procedures, immediately understood by those in the know, that assume the complicity of a group, routine adherence to *common sense*, that is to say, everything that founds "refutation" on the shrug of the shoulders, the disdainful look, the judgment-as-insult common in encounters among colleagues of similar obedience. But, as irrefutable as doxic discourse is as long as it remains within the circle of the community of belief upon which it is founded, it becomes vulnerable whenever it is foolhardy enough to place itself within the scientific logic of refutation. Indeed, ENA statistics on the distribution of overall candidates, candidates qualifying for the oral,[2] and accepted candidates, according to social, geographic, and academic origins, which Mr Kesler quotes without bothering to read, because resistance and repression are stronger than scientific fact, thoroughly refute his "refutation." They reveal the universal and universally shared culture supposedly measured by the ENA *concours* for what it is, a subculture entirely localized in social space, borne by exemplary figures who are to be found among the highest of Parisian civil servants, the very ones who, through the formally universal logic of the academic *concours*, work, entirely unknowingly, to confer universality upon it, and first and foremost in their own eyes. With undeniable success, as Mr Kesler's blindness will attest.

Tables 28, 29, and 30[3] highlight *four* successive operations of systematically biased selection or *filtering* (beyond any conscious intent on the part of the agents, of course). Given that they obey the same principle, these choices lead to the near complete elimination of certain categories (such as candidates from the working class, children of tradesmen, small-scale merchants, and minor clerical workers in industry and commerce), while other categories, which are very weakly represented in the overall population, such as children of top-ranking civil servants, executives in industry and commerce, and members of the professions,[4] see their representation increase very regularly from year to year (until they constitute the majority of the top grands corps). Whenever we are able to break down categories such as farmer, blue-collar worker, clerical worker, officer, or corporate head, as we can for 1983–5, we note that the most privileged fractions of these categories (the children of large-scale farmers with full-time employees, the children of skilled workers and foremen, office staff, high-ranking officers, or heads of large corporations) always succeed better than the rest of the category (the rare children of minor civil servants, blue-collar workers, clerical workers, and service personnel from the C [clerical] and D [typists] categories of public service all disappear between the written and oral portions of the *concours*).

The children of top-ranking civil servants (category A1) do very well at the ENA and the ENA does very well by them: proportionally high in number as candidates in the *concours*, they have always received very high grades both in the written and the oral sections, and their numbers among those admitted increase continuously over time, as if the institution were getting better at recognizing its own (we are all the more convinced of this because the children of senior civil servants (category A2)[5] who had done very well during the period from 1952 to 1958, decline in number, and the children of mid-level and subordinate civil servants never increase above very low levels, distributed according to the hierarchy). Along with the children of top-ranking civil servants, the favorites of these successive admission procedures are the children of executives in commerce and industry and members of the professions, all located in central positions in the field of power, while the candidates from the two opposite poles, the children of teachers (except those in higher education) and the children of industrial and commercial heads, seem less appreciated, the former, whose success rate is always rather low (relatively), see their numbers decline continuously over time (like the success rate of *normaliens* in the *concours*), while the fortunes of the latter fluctuate, depending on the period. The process of differential elimination is completed with rank at graduation, with the survivors from the different categories obtaining positions in high-level public service in proportion to their original social position – despite the effects of overselection. This is how sons and daughters of workers or subordinate civil servants who succeeded in the entrance *concours* are almost inevitably destined to become *administrateurs civils* and have only very low chances (increasingly low as time goes on) of acceding to the grands corps or the diplomatic corps. In contrast, the children of higher civil servants and (in the time period measured) members of the professions have a much greater likelihood of entering the grands corps, as do the children of industrialists.

Table 28 Candidates, candidates qualifying for the oral, and those accepted; external ENA *concours*; according to father's occupation (1952–1982)

	% candidates	% qualified for oral	% accepted		% candidates	% qualified for oral	% accepted
Farmers				**Civil servants B (executant positions)**			
1952–58	3.4	2.8	2.1	1952–58	7.9	4.2	2.8
1959–65	3.5	2.8	3.1	1959–65	4.2	2.7	2.9
1966–71	2.9	2.8	2.7	1966–71	5.9	5.8	4.3
1972–77	2.7	2.6	2.5	1972–77	4.4	3.7	4.4
1978–82	2.4	2.1	2.2	1978–82	5.4	3.9	2.2
Blue-collar workers				**Industrialists**			
1952–58	1.4	0.9	1.4	1952–58	4.2	5.0	6.6
1959–65	1.9	0.8	0.5	1959–65	4.3	3.4	4.3
1966–71	2.1	2.3	3.4	1966–71	3.8	5.5	5.8
1972–77	2.4	1.6	0.8	1972–77	3.6	3.4	3.1
1978–82	3.4	0.9	0.7	1978–82	9.4	8.8	8.1
Tradesmen, small commerce				**Industrial/commercial *cadres***			
1952–58	14.0	12.0	10.4	1952–58	18.3	20.3	21.9
1959–65	11.5	9.7	8.4	1959–65	20.2	21.0	22.1
1966–71	8.5	7.2	7.5	1966–71	27.3	30.1	29.4
1972–77	5.8	5.5	3.8	1972–77	32.6	33.7	36.2
1978–82	1.9	0.8	0.5	1978–82	34.8	38.0	40.3
Civil servants D (typist)				**Professions**			
1952–58	0.5	0.5	0.3	1952–58	15.0	15.3	15.3
1959–65	0.7	0.3	–	1959–65	18.5	20.3	20.6
1966–71	0.2	0.2	–	1966–71	17.1	17.0	17.2
1972–77	0.4	0.1	–	1972–77	13.7	14.4	15.5
1978–82	0.3	0.2	–	1978–82	12.9	14.2	14.7
Civil servants C (clerical)				**Senior civil servants**			
1952–58	1.7	0.7	–	1952–58	20.4	24.3	24.6
1959–65	1.8	1.3	0.7	1959–65	18.4	18.4	17.0
1966–71	1.3	1.0	0.5	1966–71	16.0	16.2	16.6
1972–77	1.6	0.6	0.2	1972–77	17.9	18.4	15.3
1978–82	0.6	0.6	0.2	1978–82	12.9	12.8	11.0
Clerical, industrial/commercial				**Higher civil servants**			
1952–58	7.0	5.2	3.5	1952–58	4.2	7.1	9.0
1959–65	6.0	7.3	6.7	1959–65	6.1	9.5	10.5
1966–71	5.6	4.0	2.9	1966–71	7.6	9.3	11.4
1972–77	9.4	8.1	7.8	1972–77	4.2	7.0	9.8
1978–82	4.3	2.1	1.0	1978–82	11.3	15.3	19.1

For the period 1952–8, the data covers all preregistered candidates; for the following periods, the data covers those who actually participated.

Source: Table constructed according to ENS statistics, reproduced in J.-F. Kesler, *l'ENA, la société, l'État* (Paris: Berger-Levrault, 1985), pp. 238–42.

Table 29 Candidates preregistered, taking the exam, qualifying for the oral, and accepted; external ENS *concours*; according to father's occupation (1983–1985)

	% preregistered (n = 3,087)	% taking the exam (n = 2,139)	% qualified for oral (n = 485)	% accepted (n = 230)
Farmworker	0.2	0.1	–	–
Farmer without employees	1.2	1.0	–	–
Farmer with employees	0.7	0.7	0.8	1.3
Semiskilled worker	0.8	0.6	0.2	–
Skilled worker	2.2	1.9	1.0	1.3
Foreman	1.1	1.1	0.4	0.4
Service personnel	0.8	0.8	0.2	0.4
Tradesman	1.5	1.3	1.2	0.8
Head small business[1]	7.4	7.5	6.6	4.8
Subordinate civil servant C and D	1.3	0.9	0.4	–
Commercial clerical	1.7	1.6	0.4	–
Office clerical	1.9	2.1	2.5	2.2
Mid-level civil servant B	3.1	3.1	2.1	3.0
Mid-level admin. manager	9.1	8.4	9.5	9.5
Technician	1.7	1.5	0.8	0.2
Noncommissioned officer	0.8	0.8	–	–
Primary teacher	2.9	3.3	2.3	1.7
Head mid-sized business[2]	1.3	1.2	0.8	1.3
Head large business[3]	1.0	1.1	2.3	3.0
Executive, engineer	23.0	22.7	21.6	20.9
Officer	0.8	0.8	0.4	0.4
High-ranking officer, general	2.3	1.9	3.1	2.6
Magistrate	0.5	0.5	0.4	–
Liberal and artistic professions	13.4	13.3	18.1	17.8
Teacher with CAPES	2.6	2.9	2.9	3.9
Teacher with agrégation	1.6	1.8	2.3	3.0
University professor	4.1	4.8	6.8	7.8
Senior civil servant	6.3	5.9	4.7	4.3
Higher civil servant	5.0	6.0	7.6	8.3
None/NR	0.7	0.4	0.4	0.4
Total	100	100	100	100

[1] Fewer than 50 employees.
[2] 50–199 employees.
[3] More than 200 employees.

Source: Statistics established by the ENA. I would like to thank R. Chelle for kindly making these data available to us.

Table 30 Corps assignment of ENA alumni on graduation, according to father's occupation (1953–1982, external *concours*) (percent)

	Affaires Étrangères	Conseil d'État	Inspection des Finances	Cour des Comptes	All grands corps	Administrateurs civils
Farmers						
1953–63	4.0	2.0	8.0	2.0	4.0	5.0
1964–73	2.2	–	3.9	5.7	3.0	6.0
1974–82	2.1	2.3	2.1	2.0	2.0	3.0
Workers, supervisors						
1953–63	–	3.0	–	–	1.0	3.0
1964–73	1.1	2.1	–	1.9	1.0	2.0
1974–82	4.2	–	2.1	2.0	1.0	5.0
Tradesmen, small commerce						
1953–63	7.0	10.0	15.0	8.0	12.0	17.0
1964–73	5.6	10.6	9.8	11.3	11.0	7.0
1974–82	4.2	2.3	2.1	2.0	2.0	7.0
Civil servants C, D						
1953–63	–	–	2.0	4.0	2.0	5.0
1964–73	–	–	–	1.9	1.0	4.0
1974–82	–	–	–	–	–	3.0
Clerical, industrial/commercial						
1953–63	6.0	3.0	4.0	2.0	3.0	11.0
1964–73	9.0	10.6	2.0	13.2	9.0	11.0
1974–82	3.1	–	–	2.0	1.0	4.0
Civil servants B						
1953–63	2.0	2.0	4.0	6.0	4.0	12.0
1964–73	3.4	4.2	3.9	7.5	5.0	6.0
1974–82	4.2	4.5	2.1	4.1	4.0	6.0
Industrialists						
1953–63	9.0	–	6.0	10.0	6.0	3.0
1964–73	4.5	4.2	3.9	3.8	4.0	3.0
1974–82	7.3	13.6	12.8	10.2	12.0	10.0
Industrial/commercial *cadres*						
1953–63	19.0	23.0	17.0	18.0	19.0	13.0
1964–73	30.3	23.4	41.2	11.3	25.0	25.0
1974–82	32.3	22.7	31.9	16.3	24.0	24.0
Professions						
1953–63	13.0	16.0	11.0	18.0	15.0	8.0
1964–73	15.7	12.8	13.7	11.3	13.0	15.0
1974–82	13.7	15.9	27.6	20.4	21.0	12.0
Senior civil servants						
1953–63	20.0	25.0	20.0	20.0	21.0	18.0
1964–73	12.3	10.6	5.9	17.0	11.0	15.0
1974–82	8.3	13.6	8.5	22.4	15.0	17.0
Higher civil servants						
1953–63	20.0	14.0	12.0	13.0	13.0	5.0
1964–73	14.6	21.3	13.7	15.1	17.0	7.0
1974–82	16.7	25.0	10.6	18.4	18.0	11.0
Independent means, no profession						
1953–63	–	2.0	1.0	–	1.0	1.0
1964–73	1.1	–	2.0	–	1.0	0.2
1974–82	–	–	–	–	–	–

Source: ENA statistics, reproduced by J.-F. Kesler, *L'ENA, la société, l'État* (Paris: Berber-Levraut, 1985), pp. 224–6.

If we leave aside the rise in the success rate of working-class candidates around 1968 and children of teachers in 1982, two rogue occurrences that do not seem ascribable to statistical accident and that may bear witness to a certain sensitivity to the times, no doubt completely unconscious, all indices combine to demonstrate the evolution towards self-enclosure of a corps whose social triumph tends to make it all the more certain of itself because, in an intellectual world often lost in awe-struck abdication before the intellectual claims of the new mandarins, nothing comes to disturb its "splendid isolation."

PART IV

The Field of Power and its Transformations

TO THE BOURGEOIS

You are the majority – in number and intelligence; so you are power, which is justice.

Some of you are learned, some landed; the glorious day will come when the learned will become landed, and the landed, learned. Then your power will be complete, and no one will protest against it.

Charles Baudelaire, Salon de 1846

1

Forms of Power and their Reproduction

How could we not recognize the enormity of our plan to compare and contrast the structure of the field of establishment schools to the structure of the field of power itself, and to attempt to demonstrate that the first is linked to the second by a relation of structural homology and, thus, by a very particular relation of causal interdependence? The abyss has never been so wide between the empirical data that would be necessary for thoroughly grounding the theory of the field of power that has gradually emerged throughout our prior historical and sociological research (the former devoted primarily to relations between the intellectual field and the field of power in the nineteenth century, the latter to artistic consumption) and those we were able to collect in a series of empirical research projects specifically on France (but, here again, how can one escape the limits of a particular place when one's very intention is to refuse to be satisfied with the vacuous universality of so-called "theoretical" discourse?).

Ars longa, vita brevis: we must resign ourselves to delaying no further in presenting a provisional and approximate description of this complex universe of objective relations of interdependence (established in and through intersecting patterns of domination) among subfields that are both autonomous and bound together by the organic solidarity of a genuine division of the labor of domination. We do so at the cost of a break with the substantialist mode of thought that upholds both theoretical disquisitions on the "dominant class" in the Marxist tradition and studies on the "elite" aimed at providing an empirical response to the question of "who governs."[1] In both cases, in fact, as in the tradition of the prosopography held dear by historians, people privilege *populations*, in other words, sets of agents susceptible to real partitions (with divisions into "fractions of the dominant class" or "sectors" of the "elite") and bound together by real and directly observable interactions or ties ("connections," for example).

It is all the more difficult to make this break because, unless one is satisfied with "theoretical" projects, one can only construct fields scientifically by relying on data that, wedded as they are to populations (management, professors, bishops, artists), call for ordinary statistical treatment. The chief virtue of correspondence analysis, when you know how to construct the data and read the results according to the logic of the relational mode of thought intrinsic to it, is that it makes it possible to discover systems of relations (among positions, among stances, and between the two spaces so defined). Although inaccessible to the unarmed intuition of ordinary experience, this space of invisible relations is more real than even the most obvious of the immediate facts that constitute commonsense knowledge, such as individuals, groups, and their characteristics, which is where realistic "typologies" stop, and even certain uses of statistics (and correspondence analysis itself), which divide populations into identified classes (by applying constitutive labels), in other words, into substantive units likely to be conceived in and of themselves. Although, at least in this case, it can only be constructed on the basis of populations and their properties, this space is the genuine principle of a simultaneously descriptive and predictive definition of these populations and these properties, redefined in relation to it, that is, relationally. It is indeed only if we think of agents and their accompanying characteristics as strictly relational entities, which arise for both individuals and groups and their properties in their objective relations with other individuals and other groups, with their own specific properties, that we are able to adequately produce and understand the system of relations of opposition and similarity that defines the space of the relevant properties and, at one and the same time, the space of the constructed individuals characterized and positioned by these properties. Unlike the simple and abstract spaces produced by ordinary statistical analysis, the spaces constructed by social science are defined by objective relations among individuals and among properties that are brought together or opposed *in all relevant respects* – from the point of view of their very relation – and are characterized by socio-logically coherent, hence, intelligible, *sets* of properties that are statistically linked (to varying degrees) and practically interchangeable. These properties only function as capital, that is, as a social *power* relation, in and through the field that constitutes them as stakes and instruments of struggle, rescuing them thereby from the meaninglessness and uselessness to which they would be just as necessarily doomed in another field or another state of the same field. More specifically, they are linked by relations, constitutive of the structure of the field, that contribute to determining their efficacy and their value in such a way that, within the field they *contribute* to defining, they are able to produce effects different from the ones they would produce in another field.

THE STRUCTURE OF THE FIELD OF POWER

The field of power is a field of forces structurally determined by the state of the relations of power among forms of power, or different forms of capital. It is also, and inseparably, a field of power struggles among the holders of different forms of power, a gaming space in which those agents and institutions possessing enough specific capital (economic or cultural capital in particular) to be able to occupy the dominant positions within their respective fields confront each other using strategies aimed at preserving or transforming these relations of power. The forces that can be enlisted in these struggles, and the orientation given to them, be it conservative or subversive, depend on what might be called the "exchange rate" (or "conversion rate") that obtains among the different forms of capital, in other words, on the very thing that these strategies aim to preserve or transform (principally through the defense or criticism of representations of the different forms of capital and their legitimacy).

The different forms of capital are specific forms of power that are active in one or another of the fields (of forces and struggles) born of the process of differentiation and autonomization.[2] Within these different gaming spaces, there arise characteristic forms of capital that function as both trumps and stakes. These different forms of capital are themselves stakes in the struggles whose objective is no longer the accumulation of or even the monopoly on a particular form of capital (or power), economic, religious, artistic, etc., as it is in the struggles that play out within each field, but rather the determination of the relative value and magnitude of the different forms of power that can be wielded in the different fields or, if you will, power over the different forms of power or the capital granting power over capital.

This struggle over the power to dictate *the dominant principle of domination*, which leads to a constant state of equilibrium in the partition of power, in other words, to a *division in the labor of domination* (at times intended and conceived as such, and explicitly negotiated), is also a struggle over *the legitimate principle of legitimation* and, inseparably, the legitimate mode of reproduction of the foundations of domination. It can take the form of real face-to-face encounters (as with "palace wars" or armed struggles between temporal and spiritual power holders) or symbolic confrontations (such as those in the Middle Ages in which what was at stake was the precedence of *oratores* over *bellatores*, or the struggles played out over the course of the nineteenth century, and still today, in which what is at stake is the preeminence of merit over heredity or gifts).

No power can be satisfied with existing just as power, that is, as brute force, entirely devoid of justification – in a word, arbitrary – and it must thus justify its existence, as well as the form it takes, or at least ensure that the arbitrary nature of its foundation will be misrecognized and thus that it will be recognized as legitimate. Of course the question of legitimacy is inscribed in practical terms in the very existence of concurrent forms of power that, in and through their very confrontation, and in the antithetical, and often irreconcilable, justifications they oppose to each other, inevitably raise the question of their own justification. It follows that *the reproduction strategies* implemented by the bearers of the different forms of capital in their efforts to preserve or increase their patrimony and, correlatively, to maintain or better their position in social space inevitably include symbolic strategies aimed at legitimating the social foundation of their domination, that is, the form of capital sustaining both their power and the mode of reproduction that is inseparable from it.

The sociodicies through which dominant groups aim to produce "a theodicy of their own privilege," to quote Weber, do not come to us in the form of a unique and fully unified discourse, as the phrase "dominant ideology" would suggest. They are so many points of view on the social world that, as the product of preference (or value) systems originating in the internalization of the structure of the chances for profit objectively inscribed in the amount and structure of one's capital, are differentiated in their grounds and their causes according to the form of capital that needs legitimating as well as its weight in the capital structure (although it is common to all sociodicies that they strive to have inscribed in the *nature* of dominants the foundation of their domination). Landed aristocrats, for example, will be more likely to look to land and blood to ground their necessity as well as their difference with respect to parvenus; new bourgeois "elites" who owe their power to *concours* and diplomas, tend to name merit or natural gifts in direct contrast to the favors and favoritism inscribed in the aristocratic tradition of patronage and clientele.

While the structure of the field of power has undoubtedly included constants throughout the most varied historical configurations, such as, for instance, the fundamental opposition in the division of the labor of domination between temporal and spiritual or cultural power holders – warriors and priests, *bellatores* and *oratores*, businessmen (sometimes called industrial knights) and intellectuals – it depends at any given time on the forms of capital implemented in the struggles for domination and on their relative weight in the structure. And, while this is a case in which the intention to combine theoretical construction and empirical verification reaches its limit, in view of the wide gap between the requirements of object construction and the available data, we can nevertheless attempt to suggest a model of the structure of the field of power as it appears in France today.

To give a first approximation of this structure, we may begin by recalling the results of a previous study (in which statistical constraints compelled us to think in terms of constructed populations) with a simplified form of the diagram of social space proposed in *Distinction* (figure 13). Comparing it to the diagrams representing the space of institutions of higher education (figure 14), we immediately see that the correspondence between the positions occupied by the different occupational categories in social space (according to the synchronically and diachronically defined value of the amount and structure of their capital) and the positions of origin of the establishment school students is nearly perfect, with very few distortions, introduced by adjustments made by the educational institution. To proceed further, we would need to attempt to construct as faithful a representation as possible of the distribution within the field of power of the different fields (and the corresponding powers) of each particular form of power, taking into account all the data likely to provide indices of relative positions, such as the intergenerational (as with so-called "mobility" phenomena) and intragenerational (such as *pantouflage*) flow between positions.

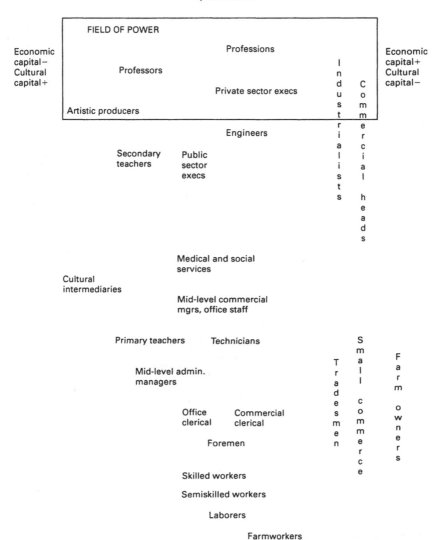

Figure 13 Social space (based on Pierre Bourdieu, *Distinction: A Social Critique of the Judgement of Taste*, trans. R. Nice (Cambridge: Harvard University Press, 1984), pp. 128–9)

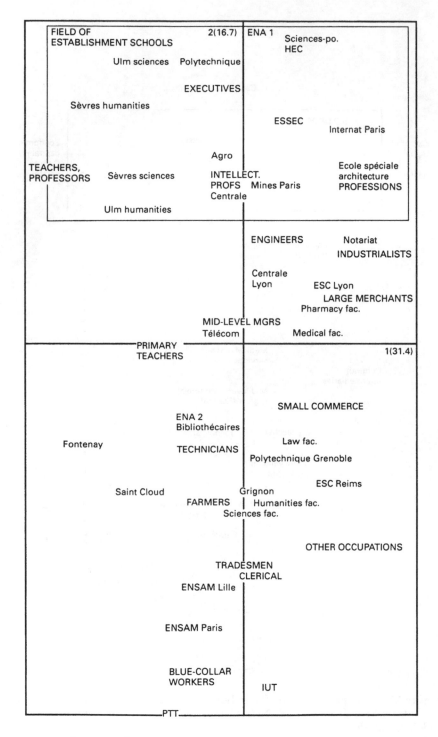

Figure 14 The space of institutions of higher education (n = 84)

In this effort, we may turn to the results of a correspondence analysis done on the entire set of populations we were able to study empirically, these being (proceeding from the economically dominant pole to the economically dominated pole) industrial and commercial heads, Inspecteurs des Finances, Mines engineers, ministry cabinet members, ministry directors, prefects, generals, teachers, and bishops, all characterized by their social origins (which were very carefully analyzed). As figure 15 illustrates, the first factor, which accounts for 31.5 percent of the total inertia, sets bishops and teachers, associated with the lowest origins (farmer, tradesman), apart from corporate heads, associated with the highest positions (board member, banker, large industrialist), and secondarily, from Inspecteurs des Finances, with higher civil servants (Mines engineers and prefects) occupying a central position. The second axis opposes, on one side, bishops – and, to a lesser degree, corporate heads – associated with origins on the side of social space characterized by the preeminence of economic capital over cultural capital (sons of farmers, tradesmen, small-scale merchants) and ties to the private sector, and on the other, generals and, to a lesser degree, Mines engineers, who are strongly associated with origins on the side of the space characterized, in contrast, by the preeminence of cultural capital and ties to the public sector (sons of officers and mid-level managers).

Although this analysis is only of limited value (principally owing to the discrepancies in the categories used for the different populations), it does

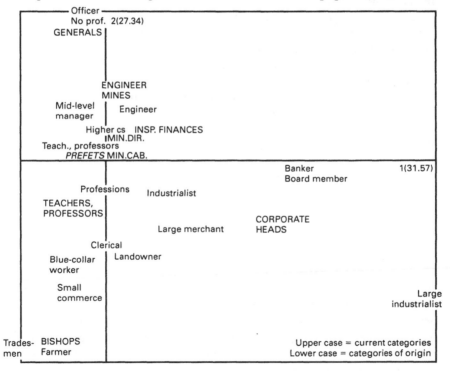

Figure 15 Positions in the field of power (correspondence analysis)

corroborate all of our previous results, both the analysis of inter- and intragenerational flows, which reveal a hierarchy among the fields, and the forms of power or capital that are generated and produced within them. The various fields are distributed within the field of power according to the objective hierarchy of forms of capital, economic and cultural capital in particular, from the economic field to the artistic field, with the administrative and university fields occupying intermediate positions. More specifically, the field of power is organized according to a *chiasmatic structure*. The distribution according to the dominant principle of hierarchization – economic capital – is, as it were, "intersected" by the distribution based on a second principle of hierarchization – cultural capital – in which the different fields line up according to an inverse hierarchy, that is, from the artistic field to the economic field. The field of higher public service owes a number of its properties to the fact that it occupies an intermediate position, which does not mean a neutral one, as is demonstated by, among other things, the fact that intragenerational displacements indisputably move toward the dominant hierarchy; shifts from the administrative field to the economic field, indeed to the private pole of this field, are frequent among higher civil servants and military dignitaries, while movement in the opposite direction is nearly unheard of.

This structural grasp of the field of power makes it possible to see that each of its constituent subfields is organized according to a structure homologous to its own, with, at one pole, the economically or temporally dominant and culturally dominated positions, and at the other, the culturally dominant and economically dominated positions. This obtains in the university field, for example, where the holders of temporal power (or, more accurately, control over the instruments of reproduction), who are often disregarded intellectually, are opposed to the holders of a recognized symbolic capital, who often have no power over institutions. It is also true of the artistic field, where, despite an acceleration in the processes of the consecration of avant-garde artists, related to an institutionalization of the anti-institutional rebellion, it is still possible to oppose those who might be called "Left Bank" artists, who are respected by their peers but are economically and temporally disregarded, to "Right Bank" artists, who combine minimal artistic prestige with sizeable economic profits.[3] And an attempt will be made to show in more detail below that the same form of opposition is found in the economic field itself, with, on one side, "technocratic" chief executives [*patrons*, also boss, Tr.], who are close in this respect to directors in the central administration and members of ministerial cabinets, who owe their position to academic capital and cultural heredity, and whose entire career falls within the public sphere (top state lycées, grandes écoles, high-level public administration, large companies with state ties), and on the other, "family" chief executives, who owe their position to their economic heritage.

The homology between the oppositions observed in different fields (the field of power, the economic field, the university field, the fields of cultural production) underlies an entire set of effects that people are prevented from seeing if they pay attention only to properties based on condition, and fail to consider the properties based on position that attach themselves to populations and their characteristics because of their location within a space of relations. In fact, in most cases, the different levels of opposition and struggle tend to be superposed, with the result being that agents, in the manner of Baudelaire condemning the "bourgeois artist" and the "bourgeois" in the same breath, may be drawn into fundamentally ambiguous and unstable alliances – such as those that develop between the dominated (relatively speaking) in the field of power and the dominated in the larger social field. The homology between the oppositions constitutive of the different fields (especially between the divisions in each specialized field and the social field as a whole) gives an objective foundation to the homology between the principles of vision and division implemented in each of them and to the generalized use of the cardinal oppositions of ordinary language (high/low, light/heavy, civilized/crude, etc.), whose semantic density and suggestive power derive from the fact that they bear all the isomorphic meanings they receive in all the different universes.

The homology between the specialized fields and the overall social field means that many strategies function as *double plays*, which, while neither expressly conceived as such nor inspired by any kind of *duplicity*, operate in several fields at once – in such a way that they are invested with all the subjective and objective attributes of sincerity, which can greatly enhance their symbolic efficacy. We will mention just one among the many possible examples, which will undoubtedly bring many others to mind by analogy: the case of the magistrates of the Paris Parlement who, in their resistance to royal power, "confuse their privileges with the public good" and, mistaking an "anachronistic court of law" for an English-style parliament, go so far as to make themselves the defenders of the "interests of the people," directly present in their mind in the guise of the "public" that observes their deliberations on "public affairs" and encourages, supports, or censures them.[4] The structural ambiguity evident in the polysemy of a discourse endowed with as many registers as there are current or potential fields of reception – a discourse we might call spontaneously polyphonic – sometimes gets separated out and exposed retrospectively. This occurs particularly in the critical situations when a choice must be made between hierarchized loyalties, or in support of reversals in symbolic power relations, both inside and outside the field, and the reforegrounding of those interests inherent in occupying a dominant position (even in a dominated position) that have remained subterraneously active in actions that on the surface are designed to shed doubt on them (processes of the sort often described in the naively finalist language of "recuperation"). And it is again within the logic of the unconscious double play (that is, through the homology between the principles of classification used in the different fields – here, the academic field and the overall social field – which enables a given pair of adjectives, such as light/heavy, to function, with different connotations, in the different universes) that the *social discrimination* implied in the most irreproachable acts of discernment is most invisibly accomplished.

STRATEGIES OF REPRODUCTION

Having thus sketched out the structure of the field of power, we must now attempt a description of its dynamics according to our knowledge of the specific properties of the different forms of capital, especially with regard to their transmission, and according to the advantages they secure for their holders in the competitive struggles which set them against each other. At the risk of oversimplifying, it can be posited at the outset that the entire logic of the struggle for power over forms of power was modified by the two great changes that affected the dominant modes of reproduction, which, already discernible within the field of establishment schools, must now be grasped within the field of power itself, that is, in the competitive struggles that set the holders of the different forms of capital against each other, particularly within the administrative and economic fields. They are, on the one hand, the increase in the relative importance of academic titles (whether coupled with property or not) with respect to property titles, even in the economic field; on the other hand, among the bearers of cultural capital, the decline of technical titles to the advantage of titles guaranteeing general bureaucratic training.

To understand how these modifications in the "exchange rates" among the different forms of capital affected the functioning of the field of power and the field of establishment schools, to which the former is dialectically linked, the first step is to grasp as such *the system of reproduction strategies* constitutive of a *mode of reproduction* and then proceed to examine how a given capital structure tends to dictate a particular mode of reproduction, characterized by a set of reproduction strategies adapted to the particularities of the forms of capital to be reproduced.

To speak of strategies of reproduction is not to say that the strategies through which dominants manifest their tendency to maintain the status quo are the result of rational calculation or even strategic intent. It is merely to register that many practices that are phenomenally very different are objectively organized in such a way that they contribute to the reproduction of the capital at hand, without having been explicitly designed and instituted with this end in mind. This is because these practices are founded in habitus, which, in the most widely different domains of practice, tends to reproduce the conditions of its own production by producing the objectively coherent and systematically characteristic strategies of a particular mode of reproduction. Just as the acquired disposition we call "handwriting," that is, a particular way of forming letters, always produces the same "writing" – that is, graphic lines that, despite differences in size, matter, and color related to writing surface (sheet of paper or blackboard) and implement (pencil, pen, or chalk), that is, despite differences of vehicles for the action, have an immediately recognizable affinity of style, or a family resemblance – the practices of a single agent, or, more broadly, the practices of all agents endowed with similar habitus, owe the affinity of style that makes each a metaphor for all the others to the fact that they are the product of the implementation in different fields of the same schemata of perception, thought, and action.

Thus, restoring to scientific analysis the unity that is inscribed in practices, the same concept of reproduction strategy can be used to describe practices that the human sciences apprehend as scattered and separate: *fertility strategies*, for example, extended long-term strategies (since the entire future of a lineage and its patrimony depends upon them) that aim to reduce the number of offspring and, hence, the number of claimants to the patrimony, strategies that may employ both direct methods, such as the various techniques of limiting the birthrate, and indirect methods, for example, postponing or forgoing marriage, which has the dual advantage of both preventing biological reproduction and excluding certain parties from the inheritance, at least in effect (this is the function of the channeling of certain aristocratic and bourgeois children toward the priesthood during the *ancien régime*, and the celibacy of the youngest son in certain peasant traditions);[5] *inheritance strategies*, which aim to ensure the transfer of the patrimony between generations with the least possible loss, among which we should locate (if this is in fact possible using traditional research methods) not only the codified measures of custom and the law, but also all the devices and subterfuges that dominants and their financial advisors are constantly inventing, which extend from the purchase of paintings to various forms of fraud; conscious and unconscious *education strategies* – one particular aspect of which is the scholastic strategies of schooled families and children – extended long-term investments that are not necessarily perceived as such and that cannot be reduced, as the economics of "human capital" would have it, to their strictly economic or even monetary dimension since they aim primarily to produce social agents both capable and worthy of receiving the group inheritance, that is, of being inherited by the group; *strategies* we might call *prophylactic*, designed to maintain the biological heritage of the group by ensuring its members continuous or intermittent preventive care; *purely economic strategies*, either short or long term, such as credit, savings, and investment activity designed to ensure the reproduction of the economic heritage; short-term or long-term *social investment strategies* that are either consciously or unconsciously oriented toward the establishment and maintenance of directly mobilizable and utilizable social relations, that is, toward the transformation, brought about by the alchemy of exchange, of money, work, time, etc., into lasting *obligations*, either subjectively felt (feelings of gratitude, respect, etc.) or institutionally guaranteed (rights); *marriage strategies*, a particular case of the preceding strategies, which must ensure the biological reproduction of the group without threatening its social reproduction through mismarriages, as well as provide for the maintenance of its social capital through alliance with a group that is at least its equal in all socially relevant respects; and finally, *sociodicy strategies*, which, as we have seen, aim to legitimate domination and its foundation (that is, the type of capital on which it rests) by naturalizing them.

Thus, working back from the *opus operatum*, from practices that reveal themselves to intuition like a data rhapsody, to the *modus operandi*, to the generating and unifying habitus that produces objectively systematic strategies, it is possible to grasp the practical relations that develop continuously among the various reproduction strategies and to understand in particular the strange solidarity among the levels of practice that, rather like the functional substitutes biologists describe, enables marriage strategies, for example, to make up for failed fertility strategies.

Indeed, given that the various reproduction strategies are implemented at different points in a life cycle in an irreversible process, they are also *chronologically articulated*, each one obliged at all times to reckon with the results of the particular strategy that has preceded it or that has a shorter temporal frame. So, for example, in the Béarnaise tradition, marriage strategies were highly dependent on a family's fertility strategies (through the number of claimants to the estate, as well as their sex, in other words, the number of offspring to be endowed with an inheritance or a compensation), on education strategies, the success of which was the prerequisite for the implementation of strategies aimed at distancing girls and younger sons from the inheritance (the former through marriage and the latter through celibacy and emigration), and on purely economic strategies aimed among other things at maintaining or increasing their capital in land, etc. This interdependence extended over several generations; a family might have to agree to heavy self-imposed sacrifices over a long period of time to compensate for the outgoings (at times in land) necessary for "dowering" an overly large family with land or money or to reestablish the material and especially symbolic position of the group in the wake of a mismarriage.

We see the same interdependence today between academic strategies and fertility strategies, and it appears, in fact, that all else being equal, opportunities for getting an education are always closely linked to a lower fertility rate. This is undoubtedly because a larger family, given the numerous expenses it must meet, tends to discourage the drive toward education, but it is also and especially because academic ambition was inscribed from the very beginning in the predisposition toward self-denial in favour of ascension that was at the root of the limitation on fertility. And just as academic strategies must reckon with the results of fertility strategies, which already incorporate the demands of academic investment, marriage strategies are undoubtedly not independent of academic strategies, or, more generally, of reproduction strategies as a whole. We need only think of the transformation of the strategies that the business bourgeoisie traditionally implemented in marrying its daughters, which, like the concomitant transformation of fertility strategies (which it undoubtedly partially explains), is correlative to a transformation of its objective relations with the educational system. With the progress in women's access to higher education, the mechanisms of self-orientation ("vocation") and selection that produce very socially homogeneous academic groups (faculté or école, discipline, etc.) have tended to insure homogamy at least as effectively, but in a much more unobtrusive manner, as family interventionism, especially family efforts at organizing directly controlled occasions for meeting mates (dances, surprise parties, debutante balls, etc.). This unexpected effect of schooling has undoubtedly contributed more than a little to encouraging families to give up their policy of control (which was difficult to implement anyway) in favor of a laissez-faire attitude, just when the system of the criteria that determined the value of their daughters in the matrimonial market, whether in terms of economic capital (dowry) or symbolic capital in respectability (virginity, appearance, etc.), was being completely redefined.[6] And the reforms in family law instituted throughout the 1970s (under the direction of Valéry Giscard d'Estaing, a president who reproduces the entire evolution of the bourgeoisie in a personal trajectory leading from the most traditional fractions, close to Pétainism, to the new bourgeoisie) are the political accompaniment, necessary for adjusting norms to practices, of a transformation of the mode of reproduction in force in the upper bourgeoisie. The new measures concerning, in no particular order, parental authority (replacing paternal authority), spousal equality in matrimonial matters, estate management, divorce, cohabitation, voluntary termination of pregnancy, etc., merely write into law a set of practices whose appearance in the new bourgeoisie had been either authorized, favored, or determined by the transformation of the mode of reproduction.[7]

Yet there is probably nothing that more clearly highlights the need to conceive of the system of strategies of reproduction as such than the example of educational investment, doomed by the division of labor among the disciplines to be the object of only partial and abstract understanding. Economists deserve obvious credit for explicitly raising the question of the relationship between the profits ensured by educational investment and those ensured by economic investment – and its evolution over time. But, in addition to the fact that their measurements of the return on academic investments only account for profits and costs in terms of money, or in units directly convertible into money, such as the cost of going to school and the opportunity cost of the time spent there, they cannot account for the relative importance given by different agents to economic and cultural investment because they do not systematically take into account the *structure* of the differential chances for profit promised to these agents by the different markets as a function of the amount and the structure of their patrimony.[8] Moreover, by failing to consider strategies of academic investment as one of a set of educational strategies and as part of the overall system of reproduction strategies, economists are condemning themselves, through an inevitable paradox, to missing the best hidden and most socially important of educational investments – the domestic transfer of cultural capital. Naive investigations into the relationship between the *ability* for studies and investment in studies become meaningless when we consider the fact that ability, or "gifts," is also the product of an investment in time and cultural capital.[9] We can see why Gary Becker, in his attempt to evaluate the profits of academic investment, could not get beyond individual monetary yield other than to investigate, following a typically functional-ist logic, either the return on educational expenditures for society as a whole (*the social rate of return*)[10] or the contribution that education makes to "national produc-tivity" (*the social gain of education as measured by its effects on national productivi-ty*).[11] This definition of the functions of education, which ignores the contribution that the educational system makes to the reproduction of social structure in sanc-tioning the hereditary transfer of cultural capital, is in fact implied from the outset in a definition of "human capital" that, despite its "humanist" connotations, remains entrenched in economism and disregards the fact that the economic and social return on academic stock depends on the social capital (also inherited) that may be put to its service.[12]

All agents and all groups do not use all the available reproduction strate-gies in the same way and to the same degree, and the system of reproduc-tion strategies actually implemented by each agent or group depends in each case on the amount and especially the structure of their patrimony. Different structures of inclinations to invest or, if you will, different *prefer-ence systems* or systems of interests are imposed upon agents, primarily through *the structure of the differential chances for profit* that investments are objectively offered by the different social markets. So, for example, the inclination to invest in scholastic work and industriousness does not merely depend on the amount of one's cultural capital; it also depends on the rela-tive weight of this cultural capital in the structure of one's heritage. This becomes clear when we compare the educational investments of clerical workers or primary school teachers to those of the heads of family busi-nesses. In contrast to the former, who tend to concentrate all their invest-ments in the academic market, the latter, whose social success does not depend to the same degree on academic success, invest less "interest" and work in their studies and do not get the same return on their cultural capi-tal. The "interest" that an agent (or a class of agents) brings to her "studies" (which, along with inherited cultural capital, on which it partially depends, is one of the most powerful factors of academic success) depends not only on her current or anticipated academic success (by anticipated is meant her chances of success given her cultural capital), but also on the degree to which her social success depend on her academic success. Of course, agents (or groups) depends less and less on their cultural capital for their reproduc-tion the richer they are in economic capital, and the economic and social return of academic capital depends in many cases on the social (or even eco-nomic) capital that allows it to acquire its full value, a dual demonstration of the dominated status of this form of capital.

Thus the structure of the system of reproduction strategies characteristic of a domestic unit depends on the relative value of the profits it can expect from its different investments according to its real power over the different institutionalized mechanisms (such as the economic market, the matrimonial market, and the academic market) able to function as instruments of reproduction that are either currently or potentially available to it as a function of the amount and the structure of its capital. It is the structure of the distribution of power over the instruments of reproduction, in a given state of the dominant definition of what is legitimately transferable and how, that determines the differential return that the different instruments of reproduction are able to offer the investments of the different agents (or classes of agents), hence determining the reproducibility of their patrimony and their social position, thus the structure of their differential inclinations to invest in the different markets.

It follows that any change in the relationship between a person's patrimony (in terms of both amount and structure) and the system of instruments of reproduction, along with the correlative transformation of the system of chances for profit, tends to give rise to a *restructuring* of the system of investment strategies. Those endowed with capital are able to maintain their position in social space (or in the structure of a given field, such as the artistic or scientific field) only at the cost of *reconverting* the forms of capital they hold into forms that are more profitable or more legitimate in the current state of the instruments of reproduction.[13] These reconversions objectively imposed by the need to keep up the value of an inheritance may be subjectively experienced as changes of taste or vocation, in other words, as conversions.

Many of the errors in judgment made by those who naively raise the naive question of "democratization" and the evolution of "social mobility" are a consequence of their failure to acknowledge phenomena of *structural shift* (describing the intergenerational passage from the status of primary teacher to that of a teacher in a collège d'enseignement général [a lesser secondary school in former system, sometimes physically attached to a primary school, Tr.] as "upward mobility," for example, when it is only an apparent move that is in fact destined to maintain the teacher's relative position). In addition, a unidimensional and linear vision of social space (with its image of the "social ladder") purely and simply obscures the fact that the reproduction of social structure may, under certain conditions, require very weak "occupational heredity" (or, if you will, very weak "rigidity"). This is the case whenever agents are only able to maintain their *position* in the social structure at the cost of a reconversion of their capital, in other words, at the cost of a change in *condition* (with the transition from the condition of small landowner to that of low-level civil servant, or from that of a minor tradesman to that of a commercial clerical worker). It is thus necessary to distinguish between *displacements within the space of a single field*, related to the accumulation, positive or negative, of the form of capital that constitutes the specific stakes in the competition that defines it in its own right, and *displacements between fields*, related to the reconversion of a given form of capital into another form, currently in use in another field, with the meaning and value of both classes of displacement being dependent on the objective relations among the different fields, hence on the conversion rates of the different forms of capital and the changes that affect them over time, following struggles among the holders of the different forms of capital.

In social universes in which the dominants must constantly change to stay the same, they necessarily tend to be divided, especially during periods of rapid transformation in the current mode of reproduction, according to the "degrees" (and the forms) of reconversion of their strategies of reproduction. The agents or groups best equipped with the forms of capital giving access to the new instruments of reproduction, who are thus the most likely and most able to undertake a reconversion, are opposed to the agents or groups most closely linked to the threatened form of capital. So, for example, in the period preceding the Revolution of 1789, the lesser aristocrats from the provinces who had neither fortune nor education – or, in the period just prior to the crisis of May 1968, teachers of disciplines directly dependent on recruitment *concours* (grammar, classics, and even philosophy) – were likely to seek to deny or to magically compensate for their economic and social regression through a conservatism born of despair. These two polar positions correspond to two forms of conservative sociodicy, the one that aims above all to legitimate the old mode of reproduction, by saying what formerly went without saying and by transforming *doxa* into *orthodoxy*, and the one that aims to rationalize (in both senses of the term) reconversion by hastening awareness of the transformations and the elaboration of the adapted strategies and by legitimating these new strategies in the eyes of the "integrists."

It is struggles of this kind within the field of power today, and even within the field of economic power, that set against each other agents and groups of agents who are differentiated by the structure of their patrimony, that is, by the profile of the distribution of the different forms (and subforms) of capital they possess, and who consequently turn toward entirely different reproduction strategies. They either give contrasting weight to economic and academic investments, or, as is increasingly the case these days, they are differentiated by the subforms of academic capital they seek to secure in making significantly increased academic investments. Yet we still see within the same economic space the coexistence of the family-controlled transfer of a hereditary right to property, as with the heads of family businesses, and the transfer of a power limited to a lifetime (founded on the academic title) more or less completely guaranteed and controlled by the school (and the state) – which, unlike property titles or titles of nobility, cannot be passed down along hereditary lines.

THE FAMILY MODE OF REPRODUCTION

For family businesses, the strictly economic strategies aimed at ensuring the development of the business are nearly inseparable from the strategies aimed at ensuring the reproduction of the family and especially its integration, one of the principal preconditions for the perpetuation of the family's power over the business. Whenever a family has complete control over an estate consisting of an agricultural, industrial, or commercial company, the strategies through which it aims to ensure its own reproduction (marriage strategies, fertility strategies, education strategies, succession strategies) tend to be subordinated to the strictly economic strategies aimed at ensuring the reproduction of its economic capital.[14] Since the same ends require the same strategies, we find constants such as a concerted effort toward homogamy and an obsessive fear of mismarriage, a strict attitude toward education and the praise of "family spirit," succession strategies aimed at avoiding the division of the estate, etc. And it would be a simple matter, in each particular case, to bring out everything that, in a given state of a given company at a given point in time, in its rise or its decline, depends upon the reproduction strategies of all the members of a lineage, from the founders on down.

It is hardly necessary to recall the extreme vigilance and rigor with which the great bourgeois dynasties managed their *matrimonial exchanges*. It will suffice to mention one case where the desire to integrate the reproduction strategies of the family group and those of the family business is particularly obvious, this being the marriages between the Gillet family of Lyons (founders of a textile dyeing company that became one of the largest French manmade textile companies, which produced the vice president, in 1972, and president, from 1973 to 1979, of Rhône-Poulenc) and the Motte family of Roubaix, one of the largest textile dynasties, which together orchestrated several considerable financial operations (such as the acquisition or absorption of other companies): Edmond Gillet, born 1873, son of Joseph Gillet, who gave a substantial boost to the family business, married Léonie Motte, daughter of Albert, who was also president of the Mines de Lens Company, while Fernand Motte, Léonie's brother, married Mathilde Balay, daughter of Henri Balay and Marguerite Gillet, sister of Edmond.

But nothing could top the case of the Michelin family for illustrating how marriage strategies and economic strategies are interwoven, how marriage strategies and financial liaisons are superposed, and how the success of marriage strategies contributes to the success of economic strategies and the continued expansion of the business. "Cousins should marry cousins so that the dowry remains in the family," recommended André Michelin (died 1931). His advice was well heeded; *endogamy*, which tends to ensure the integration of the group, enabling it to safeguard its capital as well as the secret of its business dealings and the prestige of the lineage, is a constant in the family. André Michelin and his brother Edouard married two sisters, Sophie and Marie-Thérèse Wolff. Three of Edouard Michelin's six children (Marguerite, Étienne, and Hélène) married children (Jean, Joseph, Hélène) of Jacques Callies, a naval engineer,[15] and Marie Aussédat (whose family owned the Aussédat paper mills); a fourth, Anne, married Robert Puiseux, president, then honorary president and director of the Citroën Corporation (from 1958 to 1970), co-director of the Compagnie Générale des Établissements Michelin from 1938 to 1959 and member of the supervisory board from 1959 on (three other Michelins married Puiseux). François Michelin, currently chief executive, initially co-director of Michelin and Company with his uncle, Robert Puiseux, then sole director and again co-director with François Rollier (son of Petrus Rollier and Marthe Callies, herself a daughter of Jacques Callies and Marie Aussédat), since 1968 a director of the Citroën Corporation, married Bernadette Montagne; his sister Geneviève married Rémy Montagne (a deputy from the Eure *département* and former mayor of Louviers); his other sister, Marthe, married Marie Montagne, the mayor of Mirabeau. As proof that the principle at the root of reproduction strategies as a whole can be found in the immanent necessities of the position that is to be reproduced, and in the generative and unifying habitus that they form, a high degree of endogamy goes hand in hand with a high concentration of economic activity surrounding a very particular product and the deliberate rejection of the diversification systematically practiced by financial capitalism. So, for example, François Michelin, rejecting any form of diversification that does not stem from "technical logic" and is "simply an expression of a will to power," attributes his success to the fact that his rivals, who were highly diversified and thus had a large number of "alternative solutions" at their disposal, in contrast to his company, for which "the only solution was the tire," "didn't believe in the radial tire and woke up too late," thereby enabling Michelin to capture the largest share of the market.[16]

We must consider in the same vein the fertility strategies behind the fact that very large families (those with seven or more children), completely absent from the top positions at technocratically controlled companies, are found relatively often among the heads of family companies (10 percent; with the average family numbering 3.5 children, compared to 3.1 in technocratically controlled companies and 2.6 in large public companies). Invoking the dispositions favored by Catholic ethics in matters of procreation and birth control is not enough (the explanation, in this case, would itself require an explanation). In fact, the family business frees one from any kind of limit on fertility; on the contrary, it encourages procreation, at least during the expansion phase when growth in the instrument of production corresponds to growth in the lineage, which can thus be gradually absorbed either through the creation of new branches initially financed by the parent company or by the employment of additional children as guarantors or managers. In addition, wealth in children constitutes in and of itself, and also by allowing the propagation of capital through marital alliances, a way of accumulating social capital – which we know to be made up of the sum, always potentially mobilizable, of all the forms of capital possessed by each of the members of the group.

But large families cannot remain so unless they manage to protect themselves from division and the resulting break-up of their estate. This is of course the reason for all the succession strategies aimed at preventing property from leaving the family; we know for example that the textile families of northern France in essence disinherited their daughters, through whom property might be passed on to outsiders, using the fiction of the corporation, which shelters material assets from partition. It is also, and especially, the reason for the education strategies and all the practices (such as family parties and ceremonies) aimed at creating ties of solidarity among all descendants so that the death of one of the holders of rights to the patrimony will be the occasion not of division but rather of a reorganization of the commonly held concerns. The reasons for the extreme attention given to marriage, especially to the marriages of future company heads, cannot be reduced to the desire to strengthen the business by bringing in economic capital, in the form of dowries or inheritances, and social capital, through the expansion of its network of connections. Seeking to maintain the strictest homogamy undoubtedly also stems from a concern for safeguarding the ethical dispositions regarded as the prerequisite for the economic success of the business and the affirmation of the family's social status. Admitting into the family only those women who are capable of embodying and inculcating respect for bourgeois virtues – the work ethic, an eye for saving, family spirit[17] – fulfills a function entirely similar to the *exclusivism* that leads to the choice of private educational establishments and highly selective meeting places. Indeed, family upbringing, generally quite strict, and schooling, usually entrusted to Jesuits or to English-style institutions such as the École des Roches, are expected above all to inculcate religiously underwritten ethical dispositions – especially, of course, for girls, entrusted to boarding schools such as "Les Oiseaux."

The École des Roches, in Verneuil-sur-Avre, Normandy, was founded in 1899 by Edmond Demolins, "thinker and sociologist," disciple of Frédéric Le Play, friend of the Baron de Coubertin, and a "great admirer of English pedagogical methods" (cf. his works, *Anglo-Saxon Superiority: To What Is It Due?* and *L'Éducation nouvelle*), as Jean-Claude Courbin, grandson of the founder, writes in a booklet published in 1974 on the occasion of the school's seventy-fifth anniversary ("Demolins écrivain et conférencier," in *Edmond Demolins, qui était-ce?*). This same eulogist expresses the entire educational philosophy of the heads of family businesses in a single sentence: "You had to be courageous in that day and age to undertake such a project in a French society then essentially centered around the Napoleonic lycée-barracks and the university-machine that turned out docile and more or less mediocre civil servants." At the end of the 1970s, the École des Roches numbered more than 400 boarding students, both boys and girls (about 120 of whom were foreigners), or about 20 students per class and 12 per lab; the cost for boarding per trimester for the year 1977–8 ranged from 7,205 francs for a student in the *septième* or *sixième* to 10,155 francs for a student in the *terminale*. The school's brochure describes the sumptuous Norman manor where the students live "just like at home" as follows: "A country campus whose only walls are trees, hedges, and the Iton River; sports fields, air, light, squirrels in the pines. Guichardière, les Fougères, la Colline, le Moulin. (...) Generously spaced about the grounds, Roches dormitories house between 12 and 40 children or adolescents each. They live as they would at home in personalized rooms, choosing roommates with similar interests (five or six boys to a room, two or three girls); there are study halls, game rooms, libraries, and meeting rooms. Each house has its own style, its gardens, its tennis courts, and ... its traditions. When two graduates meet, they introduce themselves as *"Pins 1924, Vallon 1907!"* Ever faithful to the glorification of physical activity that the founders, in a spirit illustrated by Coubertin, intended as a counterweight to the intellectualism of "ace test takers," the school attaches great importance to the most *select* sporting activities (the brochure pictures students fencing and, dressed in very British garb, grey slacks and a dark jacket, leaning over a private airplane sporting the school's coat of arms or leading a horse by the bridle): "Roches boasts a modern gymnasium, an equally large riding area (1,000 square metres), a large number of horses and ponies, a track, soccer and rugby fields, basketball and volleyball courts, eight tennis courts, a go-kart track, a martial arts room, a heated pool, covered in the winter, and even an airfield, all of which give its students the opportunity to participate in all the sports they love and to develop self-control, physical strength, and a sporting mind."

Such a relationship to the educational system – and especially to *public* educational institutions – is inseparable from a view of the world that gives precedence to everything that falls within the realm of the private. The rejection of public education is one aspect of an overall defiance toward the secular state and so-called "republican" social philosophy, a stance that aims to free private domains (private companies, private schools) from the clutches of bureaucratic universalism. Private education is not simply an exclusive education, whose limit is, probably quite frequently, recourse to private home tutors,[18] and a sheltered education, guaranteeing adherence to the cardinal virtues of conservative morality – work, family, and property; it is also a religious education that, through its familial appearance as much as the personalist "philosophy" that permeates it, tends to reduce the public to the private, the social to the personal, the political to the ethical, and the economic to the psychological. In short, it tends to effect a depoliticization that returns to the domain of the most irreducibly singular "actual experience" all the experiences that politicization aims on the contrary to detach from the "person" in his or her singularity in order to make them appear to be common to a class.

Thus, as long as heads of family businesses hold the power to pass down, from person to person, usually, that is, from father to son, a form of power that must be wielded personally by its holder and that requires no competence other than that which can be acquired through direct experience in the family business itself, they have no use for an institution like the school, which only grants its certificates of competence claiming universal validity in exchange for guarantees of ability that also claim to be universal. They are perfectly satisfied with a mode of reproduction in which institutions of secondary or even higher education, passage through which is merely a kind of statutory bourgeois right, are reduced to a function of legitimation. Their sense of owing their success only to their experience and their abilities, acquired on the job, through practice, and their defiance toward all forms of abstract, bookish knowledge hardly lead them to value academic titles or the institution that grants them. When the imperatives of social rank require it, they demand of the educational system only those certificates of good moral education and social distinction that private education is prepared to provide, or, if truly necessary, guarantees of technical competence that make it possible for the second-generation head to have authority over his technical managers – those conferred by the École Centrale (an institution directly set up to respond to the expectations of the traditional body of heads of businesses), for example, or by the minor engineering schools.[19]

One of their favorite topics of discussion is deploring graduates' lack of skills. So, for example, when asked about the training of his managers, Marcel Fournier, founder and chief executive of the Carrefour company, who, after completing his secondary education at the Collège de Mongré in Villefranche-sur-Saône, worked in the family notions shop, first as a "clerk," than as a "manager," before founding the Carrefour company with Denis Defforey (the first supermarket opened in Annecy in 1960), explains: "They started out as department managers in the previous stores. And (. . .) they learned on the job. We have people of all types. There are some who have only gone through secondary school, and even then, not all of them. Some have gone to business school. There are even one or two Sciences-po graduates. And they all started by working their way up the ladder (. . .). Our desire to see them move up through the ranks, starting at the manual level, certainly kept away some capable young men, the ones who put too much faith in the value of their diplomas and not enough in the value of experience" ("Facc-à-face avec Marcel Fournier," by R. Priouret, *Expansion* (June 1973), p. 221). The same views are expressed by André Blanchet, who, after studying at a professional school, which has since become the Diderot technical lycée, began at 17 at Brandt and Fouilleret, manufacturers of industrial electrical equipment, before founding Télémécanique Électrique in 1924 (with his brother Pierre, and with Jules Sarrasin, graduate of Arts et Métiers, and Michel Le Gouellec, of the Institut Électrotechnique de Grenoble): "To me, creativity is innate. Those possessed of it see new products effortlessly take shape in their hands. Of course it's better if they're engineers." If an engineer from a grande école "hasn't got the creative spirit, he won't get one from me; on the other hand, an unschooled man may have this spirit (. . .). The most creative man we ever had – he's retired now – was a former lathe operator who didn't go beyond primary school. He had an extraordinary creative gift" (cf. R. Priouret, *La France et le management* (Paris: Denoël, 1968), pp. 251–2, interview with André Blanchet).

It may be objected that language hostile to diplomas and to those who hold them is no less frequent at the other end of the space of company heads, among the enthusiastic supporters of *man development* at the topmost companies who reject the use of the diploma as the exclusive criterion for recruitment (cf., for example, J. Fontaine, "Les grandes entreprises jugent les grandes écoles," *Expansion* 109 (July – Aug. 1977), pp. 66–71). In fact, such professions of faith are contradicted in a thousand ways. For example, when asked about the value they place on diplomas as a means of gaining access to various positions in their company, these same people (who give the diploma critical weight in recruiting entry-level professional staff) grant first place, as in reality, to Polytechnique and the ENA for management positions, to the ENA and HEC for financial positions, to HEC and the ESSEC for positions in trade, to Centrale for production, and to Sciences-po for personnel administration (ibid., p. 68). And we know, moreover, that the academic properties of managerial staff overall tend to mirror very closely the properties of their chief executives, who have an increasing tendency to surround themselves with title holders (who usually have identical titles to their own) the more diplomas they themselves possess.[20]

For the heads of family businesses, the nontransferable right of succession provided by the school is merely a last resort, which they attempt to secure either when their business is threatened or when it can no longer provide jobs for all members of the family, or a substitute whose acquisition is only necessary when the right of ownership is not sufficient. Witness the statistics in table 31.

Among these 141 heads of businesses and establishments in the Rhône-Alpes region,[21] we note that academic capital, which tends to increase as ties with the founder weaken, constitutes the nearly obligatory precondition for access (in more than two-thirds of the cases) for those with no such ties. In other words, although academic capital is not absolutely essential for starting up a business, it becomes increasingly necessary when it comes to preserving or enlarging it (usually in the form of law degrees), and it is nearly indispensable for acceding to the helm once the business is fully developed.[22]

Paradoxically enough, the opportunity given to the heads of family businesses to provide positions for their children probably lies behind the decline in the number of these businesses. This is not only due to the increase in employee-related expenses that results from the artificial increase in hereditary "charges" born of the fictitious decrease in the positions earmarked for heirs more or less "capable" of filling them, but also because it enables these heads to take to the absolute limit, that is, to absurdity and failure, all reconversion of at least a portion of their heirs, through recourse to other reproduction strategies, for example, all those strategies that assume the accumulation of academic capital.[23]

Table 31   Educational background of heads of businesses in the Rhône-Alpes region, by status (percent; n = 141)

	Founder	Heir	2nd gen. + heir	No relation	Head of establ.	All
Below bac	81	50	26	19	15	40
Higher educ., non science	9	28	26	10	9	16
Higher educ., sciences	9	17	39	67	73	40
Higher educ., both		6	9	5	3	4

Source: J. Saglio, "Qui sont les patrons?" *Économie et Humanisme* 236 (July–Aug. 1977), pp. 6–11.

THE SCHOOL-MEDIATED MODE OF REPRODUCTION

In the mode of reproduction characteristic of large bureaucratic companies, the academic title ceases to be a statutory attribute (like a Rothschild's law degree) and becomes instead a genuine *entry pass*: the school – in the guise of the grande école – and the corps, a social group that the school produces apparently *ex nihilo* and, in fact, from properties that are also related to the family, take the place of the family and family ties, with the cooptation of classmates based on school and corps solidarity taking over the role played by nepotism and marital ties in businesses that have the privilege of the transfer of privileges.

We thus note that the proportion of higher education graduates among the heads of the top industrial, commercial, and banking institutions increases markedly when we go from family-controlled companies (that is, companies whose stock is largely held by a particular family) to technocratic companies (that is, companies whose capital is dispersed among a large number of organizations, businesses, or individuals) or nationalized companies. Only 3 percent of the chief executives of family-controlled companies report two or more higher education diplomas, compared to 35 percent of the chief executives of foreign subsidiaries, 73 percent of the chief executives of technocratically controlled companies, and 74 percent of the chief

Table 32   Academic capital of chief executives according to type of control (percent)

	Family control (n = 82)	*Foreign control* (n = 42)	*Technocratic control* (n = 45)	*State control* (n = 31)
Secondary schooling or higher education unfinished	21.5	10.0	4.5	3.0
Exclusively law	18.0	17.0	6.5	16.0
Engineering petite école	19.0	7.0	2.0	–
Humanities, sciences, medicine	4.0	5.0	–	3.0
Centrale, Mines Paris, Nancy, St Étienne	9.0	7.0	15.5	–
Sciences-po	15.0	10.0	38.5	36.0
HEC or other business school	7.5	19.5	2.0	–
Polytechnique only	1.0	14.5	–	10.0
Polytechnique, Mines, Ponts	5.0	10.0	31.0	29.0
Total	100	100	100	100

Because we were unable to precisely determine the type of control for 16 of the companies in the sample, the table includes only 200 companies.

executives of state-controlled companies; the first category more often went to provincial private secondary schools, principally the Collège des Roches (the percentages for provincial private schools overall being 31 percent, 18 percent, 20 percent, and 7 percent). The same pattern of differences is also found for type of title, the proportion of those with the most prestigious titles (such as X-Mines) increasing sharply as we move from "family" businesses to "public" companies.

The strategies used by the grands corps in defending their social capital obey a logic very similar to that of families – which is understandable given that, in both cases, the value of each member depends on the contribution of all the others as well as on the possibility of actually mobilizing the capital held by the group, hence on the real solidarity among the members of the group. Thus, whenever a member of the group is nominated to a prestigious position, the social and symbolic capital of all the others is enhanced and, as the saying goes, "their stocks go up." We could thus draw up a sort of summary of the overall capital of the various corps using the table of equivalences in *social stature* suggested by an experienced observer: "The president of a top national corporation 'is worth' more than a ministerial delegate or a ministry general secretary; a position as general manager of a public company is worth several jobs as division manager in the central administration."[24] It follows that grands corps capital, like family capital, cannot be left to the whims of individual initiative. It can only escape the permanent threat of devaluation and discredit if it is given constant attention and rational management – each corps has a "board of eminent members" headed by a "corps chief," or "corps conscience," who keeps watch on the choices made by *polytechniciens* and "follows the evolution of the class rank of the first and last student to choose membership in the corps."[25]

All reproduction strategies imply a form of *numerus clausus*. They in effect fulfil the functions of inclusion and exclusion that together maintain the corps at a constant size by limiting either the number of its biological products (although only the family is able to control fertility strategies in this way, within certain limits) or the number of individuals entitled to join it (in order to ensure that the latter do not exceed the availability of the positions determining membership in the corps), and by simultaneously excluding a portion of the biological products of the corps (with their consent), who are sent off toward other universes or kept in an ambiguous or reduced state. In the case of the aristocracy of the *ancien régime*, these strategies would include the celibacy of the daughters relegated to religious institutions or the dispossession of the younger sons, whose life was given over to the church. In the "familial" mode of reproduction, responsibility for these adjustments was entrusted to the family; with the school-mediated mode of reproduction, to which "technocratic" heads owe their position, the family no longer has dominion over choices of succession or the power to designate heirs.

The fundamental difference between the two modes of reproduction lies in the *strictly statistical logic* of the school-mediated mode of reproduction. In contrast to the direct transfer of property rights between a holder and the heir he himself designates, the transfer carried out by means of the school rests on the statistical aggregation of the isolated stocks of individual or collective agents, and it guarantees properties to the class as a whole that it withholds from one or another of its elements taken separately.[26] The school can only contribute to the reproduction of the class (in the logical sense of the term) by sacrificing certain members of the class who would be spared by a mode of reproduction that left the family with full power over transfer. The *specific contradiction* of the scholastic mode of reproduction lies in the opposition between the interests of the class that the school serves *statistically* and the interests of the members of the class that it sacrifices, that is, not simply the so-called "failures," but also those who hold titles that "normally" (in other words, in an earlier state of the relationship between titles and jobs) would give them the right to a bourgeois occupation, yet who cannot get their titles honored on the market, usually because they do not originate in the class. As long as the bourgeois family has control over its own social reproduction and is thus able to adjust the number of legitimate claimants to the number of available positions, the overproduction of holders of "bourgeois rights" remains an accident and tends to stay within reasonable limits, given the harsh economic consequences of this transgression. Overproduction, with all the contradictions it implies, becomes a *structural constant* when, with the school-mediated mode of reproduction, theoretically equal chances for obtaining academic titles are made available to all "heirs" (girls as well as boys, older offspring as well as younger), while the access of "non-heirs" to these titles also increases (in absolute terms) – as has been the case in France now for some 20 years or so – and a harsh form of elimination, beginning in the first year of secondary school, gives way to *a gentle style of elimination*, in other words, that is, to a progressive, continuous, and hence slow and costly process, which can only become accepted and recognized provided it allows the number of survivors from the dominated regions of social space to increase.

The strategies that the victims of this stochastic instrument of reproduction can use to fight it, whether individual compensatory strategies or collective strategies for making demands or subverting the established order (of which the May 1968 movement represents a prime example), are one of the most important factors in the transformation of social structures today. On one side lie the individual "catch-up" strategies available only to those whose social capital of inherited connections enables them to make up for their lack of titles or to get the highest possible return on the titles they do possess by choosing sanctuary occupations in the regions of social space that remain more or less unbureaucratized, regions in which social dispositions count for more than academically guaranteed specific "competences." On the other side lie the collective strategies for making demands aimed at increasing the recognition of diplomas and obtaining the compensation guaranteed in an earlier state. Both types combine to favor the creation of a large number of *semibourgeois positions*, originating either in revamped definitions of old positions or in the "invention" of new positions, and designed to save "heirs" bereft of titles from downclassing, and to give "parvenus" compensation corresponding more or less to their devalued titles.

The school-mediated mode of reproduction undoubtedly tolerates a greater distortion in social structure than the familial mode of transfer with its simple procedures of direct transfer; but, given that its transfer mechanisms are doubly hidden, once by the concealment related to aggregate statistics and then by the concealment of the direct transfer of cultural capital, which confounds the statistics, academic transfer compensates for its lesser reproductive return through an increased effectiveness in its concealment of the work of reproduction. The educational system, only apparently very similar to a stochastic system of redistribution that would inevitably lead to a redistribution of positions with each successive generation, functions with the apparent impartiality of a chance drawing that is actually systematically biased, innocently producing effects that are infinitely closer, at any rate, to those produced by the system of direct hereditary transfer than to chance redistribution.[27]

The delimitation of what can legitimately be transferred and the legitimate ways of preserving and transferring it is constantly at stake in both insidious and open struggles. Subversive critics tend to increasingly restrict the sphere of what is legitimately transferable by unveiling both the arbitrary nature of the current mode of transfer and the self-interested motivations of the sociodicies aimed at justifying it. This increase in critical vigilance (to which social science has greatly contributed) and institutional control over transfer (laws governing succession, etc.) is one of the factors that hasten the decline of efficient and economical, yet open, strategies, such as direct transfer, to the benefit of strategies that, like academic investment, effect transfer that is dissimulated, indeed entirely misrecognized as such, and thus perfectly recognized and legitimate, although at the cost of greater waste and a higher price tag.

Yet, while this mode of statistical reproduction may indeed limit a family's direct control, their dispossession remains relative. First, although the families of the top business bourgeoisie may be less well placed to take full advantage of the primarily scholastic mode of reproduction than the bourgeoisie *de robe*[28] of the professions and especially the Parisian higher civil service, they are in a position to transfer a certain amount of cultural capital and also to get the most out of the ever more numerous tailor-made educational institutions that guarantee a form of academic recognition to the dispositions they inculcate, dispositions that are relatively unpromising for success in the strictest academic competitions. Secondly, the diploma is neither a necessary nor a sufficient condition for access to all dominant positions – starting, obviously, with jobs in family businesses. And finally, although *self-made men* are increasingly denied access to the directorships of large technocratic or state-run companies (or even to positions in upper management), as we have seen, the academic title is nonetheless almost never enough in and of itself to guarantee access to dominant positions in the economic field. Witness the fact that the heads of state-run companies are nearly all from families related to the business world, by blood or otherwise.

Only 29 percent of the chief executives of technocratically controlled companies and 25 percent of those of nationalized or mixed enterprises (compared to 68.5 percent of the family chief executives) are sons of industrialists, merchants, bankers, or corporate presidents. But ties with the business world are much more important than these figures would suggest: the primary occupation of the father (for example, lawyer, academic, higher civil servant, etc.) may obscure the fact that he comes from a business family. So, for example, Edmond Hannotin, father of Marc Hannotin, honorary Maître des Requêtes in the Conseil d'État, eventually chief executive of the (technocratically controlled) Ciments Français corporation, who, if we can believe the entry in *Who's Who*, is "a lawyer in the Conseil d'État, a member of the appeals court, and a former senator," in fact served on the boards of very large banks and corporations (Crédit Lyonnais, Lyonnaise des Eaux et Éclairage, Chemins de Fer de l'Est, etc.).[29] Similarly, Jacques Donnedieu de Vabres, honorary Maître des Requêtes in the Conseil d'État, eventually chief executive of the (technocratically controlled) Campenon Bernard corporation, is the son of Henri Donnedieu de Vabres, who, classified as an "academic," was in fact a professor of great renown at the law faculté, and Edmée Beigbeder, daughter of David Beigbeder, who served on boards of numerous shipping and mining companies.[30] Robert Bizot, chief executive of Dunlop (a foreign-held company), son of Jean-Jacques Bizot, "Inspecteur des Finances" (and vice-governor of the Banque de France), comes from a long bourgeois line whose known origins go back to the sixteenth century and which has included magistrates, military officers, Inspecteurs des Finances, stockbrokers, and corporate directors. (His brother Alain has been a director of the Crédit Lyonnais since 1973; his uncle Ennemond, who married Marguerite Gillet of the well-known Lyons family, is a director for several companies in the Rhône-Poulenc group and a member of the advisory board of the Banque de France; another of his uncles, Henri, also an Inspecteur des Finances, moved into the private sector at the Comptoir National d'Escompte de Paris, over which he presided before becoming president of the Banque Nationale de Paris. Robert himself married Chantal Paul Renard, the daughter of the cheese manufacturer Paul Renard, and is a director for Fromageries Paul Renard.) Wilfrid Baumgartner, chief executive of Rhône-Poulenc in 1972 and former finance minister, is the son of Amédée Baumgartner, "surgeon," and Mathilde Clamageran, who comes from "a family of well-known nineteenth-century politicians and businessmen";[31] his grandfather, Edouard Baumgartner, had a spinning mill. He married Christiane Mercier, the daughter of Ernest Mercier, former chief engineer of the naval engineering corps, an oil and electricity magnate, who was on 24 boards of directors (as president in eight cases) and who, in 1953, was still director of the Suez Canal corporation, honorary president of Alsthom, and vice-president of the Société Alsacienne de Constructions

Mécaniques. His brother, Richard Baumgartner, married another daughter of Ernest Mercier and in 1972 was chief executive of the Société Alsacienne de Constructions Mécaniques, subsequently known as ALSPI, and the Lille-Bonnières-Colombes corporation, and director of the Compagnie Générale d'Électricité and the Compagnie Française des Pétroles. His other brother, Philippe, physician in Aix-les-Bains, married Geneviève de Lacroix and is related by marriage to the Dollfus family, which controls the textile group Dollfus-Mieg and had shares in the Société Alsacienne de Constructions Mécaniques.[32] We could cite endless analogous examples.

The marked predominance of the top Parisian bourgeoisie *de robe* in all technocratically controlled or state-controlled companies could be explained in part by the fact that – in contrast to the top and mid-level provincial business bourgeoisie, which, expecting little from academic credentials and being only slightly dependent on them, entrusted its children to private schools – it has for generations sent its children to the top lycées in the "fashionable neighbourhoods."[33] In Paris, indeed, while the most traditional elements of the business bourgeoisie entrusted their progeny to the most prestigious private schools, such as the Collège Stanislas or Sainte-Croix de Neuilly, also frequented by the offspring of the top industrial bourgeoisie and the provincial aristocracy, the modernist (and "secular") fractions of the top business bourgeoisie (that is, first and foremost, the Protestant and Jewish bourgeoisies) sent their children to the most "exclusive" public schools. An establishment like Janson de Sailly enjoyed a unique position: joined with Gerson, a private school, it enabled certain Catholic families to combine as it were the "intellectual" advantages of public education with the "moral" assurances of private education.[34] As table 33 shows, the chief executives from families in the professions or higher public service took greatest advantage of the top Parisian lycées, both the top "bourgeois" lycées like Janson and Condorcet, from which they went on in large part to Sciences-po or the law faculté, and the lycées in the Latin Quarter like Louis-le-Grand and Saint-Louis, from which they not only went on to Sciences-po but also to Polytechnique.[35] Thus these categories, distinguished by a more open relationship to the social world, found themselves in a much better position than the top Catholic provincial bourgeoisie to benefit from the opportunities for ascension and reconversion offered by the new mode of reproduction and the new route to access to positions of power opened up by the grandes écoles and especially, after the Second World War, by the École Nationale d'Administration.

FAMILY USES OF THE SCHOOL

We must nevertheless guard against reducing the opposition between the two modes of reproduction to the opposition between recourse to the family and recourse to the school. It is in fact more a question of the difference

Table 33 Secondary schooling of chief executives according to social origin (percent)

Father's occupation	Public schools						Private schools				
	Janson	Condorcet	Louis-le-Grand	Saint-Louis	Other Lycée Paris, suburbs	Lycée provinces, abroad	Collège des Roches, Normandy	Stanislas	Sainte-Geneviève	Other private school Paris	Private school, provinces, abroad
Farmer, bl. collar, clerical, mid-mgr, tradesman, sm. comm. (n = 30)	–	–	10.0	10.0	23.0	47.0	–	3.0	3.0	6.0	16.5
Exec., director, eng. (n = 26)	11.5	7.5	4.0	11.5	35.0	27.0	–	8.0	19.0	27.0	11.5
Officer, landowner (n = 16)	12.5	–	–	12.5	12.5	56.0	12.5	–	6.0	6.0	12.5
Professions, higher civ. serv. (n = 37)	24.5	11.0	19.0	5.5	19.0	16.0	–	5.5	–	8.0	8.0
Lge merchant, industrialist (n = 36)	14.5	6.0	–	3.0	17.0	29.0	9.0	6.0	3.0	20.0	37.0
Lge industr., board member, corp. head, banker (n = 57)	24.5	7.0	12.0	9.0	12.5	14.0	10.5	7.0	7.0	19.0	19.0
All	16.5	6.0	9.0	8.0	19.0	26.0	5.5	5.5	6.0	15.5	18.5

Total may exceed 100; the figures represent the percentage of chief executives from the different social classes who attended each of the schools.

between a strictly familial management of the problems of reproduction and a type of familial management that makes use of the school in certain ways in its reproduction strategies. Indeed, in addition to the fact that the school's reproductive action is based on the domestic transfer of cultural capital, the family continues to use the relatively autonomous logic of its own economy, which enables it to combine the capital held by each of its members, in order to accumulate and transfer its wealth. The new mode of appropriation of economic capital makes it possible and even desirable to establish a new form of solidarity among the members of a family. In contrast to those who possess economic heritage, who are as divided as they are united by their common claim to the appropriation of this patrimony, constantly under threat of division and dispersion according to the whims of inheritance and marriages, those who possess diversified, and largely cultural, capital have everything to gain by maintaining the family ties that enable them to benefit from the capital held by each member of the group. Thus a network of family relations can be the locus of an unofficial circulation of capital that enables the networks of official circulation to function and in turn blocks any effects of the latter that would be contrary to family interests.[36] The dialectical relationship between the official and the unofficial, between the familial and the strictly economic networks of capital circulation, here as elsewhere makes it possible to maximize the profits gained through outwardly incompatible systems of demands – combining, for example, the advantages guaranteed by prestigious academic credentials with those afforded by the protections that enable them to yield their full return, or still further, combining the secondary profits provided by matrimonial exchanges between families of company heads with the advantages gained through corporate ties. The "family spirit" and even affection that lend the family its cohesion thus contribute to securing one of the advantages that come with belonging to a family group (without expressly pursuing it as such, of course), namely, a share in the capital whose integrity is guaranteed by the integration of the family, in other words, a share in the sum of the assets of all its members.[37]

We might think of the example of the Debré family, which brings together capital in all its forms: Robert Debré, member of the Institut de France (Académie de Médecine), former professor at the Faculté de Médecine de Paris, married Jeanne Debat-Ponsan, daughter of the painter Edouard Debat-Ponsan and sister of Jacques Debat-Ponsan, recipient of the Prix de Rome in architecture. Following the death of his first wife, Robert Debré married Elisabeth de la Panouse, daughter of Sabine de Wendel (of the well-known iron and steel dynasty) who, from her first marriage to Alphonse de la Bourdonnaye, had six children, including Oriane, married to Yves Guéna, Conseiller d'Etat and former minister. Jacques Debré, Robert's brother, was a graduate of the École Polytechnique, president of the Compagnie Industrielle de Télécommunications, and director of several companies. Germain Debré, his other brother, was an architect. In the following generation, we find Michel Debré, son of

Robert Debré and Jeanne Debat-Ponsan, honorary Maître des Requêtes in the Conseil d'État, former prime minister, member of parliament, married to Anne-Marie Le Maresquier, daughter of Charles Le Maresquier, chief architect for civil construction and national palaces, member of the Institut de France, and sister of both Noël Le Maresquier, architect and member of the Institut, conservator at the Musée Condé de Chantilly, and Pierre Le Maresquier, graduate of the École Normale Supérieure, for a time cultural officer in the French Embassy in Ankara, teacher, Conseiller Technique [grade of higher civil servant, Tr.] and corporate director. Olivier Debré, Michel's brother, is a painter whose work has been exhibited in many salons, galleries, and museums, and Claude Debré, his sister, married Philippe Monod-Broca, surgeon in public hospitals, professor at the Faculté de Médecine de Paris-Sud, son of Raoul Monod, friend of Robert Debré. Jean-Louis Debré, son of Michel Debré, himself a Sciences-po graduate, is a magistrate, and was a Conseiller Technique, then Chargé de Mission in the office of Jacques Chirac. This vast web of well-heeled family relations is in no way abstract or theoretical. To quote Robert Debré: "Over the past decades, we led a very active family and social life in our cherished homes in Paris and Tours. Our children and grandchildren often came to visit. Weddings and births followed one after the other. Parents and children remained close (. . .). Later, the children of the new generation were to become more bold. Some began to question authority (. . .). We kept the tradition of gathering everyone together for Christmas dinner. There were so many descendants on both sides that, with several nieces and nephews, we would have more than 80 guests (. . .). We delighted in the personal happiness and pro-fessional success of our descendants, who were choosing widely varied paths. Some were professors of medicine or surgery, ministers or generals, and in the next genera-tion we found many diverse talents. I was perhaps most touched by the success of three of my grandchildren at the Internat des Hôpitaux de Paris."[38]

The situation in which stockholders belonging to a single family grant one of their members the right to manage the family portfolio is only one particular case (one in which the profits gained through integration are limi-ted by the particular properties of the specific capital involved) among all the *profit-sharing relationships* in which the capital accumulated by each of the members of the group through the positions held in different institu-tions and different fields – and particularly capital in social connections – is shared by all, in such a way that individuals have their own shares and all members together have the entire sum. In short, if *social capital* is relatively difficult to reduce to other forms of capital, and particularly to economic capital and cultural capital (whose return it can *increase*), without for all that being completely independent of them, this is because the capital held individually by an individual agent is increased by capital possessed *by proxy* that depends on the amount of capital held by each of the members of the groups of which that person is a member as well as the degree of inte-gration of these groups (family, corps, etc.).

The lengthening of the human biological lifespan and the correlative increase in social lifespan help to delay the moment when children inherit from their parents, putting it off to an age at which, given the decrease in the age at which people marry and have their first child, the children themselves have children who are ready to begin working and having families. It follows that the transfer of part of the patrimony tends to be subordinated to the logic of the affective ties that determine family relationships. As Hervé Le Bras has shown,[39] heirs receive an inheritance (usually between the ages of 50 and 55, that is, during the period when they "set up" their 25 to 30-year-old children) that they may either keep together or partially divide up among their children (in the form of places to live or annuities) according to their goodwill and to the degree to which their children live up to their definition of social excellence. These transformations in the economic functions of the family go hand in hand with a change in the forms of authority within the bourgeois family. The direct, overt authority exercised by the head of the family, also head of a business, keeper and guarantor of the common wealth, has been replaced by a set of relationships of affective dependence founded on "affection," "generosity," and "gratitude," and well designed to fulfill the same functions, but under cover, by generating ties that owe their essential strength to their sentimental and ethical transfiguration.

Just as the two modes of reproduction correspond to two uses of the family rather than to the exclusive use of either the family or the school, they are also distinguished by two uses of the school, or, more precisely, by a privileged use of institutions located in different regions of academic space. Whereas for one group the academic title conferred by the most academic authorities (such as the École Polytechnique) constitutes the condition *sine qua non* for entry into the field of power, the others expect educational institutions at once less academic and less selective, which strengthen inherited dispositions more than they inculcate new skills, to grant them the minimum consecration needed to consecrate vested positions. In the first case, the educational institution asserts its autonomy in the nature of the knowledge that it both inculcates and requires, knowledge that can only be acquired through a specific and specifically academic style of learning and that is worth little in worldly markets; in the second case, the school, here much like the institutions to which aristocracies of birth or money have traditionally entrusted their offspring – such as Oxford and Yale, or the École des Roches and the most exclusive Jesuit schools – bestows a consecration that, although granted by the least "academic" academic institutions, still has every appearance of the social neutrality that lends the school its more or less complete autonomy with respect to worldly demands. The social success of Sciences-po, and the ENA, its continuation, can undoubtedly be explained by the fact that these schools provided the families of the upper bourgeoisie – who were the most anxious to avoid locking themselves into the rejection of the state lycée and the grandes écoles that was seen as a sign of good breeding among the upper provincial bourgeoisie – with a way to secure academic legitimation for the transfer of their economic heritage, legitimation that, at least since the end of the nineteenth century, was tending to become increasingly necessary. And all this at the least possible academic cost: on the one hand, the entire logic of the social recruitment of the faculty and student bodies of these institutions predisposed them to recognize the particular type of cultural capital and relationship to culture and language that exclusively define the heritage of the Parisian bourgeoisie; and, on the other hand, the unacknowledged privilege that the business bourgeoisie grants to the dispositions guaranteed by the most worldly academic titles when it has the full power to choose its heirs within the family, or, failing this, within the class, tended to compensate for and readjust the adjustments the school introduces into the correspondence between social hierarchies and academic hierarchies when, as at Polytechnique, it is able to more completely assert its specific logic.

Nothing could more clearly *show* us the contrast between these two academic channels than a photo-comparison of the bodily hexis, make-up, and clothes of the adolescents who have chosen one or the other of them. Or a comparison of the architectural style of the buildings in which they get their education: on the one hand we find the monastic austerity of the great boarding schools (which were until recently exclusively male), such as Saint-Louis and Louis-le-Grand, which are completely closed in on work and study; on the other hand, the openness of the Institut d'Études Politiques, organized around a library and a vast, very modern hall, which offers a striking contrast to Louis-le-Grand's large column-bordered courtyard.[40] Or a comparison of a recorded mathematics or physics oral at the École Polytechnique with a recorded ENA oral such as the one we present here.

In the following transcribed "conversation," a perfectly typical example of the (30) exams we were able to observe in 1971, the candidate was to comment upon the following text (inaudible passages are indicated by ellipses):[41] "By contributing to the destruction of structures linked both to nature and to a rejection of historicity, the effects of big cities have been and continue to be largely negative. But what positive aspects might we bring out? First, a more abstract and calculating form of knowledge; secondly, a more varied daily life created by the many demands made on people's attention, varied conditioning, and the experience of different networks of social relations. Finally, the complexity of urban situations, which has supplanted the former determinism, gives individual freedom the chance to make of itself what it will within the margin allowed by the play of existing patterns. The rules of the game specify that freedom should also have the chance to let itself be determined according to circumstances. This line of argument does not justify the fear felt by some at the thought that urban life might neutralize creative potential by reducing everything to a kind of conformist grey. In fact, history teaches us quite the opposite: the most noteworthy individuals have come from big cities, or have at least been influenced by them, and cities have been the seat and the repository of revolutionary ideas" (Luc Thoré, *Signification du phénomène urbain*, 1965). Following the candidate's oral presentation, the "conversation" begins:[42]

First examiner: "So you seem to favor Thoré's position . . . you've shaded it somewhat, you've quoted Henri Lefebvre; how exactly would you compare the two positions?"

"I think Henri Lefebvre had a much broader view of urban planning . . . For him, a city wasn't just a collection of houses . . . cities overflow, they are vital . . ."

"So Lefebvre credits large cities with several positive attributes. Do you fully agree with him? Aren't there some things you would consider more as liabilities?"

"I think that if I had to be critical of one of these elements . . ."

"And what about the abstract and calculating knowledge?" (allusion to Thoré's text)

". . . Yes, I guess cities can make . . . the game harder, more difficult, and calculating knowledge is the necessary precondition for survival."

"It's a necessary precondition for survival, but it is good in and of itself?"

"Insofar as it extends beyond . . . I think it's a positive step."

"In your view, under what conditions can individual freedom truly flourish in a big city?"

" . . . "

"You live in a city. Do you feel that your own individual freedom is at its highest potential?"

"First I think one has to give one's own definition of freedom; I think freedom is the ability to do what you want as long as you don't limit anyone else's. According to this definition, cities give everyone greater freedom . . . Judgments people make of you are much harder to take in a village than in a city."

"Are you sensitive to what people think of you?"

"No, since I live in a city . . ."

". . . Do cities not encourage the rise of the fittest and, conversely, the crushing of the weak?"

"I don't think city life should be seen as a game between the strong and the weak; I think unequal relationships are greater in cities mainly because city dwellers are to a certain extent close and uniform . . . Furthermore, the social differences that develop among the neighborhoods of a city are perhaps less obvious than the distinctions that exist in a village. I'm thinking for example of the village chateau . . . which is still seen by some peasants as a sign of rejection . . ."

"Have you ever had the experience of living in a French village?"

"I'm only familiar with one, a small village in Burgundy . . ."

"Does it have a chateau? What is the current attitude of the residents, and I don't mean the vacationing Parisians, toward the chateau?"

"It's very strange, it's still an attitude of respect mixed with fear and defiance."

"And what does the chateau owner do?"

"He's never there, it's owned by a foreigner . . ."

"You mentioned Parly II twice in your presentation. Do you personally find Parly II to be an example of successful urban planning?"

"I think Parly II represents the coming together of two completely contradictory elements . . . I don't think town planning should be based on malls . . ."

"If you were going to build a mall, where would you locate it in relation to the town? Do you prefer malls or old-style small shops?"

"Personally, I prefer malls . . ."

"Do you feel welcome in Parly II stores?"

". . . [there is] a certain cool attitude in the men's clothing stores."

"A certain cool attitude. And do you find this same coolness in traditional small shops?"

"If I'm a regular client at a particular store, no. If I'm not . . . I feel they're trying either to attract me or to reject me."

"Do you like it when people try to attract you?"

"Personally, no."

"And you don't like attracting other people?"

". . . I think attraction is a natural thing."

"You think it's simply a matter of an inexplicable impulse?"

". . ."

Another examiner: "Do you think town planning should take the existence of social classes into account?"

". . ."

First examiner: "One final question. I'd like to draw your attention to one sentence in the passage in which the author states that cities are the seat of revolutionary change; do you yourself not know of any revolution ferment that has not had its source in large cities?"

"You mean in politics? . . . I can think of the example of . . ."

"Anything more recent?"

"In May of 1968, mid-size cities . . ."

"You don't have to be on the left to be a revolutionary . . . Do big cities favor, shall we say, conservative demands more than towns or the countryside?"

"I think that towns and villages are more likely to adopt so-called conservative demands . . ."

Another examiner: "You mentioned the famous comedian who used to talk about building cities in the countryside. Do you know his name?"

". . ."

". . . Are you interested in comedians?"[43]

"I think they're very useful . . . I like certain kinds of humor, but not all."

"In general?"

"I have a hard time understanding British humor, for example, which seems really cold to me . . ."

"Do you think humor is important in public administration?"

"Not at the office . . . but outside the office, sure."

"Would you be more likely to choose as a friend someone who thought abstractly or someone who reasoned on the concrete plane, if you were looking for the most pleasant relationship?"

". . . the concrete thinker, because . . . I don't think friendship is based on the exchange of ideas . . ."

"The rules of the game mentioned in the text, do they seem important to you, something one should respect? When you play a game, do you go by the rules? Does this annoy you?"

"Normally, when I win, I play by the rules of the game; when I play cards, for instance . . ."

"And are there rules in the game of governing?"

"I don't think the idea of rules of the game works here: there are rules, unwritten rules for functioning . . ."

Final examiner: "This passage says that important people come from cities or have been influenced by them. Can you think of any French persons of note who have not been influenced by the city?"

"I think . . . I'll mention for example . . ."

"You spoke a few moments ago about small shops. Do you change the stores you frequent often?"

". . . Considering the fact that I just got married and moved, I completely changed where I shop."

"You've mentioned the rules of the game, and in particular the fact that people shouldn't run red lights. When you're in a city, do you never go through red lights?"

"I sometimes run the yellow light."

"Yes, but when you're a pedestrian, do you cross when it's red?"

"Always."

"People say everything in France comes from Paris. You mentioned the Avignon Festival a few minutes ago, but no one ever mentions Marseilles . . . How can we explain the fact that there is a systematic devaluation of everything that goes on in the provinces?"

"I think that in any case, if this devaluation ever did exist, it's less true now . . ."

"Don't you think it's a good idea to send orchestras out from the center into the provinces?"

". . ."

"Doesn't this decentralization of culture seem a positive thing to you?"

"It's entirely positive, and it's necessary . . . I think the Jean-François Paillard orchestra should be established in the provinces and come into Paris, rather than the other way around . . ."

The apparent logic of the "conversation," with its "trick questions" and unpredictable turns, in short, the entire academic ritual of the "mental jousting match," the "a propos," the spirit of repartee, etc., conceals the true function of the examination. We need only make a list of all the information the candidate reveals, about himself, in fact, not to mention the information betrayed by his attitude, to see that the test is indeed a very personal examination, which is rescued from indiscretion (take the questions on attraction, for example) only by the frankness related to the unreality of the academic situation, and which aims either consciously or unconsciously to situate the candidate politically and socially (most of the candidate's sentences are in the first person, very often starting out with "I think").

Another candidate, asked to speak on a passage taken from Simone de Beauvoir in which she mentions one of Grimm's fairy tales, was asked if he had read Grimm and Perrault, if he thought that "it was a good idea to scare young children," if he had "read scary fairy tales" when he was a child, when he thought "children were ready to go to the movies," what he thought of Walt Disney movies, of gerontocracy, whether he knew anyone who lived in a nursing home, whether he was "generally against compromise," "what solution" he could envision for a conflict "arising during a strike in which one side was ready to give four cents when the other side wanted ten." In short, the unreality inscribed in the university game (which is evoked here through the ritual of the explication de texte) conceals both a kind of recruitment interview that combines political questions and personal questions, and a test in deportment, designed to judge "the man," as the committee puts it, in other words, that is, strictly social dispositions, such as the self-assurance needed for dodging uncomfortable questions or admitting ignorance, or the "relaxed yet respectful" attitude that allows a candidate to send a question back into the examiner's court or to respectfully interrupt him before he has finished asking it, or even to casually deflect a difficult subject by taking advantage of the approval granted in advance to the haughty rejection of the laborious inelegance of pedantic concepts and bookish knowledge ("Please don't ask me to define epistemology"). But we must quote from the preface, entitled "Committee Thoughts on Candidates' Performance," of a report on the different sections of the ENA *concours* (ENA, *Épreuves et statistiques des concours de 1969* (Paris: Imprimerie Nationale, 1970)): "Above all, candidates who most certainly studied hard, but left no time for reflection or for reading anything but *Le Monde*. They have not stepped back from their intellectual ingurgitations. They lack humor and wit; listening to them, one fears that the civil service could become a thoroughly depressing and overly serious organization. And if high-level public service and the state grands corps should become geometric places full of gloomy 'ace test-takers,' how will they create a contented France? People have forgotten that the conversation portion of the *concours* is not a test of knowledge. Knowledge is judged, let us repeat, in the technical tests. The conversation, along with the first day's essay, is a way of trying to get a feel for the candidate's human qualities, at an age when people are not yet overly concerned about concealing their true selves and when their personalities are developed yet not, we hope, entirely crystallized. As one committee member put it: 'I try to imagine whether I'd like working with the candidate I'm listening to and whether I could completely trust him.' It is thus the man that we are – ambitiously – trying to reach, not the being weighted down with diplomas and scholastic knowledge. The ability to admit one's ignorance, a relaxed yet respectful attitude, the gift of repartee, and a curious mind are all excellent qualities. We will often throw in a highly unusual or technical question so as to shake up a candidate who is either too tightly coiled up in his shell or too annoyingly conceited. This will elicit quotations from writers he hasn't read, or false refinements, or vague formulae whose imprecision gives the examiners a good idea of the vague nature of the candidate's own way of thinking."

2

Establishment Schools and Power over the Economy

Thus the two modes of reproduction coexist within the field of economic power where they represent the two poles of a continuum.[1] Everything seems to indicate that recourse to a form of academic consecration, however rudimentary, tends to be more widely, and more absolutely, the rule as the size and the age of a company increase, usually as early as the second generation (cf. figures 16 and 17). This ought not to lead to the conclusion, following a simple evolutionist schema, that the two modes of reproduction correspond to two moments in an evolution inseparable from the one that, according to some authors, leads from a mode of domination based on property and *owners* to another more rational and more democratic one based on "competence" and *managers*. The definition of the legitimate mode of reproduction is at stake, especially in struggles within the field of economic power, and it is necessary to guard against describing as the end of history what is simply a reversible state in a relation of power.

STATE BOSSES AND FAMILY BOSSES

The space of the properties of the chief executives of large companies is organized around the opposition between *state bosses*, placed at the head of large enterprises with strong state ties, either large industrial companies (nationalized companies, mixed companies, or companies dependent in large part upon government contracts) or large banks;[2] and the *private bosses* who are at the head of private banks and private industrial or commercial companies that are smaller (relatively) and less closely tied to the state.[3] The former, who are less likely to come from business families and more likely to come from families of higher civil servants or professionals, have a great deal of academic capital as well as a great deal of social capital consisting of contacts they inherit or accumulate in their passage through the civil service and ministerial cabinets. Their entire academic and professional career is placed under the sign of the *public*, large state lycées, grandes écoles, higher public service, the grands corps (particularly the Inspection des Finances,

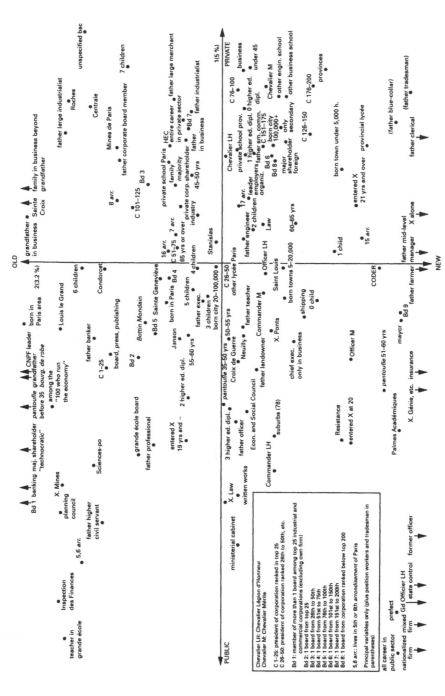

Figure 16 The space of corporate heads: correspondence analysis (plane of the first and second axes of inertia: properties)

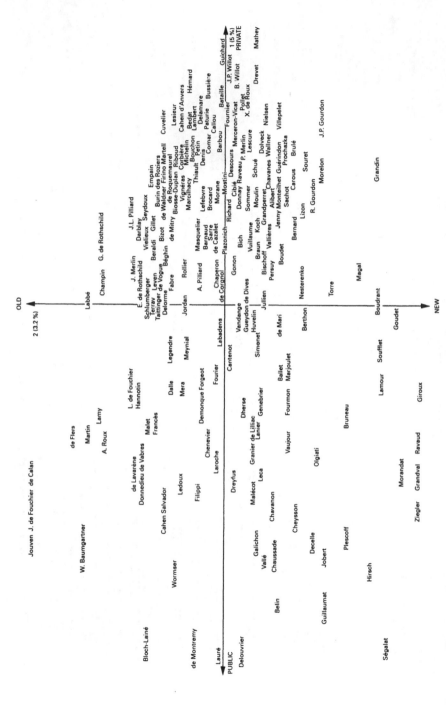

Figure 17 The space of corporate heads: correspondence analysis (plane of the first and second axes of inertia: individuals)

the Conseil d'État, and the Corps des Mines), and finally large national-level companies. The latter, heirs to large bourgeois dynasties or parvenus from the petty business or trade-practicing bourgeoisie, have had modest educations in private schools and have made their entire careers in the private sector, usually in a business owned by their family.[4]

The world of top chief executives includes a very small number of self-made men, exemplary exceptions, as rare today as ever, and as predisposed as ever to fuel the meritocratic legend of the entrepreneur as child of his own deeds. Just as the entrepreneurs of the first industrial revolution came for the most part from the ranks of the business bourgeoisie and had secondary school educations, as numerous historical studies have shown, sons of blue-collar or clerical workers today are extremely rare among top chief executives (7 of 216, or 3 percent) and are only found in second-tier businesses (we find only 2 among the top 100). Sons of small independent entrepreneurs, tradesmen, or small-scale merchants (who number 7), or mid-level managers (who number 9) occupy positions below those of the chief executives from the dominant class (this is why they are particularly well represented among the heads of foreign subsidiaries, which are most often merely appendices of multinational corporations whose true decision-making center lies outside France). Furthermore, we find practically none who are self-taught: 88 percent of the chief executives have at least the baccalauréat and most of those without a diploma have had some secondary education. The rare self-made men do not start from scratch, either. So for example, before creating Carrefour, Marcel Fournier had expanded the family business, a notions shop founded in about 1822; it was a "small business" that, as he describes it, employed "about a dozen people" when he came on the scene in 1932, two of whom were his brothers (cf. "Face à face avec Marcel Fournier," by Roger Priouret, *Expansion* (June 1973), p. 215).

Thus, on one side, we find those who are predisposed by their power over state-owned companies (such as the chief executive of Régie Renault, for example) and by their academic and social capital – constantly maintained through their participation in the important events of technocratic dialogue (state business lunches, planning councils, etc.) and consecrated by the highest official decorations (Officer or Commander of the Légion d'Honneur) – to engage in quasi-political action in the form of interventions in the upper echelons of the administration and in the political power structure. On the other side, we find those who, with many reservations about and often scorn for politics and "politicians," public service and public servants, and lacking the disposition and connections that favor exchanges with politicians and higher civil servants, rely (not without some hesitation) on appointed spokespeople and limit their political action to the level of local institutions, over which they have complete control.[5]

Private bosses often attach their *name* to *private* charitable institutions, such as clinics and day-care centers, thereby revealing their paternalistic and quasi-monarchic view of the function of business leadership. The very purpose of these institutions is defined in opposition to state and public assistance, which is both impersonal and anonymous, and hence invites no recognition, and which is likely to be viewed as a "social conquest," wrested from management's grasp through the union struggle, and not as a simple result of its benevolence. "If we established clinics, it's because one day a worker died after getting poor care at the public hospital. And if we built schools, it's because at that time there were no good schools for workers' children. We just did what the state hadn't done. And we didn't need the unions in order to do it. Unions are unnecessary in the life of a business. Unions are actually only the expression of management's shortcomings" (F. Michelin, remarks recorded by Georges Menant, *Paris-Match* 1497, Feb. 3, 1978). In Clermont-Ferrand, we find, to name but a few, a Michelin infant care center, a Michelin clinic, and a prenatal care section in the Michelin Medical Center (cf. *Guide de la santé et de l'aide sociale*, 1970). Countless stadiums and sports teams have been created or supported under the "patronage" of private *patrons*, such as the Geoffroy-Guichard Stadium (after the founder of the Casino chain) in Saint-Étienne, the Bouloumié Stadium in Vittel (from the name of the founding family of the Eaux company), or the Sochaux football team founded in 1928 by Peugeot. The same goes for housing projects, for example the Bouchon project in Nassandres in the Eure (from the name of the sugar manufacturers), etc. And people always list the cities in which all the social appurtenances are placed *under the patronage and the patronyme* of the major local employer, such as Hayange, Moyeuvre, or Joeuf, where "everything is Wendel's," or Clermont-Ferrand, where "everything is Michelin."

In quite a different way, state bosses most often support anonymous charitable organizations of, we might say, general interest. Thus Jacques de Fouchier, chief executive of the Compagnie Bancaire, Jacques Georges-Picot, honorary chief executive of the Compagnie Financière de Suez and l'Union Parisienne, Pierre Ledoux, president of the Banque Nationale de Paris, Yves Malécot, president of the Crédit Populaire de France, Jean Merlin, chief executive of the Crédit Commercial de France, as well as Antonie Riboud, chief executive of the Boussois-Souchon-Neuvesel corporation, were members in 1973 of the board of directors of the Fondation de France. This establishment, created on the initiative of the Caisse des Dépots et Consignations by the Banque de France and the largest national and private banks, saw "its goal as that of contributing to the revival of 'arts patronage' in the broadest sense of the term, in a form suited to the needs of an industrial society"; to "deprivatize" charity, as they are wont to say in these circles, by putting themselves "at the disposal of private citizens, individuals or businesses, who would like to put some of their resources into *projects for the general good* but who, neither wishing nor able to create their own foundation, to leave the matter to their heirs or executors, or to direct their monies to existing charities, are looking for an organization conceived expressly to receive and manage their gifts for the benefit of *disinterested organizations* of a philanthropic, educational, social, scientific, or cultural nature, according to their wishes" (introduction in the *Bottin administratif*, 1973 edn, p. 1021). Again in 1973, François Bloch-Lainé, then president of Crédit Lyonnais, was president of the Fondation pour la Recherche Médicale Française, whose "goal is to promote scientific medical research in all its forms."

Private bosses are firmly rooted in particular regions[6] and almost never hold positions outside the economic field. State bosses, on the other hand, most of whom have been in the civil service, ministerial cabinets, and the nationalized sector, hold important positions in establishment schools (ENA, Polytechnique, Sciences-po), and are trustees of large university research institutes, are predisposed – as much by their trajectory in the field of power as by their institutional or even personal characteristics, such as the "style" and eclectic cultivation afforded by access to different milieus and the personal connections they provide – to contribute to the development of *de jure* and *de facto* relationships between the field of economic power and the other fields constitutive of the field of power. And this positional opposition is mirrored in a dispositional opposition between the private, "discreet" men (as people are wont to say) who are the "private" heads, and the "public men," the "technocratic" heads who are eager to grant interviews, appear on television, write articles, and publish books.[7] These public men are men of connections and "public relations" whose family, lycée, and grande école connections, as well as the very trajectory that takes them from public service to private enterprise, predispose them to act as agents of connection, particularly between the public and private sectors. They are found in all institutions, committees, commissions, associations, and organizations where what we call economic policy is drafted or set.[8] They often have responsibilities – and important ones – within the CNPF [employers union, Tr.], created at the request of the state (under the name CGPF) and known to be seen by many private employers still as a quasi-official organization, always suspected of being accommodating to the state (Pierre Jouven, Ambroise Roux, and Pierre de Calan hold management positions in the organization, while François Michelin, in contrast, leaves the CNPF in May of 1968). They meet frequently at the AGREF [association of large companies for investment], created in 1969 "on the initiative of some of the most important French industrial companies and of Mr Jacques Ferry" in order to "give large companies the means to think as a group and to discuss problems specific to their situation" (excerpt from the introductory paper of the AGREF, Sept. 1977). In 1977, under the direction of Ambroise Roux, the AGREF includes 24 top companies from industry, commerce, and banking. Public chief executives are to be found in employers' federations, chambers of commerce and industry,[9] and the Centre d'Études et de Recherches des Chefs d'Entreprise [chief executive study and research center]. They very often sit on the boards of directors of the top 25 industrial and commercial companies and, showing thereby that they are an integral part of a particular mode of reproduction, they are frequently trustees of institutions of higher education, especially the grandes écoles. For example, Pierre Jouven was a trustee of the ENA (from 1964 to 1971), a member of the program advisory board of the École Nationale Supérieure des Mines de Paris, and trustee of the new University of Compiègne. Ambroise Roux, Jacques de Fouchier, François Bloch-Lainé, Pierre Moussa and Paul Delouvrier are all founding members of the national committee for the development of the grandes écoles, etc. They shun local responsibilities (they are very rarely mayors or heads of *départements*) and are nearly absent from the Commissions de Développement Écononique Régional, where private chief executives, on the other hand, rarely members of large employers' associations, are very heavily represented. The heads of technocratically controlled companies could be said to constitute the limit of the class of state bosses. Indeed, they have, to the highest degree, the largest number of the properties associated with the dominant pole, as with Ambroise Roux, for example, a kind of exemplary character that the group puts forward, perhaps less because they recognize themselves in him than because they see him as incarnating the most easily recognizable image of the legitimate chief executive.[10]

But in so dichotomizing a population that is in continuous distribution between the two poles, there is a risk that it will be forgotten that the classes described as separate for ease of presentation are divided by *statistical limits* that are not truly distinct *boundaries*. A number of state heads in fact do have ties, even family ties, with the business world and take part in local politics (as in the case of Pierre Guillaumat), while "family" heads may serve on technocratic committees or be received at the Elysée [the president's residence, Tr.] (François Michelin, for example). And, similarly, while it is true that 64.5 percent of the chief executives of large technocratically controlled companies started out in public service (18 percent are former Inspecteurs des Finances), this is also the case for 16 percent (and 4 percent) of the chief executives of family-owned companies. Still further, if 27 percent and 24.5 percent of the former have held positions in ministerial cabinets or seats on planning councils, 7 percent and 5 percent of the latter have followed a similar career path. Furthermore, in the area that most clearly distinguishes the two worlds, the mode of succession, the differences do not come down to all-or-nothing distinctions. While it is clear that prestigious academic qualifications are increasingly the rule as we move away from the familial and private pole, they are nevertheless becoming increasingly necessary for family heirs as well, and often even as soon as the second generation. It is thus pointed out that Serge Dassault, "Polytechnique and Sup Aéro graduate," son and presumed successor of Marcel Dassault, "has proved [by these diplomas] that he is more than just his father's son."[11] Succession occurs most often in favor of people who have more academic qualifications than their predecessors (we might think, for example, of the succession of Paul Richard, chief executive Thompson-Brandt, or of Sylvain Floirat). But while it is not unusual that, in order to resolve the crisis they face at the death of the head of the business, families should resort to the services of a *manager*, this manager – when he is not treated like a simple proxy holder, or like a sort of agent, "subject to dismissal *ad nutum*," as they say in this milieu where they have had a lot of contact with Jesuits –

often comes from the distinguished business world himself. It is in this light that we can best appreciate the unintended humor of the remarks made by Jean-Marc Vernes, born into high-level Protestant banking (he is chief executive of the Banque Vernes-Commerciale de Paris), in commenting on his accession in succession to Ferdinand Beghin, painting himself as a pure manager, solely concerned with the running of the company, a stranger to clan squabbles and indifferent to the defense of patrimonies: "Here, we leave dictatorship in the grand old family style to the past. My presence in this office is proof enough. What's the point of asking the heavens if the business will still be in the family in five, ten, or twenty years? What matters today is that we run it well."[12] The same basic logic is at work, despite appearances, in the replacement of Wilfred Baumgartner, the very picture of a *grand commis* [well-placed public servant Tr.] (former government minister and former governor of the Banque de France), at the head of Rhône-Poulenc by Renaud Gillet, chemical engineer (diploma from the École Supérieure de Chimie Industrielle de Lyon), president since 1966 of Pricel, a holding company in which his family has interests,[13] and board member of the Compagnie Financière de Paris et des Pays-Bas, BSN-Gervais-Danone, Eurafrance, L'Union Chimique Belge, the Société Européenne d'Horlogerie et d'Équipements Mécaniques, but also great-grandson of the founder of Rhône-Poulenc (François Gillet), where his family holds only 2.3 percent of the capital.[14]

In fact, the weight of the social capital inherited from the family is felt in all sectors of the field of economic power. The successive operations of *cooptation* that determine the selection of top executives (and to a lesser degree, the careers of ordinary managers) are armed with criteria that are never completely reducible to academic qualifications, and still less to what the latter are supposed to officially measure.

Bureaucratization obviously excludes neither the hereditary transfer of privileges nor nepotism, which can sometimes take completely open forms. So, for example, in 1974, when Jacques de Fouchier was president of the supervisory board of the Compagnie Bancaire, we find Louis-Charles de Fouchier, his brother, honorary president of Crédit du Nord and the Union Parisienne, and a member of the board of directors of the Compagnie Bancaire (and of Banque Worms), and Loïc, his nephew (son of Louis), at the head of Crédit du Nord (of which Jacques de Fouchier was a board member) and on the board of directors of Banque Worms (through a technique similar to the fosterage used by noble families long ago, the young Loïc de Fouchier began his career as an attaché to the Banque Nationale du Commerce Intérieur, going on to the Banque d'Algérie et de Tunisie before returning to the family bank).

While it is true that technocratic or bureaucratic power lasts only as long as the individual who holds it and does not get passed down from father to son, *grands commis* are able to find a way to partially dodge the bureaucratic rule against hereditary transfer in the game of exchanges of favors and influence.[15] The most prestigious diplomas, valued at this level more as guarantees of honor and good upbringing than as purely technical certificates of competence,[16] only give access to top state-controlled positions if they are associated with those rare and nearly indefinable properties that define belonging because they are the product of belonging. Thus, in the population that selects the statistical methods of academic elimination, cooptation based on the subtle criteria of membership in the establishment operates a second selection, one more specifically oriented toward the reproduction of the business world, which guarantees that the estate, which cannot always be passed down to the direct descendant, will remain in the hands of the legitimate descendants.

"THE NOBILITY OF THE BOURGEOIS CLASS"

The capacity of the academic mode of reproduction (which, as we know, allows for the familial transfer of cultural capital) to gain ground in relation to the familial mode of reproduction is limited by the fact that genetic heredity still contributes to forming, within the population of the topmost corporate heads, a genuine "elite's elite," selected, or coopted, according to the length of time their family has been in the bourgeoisie – in the end, then, according to a particularly accomplished form of the familial mode of reproduction. We indeed note that the primary opposition, between private bosses and public bosses, is mirrored by a secondary opposition that distributes them, within each of the categories defined according to distance from the state, according to *length of time* in the business world.[17] Thus, on one side, we find chief executives from the aristocracy or the top Parisian business bourgeoisie who possess all the attributes of the bourgeois lifestyle (fashionable clubs, *Bottin Mondain*, etc.), and on the other, we find the latecomers, members of more recent lineages or, in the extreme cases, parvenus from the Parisian, or even provincial, petty bourgeoisie. And this opposition corresponds perfectly to the one established according to position in the hierarchized space of economic power: bankers, "the nobility of the bourgeois class," as Stendhal saw them,[18] often originating in the Inspection des Finances, and heads of large industrial groups that are also financial powers, are opposed to industrial capitalists, "technicians" who have gone to engineering schools and often find themselves in the dominated position of civil servants of financial capitalism.

If we measure the power chief executives wield over the economic field in terms of board membership in companies other than their own (see table 34), we find that it varies very significantly according to diploma. *Polytechniciens* and Sciences-po graduates more or less equally share the seats at the 25 top-ranked companies, while most of the chief executives

Table 34 Seats on other boards of directors according to social origin and academic credentials

Father's occupation	Boards of top 25 corporations							Boards of 26th–100th							Boards of those under 100th						
	Polytechnique	Sciences-po	Engineering school	Business school	Law, humanities, science fac.	Secondary, higher ed. unfinished	Total	Polytechnique	Sciences-po	Engineering school	Business school	Law, humanities, science fac.	Secondary, higher ed. unfinished	Total	Polytechnique	Sciences-po	Engineering school	Business school	Law, humanities, science fac.	Secondary, higher ed. unfinished	Total
Farmer, bl. collar, clerical, mid-mgr, tradesman, sm. comm.	1	–	–	–	1	–	2	1	–	2	–	1	–	4	4	–	7	3	4	6	24
Exec., director, engineer	6	–	–	–	–	1	7	2	2	1	1	2	–	8	2	1	5	1	2	–	11
Officer, landowner	3	2	–	–	1	–	6	1	1	1	–	–	–	3	2	2	1	–	1	–	6
Professions, higher civ. serv.	1	8	–	–	2	–	11	4	3	1	–	–	–	8	3	8	1	1	5	–	18
Lge merchant, industrialist	3	–	1	1	–	2	7	–	–	1	–	–	1	2	2	2	8	2	5	6	25
Lge industr., board member, corp. head, banker	2	5	4	–	3	–	14	–	3	3	1	–	7	14	3	4	3	6	8	5	29
All	16	15	5	1	7	3	47	8	9	9	2	3	8	39	16	17	25	13	25	17	113

who have gone to engineering schools, business schools, law school, or no school sit on the boards of only the smallest companies (relatively). With equivalent diplomas, however, the chances for a seat on the board of a large company vary greatly according to social origin.[19]

Chief executives from the lower and middle ranges of the social scale have little chance of a seat on top-ranked boards, whatever their academic credentials. In contrast, members of the *bourgeoisie de robe* or the business bourgeoisie (who are more often members of the AGREF and more often named among "the hundred who run the economy" by *Expansion* – at a rate of 32 percent compared to 20 percent) merely need a Sciences-po diploma for membership on the boards of the 25 top-ranked companies (8 of 11 of those who are directors of one of the top 25 companies went to Sciences-po).[20] Similarly, chief executives from the top business bourgeoisie have a very good chance of serving on important boards, more or less regardless of their diploma, in contrast to chief executives from the mid-level bourgeoisie, who are found only on second-ranked boards – when they are not purely and simply denied any board representation whatsoever. This is confirmation *a contrario* of the fact that the real differences between those who hold identical titles are simply based on longstanding membership in the business world. For chief executives whose fathers were managers, directors, or engineers, and who are rich only in credentials, the chances of holding an important job vary according to diploma (six out of seven of those who are directors of one of the top 25 companies are *polytechniciens*).

Membership in fashionable clubs, which we know helps define the second dimension of the space, varies in close conjunction with social origin (see table 35). We always find more chief executives from the top legal or business bourgeoisie in the Automobile Club than those whose fathers were managers or engineers or who came from lower down the social scale. Chief executives originating in the oldest fractions (landowners or military officers) are highly represented in the oldest clubs (Jockey Club, Nouveau Cercle) and conversely absent from the newer, more "open" clubs (Rotary Club or Racing Club), the only ones available to chief executives from the dominated regions of social space. We note similar regularities for inclusion in the *Bottin Mondain*: chief executives in the middle and lower ranges of the social scale have a 28 percent chance of appearing in the register, compared to 36 percent for sons of managers and engineers, 47 percent for sons of industrialists and merchants, 65 percent for sons of bankers, corporate directors, and large industrialists, 66 percent for sons of higher civil servants and members of the professions, and 85 percent for sons of officers and landowners. Chief executives from the top business bourgeoisie are very clearly distinguished from those originating in the mid-level business bourgeoisie: they more often have noble roots on their father's side (19 percent compared to 3 percent); their wives are more often from the nobility (19 percent compared to 5 percent); they are especially often members of long-established families (47 percent had at least one grandfather in the bourgeoisie, some went even further back, compared to 10 percent of the others); they belong more often to the Automobile Club (as well as Polo de Bagatelle and the Nouveau Cercle) and less often to the Rotary Club.

Another index of social nobility, which, being public and official, is entirely different and yet equally tied to social origin, is the Légion d'Honneur. While 77.5 percent of the chief executives have the Légion d'Honneur, with 50 percent enjoying at least the rank of Officer, those from the *bourgeoisie de robe* and long-established families, who constitute the group most often found in liaison positions between the public and the private sectors, are also the ones the state most often recognizes and decorates. We find the highest rate of Commanders, Grands Officiers, and Grand Croix recipients, as well as Croix de Guerre recipients among the latter (61.5 percent for the sons of officers and landowners, 48.5 percent for sons of higher civil servants or members of the professions, compared to 27.5 percent of sons of businessmen). Chief executives from the middle and lower ranges of the social scale only exceptionally receive the highest distinctions. They are usually only Chevaliers in the Légion d'Honneur and are somewhat more often decorated with the Ordre du Mérite (25 percent as opposed to 16 percent) and especially the Palmes Académiques (17 percent as opposed to 4 percent) than the others, although they have not held more teaching positions in the grandes écoles and have had no more trusteeships in academic organizations than the others. Witness two contrasting examples: P. Lizon, chief executive of Le Matériel Téléphonique corporation (of the ITT group), whose father was a clerical worker and who went first to the Collège Arago and then to the École Nationale Supérieure d'Ingénieurs des Arts et Métiers de Paris, is an Officer in the Légion d'Honneur, a Commander in the Ordre National du Mérite, has the cross of the voluntary military services and the aeronautics medal, along with several other minor distinctions (the electronics great gold medal, the medal of honor and the gold medal of labor, the gold medal in physical education and sports, and the silver medal of the general union of electrical construction). In contrast, W. Baumgartner, chief executive Rhône-Poulenc in 1972, honorary governor of the Banque de France, former minister, has only one medal listed in *Who's Who* – the Grand Croix of the Légion d'Honneur.

The business world has its nobility, determined by seniority in business. The business *gentry* always possesses several titles to nobility. The venerability and reputation of their lineage, which is signaled by a noble or famous name and by "distinguished" manners and behavior, apt to give access to the most exceptional honors, privileges, and acquisitions, such as works of art (evidence of the taste of their owners), and the most selective groups, such as fashionable clubs, is usually linked to the seniority of the business owned, whose nobility is also a function of venerability, and to the personal connections it implies. We in fact find that the older a business is, the more likely it is to have a chief executive from one of the oldest families in the top business bourgeoisie or the top bourgeoisie (or nobility) *de robe*. In contrast, the most recently established companies, those founded after 1920, are headed at a rate that could not be due to chance by chief executives from either the dominated regions of the field of power or the petty bourgeoisie (see table 36).[21] Whenever chief executives whose fathers were members of the professions or higher civil servants, bankers, or corporate presidents are

Table 35 Club membership and Légion d'Honneur by social origin (percent)

Father's occupation	No club	Automobile Club	Maxim's Business Club	Jockey Club	Racing Club	Rotary Club	No Légion d'Honneur	Chevalier	Officer	Commander	Grand Officer Grand Croix	Total
Farmer, bl. collar, clerical, mid-mgr, tradesman, sm. comm.	82.5	7.0	–	–	3.5	7.0	17.0	36.5	26.5	20.0	–	100
Exec., director, engineer	80.0	4.0	–	–	12.0	4.0	23.0	50.0	23.0	–	4.0	100
Officer, landowner	74.0	13.0	–	13.0	–	–	27.0	6.5	20.0	40.0	6.5	100
Professions, higher civ. serv.	48.0	32.0	5.0	5.0	5.0	5.0	11.0	16.0	32.0	38.0	3.0	100
Lge merchant, industrialist	66.0	27.0	–	3.0	3.0	11.0	29.5	29.5	19.0	19.0	3.0	100
Lge industr., board member, corp. head, banker	50.5	36.0	3.5	4.0	4.0	2.0	27.0	23.0	28.5	14.5	7.0	100
All	61.5	23.5	2.0	3.5	4.5	5.0	22.5	27.5	26.0	20.0	4.0	100

Included are only those clubs whose membership could be verified from their yearbooks. The table shows the percentage of chief executives from the various social categories who are members of each of the clubs.

Table 36 Age of company and indicators of "nobility" of chief executive (percent)

| Founding date of enterprise | Length of time in business | | | | Grandfather bourg. de robe | de in name | Bottin Mondain | Jockey Club | Automobile Club | Inspection des Finances | "100 who run the economy" |
	CEO only	Father or father-in-law	Grandfather and earlier	Total							
Before 1840 (n = 24)	36.5	16.0	47.5	100	32.0	29.0	71.0	23.0	29.0	17.0	42.0
1840–1879 (n = 32)	50.0	22.0	28.0	100	19.0	28.0	75.0	3.0	31.0	28.0	22.0
1880–1899 (n = 38)	44.5	44.5	11.0	100	14.0	5.0	53.0	–	22.0	2.5	28.0
1900–1919 (n = 42)	42.5	40.0	17.5	100	10.0	5.0	47.5	2.5	19.0	5.0	14.0
1920 and after (n = 53)	58.0	32.0	10.0	100	16.0	11.0	36.0	–	19.0	6.0	7.5
All	48.0	33.0	19.0	100	16.0	14.0	53.0	4.0	23.0	10.0	20.0

For seniority in the *bourgeoisie de robe*, noble name, inclusion in the *Bottin Mondain*, etc., the table shows the percentage of chief executives who exhibited each of these properties among those presiding over companies founded (entirely or in part) during the various time periods.

found, in an apparent exception, at the helm of relatively young companies, they are companies in the most noble sectors, such as oil or electronics. With very few exceptions – which we could no doubt explain if we were to take into account each company's principal or dominant activity – the older a company is, the greater are its chances of being run by a chief executive with several of the signs and badges of nobility: a name preceded by *de*, a place in the *Bottin Mondain*, and membership in the oldest clubs (Jockey Club, of course, but also the Automobile Club) and the Inspection des Finances. When the business nobility compounds all these titles with the nobility of academic titles, it stands in a perfect position to impose the recognition of its own lifestyle, and thus the misrecognized and recognized domination of its own norms of perception and appreciation in the personal relations market where manners, tastes, accent, and deportment are negotiated and where a "person's" social value is determined. Its domination over business and academic parvenus, such as heads of second-ranked companies (often controlled by large foreign or technocratic groups), which can be witnessed, for example, in its nonreciprocal membership in their boards of directors, owes as much to the gentle violence of symbolic domination as to the harsh constraints of economic power.

It is understandable that the opposition between professional positions should once again be expressed in the properties of those who occupy them, the habitus underlying the *lifestyle* these properties characterize being the practical mediation through which the objective potentiality inscribed in the structure is achieved.[22] Just as the opposition between the two modes of control, private and public, gets retranslated into the opposition between the discreet and reticent heads of family businesses and the "public men" of bureaucratic companies, as we have seen, the opposition between the financial capitalism of banks and the industrial groups that have espoused their logic[23] and the monopolist capitalism of large industry can be found, according to a nonreflexive logic, in the contrast between the men of worldly connections and public relations, predisposed to translate financial ties into personal ties, and the technical executives, better prepared to perform the traditional tasks of authority and management needed for operations within the company (several among them are former high-ranking officers or prefects) than those of communication and "gentle" control, resting on the authority of information and monetary power, that are necessitated by the logic of financial capital.

We do not have to choose between structure and agents, between the field, which gives sense and value to the properties objectivated in things or embodied in persons, and the agents who play with their properties in the gaming space so defined, or, to come to the present case, between positions within the field of economic power and the dispositions of their occupants, or between the characteristics of a corporation (size, age, type of control, etc.) and those of its head (titles of nobility, property, school, etc.). By bringing people back into the picture, we can attempt to establish what, in the workings of economic institutions, arises only through people (we might think of the extreme example of those strangely composite groups whose sole unifying principle lies in the person of their founder, such as the Floirats, the Béghins, the Dassaults, and the Prouvosts, to name but a few). At the same time, we should not forget that at their most personal, persons are essentially the *personification* of requirements actually or potentially inscribed in the structure of a field or, more precisely, in the position they occupy within this field. This is why, from knowledge of the predominant form of capital held by a company's top management, it is possible to get an indication of the company's position in the field of economic power and its relationship both to other companies and to the state. In choosing an Inspecteur des Finances from the Parisian bourgeoisie as its chief executive, a company shows that in order to fulfill its most specific functions, it needs a chief executive who will not only be a "manager," exercising his power over the company with the aim, for example, of increasing productivity and profits, but also a spokesman who, in all his relations with representatives of other companies and especially the state, adds to the company's capital what is known as his *personal credit*, in other words, all the resources currently and potentially guaranteed by the properties attached to or even embodied in his *person*: "honor" and "distinction," "breeding" and "good manners," noble titles and academic titles.

It goes without saying that it is futile, here more than anywhere else, to try to sort out what is "functional," that is, the abilities and skills that are written into the strictly *technical* description of a job [*fonction*], from what gets gratuitously and artificially superimposed through a symbolic action aimed at producing the job description most likely to open up the most favorable market for a particular form of capital, and thus to legitimate the domination exercised by the holders of this capital. Because the definition of the role of chief executive, part of which is the ability to dictate a personal representation of the legitimate way of occupying this position, is in large part produced by the person who successfully occupies it, nothing can tell us more about the properties of the top positions in social space than the properties of those who occupy them, including those properties apparently most foreign to the strictly technical description of the job, such as the possession of a racing stable, an apartment on Avenue Foch, or a collection of paintings.

THE "ELITE"

No noble title suffices in and of itself to confer nobility in societies that claim to reject nobility. So, for example, the highest academic titles are necessary but insufficient, possible but not inevitable, conditions for access to the establishment. And wealth, when it is not accompanied by the appropriate "manners," is even less sufficient. People recall that Jacques Borel, who was sacrificed by the establishment, "couldn't succeed because he lacked both the money and the manners." In another case, most likely referring to Sylvain Floirat (second to the chief executive of the Engins Matra corporation, deputy president of Europe No. 1 Images et Son, born in Nailhac in the Dordogne), they comment that entrance into "society" assumes that one "refine one's upbringing" and "lose one's local accent."[24] The importance of the position occupied, measured in terms of a company's annual turnover, or the size of its shareholder equity, is significant, but people agree (and analysis confirms) that "you can be top man at a large corporation without being part of the establishment." This is where the nature of the business and its activities (sector) first come into play. The "noble" activities – banking, heavy industry, shipping, public service (reduced since the 1946 nationalizations to the distribution of water)[25] – are opposed to the hotel and restaurant business (Jacques Borel) and all commercial and distributional activities (with the exception of those that play up their ties to the past, such as the traditional department stores, *"ancien régime"* version of the *"grandes surfaces"*[26]), not to mention those that people would just as soon not be associated with, such as the "cosmetics" business (François Dalle) and real estate . . .[27]

In "democratic" societies, it is in the nature of "elites" to be defined statistically. Through another of those twists that statistics performs on the axiom *de omni et nullo*, all members of the group do not possess all the properties that define the group as such and, like the boundary of a cloud or a forest, using Rapoport's description,[28] the boundary of a group like the economic establishment[29] is an imaginary line (or surface) such that the density of individual bodies (droplets of condensed vapor, trees, or top executives) is above a certain value on one side, and below it on the other. We immediately see all the effects that can be drawn from this property. One can always both show off the small number of exemplary individuals who combine *all* the properties and all the titles that confer membership rights (this would be the case for Jacques de Fouchier, for example) and maintain the illusion of openness and "equality of chances" by putting forward all the cases of individuals who have all but one of them.[30] But this is not all. The fact that the various members of the group are, if not incomparable, at least *not interchangeable* (that is, they can never be entirely identified with each other in every respect, and *exceptions* can always be found for every definition) produces the subjective illusion of the mystery of the undefinable "person" and the subjective illusion of the group, which, founded as it is on the miracle of election, is nothing more than the sum of "exceptional" individuals or, as we say, irreplaceable "personalities."

All aristocracies define themselves as being beyond all definition. The business *gentry* feels and claims that it is beyond formal criteria of recognition and explicit rules of behavior. "'Consensus does not arise through rules, even unwritten ones,' as President Caplain explains, 'but from the

opinion people have of an individual's behavior.' (. . .) 'We instinctively recognize the ones who are and the ones who aren't,' a top industrial leader
states, adding that 'when you're part of the establishment, you don't talk
about the establishment.' " It is obvious that "there are truly no men of the
left in the establishment," but here again, it all comes down to the way one
behaves; and if people have nothing but scorn for the "trouble-makers"
who, in their progressiveness, betray their caste and give the game away,[31]
they are able to recognize carefully weighed attention to "social" concerns:
"M. Marcel Demonque, former head of Ciments Lafarge, 'brought tears to
the eyes of his peers' in describing his social concerns, but 'he was firmly on
the right.' " Similarly, what may be fatal to an as yet unpolished parvenu
may be pardoned in another, assured of his peers' indulgence. "This club,
with no written charter and no membership list, operating solely through
spontaneous and *instinctive cooptation*," which Jacques de Fouchier discusses and which we can picture better from the boards of directors of certain top companies (Paribas or Péchiney-Ugine-Kuhlmann, for example)
than from the most select clubs or "Century" dinners,[32] functions as a legal
authority "that claims the right to establish law and punish infractions."

It would be a mistake to think, in the name of that form of economism
that seems to be required whenever the economic world is discussed, that
these solidarities, like the affinities of lifestyle that ground them, should be
understood as cultural niceties and "music for the soul." They underlie economic choices that can be neither explained nor understood in terms of a
purely economic logic. Only a narrowly economistic vision of economic
relations can blind one to the fact that in the absence of "credit" with those
who hold power over credit, no credit can be had. Aristocratic groups – and
this is what creates their mystery and their charm for those on the inside –
have no other foundation than the apparent arbitrary of mutual recognition.
And we do mean apparent, since the principle behind all judgments about
membership or exclusion is none other than seniority in the group, in other
words, the mode of reproduction with the ability to confer on all the practices of those produced by this mode of reproduction that rare modality,
perceived as inimitable (and rightly so), which characterizes the so-called
natural distinction, the basis of all cooptations.

In these matters, it all comes down to *time*: " 'In one or two generations,
Carrefour's children will perhaps be part of the establishment.' 'Perhaps,'
for Guichard and Perrachon – born at the turn of the century – 'never got
beyond the provincial establishment.' "[33] It all comes down to time, that is,
to manners, which can only be acquired over time and which prove that one
is both able and willing to take one's time. *Speculation*, condemned especially as it is practiced by real estate adventurers, betrays a parvenu's hastiness,
in stark contrast to the slow, sure accumulation of a banker from a venerable old family. If there are areas such as real estate where it is "not very
ethical to earn money" (at least directly, for where would promoters be

without bankers?), this is because they attract "speculation in the pejorative sense" and derogation, that is, the suspicion of bribery, a form of pressure that can be dispensed with, in the name of business propriety, when one has at one's disposal the *highly euphemized* techniques of influence afforded by personal ties among honorable persons. It is also because they attract economic agents who live by the plain unvarnished truth of economic relations ("strongmen," "beasts"), in other words, people who are incapable of putting into these relations enough bad faith to conceal, to themselves as to others, their truth. Business propriety, and all the precepts that constitute the bourgeois *art de vivre* – the rejection of ostentatious spending (it is unseemly "to parade your wife around with a diamond that covers half her finger," or "to come to the office in a Rolls"), discretion ("the establishment doesn't like showy success"), reserve (one corporate head is criticized for speaking too much and appearing too often on television and at conferences), honor in one's private life,[34] and studied austerity of dress – are doubtless so many expressions of the collective bad faith through which the group conceals from itself the very foundation of its existence and its power, the originary denial of profit and the social connections it implies.

If aristocracies are never fond of parvenus, this is not simply through one of those defensive reflexes that lie behind every kind of *numerus clausus*; it is primarily because, through their overly rapid success, the necessarily fierce manner in which they achieved it, and the naively ostentatious way they assert or publicize it, these go-getter latecomers call to mind the arbitrary violence at the source of the initial accumulation. If belonging to the *establishment* is so closely linked to the seniority of one's establishment in business,[35] this is undoubtedly because symbolic capital consisting of recognition, confidence, and, in a word, legitimacy has its own laws of accumulation that are distinct from those of economic capital. As the Willot brothers say, "it's easier to get than to keep." If durable capital tends to be converted into credit, into prestige, in other words, into symbolic capital, a misrecognized, recognized, legitimate capital, it is undoubtedly not through a particular effect of maturation, but rather because capital always owes part of its capacity to endure, to perpetuate itself, and to reproduce itself to its capacity to *become recognized*, in other words, to become misrecognized as capital through conversion into better concealed forms of capital, such as works of art or education. It is also because its perpetuation is inevitably accompanied by a transformation of its owners' relationship to it, with the harsh severity of the founders, clearly reflecting the brutality of economic power relations, gradually giving way to the detachment of inherited ease.

Thus, when it comes to acceding to positions of economic power, a diploma's effectiveness is only conditional, and it is only completely effective (especially when it is of a more common, more "worldly" type) when matched with titles and qualities that it is not the school's business to inculcate or award. A much greater proportion of the chief executives with no higher education diploma, or with the Sciences-po diploma,[36] come from well-established families, either noble – and of the old nobility[37] – or related to nobility, than the Polytechnique graduates, whose families are much less deeply rooted and vested to a much lesser degree with the traditional attributes of nobility (see table 37). Sciences-po graduates are always more likely to be members of the oldest, most prestigious clubs (Jockey Club, Automobile Club, Cercle Interallié) than *polytechniciens*, who are rarely found on club lists (with the exception of the Cercle du Bois de Boulogne), even more rarely than graduates of engineering schools (principally Centrale, and Mines in Paris, Nancy, and Saint-Étienne) or business schools.[38]

For Polytechnique-educated chief executives, particularly those with origins in the provincial petty bourgeoisie, found primarily among the heads of foreign subsidiaries or newer industries, the school and the academic title are crucial preconditions for access to the field of power. For chief executives who went through Sciences-po, almost all of whom come from the Parisian business bourgeoisie (chiefly banking) or the oldest aristocracy, and who are primarily found in family or technocratic companies, the diploma awarded by a less selective educational institution[39] chiefly fulfills a function of legitimation. We thus see that even though academic titles can provide access to positions of economic power, the school-mediated mode of reproduction remains in head-to-head competition with the familial

Table 37 Length of time in business and indicators of "nobility" according to institution of higher education (percent)

| Academic credentials of chief executive | Length of time in business | | | | Grandfather in bourgeoisie de robe | de in name | | | Bottin Mondain |
	CEO only	At least father or father-in-law	Grandfather and earlier	Total		Mother	Father	Wife	
Polytechnique (n = 43)	72.5	22.5	5.0	100	15.0	5.0	–	9.0	46.5
Sciences-po (n = 45)	57.5	15.0	27.5	100	37.5	29.0	16.0	22.0	80.0
Engineering school (n = 39)	49.0	36.0	15.0	100	5.0	5.0	8.0	8.0	38.5
Business school (n = 17)	35.0	41.0	24.0	100	6.0	6.0	–	12.0	53.0
Law, humanities, science fac. (n = 39)	46.0	37.0	17.0	100	8.0	13.0	8.0	15.0	44.0
Secondary or higher ed. unfinished (n = 29)	18.0	53.0	29.0	100	14.0	14.0	17.0	14.0	52.0
All	49.0	32.0	19.0	100	16.0	13.0	9.0	14.0	53.0

For seniority in the *bourgeoisie de robe*, membership in the nobility, and inclusion in the *Bottin Mondain*, the table shows the percentage of chief executives with these characteristics from each of the educational channels.

mode of reproduction, even in sectors that are the most positively disposed to its effects, such as top bureaucratic companies. In addition to the fact that the cultural training provided by the most deeply rooted bourgeois families provides access to a large proportion of the dominant positions in and of itself, it alone provides the very particular form of cultural capital (deportment, manners, accent) and the social capital that, when combined with inherited economic capital, or even without it, give a person an advantage over rivals endowed with academically equivalent or even superior titles.

TRENDS AND STRUGGLES

This being said, the fact that even within the economic field, some positions – and this includes some of the most important – become accessible to corporate heads whose authority and power are grounded more in academic titles than property titles cannot fail to affect the social representation of the direct transfer of economic wealth. The new "business nobility" sees heads of family businesses, whose power rests on a more elementary form of social heredity, as survivors of a past era and is apt to paint them (in the Vulgate that is produced by commissions, committees, and clubs where higher public servants rub elbows with state chief executives, and is subsequently taught in political science institutes) as illegitimate holders of privileges from another age. Convinced that its own legitimacy stems not from wealth or birth, but from "intelligence"[40] and "competence," the business nobility perceives itself as an enlightened avant-garde, able to conceive, desire, and direct the change necessary to "conserve."[41]

It is understandable that under these circumstances the future of the two modes of domination and reproduction should be one of the major stakes in the self-interested prophecies by which the spokesmen for the new "elite" tend to produce the future in the guise of describing it. And it is justifiable to suspect that the "theories" that predict the inescapable decline of private enterprise and the triumph of "technocrats" over "heirs" (with David Granick) or *"managers"* over *"owners"* (with Berle and Means) are perhaps only inscribing into the logic of an irreversible and fatal evolution, which shifts one of the terms back into the past, an opposition that is constantly present and active in the economic field. The simple fact of describing the two poles of the space of economic power in language such as "before and after," "past and future," "avant-garde and *arrière*-garde," as people do without even thinking, in itself constitutes a stance in the political struggle that constantly sets these two poles against each other, a struggle whose stake is the definition of the legitimate use of economic power and of the legitimate titles granting access to this power and, more specifically, the power to define the future of the two modes of corporate domination and reproduction by defining the *political measures* most favorable to their respective interests. To speak in terms of evolution, to evoke the decline of owners and the rise of managers, is to implicitly ascribe a certain meaning to history and to describe as the end of a fatal process what might simply be a state in the power struggle that lies at the foundation of the structure of the corporate field and its changes over time.[42]

To show what is at stake in the most elementary operations of classification, and in the dichotomies that oppose, for example, *owners* and *managers* – in other words, what is at stake in an entire prophesy concerning the future of corporate management and its relationship to state bureaucracy – it is enough to quote the heads of three companies "condemned" by the new dominant vision. "We're completely removed from the preoccupations of the Paris technocrats who think that family businesses are up shit creek and, what is even more serious, that the entire textile industry has gone under" (interview with Bertrand Lepoutre, chief executive of a mid-sized textile company, Établissements Lepoutre, in A. Harris and A. de Sédouy, *Les patrons* (Paris: Seuil, 1977), p. 79). "I firmly believe that the theory that holds that everything is moving toward the concentration of big business is off the mark. My own feeling is that we'll experience a turn away from that . . ." (interview with Yvon Gattaz, chief executive of Radiall, in ibid., p. 202). The refutation of the destiny that the technocratic philosophy attempts to impose on family businesses may go as far as a refutation of the very principle claimed as a basis for this attempt, that is, a challenge to the technocratic claim to superior rationality and productivity: "These groups hardly ever turn a profit; they bring together a number of companies, any one of which can always make up for another, so they manage to maintain a nearly constant level of employment. Nothing really serious ever happens and they never have to put a lot of people out on the street. But they get a minimum out of their potential; they're almost nationalized, almost bureaucratic, and consequently very inefficient" (interview with Francine Gomez, chief executive of Waterman, in ibid., p. 33). These statements made by "private" heads find their counterpart in those of the technocrats who, like Alain Gomez, (left-wing) chief executive of Saint-Gobain Emballages, are ever-poised to recite back what they have learned at Sciences-po about the minor family heads who mistake the company till for the family till, perpetuate autocratic forms of authority and the mindset of the independently wealthy, etc. (cf. in ibid., pp. 271ff.).

There is no historical study of the evolution of industrial companies and the characteristics of their management that does not harbor an implicit or explicit stance on the question of which among the categories of companies set out in its analysis have the future on their side, and hence, which can claim to define, by means of the state, what the future of businesses as a whole ought to be. To speak of concentration and bureaucratization, to note the increase in chances for acceding to economic power through academic capital, and to establish the relationship that exists, both synchronically and diachronically, between these facts, is to tacitly suggest that the future belongs to the technocrats. To forget that statistics of change merely record the result at a given point in time of a political struggle whose stakes are the domination of the field of economic power through the seizure of the state is to furnish an additional weapon to those who have been able, by describing it as an inevitable *evolution*, to impose a *direction* inscribed as an objective potential within the logic of the field.

But it is not enough to be aware that the very question of the trend in the characteristics of corporate heads is an essentially political stake in that it conceals the question of the degree to which the holders of different properties are justified in occupying the positions they occupy and in performing their jobs as they do: for example, with more or less efficiency – legitimation through productivity – or with more or less "severity," or, on the other hand, "liberalism" – legitimation through "social policy." It is necessary to question once again the validity of statistical evidence, such as the "fact," at first glance indisputable, that between 1952 and 1972 the proportion of chief executives who either have no higher education degree or no secondary or higher education falls continuously and very sharply (see table 38).

We know that the period under consideration was marked by an entire set of restructuring measures that resulted in the (nominal) "disappearance" of some of the companies in our study and in the (nominal) growth of others, which, combined with the effects of the (real) growth of still further companies, translated into a very sharp increase in the size of the groups. The relationship between corporate growth and growth in the rate of post-secondary diplomas is in part due to the fact that the companies that were eliminated – either by absorption or decline – were those whose heads had the fewest diplomas.

Knowing that the across-the-board increase in company size is accompanied by an entire set of changes, among which we should include the change in the characteristics of chief executives, particularly the increase in their academic capital, we are justified in thinking that the increase in the rate of diplomas results (at least in part) from the increase in company size and the increase in the weight of the top companies in the economic field. The larger the company (hierarchized according to volume of shareholder equity), the more frequent (and more prestigious) the diplomas among French chief executives (1972 data); to put it more plainly, the larger the company, the less the possession of economic and social capital suffices in and of itself to guarantee access to power in the company. The proportion of chief executives who, as sons of industrialists, corporate board members, bankers, and large merchants, have had no advanced schooling decreases as the size of the company increases, going from 23.5 percent for the companies ranked between 101 and 200, to 11.5 percent for the top 100 companies.

But we may also wonder about the comparability of populations whose boundaries and composition depend completely on the defining principles adopted, when these principles have undergone profound changes during the period in question. Someone who was (or who might have been) interviewed as a chief executive in the initial period would, as director of a

Table 38 Academic credentials and social origins of chief executives of the top 100 companies in 1952, 1962, and 1972

	X (only)	X, Mines, Ponts, etc.	Other eng. school	Law	Humanities, sciences, medicine	Sciences-po	Business school	Bac., univ., no further details	No higher educ.	NR	Total
1952											
Lower and middle ranges social scale	4	4	–	1	–	–	–	2	–	–	11
Dominant class, including	6	13	14	8	4	4	–	2	5	13	69
execs, directors	1	5	3	1	1	–	–	–	1	–	12
officers, landowners	1	2	3	3	–	–	–	–	–	2	11
professions, higher civ. serv.	–	4	3	2	1	1	–	1	2	1	15
industr., bankers	4	2	5	2	2	3	–	1	2	10	31
NR	4	2	3	1	–	1	–	–	–	9	20
All	14	19	17	10	4	5	–	4	5	22	100
1962											
Lower and middle ranges social scale	1	5	2	–	–	–	1	–	–	1	10
Dominant class, including	6	20	18	7	5	8	5	3	3	5	80
execs, directors	1	3	4	2	–	–	–	–	1	1	12
officers, landowners	–	4	4	–	1	–	1	–	–	1	11
professions, higher civ. serv.	1	6	1	–	–	1	1	1	–	1	12
industr., bankers	4	7	9	5	4	7	3	2	2	2	45
NR	1	1	–	1	–	1	–	–	–	6	10
All	8	26	20	8	5	9	6	3	3	12	100
1972											
Lower and middle ranges social scale	3	1	5	2	–	–	2	–	–	–	13
Dominant class, including	1	18	16	11	3	15	7	4	5	1	81
execs, directors	–	4	4	2	–	2	1	–	–	–	13
officers, landowners	–	3	2	1	–	3	–	–	–	1	10
professions, higher civ. serv.	–	6	–	3	–	4	1	–	–	–	14
industr., bankers	1	5	10	5	3	6	5	4	5	–	44
NR	–	–	–	2	–	–	–	–	1	3	6
All	4	19	21	15	3	15	9	4	6	4	100

subsidiary, no longer count in the final period, even though his "real" position as well as that of the company he runs might not necessarily have changed significantly. On the other hand, someone counted as a chief executive may, through the game of hidden or unofficial agreements, have as factitious an independence as the head of a subsidiary who was not included; or, in the case of foreign subsidiaries, the nominal chief executive may be no more than the apparent (in the two senses of visible and illusory) manifestation of a power whose real base lies elsewhere, not to mention the case in which the declared, official chief executive is only the proxy for a genuine top officer, thus excluded from the space.[43]

What is at stake here, in fact, is the notion of a corporate group, the game of the nominal and the real, the official and the unofficial, that this notion encourages, and, at one and the same time, the question of power within the overall field of economic power and within the field of each particular group. In the survey, these questions are in part tacitly resolved in the selection of subjects, in our choice of some heads and rejection of others, which thus determines the "boundaries" of the group, in other words, the relative autonomy of the field of each company, and thus of its leadership – an autonomy that is one of the very stakes in the struggle among businesses.[44] And in fact, depending on our definition of "control," which may or may not coincide with the definition explicitly or implicitly used in the official delimitation of units, we can make the number and size of the elementary units vary considerably, and hence the nature and qualities of those who run them as well; which means that the method of division used in establishing the sample and in the coding operation inevitably prejudices the very answer to one of the questions we are attempting to resolve in comparing different states of the field – that of the "concentration" of businesses and the correlative changes in their management. In recording official delimitations, are we not merely taking and giving as a given what is actually the product of strategies? But do we not lose just as real an aspect of reality by setting up divisions based only on real ties, or at least on the most crucial among them, namely those based on the possession of capital? The nominal (that is, official) definition that agents engaged in the struggle for economic domination give themselves and attempt to give others, according to a particular definition of autonomy and dependence, is part of objective truth. "A group," according to the official definition – that is, as Michel Dollé puts it, "in the image that the interested parties themselves project" – "is any set of companies whose principal strategic decisions or goals are or may be coordinated by a single decision-making center." But observation counterposes to the obvious discontinuities in the definitions circulated by the group itself the *unbroken* fabric of the innumerable and varied ties that bind companies together and, as Michel Dollé again says, "*with a force that it is difficult to measure*," constitute them as groups – including relations between client and supplier (the subcontract is often at the basis of close and lasting dependencies), relations of technological dependence (patents), and especially financial and personal ties.[45]

It is probably not an exaggeration to say that, according to the definition of dependence used, one can create a sample of 200, 300, or 5,000 companies, or on the contrary, only consider 50 groups, or ten, or two, and at the same time, 50, ten, or two chief executives. So, for example, Paribas could be defined either as a group that "employs more than 22,000 people,"[46] or as "a financial group with direct power over an ensemble of subsidiary companies representing more than 340,000 employees of all types,"[47] or even as the center (or the brain) of an immense network over which it exercises direct and invisible "control" (not sanctioned by any official agreement or tie) through financial investment (even at a minimum level), credit, and information. The same could be said about the Compagnie Financière de Suez, whose size one can vary considerably depending upon whether one uses the most restrictive definition or whether one considers the financial entity made up of the more or less related autonomous groups that Suez either controls or has shares in (Air Liquide, Béghin-Say, the CGE, Ferodo, Lafarge, Pernod-Ricard, Wendel).[48]

These difficulties, which are not easy to overcome even in work on a particular state of the field, are obviously all compounded when it comes to diachronic comparisons. In fact, the most important changes consist of manipulations of nominal units that may be merely a ratification of preexisting ties, in other words, of a transformation of an official definition whose effects may or may not be real, such as the increase, through officialization, in the power of coordination and control held by a chief executive placed in a decision-making center. When the entire structure of the corporate field has been modified in the interval, comparing two populations of chief executives by treating each as the simple sum of separate units is to run the risk of forgetting that apparent invariability may conceal changes, while real invariability may be obscured by apparent changes. Any rigorous comparison must consequently be done structure by structure, field by field. Blindness to structure and structural changes has the result that change is reduced to a transformation of the substantial properties of individuals.[49] And the question can thus endlessly be debated as to whether corporate heads are more or less educated today than at the end of the nineteenth century. In addition to the fact that the value of a given diploma varies according to its rarity at a given moment, it is clear that what counts at each moment is the structure of the distribution of the different academic titles among the different chief executives and, more precisely, the differences recorded, at the different time periods, in the variations in this structure according to their particular origins.

Thus, for the three dates considered, 1952, 1962, and 1972, chief executives from the lower and middle ranges of the social scale or the working bourgeoisie (managers, engineers, directors) all have a higher education diploma and, with very rare exceptions, have gone to Polytechnique (or, in 1972, to another engineering school, usually Mines); almost none have done Sciences-po (we count two exceptions in 1972). In contrast, chief executives from families of members of the professions or higher civil servants all have at least one higher education diploma in 1972, a change from 1962 and 1952, and the proportion of those who have studied law or gone to Sciences-po or a business school has risen sharply. But the most important finding is undoubtedly that a number of the chief executives from the business bourgeoisie who in 1952 were relatively unlikely to have done (or who would have done little) postsecondary work (13 of 31) can still, in 1972, attain the highest positions with no higher education diploma (9 of 44), although an increasing proportion of them do have one, either a second-ranked engineering title (from Centrale, for example), or a title from a law faculté, Sciences-po, or a business school.

Given that there are no commercial companies in the 1952 sample, HEC graduates may be underestimated for that period. It is clear, however, that the rise in HEC graduates is much more marked at the management level below chief executive than at the chief executive level itself. Analyzing the careers of 908 executives working in 1977 (as chief executives, managing directors, financial managers, administrative managers, marketing directors, business managers, technical managers, and personnel directors) shows that it is graduates of HEC, the ESSEC, Sup de Co Paris, and Sciences-po (Sciences-po statistics are unfortunately mixed in with the statistics on business schools) who usually occupy the jobs of administrative manager, financial manager, marketing director, and business manager.[50]

In short, the transformation of the corporate field has been accompanied by an overall rise in the proportion of those with higher education diplomas, even among family "heirs," and by an inverse evolution for *polytechniciens* and Sciences-po or HEC graduates: the former, and especially those who did not graduate into a grand corps or do complementary studies, saw their representation diminish, while the relative proportion of the latter increased significantly (this increase, particularly dramatic among descendants of the business bourgeoisie, would be much more marked if we were to include banking as well).

Thus, analyzing the evolution of power relations over time confirms the conclusions we drew from our observation of the powers in play at a single point in time. While no one would deny that academic credentials have increasingly become the rule for all those wishing to accede to the most sought-after positions in the economic field, including heirs themselves, which might lead one to believe in the progressive triumph of the academic mode of reproduction, the fact remains that chief executives tied into the family mode of reproduction have nonetheless found ways of getting around the academic obstacle. The greatest increase involves titles that, like those awarded by Sciences-po, HEC, and even Centrale, function as instruments of legitimation that are both structurally and functionally equivalent to what the baccalauréat (or, for the provincial dynasties the most certain of their legitimacy, the simple fact of attending a Jesuit school) represented in another state of the competition and the social need for legitimation.

Describing how he found himself channeled toward Sciences-po, and especially the "humiliation" he felt at the fact that his older brother, a philosopher, advised him to go there, this Sciences-po graduate clearly reveals the institution's social image as it stood in the 1950s: "So, since all the friends I had gradually met in Paris – first at Claude Bernard, then at Janson de Sailly – were there, at least all the somewhat normal or non-math ones, I went to Sciences-po, but with a feeling of derision and great scorn for the place." And he describes his educational experience thus: "I was shocked at what I found at Sciences-po – a lack of causal reasoning, a failure to go back to the source, a refusal to sit back and take stock; all we did was descriptive work! The least little sociological analysis seemed worthy of Descartes or Kant; Sciences-po's method was really what my friend calls 'semi-education': 'Give me a "close-up" on Proust, you've got ten minutes.' "[51]

THE PRIVILEGE OF THE "BEROBED"

The advantage enjoyed in the struggle for economic power by the pretenders born into the top Parisian bourgeoisie (the top business bourgeoisie, of course, as well as high-level public service and the professions) who went through Sciences-po and the Inspection des Finances can only be fully explained if we take into account the transformations in the structure of the field of power that were triggered by a transformation of the relationship between financial capital and industrial capital, which led to a strengthening of the position held by banks and bankers within the field of economic power. Industrial companies tend to lose their financial autonomy (which, according to Jean Bouvier, was still very real at the turn of the century) with respect to large banking groups, which, owing to the invention of new ways of concentrating capital and savings, manage to control entire branches of industry without being their exclusive owners. Bankers are thus in a position to impose their vision and expectations[52] – giving priority to management questions and interpreting a company's future from a financial and accounting point of view – over those of industrialists and technicians, who are primarily interested in rationalizing technique. Within the corporate field, the increase in the power of banks also managed to strengthen financial management in relation to technical management, in other words, Inspecteurs de Finance and Sciences-po graduates in relation to those holding technical diplomas such as Mines engineers.

As they become larger and more bureaucratic, companies increasingly tend to function as a field of struggles among agents whose power, interests, and strategies depend on the amount and structure of their capital, which will either be more economic or more academic. One of the stakes in these struggles is the transformation or preservation of principles of hierarchization. Subverting the order of precedence among properties (for example, among the various grande école titles) that are expressed in the order of precedence among the bearers of these properties would amount to upsetting the balance of power within management. It can be seen that, within this logic, the cooptation among holders of identical properties that is at the source of, for example, the swarming of grande école classmates is not solely a result of personal ties developed at school or affinity of habitus, but also a consequence of the need to ensure the reproduction of the hierarchy that obtains within the company by reaffirming the invariability of the criteria of hierarchization. And it comes as no surprise that the salient properties of corporate "heads," such as graduation from a grande école or membership in a grand corps, tend to be found with nonrandom frequency among their company's personnel. The "strategies" of the corporation considered as a moral person endowed (as a collective being institutionally constituted as such) with the power to act and react to the actions and reactions of rival or allied companies and to other interest groups (financial backers, suppliers, consumers, labor unions, the government, etc.) are themselves the product of interactions that develop, on the basis of a determined set of power relations, among both individual and collective agents endowed with different capital (especially academic) and convergent or divergent interests who, whatever their title, occupy positions of power in the corporate field (stockholders – majority or otherwise – presidents, directors, managers, etc.).

We can also assume that this increased corporate interdependence can only strengthen the positions located at the center of the network of relations in the competition both within a single company and within the field of economic power, and hence attract agents of a new kind. A company's increased size results at least as often from the development of new forms of solidarity among economic units as from any autonomous development. The decrease in the relative proportion of individual companies is correlative to the appearance of a new type of moral person, such as the "common interest group," as well as an increase in the number of businesses located at the boundary of the private and public sectors and the development of more diversified and more complex relations among elementary economic units: competitive relations among independent companies, but also administrative relations among companies belonging to the same group, relations of dominance among companies that are formally distinct but joined by financial ties, "personal ties" among companies belonging to different groups, or still further, the domination of a market, which makes it possible for a large integrated company to guarantee itself the equivalent of bureaucratic control over the smaller companies it buys from. These transformations in the structure of the economic field tend to increase the *de facto* interdependence among companies, thus substituting for the former mechanical solidarity among businesses and entrepreneurs that fit into a "common type," as Durkheim would say, an *organic solidarity*, founded on the complementarity of their interests and on complex (and sometimes circular) networks of domination.

In the competition that opposes them on the one hand to family heads, whether founders or heirs, who are up against all official discourse and the policies it inspires, and on the other, to technicians, products of their scholarly works, whose virtues are a bit too military for the needs of the new mode of domination, financial managers seem to be in the best position to ensure the victory of their vision of the economic and social world.[53] The increase in *de facto* and *de jure* corporate interdependence, especially increased relations between the private and public sectors and with foreign companies,[54] probably plays no small part in the added value conferred on graduates of Sciences-po and the ENA. These two schools – especially through their social recruitment, but also through the social philosophy they inculcate and the premium they put on the ability to discuss and to negotiate, on mastery of foreign languages, and on the guarded manners of the higher civil servant (in direct contrast to the energetic and bully-like brutality of the combat corporate executive) – indeed constitute one of the laboratories of the new style of sociability called for by the changes in the structure of the economic field.[55]

The heads of the top 100 companies were much less likely in 1952 than in 1972 to be on ad hoc committees or commissions (the number of which increased during the Fifth Republic), to have held high-level public service positions, or to have spent time in ministerial cabinets. In addition, while it was graduates of the scientific grandes écoles (especially *polytechniciens* from the Corps des Mines) who held a monopoly on connections with bureaucratic authorities in 1952, in 1972 we tend to find corporate heads from families of civil servants or members of the professions (who have often spent time in a grand corps, principally the Inspection des Finances, and ministerial cabinets) on planning councils and especially on restricted committees where higher civil servants with ties to the business world rub shoulders with representatives from the private sector who often have close ties to high-level public service.[56]

The top state chief executives (at the time of our survey, this would include, for example, Pierre Jouven, Wilfrid Baumgartner, Ambroise Roux, Roger Martin, Pierre de Calan, and Jacques de Fouchier), especially those with origins in the top *bourgeoisie de robe* (high-level public service and the professions) and also, but to a lesser degree, the old fractions of the bourgeoisie (officers or landowners), were "predestined," as it were, to occupy positions located at the *intersection* between the public and the private sectors or, better still, between banking, industry, and the state, the very locus of power today. Everything combines indeed to prepare these "men of connections"[57] to occupy these eminent positions (top corporate banks, public energy and transportation companies, mixed companies, etc.) where, in an atmosphere of both complicity and conflict, large state markets and the public subsidy of so-called "grassroots" or "high tech" industries are negotiated, and where political decisions (on credit, housing, etc.) likely to provide new areas of investment and new sources of profit are hammered out.

As members of families with ties to several social universes (the professions and business, for example), with an often eclectic education (science and the law, for example), these men found themselves faced with a wider space of possibilities[58] than the one available to businessmen whose origins were in the business world (Guy de Rothschild, Stanislas Darblay, Tristan Vieljeux, Renaud Gillet, Pierre Champin, etc.).[59] More often born in Paris or the surrounding area, with wider experience of the (relatively) more diverse and more open world of the top lycées, followed by the grandes écoles and the grands corps (especially the Inspection des Finances and Mines), they were connected to the business world from the very start of their careers, either as members of a ministerial cabinet, usually in the Finance Ministry or the Ministry of Industry, or as deputy directors in these same ministries, thus acquiring, when it had not already been passed on to them from their family, the vast network of connections that enabled them to cross over to the private sector [*pantouflage*] very early on. (See table 39.)

But this is not all. Belonging to an old noble family or a long-established bourgeois family by definition implies the possession of social capital in the form of relations (kinship or otherwise), which are always partially transferable. What is

Table 39 Career and ties to the state according to social origin (percent)

Father's occupation	Career						Ties with the state				
	Private sector only	Pantouflage before age 35	Pantouflage at 35–50	Pantouflage at 51 and over	Public sector only	Total	Inspection des Finances	Conseil d'État	Cour des Comptes	Préfectural corps	Ministerial cabinet
Farmer, bl. collar, clerical, mid-mgr, tradesman, sm. comm.	74.0	4.0	7.0	4.0	11.0	100	3.0	–	–	–	13.0
Exec., director, engineer	64.0	4.0	24.0	4.0	4.0	100	4.0	–	4.0	–	27.0
Officer, landowner	36.0	7.0	21.0	7.0	29.0	100	27.0	6.5	–	6.5	47.0
Professions, higher civ. serv.	25.0	22.0	22.0	14.0	17.0	100	22.0	19.0	3.0	5.5	43.0
Lge merchant, industrialist	75.5	11.0	2.5	5.5	5.5	100	3.0	–	–	3.0	5.5
Lge industr., board member, corp. head, banker	82.0	5.5	3.5	–	9.0	100	7.0	2.0	–	2.0	11.0
All	64.0	9.0	11.0	5.0	11.0	100	9.5	4.5	1.0	2.5	21.0

For the grands corps and ministerial cabinets, the table gives the percentage of chief executives from the different social classes who have been in each.

more, it provides a thousand ready ways to increase this capital: first, because, in these matters more than anywhere else, capital attracts capital, and because belonging to a prestigious lineage, symbolized by a famous name, provides relations in and of itself (marriages, friendships, connections, etc.); secondly, because overt *placement* strategies,[60] such as those that lead people to join groups of similar rank and avoid inferior groups, tend to favor the development of socially homogeneous relations; and finally, because early inclusion in a universe that attaches great importance to social life [*la "vie de relations"*] (parties, family ceremonies, such as birthdays, etc.) and places a high value on institutions and occasions designed to establish or maintain social relations (New Year's greetings, social calls, etc.) is very likely to inculcate both the propensity and the aptitude (for example, in the form of a very special type of memory for names and genealogies) for cultivating relations as well as a "sense" of appropriate ties.[61] It would be necessary to examine in the same way all the advantages associated with Parisian birth and residence in this highly centralized social universe, not only from the economic and political point of view, but also and most importantly from the cultural and "worldly" point of view (see table 40).[62] The importance attached to place of residence can be understood not only in the value attached to one's *address*, one sign of nobility among others, but also in the importance that being at the very heart of "society" takes on for one's social life (parties, dinners, encounters). Thus, among the chief executives (almost all of whom live in Paris or the surrounding area and a great many of whom live in the sixteenth *arrondissement* [upper-class neighborhood, Tr.]), those who went to Sciences-po, especially those from the bourgeoisie or the *noblesse de robe*, more often live in the first seven *arrondissements*, particularly the sixth and seventh, traditional aristocratic neighborhoods where the top ministries were set up (while *polytechniciens* more often live in the stylish suburbs – Neuilly, Saint-Cloud, Versailles, etc.).

As large holders of cultural capital (they hold the most prestigious academic titles), symbolic capital (often noble, they enjoy *honors* both public, such as the Légion d'Honneur, and private, such as membership in the most exclusive clubs), and social capital (either inherited directly from their family or acquired through marriage, attendance at a top lycée or grande école, tenure in a ministerial cabinet, or service on the board of directors of a top-ranked company), the chief executives from the Parisian *bourgeoisie de robe* and *noblesse de robe*, from which the new state financial oligarchy is primarily recruited, are the *personification*, as it were, of a particular state of the structure of the field of economic power.[63] This is not only because they have all the properties needed to bring out the potential of that part of the necessity of the field that is achieved through agents, and only through agents, that is, in the relationship between the network of financial relations and the network of "personal relations," in the broadest sense; but also because they hold titles of all kinds, both those that actually provide access to the positions they occupy, such as property titles and titles of nobility, and those that legitimate this occupation. The primary function of the titles conferred by the most worldly educational institutions might thus be to encourage people to impute to the competence these titles are taken to

Table 40 Place of birth and residence according to institution of higher education (percent)

Academic credentials of chief executive	Place of birth						Residence									
	Paris + Paris area	Over 100,000 inhabitants	5,000–100,000 inhabitants	Under 5,000 inhabitants	Abroad	Total	Paris, I to VI	Paris VII	Paris VIII	Paris XVI	Paris XVII	Paris, other arr.	Neuilly	Suburbs	Provinces	Total
Polytechnique	37.0	14.0	28.0	12.0	9.0	100	9.5	2.0	7.0	36.0	5.0	2.0	21.5	12.0	5.0	100
Sciences-po	64.5	4.5	20.0	–	11.0	100	14.0	21.0	5.0	30.0	5.0	–	11.0	9.0	5.0	100
Engineering school	33.5	20.5	10.0	26.0	10.0	100	3.0	18.0	3.0	34.0	5.0	3.0	8.0	13.0	13.0	100
Business school	47.0	23.0	12.0	12.0	6.0	100	–	12.5	25.0	25.0	–	6.0	12.5	6.0	12.5	100
Law, humanities, science fac.	39.0	20.5	10.0	20.5	10.0	100	8.0	5.0	13.0	24.0	5.0	5.0	24.0	–	16.0	100
Secondary school or higher ed. unfinished	35.0	24.0	17.0	17.0	7.0	100	–	14.0	3.5	38.0	7.0	–	3.5	3.5	31.0	100
All	43.0	16.5	17.0	14.0	9.5	100	7.0	12.0	8.0	31.5	5.0	2.5	14.0	8.0	12.0	100

guarantee what is in reality an effect of the set of secondary properties they designate by implication (such as social capital in the form of school acquaintances or the "authority" and "self-assurance" of the academic "elite") or that are statistically associated with them (such as the "distinction" that accompanies longstanding membership in the bourgeoisie).

The facade of pure technical rationality erected by the top management class, and the state financial oligarchy that dominates it, especially for external consumption, by making competence, understood as a guarantee of efficiency and productivity, the be-all and end-all of values, effectively masks the true preconditions for access to dominant positions. The criteria operative on the inside are diametrically opposed to the rational modernist image that the great technocratic parade presents to the outside world. This managerial "elite" that claims to be completely future-minded finds the true principles of its selection, as well as the practical justifications for its privileges, in the past, in history, and in the antiquity of its vested interests. It has not been sufficiently brought out that, by means of a *concours* that, like ENA's, consecrates very particular dispositions (as far removed from those supposedly required of an industrial head as from those expected of a researcher or an intellectual), an entire set of social categories formerly on the margins of industrial development and scientific progress – large-scale owners, higher civil servants, military dignitaries, top magistrates – returns to the scene; and that we have probably never seen so many bearers of noble or ennobled names in the highest echelons of the state.

Making the length of time one has been in power the (hidden) principle behind hierarchies of power is not just to impose the probation time necessary for parvenus both to assimilate themselves by assimilating the ways of behaving that need a long period of time to become deeply ingrained, and to become assimilated, among other ways, through marriage or acquaintanceships, which in all milieus at all times constitute one of the surest ways of *policing* latecomers. Placing this assimilative effort under the sign of the past, the old ways, and the established order of which the "old guard" are both guarantors and guardians is to place an insurmountable obstacle in the way of the impatience of the newcomers. There is no barrier more insurmountable than time ("Time, the mark of my powerlessness," as the philosopher said, unaware of just how right he was), and all social bodies use it to maintain *an order of succession*, as Leibniz said in reference to time, in other words, to maintain the distances that must be kept, as we say, because they are constitutive of the social order – those that separate tenants and claimants, fathers and sons, owners and heirs, masters and disciples, predecessors and successors, so many social ranks that are very often distinguished by nothing but time. This is what is concealed by the ritual debate over *owners* and *managers* when people confine their consideration to property titles.[64] The process through which the top economic establishment assimilates some of its *grands commis* or through which some of its *grands commis* in turn assimilate themselves into it (when their origins are elsewhere) cannot be measured solely in terms of economic indices such as the possession of shares or seats on boards of directors.

And these indices themselves, if we take them seriously, are enough to call into question the idea that *managers*, authorized solely by their competence, are gradually replacing owners. We see in fact that chief executives of top public companies, who thus conform most closely to the ordinary image of a *manager*, are just about as likely as family chief executives to hold a significant number of shares and are often from families who have been in business for a long time. We also note that a good number of the heads of top corporations are also heads of smaller subsidiaries and thus hold "property rights." Finally, we see that, without having to dip into the company till like family chief executives (as *managers* see them), most *managers* receive rewards taken directly out of company profits, "bonuses," housing, cars, and services, especially in the form of vacations or business meals.[65]

In short, ignoring the forms of integration into the establishment that do not necessarily derive from capital participation and confusing a transformation of the mode of reproduction with a transformation of the mode of appropriation of capital and profits add up to succumbing to the myth of the "democratization" of capital or, as Keynes put it, "the tendency of big enterprise to socialize itself,"[66] which finds natural support in the myth of "school democratization."[67] Everything – the logic of the mechanisms of academic reproduction that, among other things, effectively conceal their own efficacy, the inertia of the taxonomies that, in continuing to contrast private income with salaries, prevent one from recognizing, under the irreproachable appearance of a salary, income from capital that is inseparably economic, cultural, and social, and the infusion of the ideology of "public service" that joins with the illusion of academic neutrality to substitute the academic title for the property title as a legitimate instrument for the appropriation of the profits of economic capital – combines to make the company heads of the present, and especially those of the future, no longer appear to be the heirs to a fortune they did not create, but rather the most exemplary of self-made men, appointed by their "gifts" and their "merits" to wield power over economic production in the name of "competence" and "intelligence."

The public service ethic that higher civil servants and "technocratic" heads love to profess undoubtedly finds some objective foundation in the inherited dispositions of a family milieu that, both in the case of the *bourgeoisie de robe* and the salaried portions of the petty bourgeoisie, hardly encourage an interest in business or the worship of money. Everything indeed occurs as if individuals with origins in these regions of social space were only able to brave the business world after a legitimating detour through education and public service, a route that leads them to manage already established businesses rather than to establish new ones, with all the risks and compromises these may involve. In a draft of a book on Jacques de Fouchier,

Merry Bromberger describes his original family milieu thus: "He was born on 11 June 1911 in Pecq (Seine-et-Oise) in a highly regarded villa surrounded by old trees, the son of Louis de Fouchier, president of chambers at the Cour des Comptes. In those days, the Cour des Comptes was the most highly respected of all the government corps. The president of chambers was a magistrate of elegant bearing, but full of zest for life, a man who loved the theater, and wit, and who appreciated an honorific occupation that left him leisure time (. . .). Money was despised, and the desire for money was seen as a moral defect" (press archives of the Compagnie Bancaire).

Few ruling groups have ever brought together so many principles of legitimation of such diversity, which, although apparently contradictory (such as the aristocracism of birth and the meritocracism of academic success or scientific competence, or the ideology of "public service" and the cult of profit disguised as the worship of productivity), combine to inspire in the new leaders the most absolute certainty in their legitimacy. The top bourgeoisie, that ensemble of nearly exclusively Parisian lineages, bankers, industrialists, top state chief executives, and top *bourgeois de robe*, among whom the ensemble of positions of economic and political power are redistributed at the mercy of "vocations" and cooptations, with apparent discontinuities in the mechanical chain of successions – a banker's son may become a professor at the law faculté, while the son of a professor of medicine may become a state chief executive – tends to wield in all domains of practice a power equivalent to the power over economic capital that is secured by its capacity to mobilize financial capital. The interpenetration of the public and private sectors, and the coexistence of the family mode of reproduction and a school-mediated mode of reproduction adjusted by the game of cooptation – which share in making the bourgeois culture and *art de vivre*, rather widely recognized as realizations of human excellence, the precondition for access to economic power – combine to make the historic combination thus realized a highly euphemized and sublimated form of power, which ordinary denunciations leave untouched, failing as they do to challenge the foundations of people's belief in it.[68]

3

Transformations in the Structure of the Field of Power

The changes that have occurred in the field of economic power, and especially those resulting from the fact that access to dominant positions in the economic field has increasingly tended to depend on academic titles, even specially bred ones, have given rise to a profound modification in the structure of the relations of power within the field of power. In the economic field itself, the concentration in the means of economic production was accompanied by a concentration in the means of cultural production, which has defined the conditions for a new use of cultural capital. *Bourgeois employees*, a group whose development goes hand in hand with the spread of corporate bureaucratization, express in their strategies the contradictions inherent in the possession of a form of capital that, with few exceptions, can no longer guarantee economic profits (especially in its role as an instrument for the specific appropriation of cultural capital materialized as instruments of production) except within organizations of cultural production that have the economic capital necessary to gather cultural producers together and guarantee them the salaries and increasingly costly instruments of production that are essential to their productive activity. This is what distinguishes bourgeois employees (engineers, researchers, teachers, etc.) from members of the professions, who, as self-employed professionals, can put their embodied capital to use and earn profits from it with no external capital input (or at the cost of just a limited amount, in any case).[1] As holders of a form of capital whose use depends on the possession of economic capital, bourgeois employees, and more generally, those known as *cadres*, are doomed by the ambiguity of their position to a profound ambiguity in their stances. The advantage they enjoy as holders of cultural capital over those who are bereft of it moves them closer to the dominant pole of the field of power, without necessarily placing them close to the dominated in social space, while the subordinated position of this kind of capital distances them from those who, being possessed of economic capital, have control over the use of their capital. The change in the structure of intellectual establishments (which is itself governed by the change in industrial establishments) and the increased complexity of technology combine to force many holders of cultural capital to abandon their status as unattached cultural producers or small independent inventors for that of salaried cultural producers, integrated into research teams endowed with expensive equipment and involved in long-term projects.[2] This process of relative dispossession, which first took place in the domain of the exact sciences, where it led to a very high concentration of producers in large public and private companies, now affects the domain of the human sciences, where the development of publicly sponsored research (the institutional prosperity of which varies inversely with its autonomy vis-à-vis external constraints or demands) and applied research designed to serve large public and private bureaucracies drive the intellectual trades back toward the most traditional academic disciplines, such as philosophy and the arts.

The development of vast collective units of cultural production (research organizations, think tanks, etc.) and distribution (radio, television, film, journalism, etc.) and the correlative decline in independent intellectual producers in favor of salaried categories have given rise to a transformation both of the relationship that the producers (henceforth inscribed in hierarchized ensembles and vested with rationalized careers) maintain with their work and of their aesthetic and political stances. Intellectual work performed collectively, within technically and socially differentiated and often hierarchized units of production, and largely dependent on past or present collective work and costly instruments of production, can no longer surround itself with the charismatic aura that used to cloak the traditional writer, artist, or philosopher, as small independent producers laboring solely with their cultural capital, apt to be perceived as a gift from heaven. The objective and subjective demystification of "creative" activity that correlates with this transformation in the social conditions of production particularly affects intellectuals and artists working in cultural distribution (radio, film, television, journalism), who, in addition, cannot fail to sense the contradiction between the aesthetic and political attitudes called for by their inferior and marginal position in the field of production and the objectively conservative functions (from both the aesthetic and political standpoints) of the products of their activity.

These structural changes have been accompanied by upheavals in the relative market values of the different subforms of cultural capital. The official price quoted for the traditional humanities, whose value derived less from their professional utility or economic profitability than from the limited nature of their distribution, and hence their power to confer distinction, has tended to diminish in favor of that of cultural capital in its scientific, technical, and especially bureaucratico-political form; the economic profitability of the latter has been ensured by the increase in new demands for symbolic services, and its symbolic profitability has tended to increase in concert with the change in the relative weight and prestige of the traditional compared with the new fractions of the bourgeoisie (doctors, lawyers, etc., versus managers, advertising agents, etc.).

Cultural producers, henceforth denied a monopoly on academic capital by the importation of the academic title even into milieus traditionally foreign to the school and to culture (according to the old antinomy between the artist and the "bourgeois") or reduced to a monopoly on forms of cultural capital that have suffered a significant devaluation in all but the academic market (such as the classics), come up against the holders of economic capital who, shored up by a temporal success guaranteed, at least in their own eyes, by an academically attested competence, attempt to extend their hold over the field of cultural production in three ways. First, they intervene either personally or through their "organic intellectuals" in struggles over the imposition of a new definition of legitimacy for cultural capital and intellectuals. Secondly, they mount a practical challenge to the university's monopoly on establishing the hierarchy of rank, using educational institutions staffed by teachers who, in their great majority, are either born into the economic field or hold secondary positions in it (as is already the case at Sciences-po and HEC). Finally, they favor the establishment of institutionalized controls on cultural production, particularly scientific research. One sign of this process is the appearance, alongside administration "scientists," of science administrators with origins in public administration or scientific research, and often adjudged to be of little value in their respective universes, who impose upon researchers constraints and hierarchies that are foreign to the specific logic of the scientific field. Another is the development of a veritable *state patronage*, which enables high-level cultural officials and their contacts in the art world (such as directors of museums or large institutions of cultural promotion) to impose their norms in the artistic field.

This heightening of external pressures and demands has given rise to an increase in the tensions within the field of cultural production. The division (as old as the intellectual field) between production for the sake of producers and production directed to an outside demand, which implied a form of agreement on the areas of disagreement (the so-called right-wing or "Right Bank" intellectuals affirming their recognition of the values and the value of the so-called left-wing intellectuals in and through the very weapons they used to fight them), has increasingly tended to give way to a radical antagonism between two categories of producers each of which refuses to recognize or acknowledge the existence of the other. In contrast to the old-style intellectuals, who can only assert their existence, identified with their autonomy, by renouncing more radically and more ostentatiously than ever all compromise with the economic world (and all its corresponding profits) and by exasperated declarations of their irreducibility, both on the strictly intellectual plane and on the political plane, there arise henceforth the managerial intellectuals, or the intellectual managers, who, as holders of forms of cultural capital recognized in the economic field, accept the status of bourgeois employee, ready to satisfy a demand for a new kind of intellectual service. We can see why certain institutions, such as the INSEE, finding themselves in a doubly legitimate position, both governmental and scientific, and certain disciplines, such as economics, and perhaps especially sociology, located at the intersection of the intellectual, political, and economic fields, should be the locus of particularly lively confrontations between different ways of conceiving or incarnating the role of cultural producer. The choice is clear indeed, although rarely distinguished: either accept one of the two social functions imparted by the new social definition to cultural producers, that of the expert, charged with assisting the dominants in the management of "social problems," or that of the professor, locked away in erudite debate on academic questions; or efficiently (that is, using the weapons of science) assume the function that was for a long time fulfilled by the intellectual, that is, enter the political arena in the name of the values and truths acquired in and through autonomy.

Appendix 1

The Field of Economic Power in 1972 (Correspondence Analysis)

SAMPLE AND INDICATORS USED

This analysis is based on a systematic examination of data gathered, beginning in 1972, on the chief executive officers of the top 200 industrial and commercial companies in 1972 ranked according to shareholder equity (cf. the list of the top 5,000 companies published by *Entreprise* in November of 1972), to which were added the CEOs of nationalized or semipublic utilities (EDF, RATP [greater Paris public transportation system, Tr.], etc., who numbered 9) where shareholder equity was at least 102,361,000 francs (capital held in 1972 by Presses de la Cité, the 200th company) and the CEOs of the largest banks (20) and insurance companies (12). It was only possible to use 216 (or 90 percent) of the 241 CEOs because data on the other 10 percent proved to be too *sketchy*.[1] Identical data were also gathered on the CEOs of the top 100 industrial companies in 1952 and 1962 for the purpose of historical comparison.

In addition to demographic information (date and place of birth, number of children, place of residence), we analyzed[2] a set of data on their *family*, such as father's occupation, the length of time the family had been in the business world or the *bourgeoisie de robe*, mention in the *Bottin Mondain*; their *secondary and post-secondary schooling*, at one of the top Parisian lycées (Janson, Condorcet, Louis-le-Grand, Saint-Louis), another lycée in Paris or the provinces, or at a private school (École des Roches, Stanislas, Sainte-Croix de Neuilly, Sainte-Geneviève, etc.), the number of higher education diplomas, the diploma(s) obtained, and, for Polytechnique and the Institut d'Études Politiques, the age at which the diplomas were awarded; their *career*, including changes in sector and particularly, for those who moved from the public to the private sector, the age at which the move was made, tenure in the grands corps (Inspection des Finances, Conseil d'État), the prefectural corps, or the military; their *positions of economic power*, such as service on boards of directors in industry and banking (by importance), responsibilities held in the CNPF and the various employers' federations, name among "the hundred who run the economy" (published by the monthly *Expansion*); their past and present *service on commissions and in organizations* belonging to other fields (political, administrative, academic, or intellectual), planning councils, the Economic and Social Council, grande école or university teaching, trusteeships in the university field, the press, or publishing, service on commissions on regional economic development, positions as mayor or head of *département*; major *decorations*, as signs of official recognition for services rendered and ties to other fields – the Légion d'Honneur, Médaille de la Résistance, Croix de Guerre, Ordre du Mérite, Palmes Académiques, Médaille du Commerce; and finally, data concerning their *company*, its status (private, mixed, etc.), mode of control (family, foreign, technocratic, or state), principal sector (banking, insurance, industry, business, public utilities, transportation), and importance (according to the amount of shareholder equity).

We chose to treat as illustrative variables the indicators for which the available data either were not exhaustive or could not be verified for a portion of the CEOs (from between 10 and 30 percent, depending), such as the fact that a CEO may possess a significant number of shares in the company he heads, or that he has held a position as engineer or manager in the company, his religion, the degrees he has earned abroad (particularly in the United States), his sporting activities (skiing, tennis, golf, riding, yachting, flying, etc.), his club memberships (Nouveau Cercle, Polo de Bagatelle, Rotary Club, Racing Club de France, Automobile Club de France, Maxim's Business Club, Travellers Club, Cercle Interallié, Cercle du Bois de Boulogne, Jockey Club), and the founding date of his company. We also used as supplementary variables indicators that only measured part of the phenomenon that we wanted to study, for example, indicators of political opinions or attitudes (in the broad sense), such as membership in various sorts of employers' groups – ACADI [association of industrial executives for economic and social progress]), AGREF, Centre de Recherches et d'Études des Chefs d'Entreprise, Entreprise et Progrès (we were in the end unable to gain access to complete lists of the members of the UNICER [union of corporate heads and executives] or the Centre Français du Patronat Chrétien [French center for Christian employers]). We also used as illustrative variables data on the particle *de* in the father's, mother's, and wife's names because these data were only relevant for a relatively small percentage of the CEOs (13 percent have a *de* in their name) and because mention in the *Bottin Mondain* and especially length of time in the bourgeoisie and the business milieu were more relevant and less restrictive indicators of access to "society." The properties that were limited to a small number of CEOs (5 or fewer) were also treated as illustrative variables, even when they were important indicators that we had carefully verified. This is primarily the case for a tour in the Cour des Comptes (2 CEOs), political office, such as parliamentary deputy or senator (4 CEOs), or particular forms of a variable (for example, the CEOs who are sons of blue-collar workers or tradesmen, 2 of each).

SOURCES

As public figures, the heads of top companies may agree, on different occasions and with different interlocutors, to reveal information that they would not willingly grant to the first researcher to come along.[3] This is why, as long as we gather together the various sparse bits of data and control them by collating sources and, whenever possible, including direct questioning or informant interviews, we stand to learn more, more fully, about the essential questions this way than we would from a direct survey.[4] We thus complemented and controlled the data collected through a methodical study of written sources with a systematic set of informant interviews (journalists from the economic press, authors of biographical yearbooks, managers and CEOs of large and mid-sized companies, leaders of employers' organizations, clubs, etc.); we also consulted INSEE researchers well versed in corporate studies, to whom this work is indebted.

Even though the list published by *Entreprise* in 1972[5] is not without its gaps and imperfections,[6] it proved to be the one that best enabled us to study the field of economic power, its transformations, the conditions for entry into the field, and the power struggles among business leaders, for the very reason that it "shows a group's true strength while breaking its principal activities down into distinct producer and commercial units" (subsidiaries are not counted when the larger group has already been mentioned).[7]

Given that our study of the *boards of directors* of a sample of 30 companies of varying size, sector, and mode of control established that the members of these boards usually share a larger number of characteristics with the CEO, especially social and academic characteristics, it did not seem necessary to extend our analysis to all board members of all the companies in the study. On the other hand, in order to gain a complete understanding of the laws governing transformation in the corporate field, we would need to do a direct survey of *all the directors of a carefully chosen sample of companies*. Indeed, the data to which we might have access using the methods of our study on CEOs are insufficient here, especially for the companies which are relatively the smallest.

The data collected on the history of the largest companies, their development, recent transformations, and financial and personal ties, come mainly from DAFSA publications "Fiches synthéthiques par sociétés," "Études de groupes," from the *Annuaire Desfossés-SEF* (Paris: Cote Desfossés and DAFSA), various board reports (a large collection of which can be found at the library of the Chambre de Commerce et d'Industrie in Paris), and from literature put out by the Office National de la Propriété Industrielle.[8] We also did a secondary analysis of the data published in *Expansion*, 84 (Apr. 1975), on the "social policy" of the top 50 companies.[9]

In order to relate the space of the properties of chief executives and the space of the properties of companies in a more precise way, we endeavored to gather a set of data for each of the companies under study on its job structure, skill level of labor, diploma structure (level and type of diploma), evolution (growth, stagnation, decline), productivity, "social policy," etc., for the three to five preceding years. Given the current state of data collection methods, this project seemed too ambitious (considering the means we had at our disposal). At this point in our research, we had to limit ourselves where companies with several variables were concerned: principal sector, status (private company, mixed company, or public industrial and commercial company),[10] mode of control (state, technocratic, foreign, family),[11] founding date, or, in the most frequent case (the groups established through consolidations or mergers), the founding date of the oldest company in the group (for Saint-Gobain-Pont-à-Mousson, for example, we used the founding date of the Manufacture de Saint-Gobain, 1695).

For each CEO in the sample, we collected a set of data from different sources, which we systematically collated and controlled. *Who's Who in France* (Paris: Jacques Lafitte) is currently the best and most complete source of biographical information, but it has inevitable gaps and imprecisions. So, for example, we know from frequent use of the guide that while most CEOs give precise information on membership in a grand corps, decorations, and national and local political office, the same cannot be said for secondary school, membership in professional organizations, on planning councils, or clubs, or past teaching experience, etc. In addition, the data in the 1953–4 edition were often much sketchier than in the later editions (30 of the 82 CEOs of the top 100 companies in 1952 who were included in *Who's Who* did not give their father's occupation). Finally, data on their careers are often fragmentary (many CEOs do not start their careers until they are about 40 or 45), and the probability of getting one's name in *Who's Who* is much greater today than it was in 1954 (the number of entries went from somewhere above 5,000 in 1953–4 to over 20,000 in 1976).[12]

We also based our work on biographical information collected in a systematic examination of specialized publications (*Expansion, Entreprise, Le Nouvel Écono-miste, La Vie Française-l'Opinion*) and dailies and weeklies (*Le Monde, Le Canard Enchaîné, L'Express, Le Point, Le Nouvel Observateur*, etc.). Press files on CEOs and companies put together by *Le Monde, Expansion*, and the library of the Paris Chamber of Commerce and Industry were a source of complementary data.

The data we got from the specialized press and *Who's Who in France* were complemented and verified through a systematic examination of the information available in various yearbooks: *Nouveau dictionnaire national des contemporains*, vols 1–5 (Paris: Ed. du Nouveau Dictionnaire National Contemporain, 1961–8); *Biographies de personnalités françaises vivantes* (Paris: La Documentation Française, 1967); *Bottin Mondain. Tout Paris. Toute la France* (Paris: Didot-Bottin, annual edn), which enabled us to fill out our data on ownership of residences, clubs, sports, and, of course, kinship.

For the CEOs in 1952, we also consulted the *Dictionnaire biographique français contemporain* (Paris: Pharos, 1954–5), and H. Temerson, *Biographies des principales personnalités françaises décédées au cours de l'année 1962*, published by author (Paris, 1962) (see also the editions of 1956, 1957, 1960, 1961, 1962, and 1963, all by the same author). We also went through *obituaries* and *booklets* written by close relations in "homage" to recently deceased CEOs.[13]

For CEOs having served in high-level public service and ministerial cabinets, we used the yearbooks of the Société Générale de Presse, particularly the *Annuaire des cabinets ministériels*, the *Annuaire du Conseil d'État*, and the *Annuaire de l'Inspection des finances*.

For involvement in different organizations and commissions we relied on the *Bottin administratif et documentaire* (Paris: Didot-Bottin, annual edn).

For municipal functions, we used the *Annuaire national des maires des communes de France*, 2nd edn (1974–5), from 30, rue René-Boulanger, Paris.

For involvement in the various employers' organizations, the *Annuaire officiel du CNPF* (Trappes: Ed. UFAP, 1974); *Annuaire 1977*, ACADI; *Bulletin no. 320 (spécial)*, ACADI; *Annuaire du Centre des jeunes dirigeants d'entreprise* (Paris, 1974); and lists of AGREF members and the executive committee of Entreprise et Progrès.

For decorations, especially the Légion d'Honneur, *le Ruban rouge: Annuaire des membres de la Légion d'honneur*, which was replaced in 1968 by *La Légion d'hon-neur: Annuaire des nominations et promotions dans la Légion d'honneur* (Paris: Association des Membres de la Légion d'Honneur, Société Nouvelle Mercure).

We found information on the organization of Protestant and Jewish communities, their works and associations, and the names of their primary leaders or decision-makers in *La France protestante (métropole et outre-mer)* (Valence: Fédération Protestante de France, 1977), and the *Guide juif de France* (Paris: Ed. Migdal, 1971). There being no listings of eminent Catholic, Protestant, or Jewish families, however, we turned to various informants to determine the religion of origin of the CEOs in our sample.

For higher education diplomas, the age at which they were awarded, and teaching activity, we complemented and verified the data we had collected using the alumni publications of the different grandes écoles: Centrale, ENA, ENS, HEC, Institut d'Études Politiques, Polytechnique, etc.

Finally, we were able to verify statements about membership in various clubs through the yearbooks of the Automobile Club of France, the Jockey Club, Maxim's Business Club, the Racing Club of Paris, and the Rotary Club (we were unable to verify membership in the other clubs).

Because published information on family background was often inexact and incomplete (both in the specialized press and the yearbooks), we attempted to precisely determine the connections between the various families and the business world as well as how longstanding these ties were, the extent of the network of family relations (the study of marriages being a central focus), and the length of time the family had belonged to the bourgeoisie (primarily for the families with few ties to the business milieu) and the nobility.[14] To this end, we examined the following guides: A. Delavenne, *Recueil généologique de la bourgeoisie ancienne*, vols 1 and 2 (Paris, 1954–5); *Dictionnaire de biographie française*, editing team headed by J. Balteau, M. Barroux, M. Prevost, and then by Roman d'Amat (Paris: Librairie Letouzey et Ané), 13 vols published (installment 80, published in 1976, covers Forcemagne to Forot); *Dictionnaire national des contemporains*, vols 1–3, directed by Nath Imbert (Paris: Ed. Lajeunesse, 1936–9); E. de Sereville and F. de Saint-Simon, *Dictionnaire de la noblesse française* (Paris: La Société Française du xxe Siècle, 1975); P. Dugast-Rouillé, *Le nobiliaire de France (actuel). Résumé pratique sans généologie ni armes ni devise. Noblesse de France. Noblesse d'origine étrangére* (2 vols, Nantes, 1972–3); *Qui êtes-vous? Annuaire des contemporains* (Paris: Librairie C. Delagrave, 1903; last edn, 1933); *Qui est-ce? Ceux dont on parle* (Paris: Ed. de la Vie Moderne, 1934). Cf. also, for industrialists of the Nord–Pas-de-Calais region, *Le livre des familles. Généologies Nord–Pas-de-Calais* (Lille: Annuaires Ravet-Anceau).

We also drew a good deal of information from the following texts: E. Beau de Loménie, *Les responsabilités des dynasties bourgeoises*, vol. 1: *De Bonaparte à Mac Mahon*; vol. 2: *De Mac-Mahon à Poincaré*; vol. 3: *Sous la Troisième République, la guerre et l'immédiat après-guerre*; vol. 4: *Du cartel à Hitler (1924–1933)* (Paris: Denoël, 1943–73); H. Coston, *Dictionnaire des dynasties bourgeoises et du monde des affaires* (Paris: Ed. Alain Moreau, 1975); A. Hamon, *Les maîtres de la France*, vol. 1: *La féodalité financière dans les banques*; vol. 2: *La féodalité financière dans les assurances, la presse, les administrations, le Parlement*; vol. 3: *La féodalité financière dans les transports, ports docks et colonies* (Paris: Ed. Sociales Internationales, 1936–8); and finally the magazine *Crapouillot*, primarily *Les 200 familles* (Mar. 1936), *Les gros* (1952), *Les beaux mariages* (Apr. 1961).

To complement and verify the data gathered from the sources listed above, we asked press offices, public relations offices, and secretarial offices to furnish us with resumés, which in more than one case created an appreciably different image from the one gained from reading biographical entries in yearbooks such as *Who's Who*, whose questionnaire dictates a certain definition of the relevant properties and creates an artificial homogeneity. So, for example, the entry on the career of Antoine Riboud submitted by the public relations department of BSN-Gervais-Danone, the company he heads, stresses the various undertakings he initiated (takeover bid against Saint-Gobain, mergers, diversification of the group's activities), but gives practically no information on the different stages of his career, his membership in associations, etc. In contrast, the biography of Michel Firino Martell, president of the directorate, then of the supervisory board of Martell et Co., stresses his membership in numerous professional and local associations that are not mentioned in the biographical yearbooks. The resumé of François Dalle, CEO of L'Oréal, devotes a lot of space to his publications – articles (including those published in *Le Monde*), books, symposia presentations, etc. – while *Who's Who* only mentions one of them. The resumé of Benno Vallières, CEO of the Électronique Marcel Dassault corporation, "confidence man" of Marcel Dassault, who placed Vallières at the helm of his company when he began his political career and was elected to parliament, stresses his military achievements and activities, particularly during the Second World War, while nothing in *Who's Who*, aside from the mention of one decoration, would even hint at the extent of these activities.

In analyzing attitudes and opinions, we examined, in addition to the great many interviews published in the specialized press, a number of works that included interviews with management, such as: J. Bassan, *Les nouveaux patrons* (Paris: A. Fayard, 1969); J. Baumier, *Les grandes affaires françaises. Des 200 familles aux 200 managers* (Paris: Julliard, 1967); J. Chancel, *Radioscopie* (Paris: R. Laffont, 1971–2) (vol. 1 includes an interview with Sylvain Floirat, vol. 2 an interview with Marcel Dassault); A. Harris and A. de Sédouy, *Les patrons* (Paris: Seuil, 1977); R. Priouret, *La France et le management* (Paris: Denoël, 1968); J.-P. Roulleau, *Les champions de l'expansion, une nouvelle race de dirigeants* (Paris: Cercle du Livre Economique, 1969).

For our analysis of the stances of the various sectors of upper management,[15] we looked at works written by CEOs or former CEOs: especially, F. Bloch-Lainé, *Profession: fonctionnaire* (Paris: Seuil, 1976); F. Bloch-Lainé, *Pour une réforme de l'entreprise* (Paris: Seuil, 1963); P. de Calan, *Renaissance des libertés économiques et sociales* (Paris: Plon, 1963); P. de Calan, *Les jours qui viennent* (Paris: Fayard, 1974); P. de Calan, *Le patronat piégé* (Paris: La Table Ronde, 1977); J. Chenevier, *Parole de patron*, interview with Jean Bothorel (Paris, Ed. du Cerf, 1975); F. Dalle and J. Bounine-Cabalé, *L'entreprise du futur* (Paris: Calmann-Lévy, 1971); M. Demonque and J.-Y. Eichenberger, *La participation* (Paris: France-Empire, 1968) (preface by J. Chenevier); R. Devillelongue, *Péchiney Ugine Kuhlmann, Pourquoi?* (Paris: Stock, 1977); P. Dreyfus, *La liberté de réussir* (Paris: J.-C. Simoën, 1977); Claude Neuschwander, *Patron mais . . .* (Paris: Seuil, 1974); F. Sommer, *Au-delà du salaire* (Paris: R. Laffont, 1966); R.-J. de Vogué, *Alerte aux patrons. Il faut changer l'entreprise* (Paris: Grasset, 1974).

RESULTS

The first factor reveals a first dominant principle of division (it represents 5 percent of the total inertia, compared to 3.2 and 3 percent, respectively, for the second and third factors): it counterposes everything *public*, or tied to the "public sector," the state, and public schooling and its official sanctions, to everything *private*, private property – with little dependence (at least publicly) on state credit either economically (credit) or symbolically (official decorations, service on commissions, etc.) – private schooling, etc. The opposition between the CEOs who have spent their entire career in the private sector and those who have spent all or part of their career in the public or nationalized sector accounts for the greatest portion of the variance in the first factor (8.4 percent), to which we should add all indicators of ties to the state, primarily tenure in ministerial cabinets (5.6 percent), the Inspection des Finances (3.3 percent), the Légion d'Honneur (5.3 percent), control of the company by the state or by one or several families (7.4 percent), and the company's status – private, mixed, or state (5.1 percent). Academic capital also makes a significant contribution to the constitution of the first factor, with, on the one hand, the number of diplomas in higher education (4 percent), on the other, the particular diploma possessed (5.9 percent) (the Sciences-po diploma alone, found frequently among the CEOs who have come up through the public sector, accounts for 2.2 percent of the variance). Finally, the occupational category of the father, through the opposition between the CEOs whose father was a higher civil servant or a member of the professions and those whose father was a commercial or industrial head, plays a significant role in the definition of the first factor (4.1 percent).

It is interesting that indicators of relations with other fields (administrative, university, etc.), such as service on planning councils, teaching in a grande école or university, membership on boards of trustees for the grandes écoles or university or para-university bodies (Institut Pasteur), publishing books (the absolute contributions of these being less significant than all the preceding indicators), should all be more fully explained by the first factor than by the subsequent factors. Toward the "private" pole, that is, on the side of the positive values of the first axis, we find ownership of a significant portion of shares in one's company, former directorship in this same company, participation in stylish and worldly sports, and membership in clubs. (We should not be surprised to find that the Cercle Interallié and the Cercle du Bois de Boulogne are exceptions. The Cercle Interallié has always been open to higher civil servants; the Cercle du Bois de Boulogne includes politicians.) Indications seem to be that the CEOs who have spent their entire careers in the private sector consider exterior signs of society life to be more important than those who have not. They more often mention their membership in clubs in biographical yearbooks, and, as we were able to verify, proportionally more of them are members. They are also the most likely to mention and in fact to participate in the most stylish and worldly sports (golf, riding, yachting). In contrast, as can be seen from, among other things, the extreme discretion in *"grands commis"* autobiographies (Pierre Dreyfus, François Bloch-Lainé, etc.), the image that these great servants of the state, these high-level officials identified with their jobs, create and wish to promote to others excludes all indulgent reference to the innermost aspects of the individual and details of his personal life (so, for example, less often involved in sports, especially those considered fashionable, than the "private" bosses, the "public" men are in any case less likely to mention them).

In the case of individuals, the most striking opposition lies between commercial corporate heads, either founders or direct heirs, whose entire career has been in the family business and who have not gone beyond secondary school, and top business leaders in the public sector, who often come from families from the petty bourgeoisie or the dominated regions of the field of power, and owe their position more to the academic and social capital they have acquired through their studies and their career than to inherited economic and social capital, and who occupy an intermediate position between CEOs and higher public servants (or politicians). We find, on the one hand, for example, Pierre Guichard, president of the board of directors of Établissements Économiques du Casino (Guichard-Perrachon et Cie), son of Geoffroy Guichard, founding director of Établissements Économiques du Casino, and Antonia Perrachon, who was born in Saint-Étienne and lives in Saint-Étienne, was educated at the private École des Roches, and has his baccalauréat; the Willot brothers, or two of them at least, Bernard and Jean-Pierre (son of Pierre Willot, industrialist),[16] CEO and chairman respectively of the Bon Marché corporation, the former also president of the directorate of the A la Belle Jardiniére land corporation, the latter CEO of the A la Belle Jardinière corporation, both of whom went to private schools in Roubaix, then to the Roubaix technical institute; or still further, Henri Pollet, president of La Redoute corporation in Roubaix, who, after studying at Notre-Dame-des-Victoires in Roubaix, received his law degree from Lille. At the opposite end of the space, we find Maurice Lauré, president of the Société Générale, son of Prosper Lauré, battalion chief, who did his secondary schooling first in high schools in Rabat and Saigon, then the Lycée Saint-Louis in Paris, going on to the École Polytechnique and the law faculté in Paris; starting out as an Inspecteur des Finances, he then became Conseiller Technique for Maurice Petsche (Secretary of the Treasury), taught at the ENA and subsequently became director of financial services and programs at the Ministry of the Armed services, and then director of Crédit National, before being appointed managing director and then very quickly president of the Société Générale. Or Paul Delouvrier, president of Électricité de France, son of a banker, student at various private schools, then the École Libre des Sciences Politiques and the law faculté, Inspecteur des Finances, several times ministerial cabinet director, delegate general to the government in Algeria from 1958 to 1960, district delegate general for the Paris region, then prefect of the Paris region, teacher at the Institut d'Études Politiques, member of the board of the Office de la Radio-Télévision Française from 1970 to 1972, and Grand Officier of the Légion d'Honneur.

The second factor corresponds to another principle of division, which opposes the CEOs primarily according to the length of time their family has been in the upper bourgeoisie (*de robe* or business) and their power over the economy (which is correspondingly greater the greater their inherited social capital), and secondarily according to the basis of this power, either predominantly industrial or predominantly financial. The length of time the family has been in the *bourgeoisie de robe* or the business bourgeoisie (especially Parisian) accounts for 9.4 percent and 5.8 percent of the variance in the second factor, respectively, the occupational category of the father for 7.6 percent, mention in the *Bottin Mondain* for 2.5 percent, and place of birth (either Paris and surrounding area or the provinces), 3.1 percent. Other important contributions to this factor are service on the boards of directors of the top industrial companies (6.6 percent) or the largest banks (4.4 percent) and the age at which the individual moved into the private sector (5.4 percent), which we know to be younger as social origins rise. Finally, the second factor opposes the CEOs of technocratically controlled companies (or groups) to the CEOs of nationalized companies (7.8 percent of the variance), and the CEOs of banks to the CEOs of public utilities (4.9 percent). Properties such as having gone to a provincial high school, graduating from Polytechnique into a second-ranked corps (Génie Maritime, for instance, rather than Mines), having spent part of one's career in military service, or receiving the Palmes Académiques, which are more fully accounted for by the second factor, are all located on the side of the negative values of the second axis, in contrast to properties such as holding important positions in the CNPF (and not only in an employers' federation) and inclusion in the list of "the hundred who run the economy" (an indicator of "visibility"). And it is probably no accident that the greater or lesser period of time the line has been part of the bourgeoisie or in business usually corresponds to the age of the business itself, and hence its greater or lesser nobility. Using the founding date of the company as an illustrative variable shows that the chief executives whose families have belonged to the *bourgeoisie de robe* or the business bourgeoisie for several generations are heads of the oldest companies, those founded in the early nineteenth century or before; we also find that club membership (except the Rotary Club and the Racing Club, which are much more open and have a much larger membership) is almost always related to long-standing membership in the bourgeoisie. We thus find on one side, Guy de Rothschild, great-grandson of James de Rothschild (head of the branch of Rothschilds), CEO of Le Nickel corporation (ranked 19th in 1972 by *Entreprise*), CEO of Banque Rothschild, member of the Nouveau Cercle, the Automobile Club de France, and the Cercle Interallié, owner of a stud farm and racehorse stables, etc.; Pierre Champin, son of Marcel Champin, who founded the Compagnie de l'Omnium Français des Pétroles in 1920, and who sat on 22 boards, whose first wife was Marguerite Pereire (of the well-known business and banking family), CEO of the Denain Nord-Est Longwy group (ranked sixth by *Entreprise* in 1972), a group that arose out of a slow movement toward integration that in the end brought together companies that were all over 100 years old (Forges d'Anzin, founded in 1836 by Talabot, Forges de Gorcy, founded in 1837 by J. Labbé, etc.).[17] And, at the other extreme, Georges Goudet, graduate of the École Normale Supérieure, officer of the Palmes Académiques, who, after a career as a professor at the science faculté in Nancy, became managing director then CEO of the Compagnie Générale de Constructions Téléphoniques (ranked 148th in 1972), founded in 1892, acquired in 1925 by the American corporation ITT; and Roger Boudrant, son of Jean Boudrant, farmer, graduate of the École Polytechnique, who acceded to the presidency of the Compagnie Parisienne de Chauffage Urbain (ranked 186th in 1972), founded in 1928 and controlled by the state, after having been an engineer at the Société d'Électricité de Paris and director of production and shipping at Électricité de France. We see on the plane where the first two axes of inertia are projected that the CEOs located in the lower left-hand quadrant are in a way the most removed, we might even say the most cut off from the field of economic power. Having frequently spent their entire career in the public or nationalized sector, they hold no other position on boards of directors (while they hold the position of mayor, member of parliament, and senator more often than all the others) and their access to the field of economic power appears to be a reward for the services they have rendered as high-level public or political officials (we find the highest percentage of prefects and military men, and of recipients of the Médaille de la Résistance, within this group).

The third factor opposes those who owe their social success to their academic success, essentially *polytechniciens* from the petty bourgeoisie and the dominated regions of the field of power (engineers), chiefly found in industrial companies, to those for whom academic credentials represent above all the legitimation of a position already held, principally Sciences-po graduates, more often from the upper Parisian bourgeoisie (bankers and large industrialists), and those who have only gone through secondary school (the academic title accounts for 11.8 percent of the variance, the age at entry into Polytechnique, a very good index of academic success, for 9.1 percent, father's occupation for 9.5 percent, and length of time in the bourgeoisie and in business for 6.9 and 7 percent). The projection of supplementary variables enables us to glimpse the opposing lifestyles in which this opposition between social trajectories and relationship to the educational system is expressed: on one side, we find skiing and tennis, more specifically "athletic," we might say, and less "worldly" sports (at least at the time of our survey) than golf, riding, or yachting, which we find on the other side; on one side, the least stylish clubs, the Rotary and Racing Clubs (or the Cercle du Bois de Boulogne, to which people can take their families) and, on the other, the Automobile Club, Polo de Bagatelle, the Cercle Interallié, the Jockey Club, or the Nouveau Cercle.

Appendix 2

Positions in the Field and Political Stances

In the absence of data that would allow positions in the corporate field as it has been described to be related directly to political stances, and especially to corporate social policy and to management strategies for handling social conflict, we have conducted an analysis of an *Expansion* survey on the top 50 French companies, solely with the purpose of making the proposed "model" more specific.[1] The principal division counterposes nationalized or mixed companies (Air-France, Banque de France, Banque Nationale de Paris, EDF, RATP, Assurances Générales de France, Elf-France, Compagnie Française de Raffinage, etc.) to private companies, which are often under family control or tied to foreign groups (Michelin, Hachette, Dollfus-Mieg, Agache-Willot, Citroën, Honeywell Bull, etc.). As the state pole is approached, there is an increased frequency in paid union representation, permission to distribute tracts at the workplace during working hours, extensions to the terms of personnel representatives above the legal minimum, equal representation in examining personnel advancement files, access to individual salary information for employees' elected representatives, etc.; the "private" pole, on the other hand, is associated with the lowest salaries, the highest rate of resignations and work-related accidents, the latest retirement, and the lowest level of funds set aside for employee development (see figure 18).[2]

A secondary opposition separates companies according to the *form* that, in a given state of power relations, they manage to give the *inevitable concessions* that this power structure imposes upon them. More precisely, it divides companies that pay more in *symbolic rewards* from those that are forced to make more directly material concessions. On one side, we find noble and longstanding enterprises, such as banks and insurance companies (Banque Nationale de Paris, Assurances Générales de France), as well as "advanced technology industries," with large educational investments, such as electronics companies (Honeywell Bull, IBM, Schlumberger) and chemical companies (Roussel-Uclaf, L'Oréal), companies whose leaders often have ties to Entreprise et Progrès, whose top management frequently went to Sciences-po or a management school, and whose employees include a relatively high proportion of managers and white-collar staff. On the other side, we find large public utilities (SNCF, RATP) and both heavy and traditional industry, which have adopted the most modern division of labor,[3] such as the coal (Les Houillères), automotive (Renault, Michelin), and textile industries (Dollfus-Mieg, Agache-Willot, etc.), whose employees include a large proportion of blue-collar workers,[4] and whose executives and managers have usually gone to engineering school (automotive, public utilities) and are members of the ACADI, or who have few diplomas (textile) and have often suffered from economic crisis. The closer we get to the *neopaternalistic pole*, the greater the frequency of informative meetings organized for all personnel, the greater the "general education" portion of worker training, the greater the chances women have for reaching management positions, and the greater the flexibility in working hours. At the same time, however, we find a greater number of firings, a greater inequity in salaries, fewer paid syndicalists, a decrease in time allowed to personnel representatives beyond the strict legal minimum, an increase in the dif-

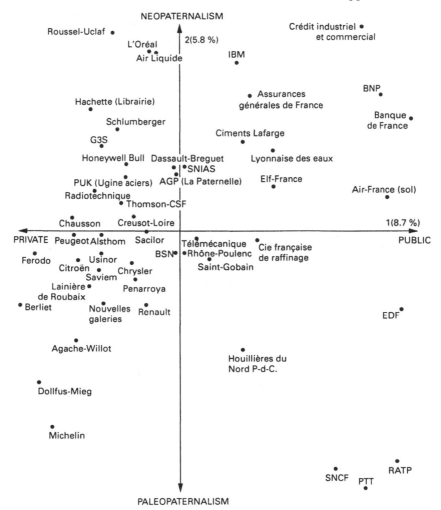

Figure 18 Conflicts over conflict management

ficulty external union leaders encounter in participating in company meetings, a higher rate of daily absenteeism, and less arbitration in conflict resolution.[5]

Everything thus takes place as if, under certain conditions – to be sought as much in the properties of the company as in the properties of the chief executives – "social policy" had succeeded in securing itself a certain freedom with respect to the constraints inscribed in the power relations, by offering symbolic rewards as a substitute for real advantages (which seems to constitute a good objective definition of the *management* of social conflicts). But care must be taken not to forget that an employer's freedom to play with the form of domination adopted undoubtedly depends largely on the *form of the struggles* in the company, expressing itself, among other ways, in the particular traditions of the dominant union, and depending largely on production methods and the correlative division of labor.[6]

In short, it could be that the stances employers adopt in matters of "social policy" depend on their company's particular situation with regard to social conflict, in other words, its status (public or private), its sector (and the nature of its product), the structure of its personnel in terms of the hierarchical division of responsibilities and the weight of its cultural capital, as well as gender, its structural and circumstantial position in economic competition (monopoly or competitive, on the rise or in decline) and, as a consequence of all this, on union power, as well as the employers' own individual dispositions, related to their social and academic trajectory (the opposition between Sciences-po or management school graduates and *polytechniciens*, for example) – given that the mechanisms governing orientation, "vocation," and cooptation ensure that the different company heads, along with the relatively "authoritarian" or "diplomatic" dispositions they bring to their position, are not randomly distributed among the different positions. It goes without saying that the freedom granted to the gentle violence of symbolic strategies depends not only on the intensity – to some extent structural – of employee struggles (employers who tend toward dialogue are found more often in the regions where struggles are the least intense), but also on the situational intensity of these struggles; the secondary opposition, between mild and harsh forms of riposte, disappears when struggles become more intense and more generalized.

If we confine ourselves to definitions of the way in which domination can be exercised, definitions which, in agents' minds, are nearly indiscernible from the definition of the foundations of the legitimacy of domination, we find three major classes of contrasting attitudes, in which we immediately recognize familiar classes of positions in the field of economic power. On the one hand, there is the gentle, that is to say, highly euphemized, method of management, which implements the entire arsenal of more or less scientifically guaranteed modern techniques borrowed from America ("job enrichment," "social indicators," "flextime," "employee advisory committees," "direct voicing of concerns," etc.);[7] on the other, there is the blunt method, in the old style, which implies the overt imposition of structures of patriarchal and paternalistic authority, the highest realization of which is military hierarchy. These two methods of wielding power are similar to two definitions of the function of a company head. On the one hand, we find *"chargés d'affaires"* who put the network of relations they have inherited, maintained, and developed, and their correlative aptitude for diplomacy, to the service of the company and are predisposed to handle external public relations with other companies and the government as well as internal public relations, euphemized variants of the old techniques of authority through which order is maintained within a company, at least during normal periods, and which are related to the aristocratic laxness of a paternalism that is both distant and easy-going. On the other hand, we find "leaders by divine right," entirely confident in their mission and determined to carry it out without making any other concessions beyond those they impose upon themselves in accordance with a patriarchal image of their role. This figure of a company head is fully realized by some of the "private" bosses, armed with both the confidence they gain through their property titles and the meritocratic clear conscience of the *self-made man* (for which the tradition that consists of having heirs go through all the steps in the hierarchy, although at a faster rate than the rest, undoubtedly goes a long way toward providing an ample substitute).[8] But it also has its "state" variant, in the form of those *polytechniciens* who find in the elitist self-certainty characteristic of the winners of top *concours*, combined with the clear "guilty conscience" of high-level Catholic bourgeois (with their Saint-Geneviève diplomas), the grounding for a bluntly exercised form of authority;[9] this is especially the case for those originating in the petty bourgeoisie, who feel that their position results solely from their gifts and personal characteristics.

While the brute paternalism of the leader by divine right is rarely discussed and gives rise to little theorization, even in the most conservative employers' associations, enlightened modernist conservatism and authoritarian technocratism find institutional expression in two associations of very different styles: the Association des Cadres Dirigeants de l'Industrie pour Le Progrès Social et Economique (ACADI) and Entreprise et Progrès. Founded in 1946 during a period of great social tension by a group of *polytechniciens*, together with churchmen, the ACADI includes mostly *polytechniciens* (more than half of its leaders are X alumni, as is 57 percent of its membership), a good portion of whom work for companies like EDF, the SNCF, the Compagnie Française de Raffinage, Rhône-Poulenc, and Ciments Lafarge, all of which are located toward the public pole (upper and lower left-hand quadrants).

In 1977, the ACADI had 501 members (up from its original 300). It is not associated, nor did it request to be associated, with the CNPF. It organizes get-togethers, conferences, and working committees and publishes a monthly newsletter. It sees itself as open and non-denominational, even though Catholics undoubtedly number heavily among its members. For 15 years, many Christian members of the ACADI met annually to talk over social problems, with church officials, and, especially at the beginning, with worker priests, such as the Fathers Magan (Jesuit Superior), Loew (OP), and Ancel (Superior of the Prado). Among ACADI members mentioned in *Who's Who* are numbered 54 percent *polytechniciens* (most of whom graduated into a grand corps), 9 percent Central or Mines graduates, 7 percent graduates of another engineering school, and 8 percent Institut d'Études Politiques alumni; 7 percent have a law degree, 3 percent another higher education diploma (only 1 percent do not list education). Nearly all have roots in dominant positions (85 percent); 27 percent are sons of industrialists, merchants, bankers, and corporate directors, 31 percent are sons of engineers, corporate heads, managers, and teachers, and 8 percent are sons of officers; only 19 percent are sons of higher public servants and members of the professions.

Founded a short time after 1968 (in March of 1970), Entreprise et Progrès brings together corporate leaders who are for the most part, at least at the level of the management committee, sons of industrialists, merchants, or corporate directors, who have very often gone to law school, HEC, or Sciences-po (never to Polytechnique), and who manage businesses located toward the private pole. Resulting from the merger of the Groupement pour L'Étude de la Réforme de l'Organisation Patronale [group for the study of the reform of management organization], whose membership consisted of presidents of large companies and whose activities were organized by François Dalle, Jean-Louis Descours, Francis Gautier, and Jacques Ehrsam, and the Centre National des Dirigeants d'Entreprise [national center for corporate heads], whose membership consisted of chief executives, headed by José Bidegain, Entreprise et Progrès "brings into contact companies that have felt the need to share their ideas and their research on the corporation and its true role in the national economy" (excerpt from the introductory brochure of Entreprise et Progrès). In contrast to the ACADI, it is in fact companies, not individuals, that belong to Entreprise et Progrès, with member companies appointing the executives who will represent them on the committees. (See also table 41.)

At the level of stances and manifestos, the differences are subtle. In both cases, the cult of Man is professed, but on one side they use the somewhat rough inflections of a military or boy-scout version of Christianity and on the other they put forward modernist proofs adduced for an enlightened science of *management*. The former speak of classes and inequality, and, contrasting in all meritocratic good faith "legitimate and globally beneficial inequalities" (with "intelligence" and the diploma in mind) to inequalities "that result merely from routine and the abuse of power" (with "private" bosses in mind), they insist, with the assuredness of academic laure-

Table 41   Social origins and academic credentials of leaders and members of the ACADI and Entreprise et Progrès (numbers)

	Entreprise et Progrès executive committee	*ACADI board of directors*	*ACADI, all members**
Father's occupation			
Lower and middle of social scale	1	1	8
Exec., director, engineer	2	8	32
Officer, landowner	–	2	8
Professions, higher civ. serv.	1	4	18
Industr., merchant, banker	11	12	27
No information	9	3	7
Total	24	30	100
Diploma			
Polytechnique, Mines	–	8	21
Polytechnique, Ponts	–	4	9
Polytechnique (only, or other school)	–	5	27
Other engineering school	3	5	16
Law, economics	6	2	7
Sciences-po	4	2	8
HEC, other business school	6	1	8
Other	–	–	3
None	1	–	–
No information	4	3	1
Total	24	30	100

* Study done on sample of 100 members.

ates, that "inequalities are a necessary condition for progress" and that leveling "would give rise to a stagnant, lazy, and irresponsible society"; the latter, who would not use this rather old-fashioned language, raise the issue of the quality of life, call for the "recognition of the dignity of the working man," show concern for the "excluded," and rely on "dialogue" to ease "inevitable tensions." The former, who define themselves in all domains as heads, leaders, even in "dialogue," and who, in the name of their devotion to "service for the common good," see themselves as "motivators, tireless driving forces for reform," speak in much more overtly political tones. They denounce the "totalitarian route" and "totalitarian reforms," and call more clearly for a "system of rights." The latter see themselves less as "heads" than as "moving forces," who are anxious to establish "bridges" between the private and public sectors and create a "climate of confidence among corporate heads and public officials," who rely entirely on innovation and the introduction of new techniques. The above quotes are taken, for the ACADI, from a September 1977 declaration presented to the press by the association on the occasion of the thirtieth anniversary of its founding (*ACADI Bulletin* 323, Sept. 1977) and, for Entreprise et Progrès, from the association's descriptive brochure. We would be safe in betting that the former are more often *Figaro* readers, close to Chirac and Gaullism, and that the latter are more often readers of *Le Monde*, close to Giscard d'Estaing and "advanced liberalism." One thing is certain, and that is that Entreprise et Progrès, representing management's avant-garde, is essentially distinguished from the ACADI in matters of *form*, the form of their discourse, of course, which is one among many strategies of domination, but especially in the form of dominance relations they employ, or, if you will, the forms that must be used in asserting this domination.

Appendix 3

A Day in the Life of a VIP

This account[1] of an ordinary day ("rather representative") in the life of a top "state" boss is interesting in that it provides, in addition to numerous indications of a lifestyle (breakfast in bed served by a maid in a black dress and white apron, sedate bourgeois apartment building, paintings by famous masters, an affectedly simple car, a Renault 5, no driver, a sense of both the value of time, listening to the news while shaving, for example, and punctuality, France-Musique, English cassettes, once again saving time, international relations, the *Herald Tribune*, distance from politics and internationalism, business tourism, etc., etc.), a kind of *job description*, and a rather rigorous one at that, as well as an exact description of *the space of the social network* mobilized in practice in the course of a single day. The job that consists first of all in silently listening to reports (skill required: "knowing how to listen") given by colleagues who expect nothing more than this disposition to availability ("you're going to smile at my ignorance"), felt to be all the more valuable because it comes from a man who is overwhelmed with similar activities (as can be seen from his appointment book, already filled with meeting requests for the upcoming two months . . .). The *extraordinarily homogeneous* space of relations: everyone, barring the maid and the secretary, comes from the same milieu, the same schools (as shown by the information added in quotation marks on the academic credentials and social origins of the people with whom he comes in contact); the other chief executives seen that day who are among the top 200 (names marked by an asterisk), with the exception of Paul Delouvrier, all fall on the side of the positive values of the second axis.

• •

7:45 a.m.   Coffee, toast, jam. Today Roger Martin decided against his usual breakfast in bed, served by a maid in a black dress and white apron. His apartment, on the top floor of a building on the Rue d'Assas – freestone, clanky old elevator – is bright, comfortable, and modest in style. A few spots of color in among the beige and ecru: paintings, of the sort that stir up memories. His favorite: *Envol de flamants roses*[2], a wash drawing by Marchant, almost abstract in style, but recalling "scenes you see in the Camargue."

• •

8:30   Roger Martin drives his own navy-blue Renault 5. We have made him late, but it will be the last time he will be late today; this man is punctuality itself. He listens to the news while shaving, on RTL or Europe, "it's convenient, short, quick." In the car, he prefers France-Musique or English language cassettes. "I need to improve my English." Next to him on the seat, the only newspaper he takes with him: the *Herald Tribune*.

Avenue Hoche, the modest building that was once pied-à-terre for the provincial Pont-à-Mousson has not changed. From the underground parking garage, an elevator takes him up to the fifth floor, where, behind a door no different from all the rest, the presidential office offers up its 20 square meters of nearly spartan severity.

8:55   The secretary calls on the phone and stops in. A quick look at the day's calendar: it will be a rather representative "Parisian" day. A few files for the day's scheduled interviews and meetings; the mail.

9:15   The chauffeur slams the door of the [Peugeot] 604. Roger Martin is on his way to a Rhône-Poulenc board meeting. At 9:29, he hurries toward the Avenue Montaigne entrance, he just misses being late. An hour and a half later, Antoine Riboud* is the first to come out into the courtyard; he jumps into his black Renault 5 Alpine.
Roger Martin follows, accompanied by Pierre Jouven*, of Péchiney. He hates meetings but makes an exception for a few boards. "You meet some really interesting people in these meetings." Did he actively participate in this one? "They were going over the general situation at Rhône-Poulenc. I listened."

11:05   Back at the office. A few free minutes, a smile (. . .). The head of the travel department arrives. Roger Martin is going to take advantage of a meeting in Australia to go around the world and visit several subsidiaries and delegations of the group in Asia and the US.

11:20   Arrival of Jacques Beigbeder, chief financial officer [graduate of the École des Mines and Sciences-po].
"Would you like some coffee?"
"Thank you. We've done a study on the image of specific banking establishments in our financial departments . . ." The two men greet each other quite formally, but appear to be picking up a recently interrupted conversation. Questions and answers are often expressed in half-sentences, and refer to preceding conversations. The important points are contained in notes that Roger Martin shuffles through, then puts in his briefcase. "I'll read them later lying down."
The secretary returns with an urgent meeting request. Roger Martin: "Could we hold it in Rome?" He looks through his appointment book, comes up against appointments such as a Croix du Mérite award ceremony or a trip to New York; finally, after five minutes, he finds a free spot. Two months away.

12:00   The daily ritual of the "informational meeting." Group executives present in the building have a round table meeting to exchange information informally. Roger Martin goes over a few difficulties Rhône-Poulenc is currently experiencing: has the group had similar experiences? The executives involved reassure him. Edmond Pirlot de Corbion [graduate of the École Nationale Supérieure des Mines de Paris, vice CEO of the Compagnie de Saint-Gobain-Pont-à-Mousson, president of the Saint-Gobain Industries corporation from 1970 to 1975, board member for many companies in the group, son of André Pirlot de Corbion, lawyer] has just met with a South Korean representative; does this interest anyone? One, two, three hands go up. They continue around the room.

••

12:50 p.m.   Roger Martin arrives at the restaurant on the top floor, where managers of the insulation division are awaiting him. Once or twice a year, each division in the group has lunch here; opportunity to meet the *staff* and *line*.

••

1:00   Roger Martin sits down (. . .). The conversation gets started; each brings the others up to date on his activities.

Roger Fauroux [graduate of the ENS and the ENA, CEO since 1975 of Saint-Gobain Industries, son of Théo Fauroux, lycée headmaster] sparks laughter by quietly correcting Jacques Chevenard [graduate of the ESSEC, head of the insulation division of Saint-Gobain Industries, president of the Roclaine corporation, son of Pierre Chevenard, Mines engineer, member of the Institut] who speaks of certain industrial establishments as being "horribly" polluting. Roger Martin says little. A few questions, on long-term projections, or on technological research, one particular X and École des Mines alumnus starting out by saying, "You're going to smile at my ignorance . . ."

••

2:45   "Thank you all for coming. Our congratulations. You are true industry professionals, from mastering specific technologies to spreading these technologies all over the world."

••

3:00   Back in his office. Jean-Louis Beffa [Polytechnique and École des Mines graduate, director of strategic planning at the Compagnie Saint-Gobain-Pont-à-Mousson, son of Edmond Beffa, engineer], one of the closest advisors to the president, presents him with a report on the paper industry in preparation for an upcoming meeting with Hugues de L'Estoile [director general for industry to the Ministry of Industry and Research since 1974, graduate of Polytechnique and the École Nationale Supérieure de l'Aéronautique, son of General Maurice de L'Estoile] on the restructuring of the sector (where the group is represented by Cellulose du Pin). Solutions do not seem to be forthcoming: "like trying to fit a circle into a square," Roger Martin mumbles.

••

3:30   Christian Dambrine [head of the fireproof products department since 1975, president of the Quartz et Silice corporation since 1976, graduate of Polytechnique and engineer in the Maritime Corps] comes in to tell Roger Martin about a personnel problem.

••

3:55   Mail to sign. Roger Martin waits for two executives from Morgan Stanley International, one of which is the president from New York. He does not yet know the reason for their visit.

••

4:07   The men arrive. Roger Martin crosses his office to shake their hands. He explains, in French: "The *Expansion* journalists are curious to know how a president spends his days." The Americans laugh . . .

....

5:00   Roger Martin leaves for a physical therapy appointment.

....

6:45   Outside the central offices of EDF, where there is to be a board meeting of the Foundation pour le Cadre de vie (. . .).[3] Roger Martin is soon joined by a small cohort of high-flying chief executives. Paul Delouvrier*, host for the evening, is there, as are Renaud Gillet* [Rhône-Poulenc], Jean-Léon Donnadieu [Boussois-Souchon-Neuvesel], Ithier de Roquemaurel* [Hachette], François Bizard [Inspecteur des Finances, BP board member, son of Léon Bizard, teacher], Pierre Ledoux*, Gérard Llewellyn [assistant general manager of the Banque Nationale de Paris, board member of several corporations, graduate of Sciences-po, son of Edgar Llewellyn, banker], Henri Schulz-Robellaz [board member of the Peugeot corporation, graduate of the École Nationale Supérieure des Mines de Paris, son of Pierre Schulz, stockbroker]. Seated across from Roger Martin, Philippe Viannay summarizes the foundation's activities. A surprising encounter: Viannay, the extrovert involved in a hundred activities (Les Glénans,[4] the press, the center for journalistic training), and Roger Martin, the man of reflection (. . .). They are nevertheless the two promoters of this foundation, whose objective it is to work out a reconciliation between industry and its environment. A major topic for Roger Martin, who stresses it once again, after an hour and a half of attentive silence behind his smooth professor's hands.

....

8:30   Paul Delouvrier invites the members to a cold buffet dinner.

....

10:30   The blue R5 [Roger Martin's] makes its way toward the Rue d'Assas.

Appendix 4

Elective Affinities, Institutionalized Connections, and the Circulation of Information

The amount of social capital as a *portfolio of connections* becomes all the greater the more numerous, stable,[1] and profitable these connections are (in other words, the greater the capital possessed by institutions – boards of directors, for example – or the individuals to whom they give access), and in many cases, the better *hidden* this capital is as well. Many connections are only effective because people are not aware of them; many are even clandestine. This is the case for most relatively distant family relations and, given the difference in names, all relations established through women (the image of neutrality, which higher public servants and politicians wish to create, owes part of its social credibility to the fact that only a few are aware of most of the family ties that often link higher civil servants and politicians to the top business bourgeoisie). Financial ties (between banks and the companies in which they hold shares or to which they grant significant credit, for example) are thus almost always coupled with personal ties through which they become both fully realized and trans-figured. Indeed, given that the individuals involved are the product of very similar social conditions of production, the sole foundation of these connections seems to be the one principle recognized by the most legitimate co-elections: friendship or attraction based on the affinity of tastes and lifestyle that arises in the homogeneity of habitus. So, for example, in the merger of Péchiney and Ugine-Kuhlmann, news-papers could celebrate the reunion of the heads of the two merged companies, P. Jouven and P. Grézel, childhood friends, tennis partners, and neighbors.[2]

To demonstrate the effect of the affinity of lifestyles, which, given the correspon-dence between positions and dispositions, is inseparable from an affinity of objective positions, and to make visible to the very people who pretend to doubt it the practi-cal unity of the establishment that dominates the economic field of power, it would be necessary to draw up both the impossible diagram of the ensemble of acquain-tances ensured by the homogeneity of the group as a whole as well as its concentra-tion in limited places (schools, clubs, etc.), and the diagram of the network of *institutionalized relations* that, expressly maintained by institutions either directly or indirectly geared toward this end (boards of directors, clubs, associations, "unions," professional groups, commissions – the Commission du Plan [planning council, Tr.], etc. – committees, etc.), combine with financial and technical relations and, through the logic of institutionalization, reinforce the effects of the affinity of habitus and lifestyles. As we are unable to encompass this network in its entirety, we can instead examine on the one hand the configuration produced within the space of corporate heads by the body of personal connections (defined solely by membership on boards of directors) of several chief executives located in different quadrants of the space, and on the other the network of personal connections whose center is the boards of directors of companies headed by the differently situated CEOs. Guy de Rothschild is particularly representative, on this point as on many others, of the great private dynasties (upper right-hand quadrant of the correspondence analysis diagram), the heads of which almost always sit on the boards of companies in the same universe, as personal ties tend to duplicate financial ties very exactly, and sometimes, but more rarely, on those of top public companies (upper left-hand quadrant of the chart), but never, except by proxy, on those of lesser-ranked private companies. In 1972 (see tables 42 and 43), Guy de Rothschild is thus CEO of the Banque Rothschild-Paris, CEO of Le Nickel corporation, board member of Penarroya, La Saga, Francarep, Compagnie du Nord, Rothschild Intercontinental Bank Ltd, London, N.M. Rothschild and Sons Ltd., London, the Rio-Tinto Zinc corporation, London, etc., in other words, establishments that are all to varying degrees controlled by the Rothschild family; and, although he himself is not a board member of any company whose chief executive is located in the other quadrants, Michel de Boissieu, Banque Rothschild board member, general manager of the Compagnie du Nord (from 1967 to 1973), and Jacques Getten, assistant general manager of Banque Rothschild, and then of the Compagnie du Nord, represent the Rothschild group on the board of directors of the SNCF, which continues to pay out to former railroad companies (PLM [Paris-Lyon-Marseille; now strictly hotel business, Tr.], Compagnie du Nord) a fixed rate of 6 percent interest on non-amortized shares (see P. Allard, M. Beaud, A.M. Lévy and S. Liénart, *Dictionnaire des groupes industriels et financiers en France* (Paris: Seuil, 1978), p. 148).

The relatively atypical position of Antoine Riboud can be seen from the fact that, in contrast to the chief executives located in the same quadrant (Guy de Rothschild, Ferdinand Béghin, etc.), he is associated not only with companies in the Boussois-Souchon-Neuvesel group, but also with the Compagnie Financière de Paris et des Pays-Bas, the Rhône-Poulenc corporation, Crédit Lyonnais, etc. (in other words, companies whose CEOs are in the upper left-hand quadrant of the diagram).

CEOs belonging to the state financial oligarchy (upper left-hand quadrant) generally boast a large number of important connections, and the boards on which they serve are almost always headed by CEOs occupying dominant positions. So, for example, Ambroise Roux sits on a number of corporate boards whose presidents are all in his immediate neighborhood: Pierre Jouven, Péchiney-Ugine-Kuhlmann, Jacques de Fouchier, Paribas, Christian de Lavarène, CIC [Credit Industriel et Commercial], and Jean-Louis Pilliard, La Radiotechnique. The same is true for Wilfrid Baumgartner, CEO of Rhône-Poulenc in 1972, with a seat on the boards of Péchiney-Ugine-Kuhlmann (whose president was Pierre Jouven, situated in the upper left-hand quadrant), Chargeurs Réunis, Denain-Nord-Est-Longwy, the Peugeot corporation (whose presidents were, respectively, Francis Fabre, Pierre Champin, and Maurice Jordan, all in the upper right-hand quadrant), the Compagnie Française des Pétroles (René Granier de Lilliac, lower left) and for Jacques de Fouchier, president of the Compagnie Financière de Paris et des Pays-Bas, president of the supervisory board of the Compagnie Bancaire, with a seat on the boards of Péchiney, BSN, Thomson-Brandt, the Compagnie Française des Pétroles, Schlumberger, etc., the apparent exceptions arising in a few cases of discordance between the properties of the company and those of the CEO (such as Paul Ricard, lower right-hand quadrant, CEO of Thomson-Brandt, graduate of Arts et Métiers, who made it to the top of a large company the board of which was composed nearly exclusively of members of the establishment, or René Granier de Lilliac, located in the lower left-hand portion of the diagram, son of an engineer and CEO of the Compagnie Française des Pétroles, whose board was likewise primarily made up of members of the establishment).

Table 42 A sampling of boards of directors in 1972

		Bottin Mondain	Business bourgeoisie	Bourgeoisie de robe	Officer, landowner
Kodak-Pathé*	Paul Vuillaume				
	Jean Marot		X		
	Georges Roques				
	Bernard Blanchard	X			X
	Pierre Clément				
	Jacques Ladreyt				
	Jean Ganot				
	Lucien Vacher				
Société F. Béghin	Ferdinand Béghin	X	X		
	Jean-Marc Vernes	X	X		
	Edouard Archambeaud**				
	Claude Descamps		X		
	François d'Epenoux**	X			
	Marcel Kilfiger				
	Pierre Malle	X	X		
	Etienne Pollet	X	X		
	François Pollet	X	X		
Compagnie Générale d'Électricité	Ambroise Roux	X	X	X	
	Raymond Pelletier		X		
	Pierre Abbé**				
	Robert Baboin	X		X	
	Richard Baumgartner	X	X	X	
	Paul Huvelin	X	X		
	Pierre Jouven	X		X	
	Guy Marcille	X		X	
	Jean Matheron		X		
	Georges Pébereau			X	
	Jérôme Richer				X
	Claude Marcilhacy	X		X	
Compagnie Bancaire (supervisory board)	Jacques de Fouchier	X		X	
	Jacques Brunet	X		X	
	François Bloch-Lainé	X	X	X	
	Jacques Burin des Roziers	X	X	X	
	Amaury de Cazanove	X			X
	Jacques Ferronnière	X	X		
	Louis-Charles de Fouchier	X		X	
	Roland Labbé	X	X		
	Christian de Lavarène	X			X
	Jean-Maxime Robert	X			X
	Jean Reyre	X	X		

* Only French board members have been listed.
** Board members on whom there is little data.

Related to other board member	No higher education	Sciences-po	Inspection des Finances	Commander, Gd Officier Légion d'Honneur	Polytechnique	Mines	Ponts	HEC	Entire career in company	Father eng., petty bourgeoisie	Chevalier du Mérite
								X	X	X	
								X			X
								X	X	X	
									X	X	X
								X	X	X	X
									X		
X	X			X					X		
	X										
X	X								X		
					X					X	
X									X		
				X	X		X				
					X				X		
					X						
					X	X					
					X						
X			X		X						
			X		X	X					
X					X		X				
					X		X				
								X	X		
									X		
X		X	X	X							
		X	X	X							
		X	X	X							
		X									
	X										
X		X	X								
		X									
		X		X							
		X	X	X							
		X	X	X							
		X							X		

Table 43 A sampling of portfolios of connections

Jacques de Fouchier	President of chambers in the Cour des Comptes	Sc.-po, Insp. Fin.
Roger Martin	Industrialist	Polyt., Mines
Wilfrid Baumgartner	Surgeon; father-in-law president Union Électricité, CFP, etc.	Sc.-po, Insp. Fin.
François Bloch-Lainé	Banker, partner-manager Banque Lazard	Sc.-po, Insp. Fin.
Michel Caplain	Engineer	Sc.-po, Insp. Fin.
François de Flers	Playwright, member Académie Française	Sc.-po, Insp. Fin.
Paul Huvelin	Wine merchant; father-in-law president Soc. Gén. d'Entreprises	Polyt.
Pierre Jouven	Architect, top prize Expo 1937	Polyt., Mines
Christian de Lavarène	Officer	Sc.-po, Insp. Fin.
Jean Reyre	Merchant	Sc.-po
Ennemond Bizot	Inspecteur Général, Financies; father-in-law board Cr. Lyonnais, Us. Ch. du Rhône	Polyt., Mines
Pierre David-Weill	Partner Banque Lazard, director Banque de France	?
Jacques Georges-Picot	President Société Générale, Crédit Industriel et Commercial	Sc.-po, Insp. Fin.
Renaud Gillet	President Créd. Ind. Textiles Artificiels, board Rhône-Poulenc, etc.	École Chimie Ind. Lyon
Dominique de Grièges	Engineer	Sc.-po, Insp. Fin.
Roland Labbé	Foundry director	Sc.-po
Emmanuel Lamy	Vice president Établissements Kuhlmann	Sc.-po, Insp. Fin.
Pierre Ledoux	Merchant	HEC, Insp. Fin.
Ambroise Roux	President Compagnie Générale d'Accidents (insurance)	Polyt., Ponts
Richard Baumgartner	Surgeon; father-in-law president Union Électricité, CFP, etc.	Polyt., Génie
Henry Bizot	Inspecteur Général, Finances	Law, Insp. Fin.
Jacques Burin des Roziers	Director Providence-Accidents	École St L. de Gonzague
Lazare Carnot	Founder Viscose Française, La Cellophane, etc.	Mines de Paris
Pierre Celier	Banker; father-in-law foundry director	Law, Insp. Fin.
Louis Dherse	Intendant Général	Polyt., Ponts
Francis Fabre	Shipowner/outfitter, president Cyprien-Fabre, board Chargeurs Réunis, etc.	Sc.-po
Jacques Ferronnière	Banker	Sc.-po, Insp. Fin.
Jean Forgeot	Veterinarian	Law, Insp. Fin.
Pierre Grézel	Engineer, tobacco	Polyt., Mines
Jacques Merlin	Shipowner/outfitter	Inst. Ste Croix Neuilly
Emmanuel Monick	?	Sc.-po, Insp. Fin.
Gustave Rambaud	Teacher at the École Centrale de Lyon	Polyt., Mines
Antoine Riboud	President Société Lyonnaise de Dépôts et Crédit Industriel	École Sup. Comm. Paris
Philippe Thomas	Industrialist	Polyt., Insp. Fin.
Arnaud de Voguë	Vice president St Gobain, president L'Urbaine insurance, etc.	Humanities

This table gives the social origins and routes taken by the members of the boards of directors of 20 banks or large industrial companies (included among the largest most "noble" establishments in 1972). Board members were chosen who had seats on at least two of these boards and they were ranked according to the number of positions held. Abbreviations: P = President; HP = Honorary President; VP = Vice President; B = Board member; M = Member; PC = President of commission.
* "100 who run the economy": Members whose names appear on the list published by *Expansion* (Sept. 1972).
** The consultative committee for the production of nuclear-based electricity was created by the Commissariat à l'Energie Atomique; members were named for a term of four years by the order of May 11, 1971.
*** The national committee for the development of the grandes écoles was set up in October 1970 by "corporate executives, grandes écoles directors, and alumni representatives." It is defined as "a group of men and women who wish to safeguard and improve this particular form of higher education so as to make it more efficient still" (cf. Comité National pour le Développement des Grandes Écoles, "Les partis politiques et le sort des grandes écoles," Feb. 1978, p. 2).

Cie Financière Paris-P. Bas	Cie Financière de Suez	Crédit Ind. et Commercial	Crédit National	Compagnie Bancaire	Banque Nationale de Paris	Crédit Lyonnais	Société Générale	Pechiney-Ugine-Kuhlmann	Saint-Gobain Pont-à-Mousson	Cie Générale d'Électricité	Rhône-Poulene	Cie Francaise des Pétroles	Boussois-Souchon-Neuvesel	Thomson-Houston	Denain-Nord-Est-Longwy	Lyonnaise des Eaux	Esso-Standard	Schneider	Wendel-Sidelor	"100 who run the economy"*	AGREF	CNPF	Comm. Prod. Énergie Nucl.**	Comité Nat. Dével. G. Écoles***	Fondation de France
P		B	B	P			B					B	B	B						X	M			M	B
	B	B				B		P		B				B					VP	X	M				
							B			P	B			B						X					
		B	B		P		VP							B						X	M	PC			
B	B						B					B						B							
	B						B		B	B		VP								X	M	PC		M HP	
		B						P		B	B										M				
B		P	B	B				B					B								M				
B			B					B				B								X					
	HP	VP						B													M				B
B	VP							B					B							X	M				
	VP	B						B					B			B									
	B	B	P						B				HP							X	M				B
	B		B		P			B												X	M	VP	M	M	
	B	P			B			B			B												M		
	B			B			B														M				
	B		B		P						B														
B																B		B		X					
		B		P														B	B		M				
		HP						B	B			B								X				M	
HP															B					X					B
B												P					B			X	M			M	B
	B			B			VP	HP													M				

It is very rare that the CEOs of second-order private companies or subsidiaries of foreign companies (lower right-hand quadrant) would have access to the boards of companies located in other quadrants. The CEOs of companies directly dependent on a foreign group (Kodak, Shell, etc.), along with those who have only recently entered the field of top companies (Leroy-Somer, Bic, etc.), sit on only a small number of boards, almost all of which are of second rank. So, for example, Paul Vuillaume, CEO of Kodak-Pathé, was on no other boards, and Léonard Carous, CEO in 1972 of Shell Française and Shell Chimie, was on the board of Shell-Gabon, the Société d'Investissements et de Travaux Publics, the Société pour l'Utilisation Rationnelle des Gaz, and the Institut Français du Pétrole, des Carburants et Lubrificants. Similarly, the Baron Marcel Bich, founder of the Bic corporation, sits on no other boards, and Georges Chavanes, president of the directorate of Leroy-Somer, Inc., was also president of the supervisory board of the SERAP (company within the Air Liquide group), and in 1975 became a boardmember of a regional bank (Crédit Industriel de l'Ouest).

CEOs of nationalized companies generally only serve on the boards of other government-controlled companies: Pierre Dreyfus, CEO of the Régie Nationale des Usines Renault in 1972, was also president of the Société des Aciers Fins de l'Est (a subsidiary of Régie Renault). René Ravaud, CEO since 1971 of the SNECMA corporation [aeronautics industries, Tr.], 85 percent controlled by the state, was on the board of the CNMP Berthiez corporation (subsidiary of the SNECMA) and CFM International, Inc., another SNECMA subsidiary.

Exactly the same logic is found in examining the composition of boards of directors. So, for example, in 1972 the president of the board of the F. Béghin corporation was Ferdinand Béghin, born in the northern town of Thumeries, son of Henri Béghin, sugar industrialist, secondary schooling completed at the Lycée Janson de Sailly, no further education. Four other members of the board (at least four; we have no information on Edouard Archambeaud) are related to the president: Pierre Malle married Françoise Béghin, sister of Ferdinand Béghin; Claude Descamps married Jenny Béghin, daughter of Joseph Béghin; Étienne and François Pollet belong to a well-known northern family that also has ties to the Béghins (Étienne Pollet married a daughter of Joseph Béghin). With the exception of Marcel Kilfiger, son of a civil servant and alumnus of Polytechnique, most of the board members have few diplomas (Jean-Marc Vernes, CEO of Banque Vernes, who went to Janson, has only the baccalauréat; Claude Descamps went to the Faculté Catholique de Paris and has no higher education degree). Only Jean-Marc Vernes and Claude Descamps sit on the boards of other dominant companies, with the other board members either holding no other seats or only sitting on second-ranked boards.

On the board of directors of Kodak-Pathé, whose president in 1972 was Paul Vuillaume, HEC graduate, son of Louis Vuillaume, grocer, whose entire career was spent in the business, we find five American members, all of whom are on the board of the Eastman Kodak Company, and in addition to Paul Vuillaume himself, seven French members. Among the latter we find three sons of engineers, one merchant's son, one general's son, and one son of a corporate director (we were unable to establish the origins of the final member, since deceased); four of them went to HEC, three to less prestigious engineering schools, and one to law school. They have almost all spent their entire careers at Kodak, as "in-house executives," as it were, and serve on no other boards. We can undoubtedly see signs of a certain affinity in their lifestyles in the fact that five of them live in relatively marginal neighborhoods (the twelfth, fifteenth, and twentieth *arrondissements*, Fontenay-sous-Bois, Garches), and that none has a very rare official decoration, whereas five are Chevaliers du Mérite.

The board of directors of the Compagnie Générale d'Électricité, presided over by Ambroise Roux, École Polytechnique alumnus, includes no fewer than eight other École Polytechnique graduates (Raymond, Pelletier, Pierre Abbé, Robert Baboin, Richard Baumgartner, Paul Huvelin, Pierre Jouven, Jean Matheron, and Georges Pébereau) out of a total of 12 members; two graduated into the Corps des Mines, two, like Ambroise Roux himself, into the Corps des Ponts. Two, in addition to Ambroise Roux, went to the Collège Stanislas. All have origins in either the top *bourgeoisie de robe* or the top business bourgeoisie.[3]

Nine of the 11 members of the supervisory board of the Compagnie Bancaire in 1972 were Sciences-po graduates, including the president Jacques de Fouchier himself; six, including Jacques de Fouchier, were *Inspecteurs des Finances*. Often belonging to the nobility and old bourgeois families *(de robe,* business, or military), they are all mentioned in the *Bottin Mondain* and have the top decorations (six are at least Commanders in the Légion d'Honneur).

We could give example after example. It will suffice to add that this affinity of origins, training, and lifestyle is not without consequence at the level of political choices and opinions. So, for example, the board of directors of Boussois-Souchon-Neuvesel, the president of which is Antoine Riboud, son of a banker, ranked last at his graduation from the École Supérieure de Commerce de Paris, with a reputation as a nonconformist (at the 1972 CNPF convention in Marseilles he gave a report on "quality of life" and advocated the development within each company of a "five-year social and human plan to set objectives for Being to the exclusion of demands for Having, that is, salaries"; B. Brizay, *Le patronat* (Paris: Seuil, 1975), pp. 188–91), is mostly made up of members from the business bourgeoisie, often from Lyons, who did not attend the top grandes écoles; we also find Francis Gautier, son of a corporate director, who went to law school and the HEC and who is a member of the management committee of Entreprise et Progrès, Philippe Daublain, Agro graduate, son of a farmer, and president of the Centre Français du Patronat Chrétien, and Jérôme Seydoux Fornier de Clausonnes, who went to the École Nationale Supérieure d'Électronique de Toulouse, whose father, a corporate board member, was a friend of the Ribouds, and whose mother, Geneviève Schlumberger, belongs to a well-known business family, and who is considered in business milieus to be a supporter of François Mitterrand (*Le Point*, 13 May 1974).

The same logic often presides over the composition of committees or commissions with close ties to the state. So, for example, the committee on industrial development created in 1966 to oversee the operation of the Fifth Plan in the area of industrial development, the chairman of which was François-Xavier Ortoli, ENA graduate and Inspecteur des Finances, was made up exclusively of grandes écoles alumni, most of whom graduated into the grands corps. Of 14 members, we found eight Inspecteurs des Finances and four *polytechniciens* from the Corps des Mines. The committee on nationalized companies, chaired by Simon Nora, Inspecteur des Finances, probably because of its relatively less prestigious mission (it was "to analyze the activity of public companies," rather than "forming opinions on the desirable evolution of the various sectors of French industry"), included fewer members of the Inspection des Finances or the Corps des Mines (4 of 11), whereas we found two Conseillers from the Cour des Comptes, one Maître des Requêtes from the Conseil d'État, one ministry director, etc. The public administration committee, chaired by Claude Lasry, former Conseiller d'État, included three Conseillers d'État (out of eight members).

The tendency toward economism must not cause us to underestimate the importance of personal connections (particularly those officialized by boards of directors) in the functioning of economic power, especially in the banking world. Information, especially information on power – for example, knowing the capital ownership structure of a particular institution – is a source of power in and of itself. We may concur with Jacques de Fouchier when he comments that cultural, or, to use a broader term, informational, capital plays a crucial role in the power of banks, which have the economic capital to be able to concentrate their informational capital; and that the domination of banking capital over industrial capital that defines financial capital is partially due to the fact that banks are able to accumulate the economic information that enables them to rationally direct economic strategies, by combining the scientific knowledge provided by various rationalized and organized instruments of research (brain trusts, think tanks, etc.) and by economic "experience" in all its guises: the experience provided by contact with borrowers who are required to furnish guarantees, that is, information, among other things; the experience brought by the state *grands commis* called over to the other side; and the experience that comes from "personal connections" and service on boards of directors, commissions, and especially select committees charged with "study missions" (the Rueff-Armand committee, for instance). Like the power of economic capital as described by François Perroux, the power of cultural capital, under certain circumstances, can also be a form of power over capital: "A corporate bank is almost a cybernetic ensemble, able to collect and analyze the greatest possible amount of information and take full advantage of it: information on the general economy, not merely on a national level, but on a worldwide level; information on conditions of investment in the short, medium, and long term in each industrial sector; information on individual businesses; information on people, ideas, and technology."[4] Because of the informational capital mobilized by its brain trust, a concentration of embodied cultural capital that makes economic capital possible and helps to give power over economic capital, and because of the connections that it can thus establish and maintain, which extend well beyond the limits of the group defined solely in terms of financial interests, the corporate bank, with a moderate *symbolic* financial investment, is able to dominate industrial companies. And it can do so in the gentlest, most unobtrusive, least visible, yet most *economical* way imaginable, and come to control, for example, their management, or even choose their directors.

Thus Jacques de Fouchier explains that "the group is made up of all the businesses in which the bank took an interest, the ones it provides its services to, the ones it keeps a position in. It's a complex network of influences that actually go both ways, where human relations, memories, habits, and interests each play a role that it is difficult to calculate." If this is so, it is because, as a counterpart to its symbolic services, which cannot be reduced to financial credit, the bank secures shares whose importance cannot be measured in financial terms: "We hold shares in many French companies, but they're not the source of most of our income. They're more the sign of the position we have acquired in one or another business subsequent to providing our services. In general, we keep only a *moderate* level of investment, and often a *board membership*; but by joining these businesses to a *group of relations* that is continuously strengthened and enlarged, we gain from their very vitality, keeping their accounts current, participating like a file leader in their financial operations as well as their credit operations." This is to say that the bank's "control" goes well beyond the lowest limits specified for "minority control" when only the strictly economic dimension of domination is taken into account.[5] And, in fact, through a typical effect of specifically cultural domination (which it is interesting to find, beyond simplistic dichotomies, deep within the realm of economic power), companies can be "held" as efficiently through cultural credit (credit also being a form of authority) as through financial credit.

"Investments in grey matter, in representations, and in negotiations," to quote Jacques de Fouchier once again, and the capital consisting of personal connections and information that can be accumulated and put to work because of these investments make it possible to deploy the strictly financial strategy of limiting capital investment to what is strictly necessary in order to secure the "privileged position of foreman of the financial machinery," in other words, the strictly cultural power that highly performative information wields over the dominated company, and to maximize thereby the power of control likely to be gained with a minimum of financial expenditure.[6] It becomes clearer why academic capital and everything associated with it should be at the basis of the opposition between the bankers located at the two ends of the space of banking, symbolized by Jacques de Fouchier and Guy de Rothschild, the latter of whom remarked one day to Roger Priouret that "he had never understood how one could be a good *manager* for the Banque de Paris et des Pays-Bas and for the company in which Paribas held shares at one and the same time."

PART V

State Power and Power over the State

If he should feel only the ingratitude of the masters of Fortune, he will get all the more satisfaction from his reputation, for it will be the only good he will have acquired in his service to the State; happy to have done more for the Fatherland than the Fatherland has done for him, and to count all its Citizens among his debtors!

Let's admit it nonetheless; a magnanimous heart easily goes beyond the service of its own particular self-interest. But it is necessary at very least that a gentle and virtuous hope of providing this public good, which is everything to him, inspire him, sustain him, and strengthen him in the honorable but difficult service to the Fatherland.

D'Aguesseau, *L'amour de la patrie*, Mercuriale XIX

Tyranny consists in the desire to dominate everything regardless of order.

In the various departments for men of strength, beauty, sense and piety, each man is master in his own house but nowhere else. Sometimes they meet and the strong and the handsome contend for mastery, but this is idiotic because their mastery is of different kinds. They do not understand each other and their mistake lies in wanting to rule everywhere. Nothing can do that, not even strength: it is of no effect in the learned world and only governs external actions.

Pascal, *Pensées*, 332

Part V

State Power and Power over the State

The discomfort caused by the scientific analyses that brought to light the role of the educational institution in the preservation of the social order was just as acute for the defenders of the public sector school, as fervent zealots of the republican cult of the "school as liberating force," as for its adversaries, whose suspicions and accusations had given it the stamp of progressivism. It is usually in the name of a comparison, nearly always implicit, between the defects of the *ancien régime* and the virtues of academic meritocracy that people have viewed the implacable findings of sociology as the expression of a kind of irresponsible ultraradicalism, which clothes in the garb of utopian egalitarianism a kind of "the worse the better" politics, liable to drive the republican primary school teacher to despair.[1] As a confused amalgam of edifying stories – that of the three-stage social ascension from peasant grandfather to schoolteacher father to *normalien* son, that of the President of the Republic of modest beginnings, or that of the defeat of nepotism and favoritism at the hands of the anonymous *concours* – the myth of the liberating school, just like belief in nobility, was based on birth and nature, but restored beneath a democratic facade of an ideology of natural gifts and individual merit. It was inscribed in practice in the deepest regions of the educational institution, both in the traditions and rules of pedagogic methods and in the convictions and dispositions of teachers, with variations according to scholastic level.[2] People could thus in all equanimity think of academic nobility as being entirely different from blood nobility while still granting it all the properties attributed to dominant groups whose domination is legitimated by birth, in other words, by virtue of their essence[3] – starting with the precocity that, seen as the sign *par excellence* of "gifts" and reinforced by human hothousing,[4] authorizes the rapid access to power of those who are destined to it by birth, that is, from birth: "To be of noble birth is a great advantage," as Pascal said long ago. "At the age of 18 it places a man within the select circle, known and respected, as another would have merited it at 50. It is a gain of 30 years without trouble" (*Pensées*, 322).

All this hardly predisposed analysts to grasp the true nature of an educational institution to which, whether as heirs or wonder children, they are always intimately bound. How indeed could they have thought of the new academic "elite" as a nobility when everything encouraged them to see it in opposition to the former aristocracy, in the name of the antithesis, a newly established category of republican understanding, between "birth" and "merit"? They thus had to break with this entire universe of more or less unconscious representations, all the more insidious for its aura of progressivism, in order to be able to gradually discover that the transmission of sometimes universal and emancipatory knowledge, such as scientific knowledge, also accomplishes a magical (or religious, in the Durkheimian sense) act. The lay school, often anticlerical, institutes social breaks, acts of consecration or ordination that, like dubbing as described by Marc Bloch, and all rites of institution, institute *orders*, or, in Weber's language, *Stände*, bodies separated from the commonplace, like the blood nobility of earlier times, and therefore sacred.[4]

STATE MAGIC

Corps instituted by academic selection, while they do share some of the properties of ethnic groups, castes, and lineages, differ from them in significant ways. Although they fulfill functions very similar to those of the family, to which they join their efficacy, they are profoundly different in their mode of reproduction, and perhaps especially in the tie that, through the academic title, binds them to the state. Similar in this to the noble title, academic titles indeed guarantee their authors a legal monopoly protected by the state, that is, juridically guaranteed by the state's authority over certain positions. The bureaucratic authority that makes these titles the precondition for access to public service positions has the power to guarantee the perpetuation of their rarity, and hence, their value, and to protect their holders from the threat of devaluation and crisis that results from an overproduction of title holders. However, while academic titles, like noble titles, are "privileges," as in the *ancien régime*,[5] unlike them they do not constitute *property* that can be bought and sold, or passed down to descendants; their acquisition and use are subordinated – to varying degrees – to the acquisition of technical competences.[6]

In contrast to less polished systems, based on the direct and open patrimonial transfer from father to son,[7] the mode of reproduction based on the educational institution, a combination of strategies and instruments of reproduction without precedent and thus, as it were, incomparable, obeys a statistical logic. It follows that some of the information contained in the structures constitutive of the social order is inevitably lost in the crossgenerational transfer, despite the innumerable acts of ordination performed by the participants in the academic race, be they classifiers or classified. The security of the dominants as a group does not preclude the failure of one or another of them taken as an isolated individual. This regime of reproduction would thus be under constant threat from the specific crises resulting from the rebellion of those excluded from the inheritance[8] if this threat were not counterbalanced by an extraordinary increase in the dissimulation of the processes of transfer, thus in the misrecognition of the arbitrary nature of the established order and its perpetuation, and hence in the recognition granted to such an order.

Yet the enchanted perception of the functioning of the school expressed in the myth of the school as a liberating force cannot simply be imputed to the obscure efficacy of statistical mechanisms that can only be revealed by scientific analysis, armed with statistics; it also stems from the essential ambiguity of the academic title and its effects. So, for example, while the academic title plays a crucial role in the reproduction of the social order, it also offers the dominated who manage to appropriate it one of the surest guarantees against unchecked exploitation. As an officially recognized right, it protects its bearers, at least in those job markets most closely controlled by the government, against the other privileges, or at least it limits their effects.

But it so happens that today this phenomenon is seen as a formidable factor of social conservation. And that the top academic nobility, through one of those extraordinary instances of blindness that results from nonreflexive lucidity, denounces the privileges that the lesser academic nobility gains from its "patent of education," to use Weber's phrase, especially in state-controlled markets. In fact, the top academic nobility is a state nobility. It is in league with the state, whose "higher interests" it serves – in the name of the concept of devotion to "public service" – insofar as in so doing it serves its own interests. There is thus indeed a relationship between the academic title and the great state bureaucracy, but it is not as simple and one-sided as Max Weber leads us to believe when he sees in the process of the rationalization of training, and especially the rationalization of selection (with specialized examinations), a dimension (or result) of a process of rationalization of forms of government that tends to eliminate from official business "love, hatred, and all purely personal, irrational, and emotional elements which escape calculation," and leads, through the delimitation and specialization of tasks, to the figure of the *specialist*, "personally detached and thus, strictly objective."[9]

Without entering into a full-fledged critique of Weberian analysis, we may note that in the interstices of the text in which he develops his central thesis, the only one most commentary has addressed, Weber hints at properties or effects of the examination and academic qualifications that cannot easily be integrated into his model. Thus, while the *ambiguity* of the academic title as analyzed above seems to have escaped him, it does appear between the lines when he mentions, without really accounting for them, the ambivalent reactions to which this ambiguity gives rise in what he simply calls "democracy." "'Democracy' takes an ambivalent attitude also towards the system of examinations for expertise, as it does towards all the bureaucratization which, nevertheless, it promotes." On the one hand, he goes on, it approves of the replacement of the domination of persons of distinction by that of "the qualified" (*Qualifizierten*) from all social classes; on the other hand, it fears and fights against the development of a privileged "caste" originating in the examination and the academic title (*Bildungspatent*).[10] And, further on, this time making the point explicit, he goes so far as to establish similarities between the academic title and the noble title of the past.[11] But these observations, along with many others, are simply juxtaposed to the central thesis they contradict; in such a way that he skirts the issues that a genuine comparison would raise.

We must thus make a radical break with the unilateral representation of the academic title and bureaucracy, thus of their relationship, as proposed by Weber (nearly as positively disposed toward the idealized vision that the state nobility has of itself as a "universal class" as Hegel) and restore to analysis the profound ambiguity of institutions that conceal behind a mask of "modernity" and rationality the efficiency of social mechanisms ordinarily associated with the most archaic societies. The academic title is indeed the manifestation *par excellence* of what must be called, through a seemingly strange juxtaposition of words, *state magic*: the conferring of a diploma belongs to the class of the acts of *certification* or *validation* through which an official authority, acting as an agent of the central bank of symbolic credit – the state – guarantees and consecrates a certain state of affairs, a relationship of *conformity* between words and things, between discourse and reality – with, for example, the stamp and the signature that authenticate an act or a document as attested and true, a copy as genuine, a document as valid, a warranty as good. These acts of official recording, in the guise of taking note of a *de facto* situation (a relationship between two people, occupying a certain position, being ill or disabled, etc.), cause this situation to undergo a genuine ontological promotion, a transmutation, a change of nature or essence. Operations of regularization, such as recognizing a child, or, quite simply, recording its birth, or marriage, or still yet, confirming someone in a temporary or "acting" position, are so many bureaucratic manoeuvres that, in a way, change nothing, and, in another sense, change everything, specifically, the collectively attributed meaning and publicly recognized social value of the act or thing in question, with very real consequences: the right to an inheritance, to dependents' allowances, to disability pensions, to sick leave, etc.

The academic title is a public and official warranty, awarded by a collectively recognized authority, of a competence whose technical and social boundaries and proportions can never be disentangled or measured, but which is always independent of subjective, partial evaluations (those of the bearer himself or his close relations, for example). The attributions (in the sense of powers, prerogatives, or privileges) and the statutory attributes ("intelligence," "knowledge," etc.) that it assigns its bearer are endowed, by very virtue of the transcendence of the social, with an objectivity and a universality that impose them on everyone's perception, including that of the bearer himself, as being inscribed in a socially guaranteed nature or essence, implying rights and responsibilities. The educational institution is thus one of the authorities through which the state exercises its monopoly on legitimate symbolic violence. By imposing the legitimate perspective on each agent, through the act that either consecrates him (as a *polytechnicien*, an *agrégé*, etc.) or condemns him (as being excluded from the class of title holders), the *academic verdict* reconciles agents, at least partially; without putting a definitive end to the struggle of every man for himself for the monopoly on the legitimate point of view, it institutes an eminent point of view, with which all others must reckon, even if this is only in contesting it.

THE "BEROBED" AND THE INVENTION OF THE STATE

If the academic title is linked to the state, it is thus as a privilege symbolically instituted and guaranteed by the state, that is, as a "right to the exclusive exercise of a certain function and the benefit of a certain income,"[12] a right that is intimately tied up with the state, both in its historical development, as David Bien has shown, and in its operation. And this is, as it were, by definition: the guarantee ensured to any form of capital – whether in the guise of currency or a universally valid academic title – is undoubtedly one of the most important, if not the most obvious, effects of the existence of the state as a public treasury of material and symbolic resources guaranteeing private appropriations.

It is thus possible, by relating historical works from two separate areas of the discipline, describing the invention of the state or the grands corps and the parallel development of an entire array of new kinds of educational institutions (academies, collèges, boarding schools), to formulate the hypothesis according to which the state nobility, initially in the guise of the *noblesse de robe*, and the academic title, as a "patent of education" guaranteeing privileges, were born of correlative and complementary inventions. The state nobility, whose power and authority, both in their punctual efficiency and their reproduction, are founded, to a great and ever-increasing degree, on the academic title, is the product of an inseparably practical and symbolic construction operation aimed at instituting positions of bureaucratic power that will be relatively independent of the previously established temporal and spiritual forms of power (knights [*la noblesse d'épée*, noblemen of the sword Tr.], the clergy, etc.) and creating a hereditary body of agents entitled to occupy these positions in the name of a competence sanctioned by educational institutions expressly designed to reproduce it.

It is indeed not enough merely to establish that university populations increased significantly between the mid-sixteenth and mid-seventeenth centuries in various European countries, and to relate this expansion to the development of church and state bureaucracies.[13] Nor is it enough simply to follow this parallel evolution over a long period of time – in France's case, starting with the development in the early sixteenth century of the academies that gave noblemen access to the book learning formerly limited to clerics and *robins*,[14] or, a century later, the first rise of the socially very selective collèges that, on the model of Louis-le-Grand, prepared students for the great military and bureaucratic offices,[15] and moving up to the years 1760–70 (after the expulsion of the Jesuits), which saw an increase in the number of boarding schools associated with the most prestigious collèges, which, primarily due to their high cost, catered to students from very comfortable milieus, particularly (alongside the sons of noblemen and officers) a large proportion of sons of office holders and members of the professions.[16] It would also be necessary to examine the formation of the state grands corps and, more specifically, the new system of reproduction strategies that lay at the foundation of their existence and their subsistence, a system in which education strategies, the only ones capable of securing specific competence and legitimacy, were granted an ever-increasing role over time, alongside marriage strategies (analyzed by Françoise Autrand for "the people of the Paris Parlement"[17]) and the symbolic strategies necessary for inventing and imposing both the notion of a *noblesse de robe* and the new system of perceptions that gave it a privileged relationship to the state, such as the idea or the ideal of "public service."[18] Undoubtedly dating back to the beginning of their corps, the interest parliamentarians took in cultural and educational matters,[19] already evident from the fact, among others, that the physical establishment of the universities was tied to the location of the Parlements,[20] came to full fruition in the years 1760 to 1789 (when boarding schools were flourishing) with the educational plans presented in the different Parlements of the kingdom and the propositions of Chrétien-François de Lamoignon (in 1783) and Rolland d'Erceville.[21] And the solidarities that develop among schoolmates and the affinities associated with a common education and title undoubtedly also played a role, alongside family ties, in the creation of an entirely new kind of esprit de corps.[22]

What was at stake in the competition pitting noblemen of the robe against noblemen of the sword, the *robin* and book learning against the knight and chivalrous education, as well as against the cleric, a man of the book like the *robin*, but one prevented from hereditarily transferring his powers and privileges, was the autonomization of a bureaucratic field and, correlatively, the constitution of corps founded on a completely new combination of principles of domination and the legitimation of domination: cultural capital as with the clergy; heredity and the transferability of wealth, as well as devotion to public service, as with the nobility. It was the progressive rise of a new order, whose constituent elements fell into place at the end of a series of partial inventions and transformations – such as, for example, the transition from the purchase of offices legitimated by the acquisition of a minimal competence to the academic acquisition of titles granting rights to certain positions. We see that, contrary to what has sometimes been claimed, through an error equivalent in its principle to the one made by the proponents of the "liberating school" regarding the relationship between noble titles and academic titles, "the world of the Parlement was not built through the elimination of the nobility,"[23] but that, on the contrary, it annexed the most fundamental aspect of the former nobility and integrated a significant proportion of its members. To quote from Françoise Autrand's description of the original combination of properties thus assembled by the *noblesse de robe*: "Originating in chivalrous families or sons of those raised to the peerage, but all men of law rather than men of war, the parliamentarians formed a new nobility. But are we justified in speaking of a new nobility because members of the Parlement wielded the pen rather than the sword, wore lined hoods rather than helmets and, in place of armor, put on the royal red coat? Are we justified in completely assimilating nobility and knighthood? In fact, from its very origins, nobility contains a notion that makes it possible for it to include within its ranks the parliamentary corps: the idea of public service. Whether new or old, noblemen 'faithfully and constantly serve' the king, carrying out 'the service that noblemen must perform for him and for the public good.' Nowhere outside of the Parlement, especially since the early part of the fifteenth century, was this aspect of nobility more fully emphasized. 'To live nobly' was 'to serve the king,' 'in his wars' or otherwise. If *public service* is the hereditary vocation of the nobility, *service to the state* is the soul of the parliamentary body."[24]

The *noblesse de robe*, of which contemporary technocrats are the structural heirs (and sometimes the descendants), is a body that created itself by creating the state, a body that, in order to build itself, had to build the state, that is, among other things, an entire political philosophy of "public service" as service to the state, or to the "public" – and not simply to the king, as with the former nobility – and of this service as a "disinterested" activity, directed toward universal ends. "Service to the king" is an attribute inscribed as it were in the social definition of nobility, as the equation "to live nobly" is "to serve the king" reminds us. It is a destiny that the nobility has neither to choose nor to create since it is incumbent upon it by birth, an ascription imposed upon it as a given if it is truly what it is, that is, what it must be, and if it wishes to "maintain its rank," that is, realize its essence. In contrast, "public service" as devotion to the state is less an inheritance than a deliberate choice of vocation, a consciously assumed occupation (*Beruf*) that presupposes particular dispositions and talents as well as special skills acquired through study.

The transition from one to the other can thus only be made through a collective conversion of minds and a full-scale inventive effort located in the realm of perceptions no less than in organizations. This is why we cannot truly understand such a mutation unless we restore to historical analysis everything that is usually left to the historians of ideas, religion, and the church (again so many separate specializations), and recall all the political theories, both well known and obscure, that have been produced (often on the occasion of theological or ecclesiastical debates that inextricably combine political and religious passions and corporate interests) by successive generations of the state nobility, from the royal jurists of the Middle Ages to the Girondin lawyers, and well beyond (if we think of the great Gaullist reformers of the Fifth Republic), taking in along the way all the politico-religious doctrinarians created by the parliamentary body: Jansenists, Gallicans, etc. In struggling for the recognition of their corps, which they are spontaneously led to see as universal, parliamentarians, from the sixteenth-century jurists who laid the foundations of modern political philosophy to those who, throughout the eighteenth century, developed a number of notions that would lead to the French Revolution, by way of the Girondins, made a critical contribution to the construction of the official perception of public service as disinterested devotion to the general interest.

What thinkers as far back in time as Louis le Caron or Louis le Roy and Chancellor d'Aguesseau have in common, allowing us to place the latter under the label of the "civic humanism of civil servants"[25] that was coined for the former, is their willingness to take civic duties seriously and to make knowledge an indispensable guide for conduct in the city. They propose to found a philosophy of civic responsibility (the philosopher, writes Louis le Caron in his *Dialogues* of 1556, is "in love with the public good") and they are opposed to the "individualists" who, like Montaigne, Charron, or François de la Mothe le Vayer, radically separate the public and the private – according to the formula *intus ut libet, foris ut moris est*. Expressing the specific interests of groups who wish to exercise power in the name of competence, these inventors of civil virtue defend a philosophy that claims to be resolutely political. Rejecting the "retreat" into libraries, they propose to found a set of civic duties befitting those who must exercise civil responsibilities for the sake of the entire nation.

And it is again in basing his ideas on that other parliamentary tradition, the Jansenist school of the Domats or the Nicoles, who develop, in line with the idea of *raison d'état*, the notions of private interest (or "self-interest") and public interest, as "enlightened self-interest," indiscernible from charity, that Chancellor d'Aguesseau attempts to assert the autonomy of a genuine public service, at once in relation to royal power, in the name of the constitutionalist tradition, in relation to the church, in the name of the specific competence of the jurist, in relation as well to hereditary nobility, which owes its position to a mere accident of birth, and finally, in relation to the "public," which, although constantly invoked, cannot be maintained as a principle of exclusive legitimation without reducing the Parlement to the subordinate status of a simple body of representatives of the nation.

And we must quote this great parliamentarian, undoubtedly one of the first incarnations of the modern technocrat, whose origins were in two great parliamentary families, the Daguesseaus and the Talons, and who was related by marriage to a third, the d'Ormessons,[26] from his famous speech of 1693 on "the independence of the *avocat*," often quoted but probably never truly read, where he attempts to found both a new form of capital and a new form of legitimacy by praising the demanding and liberating tasks of public service: "In this nearly general subservience of all stations, an Order as old as the magistrature, as noble as Virtue, as necessary as Justice, is distinguished by a singular character; and alone among all the states, it abides in the happy and peaceful possession of its independence. Enjoying freedom without being useless to the fatherland, it *devotes itself to the Public* without being its slave; and condemning *the indifference of the philosopher*, who seeks independence in inactivity, it pities the misfortune of those who only go into public service because they have lost their freedom (. . .). Happy to be in a state where making one's fortune and fulfilling one's duty are but one and the same thing; where *merit* and glory are inseparable; where a man, *as the sole author of his elevation*, holds all other men in a state of dependence on his *lumières*,[27] and forces them to pay homage to *the unique superiority of his genius!* All those distinctions founded merely on the *accident of birth*, those great names that flatter the pride of common men, and dazzle even the learned, become useless supports in a profession whose *virtue* creates its *nobility* and in which men are esteemed not by what their fathers have done, but by what they themselves have done (. . .). *Merit* (. . .) is the only good that can never be bought, and the public, always free in its suffrage, never sells glory – it gives it. It is not an obligatory tribute paid to Fortune out of propriety or necessity: it is a *voluntary* homage, a natural deference that men show toward virtue. (. . .) All your days are marked by *the duties you perform for Society*. All your occupations are exercises in rectitude and integrity, justice and religion. The Fatherland profits from every moment of your life; its even gains from your leisure and benefits from the fruit of your repose. The *Public*, aware of the value of your time, dispenses you from the duties it requires of other men (. . .)."[28] The Public, constantly invoked throughout this speech, with variable meanings, is that powerful abstract ally that, as a disinterested guarantor of the disinterestedness of the magistrate ("the Public scorned these venal souls") and as a universal security for the universality of his acts, enables him to assert his autonomy in relation to all true forms of power.

This speech, which would merit full quotation, condenses all the themes of the new sociodicy – merit associated with gifts, criticism of birth and venality, faith in *les lumières* and science, and especially the glorification of disinterestedness and devotion to the public (in the dual sense of the commonwealth, or common good, and public opinion), thus established as a justification *par excellence* for power. What gives this speech its current or timeless quality (a Jacobin Gaullist or socialist ENA graduate from the "liberating school" could well make this speech today) is the fact that, in order to constitute and legitimate itself, the state nobility had to immediately inscribe in its system of justifications – primarily in view of the nobility of the sword, to which, we might add, it was assimilated, Daguesseau becoming d'Aguesseau – elements that would not yield their full return until a later stage in the development of the new mode of reproduction. This is the case, for example, with their confidence in talent and merit, and thus in the reproductive capacities of the educational institution, a confidence that, although shaken for a time (witness the anxiety experienced by the bourgeoisie at the end of the nineteenth century at the possibility of universal mandatory schooling), is restored in the very form that d'Aguesseau gave it, when, as today, with the logic of the transfer of cultural capital fulfilling its function perfectly, people are again able to find in "gifts" the justification for the academic distribution of titles, and thus of powers and privileges. The ambiguity of this entire constellation of practices and perceptions stems from the fact that it clearly expresses the interests of people who are intimately bound up with the state, with the "public," and particularly with the diploma (which is precisely what opens the door to the public service market), and who occupy a dominated position within the field of power, just like the *noblesse de robe* in relation to the *noblesse d'épée* during the initial phase – and perhaps still today, as a result of differing origins, technocrats of the left in relation to technocrats of the right.[29] These dominated dominants are only able to enhance their interests by associating them, perfectly innocently, with causes that appear to them to be universal, such as emancipatory science, or, in other times, the liberating school. There is in fact no reason to be surprised – unless we were to believe in miracles, and in the possibility of an unmotivated action or an action with no other motivation than the resolution of pure will – and still less to be upset that those who make themselves the disinterested defenders of universal causes might, without even being aware of it, have an interest in disinterestedness.

THE LENGTHENING OF THE CIRCUITS OF LEGITIMATION

While there is probably no leading group that has accumulated more insurance – property titles, academic titles, and, sometimes, noble titles – than the great state nobility, there is no group that has to provide as much insurance either, especially in the area of competence and devotion to the universal. There is thus nothing that can be said about this nobility that is not two-sided. While technocrats, as unwitting Hegelians, spontaneously lay claim to the privileges of the "universal class," they are obliged to invoke the universal in order to exercise their domination, and they cannot avoid being caught in their own game and having to subject their practice to norms with claims to universality. They believe themselves to be the necessary agents of a necessary policy, capable of making the populace happy in spite of itself, and they are, for example, convinced that the "managerial revolution," in reforming the organization and decision-making procedures of large private companies, will spare them a revolution in the area of property rights. Yet they feel just as keenly the need to think in a "social" perspective, to conduct themselves as agents of the state more than as businessmen, and to base their decisions on the "neutrality" of "expertise" and the ethics of "public service." Similarly, the temptation to self-legitimation that leads some of the new mandarins crowned for their cultural competence to use this competence to crown and legitimate themselves carries with it an obligatory recognition of strictly cultural forms of power and is counterbalanced by the complexity in the competition for the production and imposition of principles of vision and division of the social world, a complexity that stems from the unprecedented differentiation of the field of power and raises in profoundly altered terms the question of the legitimation of power.

Domination must gain recognition, that is, it must be known and recognized for what it is not. The tautology "the dominants are those who dominate" (or "power relations are relations of force") functions as a denunciation, and if dominants were ever to use it for themselves, it would sound like a self-destructive confession. This is to say that in contrast to raw power, which acts according to mechanical efficiency, all genuine power acts as symbolic power, the basis of which is, paradoxically, *denial*.[30] It carries with it a demand for recognition that is a demand for misrecognition, addressed to an autonomous agent in a position to grant to power what it grants to itself – that is, that it is not a simple arbitrary imposition – but which has no value or social efficacy unless conceded by an independent power. The chances that the act of recognition will be recognized as legitimate, and that it will be able to exercise its power of legitimation, are increased the less it appears to be determined by external physical, economic, political, or affective constraints (hence the more "authentic," "sincere," "disinterested," etc., it appears) and the more it appears to be exclusively inspired by the specific grounds of an elective submission, and thus the greater the degree to which its author possesses the legitimacy demanded by the power in search of legitimation.

In other words, the symbolic efficacy of an act of legitimation increases concomitantly with the ratio of the recognized independence of the consecrator to that of the consecratee, and with his statutory authority as well (which is always linked, through a relation of circular causality, to his autonomy). It is nearly nonexistent in the case of self-consecration (Napoleon taking the crown from the hands of the pope to crown himself) or self-praise (writers writing their own panegyrics, or Ford saying that

Fords are the best cars); it is weak when the consecration is carried out by mercenaries (hired clappers at the theater, advertisers) or accomplices, or even close relations or acquaintances, whose judgments are suspected of being based on complaisance ("my son is the smartest"); it is also weak when the acts of recognition (homages, prefaces, reviews, etc.) are the object of exchanges that become all the more transparent, and correspondingly less symbolically effective, the shorter the circuits of exchange and the intervals between the acts of exchange; it reaches its highest level when all real or visible relations of material or symbolic interest between the agents or the institutions in question disappear and when the authors of the acts of recognition are themselves more highly recognized.

The principle according to which the autonomy of a celebrator is the precondition for the symbolic efficacy of an act of celebration is not a norm established by the analyst – even on the basis of anthropological universals – but a *positive law* of the way social universes work. Agents implement this principle in the real world in evaluating the validity of practices of consecration – literary criticism, for instance – and it is at the source of strategies that work to conceal strategies of either direct or mediated self-celebration. The most typical of these strategies, drawn from an analysis of the phenomenon of return favors in the area of the criticism of written works, all of which aim to conceal the relationship between the praiser and the praised, can be exemplified as follows: let a period of time go by between celebration and countercelebration (A praises B in January and B praises A in June); change audience by changing medium (A praises B in daily newspaper X; B praises A in weekly newspaper Y or on the radio); substitute individuals – the author initially praised can carry out her counterpraise under a pseudonym or through a writer she is related to by an invisible tie, a woman writing under her maiden name, a friend, lover, disciple, proxy, or henchman, etc.; give an invisible counterbenefit in the form of a university position, a vote in an election, etc., rather than a book review; accumulate capital consisting of potential countercelebrations by praising an individual (the editor of a daily or weekly newspaper, the writer of a column, the leader of an intellectual lobby, etc.) who has the power to determine celebrations. All of these procedures may be combined and accumulated, lending every appearance of freedom to exchanges almost as perfectly regulated as matrimonial exchanges in traditional societies. This is how the holders of top positions of temporal power in the journalistic field are able to exert their influence over the entire field, obtaining the submission of a portion of those who hold symbolic power in the intellectual field, who in turn obtain more or less required compliments.[31]

The fundamental law of the economy of legitimation might be written thus: given that the symbolic efficacy of a legitimating discourse varies in direct proportion to the real or visible distance (independence) between the praiser and the praised, and that the distance between their corresponding points of view tends to vary in inverse proportion to this distance, an agent or institution wishing to perform an act of symbolic promotion (propaganda, advertisement, etc.) must inevitably find an optimum between seeking the maximization of the celebratory content of the message and the maximization of the (visible) autonomy of the celebrator, thus of the symbolic efficacy of the celebration. This logic, which governs the practical choices advertisers make between open, direct advertising strategies and the more indirect, less obvious strategies of public relations, also governs the various strategies to which the different categories of dominants have recourse in order to produce the "theodicy of their privilege."[32] Driven by their distrust of things intellectual as well as their concern for conserving the energy required for dissimulation, the integrists of the old guard (for example, "shock CEOs") produce a message heavy in conservative content but weak in symbolic efficacy, at least outside their universe. In contrast, the modernist fraction subscribes to a discourse weak in informative content but strong in dissimulation, hence in symbolic efficacy. They know how to hide behind spokespeople who are all the more effective because they do not appear to others or to themselves to be such and who may even achieve the gains in symbolic efficacy that their independence secures for the conservative message at the risk of symbolic contestation. Thus, given that energy [*force*] must be expended in order to bring about the recognition of power [*force*][33] and that there is necessarily a division of the labor of legitimation, it is understandable that the amount of social energy expended should tend to increase with the symbolic efficacy of the legitimation, which is related to the length and complexity of the networks of interlegitimation.

In short, there is at least one case in which it is false to say that one is never better served than by oneself: whenever an individual or group – a power, in any case – is to contribute to its own legitimation. Consequently, the logic of "enlightened egoism," discussed by de Tocqueville, recommends going beyond the tendency all power holders have to perform their own celebration and to avoid thereby both the expense and the risk of misappropriation inherent in the inevitable delegation of the symbolic work of legitimation.[34] The prince is only able to get truly effective symbolic service out of his painters, his poets, or his jurists insofar as he gives them the capacity to legislate within their domain. Although apparent autonomy or misrecognized dependence may have the same effects as real independence, symbolic efficacy, the precondition for which is a degree of autonomy for the legitimating authority, has as a nearly inevitable counterweight the proportional risk that this authority may appropriate his delegated power of legitimation for his own benefit. Thus, from the very first instance of a corps of professional jurists, in twelfth-century Bologna, the ambiguity of the relationship of dependence in and through independence that binds cultural power to temporal power is abundantly clear. As Kantorovicz has convincingly shown,[35] while the autonomization of the law effectively guaranteed the prince new powers, which were more hidden, and more legitimate, founded as they were on the authority gained by the juridical tradition and its guardians *in challenge to him*, it was also at the source both of the demands made on him by the jurists and of the power struggles in which those holding the monopoly on the legitimate manipulation of texts could invoke the specific legitimacy of the law against the arbitrariness of the prince.

As autonomous fields multiply and the field of power diversifies, there is a move away from political indifferentiation and *mechanical solidarity* among interchangeable powers (such as clan elders or village leaders) or elementary forms of the division of the labor of domination into a small number of specialized functions (such as warriors and priests), away from simple systems dominated by one principle or the other, which include hierocracy and caesaropapism, and even the hereditary monarchy of divine right, systems doomed to open conflicts between temporal and spiritual authority.[36] No longer incarnated in persons or even in particular institutions, power becomes coextensive with the structure of the field of power, and it is only realized and manifested through an entire set of fields and forms of power united by a genuine *organic solidarity*, and thus both different and interdependent. More precisely, power is primarily wielded invisibly and anonymously, through "mechanisms" such as those that achieve the reproduction of economic and cultural capital, in other words, through the apparently anarchical, yet structured, actions and reactions of *networks* of agents and institutions that are both in competition and complementary, and involved in increasingly long and complex circuits of legitimating exchanges. The simple relation between pairs of antagonistic and complementary powers, such as *oratores* and *bellatores*, gives way to complex relations among fields and, in particular, to the relations between the university field and the bureaucratic field as analyzed above, as well as to relations between these two fields and the economic or political field; in other words, it gives way to relations among universes that all function as the loci of highly dissimulated reproduction mechanisms, founded on operations of classification, and thus all manage to durably protect the interests of the dominants while officially rejecting all forms of hereditary transfer.

Is it possible to characterize the overall process we have just described, the culmination of which is the lasting reign of the school nobility and the state nobility, without subscribing to the views, usually superficial and unilateral, that are proposed in struggles on the subject of the social world and merely borrowed by researchers (even the best of them) in more or less euphemized form when they resort to concepts such as "democratization," "rationalization," "modernization," etc.?[37] To be sure, with legitimation circuits becoming increasingly long and complex, the symbolic efficacy of the prevailing mode of domination tends to increase, and physical coercion and repression tend to give way to the milder dissimulated constraints of symbolic violence, with the police and the prison system, privileged by adolescent denunciation and its extensions in scholarly discourse, becoming much less important in the maintenance of the social order than the school and authorities of cultural production. And, while there is progress in "rationalization," it is in the sense of Freud, more than Weber;[38] the mechanisms that tend to "rationalize" practices and institutions, by layering them with justifications likely to conceal their arbitrariness, become increasingly effective. Per contra, the cost of the social energy expended for legitimation increases, as do the threats of crisis that result from the fact that the organic solidarity between the agents and institutions engaged in the labor of domination is both more complex and more fragile. But, most importantly, the ever-increasing role played by the educational institution in the reproduction and legitimation of power, even in the economic order, gives a particularly sharp edge to the *legitimation antinomy* universally encountered by temporal power holders in their relationship with those whose power is associated with the possession of one or another form of cultural capital. The latter, be they clerics or laypersons, are always tempted to use to their own advantage the autonomy that the dominants are compelled to concede to them because it creates the very value of the consecration and legitimation that their "spiritual" interventions in the "temporal" order are able to grant ultimately only in direct proportion to their supposed independence.

"Progress" in symbolic efficacy, which correlates with the increased complexity of the circuits of legitimation and, most especially, with the intervention of the mechanisms of the educational institution, as complicated as they are concealed, is counterbalanced by the considerable increase in the potential for subversive misappropriation of the specific capital associated with being in one or another of the fields resulting from the process of differentiation. The interests inscribed in the different positions within the field of power (specific or, as is sometimes said, class interests) are relatively independent of the generic interests associated with membership in the field of power, which they may obscure from agents' view. It thus may happen that the interests associated with the dominated positions in the field of cultural production lead to subversive alliances, capable of threatening the social order. This occurs when, in the cognitive struggles over the social world, the professional producers of principles of vision and division, globally located in dominated positions in the field of power (or at least those among them who, as second-degree dominated, occupy a lower position in the field of cultural production), engage their cultural capital in struggles that they more or less completely or more or less durably identify with their own struggles in the field of power; when, in other words, certain cultural producers (defrocked priests of the millenarist movements of the Middle Ages, revolutionary intellectuals, etc.) symbolically abandon the camp of the dominants from whom they derive their power of symbolic construction in order to lend to the dominated their power to constitute the social order, thus providing them with the means of mobilizing the potential power that the current symbolic systems were helping to contain.

This new form of division of the labor of domination, along with the particular risks it involves, is what makes all the solidarities that transcend the divisions linked to the existence of multiple fields and principles of hierarchization so important – solidarities such as family ties, for example, the foundation of networks of exchanges and alliances that play a crucial role in struggles for power within the field of power and in the perpetuation of the "great bourgeois dynasties" over time and across regimes. It is undoubtedly because these high-placed families manage to control dominant positions in different fields that they manage to survive changes of regime and political crises that, as Syme has shown for ancient Rome, simply substitute one network of connections (family or school) for another.[39] But, in addition, like all mechanisms, institutional or otherwise, that favor exchanges between the various fields, and hence their integration – salons and clubs, as well as commissions, committees, and colloquia, where representatives of the different universes get together – such solidarities help to maintain the minimum cohesion necessary for getting the collective interests of the dominants to prevail over the divisive interests associated with each field. And the denial of calculation and instrumentality that is essential, in exchanges among dominants, for transmuting economic transactions into symbolic actions (substituting a gift for a salary, for example) manages to strengthen the unity of the group simply by reaffirming it while asserting the insubstitutability of the goods and services exchanged, and thus the incommensurability of the various forms of capital.

All this is to say that the question of the unity or the division of the "dominant class," which has given rise to so much debate, has little meaning. The organic solidarity that unites the different powers and agents engaged in the different fields is a principle of both unification and division, the foundation of exchanges that enable the development of two-way relations of obligation and recognition (each of the partners in an exchange being dominant in one respect and dominated in another) as well as constant struggles for the power to impose the dominant principle of domination – and hence, either the preservation or the transformation of the structure of the forms of power within the field of power. The strictly political struggles whose stake is power over the state, and, at one and the same time, over the rules and procedures that contribute to determining the relations of power within the field of power and controlling their manipulation, must not cause us to forget the subterranean struggles constantly being played out in the apparent anarchy of reproduction strategies, as well as in the collective struggles among corps, interest groups, parties, etc., which, like today's struggles over the preservation or transformation of the educational institution, or, more precisely, over the structure of the field of educational institutions charged with the reproduction of the field of power, profoundly and durably affect the relations of power within the field of power and contain the true principle of stances in political struggles for power over the state.

It is clear that whatever their grounds or motives, these struggles among dominants necessarily add to the field of power a bit of that universal – reason, disinterestedness, civic-mindedness, etc. – that, originating as it does in previous struggles, is always a symbolically effective weapon in the struggles of the moment. And, while taking care not to pronounce the kind of judgments on the comparative merits of one or another regime that are often identified with "political philosophy," we may advance the notion that progress in the differentiation of forms of power is constituted by so many protective acts against *tyranny*, understood, after the manner of Pascal, as the infringement of one order upon the rights of another, or more precisely, as an intrusion of the forms of power associated with one field in the functioning of another. Not only because the dominated can always take advantage of or benefit from conflicts among the powerful, who, quite often, need their cooperation in order to triumph in these conflicts, but also because one of the principal weapons in these struggles among dominants is the symbolic universalization of particular interests that, even if it is undertaken for the purpose of legitimation or mobilization, inevitably leads to the advancement of the universal.

Translator's Appendix

A list of the schools as they were at the time of survey can be found in table 8 on p. 133.

GLOSSARY

ACADI Association des Cadres Dirigeants de l'Industrie pour le Progrès Social et Economique, association of industrial executives for economic and social progress

accessit honorable mention

administrateur civil member of general corps of civil servants (that is, not grand corps)

administration, administrative refers to civil service unless otherwise specified

AGREF Association des Grandes Entreprises Françaises Faisant Appel à l'Épargne, association of large companies for investment

agrégation highly select national examination, virtually guaranteeing those who succeed (referred to as *agrégés* or *agrégées*) a teaching position in secondary or higher education

baccalauréat national competitive examination taken at the end of high school, serves as pass to university entrance

BEP brevet d'enseignement professionnel, vocational high school diploma

BEPC brevet d'études du premier cycle, junior high school diploma

Bottin Mondain society directory

BS/brevet supérieur certificate in earlier system for those leaving school at 15

cadre manager, executive, corporate professional staff

CAP certificate d'aptitude professionnelle, earned following vocational classes plus work internship

CEG collège d'enseignement général, in earlier system, secondary school parallel to and of lesser rank than lycée

CEP certificate d'études primaires, in earlier system, primary school certificate

CNPF Conseil National du Patronat Français, national employers' union

CODER Commissions de Développement Économique Régional, commissions on regional economic development

collège first "cycle" of public secondary school, junior high school; also select private secondary school

concours national competitive examination

Concours Général annual national competition in which lycée students are invited to compete for a *prix* (first prize) and *accessits* (honorable mention) in a variety of subjects

Conseiller d'État top rank in Conseil d'État

culture culture, Culture, education, upbringing, knowledge, learning, and all of the above

culture générale wide-ranging knowledge and sophistication

cycles see chart of school system below

DAFSA Société Anonyme de Documentation et d'Analyse Financière, documentation and financial analysis corporation

de robe, robins, "berobed" refer to the division of the nobility marked by its robes, i.e. the legal professions

DEA diplôme d'études approfondies, research degree leading to doctorate

DESS diplôme d'études supérieures spécialisées, specialized degree preparing for entry into working world

DEUG diplôme d'études universitaires générales, associate's degree

EDF Electricité de France

facultés various schools making up the public university system

general inspector higher public servant charged with teacher evaluations, curriculum decisions, etc.

grande école see note 2 to Prologue, p. 396

grand commis high-level civil servant

grande porte route leading to the most prestigious schools, careers, etc.

grands corps highest level of corps in French administrative system, goal of graduates of the grandes écoles, often used as a springboard to high-level positions in the private sector. Major technical corps are Mines, Ponts et Chaussées, and Eaux et Fôrets; the major nontechnical corps are the Conseil d'État, the Inspection des Finances, and the Cour des Comptes, with the Prefectural Corps following next in the hierarchy.

hypokhâgne first year of humanities preparatory class

INSEE Institut National de la Statistique et des Études Économiques, national institute of statistics and economic research

Inspecteur des Finances member of Inspection des Finances

Institut de France highly prestigious body composed of the Académie Française and the Academies of Letters, Medicine, Science and Social Sciences

khâgne humanities preparatory class

licence three-year university degree, equivalent to Bachelor of Arts in US or UK

lycée second "cycle" of public secondary school, high school

Maître des Requêtes second rank in Conseil d'État

mention honors on baccalauréat, in the form of comments such as "good" or "excellent"

normalien student or graduate of l'École Normale Supérieure

pantouflage passage from public to private sector

patron boss, head of business, business owner, employer

petite école less prestigious professional school

petite porte route leading to less prestigious schools, careers, etc.

polytechnicien student or graduate of l'École Polytechnique

preparatory classes   postsecondary institutions for students planning to compete in entrance examinations to the grandes écoles, often housed within lycées

prix d'excellence   awarded to first-ranked students at end of school year

RATP   Réseau Autonome des Transports Parisiens, greater Paris public transportation system

section   hierarchized tracks in school system, see note 6 to Prologue, p. 396

sévrienne   student or graduate of École Nationale Supérieure de Sèvres, for women

sixième, **etc.**   levels of secondary school, see note 6 to Prologue, p. 396

SNCF   Société Nationale des Chemins de Fer, national railroad system

taupe   preparatory class in the sciences

UNICER   Union des Chefs et Responsables d'Entreprise, union of corporate heads and executives

SIMPLIFIED CHART OF THE CURRENT FRENCH EDUCATIONAL SYSTEM

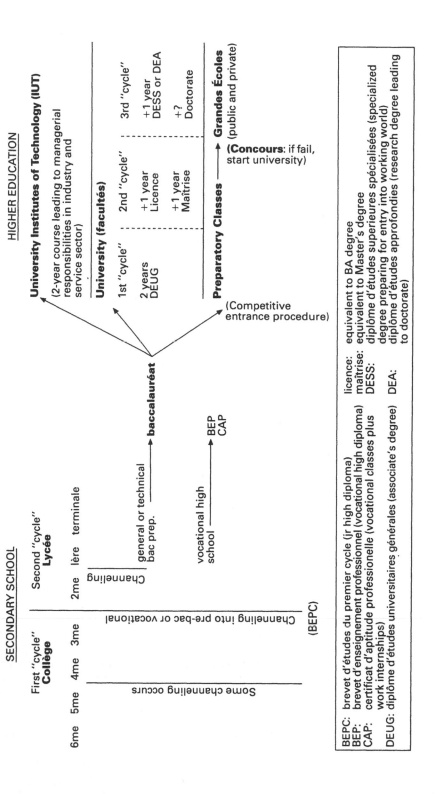

SECONDARY SCHOOL

First "cycle"
Collège

6me 5me 4me 3me

Some channeling occurs

Channeling into pre-bac or vocational

(BEPC)

Second "cycle"
Lycée

2me 1ère terminale

Channeling

general or technical
bac prep. → **baccalauréat**

vocational high
school → BEP
CAP

(Competitive
entrance procedure)

HIGHER EDUCATION

University Institutes of Technology (IUT)

(2-year course leading to managerial
responsibilities in industry and
service sector)

University (facultés)

1st "cycle"   2nd "cycle"   3rd "cycle"

2 years   +1 year   +1 year
DEUG   Licence   DESS or DEA

    +1 year   +?
    Maîtrise   Doctorate

Preparatory Classes → **Grandes Écoles** (public and private)

(Concours: if fail,
start university)

BEPC: brevet d'études du premier cycle (jr high diploma)
BEP: brevet d'enseignement professionnel (vocational high diploma)
CAP: certificat d'aptitude professionelle (vocational classes plus
      work internships)
DEUG: diplôme d'études universitaires générales (associate's degree)

licence: equivalent to BA degree
maîtrise: equivalent to Master's degree
DESS: diplôme d'études superieures spécialisées (specialized
          degree preparing for entry into working world)
DEA: diplôme d'études approfondies (research degree leading
          to doctorate)

Notes

The epigraph to the book can be glossed as follows:

> With their pockets full of money, ennobled children,
> From the college, in a single leap, soar to the fleur de lis.
> There, whistling, singing, thinking about their mistresses,
> Armor-plated with ignorance and proud of their riches,
> These 20-year-old Catos go about randomly
> Making unappealable decisions on various matters.
>
> *The uncovered pot of roses,*
> *or Parlement unveiled, 1789*

Prologue   Social Structures and Mental Structures

1   In a previous work, which prefigured some of the most typically constructivist research that amateurs of academic classification sometimes like to oppose to *Reproduction* (I am thinking, for example, of A. Cicourel et al., *Language Use and School Performance* (New York: Academic Press, 1974)), it was shown how teachers and students tacitly agree to accept a communication situation that, when the strict technical return is measured, seems completely dysfunctional. Teachers act as though they are being understood and, in any event, take care to avoid any evaluation of their students' understanding, while students behave as though they are understanding and elude the very question of the intelligibility of magisterial discourse (cf. P. Bourdieu, J.-C. Passeron and M. de Saint Martin, *Academic Discourse* (Cambridge: Polity Press, 1994)). [For *Reproduction*, See Pierre Bourdieu and Jean-Claude Passeron, *Reproduction in Education, Society and Culture* (1970), trans. R. Nice (London: Sage, 1977), Tr.]

2   The grandes écoles are elite graduate or professional schools, entrance into which is determined by national competitive examination (*concours*) following one to four years of postsecondary studies designed expressly in preparation for the *concours*. Tuition and fees for those accepted are paid by the government, and students receive a stipend as well. The grandes écoles as a whole are opposed to the facultés, the schools that make up the university system, which accept anyone who has passed the baccalauréat exam taken at the end of high school. One might think of the Ivy League schools in the US or Oxford and

Cambridge in the UK as similar training grounds. A list of the grandes (and not so grandes) écoles treated in the book can be found in table 8 on p. 133, but the most prestigious are the École Normale Supérieure, which trains secondary and higher education teachers, Polytechnique, which trains future high-level technical civil servants, the École des Hautes Études Commerciales, for business studies, and the École Nationale d'Administration, which prepares its students for higher civil service and cabinet positions.[Tr.]

3 Since the present work is here to affirm it, I will not repeat my absolute rejection of sectarian rejections of one or another research method – so-called qualitative approaches for some, who swear only by discourse analysis or direct observation; survey questionnaire and statistical analyses for others, who do not want to hear about anything other than a highly codified and very narrow use of statistics. The most elementary techniques in the sociology of science would suffice to establish that the denunciations certain ethnomethodologists hurl at sociologists – who are purely and simply identified with a certain way of conceiving of social science, no doubt dominant in the American establishment – owe their mobilizing efficacy to the fact that they allow many sociologists to convert certain deficiencies in their training into an elective rejection. They would likewise reveal that the scorn of methodologists for anything that diverges, however slightly, from the narrow canons they have erected as an absolute measure of rigor often serves to mask the routine platitude of a practice devoid of imagination and almost always lacking in what must constitute the genuine precondition of genuine rigor: the reflexive criticism of one's own techniques and procedures of analysis.

4 Among the strategies used to resist scientific analysis, one of the most infallible consists in destroying the very purpose of the enterprise of objectivation by reducing the distanced description – which, since it presupposes a suspension of belief (or better yet, of the doxic adherence characteristic of the ordinary attitude), is destined to appear disillusioned and sometimes close to derisive – to the status of "critique" in the everyday sense, if not to that of satire or gossip. This reduction is all the easier, and all the more likely, when the effort required to communicate a sense of the necessity of the practices or institutions objectivated has every chance of being misunderstood – when it is not purely and simply perceived, through a reversal of the previous error, as a typically functionalist attempt at legitimation. The problem for science becomes most acute when it deals with social worlds such as the university field or the intellectual field, which are characterized by a claim to a monopoly on their own objectivation and in which agents multiply the partial objectivations of their adversaries and the quasi-objectivations of their own properties and excel in the elaboration of that "near truth" that undoubtedly constitutes the most formidable defense against the unveiling of truth.

5 Here I concur with Gilles Deleuze in his analyses of freedom as the "expansion of consciousness" (G. Deleuze, *The Fold: Leibniz and the Baroque* (1988), trans. T. Conley (Minneapolis: University of Minnesota Press, 1993)), albeit via a different route. Paradoxically, there are those who would stigmatize as "deterministic" analyses that, by working to enlarge the space open to consciousness and clarification, offer those being studied the possibility of liberation (teachers in the present case, for example).

6 After two or three years of preschool and five years of primary school (ages 6 to 11), students enter the *sixième*, proceeding through the *cinquième*, the *quatrième*, the *troisième* (which constitute the "first cycle" of secondary school), moving on through the *seconde*, the *première*, and finally the *terminale* (the "second cycle"). At the end of the *seconde*, students who plan to take one of the several general or technology baccalauréat examinations at the end of their secondary education are channeled into separate, hierarchically ordered *sections*, or tracks. [Tr.]

7 Cf. P. Bourdieu, *Distinction: A Social Critique of the Judgement of Taste* (1979), trans. R. Nice (Cambridge: Harvard University Press, 1984), and "Social Space and the Genesis of Groups" (1984) *Social Science Information* 24:2 (1985), pp. 195–220.

8 I am thinking here in particular of my analysis of the structures of professorial perception and the pained and indignant reactions it triggered (cf. chapter 2 below).

PART I   ACADEMIC FORMS OF CLASSIFICATION

A preliminary version of part I was coauthored by Monique de Saint Martin.

Chapter 1   Dualistic Thinking and the Conciliation of Opposites

1 The Concours Général is a national competitive examination in which high school students are invited to compete for a *prix* (first prize) and *accessits* (honorable mention) in each subject. [Tr.]

2 Address of the Institut des Sciences Politiques, whose graduates often go on to hold high-level civil service positions. [Tr.]

3 The *prix d'excellence* is awarded to students at the top of their class at the end of the year. [Tr.]

4 The agrégation is a highly select national examination, and it virtually guarantees those who succeed in it a teaching post in secondary or higher education. [Tr.]

5 Preparatory classes are post-secondary institutions for students planning to compete in entrance examinations to the grandes écoles. Sections preparing for the entrance examination at "intellectual" and teaching schools such as ENS are called *khâgnes*. Sections preparing students for entry to Polytechnique and other science and engineering schools are known as *taupes*, while those leading to entry into HEC and lower-ranked business schools are nicknamed *épices*. [Tr.]

6 The word *culture* in French has a wide range of meanings, including culture, Culture, education, upbringing, knowledge, and learning, and can be used to mean all of these at once. [Tr.]

7 When asked about the factors contributing to their success, 50 percent of the prizewinners in French mention "talent," compared to 40 percent of the winners in Latin/Greek and 6.5 percent of the winners in the natural sciences. For

"methodical and regular work," these proportions are, respectively, 25 percent, 40 percent, and 46.5 percent. For 50 percent of the prizewinners in French, the ideal teacher must be creative. Among the prizewinners in geography, 17.5 percent (19.5 percent for the ensemble of historians and geographers), compared with, most notably, 40 percent of the winners in the natural sciences, require that the teacher be above all "earnest," a quality never mentioned as important by the winners in French. The prizewinners in Latin/Greek demand that the teacher be erudite in 10 percent of the cases, compared to none among the winners in French and 5 percent among the winners in philosophy, history, and geography.

8   The same contrasts can be found in the domain of radio and television. While the prizewinners in the noble disciplines listen most often to "cultural" stations (France-Musique and France-Culture), the prizewinners in geography and especially the natural sciences listen frequently only to the more popular stations (France-Inter and the peripheral stations). Likewise, in sports, the prizewinners in philosophy stress the intellectual or aesthetic functions of the practice, while the prizewinners in geography or the natural sciences insist on its moral functions.

9   The academic productions of these prizewinners are treated as literary events. As with inaugural speeches from the Académie Française [elite body of distinguished literary figures charged with maintaining the standards of the standard language, Tr.], the best French essays from the Concours Général and the baccalauréat were traditionally published by literary journals (such as *Figaro Littéraire* and the literary supplement to *Le Monde*).

10   According to Lalande's dictionary, the adjective "personal" [*personnel*] has only recently been used in the laudatory sense of "original, resulting from genuine, sincere thoughts or feelings, and not from either memory or imitation" (this meaning is not found in either Littré or Darmesteter, Hatzfeld and Thomas) and only "in literary and artistic criticism and pedagogy" in order to describe "ways of thinking, feeling, and expressing oneself."

11   Cf. appendix 3, p. 60. The prizewinners in French, philosophy, and also languages (especially English) include a large number of girls, often from intellectual and practicing Catholic circles, who hold particularly strongly to literary values and to the charismatic representation of intellectual activities. The boys, who receive the *prix d'excellence* much more often, are represented to a much higher degree in the scientific disciplines and in the less "noble" humanities (classics, history, geography, and natural sciences) and more often expect to reach positions of power. (If this is indeed the meaning of the opposition between the sexes as manifested in academic logic, we might expect that the feminization of the teaching profession, particularly in humanities departments, will be accompanied by an increase in the atmosphere of high spirituality that used to dominate this type of study).

12   The first year of a preparatory class in the humanities. [Tr.]

13   It should be noted that the system of differences among disciplines that emerges from our analysis of the properties of Concours Général prizewinners can also be found at other levels of the *cursus* (professors in the university of Paris, in particular: cf. P. Bourdieu, *Homo Academicus*, (1984), trans. P. Collier (Cambridge: Polity Press, 1988)).

14   P. Ariès, *Centuries of Childhood: A Social History of Family Life* (1960), trans. R. Baldick (New York: Knopf, 1962).

15   Hence the many gaps and discordances between consciously controlled political or pedagogical discourse and those *word alliances* produced by the absurd combination of the *slogans* of the political superego and *words that betray* one's *habitus*, a lapse that reveals poorly suppressed dispositions.

16   The following is a characteristic example: "Combination of *carelessness* and *jargon* that encompasses both the effrontery of fashionable words and vulgar solecisms. This clash is as unpleasant as *the sight of imitation jewelry against dirty skin.* How is it that the most intelligent among our candidates are not themselves *shocked*? How, in their eyes, can the occasionally accurate and subtle thoughts they develop be expressed in such a *grating* and often so *low* a way?" (literature agrégation, men, 1959).

17   Likewise, among *khâgne* students, children of blue-collar workers are the least inclined to consider talent to be a critical factor in success and are, on the contrary, the most likely to rank careful and regular work as the most important factor (at the rate of 44 percent – similar to children of mid-level managers and teachers, at 45 percent, and in contrast to children from privileged families, at 35.5 percent).

18   G. Gusdorf, *Pourquoi des professeurs?* (Paris: Payot, 1963), pp. 10, 49, 105 (emphasis added).

Chapter 2   Misrecognition and Symbolic Violence

1   Given the semi-"private" nature of this material, we were unable to gather similar data on other classes or determine with absolute certainty what part the individual characteristics of the particular institution, its patrons (women), and the teacher may have played in our study. Everything does, however, appear to confirm the generality of the classificatory principles used, especially in view of our analysis of *concours* reports.

2   J. Bertin, *Sémiologie graphique, les diagrammes, les réseaux, les cartes* (Paris and The Hague: Mouton and Gauthier-Villars, 1967).

3   The French grading system functions on a 20-point scale, roughly corresponding to the US system as follows: 0–3/F; 4–6/D; 7–9/C; 10–11/B; 12/A−, B+; 14–15/A; 16–20, A+. [Tr.]

4   Translated from "correct sans plus," and appearing above as "Ok." [Tr.]

5   Given the poor quality of the photographs accompanying the reports, we had to give up the idea of relating the adjectives chosen to the perception the teacher may have had of her students based on their appearance.

6   Recollecting student social origins is an automatic part of scholastic routine, and most teachers almost certainly make no use of facts that are probably forgotten almost as soon as they are recalled. In any event, social origin as such is never used as a basis for academic judgment or, more generally, for practical evaluations. A good number of the obituaries analyzed below (16 of 50), in spite of the conventions of the biographical genre, thus make no mention of social origins, and the authors of these orations, even though they were very close to the people they are describing, often say they had to do research expressly in order to be able to make this information available.

7 We will willingly agree with Lacan that "Chamfort's dictum that 'you can bet that any public idea, any received convention, is foolish, for it has appealed to the majority' will certainly appeal to all those who consider themselves exempt, that is, precisely, the majority (J. Lacan, *Écrits* (Paris Seuil, 1966), p. 21). As long as we add an important distinction that the analyst is forgetting – through a scotomization that no doubt underlies the charm wielded by analysis: "the majority" . . . of those that the social world and the educational institution treat as the *happy few*.

8 More generally, we should mention the stated and tacit devaluation of everything that arose from what used to be called, after Cicero, the *plebeia philosophia*, in other words, all the "vulgar" doctrines, such as materialism or empiricism, along with those too akin to "common sense." Among numerous other indices, this devaluation can be seen in the fate that befalls all the somewhat unpolished philosophers in courses and textbooks (philosophers sentenced to the first sections of essays and easily topped – such as Hume, Comte, or Durkheim) and in the hundreds of ways there are of discrediting the rigor and down-to-earth awkwardness of scientific discourse, from ritual excommunication and defamatory anathema ("scientism," "psychologism," "sociologism," "historicism") to transfiguring annexation.

9 The last judgment that the group makes of one of its members through a duly mandated spokesperson (responsibility for the eulogy is given to a classmate, and it is only in very exceptional circumstances that it is granted to anyone else, and then only to a *normalien*, which is likewise the case for the committee administering the entrance exam) is always the product of a collective effort, and sometimes the signs of this are evident, as when the author compiles or integrates information and opinions provided by numerous informants. (The group controls the work of symbolic, as well as ethical, production – and if need be, the struggles occasioned by the obituary over the appropriation of the symbolic capital accumulated around the name of the deceased – by controlling access to the role of legitimate group spokesperson on this particular occasion.)

10 Obituaries only mention accents when they deviate from the norm, and then only southern accents. "His rough Pyrenean accent, rolling his r's and accenting certain consonants" (obituary of G. Rumeau, born in Arbéost, Hautes-Pyrénées, son of primary school teacher, *Annuaire ENS*, 1962, p. 42); 'A thick voice that resonated with local sound' (obituary of A. Montsarrat, born in Castres, Tarn, *Annuaire ENS*, 1963, p. 51). Pronunciation is probably the example *par excellence* of a way of being that forever and often indelibly calls to mind its mode of acquisition and thus functions as a very powerful instrument of social marking.

11 Most of the alumni studied were born between about 1880–1890 and were in the workforce between 1905 and 1955. It naturally follows that the image of the *normalien* that emerges in these obituaries corresponds to a relatively old state of the system. Research we were able to do only after the obituary analysis had been completed revealed that the alumni whose social origins are absent from the obituaries are not distinguishable in any significant way in this respect from the remainder of the population under study (six have origins in the middle classes, five in the upper classes, five unknown) and that the terms used to describe them strictly obey the laws derived from our analysis. (A subsequent

look at archival documents even uncovered a very strong correlation between recorded academic judgments and the judgments contained in the obituaries.) The alumni granted obituaries do not seem to be distinguishable from deceased alumni as a whole, except perhaps for their attachment to the school. It thus seems that there is a higher proportion of lifelong school supporters among the obituary subjects than among the others. Finally, indications are that the relationship between the author and the subject of an obituary is not random, and that they generally share social origins (roughly defined), discipline, and type of career.

12   Of the 15 alumni from the lower echelons of social space, 12 became secondary school teachers or higher secondary school teachers (*khâgne* and *taupe*); only three became professors of higher education, and then only in disciplines held to be inferior at this level (modern languages, chemistry) and often in the provinces. On the other hand, of the 19 alumni from the upper echelons, only two became secondary school teachers, while two went into diplomacy, two became writers, and 13 became professors of higher education, mainly in Paris, and, for four among them, at the Collège de France.

13   A higher civil servant charged with judging the performance of secondary school teachers, making curriculum decisions, etc. [Tr.]

14   The Collège de France is a prestigious institution of higher education falling outside the main university system. It confers no degrees, but offers lectures and seminars, its professors ranking among the best known in the country. [Tr.]

15   Thus, the humorous poem entitled "The Little *Normalien*," which, in a self-deprecating tone very characteristic of the neutralizing effect of the "nearly true," successfully evokes the modal trajectory of the *normalien*, closes with a stanza that reveals the truth of the praise of "modest" people:

VII

After his death, his *cacique*
Visited his graveside,
And in a melancholy tone
Spoke these words:
He was a good husband, a good father,
A good citizen as well,
But his particular virtue
Was that he had great wit
Our friend, etc.

(P. Roussel, *Le livre des cubes*, quoted in A. Peyrefitte, *Rue d'Ulm, Chroniques de la vie normalienne* (2nd edn, Paris: Flammarion, 1963), pp. 316–19.) [*Cacique* is the student with the highest grade on the entrance examination, Tr.]

16   Never praised as a quality worthy of pursuit in and of itself, obscurity can only be recognized in the guise of the positive characteristics it is thought to require: a disdain for honors and a rejection of the pursuit of success outside the university. To wit, this sentence tossed out about 20 years ago by a professor at the

Sorbonne to a candidate known outside the milieu for his philosophical writings and also as a journalist and essayist: "You are too well known."

17 Graduate of the former École Normale Supérieure de Sèvres, limited to women. [Tr.]

18 From the obituary of Jules Romains, *Annuaire ENS*, 1974, p. 43.

19 The French Institute encompasses the Académie Française and four other academies: Letters, Medicine, Science, and Social Sciences. [Tr.]

Appendix 2

1 Age is calculated from the first of January for the general student population; for the prizewinners, it is calculated from the first of June. The age gap between prizewinners and students at large is therefore slightly greater than it appears here.

2 Prior to the post-1968 reforms, the lycée began at the *sixième*; those who did not qualify would do four years of complementary schooling before being given the chance to rejoin the lycée track. [Tr.]

3 The proportion of students with upper-class backgrounds is still greater among the prizewinners in mathematics and physics in the sciences, and among the winners in French and the classics in the humanities. We know that these students are more often headed toward the preparatory classes than prizewinners in the other disciplines (74 percent express their intention to enter higher education by way of the preparatory classes, with the remaining 26 percent entering the universities, even though the preparatory classes include only about one-twentieth of all students enrolled in higher education.)

4 We observe an analogous situation in the preparatory classes. So, for example, in *khâgnes*, 28 percent of working-class students have received six or more *prix d'excellence*, compared to 15.5 percent of middle-class students and 14.5 percent of upper-class students.

5 Brevet d'etudes du premier cycle, earned on passing an examination at the end of the *troisième*. [Tr.]

6 Almost all of the working-class winners seem to have had specific advantages, whether taking up the interrupted trajectory of their father ("My father was studying to be an engineer, but because his parents were ill, he was unable to continue" – son of printing press operator, CAP [vocational school diploma], grandson of semiskilled laborer), benefiting from the relatively high level of their mother's education, or "rubbing shoulders" with a successful older sibling ("Thanks to my sister, I was able to learn what she had learned sooner and more easily" – daughter of builder whose sister was preparing for the ENS in Fontenay).

7 To demonstrate the atypical character of these families of "farmers," we can point out that 38 per cent of winners originating in farming families practice a "noble" sport (tennis, riding, fencing, sailing, or skiing), a rate below that of the children of professionals (58.3 percent), but about equivalent to that of the children of executives (42 percent) and teachers (38 percent), and clearly higher than that of the children of primary school teachers (22 percent), mid-level managers (27 percent), clerical workers and tradesmen (22 percent), and blue-collar workers (4 percent).

8 We observe the same sort of differences, although to a lesser degree, between science and humanities *normaliens*.

9 The same regularities can be seen among the prizewinners who took the exam in more than one subject. More often science oriented than humanities oriented, they come from families with greater advantages of social class (70 percent, compared to 56.5 percent of those who only competed in one subject) and education (the fathers of 52.5 percent have at least the licence, compared to 41 percent for the others).

PART II THE ORDINATION

Chapter 1 The Production of a Nobility

1 *Titre* means both title (in the sense of nobility or property) and diploma or credentials. In order to privilege Bourdieu's notion of academic nobility, I have used "title" rather than "diploma" in most cases. [Tr.]

2 The (necessarily *paradoxical*) strategies of initiating breaks, which are imperative whenever it comes to destroying the seemingly self-evident facts of *doxa*, are bound to have appearances against them. So someone is certain to surface to make an appeal to *good sense* against this challenge to common sense or to reaffirm that it is *also* necessary to give the technical efficacy of scholastic action its due (following a strategy analogous to the ones that consisted in reminding everyone that economic capital *also* played a role in educational elimination or that the dominated *also* put up a form of "resistance" to academic imposition).

3 "The Yellow and the Red," Polytechnique alumni periodical. [Tr.]

4 M. Corday, Preface to R. Smet, *Le nouvel argot de l'X* (Paris: Gauthier-Villars, 1936) (see also "An Enchanted Experience" in the appendix below, p. 125).

5 Bertrand Russell aptly describes the conformity resulting from elitist traditions, ordinarily associated with petitions of originality and freedom: "those who have been taught from an early age to fear the displeasure of their group as the worst of misfortunes will die on the battlefield, in a war of which they understand nothing, rather than suffer the contempt of fools. The English public schools have carried this system to perfection, and have largely sterilized intelligence by making it cringe before the herd" (B. Russell, *Education and the Social Order* (London: Allen and Unwin, 1932)).

6 Here we reach the limits of what a survey questionnaire and statistical analysis can apprehend. No doubt we were somewhat naive in hoping, even through the use of indirect questions devised as subtly as possible, to grasp what defines, in their practical truth (which agents themselves are often unaware of), ways of conceiving, organizing, and accomplishing academic work and the view of education and intellectual practice implicated therein.

7 "I give the students a corrected outline of each paper. The rest is taught by example; they see how I teach my course. My former students used to be amused by what they would call 'my art of the transition' " (*khâgne* history teacher).

8 "I start from (. . .) the idea that the students who are here have chosen to be

here because they are worthy of being here. If they don't make it, that's their problem; they'll make up for it later. I have complete confidence in them . . . I don't feel the same sense of responsibility that I do up in front of a *seconde* class, where you can't let the ones who slip get too far behind. But here, in spite of everything, I don't feel so bad about holding them to tough standards" (*khâgne* literature teacher).

9 F. Charmot, *La pédagogie des jésuites* (Paris: SPES, 1943), p. 221.

10 "The administration structures lycée life with an eye toward the *concours*: for example, no going outside after lunch for day students; there's no time to waste. If a teacher is absent, the monitor who comes to tell the students and assign them their work says at the end, 'OK now, you have two hours to work, no wasting time' " (*khâgne* student, age 20, Fénelon).

11 This is undoubtedly a characteristic trait of most "elite schools." So, for example, according to the National Opinion Research Center ("Report to the National Center for Education Statistics under Contract," no. 300–78–0208, NORC, Chicago, Nov. 1980, pp. 8–9), two-thirds of American prep school students say they have to write essays, poetry, or stories "frequently," in contrast to only one-quarter (27 percent) of public high school students.

12 The gap between university and preparatory class statistics would probably have been even greater if, rather than limiting our comparison to the most directly comparable disciplines (classics, mathematics, and physics), we had turned to disciplines such as sociology, psychology, or foreign languages.

13 The "*topo*", also known as "*pécu*," or PQ, is an elementary unit of discourse, usually taken from published lectures or textbooks, sometimes made up ad hoc by the user himself, that can be inserted into the most varied discursive ensembles at the cost of only a few necessary adjustments and alterations. A good *topo* is defined by its capacity to be reused on different occasions, and indeed, even in the different essays of a single concours (philosophy, French, and history, for example). The ability to "use *pécus* ad infinitum," openly admitted by *khâgne* students, consists in mastering the *ars combinatoria* that enables them to create endless discourses by "stringing *pécus* together."

14 Asked about the tools they used in preparing their final essay, *khâgne* students at Louis-le-Grand more often mention survey textbooks (Lagarde and Michard, Chassang and Senninger, Castex and Surer), Bordas anthologies, and Larousse abridged editions than critical works or original texts.

15 *Cadre* is a general term meaning manager, executive, high-level professional, or professional staff; qualified by *moyen*, it can be rendered by *mid-level manager*; qualified by *supérieur*, the equivalents include *upper-level manager* and *executive*. [Tr.]

16 Term meaning "marked by breadth of knowledge and sophistication." [Tr.]

17 Cf. J. Wellens, "The Anti-Intellectual Tradition in the West," *British Journal of Educational Studies* 8:1 (Nov. 1959), pp. 22–8, and also L. Stone, "Japan and England: A Comparative Study," in P. W. Musgrave (ed.), *Sociology, History and Education* (London: Methuen, 1970), pp. 101–14.

18 "Today, the former facultés are no more than the midwives of the revolution. They turn out neither the business professionals nor the scientists our country needs. They graduate failures and agitators. Shall I give you an example? At Paris-VII, first-year classics and modern literature students have to submit to a

veritable brain-washing. The syllabus of the core required course offers Marx, Lenin, and Mao Tse-tung as main dishes. Which is to say that at Paris-VII students cannot study Montaigne, Molière, Racine, Hugo, or Baudelaire with any hope of passing if they haven't successfully recited their lessons on Marx, Lenin, and Mao. It's an outrage. At this university, and perhaps others, a German (whose political economy is these days about the equivalent of Diafoirus' medicine), a Russian (who never taught anything except how to destroy our civilization and our liberties), and a Chinese man (whose thinking would have been rejected by Tabarin's *Almanac*) are hereafter the required introduction to the great thinkers and writers of our country. Anyone who has not had their head filled with the balderdash of the Chinese man, the Russian, or the German will not receive a diploma from the French state" (P. Gaxotte, "Recours à la reine," *le Figaro*, July 25–6, 1970).

19   Cf., for ENS, A. Peyrefitte, *Rue d'Ulm, Chroniques de la vie normalienne* (2nd edn, Paris: Flammarion 1963), pp. 289–405, and, for Polytechnique, Smet, *Le nouvel argot de l'X*.

20   J.-P. Sartre, *Critique of Dialectical Reasoning: Theory of Practical Ensembles* (1960), trans. A. Sheridan-Smith, ed. Jonathan Ree (Atlantic Highlands, N.J.: Humanities Press, 1976), vol. 1.

21   É. Durkheim, *The Evolution of Educational Thought: Lectures on the Formation and Development of Secondary Education in France* (1938), trans. P. Collins (London: Routledge and Kegan Paul, 1977), p. 257.

22   "I think we teach them to work quickly, to cover material in a limited amount of time" (*khâgne* French teacher). "A teacher's importance comes from the framework he provides. He's more useful in what he gives us to learn than in what he teaches us" (*khâgne* student, 20, Louis-le-Grand).

23   Certificat d'aptitude au professorat de l'enseignement secondaire, a national secondary school teaching certificate, awarded according to the results of a *concours*. [Tr.]

24   When asked whether they would at one time have liked or would now like to move into higher education, most answer in the negative: "I hate the customs and the mystifications of higher education. Careers aren't based on 'merit,' but on cooptation" (*taupe* mathematics teacher). "I prefer more controlled students who have, it seems to me, chosen their option, like my preparatory class students" (*taupe* mathematics teacher). "In a university, you don't get to know your students. That's not teaching" (*taupe* physics teacher). "No, because I like teaching and don't like specialization" (*khâgne* literature teacher).

25   "I've underlined homework grades in blue for the *cubes* [students doing a third year, Tr.] and in red for the *bicas* [students doing a fourth year, Tr.]. Every year I of course have everyone's *concours* grades, both written and oral, and I carry the *concours* grades over to another page for the ones who have qualified for the oral. In addition, we have the forms from the 'trial run' that marks the passage from first to second year of the *khâgne*, and each trimester the general class ranking, with the coefficient of the *concours* per subject. See, the averages for the essays in red, and for languages in blue; I have what amounts to a type of histogram, with both total and rank" (*khâgne* philosophy teacher).

26   They can thus resurrect the most typical practices of the Jesuits, such as this

taupe teacher who asks each of his students to act as keeper of the others: "It is understood that each student should tell me the name of the student next to him when that student is absent. I trust them in this and they can't fool me for very long" (*taupe* mathematics teacher).

27 A twentieth-century philosopher who trained generations of students at Henri-IV. [Tr.]

28 Cf. G. Fauconnier, *Mental Spaces: Aspects of Meaning Construction in Natural Language* (1984; Cambridge: MIT Press, 1985).

29 Here the reader will no doubt have recognized an exemplary expression of *amor fati* as a convergence between the objectivated institution and the embodied institution. (See also "The Eternal Return" in the appendix below, p. 127).

30 There is no clearer sign of the structuring force of the schemata of thought produced and reproduced by *khâgnes* than the functioning of the French intellectual field, which owes its very high degree of integration not, as the stereotype would have it, to its Parisian concentration, but to the effects of a homogeneous and homogenizing socialization. The poorest essayist is sure to meet with the approval of journalists and editors, not to mention philosophy or literature professors, as soon as he publishes anything on one or another of the canonical topics: determinism and freedom, structure and history, consciousness and unconsciousness. So-called "worldly" success stories are often based on this kind of perfect accord between texts and the academically constituted expectations of the tastemakers.

31 So, for example, we saw students in a preparatory class in Paris in 1970 "go on strike in order to get more done," as *Le Monde* reported it.

32 Cf. J. R. Levenson, *Modern China and its Confucian Past* (New York: Anchor Books, 1964), p. 31.

33 There used to be two levels of doctorate, this being the lower. [Tr.]

34 Cf. A. Charlot et al., *Les universités et le marché du travail* (Paris: La Documentation Française, 1977).

35 Examiners who tend to ask difficult questions. [Tr.]

36 In the preparatory classes, group integration is created around academic activity. Resting on a primary solidarity arising from a common condition, it creates an academically defined group that is forever united by strong ties (after entering a grande école and beyond). In the universities, integration is based on secondary solidarity (religious associations, political parties, unions, mini-groups) and takes the form of symbolic integration into an intellectual role rather than real integration into a group of schoolmates driven by a common goal and caste consciousness.

37 The pedagogic practices of university professors (and undoubtedly preparatory class teachers as well) vary according to discipline, as well as career path and the slope of the future trajectory foretold thereby (which can be grasped by looking at the position held at a given age). So, for example, the most scholastic pedagogic practices are found most particularly among teachers in the most classical disciplines who, after many years in secondary education, were recruited by the universities during the period of expansion.

38 Hence the difference between these two typical statements regarding student lateness, one from a full professor and the other from a lecturer. "Their attention to courtesy is minimal; all I ask is that they not make too much noise"; "I

don't keep latecomers out; we're not in primary school here." The first, with a weary pessimism, requires his students to comply with the basic rules of common courtesy; the second believes that his liberalism distinguishes him completely from primary school teachers.

39 Cf. P. Bourdieu, *Homo Academicus* (1984), trans. P. Collier (Cambridge: Polity Press, 1988), pp. 128–58.

40 This is one of the most important differences between universities and preparatory classes. More highly selected, preparatory class students are much more homogeneous than university students, both socially and academically. Some 86.5 percent of A' *taupe* students and 84 percent of *khâgne* students have received honors on the baccalauréat. Almost all *khâgne* students (95 percent) have followed classical tracks. Measuring their ability to manipulate and understand academic language has shown not only that *khâgne* students achieve better results than university students, but also that the distribution of grades earned by *khâgne* students in a word definition exercise diverges sharply from the normal curve in showing no low or very low grades (cf. P. Bourdieu, J.-C. Passeron, and M. de Saint-Martin, *Academic Discourse* (Cambridge: Polity Press, 1994)). It follows that preparatory class teachers are spared one of the most difficult problems in teaching (especially evident in science facultés) – the *extreme disparity in student preparedness*.

41 The same paradoxical relationship can also be observed in Great Britain and the United States, where private schools boast teachers who are completely devoted to their students and their institution (so much so that people have spoken of their *double duty*), but usually very poorly paid and originally from modest backgrounds.

Chapter 2   A Rite of Institution

1 These expressions are taken from Durkheim's description of the effects of the "negative cult" – or asceticism (cf. E. Durkheim, *The Elementary Forms of the Religious Life* (1915), trans. J. Swain (New York: Free Press, 1965), p. 309).

2 "We go down to the Sorbonne in groups; they say patricians never risked being alone in the Subura. We sit in the highest rows in the lecture hall. Everyone fears the sarcastic remarks we whisper back and forth. We don't bother doing homework either. We'll take criticism, criticism is easy . . ., but grades, no way' (J. Bompaire, in A. Peyrefitte, *Rue d'Ulm, Chroniques de la vie normalienne* (2nd edn, Paris: Flammarion, 1963) [The students are echoing the French expression: criticism is easy, but art is difficult, Tr.]

3 "A knight was not merely 'made'; he was 'ordained.' (. . .) The whole body of dubbed knights constituted an 'order': *ordo* (. . .). In the vocabulary which Christian writers had borrowed from Roman antiquity, an *ordo* was a division of society, temporal as well as ecclesiastical. But it was a regular, clearly defined division, conformable to the divine plan – an institution, really, and not merely a plain fact" (M. Bloch, *Feudal Society* (1940), vol. 2, trans. L. A. Manyon (Chicago: University of Chicago Press, 1964), p. 314).

4 O. Lattimore, *Inner Asian Frontiers of China* (Boston: Beacon Press, 1962), p. xlvi.

5 Cf. R. H. Wilkinson, "The Gentleman Ideal and the Maintenance of a Political

Elite, Two Case Studies: Confucian Education in the Tang, Sung, Ming and Ching Dynasties and the Late Victorian Public Schools, 1879–1914," in P. W. Musgrave (ed.), *Sociology, History and Education* (London: Methuen, 1970), p. 130.

6 The reader may be inclined to think that preparatory classes and universities are not being treated equally here and to attribute these differences to this sociologist's mood and unequal relationship to the two objects. This would be to forget that, given that the degree of symbolic entrenchment of the two institutions is very unequal (as witnessed by the profusion of celebratory texts on the preparatory classes and the grandes écoles), scientific procedure must somehow make the rhetorical force of the break being made proportional to the probable resistance that the analyses offered are likely to meet, especially in readers who are the most closely connected to the dominant institutions (at the risk, obviously, of pandering to the latent resentment that haunts not so much those who are connected to the dominated institutions as those who have rubbed elbows with the dominant institutions to no avail, whose paradigm is the "top rejected candidate"). Having said this, we should note that the sociologist accomplishes the same task in either case: demonstrating what *determines* these behaviors – tearing them away from the realm of the arbitrary by recreating the universe of constraints that make them what they are – without justifying them.

7 All of these effects, which simply become more visible at this high level of the *cursus*, where the break between the survivors and the unsuccessful is marked in a formal way, obtain at every other critical point in an academic career as well, that is, whenever a relatively significant operation of selection divides a population into hierarchized classes (*section* C [sciences, most prestigious, Tr.], other *sections*, etc.) – for example, the selection that used to be made at the beginning of the *sixième*, but now occurs at the beginning of the *seconde*.

8 This effect, which leads some categories of agents to seek and to love the professorial station in and of itself, partially resolves the contradiction involved in keeping those with the power to bestow the rarest titles, giving access to the highest positions, in this economically and socially inferior position (according to the paradigm of the pedagogue slave).

9 We know that, in general terms, father's occupation is an imperfect indicator of original social status; the latter can only be identified with some accuracy if we take into account indicators of the status of members of both sides of the family (father and paternal grandfather, mother and maternal grandfather) at different points in their trajectory (at least for the father) as well as that of any siblings, as we have attempted to do in all our studies. So, for example, mothers of *khâgne* students often (and increasingly often the lower the father's position in the academic and social hierarchy) originate in a slightly higher social class than the fathers and are endowed with somewhat greater cultural capital, particularly in literature and the arts. The following are a few examples from the *khâgne* at Louis-le-Grand. First case: father, industrialist, owner of pill manufacturing company, pharmacy degree; paternal grandfather, railroad worker; mother, *artist, painter*; maternal grandfather, architect, graduate of Beaux-Arts. Second case: father, engineer, baccalauréat; mother, *civil servant in the national museum service*, baccalauréat and two licences; maternal grandfather, physics teacher. Third case: father, unemployed, passed first half of baccalauréat [in

French literature, Tr.]; mother, doctor, *interne* in public hospitals in Paris [chosen by *concours*, Tr.]; maternal grandfather, independent means. Fourth case: father, PTT inspector, CEP mother, *legal consultant*, licence in law. Fifth case: father, bank employee, CEP; mother, *primary school teacher*, baccalauréat. Sixth case: father, telephone installer, CAP; mother, *medical secretary* for Social Security. Seventh case: father, clerical worker; mother, *educational guidance counselor*, licence in psychology. Having said this, we should stress that social origin, as exact as its measurement might be, remains only an *indicator* and is not an explanatory principle. It enables us to identify different forms of the transfer of cultural capital.

10   The enchantment engendered by a universe that, being apparently and partially free of ordinary forms of social discrimination (such as racism), seems like some sort of miraculous exception undoubtedly reaches its paroxysm in the case of students from stigmatized groups (which partially explains why both Jews, no matter what their milieu – and most particularly during the heroic period of the republican school [Third republic, 1870–1914, initial period of public education, which was to be "secular, mandatory, and free of charge," Tr.] – and colonized peoples, the latter to an extreme degree, have often demonstrated a militant enthusiasm toward the "liberating school" that is not unlike that of the oblates. See the account of Léopold Sédar Senghor in the appendix below, pp. 125–6).

11   We should analyze in this light the *correction* of regional accents, a process that accompanies the march toward consecration and that is one of the most visible signs of *social division*. By using legitimate pronunciation as an implicit selection criterion and by tacitly but no less firmly prescribing the *correction* of pronunciation (as well as syntax), by making a break from one's native region the necessary condition for success (we are all familiar with the privilege enjoyed by Parisian preparatory classes), "elite schools" tend to produce a so-called "national elite," in other words, a group cut off from its local ties.

12   We have seen that among Concours Général prizewinners, the middle-class students who have earned honors in the classics are distinguished from the other prizewinners – and especially from the winners in French from the dominant class – by a series of characteristics that are in fact so many differences between themselves and their class of origin. So, for example, they come from small families, and almost all of them learn to read before starting school. They are also the ones who manifest the most complete identification with the institution. Most intend to enter the preparatory classes and rank highest the occupations of teacher and researcher.

13   Cf. J.-P. Sartre, foreword to P. Nizan, *Aden Arabie* (1960), trans. J. Pinkham (New York: MR Press, 1968).

14   Seen in this way, the more or less autobiographical narratives of writers from the dominated regions of social and geographical space constitute incomparable sociological documents as first-hand accounts of the subjective *experiences* related to these social trajectories (and not of the corresponding "realities") that are in fact more reliable, being more naive, than we might think.

15   We might also include in the class of rites of cloture the ritual of the doctoral dissertation or the inaugural lecture, cousin of the medieval *inceptio*, an inaugural act of teaching that marked the end of the *trials* of the years of apprentice-

ship in the guilds (occasionally still evoked in the language of Anglo-Saxon university diplomas by the expression *periculo facto*, "having braved the trials"; cf. W. J. Ong, "Latin Language Study as a Renaissance Puberty Rite," in Musgrave, *Sociology, History and Education*, pp. 232–48).

16 A. Hermant, *Monsieur Rabosson* (Paris: Dentu, 1884), quoted in Peyrefitte, *Rue d'Ulm*, p. 96.

17 Cf., for example, R. M. Marsh, *The Mandarins: The Circulation of Elites in China, 1600–1900* (New York: Free Press, 1961).

18 Poem written in 1768 by Yüan Mei for Teng Shih-min, his examiner for the *chin-shih* exam (cited by Robert Marsh, *ibid.*, p. 8). A remarkable account can also be found in J.-F. Billeter, "Contribution à une sociologie historique du mandarinat," *Actes de la Recherche en Sciences Sociales*, 15 (1977), pp. 3–29.

19 Among the conditions for the functioning of academic rites of consecration we should also take into account the body of hagiographic literature surrounding the grandes écoles, the printing of complete lists of the names of students who have passed the top *concours*, *concours* essay topics, and occasionally the best essays, etc. in the most popular semi-official papers.

20 M. Weber, *Economy and Society* (1921–2), vol. 2 (New York: Bedminster Press, 1968).

21 É. Durkheim, *The Elementary Forms of the Religious Life* (1912; New York: Free Press, 1976), p. 313.

22 Weber, *Economy and Society*, vol. 2. In this sense, preparatory classes and grandes écoles are less different than we might think from institutions as visibly dedicated to a function of consecration as the Maori "sacred schools" reserved for the children of the nobility (cf. R. H. Lowie, *Social Organization* (1948; New York: Holt, Rinehart and Winston, 1960), p. 197) or the Japanese boarding schools of the Tokugawa era that took only the eldest sons of the great Samurai families (cf. R. R. Dore, *Education in Tokugawa Japan* (London: Routledge and Kegan Paul, 1965) or still yet, the boarding schools of Victorian England (J. Wakeford, *The Cloistered Elite: A Sociological Analysis of the English Public Boarding School* (London: Macmillan, 1969)).

23 "The *khâgne* pranks, much more innocent than those of similar groups, were not without their witty side: I remember one particular poetry *concours*, for which I was counting heavily on a little piece in the style of André Chénier, where I came out looking really stupid. The rule, kept secret by the committee until the contest results were announced, was that the prize would be given to the most chaste of the poems. Other practical jokes seemed to be designed to quell enthusiasm and hopes, to cut us down a peg. The upper classmen forbade us to talk about the École Normale *concours*; the only term we could use was *concours* for the *Bourses de licence* (scholarships given out as consolation prizes to the top unsuccessful candidates [who would then have to enter the university system and begin working toward the licence, Tr.])" (J. Prévost, *Dix-huitième année* (Paris: Gallimard), quoted in Peyrefitte, *Rue d'Ulm*, p. 83).

24 Durkheim, *The Elementary Forms of the Religious Life*, p. 316.

25 Just as the ethical control imposed upon girls may be carried out via the indirect routes of an aesthetic discipline (forbidding "vulgar" clothing, make-up, manners), control over a boy's sexuality may be carried out through the temporal discipline of academic life.

26 "The popular image of prep schools as oases of learning and/or schools for snobbery is naive; prep schools are hard places, where literally from dawn to dusk each person's life is so regulated that freedom must be won by stealth." (P. W. Cookson Jr and C. Hodges Persell, *Preparing for Power, America's Elite Boarding Schools* (New York: Basic Books, 1985), pp. 19–20).

27 Cf. Wilkinson, "The Gentleman Ideal"; Ong, "Latin Language Study" F. Campbell, "Latin and the Elite Tradition in Education," in Musgrave, *Sociology, History and Education*, pp. 249–64.

28 Here let us quote a scientist who was in a particularly good position to evaluate the strictly technical efficacy of current mathematics teaching: "Having for several years directed a research training institute for engineers, I deeply sense the failure of our educational system, especially in the pre-baccalauréat year and the preparatory classes. I am convinced that the mass introduction of modern math, and more generally, of a certain deductive and formalist approach, is a catastrophe for the creativity of our young people. Whether you're trying to create a synthetic diamond, patent a new microchip, or intelligently test a pharmaceutical product, it's not through theorems that you're going to get anywhere. More generally, I think that the dogmatism instilled in secondary school students poses a serious threat to the future of our society" (P.-G. de Gennes, Gold Medal Acceptance Speech to National Scientific Research Center (CNRS), 5 March, 1981, p. 4).

29 Lord Plummer, "Speech to the old Etonians," quoted in B. Simon and I. Bradley (eds), *The Victorian Public School: Studies in the Development of an Educational Institution* (Dublin: Gill and Macmillan, 1975), p. 23.

30 We find several examples of passages intended to justify "the time spent on sunlit cricket squares and muddy football fields" in J. A. Mangan, "Athleticism: A Case Study of the Evolution of an Educational Ideology," in Simon and Bradley, *The Victorian Public School*, pp. 146–67, esp. p. 154.

31 The alumni ("old boys") play a crucial role in this mechanism of the circular reinforcement of belief. They indeed have no choice but to justify the ends and means of a pedagogic action to which their own excellence is linked (following this line of reasoning: we are excellent because the education that produced us is excellent; moreover, the education that produced us is excellent because we are excellent).

32 In other words, the oft-measured effect of academic sanctions, being assigned to a "strong" or "weak" group, for example (cf. R. A. Rosenthal and L. Jakobson, *Pygmalion in the Classroom: Teacher Expectation and Pupils' Intellectual Development* (New York: Irvington, 1992)) is just one manifestation among many of the effect continually produced by the entire educational system and, more generally, by any institution of consecration oriented toward the production of a *nobility* or, if you will, a legitimate elite. This is what is missed by those who claim to be measuring the statistical relationship between a researcher's prestige and the prestige of his academic credentials, leaving aside the effects of his productivity. They proceed as if productivity and current prestige were independent of one another and especially of the original credentials, when in fact, through the *aspirations* they authorize and the *obligations* they imply, credentials command a level of productivity that increases as they become more scarce (cf. P. Bourdieu, "Le champ scientifique," *Actes de la*

Recherche en Sciences Sociales, no. 2–3 (June 1976), pp. 88–104, especially p. 94).

33 R. H. Wilkinson discusses the "psychological effects" of the "elite style" on the individual, particularly the heightening of self-esteem and self-assurance (cf. Wilkinson, "The Gentleman Ideal," pp. 126–42, esp. p. 133).

34 P. Gréco, in Peyrefitte, *Rue d'Ulm,* p. 276.

35 H. Bellaunay, in ibid. pp. 185–6. To be surprised that sociology could find so many illustrations among the writings of *normaliens,* and to conclude either that the latter are particularly clear-minded individuals or that sociologists are particularly sympathetic toward them would be to ignore the specific form of mystification that the institution produces in this case – in other words, the relationship of recognition/misrecognition that it encourages in its chosen people. Like student practical jokes (or student heckling), which borrow the instruments for an indulgent protest against the institution from the most prestigious institutional traditions, mystifying demystifications again betray an enchanted complicity, up to and including the very intention to disenchant. This is why they respond even better than the stale panegyrics of canonical tradition to the twofold interrogation of a research project aimed at establishing both the objective functions of the institution and the mechanisms it uses to conceal them.

36 The ritual walk on the roof would not hold such importance in *normalien* mythology if this urban mountaineering were not also closely associated with the Rastignacian ambition fostered by the institution. Witness the following typical descriptions: "standing up there on the roof, filled with the sense of *exhilaration and power that heights can give,* we could see the entire southern half of Paris and its veiled horizon, broken here and there by domes, spires, clouds, and chimneys" (P. Nizan, *The Conspiracy* (1938), trans. Q. Hoare (New York: Verso, 1988), quoted in Peyrefitte, *Rue d'Ulm,* p. 59). "Also a good place to walk for *ambitious daydreaming*" (J. Romains, *Men of Good Will* (New York: Knopf, 1934), quoted in Peyrefitte, ibid., p. 63). "Leading the lives of alley cats up there on the famous École roof, they *pondered over the destinies of Herriot [politician], Tardieu [politician], Jules Romains [writer], Giraudoux [writer]*" (P. Guth, *Jeanne la mince et l'amour* (Paris: Flammarion, 1962), quoted in Peyrefitte, ibid., p. 87); emphasis added.

37 The *Nouvelle Revue Française* is the most prestigious literary journal. [Tr.]

38 P. Gréco, in Peyrefitte, *Rue d'Ulm,* p. 275. [In other words, how many "unsuccessful" careers for every "success story"?, Tr.]

39 J. Prévost, in ibid., p. 316.

40 Here we would want to analyze the motivations that might lead members, in talking about a famous person, to say that they knew him, or that they went to the École Normale with him, or simply that the person was an X. The *profit sharing* that can be gained through such statements (both subjective and objective profits) is part of the advantages guaranteed by the possession of social capital.

41 E. Aronson and T. Mills, "The Effects of Severity of Initiation on Liking for a Group," *Journal of American Social Psychology* (1959), pp. 177–81; H. B. Gerard and G. C. Mathewson, "The Effects of Severity of Initiation on Liking for a Group, a Replication," *Journal of American Social Psychology* (1966), pp. 278–87.

Chapter 3   The Ambiguities of Competence

1   The clearest demonstration of this power of symbolic imposition is the dearth – we might even say the *absence* – in the scientific literature of analyses of the most specific practices of the academic world, particularly the ones that best reveal or betray the structures of the university unconscious. This is undoubtedly because, in this case, objective analysis inevitably implies self-analysis (it is no accident that the exceptions are almost always found among historians – Levenson, Ringer, etc. – for whom the task is made easier by temporal and occasionally cultural distance). A critical eye, which is constitutive of the scientific mind, in effect operates a *desacralization* of its object, which earns it the stamp of betrayal in the eyes of the clerics. There is the additional feature that the degree of initiation into the secrets of the curia is in direct proportion to the degree of membership in the innermost circles of the sacred, which is itself of a piece with the degree of investment in the most intimate beliefs of elite groups, and hence with the tendency (usually attributable to the unconscious) to remain silent about these secrets (although it is also a privilege of the inner circle to be able to take liberties with common belief that are prohibited to common mortals). In short, "select" groups are protected from analysis by the fact that those who know do not tell and those who tell do not know – or more precisely, by the fact that attempts at critical analysis are often produced by those on the fringe or by outsiders.

2   *Compétence* has been translated in most cases as *competence* rather than *skill* to capture the legal sense Bourdieu is bringing out. [Tr.]

3   Forcing the expression somewhat, we might write that the "liberating school" is the new opiate of the people. Which would at least have the virtue of showing just how far off the mark those who are still brandishing the flag of laicity really are. One battle can (serve to) mask another. The type of sociology that demonstrates that boundaries and battlefronts have shifted puts those who are still fighting the last war in a precarious position, arousing unequivocal feelings in the defenders of order and ambivalent feelings in the partisans of progress.

4   Cf. P. Bourdieu, "Les rites d'institution," *Actes de la Recherche en Sciences Sociales* 43 (June 1982), pp. 58–63.

5   We thus understand the importance of the *publication* of the results of the top *concours* (in the *Journal Officiel*, as well as in the important semi-official papers), which (like the publication of marriages in another order) makes a *change in social state* official.

6   In the article referred to above (cf. note 4), I attempt to show that contrary to the primary representation reinforced by the expression "rite of passage," the rites that I prefer to call rites of institution separate boys who have been put to the test, not from younger boys (the not yet circumcised), but rather from all women, who are not subject to the ritual that constitutes a privilege *in and of itself* (even if it takes the form of a grueling ordeal, such as, in our societies, military service or the preparatory classes).

7   The question of whether the monopoly held by the academic nobility is related to the monopolization of technical skills to a greater or lesser degree than it was for nobilities of the past is not obviously pertinent. Nor is it obvious that science can provide an explanation, despite what might be thought by the defen-

ders of the meritocratic-technocratic vision who believe in the progress of "rationality" and the substitution of *achievement* for *ascription*.

8   Here are two examples: "How can we prevent these young people from harboring dangerous illusions, sparked by the presence of the *word 'superior'* in the diplomas they will be awarded? The deletion of *this word* would eliminate all the difficulties mentioned heretofore" (M. Lehmann, "Compagnie générale d'électricité," *L'Expansion de la Recherche Scientifique* 14 (Oct. 1962); emphasis added). And another, more simply: "If the DEST [diplôme d'études supérieures techniques] can be assimilated, combined with these other diplomas, particularly the chemistry or physics technician's diploma, then we have no problem with it, quite the contrary, in fact, as long as it is earned through technical or higher education, if the higher education system really sees itself getting involved in that. But we'd be uneasy about any title awarded at a level above that of existing diplomas" (M. Arnaud, "Union des industries chimiques," ibid.).

9   "In-house," that is, trained solely on the job; the holder must keep within the bounds dictated by a specific *concours*. [Tr.]

10 We realize that it is impossible to make a single overarching value judgment on the role of the educational institution. It is an instrument for reproduction, and it also fulfills a function we might call "democratic" in that it guarantees a minimum of rights to employees in their transactions with the economically powerful. In any event, we can be sure that the dominated have, certainly in global terms, an interest in the rationalization of both required skills and the manner in which they are taught and evaluated, as well as that of the definition of the attributes guaranteed by titles.

11 Proof of the counterproductive effects of subordinating the technical imperatives of production to the social imperatives of reproduction can be seen in the discrimination Jews suffered at the hands of the three most prestigious American universities (Harvard, Yale, and Princeton) at a time when their technical abilities (related to their favorable predisposition toward intellectual matters, among other things) would have been particularly indispensable for scientific and economic development (cf. J. Karabel, "Status-Group Struggle, Organizational Interests and the Limits of Institutional Autonomy: The Transformation of Harvard, Yale and Princeton, 1918–1940," *Theory and Society* 13:1 (Jan. 1984), pp. 1–39). Similar effects, of which social science is the primary victim, can be observed more generally in the way the dominated are treated.

12 The job market is but one among many loci of these constant struggles and transactions regarding social identity.

13 INSEE is the National Institute of Statistics and Economic Research. [Tr.]

14 Both bureaucratic taxonomies, produced through negotiation and constantly subject to distortions imposed by pressure from the various groups involved, and, even more so, the less codified taxonomies conveyed by ordinary language have practical functions. In social coding, words have consequences; being certified as disabled or ill entitles one to a pension or to time off. If a single word gets left out of an official job description, people might have to perform duties they would rather not be responsible for or, conversely, they may not be authorized to carry out a duty they would like to be theirs.

15   We thus see more clearly what is implied in reducing science, with the
ethnomethodologists, to a simple *enregistrement* (a word that aptly translates
the term *account*, so dear to Garfinkel) of accounts in the usual sense,
understood as a verbal device that constructs the world. This methodological
postulate, closer to the positivist tradition than to the true spirit of phenomenology, leads the researcher to accept facts as they appear, in other words, in
their *preconstructed* state (rather like a clerk in a registrar's office), rather than
to break with things as they appear in order to reconstruct the social conditions
that have made them possible and the historical laws governing their construction.

Part III   The Field of the Grandes Écoles and its Transformations

Chapter 1   A State of the Structure

This chapter was coauthored with Monique de Saint Martin.

1   Cf. appendix 1 below, "A Discourse of Celebration," pp. 230–1.
2   The following is an example of this type of tacit reference, taken from the
report of the Polytechnique alumni association committee, chaired by Pierre
D. Cot, which appeared in the October 1968 issue of *La Jaune et la Rouge*, the
alumni periodical. "A legal and administrative education, even if it is tinted with
qualitative economics [a transparent allusion to the education received at
Sciences-po and the ENA], will no longer be enough for higher civil servants"
("Le rôle des grands corps d'ingénieurs dans la société moderne française," *La
Jaune et la Rouge* 230 (Oct. 1968), pp. 18–19).
3   Cf. W. V. O. Quine, "Epistemology Naturalized," in *Ontological Relativity
and Other Essays* (New York: Columbia University Press, 1969).
4   Less prestigious professional schools. [Tr.]
5   For a description of the method used in constructing the structural sample of
establishments and an overview of the administration of the survey, see appendix 2, pp. 232–44.
6   The former "great" door leads to the top schools, jobs, etc., and the latter
"minor" door to less prestigious schools, careers, etc. [Tr.]
7   Cf. C. Thélot, *Tel père, tel fils? Position sociale et origine familiale* (Paris:
Dunod, 1982).
8   We need only think of the cases in which occupational heredity is accompanied
by structural regression – for example, when the son of a primary school
teacher becomes a primary school teacher during a period when the entire
structure is shifting upward.
9   The quotation marks are there to remind the reader that we are not talking
about the conscious choices of a rational subject, but rather about the (often
unconscious) operation of a "practical sense" of *placement* [also *investment*,
allowing one to "place oneself" as in the job market, the stock market, betting,
physical positioning, political stances, etc., as well as the educational system,
Tr.].

10 The difficulty people may have in truly comprehending the complex processes responsible for these effects and the complex theory of action that must be constructed, at odds with all the habitual ways of thinking, in order to make sense of them, accounts for the fact (without excusing it) that, in spite of all statements to the contrary, the analysis revealing them should regularly be reduced to a form of conspiracy theory (especially by those disturbed by the revelation) or, in an equally narrow-minded variant, to a utilitarian theory of carefully considered self-interest.

11 The grands corps are the elite corps of the French administrative system, whose members, recruited on graduation from the grandes écoles and granted a title for life, often go on to hold ministry positions and high-level jobs in the private sector. The major technical corps are Mines, Ponts et Chaussées, and Eaux et Fôrets; the major nontechnical corps are the Conseil d'État, the Inspection des Finances, and the Cour des Comptes. [Tr.]

12 The statistical laws that define each of the classes of order produced by the educational system merely characterize individuals as members of a class. In an apparent violation of the axiom *de omni et nullo*, the individual object is undetermined, the class is determined. Or, to be more precise, the individual object is only defined negatively, the limits of its indeterminacy being none other than the limits of the class. We thus come to understand the importance that the extreme possibilities take on in the subjective estimation of opportunities. Everything indeed happens as if, among objectively possible (and unequally probable) trajectories, agents' spontaneous statistics tended to favor the extreme values (for example, in "The Ballad of the *Khâgne* Student," the writer or ambassador and the high school teacher).

13 We chose to treat individual institutions rather than groups of institutions: for example, in Lyons, rather than using all the engineering schools in the city, we included one engineering grande école, the École Centrale Lyonnaise, and a few less prestigious engineering schools of differing status and specialization, the École Supérieure de Chimie Industrielle, the École Catholique d'Arts et Métiers, and the École Française de Tannerie. In the subfield of institutions leading to professions in art and architecture, we included an architecture school in Paris, the École Spéciale d'Architecture, and two non-Parisian architecture schools, in Nantes and Toulouse, rather than all architecture schools as a whole. Nevertheless, when we wanted to indicate general positions that function as *points of comparison*, we used aggregates, as in the case of the humanities and science preparatory classes for the grandes écoles, for example, which are represented by only two points (*khâgne* and *taupe*), as well as the Instituts Universitaires de Technologie and the different facultés – law and economics, sciences, humanities, medicine, and pharmacy (which, if we had wanted to be completely rigorous, we could have or should have broken down by city).

14 That is, accounts for 31.4 percent of the deviation from the mean. [Tr.]

15 These offer two-year courses, admission to which is selective, aimed at enabling students to obtain managerial responsibilities in the industrial and service sectors. [Tr.]

16 Projecting the supplementary variables shows that the first axis also opposes students according to regional origins. Those whose parents live in or around Paris are located on the side of the dominant institutions (on the right-hand side

of the diagram) while those whose parents live in the provinces are located on the side of the dominated establishments (on the left-hand side of the diagram).

17 We will only analyze the first factor here, even though, as we shall see below, the second factor gives a first approximation of the structure that is fully revealed in the second analysis (which includes a greater number of properties for the students at each establishment, particularly indices of scholastic success).

18 We find the same opposition between the older, more noble, and better frequented École Nationale des Chartes and the École Nationale Supérieure des Bibliothécaires, both of which we treat as illustrative variables.

19 The École de la Magistrature and the Institut d'Études Judiciaires are actually farther from the ENA and Sciences-po than it appears from the diagram. They in fact include a high percentage of children of mid-level public sector executives, and on the contrary, very few children of private sector chief executives or higher civil servants, in contrast to the ENA and Sciences-po (we were unable to distinguish the different fractions of executives, however).

20 There does exist one apparent exception that can be explained if we note that academic properties were not taken into account in the construction of the space: the École Spéciale de Mécanique et d'Électricité. This institution – neither a specialized professional school, nor a comprehensive grande école, but rather a sanctuary school counting among its students a large percentage of sons of executives and members of the professions with relatively poor scholastic records – is located near the top grandes écoles.

21 These schools indeed have the highest proportion of sons and daughters of blue-collar and clerical workers (43.1 percent at the École de Tannerie de Lyon, 39.3 percent at the ENSAM de Lille, 34.5 percent at the École des Arts et Industries Textiles de Roubaix, in contrast to only 7.7 percent at Polytechnique, or 7.5 percent at the École des Mines de Paris).

22 It is extremely rare for a student to enter both *concours* simultaneously.

23 This entire set of mechanisms is called into question today due to the general rise in the level of schooling, which has shifted the break that used to be made at the beginning of the *sixième* to a much higher level (the *seconde*). It follows that the boundary between the *grande* and the *petite portes* has undoubtedly never been as noticeable or as strategic as it is today.

24 In both cases, the third factor opposes the various schools principally in terms of their curriculum and the corps they feed. Here the schools that offer "general" preparation for positions in *government* (ENA, first and second *concours*, IEP) are opposed to the schools that provide a relatively specialized advanced *technical* training: ENSIAA, Mines de Saint-Étienne, Agro. Obeying the same logic, this factor differentiates students with a classical *literary* secondary education (including Latin, Greek, and/or modern languages) from students with a *scientific* and/or technical background. (When the first factor disappears in the third analysis, which focuses on the grandes écoles alone, this factor of differentiation quite logically moves from third to second place.)

25 A series of statistical tables based on our survey of the top grandes écoles can be found in appendix 3, p. 245.

26 When we treat the entire set of 15 top-ranking and second-order grandes écoles as principal variables, the first factor opposes the schools exactly as it did in the preceding analyses, that is, not according to the structure of their students' capi-

tal, but according to the total amount of this capital. Thus, on one side, we have the schools with the most "bourgeois" student body (HEC, IEP, ENA) and, on the other, the schools with a relatively large proportion of middle-class students (Fontenay and Saint-Cloud). The second factor then opposes the schools primarily in terms of their students' academic capital.

27 At the time of our survey, there were very few women, except at Sèvres and Fontenay, which are exclusively female and which principally lead to the teaching profession. Where women were found, it was generally at the various Instituts d'Études Politiques (20 percent overall in Paris, but only 10 percent of students specializing in public service), the ENSAE, second division (23.5 percent, compared to 10 percent for the first division), the École de Physique et Chimie (13.5 percent), and the École d'Horticulture (7.4 percent) and Grignon (3 percent). Everywhere else, there were never more than 2 percent women (except in the second *concours* at the ENA, where the figure was 5.5 percent).

28 P. Bourdieu, *Distinction: A Social Critique of the Judgement of Taste* (1979), trans. R. Nice (Cambridge: Harvard University Press, 1984).

29 If we use data on salary levels to construct a hierarchy among the schools based on the market value of their diplomas, we find that Polytechnique alumni earn the highest salaries directly after graduation (above HEC), but that since 1969, when *Expansion* began its surveys, the gap has continued to narrow.

30 On the ties between the École Centrale and management, see M. Lévi-Leboyer, "Le patronat français a-t-il été malthusien?," *Le Mouvement Social* 88 (July–Sept. 1974), pp. 1–49, and J. H. Weiss, *The Making of Technological Man: the Social Origins of French Engineering Education* (Cambridge: MIT Press, 1982), p. xvii.

31 So, for example, according to a survey conducted by the Union Nationale des Diplômés des Écoles Supérieures de Commerce on about 2,000 graduates of business schools, the salaries of alumni of the 17 ESCAE (Écoles Supérieures de Commerce et d'Administration des Entreprises) decrease after age 40, while the salaries of graduates of HEC, the ESSEC, or the ESCP continue to rise (cf. *Trait d'Union, ESC* 31 (July 1972), p. 22).

32 Cf. P. Beaudeux, "La cote des débutants," *Expansion* 287 (June–July 1986), pp. 142–3.

33 R. Alquier, in *L'Usine Nouvelle* (Spring 1967), p. 25 (emphasis added).

34 This is only absolutely true for men, who are more thoroughly dominated than women by the principle of division that favors them. In fact, the objectivated and embodied structure of the division of labor between the sexes tends, for women, to strengthen the temporally dominated pole of every alternative, all else being equal.

35 Baccalauréat honors or nominations to the Concours Général become all the more necessary for students wishing to enter the preparatory classes the more prestigious the school and the higher its success rate in the top *concours*. (The admissions committee for first-year *taupe* classes in a top Parisian lycée based its decisions in the 1970s on the calculations of one of its members, according to which success in the *concours* was very closely related to the comment received on the baccalauréat, in order to minimize the effects of other criteria (such as the supposed rank of the establishment) and favoritism and private influence.)

36 We know that the proportion of women, Jews, and newcomers from the domi-

nated regions of social space (this no doubt includes homosexuals as well) increases in the university field when we move from the temporally dominant regions to the temporally dominated regions, a tendency we also note within the subfield of arts and humanities facultés (cf. P. Bourdieu, *Homo Academicus* (1984), trans. P. Collier (Cambridge: Polity Press, 1988) pp. 40–51).

37 Cf. in particular *Anglo-Saxon Superiority: To What Is It Due?* (1897), trans. L. Bert (Freeport, N.Y.: Books for Libraries Press, 1972), and *L'éducation nouvelle, l'école des Roches* (Paris: Firmin-Didot, 1898).

38 It will suffice to cite one example of the position of the conservatives who fought against compulsory education, which they viewed as a challenge to the authority and the rights of the family and as the seizure of children by the state: "It is still the interests of the working-class child that are usually invoked, but, in the thinking of the reformers, they are used to strengthen the so-called 'state control' idea. So, for example, they will argue both that a child is his own person and that the state nevertheless has the right and the duty to take possession of him. (. . .) For these people, national interests merge with the interests of the child, thus justifying the state's pressure on the family in imposing compulsory education, guaranteeing in return that it will be free" (L. Delzons, *La famille française et son évolution* (Paris: Armand Colin, 1913), pp. 151–2).

39 This antagonism is found within the field of economic firms itself, particularly in the opposition between employers whose power is wielded in opposing sectors of the economic field (in other words, in private companies or in companies that are more or less closely tied to the state) and is very unequally dependent on academic capital.

40 L. Pinto, "L'école des philosophes, la dissertation de philosophie au baccalauréat," *Actes de la Recherche en Sciences Sociales* 47–8 (June 1983), pp. 21–36.

41 The name *"fisticis,"* by which HEC students refer to themselves, apparently derives from the phrase "le fils est ici!" [the son is here], which they are in the habit of shouting out whenever they hear the name of a top industrial or commercial firm.

42 Sons of officers are the most likely to enter the Armement corps. Sons of engineers are divided nearly equally among all applied engineering schools and all careers.

43 We would like to thank Alain Desrosières and Laurent Thévenot for having made these data available to us.

44 As we were able to show in detail for the very homogeneous population of *normaliens*, who have an extremely high rate of endogamy, we know that matrimonial strategies are the product of this principle as well, with endogamy circuits tending to be organized in terms of the structure of social space as established in *Distinction* (cf. A. Desrosières, "Marché matrimonial et classes sociales," *Actes de la Recherche en Sciences Sociales* 20–1 (Mar.-Apr. 1978), pp. 97–107).

45 L. J. D. Wacquant, "Production scolaire et reproduction sociale: HEC, 1881–1981, l'autre histoire d'une Grande École," MA thesis, University of Paris X-Nanterre, 1983.

46 The interpenetration of family traditions and school traditions is the highest at Polytechnique: 51 percent of *polytechniciens* have heard of the school before the *troisième,* from their families in fact, compared to only 26 percent of

normaliens, 24 percent of HEC students, and a minute portion of ENA students. It is also at Polytechnique that the rate of alumni offspring is the highest (9 percent) as well as the most paraded. *La Jaune et la Rouge*, the alumni review, publishes statistics on the number of sons, grandsons, and great-grandsons of alumni among its students and is apt to mention family ties among alumni as well (in wedding announcements, for example). The students are well versed in the names of famous graduates. All of these indices, as well as the acuteness of their memories, seem to indicate a *high degree of integration*.

47 *Normaliens* are probably the least "Parisian" of all grandes écoles students. At the start of the *sixième*, only a third were living in Paris or the surrounding area, another third lived in a city of over 100,000 residents, and the final third were from small cities or the countryside.

48 Differences in terms of social origin seem less pronounced at Polytechnique in the area of theater-going, concert-going, and bridge-playing, particularly because working-class students at Polytechnique, who are very highly selected, go to plays and concerts more frequently than at the other schools.

49 A detailed analysis of the rates at which different social categories are represented at the various stages in the selection process of ENA students can be found in appendix 4, pp. 255–60.

50 Given that the ENA is of recent origin, at the time of our survey there were as yet no family dynasties, but ties with Sciences-po were very strong: 9 percent of ENA students were sons of a Sciences-po graduate.

51 Had his intentions been scientific rather than apologetic, Jean-François Kesler would not have sought the ways in which ENA students are like French people as a whole ("ENA students vote like other French people (. . .) and were not connected to the UDR State or the UDF State"; J.-F. Kesler, *l'ENA, la société, l'État* (Paris: Berger-Levrault, 1985), pp. 409–17), but rather *what distinguishes them* from other grandes écoles students, in the political arena as in other domains.

52 The question read as follows: "Who are the five people you would most like to have come to give a talk at your school?" (By using the term "talk" [*conférence*], we were introducing a certain bias in favor of persons tacitly judged as qualified to perform this strictly *cultural* activity.) The probability of response varies greatly by school: it is highest at HEC and Polytechnique (84 percent and 82 percent) and lowest at Ulm-sciences and Sèvres-sciences (only 51 percent and 38 percent). Nonresponses may be accompanied by an avowal of incompetence (especially at Sèvres-sciences, Ulm-sciences, and Agro); but they may also be a sign of scorn for the question, particularly at Ulm ("stupid question"; teacher's son, Ulm-sciences), or a rejection of the practice ("I don't believe that talks given by eminent figures are useful"; son of mathematics teacher in technical education, Ulm-sciences).

53 A few students (nearly all from the petty bourgeoisie) stand out from the rest in naming more intellectuals, artists, and writers than the others (two examples: "Couve de Murville, Niemeyer, Dali, Sartre, Beuve-Méry"; "Sartre, Pisani, Mendès France, Godard, Malraux"). The students who have entered through the civil servant *concours* propose left-wing politicians somewhat more frequently than their classmates from the student *concours*; Mendès France is named by more than half of the respondents, who occasionally propose "a

union leader" (without giving a name). Their choices show a bit more evidence of humanist and Third World concerns: Josué de Castro and Don Helder Camara are given by one student, son of an engineer. Here is a further example of a very unlikely list for a (student *concours*) student: "L. Pauling, J. Rostand, Steinbeck, Fidel Castro, Mendès France" (son of clerical worker). And another: "Mendès France, J. Vilar, A. Fabre-Luce, J. Rostand, M. Debatisse" (son of clerical worker). The choices made by the students at the Institut d'Études Politiques (particularly those majoring in public service) closely resemble those of the (student *concours*) students at the ENA.

54 A small minority of students originating in the liberal or intellectual professions propose names closer to the intellectual pole: for example, "Althusser, Barthes" (son of physician); or "Mao Tse-tung, Fidel Castro, Althusser, J.-P. Sartre, General Diop" (son of Protestant minister); or "Giscard, Mendès France, J.-P. Sartre, Lévi-Strauss, Robbe-Grillet, Bresson" (son of architect).

55 We would undoubtedly get a better understanding of the alchemy of *recognition* if we could do a comparative analysis of the oral sections of the various *concours*. To remain within the limits of practical comparability, we would need to contrast the ENA oral, for example, which requires mastery of a complex social situation, wavering between official interview, cocktail or dinner party conversation, and administrative committee report, with the École Normale oral, more like an oral presentation of a written exam, in the style of a "lecture," which requires rather more the virtues of clarity and conviction than the skills of a clever politician and presence of mind. We would then see that discourse analysis, which is today often reduced to an analysis of texts, should take the form of a methodical establishment of relations (analogous to what we did above with the choices of speakers) between the space of discursive stances and the space of the positions held by the producers and the recipients of the discourse – in the present case, in other words, the entire field of the grandes écoles and its relations to the field of power.

56 The fraternities and sororities of the Anglo-Saxon university, like French alumni associations, represent the institutionalized form of these ties.

57 The progressive invention, throughout the seventeenth and eighteenth centuries, of a new framework for noble and bourgeois adolescents – the boarding collège – made adolescence the age of friendship *par excellence* (cf. M. Aymard, "Friends and Neighbors," in P. Ariès and G. Duby (eds), *A History of Private Life*, vol. 3, trans. A. Goldhammer (Cambridge: Belknap Press of Harvard University Press, 1989), pp. 447–91).

58 As we can plainly see in instances of transfers to the private sector, this social capital, along with the informational capital acquired during stints in high-level administration is undoubtedly one of the most important determinants of the value of certain titles.

59 Mentioning a few proper names would suffice to demonstrate the explanatory force of our model, but lest these analyses appear to be *ad hominem* attacks whose point of departure is the individual case they in fact enable us to understand, I will simply refer those who might be anxious for evidence and illustration to pages where they will find descriptions of several exemplary deviant trajectories and accounts of how these "teachers' kids," lost among the "*fisticis*," experienced their education, their classmates, their future careers, etc. (M.

Nouschi, *Histoire et pouvoir d'une grande école, HEC* (Paris: Robert Laffont, 1988), pp. 216–31).

Chapter 2 A Structural History

1 According to a June 1987 poll of 500 graduates of Polytechnique, the ENA, HEC, the École Supérieure de Commerce de Rouen, and the École des Mines de Nancy, all of whom had worked in a company for more than five years, ENA alumni were the most likely to express the opinion that the grandes écoles system "does not provide training sufficiently adapted to the modern world" (at 65 percent, compared to 62 percent at Polytechnique and 39 percent at HEC) and that it is "a cause of stagnation in French society" (37 percent, compared to 17 percent and 18 percent). None of which, however, precludes their congratulating themselves more than all the others on the existence of the grandes écoles, absolutely essential "for providing France with the elites that the university does not produce" . . . (cf. J. J. Gurviez, "Miroir, mon beau miroir, sommes-nous encore les meilleurs?" *Expansion*, Sept. 11–24, 1987, pp. 171–3).

2 Cf. R. J. Smith, *The École Normale Supérieure and the Third Republic* (Albany: State University of New York Press, 1982).

3 Establishments that combined disparate categories in their reporting (primary teachers and mid-level managers, for example, or higher-level teachers and executives), which include HEC, Supelec, the ENSAE, the École des Mines de Saint-Étienne, etc., had to be used as supplementary variables.

4 The projection of the schools used as supplementary variables confirms these analyses for the first factor; the secondary opposition cannot be shown because the statistical data we considered do not distinguish between children of engineers and teachers and children of executives.

5 Study group on image and selection at Dauphine, *Paris IX-Dauphine: entre l'image et la réalité*, MS, Paris, May 1987.

6 While the number of students entering Polytechnique increases only slightly over time, and the number at Ulm has risen considerably since 1956, and while, after a marked rise between 1966 and 1976, the number of students entering the ENA reaches a plateau, Saint-Cloud experiences continuous and rapid growth (overtaking Ulm in 1966). Among the scientific schools, the increase at the lesser-ranked Centrale is similar to that at Saint-Cloud (the number of students enrolling seems to vary overall in relation to the number of students admitted).

7 Their curricula are very similar and they share preparatory classes.

8 "The change to a three-year course further deepens the gulf. As the only business school to have such a long program, it maintains the practice of accepting advanced business school graduates into the second year. They have to do an additional year. They're not actually increasing or deepening their knowledge, they're beginning a new education. In 1948, the École Supérieure de Commerce de Paris extends its program to three years, and two years later, the others follow suit. Aware that few students, after three years of study, would want to go through another two to get a second diploma, even a more prestigious one, the administrative committee proposes that the best École Supérieure de Commerce students, provided they are nominated by their schools, attempt the

concours a year before their graduation. The schools concerned put up such an outcry that the measure could not go through; it would turn these schools into a screening ground for HEC, depriving them of their best students while offering them nothing in return" (M. Meuleau, *Histoire d'une grande école, HEC, 1881–1981* (Paris: Dunod, 1981), p. 109).

9 Following a logic altogether analogous to the one that governed the founding of the École Libre des Sciences Politiques in the last century (cf. D. Damamme, "Genèse sociale d'une institution scolaire: l'École libre des sciences politiques," *Actes de la Recherche en Sciences Sociales* 70 (Nov. 1987), pp. 31–46). There is probably no better illustration of the power of conservative forces and their ability to get around the juridical or technical obstacles placed in their way than a comparison between the reality of the ENA 40 years after its founding and criticism of the system of civil service recruitment it was meant to replace (cf. G. Thuillier, *l'ENA avant l'ENA* (Paris: PUF, 1983), pp. 234–56, and especially M.-C. Kessler, *La politique de la haute fonction publique* (Paris: Presses de la Fondation Nationale des Sciences Politiques, 1978, pp. 35cff)).

10 We would also need to determine the set of factors that favored the process of circular reinforcement through which the success of alumni in the political and administrative field enhances the school's symbolic capital, while the school's accumulated influence improves students' chances for success in the competition for power: for example, the transformations in the economic field and the primacy given to financial and commercial positions over technical positions, and the transformations in the political field and the relationships between civil servants and party men. As Jean-Claude Thoenig observes, the concentration of power in the hands of "technocrats" (he has the Ponts et Chaussées corps in mind, but his observation is equally valid for the ENA) increased markedly during the Fifth Republic (cf. J.-C. Thoenig, *L'Ère des technocrates* (Paris: Ed. d'Organisation, 1973)).

11 Law facultés (the social status of whose students fell while its female population rose) should have been included in the model; they were in fact affected by the creation of the ENA more than all other facultés. In setting itself up in a relationship with law facultés homologous to the one between Polytechnique and the École Normale and science and humanities facultés, the ENA brought about a structural devaluation of the institution, the titles it grants, and even the professions for which it prepared its students (due to the increased weight of institutions dominated by ENA alumni, for example, such as the Conseil d'État and, in the juridical field, the Constitutional Council).

12 As the official HEC historiographer writes, today "only the École Supérieure des Sciences Économiques et Commerciales (ESSEC) can challenge its preeminence, a fact that leads some corporate heads to say that HEC is resting comfortably on its laurels because it has not been pushed." And further on: "The success of the École Supérieure des Sciences Économiques et Commerciales does concern HEC, but it comforts itself by noting that students who succeed in both *concours* choose HEC" (Meuleau, *Histoire d'une grande école, HEC*, pp. 107, 109).

13 The "research" option, created in 1959 to allow students wishing to become researchers without entering a corps to continue their studies without having to pay the school back for their tuition (provided they complete a science doctor-

ate within a period of six years), was tremendously popular, attracting up to a fifth of all students (cf. G. Grunberg, "L'École polytechnique et ses grands corps," in *Annuaire international de la fonction publique, 1973–1974* (Paris, International Institute of Public Administration, 1974), p. 388 n3).

14 That is, well before the critical outpour of 1973–4. (The reader will find a detailed chronicle of criticism of the ENA based on exhaustive media research in Kessler, *La politique de la haute fonction publique*, pp. 67–109.)

15 We thus have an entire series of commissions referred to by the name of their chair: the Couture Commission, 1962; the Guillaumat Commission, 1963 (report to the Minister of Defense); the Boulloche Commission, 1963 (on the grandes écoles), the Nardin Commission, 1964 (on the Collège des Techniques Avancées); the Long Commission, 1967 (on steering *polytechniciens* toward research); the Couture Commission, 1967; the Cot Commission, 1968 (on the role of the grands corps of engineers); the Lhermitte Commission, 1968 (for grandes écoles reform). To which we should also add the various reports of the Polytechnique alumni association and the École Polytechnique, especially the Report on the Profile of *Polytechniciens* (1967), the Pedagogy Report (1968), and all the alumni opinions published in *La Jaune et la Rouge*.

16 Quoted by Grunberg, "L'École polytechnique et ses grands corps," p. 492.

17 Cf. for example, "Le profil du polytechnicien de 1975–1980," *La Jaune et la Rouge* 225 (Apr. 1968), pp. 11–17.

18 Report of the Polytechnique alumni association committee chaired by P. D. Cot, "Le rôle des grands corps d'ingénieurs dans la société moderne française," in *La Jaune et la Rouge* 230 (Oct. 1978), pp. 7–45 (p. 9); emphasis added.

19 Ibid., pp. 18–19.

20 Ibid., p. 22.

21 Ibid., p. 33.

22 Ibid.

23 J. Majorelle, "Réflexions sur l'X," *La Jaune et la Rouge* 232 (supplement) (Dec. 1968), pp. 49–62 (p. 51).

24 Lhermitte report, *La Jaune et la Rouge* 232 (supplement) (Dec. 1968), pp. 67–112 (p. 87).

25 Cf. J. Ullmo, "La réforme de l'école et le nouvel enseignement de science économique," *La Jaune et la Rouge* 242 (Nov. 1969), pp. 9–11.

26 Cf. M. Berry, 'L'enseignement de la gestion aux élèves-ingénieurs: de l'expérience de l'Ecole des mines à celle de l'Ecole polytechnique', *La Jaune et la Rouge* 305 (Oct. 1975), pp. 17–24.

27 HEC, which is given the great majority of the commercial and financial positions (even by ENA students), is ranked second, just behind their own school, by both *polytechniciens* and ENA students. Polytechnique, which gets the vast majority of the technical positions, and refuses them, passing them off to minor schools (Centrale or Arts et Métiers), gives itself a greater proportion of the management positions than HEC and especially the ENA do, but the gap is not as wide as at the ENA.

28 This gap is especially evident in the judgments made by alumni of second-ranked schools, such as the ESSEC or the École des Mines de Nancy, who, by overwhelmingly giving the management positions to HEC and Polytechnique, show that they strongly recognize academic hierarchies.

29   Between 1960 and 1982, the examining committee for the external *concours* had 11 members, only half of whom were teachers (5 or 6 depending on the year, mostly subordinate professors from law facultés). In 1983, the number was raised to 13, of which about a third have been teachers (4 or 5). The remainder of the committee is made up of one-third higher civil servants and another third corporate directors. Since 1982, committee chairs have included university professors, higher civil servants (high-ranking members of Cour des Comptes and Conseil d'État), and journalists.

30   The transplants were usually students from the upper categories who had failed the *agrégation*. In the 1970s, following the upheaval of 1968 and the appointment of a new director, and with the decline in far left-wing movements, the issue of the closed nature of academic careers is raised. The first calls for equivalence with the ENA are heard in 1973.

31   On the morphological changes in the teaching profession and their effects, see P. Bourdieu, *Homo Academicus* (1984), trans. P. Collier (Cambridge: Polity Press, 1988), ch. 4.

32   As Robert J. Smith has shown, the École Normale never really played the role of talent scout, as the ideology of the "liberating school" would have it, and the number of sons of farmers, blue-collar workers, and minor clerical workers has always been low. Another structural constant, the proportion of sons of commercial and industrial heads, is incomparably lower than that of the sons of secondary or higher education teachers, civil servants in education, or even primary teachers (cf. Smith, *The École Normale Superieure*).

33   According to our secondary analysis of the data given in A. P. Emmenecker and R. Paturel, *Étude démographique des élèves des Écoles normales supérieures*, DES thesis in economics, Paris, Oct. 1971.

34   Cf. G. Bonet and J.-M. de Forges, "La condition des universitaires en France," *Commentaire* 38 (Summer 1987), pp. 332–44.

35   The ministerial decree of 28 July 1985, which provided that four *normaliens* should be directly accepted into the ENA every year, touched off a call to arms, especially from the ENA alumni association (cf. *Le Monde*, 20 July and 20 Sept. 1985; *Le Figaro*, 18 Sept. 1985), which filed an appeal with the Conseil d'État. Also to be noted was the violence of the reactions to the "third route" [open to union organizers, local politicians, and community service personnel, Tr.] instituted in 1983 (even among ENA alumni in the Socialist Party).

36   Among these misguided strategies, in addition to demands for equivalence and encouragements to prepare for the ENA (or even Sciences-po), have to be included all the institutional creations aimed at "opening the École Normale up to the business world" (such as the ENS association for research and development, the ENS institute for expertise and forecasting, and the group for industrial careers and connections), which, about as topical as a group of Chinese communists at HEC in former times, are destined to appear out of place and out of phase both in the intellectual universe and in the business world, where the ENS has maintained a very high reputation (which explains why no one thinks of ENS for the applied sciences).

37   If *normaliens*, who were competing in large numbers, especially after 1976, are increasingly tending to forgo the ENA *concours*, this is undoubtedly because the length of active civil service duty required for participation in internal *con-*

cours was lengthened by the 1982 reform, and because the years spent in preparation or training at the École Normale no longer count, these being so many restrictions on the advantages statutorily granted to *normaliens*. It is also because a new and heavily weighted test was added to the *concours*, giving central administration *attachés* an advantage over teachers (candidates must prepare a note addressed to the prime minister or other leading public figure after reviewing a set of documents).

38 At the risk of provoking outrage with this show of amateur sociologism, I must confess that I am inclined to think that the success enjoyed by the Leninist variant of the phantasm of the philosopher-king at the École Normale during the 1970s was able to provide an undoubtedly somewhat unexpected outlet for the socially constituted "will to power" that the "new *normaliens*" had imported into the institution and that has since found several opportunities to surface in more direct guise. This hypothesis has the virtue of making sense of the political reversals, experienced and described as incomprehensible – and hence eminently excusable, indeed, admirable – that led a number of "strays" to move from a revolutionary authoritarianism, as terrorist in bent as it could be considering the conditions available to their dispositions (the communists of the 1950s and the "Chinese" of the 1970s), to much less contorted forms of exercising the will to power.

39 Cf. Bourdieu, *Homo Academicus*.

40 The reader will find an attempt at reconstructing the matrix of this vulgate, expressed in interchangeable fashion in technocratic essays, in P. Bourdieu and L. Boltanski, "La production de l'idéologie dominante," *Actes de la Recherche en Sciences Sociales* 2–3 (June 1976), pp. 9–31. A quick examination of the work produced by ENA alumni over the past five years reveals quite a consistency in the themes (always subjects closely connected to current political issues, such as immigration, liberalism, nationalizations, the "excluded," etc.), style, and appearance (their books are always very short, never going beyond 200 pages, and in large type) of the ENA alumni "philosophy."

41 R. Fauroux, "Alain Minc ou le révolté," *Le Monde*, 23 Sept. 1987, p. 2.

42 The strategy consisting in predicting the end of intellectually dominant schools of thought is quite common (we see it already in the Huret study on naturalism). Both the pretenders on their way out and their unsuccessful adversaries agree to mask behind apparent statements of fact ("structuralism is over") wishes that are veritable symbolic murders ("bring on the end of structuralism!").

43 As in the case of the UDF and the RPR [Union Démocratique Française and Rassemblement pour la République, both conservative political parties, Tr.], a large number of socialist political personnel graduated from the ENA, but, it would appear, *at a lower rank*. The ENA graduates in the Socialist Party, who are undoubtedly more likely to be from families of teachers, seem to have had a less "brilliant" and later success story than those in the UDF or the RPR, especially the latter. These generalizations, based on a quick analysis of the careers of former ministers of the different parties, would need methodical verification, but they are corroborated by the observations of Pierre Gaborit and Jean-Pierre Mounier on ministerial cabinets (cf. P. Gaborit and J.-P. Mounier, "France," in W. Plowden (ed.), *Advising the Rulers* (Oxford: Blackwell, 1987), pp. 92–123).

44 On the generalization of recourse to the school as an instrument of reproduc-

tion, see P. Bourdieu, *Distinction: A Social Critique of the Judgement of Taste* (1979), trans. R. Nice (Cambridge: Harvard University Press, 1984); on the transformations of the mode of reproduction of the business bourgeoisie, see the discussion beginning on p. 272 below.

45 Although it too is related to the increase in academic competition, the case of sons of members of the professions or higher civil servants who choose a school like HEC, whose student body used to be primarily made up of sons of industrial and commercial heads and private sector executives, is in fact distinct. According to a mechanism that can be seen more clearly still in choices among scientific schools, where the results of hierarchized *concours* determine "vocations," the logic of choosing among socially as well as *academically* hierarchized institutions leads these young people to prefer an institution that, even if it leads them to occupations that are little prized in their universe, is still perceived as a "grande école," and hence incomparably more prestigious than Sciences-po, for example. (The proportion of sons of members of the professions increases from 7 percent in 1950 to 11 percent in 1960, 10 percent in 1970, and 15 percent in 1980; the portion of sons of higher civil servants increases from 2 percent in 1950 to 4 percent in 1960, 6 percent in 1970, and 9 percent in 1980; cf. Meuleau, *Histoire d'une grande école, HEC*, p. 117.)

46 It appears that the new schools experienced a particularly sharp increase. So, for example, the number of candidates to the École Supérieure de Commerce de Lyon, which had just been renovated, rose from 184 in 1968 to 2,688 in 1981, while the number of students accepted went from 72 to 175.

47 J. Marceau, *A Family Business? The Making of an International Business Elite* (New York: Columbia University Press, 1989).

48 Between 1949 and 1969, growth in foreign trade increased at an annual rate nearly twice that of the gross national product, while during the first half of the century, imports and exports had increased at an average rate close to that of production. Despite a marked slowdown between 1951 and 1957, the expansion of trade continued apace during the period from 1949 to 1969. Overall trade increased by a factor of five, which translates into an average annual rate of 8.4 percent (cf. J. J. Carré, P. Dubois, and E. Malinvaud, *French Economic Growth* (1972), trans. J. P. Hatfield (Stanford: Stanford University Press, 1975). The same years witnessed an accelerated development in the service sector and its occupations and an increase in nonproduction jobs in manufacturing firms.

49 M. Gollac and B. Seys, "1954–1982. Les bouleversements du paysage social," *Économie et Statistique* 171–2 (Nov.–Dec. 1984), p. 154.

50 Cf. L. Thévenot, "Les catégories sociales en 1975. L'extension du salariat," *Économie et Statistique* 91 (July–Aug. 1977), p. 30.

51 Cf. ibid., pp. 23–4.

52 Quoted by J. J. Gurviez and P. Beaudeux, "Salaire des cadres, 1984," *Expansion* 240 (8–21 June 1984).

53 Ibid.

54 B. Girod de l'Ain, *L'évolution des écoles de gestion* (Paris: Université de Paris IX-Dauphine, 1976).

55 There is considerable similarity between private collèges and the new private schools of management, as well as, undoubtedly, the less prestigious sanctuary schools such as Breguet and Sudria. For graduates of these institutions, the

preparatory classes for the most competitive grandes écoles seem "hellish," places to be avoided at all costs, because "they make you work like dogs." In contrast, business and management schools offer a seemingly much more "open" and "comprehensive" education.

56 Cf. H. LeMore, "Classes possédantes et classes dirigeantes. Essai sociologique sur l'École des hautes études commerciales," 3rd cycle dissertation, EHESS, Paris, 1976, pp. 33–55; Meuleau, *Histoire d'une grande école, HEC*. The near homonymy of acronyms, which leads to the desired confusion between the imitation article and the authentic article, is one of the bluffing strategies through which the new institutions – the École des Hautes Études Polyrelationnelles, HEP, for example – attempt to promote themselves, thus contributing to the inflationary spiral of aspirations and nominal rewards.

57 These figures are meant to give an idea of the evolution of management schools as a whole, and only serve as an indication. Boundaries are in fact extremely fluid within this sector, and unlike the case of engineering schools, no title commission exists to determine which schools are entitled to grant the title of "manager." Our data are taken principally from *l'Annuaire national des écoles de commerce et des formations supérieures à la gestion* (Paris: Génération, 1984); H. de Bodinat, "Les écoles de gestion au banc d'essai," *Expansion* 63 (May 1973), and "Le guide Michelin des écoles de gestion," *Expansion* 122 (Oct. 1978); Girod de l'Ain, *L'évolution des écoles de gestion*; B. Magliulo, "Les grandes écoles de commerce et de gestion et les autres formations à la gestion comptable," *Profils Économiques* 8 (Apr.–May 1982); Y. Ménisez, "L'enseignement de la gestion en France," *Notes et Études Documentaires* 4529–30, 24 Sept. 1979.

58 The discussion which follows dealt with the schools at the time of our original investigation and no doubt there have been changes in the intervening years.

59 B. Girod de l'Ain, V. Eyrignoux, and P. Eyrignoux, "*Institut de préparation à l'administration et à la gestion (IPAG),*" Mimeograph, université Paris IX/Dauphine, Paris, 1976, p. 6.

60 In 1975, "90 percent of IPAG students were from managerial or professional families," cf. ibid., p. 2b.

61 European Business School, "Concours d'entrée en premierè année," introductory booklet, Wednesday, 30 May 1984, p. 4.

62 Taken from the instruction sheet passed out to members of the examining committee of the ESCAE in Grenoble in June 1985 during a preparatory meeting on the school's entrance oral.

63 Institut de Préparation à l'Administration et à la Gestion, introductory brochure, IPAG, Paris, 1983, p. 17.

64 " 'Château EDHEC 84': un jeu pour accueillir les nouveaux élèves," *Le Monde*, 29 Nov. 1985, p. 29. The game's author, M. de Milleville, a computer teacher, explains: "We want to make a clean break with the teaching methods the students experienced in the preparatory classes"; they must "constantly calculate the broad-reaching consequences of their decisions."

65 This is the same logic that led the École Supérieure de Commerce de Paris to withdraw in 1968 from the unified and uniform group of the Écoles Supérieures de Commerce et d'Administration des Entreprises (ESCAE), which they had agreed to join after the war in return for state aid, in order to specialize in a

"resolutely practical education in keeping with corporate needs" (Meuleau, *Histoire d'une grande école, HEC*, p. 109).

Appendix 1

1   The École Polytechnique had already been the subject of several works: A. Fourcy's *l'Histoire de l'École polytechnique* dates from 1828. François Arago, who taught at Polytechnique, also wrote several books about the school.
2   The publication in the 1930s of a collection entitled "Nos grandes écoles," which includes works on the École Normale and Polytechnique, as well as Centrale, Navale, and Saint-Cyr, gives first-hand accounts of the famous schools of the day.
3   A. Peyrefitte, *Rue d'Ulm, Chroniques de la vie normalienne*, (2nd edn, Paris: Flammarion, 1963); J. A. Koscuisko-Morizet, *La "mafia" polytechnicienne* (Paris; Seuil, 1973).
4   J.-L. Bodiguel, *L'École nationale d'administration: les anciens élèves de l'ENA* (sociology) (Paris: FNSP, 1978); J. Freches, *L'ENA: voyage au centre de l'État* (Paris: Conti-Fayolle, 1981); J.-F. Kesler, *L'ENA, la société, l'État* (Paris: Berger-Levrault, 1985); M.-C. Kessler, *L'École nationale d'administration: la politique de la haute fonction publique* (history) (Paris: FNSP, 1978); J. Mandrin, *l'Enarchie ou les mandarins de la société bourgeoise* (Paris: La Table Ronde de Combat, 1968), new edn 1980; M. Schifres, *L'Enaklatura* (Paris: J.-C. Lattès, 1987); G. Thuillier, *L'ENA avant l'ENA* (Paris; PUF, 1983); O. Vallet, *L'ENA toute nue* (Paris: Moniteur, 1977).

Appendix 2

This section was coauthored by Monique de Saint Martin.

1   Pierre Bourdieu, *The Inheritors: French Students and their Relation to Culture* (1964) trans. R. Nice (Chicago: University of Chicago Press, 1979). [Tr.]
2   In order to grasp the secondary opposition between general and technical education, which is nonetheless of primary importance within the educational system, it would have been necessary to include the École Nationale Supérieure de l'Enseignement Technique in our survey, thus making it possible to investigate the opposition between the École Normale Supérieure (Ulm) and the ENSET. Even so, we can nonetheless observe the functioning of homologous oppositions, either in the subfield of engineering schools (the opposition between Polytechnique and the École Nationale des Arts et Métiers de Lille, for example), or in the subfield of higher public service (the opposition between the ENA and the École des PTT).
3   There are no socially low and academically very high engineering schools.
4   Members of the Bureau des Étudiants are active in organizing leisure and cultural activities, lectures, conferences, etc.; it offers experience in organizing and "networking," and is a plus for one's resumé. [Tr.]
5   The survey was not conducted in the "petites écoles" that either recruit at the baccalauréat level or run their own preparatory courses (Angers, Purpan, Beauvais, Lille, Institut Technique de Pratique Agricole in Paris, Ingénieurs des Travaux Agricoles de Bordeaux), or in specialized schools with relatively small

student bodies (tropical agronomy, fatty materials science, dairy industry and economics). We may, however, consider this last category to be represented in the study of the ENSIAA at Massy.

6 I will only remind the reader here that, as I have already indicated elsewhere, the multidimensional space we are attempting to construct (shown in the correspondence analysis diagram) is an isomorphic representation of the field of the grandes écoles that establishes among the various elements (agents or institutions and properties) of the two spaces a bi-univocal correlation such that the ensemble of relations among agents and properties has the same structure in both.

7 This problem arises whenever it comes to studying a sector of social space, an "occupation," for example: the inclination to privilege indigenous questions means that the questionnaire, which is necessarily limited, is likely to provide an overabundance of information on internal principles of division – on matters of politics, unions, professional practices, etc. – without enabling us to characterize the group as a whole, thus to truly understand the practices based on the group's *differential position* in social space or even, consequently, the different ways the group itself refers to this position.

8 We received no grant money for this study: retrospective funding (which was used to cover coding expenses) was received as part of a study on the administration carried out at the behest of the budget management office of the Ministry of Finance. A grant from the Ministry of Education, under the rubric of "transitions in the educational system," enabled us to conduct supplementary interviews (principally at the new business schools) and to run statistical analyses in 1984 on the data on establishments of higher education.

9 We are very grateful to these and to the many other individuals who made this research possible, school directors, staff, and administrators who authorized our survey and supported the different stages of the research, teachers who helped administer the questionnaire, students who organized the survey in their schools, gathered data, and made very valuable observations on life at their school, librarians, archivists, secretaries, persons in charge of administrative departments in the different schools or in the Ministry of Education who provided us with the necessary files, documents, and data, as well as all those who agreed to be interviewed. We would also like to thank Salah Bouhedja, who undertook the computer data analysis, and Rosine Christin and Claire Givry, who researched documents provided by the various establishments and conducted some of the interviews with institutional heads and other members of staff as well as with grande école and university students in the Paris and Lyons-Grenoble areas. Of the works stemming directly or indirectly from this project, the dissertation written by Henri Le More (H. Le More, "Classes possédantes et classes dirigeantes. Essai sociologique sur l'École des Hautes Études Commerciales," 3rd cycle doctoral dissertation, Paris, 1976, 301pp.) gives the best idea of the initial project: to come up with a set of methodically articulated monographic studies based on an analysis of the structure of the relations constitutive of the field of institutions.

10 The logic of collective discussion of the questionnaire would have led to the indefinite addition of specific questions that would not have lent themselves to general comparison (the pressure toward specification was particularly strong

in the case of the subtly hierarchized universe of the scientific schools that we would have liked to have been able to distinguish). But at the same time, given that most of the participants were defined by their particular relationship to one or another of the schools under study, they tended to form a space reminiscent of the object analyzed, and the confrontation of points of view thus defined constituted a first step toward objectivation, and scientific control.

11 Without subscribing to the myth according to which each grande école is distinguished by customs, rites, and beliefs reserved for the initiated, which graduates love to evoke with complicitous looks and knowing smiles, we do have to recognize that each school has its own history and is therefore unique. It was thus necessary to use in-house informants to foster contacts and assist in discerning what was or was not important from the indigenous point of view.

12 Among the monographs on individual schools, which vary in quality, we can cite (in chronological order): T.-B. Bottomore, "La mobilité sociale dans la haute administration française," *Cahiers Internationaux de Sociologie* 13 (1952), pp. 167–78; G. Grunberg, *Les élèves de l'École Polytechnique 1948–1967* (Paris: Centre d'Études de la Vie Politique Française, 1970), 107pp.; J. Marceau, "INSEAD, the Social Origins, Educational Experience and Career Paths of a Young Business Elite," final report for SSRC grant, 1973–5, 118pp.; J.-L. Bodiguel, *L'École nationale d'administration, les anciens élèves de l'ENA* (Paris: Presses de la Fondation Nationale des Sciences Politiques, 1978), 271pp.; M.-C. Kessler, *L'École Nationale d'Administration: la politique de la haute fonction publique*, preface by M. Debré (Paris: Presses de la Fondation Nationale des Sciences Politiques, 1978), 299pp.; T. Shinn, *L'École polytechnique, 1794–1914* (Paris: FNSP, 1980), 263pp.; J. Marceau, *A Family Business? The Making of an International Business Elite* (New York: Columbia University Press, 1989); M. Meuleau, *Histoire d'une grande école, HEC 1881–1981* (Paris: Dunod, 1981); T. Shinn, "Des sciences industrielles aux sciences fondamentales. La mutation de l'École supérieure de physique et de chimie (1882–1970)," *Revue Française de Sociologie* 20 (1981), pp. 167–82; J.-N. Luc and A. Barbé, *Des normaliens, Histoire de l'École normale supérieure de Saint-Cloud* (Paris: FNSP, 1982); J.-F. Kesler, *l'ENA, la société, l'État* (Paris: Berger-Levrault, 1985), 584pp. Certain works on the "elites" or the "ruling class" cover the grandes écoles as a whole, but are not based on specific surveys (cf. E. Suleiman, *Elites in French Society: The Politics of Survival* (Princeton: Princeton University Press, 1978); P. Birnbaum, C. Barucq, M. Bellaiche, and A. Marié, *La classe dirigeante en France. Dissociation, interpénétration, intégration* (Paris: PUF, 1978), esp. ch. 4).

13 The work of Christophe Charle on the history of the dominant class at the end of the nineteenth century falls in with this line of thinking (cf. C. Charle, *Les élites de la République: 1880–1900* (Paris: Fayard, 1987)).

14 Given our firm grasp of nearly all the relevant positions, we were able, by means of a single, yet very powerful indicator – the social origins of students – to construct the space of institutions of higher education and to determine the position occupied in this space by establishments we were unable to survey, such as the École de la Magistrature and the Internat de Médecine.

15 Unions were very important at the ENS during this period, and a great majority of students belonged to either a student union (UNEF) or a teacher's union

(SNES, SGEN), usually both (even when they did not attend the meetings or assemblies) [unions with varied left-wing stances, Tr.]. We can use the example of Ulm, which in 1965–6 included about 160 UNEF members, 100 SNES members, and 95 SGEN members (almost all of whom were also members of the UNEF), out of a population of about 320 students, which comes to about two-thirds of the student body (however, only about 100 students voted in the elections). At Saint-Cloud there were about 180 UNEF members out of about 360 students. At Sèvres, unions were somewhat less important, relatively, than at Ulm: there were 102 UNEF members, 65 SNES members, and 27 SGEN members out of a total of about 230 students.

16 Another possible distorting factor is that the students may have feared that those running the study would see their answers. The anonymity was rather easy to see through (especially using a student's rank at entry). Some wrote on their questionnaires things like, "You say this questionnaire is anonymous. So how is it that you could come up and ask me for it again?" At Ulm-humanities, we observed a very violent protest against the fact that anonymity was not guaranteed. At Ulm-sciences, on the other hand, one student wrote, "It's not true that these are anonymous, but it doesn't matter."

17 There is no question that some of the properties of the population studied are linked to chance events in the administration of the survey. So, for example, at the Agro in Paris, the questionnaires were distributed by nine student council members or *section* heads in May and June of 1966, in other words, after many of the students had already left for the summer. It was thus necessary to resume in October of 1966 and to undertake a new survey at the beginning of 1967 for those students who had entered in October of 1966. Similarly, we found that in most of the agronomy schools, the third-year students, who are often away during the third trimester (the period during which we administer the survey), responded too infrequently to be used in the analysis.

18 We gave our word to the ministry officials who furnished us with the data used in describing the field of the institutions of higher education in the 1960s and the 1980s that we would not specifically name the schools in question.

19 At the Écoles Nationales Supérieures Agronomiques, students whose fathers were farmers or farm owners were asked to indicate the acreage of the land worked.

20 At the same time we undertook a series of studies on those regions of the field of power most directly linked to the field of the grandes écoles: the field of higher public service, the field of large public and private corporations, the university field, the intellectual field, and the religious field. Unless one is satisfied, as are some, with hasty examinations of unreliable sources, such as *Who's Who*, it takes a long time to enter into the specific logic of each universe and to get access to authentic information that, in these upper strata, is not given out to just anybody.

21 The years 1966 and 1967, which encompassed the major portion of our surveys, have a strategic value: in them we witness the final state of the old university (as in the study on professors in higher education) as well as an indication of things to come.

22 Cf. P. Bourdieu, "Cultural Reproduction and Social Reproduction," in R. Brown (ed.), *Knowledge, Education, and Social Change* (London: Tavistock,

1973); "Épreuve scolaire et consécration sociale, les classes préparatoires aux grandes écoles, *Actes de la Recherche en Sciences Sociales* 39 (Sept. 1981), pp. 3–70.

23 In 1969 we developed a program for correcting the sample according to year, discipline, and father's occupational category for the ENSs, and year and father's occupational category for the other schools. But, in addition to the fact that this concern for statistical representativity was not necessary, since we never have concurrent results on all the schools together, mathematical correction sometimes managed to introduce errors more serious than the ones it was supposed to correct, and in any case, it merely *concealed* the distorting factors, through a kind of falsification, without actually eliminating them. Rather than giving ourselves the illusion of perfection by giving in to purely formal manipulations, it seemed preferable to keep a clear mind about the distorting factors (which do not all have the same source in the different institutions), and to purely and simply exclude from our analysis those populations whose response rates fell below a certain threshold. The only exceptions were the Écoles Normales de Saint-Cloud and Fontenay, which were important for our comparison, and where we were able to get a precise picture of the sources of the distorting factors by examining school files. (For the correspondence analysis, we used the data collected in our survey as principal variables, and the data from our study of school files as secondary variables. For both Fontenay and Saint-Cloud, the points that correspond to our data and the points that correspond to theirs are very close.)

24 Cf. in particular D. Merllié, "Une nomenclature et sa mise en oeuvre: les statistiques sur l'origine sociale des étudiants," *Actes de la Recherche en Sciences Sociales* 50 (Nov. 1983), pp. 3–48.

Appendix 4

1 J.-F. Kesler, *L'ENA, la société et l'État,* (Paris: Berger-Levrault, 1985), p. 243.

2 Through their performance on the written section. [Tr.]

3 Note that the columns on the tables refer to progressively more selected groups: for example in table 28 of 100 *candidates* to the ENA between 1952 and 1958 (col. 7), 4.2 percent are sons of higher civil servants [*hauts fonctiónnaires*] (Category A1), 20.4 percent are sons of senior civil servants [*fonctionnaires supérieurs*] (category A2), etc.; then, of 100 qualifying for the oral (col. 2), 7.1 percent are sons of higher civil servants; and so on.

4 The gaps, which are already impressive when we consider the *percentages* of each category in each of the populations under consideration (candidates, candidates qualifying for the oral, and candidates accepted), would be infinitely greater if we could take into account the very unequal sizes of the different categories (or the percentages they represent in the overall population) and compare the *likelihood* of their presence. The top category of civil servants (A) (central administrative directors, prefects, ambassadors, generals, Conseillers d'État, inspectors general of the Inspection des Finances, engineers general in Mines, in Ponts et Chaussées, etc.) is extremely limited (probably less than 5 percent of all civil servants). The B [executant positions], C [clerical], and D [typists] categories of civil servant make up 32.4 percent, 35.1 percent, and 5.8

percent, respectively (cf. "Effectifs des fonctionnaires civils par ministère et par catégorie hiérarchique," *in La fonction publique de l'État en 1984* (Paris: La Documentation Française, 1984), pp. 134–5).

5 Civil servants who have risen in the ranks but remain subordinate to "higher civil servants." [Tr.]

PART IV THE FIELD OF POWER AND ITS
TRANSFORMATIONS

Chapter 1 Forms of Power and their Reproduction

1 From the title of a famous book: R.A. Dahl, *Who Governs? Democracy and Power in an American City* (New Haven: Yale University Press, 1965).

2 The emergence of a field of power goes hand in hand with the emergence of a number of relatively autonomous fields, and thus with a differentiation of the social world (which we must take care not to confuse with a process of stratification, although it does lead to the establishment of social hierarchies). This process has previously been analyzed by Durkheim, who, extending the work of Spencer, for whom the universe goes "from the homogeneous toward the heterogeneous," sets against Bergson's "unitarist vitalism" the evolution that leads from the "primitive state of nondivision" in which the "diverse functions" are already present but "in a state of confusion" (religious life, for example, combining rites, morality, law, art, and even the beginnings of a science) to the "progressive separation of all these diverse yet primitively blended functions": "secular and scientific thought became separated from mythical and religious thought; art became separated from worship; morality and the law became separated from rites" (cf. in particular, E. Durkheim, *Pragmatism and Sociology*, trans. J. C. Whitehouse (New York: Cambridge University Press, 1983). Durkheim sees in this confusion of different forms of activity an obstacle to the full realization of any one of them: "Primitively, all forms of activity, all functions are assembled together, as each other's prisoners: they are obstacles to each other; each prevents the other from completely realizing its nature." If Weber hardly notes an advance away from primitive lack of differentiation, he does show, at least for the economy, that the appearance of separate domains is accompanied by the institution of a specific legality, manifested by a constitutive *as such* (the economy as such, etc.).

3 According to the INSEE, which uses a broad definition of the category, artists are very similar to mid-level managers in terms of both income and schooling; but it is clear that for artists, cultural capital is not measured solely in terms of academic credentials. We learn furthermore that, as we have noted elsewhere, a very high percentage of artists are unmarried (21 percent of the men and 36 percent of the women) and that they have a particularly high rate of illegitimate children (two-thirds of whom are recognized by their fathers). All signs of the lasting nature of the artist lifestyle (*Données Sociales* (1984), p. 16). [The Left Bank and Right Bank, the areas of Paris south and north of the Seine River, have taken on metaphorical meanings in political and social terms, Tr.]

4 Cf. in particular, F. Bluche, *Les magistrats du parlement de Paris au XVIIIe siè-*

cle (1715–1771) (Paris: Belles Lettres, 1960), pp. 284–9, 296. All observers, from the writers of the sixteenth century (such as Claude de Seyssel in *The Monarchy of France*, trans. J. H. Hexter (New Haven: Yale University Press, 1981) to present-day historians, have stressed the ambiguous role of the *noblesse de robe*, especially in the political realm (cf. in particular, R. Mousnier, *La vénalité des offices sous Henri IV et Louis XIII* (Rouen: Maugard, n.d.), p. 53 and especially pp. 83–9, and also Denis Richet, *La France moderne: l'esprit des institutions* (Paris: Flammarion, 1973), p. 102; B. Porchnev, *Les soulèvements populaires en France de 1623 à 1648* (Paris: Sevpen, 1963); finally and above all, J. H. M. Salmon, "Venal Office and Popular Sedition in Seventeenth-Century France: A Review of a Controversy," *Past and Present* 37 (July 1967), pp. 21–43, which includes a summary of the arguments that arose over this matter, principally between Mousnier and Porchnev). For a discussion of the analogous effects that result from the propensity of the dominated in relatively autonomous fields (lower-ranked clergy in the church, lecturers in the university, etc.) to universalize their internal struggles by identifying them with the struggles of the dominated in general, very often by resorting to an extended and approximate usage of the buzzwords of the day – "democratization," for example – see P. Bourdieu, *Homo Academicus* (1984), trans. P. Collier (Cambridge: Polity Press, 1988), pp. 177–9.

5   On the social functions of the celibacy of the younger sons in the Béarnaise tradition, see P. Bourdieu, "Marriage Strategies as Strategies of Social Reproduction" (1972), in R. Forster and P. Ranum (eds), *Family and Society: Selections from the Annales* (Baltimore: Johns Hopkins University Press, 1976). On the functions of the celibacy of priests during the *ancien régime*, see F. Y. Besnard, *Souvenirs d'un nonagénaire* (Paris, 1880), vol. 1, pp. 1–2, cited in E. G. Barber, *The Bourgeoisie in Eighteenth Century France* (Princeton: Princeton University Press, 1967), p. 126.

6   Similar observations have been made in the United States, where the increase in overall schooling related to heightened academic selection (which helps to maintain the social homogeneity of each institution and each educational level) tends to compensate for the greater freedom young people enjoy in choosing a mate (cf. B. K. Eckland, "New Mating Boundaries in Education," *Social Biology* 17: 4 (Dec. 1970), pp. 269–77).

7   A secondary analysis of a set of polls has shown that the most economically and culturally privileged categories systematically proved to be more "liberal" in questions of morality, principally familial and sexual morality, than all the other categories, while remaining more conservative politically (on the issue of the right to strike, for example).

8   Cf. in particular, G. S. Becker, *Human Capital* (New York: Columbia University Press, 1964).

9   Ibid., pp. 63–6.

10   Ibid., p. 121.

11   Ibid., p. 155.

12   If I must repeat these criticisms, which were formulated a long time ago (cf. P. Bourdieu, "Avenir de classe et causalité du probable," *Revue Française de Sociologie* 15 (Jan.–Mar. 1974), pp. 3–42), it is because certain adepts at *"fast reading"* insist upon likening my analyses to those of the economists and socio-

logists who, along the lines of Becker, refuse to entertain the notion of any other principle of practice than that of *self-interested calculation*, and who, with the help of a few "philosophers," are putting the old ghost of *homo economicus* back on today's stage.

13 This is the principle underlying social phenomena of a very different scale and nature, such as the reconversion of a landed aristocracy into a government bureaucracy, or, at the other extreme, the reconversion of part or all of one scientific discipline into another, or of one literary or artistic genre into another (in this case, the gap between objective truth and subjective truth is at its widest, as it must be, since reconversion can only succeed, that is, produce its symbolic effect, if it is experienced and perceived as a conversion).

14 Nearly everything that has been written about farming families could be repeated here in reference to industrial families (cf. Bourdieu, "Marriage Strategies as Strategies of Social Reproduction").

15 Joseph Callies, initially engineer at Papeteries Aussédat, goes on to become chief executive of the Compagnie des Machines Bull and director of Papeteries Aussédat-Rey.

16 Cf. P. Michelin, in A. Harris and A. de Sédouy, *Les patrons* (Paris: Seuil, 1977), pp. 245–50.

17 For a discussion of this "bourgeois morality" and the role of women in its perpetuation, see J.-L. Dansette, *Quelques familles du patronat textile de Lille-Armentières, 1789–1914* (Lille: E. Raoust, 1954), passim.

18 Private tutorship is spontaneously brought up by two of the *patrons* interviewed by André Harris and Alain de Sédouy – Ferdinand Béghin and François Ceyrac. In the words of the latter: "My father's family had a home tutor and my grandfather's thirteen children were all taught by her before going on to Sacré-Coeur or to a Jesuit school. My mother considered it quite naturally indecent for her children to go to primary school! I had the same teacher at home until I went into the *troisième* at the Jesuit school in Sarlat where my father and grandfather had gone before me" (F. Ceyrac, in Harris and de Sédouy, *Les patrons*, p. 47).

19 The École Centrale, which until 1866 took in young people from "comfortable backgrounds" (80 percent), principally industry, with no concern for selection, and prepared them – through an education in which the abstract sciences were given no more than 15 percent of total class time, compared to 37 percent at the École Polytechnique – for careers in industry (40 percent of the student body between 1829 and 1885), the railroad (27 percent), and public works (9 percent), or for positions as consulting engineers (16 percent) or teachers (4 percent) (M. Lévy-Leboyer, "Le patronat français a-t-il été malthusien?" *Le Mouvement Social* 88 (July–Sept. 1974), pp. 1–49), continued to recruit mainly within the business bourgeoisie even after the institution of an entrance *concours*. For example, between 1900 and 1925, 77.9 percent of the students were from "comfortable backgrounds" (the independently wealthy, business owners, industrialists, merchants, the professions), compared to 45.4 percent at the École Polytechnique in 1925.

20 The *cluster* phenomena fostered by cooptation among the graduates of any one school, which mean that the succession struggles involving a particular chief executive position often mobilize the entire set of executives from different aca-

demic backgrounds, who take a direct interest in the success of one of their own, can be observed more or less everywhere. So, for example, at Saint-Gobain-Pont-à-Mousson, where the chief executive in 1972 was Roger Martin, *polytechnicien* and engineer in the Corps des Mines, we find among the 16 directors that same year five *polytechniciens* (three of whom entered the Corps des Mines upon graduation) and two graduates of the École Normale Supérieure d'Ulm (one of whom had also gone to the ENA). In contrast, at Boussois-Souchon-Neuvesel, whose chief executive, Antoine Riboud, willingly boasts that he was last in his class at the École Supérieure de Commerce de Paris, of the 16 directors, we find only one *polytechnicien* and no École Normale Supérieure or École Nationale d'Administration graduates. At the Kodak-Pathé corporation, whose chief executive, Paul Vuillaume, is an HEC graduate, five of the nine directors graduated from HEC as well, and the management team includes not a single graduate of Polytechnique, the ENA, or the ENS. Here again, we could give example after example.

21 See further, J. Saglio, "Qui sont les patrons?" *Économie et Humanisme* 236 (July–August 1977), pp. 6–11.

22 Our own survey confirms this hypothesis: the rate of chief executives with degrees in higher education rises sharply when we go from family-controlled companies to technocratic or nationalized companies.

23 A reconversion that is all the more difficult because it implies a conversion of the entire traditional view of the business, particularly faith in on-the-job training and the disdain for higher education that, in more than one case, makes it unthinkable. "The textile families of the North were very prolific and had maintained the tradition, developed during the nineteenth century, of welcoming sons and sons-in-law into the business. This attitude, which made sense in times of expansion when management positions were in increasing supply, with the creation of new establishments, became very dangerous when it was necessary to reduce the number of units of production" (M. Battiau, "Les industries textiles de la région Nord-Pas-de-Calais," vol. 2, Ph.D. diss., Lille, 1976, p. 417). Further on, the same author describes the paralyzing effect that stockholders, often quite numerous, had on company management, stockholders who were sometimes made partners to management in order to avoid conflict: "We found ten, perhaps 15 or more cousins who were partners; each branch of one of the families became the guardian of a particular area, we might even say fiefdom. They easily ended up with a glut of managers" (p. 418).

24 J. A. Kosciusko-Morizet, *La mafia polytechnicienne*, op. cit., p. 99.

25 Ibid., p. 125.

26 For a discussion of statistics and the axiom *de omni et nullo*, see G. Bachelard, *The New Scientific Spirit* (1934), trans. A. Goldhammer (Boston: Beacon Press, 1984).

27 The anonymous *concours*, central to the ideology of equal opportunity that has become one of the foundations of bourgeois legitimacy, is contrasted to hereditary transfer, to recruitment on the basis of connections, to nepotism, and to all mechanisms of cooptation founded on acquaintances, just as the free choice (arising through chance meetings at the university and at the mercy of the affinity of habitus) of a spouse endowed with socially matched characteristics by the social homogeneity of groups carved out through the logic of "vocations" and selection is contrasted to arranged marriages.

28   *De robe* and *robins* refer to the division of the nobility marked by its robes, i.e. the legal professions. [Tr.]

29   Cf. A. Hamon, *Les maîtres de la France* (Paris; Ed. Sociales Internationales, 1936–8), vol. 1, pp. 46–7. [Maître des Requêtes is a middle rank, between Auditeur and Conseiller d'État, Tr.]

30   Cf. ibid., vol. 3, p. 152.

31   Ibid., p. 109 (on the Clamagerans, vol. 1, p. 78, and on Ernest Mercier, pp. 100–1).

32   H. Claude, *Le pouvoir et l'argent* (Paris: Ed. Sociales, 1965), pp. 22–3.

33   Cf. R. Anderson, "Secondary Education in Mid Nineteenth-Century France: Some Social Aspects," *Past and Present* (1971), pp. 121–46.

34   "The Collège Gerson was symbiotically linked to the Lycée Janson de Sailly. This arrangement pleased Catholic families, who were thus assured of a religious environment at the collège and a high quality education at the lycée, (. . .). You got a good education at Gerson-Janson. Among the classmates I can remember, Robert Gérard, Ennemond Bizot, and Georges de Montalivet went to X, Henri Beau, Christian de Jumilhac, and Henri de Gouvion-Saint-Cyr went to Centrale, René Bachelier entered Eaux et Forêts, Henri Blanche entered Navale, Jacques Georges-Picot and Jacques Lagrenée entered the Inspection des Finances, Jean Delorme went into Mines, René de Kainlis went into chemistry, and Philippe Renaudin chose the Conseil d'État" (Duc de Brissac, *En d'autres temps, 1900–1939* (Paris: Grasset, 1972), pp. 140, 146–7).

35   The hierarchy of secondary schools, with first place going to the top bourgeois lycées (Janson, Condorcet), followed by the top lycées of the Latin Quarter, then the other Paris lycées, and finally the provincial lycées, corresponds *grosso modo* to a series of hierarchized channels open to populations that are themselves socially hierarchized.

36   C. S. Wilson and T. Lupton ("The Social Background and Connections of Top Decision-Makers," in K.W. Rothschild (ed.), *Power in Economics* (London: Penguin, 1971), pp. 220–48) register surprise at the fact that blood relations should have remained very important in spite of the change in corporate structure; what they are missing is that this restructuring is precisely what makes the maintenance of personal relations so vital.

37   As with highly diversified investment portfolios, capital held in different forms by different yet interdependent persons gives them advantages regardless of all changes made to the rules of the game. This, as historians have shown many times over, is probably what explains how wealthy families can come through revolutions and changes of regime unscathed.

38   R. Debré, *L'honneur de vivre* (Paris: Hermann et Stock, 1974), p. 454.

39   H. Le Bras, "Parents, grands-parents, bisaïeux," *Population* 28:(1) (Jan.–Feb. 1973), pp. 9–37.

40   This austerity, part grandeur, was expressly sought by the architects of the great lycées built at the end of the nineteenth century, such as the Lycée Montaigne, the Lycée Victor-Hugo, and the Lycée Lakanal, all built between 1882 and 1886, about which Françoise Boudon writes: "The government wanted to build a lycée that would be a model both in its general layout and its amenities (. . .). The plans were very important. The school was to house 700 boarders, and they decided to set up outside Paris in a nine-hectare park filled with magnificent

trees (. . .). These little decorative details are not enough to dispel the austerity the lycée buildings exude. This austerity was intended by the architect, and was to be offset by comfortable interiors. In the rationalist spirit of someone like Baudot, combining a grand and beautiful simplicity in architectural design with a truly refined interior is the very aim of modern architecture, which rejects the superfluous in its overarching concern for human well-being" (F. Boudon, "Recherche sur la pensée et l'oeuvre d'Anatole de Baudot, 1834–1915," *Architecture, Mouvement et Continuité* (Mar. 1973); the reader might also refer to Paul Chemetov, *Architectures, Paris*, 1848–1914 (Paris: Secretariat d'État à la Culture, 1977), especially pp. 55–6 on the Collège Sainte-Barbe, p. 62 on the Lycée Montaigne and its winter garden, and p. 55 on the Lycée Lakanal). We will note that the attention that has been given to the question of the (indisputable) functions of surveillance in recent years, following Michel Foucault, out of a somewhat naive interest in the most visible aspects of "repression," has led people, in this area as in many others, to miss much more fundamental, and less visible, aspects of the exercise of symbolic domination (on the function of surveillance, we might, for example, quote the architect of the Lycée Racine: "The entire street level of the building is taken up by the headmistress's apartment. Her office is at P, and from there she can watch the students coming and going on the street side while she keeps an eye on what is going on in both the central courtyard and the classrooms. This room connects to a waiting room and then directly on to a reception room Y. At X, over the loggia, there is a balcony that also lets her see what is going on." P. Gout, "Lycée Racine," in *Encyclopédie d'architecture*, 4th series, no. 22, May 15, 1889).

41 The (15) sessions we were able to observe in the *concours* for candidates already holding public service positions (who are usually from the petty bourgeoisie) are formally identical to those of the first *concours*. However, the committee members (who are not the same in the two *concours*) often display a protective attitude toward the candidates, and the interest they take in them always seems a bit forced, a bit condescending, as if on command. They say things like, "Perhaps you will one day be a higher civil servant," or "you've spoken well," and they pretend to think that their mistakes raise interesting questions. They ask questions of a more scholastic nature, closer to the kind one might find in a poll (for example: "You work for the internal revenue service. Do you think that compulsion plays a role in the organization you work for in its relations with the taxpayers? Do you think this is a good thing, or do you think one could set up a tax bureau as Spinoza would, in other words, giving taxpayers a sense of freedom?" And their answers, always markedly different from the somewhat nonchalant ease with which the "virtuosos" of the first *concours* reply, express above all their goodwill and their concern for answering well: "I think that greater taxpayer participation, better organization, particularly in the minds of the administration, would do wonders to make many things go much more smoothly. I especially think that they could do more toward helping taxpayers understand what lies at the basis of the tax system . . .; without taxes, I don't think there could be a state."

42 The part of the examination called the "conversation" is one of the major aspects of the oral portion of the ENA *concours*. Following the candidate's ten-minute oral presentation on a particular passage, one of the members of the

committee engages him or her in conversation. After another ten minutes or so, the other committee members (who generally number about three or four) may also join in.

43 Humor, the manifestation *par excellence* of "keeping one's distance from one's role," undoubtedly the bourgeois disposition *par excellence*, is one of the first things on an examining committee's list of expectations.

Chapter 2   Establishment Schools and Power over the Economy

This chapter was coauthored by Monique de Saint Martin.

1 See appendix 1 on p. 340 for a description of the survey and its analysis (construction of sample, indicators, coding, sources, etc.), as well as a detailed description of our results.

2 We will refer to state heads or state bosses to designate chief executives who, even when they are not in public service, are closely tied to the state through their education, their careers, and above all their position, which gives them the opportunity, at least for the most powerful among them, to influence government policy in favour of the interests they represent.

3 The majority of orders placed by the government and by state-held companies are concentrated in a small number of sectors (electric and electronic construction, naval and aeronautical construction, oil and natural gas production, mechanical construction) and in large companies. Businesses with 2,000 employees or more, whose sales in 1974 represented 49 percent of total industry sales, were awarded 68 percent of government contracts that same year (to which should be added, as the authors of the study suggest, the orders filled by subsidiaries with fewer than 2,000 employees). Government contracts are, moreover, very regular, at least for the largest companies, the regularity in the choice of suppliers being less steady for businesses with fewer than 2,000 employees (cf. E. Mathieu and M. Suberchicot, "Marchés publics et structures industrielles," *Économie et Statistique* (Jan. 1978), pp. 43–54).

4 Everything leads us to believe that we would find in the characteristics of the wives of these men the oppositions that structure the entire field. Thus, for example, according to a study done in 1967 on 159 chief executives of the top 500 companies, more than half (57.3 percent) of the chief executives of the smallest companies, which tend to be family businesses, married daughters of chief executives, compared to only 21.2 percent of the heads of the largest companies (cf. D. Hall and H. C. de Bettignies, "L'élite française des dirigeants d'entreprise," *Hommes et Techniques* (Jan. 1969), pp. 21, 23). As far as can be judged from the limited data it was possible to gather on the population in question, it seems that at the level of heirs to large dynasties, the strategies are modified, and wives frequently belong to the *bourgeoisie de robe* – as if the need to strengthen economic ties through marital alliances were becoming less and less critical as the generations pass and the group increases in size.

5 "Private" heads are much less often decorated and receive less prestigious decorations (they are usually merely chevalier of the Légion d'Honneur or recipients of the Ordre du Mérite). Everything leads us to believe that the possession of these official signs of recognition for services rendered is a good indicator of a person's relationship to all things public and official. Thus Dansette remarks

in passing that "the decorations were relatively few among the textile bour-
geoisie, generally far removed from the spheres of public appointments" (J.-L.
Dansette, *Quelques familles du patronat textile de Lille-Armentières, 1789–1914*
(Lille: E. Raoust, 1954), p. 745 n23).

6   Affinities can thus be found related to regional proximity and religious group.
    "If we diagram the pattern, we can see an Alsace-Franche-Comté-Lyons-
    Marseilles axis that shows the assets of the eastern Protestant bourgeoisie (the
    Schlumbergers, the Peugeots) and the capital controlled by the bourgeoisie of
    Lyons (the Gillets) and Marseilles (the Fabres of Chargeurs Réunis) around
    Lazard and Paribas. In these constellations of capital, marital ties, the 'circula-
    tion of women and goods' (. . .) count as much as classic personal and financial
    ties" (P. Allard, M. Beaud, B. Bellon, A.-M. Levy, and S. Liénart, *Dictionnaire
    des groupes industriels et financiers en France* (Paris: Seuil, 1978), p. 18).

7   The chapter dedicated to François Michelin in A. Harris and A. de Sédouy's *Les
    patrons* (Paris: Seuil, 1977), pp. 245–50), which describes their failed attempt to
    get an interview, is entitled "A Discreet Man." Similarly, there is not a single
    portrait of the business bourgeoisie of Lille, Lyons, Bordeaux, or the provinces
    that does not bring out the privacy and discretion that the old bourgeoisie has
    made into a technical and ethical principle – witness the remark of one of the
    Mulliez-Phildars in response to a request for an interview: "Good doesn't need
    talking about; talking never leads to anything good [*Le bien ne fait pas de bruit,
    le bruit ne fait pas de bien*]." Remarks reported by Philippe Labarde, economic
    correspondent for *Le Monde*.

8   On the "interpenetration" of higher civil servants and heads of state banks or
    businesses in the commissions that led to the elaboration of the new housing
    policy in the mid-1970s, see P. Bourdieu et al., "Eléments d'une analyse du
    marché de la maison individuelle," MS, Centre de Sociologie Européenne, Paris
    1988.

9   Top chief executives count for nearly one-third of the directors of chambers of
    commerce and industry, whose influence on economic and political life, as well
    as on teaching and education, is well known (in particular, they control the
    HEC and several other business schools).

10 "Through his duties as vice president of the CNPF, his multiple public spon-
    sorships, his praise of profit and 'free-wheeling liberalism,' his ties to the politi-
    cal world, [Ambroise Roux] is one of the most prominent French business
    leaders" (*Le Monde, Dossiers et Documents* supplement, Nov. 1977). Compare,
    for example, this opinion concerning Henri de Wendel: "that man who has no
    experience in relations with the press" (R. Priouret, *Expansion* (July–
    Aug. 1971).

11 H. Jannic, "Les grandes successions," *Expansion* 52 (May 1972), pp. 94–101.

12 Ibid.

13 A. Jemain and J.-P. Robin, "Pricel: la base des Gillet," *Enterprise*, 2 Nov. 1973,
    pp. 85–6.

14 R. Priouret, "Rhône-Poulenc: l'ampleur de la crise," *L'Express*, 1 Dec. 1975,
    pp. 80–3; cf. also R. Priouret, "Face-à-face avec Renaud Gillet," *Expansion*
    (April 1975), pp. 157–69.

15 Among the privileges granted to "*grands commis*" should be included that of
    the freedom to influence, if not to determine, the choice of their own successor.

We might look in particular at what Pierre Dreyfus, former chief executive of Régie Renault wrote about the circumstances of his own appointment and the appointment of his successor (P. Dreyfus, *La liberté de réussir* (Paris: J.-C. Semoen, 1977), pp. 40–3, 175–6).

16 "Roger Martin, chief executive of Saint-Gobain Pont-à-Mousson, made the point to his classmates once and for all: 'Of everything I was taught, both at the École Polytechnique and the Ecole des Mines, I can solemnly attest that I never used any of it.' What an engineer or a manager really needs to know he will learn on the job and only on the job. And he needn't worry, the company knows it and will help him. If fancy diplomas still have prestige, it is primarily because they are a favorable prediction of those positive character traits considered to be of highest importance. After all, getting into Polytechnique proves that you were capable of enduring two or three years of really hard work" (J. Fontaine, "Les grandes entreprises jugent les grandes ecoles," *L'Expansion* 109 (July–Aug. 1977).

17 It is no accident that length of time in a position becomes increasingly important (along with everything marking it, manners, lifestyle, etc.) as we approach the summit of the social hierarchy. We see that for individuals who have reached the same endpint, in other words, the end of the race, difference is reduced to seniority, that is, to rank based on time of arrival in the position, which survives in the degree of self-assurance and ease with which it is occupied.

18 "The bankers are at the heart of the State. The bourgeoisie has replaced the Faubourg Saint-Germain, and the bankers are the nobility of the bourgeois class" (quoted without source by T. Zeldin, *France 1848–1945*, vol. 1 (Oxford: Clarendon Press, 1973), p. 77).

19 We know that academic credentials – and more than any other, the title of grande école graduate – are worth only what their holder is worth. The "social success" of the graduates of a particular school varies very significantly according to a set of variables that are not independent of the students' original social milieu. We have shown this above for *normaliens*, whose past success, even at the university, remains tied to their social origins. Similarly, as we have seen, the incomes of HEC graduates vary at least as much according to the way they got the position they hold, in other words, in fact, according to their original milieu, as to their class rank at graduation (which is far from independent of social origins).

20 The relatively high number of chief executives from the *bourgeoisie de robe* who are not members of any board, or only serve on the boards of second-ranked companies, is due to the fact that a high proportion head large state-run companies.

21 J.-P. Courthéoux shows clearly for the steel industry how the seniority of the social milieu of the entrepreneur and the seniority of the business go hand in hand. "The Audiffret-Pasquiers, Foulds, Girod de l'Ains, Hélie d'Oissels, Lacazes, Mallets, Périers, de Nervos, Petiets, Roederers, and de Wendels, who distinguished themselves during the first industrial revolution," either managed or were directors in 1960 of "one or several steel industry firms, and not the least among them." He goes on to say that "the prestige resulting from the longstanding nature of their stature and their positions would not have been

enough to consolidate the economic and social power of such dynasties had they not secured influential contacts, primarily by coordinating their industrial functions with their political, public, academic, and honorific functions, or, in other words, by combining their economic and social functions" (cf. J.-P. Courthéoux, "Les pouvoirs économiques et sociaux dans un même secteur industriel: la sidérurgie," *Revue d'Histoire Économique et Sociale* 38:3 (1960), pp. 339–76).

22   This correspondence between positions and the dispositions of their occupants can be observed at the level of social space as a whole no less than within particular fields (religious, university, etc.), with the exceptions – that is, the cases of discordance – themselves being intelligible through reference to the usual concordance, especially in their effects. We know that agents placed in positions where the fit is "off" are often those who come up with innovative, indeed subversive, ideas.

23   So, for example, industrial groups, such as Péchiney-Ugine-Kuhlmann (whose president in 1972 was Pierre Jouven) or the CGE (whose president was Ambroise Roux, *polytechnicien* and engineer in Ponts et Chaussées, with business connections originating in his family – his father served on corporate boards and was president of the Compagnie Générale Accidents; his grandfather was a physician), indeed have "objectives that are more financial than industrial." "The CGE was founded by financiers, not technicians. The technical aspect of the company has always been handled with profit in mind" (A. Roux, interview in *Entreprise*, 1967).

24   This quote, like the following, is taken from an article that would merit full quotation. It is one of those hagiographic texts (grandes écoles alumni "golden books" such as Peyrefitte's *Rue d'Ulm*, literary interviews, etc.) in which the innocence of the celebrants combines with the conceit of the celebrated to clearly reveal the most objective and most intimate truth, which is hotly protested whenever it is revealed by scientific analysis (cf. R. Tendron, "Establishment: les intouchables," *Le Nouvel Économiste* 102, 17 Oct. 1977, pp. 66–72).

25   Jacques de Fouchier, president of the Banque de Paris et des Pays-Bas, François de Flers, chief executive of the Banque de l'Indochine et de Suez, Pierre Champin, chief executive of the Denain Nord-Est-Longwy corporation, Ambroise Roux, chief executive of the CGE, Francis Fabre, chief executive Chargeurs Réunies, Tristan Vieljeux, chief executive of the Société Navale Chargeurs-Delmas-Vieljeux, are well at the top of the second axis in figure 17, p. 302).

26   Unlike the chief executives of most commercial firms, Jean Vignéras, president of Au Printemps corporation, is located in the upper portion of the second axis. [*Grandes surfaces* are large, modern, discount department stores, Tr.]

27   The rare chief executives who do not have the Légion d'Honneur (22.5 percent) are found in the least noble activities (commerce, beverages) at the head of second-ranked subsidiaries of foreign companies or companies under the direct control of an important group.

28   E. Rapoport, in R. R. Grincker, *Toward a Unified Theory of Human Behavior* (New York: Basic Books, 1956).

29   That is, *grosso modo*, the two upper quadrants of the space defined by correspondence analysis (the same thing can be said for the boundary of the groups defined by their proximity to the two poles of the field, as we have seen).

30 Statistics being inscribed in the very functioning of the social world, statistical analysis should not limit itself solely to the technical realm. Failing to grasp the social implications of statistics and the statistical implications of social reality – a further example would be the debate over objective probabilities and subjective probabilities – carries the risk of engaging in sociology without knowing it, producing bad sociology every time.

31 Among these "killjoys" we might cite the case of Lucien Pfeiffer, chief executive of Prétabail since 1965. Having broken into the world of banking through the leasing business, this son of a small businessman and graduate of HEC, full of "left-wing" ideas (he was editor of *La Vie Catholique Illustrée* from 1959 to 1961) and member of the Entreprise et Progrès association and the center for young corporate managers, ran counter to all establishment conventions (cf. *Expansion* (Jan. 1976), p. 36 and J.-P. Roulleau, *Les champions de l'expansion, une nouvelle race de dirigeants* (Paris: Cercle du Livre Économique, 1969).

32 It should be pointed out that most of the members of the establishment (located at the top of the second axis) neglect to mention their club membership in *Who's Who*, no doubt intending to show by this that they are above such forms of association. To wit: "I'm not at all conventional, I'm not the least bit snobbish; I don't give a shit about those things, they can all go to . . . If I'm president of the Polo de Bagatelle club, it's out of tradition, duty! (. . .) My wife never sets foot in the place; when I say 'you have to come because they're giving an award in memory of my father,' she says, 'you can take one of your daughters, but leave me home, that kind of thing just bores me to death'" (interview with Elie de Rothschild, president of Polo de Bagatelle). ["Siècle," or "Century," dinners are attended by those who will "make their mark on the century," Tr.]

33 A. Duffau, "Le palmarès des fusions!" *Expansion* (Mar. 1974). "In reference to Raymond Sachot [tradesman's son, law graduate, Harvard graduate], who appeared for a time like the great federator of the food industry, one banker is quoted as saying: 'He tried to go *too fast* and didn't always get along with his bankers. Paying for his acquisitions in shares, he'd then go about issuing new classes of stock. But he changed bankers too often. As soon as one parcel of shares was invested, he'd piss out a hundred others.' This is why Raymond Sachot's success was so short-lived, and why he had to merge his group with James Goldsmith's nebulous multinational" (ibid.; emphasis added).

34 "A top president found himself *persona non grata* at the table of the governor of the Banque de France for two years because he had gotten a divorce under delicate circumstances. Having mistresses, and even appearing in public with them, is not frowned upon, but 'one should never go so far as to create a scandal'" (R. Tendron, "Establishment: les intouchables").

35 Both length of lineage and length of standing of the individual himself; the precocity of the move from the public service to the private sector, which expresses that familiarity with the business world that favors the propensity toward and the likelihood of making the change, greatly contributes to defining membership in the establishment.

36 The third factor opposes a set of chief executives who owe their social success to their academic success (where *polytechniciens* dominate) to a set of chief executives who have either gone to Sciences-po (the case for the Baron Elie de Rothschild, chief executive of the PLM company, Wilfrid Baumgartner, chief

executive of Rhône-Poulenc in 1972, and Christian de Waldner, chief executive of IBM, son of a member of several corporate boards) or have no advanced diploma (such as Edouard de Cazalet, chief executive of the Société Marseillaise de Crédit, son of a banker, graduate of Janson, Jacques Corbière, chief executive of Gervais-Danone in 1972, son of an industrialist and great-grandson of Charles Gervais, "the creator of the dairy industry in France," graduate of the École Fénelon and the Lycée Condorcet who did not go beyond the baccalauréat, and Ferdinand Béghin, chief executive of Béghin-Say, son of a sugar manufacturer and graduate of the Lycée Janson.)

37   It should be noted that the chief executives who went to Sciences-po and have a *de* in their name appear more often in dictionaries of nobility than those who followed other channels (cf. especially Dugast Rouilly (ed.), *Le nobiliaire de France (actuel)* (2 vols, Nantes, 1972), or E. de Sereville and F. de Saint-Simon, *Dictionnaire de la noblesse française* (Paris: La Société Française du XXe Siécle, 1975).

38   Chief executives who graduated from business schools (often from families who have been in business for several generations) or engineering schools such as Centrale or Mines very often join clubs (especially the Automobile Club) and practice the most worldly sports, golf and yachting, for example.

39   We know that Sciences-po students have a much lower academic success rate (measured by *mentions* on the baccalauréat or nominations to the Concours Général) than students in the preparatory classes for the grandes écoles (both *khagñes* and *taupes*) and, *a fortiori*, at Ulm and Polytechnique.

40   People always speak of Ambroise Roux as having "superior intelligence." Identifying intelligence with success in *concours*, people are apt to remember rank in these competitions. So, for example, they never fail to point out that Jacques de Fouchier was the top candidate accepted into the Inspection des Finances. Following their convention in Marseilles in October of 1972, CNPF executives were thrilled, as Bernard Brizay writes, "to see this confession published in the PSU [Parti Socialiste Unifié; left of socialist party, Tr.] newspaper, *Tribune Socialiste*: '*That* capitalism is intelligent' " (cf. B. Brizay, *Le patronat, historire, structure, stratégie du CNPF* (Paris: Seuil, 1975), p. 192).

41   The opposition between family businesses and large modern companies open to social progress is quite naturally inscribed in the long series of *commonplaces* produced in the *neutral places* created by the new economico-bureaucratic "elite's" vision of the world: past (obsolete)/future, closed/open, local/national, traditional/modern, etc. (an analysis of the structure and functions of this reconverted conservatism can be found in P. Bourdieu and L. Boltanski, "La science royale et le fatalisme du probable," *Actes de la Recherche en Sciences Sociales*, no. 2–3 (June 1976), pp. 39–55).

42   Many academic debates on trends in the social world or in this or that aspect of it oppose thoroughly unresolvable theses (unresolvable, at least, given the means implemented) that are so many prophesies claiming to be self-verifiable, that is, so many acts of symbolic power that aim to usher in the future best suited to the interests of the prophet, by foretelling it, and to magically condemn the opposing possibility, through a sort of malediction.

43   The position held within the space of power by Benno Vallières, chief executive of the Société des Avions Marcel Dassault/Breguet Aviation, is easily accounted

for when it is realized that, like the chief executives of subsidiaries of large foreign companies, he is confined to management tasks, as can be clearly seen in what the true top man, Marcel Dassault, says of him: "M. Vallières has proved to be a first-rate industrialist and an excellent businessman, demonstrating all the necessary technical qualities. He's the one who discusses markets with the government and the suppliers; he's the one who sets salaries" (cf. H. Jannic, "Les grandes successions," *Expansion* 52 (May 1972), pp. 94–101).

44 The question of elementary units is a particular case of the very general question of the existence of groups, the relationship between the nominal and the real, between the official and the unofficial, and between institutionalized and juridically guaranteed boundaries and real limits. As in the case of kinship relations, the truth in this case lies neither in the official definition, which may have several functions (tradition, brand image, etc.), nor in the real definition – among other reasons because, in the very case in which the "fusion" is as complete as possible, each of the former units retains an autonomy that stems from its unique history and tradition.

45 M. Dollé, Editorial, *Économie et Statistique* 87 (Mar. 1977), pp. 3–8.

46 "Le dossier des nationalisations," *Le Monde, Dossiers et Documents* (Nov. 1977).

47 P. Allard, M. Beaud, B. Bellon, A.-M. Lévy, and S. Lienart, *Dictionnaire des groupes industriels et financiers en France* (Paris: Seuil, 1978).

48 Ibid.

49 The same observations could be made for any historical comparison treating agents defined by the positions they occupy within a field as populations (bishops, higher civil servants, artists, writers, etc.).

50 Cf. P. Beaudeux, "Le prix des cadres," *Expansion* (June 1977), pp. 125–56.

51 D. Toscan du Plantier, in Harris and de Sédouy, *Les patrons*, p. 347.

52 See in particular J. Bouvier, "Capital bancaire, capital industriel et capital financier dans la croissance française au XIXe siécle," *La Pensée* 178 (Dec. 1974), pp. 3–17.

53 Although the data are lacking for directly establishing the relationship between positions in the field and political stances, particularly the strategies used in the management of social conflict, the results of a survey carried out by *Expansion* (April 1975, pp. 78–97) on the social characteristics of 50 companies reveal, at the level of "social policy," the same fundamental opposition that we found in the corporate field between large public companies, more open to trade unionism, and private companies, as well as a secondary opposition between a modernist neopaternalism, often practiced by Sciences-po and business school graduates, and a starker paternalism, more generally associated with *polytechniciens* (see appendix 2, p. 350).

54 Only 37 percent of companies with between 20 and 49 employees do any exporting, compared to 60 percent of those with between 100 and 199 employees, 80 percent of those with between 500 and 4,999 employees, and more than 90 percent of those with at least 10,000 employees (R. Brocard and J.-M. Gandois, "Grandes entreprises et PME," *Économie et Statistique* 96 (Jan. 1978), pp. 25–41).

55 Endowed with a set of skills of a new type, such as familiarity with foreign languages and a practical knowledge of the corporate field and marketing and

advertising techniques, chief executives from schools such as HEC or the Institut Européen d'Administration des Affaires (INSEAD) are predisposed to seek positions in multinational corporations. In many ways, they contrast with those who went to engineering schools, whose interests tend toward production rather than commercialization, and internal management rather than market research.

56 These are the ones journalists are the most apt to name in their honor rolls of the powerful ("the hundred who run the economy").

57 Refer to appendix 3 (p. 356) for a description of a typical day in the life of a VIP.

58 So, for example, Jacques de Fouchier won the Académie Française poetry prize at the age of 16 and, according to Merry Bromberger, was "tormented by his desire to write" (press archives of the Compagnie Bancaire). Similarly, when asked about his secondary loves, Ambroise Roux "doesn't name gardening, golf, hunting, or yachting, he talks about surrealist literature and abstract painting" (J. Baumier, *Les grandes affaires françaises* (Paris: Julliard, 1967), p. 145).

59 Chief executives with origins in the top business bourgeoisie occupy an intermediate position in all respects between those from the *bourgeoisie de robe* and those from the mid-level business bourgeoisie. What distinguishes them from the latter, who, like them, have spent their entire careers in the private sector more often than chief executives from the *bourgeoisie de robe*, is that they are more often Parisian (53 percent versus 32 percent), are somewhat less likely to have gone to private schools and more likely to have gone to Paris lycées, and especially that they have more often been through grands corps and ministerial cabinets before becoming heads of private companies.

60 See note 9 to part III, chapter 1 (p. 414 above). [Tr.]

61 The combination of a lack of inherited social capital and a weak inclination to acquire such capital means that members of the high-level public service with origins in the dominated regions of social space have very little chance of moving into the private sector. If they do manage to switch over, it is only very late, at the end of their careers, at which time they move into quasi-bureaucratic positions. Chief executives who are sons of engineers or managers, being more likely to have gone through the grandes écoles and the grands corps, undoubtedly have their school connections to thank for the fact that they have more often been members of ministerial cabinets and have moved into the private sector at a younger age than chief executives from the middle or lower categories, who are often former engineers from the Génie Maritime [naval corps], Houillères [coal industry], or EDF, rather than the grands corps.

62 While most of the chief executives were born in Paris or a major city, those who went to Sciences-po or a business school are the most likely to have been born in Paris or the surrounding area (conversely, no Sciences-po student was born in a town of fewer than 5,000), whereas the *polytechniciens* tended to come from mid-sized cities, and graduates of other engineering schools were quite likely to have grown up in small communities.

63 An analysis of institutional ties (principally boards of directors) and their different functions can be found in the economic information assembled in appendix 4, p. 360.

64 The censorship effected by the division of labor between economists and socio-

logists has meant that studies done by economists in response to the question raised by Berle and Means's famous study (A. A. Berle and G. C. Means, *The Modern Corporation and Private Property* (New York: Macmillan, 1933), among which we can mention those of Chevalier (J.-M. Chevalier, *La structure financière de l'industrie américaine* (Paris: Cujas, 1970) and Morin (F. Morin, *La structure financière du capitalisme français* (Paris: Calmann-Lévy, 1974), do not take into account the *personal* properties of corporate heads (for example, the ties that bind them to the business milieu through birth or marriage) or all the forms of *social control* (as opposed to economic control) through which the incorporation of *managers* is ensured.

65 On the other side, "family" chief executives, even when their business is small and managed in the traditional style, tend increasingly to keep a portion of their profits for themselves in the form of a salary, as can be seen from the fact that between 1956 and 1970 the percentage of the incomes of industrial and commercial heads derived from salary and pensions went from 12.9 to 31.3 percent (cf. G. Banderier and P. Ghigliazza, "Les revenus des ménages en 1970," INSEE Documents M40, Paris, Dec. 1974, pp. 128–9).

66 J. M. Keynes, "The End of Laisser-Faire" (1926), republished in *Essays in Persuasion* (London: Macmillan, 1931), pp. 314–15.

67 A single example will suffice, as a genuine *concentrate* of the new sociodicy, an example entitling its author to the prize of modern "Pindar of manufacturers," awarded in the past by Marx to Andrew Ure, intrepid laudator of *managers*, "the soul of our industrial system" (K. Marx, *Capital*): "Thus the traditional bourgeoisie, tied to the possession of things, is evolving into a capital-less neobourgeoisie whose base is expanding through the extension of the tertiary industries. In short, inherited property is tending to give way to merited property (insofar as diplomas sanction merit) – but what could be more personal than such property?" (A. Piettre, "La propriété héritée ou méritée?," *Le Monde*, Jan. 1978).

68 Motivated by resentment converted into ethical indignation against "profiteers," "rogues," and "exploiters," the ordinary denunciation of "fatcats," "industrial and financial magnates," and "the top 200 families," one of the favorite themes of the petty bourgeois political tradition, both of the far right and the far left, is apt to fall into what it denounces at the first opportunity, because, blind to its own truth, it remains dominated, at its very foundation, by what it is denouncing. Can we be sure, indeed, that the indignation expressed (sometimes collectively, such as in 1968) in the dominated regions of the field of power against the meritocratic claims of the new economic leaders and against the elitist exaltation of competence owes nothing either to the anger felt by disappointed heirs toward an educational institution unable to recognize them or to the meritocratic indignation of the holders of rare titles convinced that they have not received just recompense for their bourgeoisie certificates?

Chapter 3 Transformations in the Structure of the Field of Power

1 In fact, the professions are less independent than it appears. The profits procured by their cultural capital depend on a state-guaranteed monopoly on the production of producers, thus on control of the educational system, and they

experience crises when there is an increase in the production of diplomas, and hence in the supply of services.

2   In the past, invention required creative abilities rather than formal education, and it was thus a risky business. This was due to the *rudimentary state of science and technology*, which were easier to master. The simplicity of scientific knowledge was matched by *simple equipment*; inventors of modest means could equip their own labs without the assistance of patrons, or with the support of a single individual. Today, as the decrease in the proportion of independent researchers among patent holders shows, invention implies conditions that are now rarely met outside large research organizations.

Appendix 1

1   The chief executives eliminated all belong to the smallest companies (relatively), do not get mentioned in specialized publications, do not appear in biographical yearbooks, and, when approached, refuse to give personal information to the authors of yearbooks or to researchers. The data it was possible to collect indicate that they are more likely to have gone to engineering schools (Centrale, Mines, or second-ranked schools) than to Sciences-po or business schools, and that they have made their entire career in the private sector and would probably be located for the most part in the lower right-hand quadrant of the correspondence analysis diagram.

2   The analysis of the multiple correspondents presented below was carried out using the MULTM program developed by Ludovic Lebart, whose text the reader may consult for a description of the procedures involved (L. Lebart, A. Morineau, and N. Tabard, *Techniques de la description statistique. Méthodes et logiciels pour l'analyse des grands tableaux* (Paris: Dunod, 1977)). We would like to express our sincere thanks to Ludovic Lebart for helping us master the intricacies of his method. For a list of data sources, see the section starting on p. 341.

3   "Corporate heads, like all bourgeois, will only willingly speak with some degree of confidence to those they consider to be equals within their sphere. It is painfully obvious that sociologists do not meet these criteria. Thus the protocol governing interviewing procedures is more strict here than in most other social milieus. The skepticism considered to be good form where the social sciences are concerned is compounded by the fact that the interviewee *is used to enjoying a position of authority and dominance in conversations*, which further restricts the researcher's margin of freedom." (J. Lautman, "Fait social et questions sociologiques: à propos du syndicalisme patronal," *Le Mouvement Social* 61 (Oct 1967), pp. 65–76; emphasis added.)

4   What sociologist would ever be granted the right to photograph Roger Martin and follow him throughout a typical workday (*Expansion*, May 1977), attend even an "exhibition" meeting of the CNPF (cf. A. Harris and A. de Sédouy, *Les patrons* (Paris: Seuil, 1977), pp. 211–14), and interview François Michelin (*Paris-Match*, 3 Feb. 1978), etc.?

5   Cf. *Entreprise*, 31 Nov. 1972, 22 Sept. and 3 Nov. 1962, and, for 1952, J. Houssiaux, *Le pouvoir de monopole* (Paris: Sirey, 1960), pp. 242–7.

6   We might wonder why, for example, after classifying the Shell France corpora-

tion, headed by Léonard Carous, in 10th position, the Shell Chimie corporation, under the direction of the same Léonard Carous, should be in 74th position. Conversely, it is surprising that we should not find the International Harvester corporation or the Richier corporation on the list.

7 Cf. "Comment utiliser un dossier," *Entreprise*, Nov. 1972, p. 5. According to the official definition (the one used by DAFSA [documentation and financial analysis corporation] compilers), "subsidiaries" are those companies whose "parent company" holds 50 percent of their capital. This explains why Cellophane, a subsidiary of Rhône-Poulenc, which in 1972 held more than 50 percent of its capital, is on the list, but not ranked, and why its CEO is not included in the sample. In contrast, Laboratoires Roger Bellon is ranked, even though in 1972, the date of the survey, Rhône-Poulenc held 45.1 percent of its capital (51.8 percent in 1977). In choosing to use this ranking, we are not making any claims about whether or not Laboratoires Roger Bellon was a subsidiary of Rhône-Poulenc in 1972.

8 A very useful list of various sources (public or otherwise) can be found in "Les statistiques d'entreprises, Sources," *Les collections de l'INSEE*, E44 (Mar. 1977). Data on the history of the various firms can be found in J. Boudet, *Le monde des affaires en France de 1830 à nos jours* (Paris: Soc. Ed. de Dictionnaires et Encyclopédies, 1952). Very useful historical notes and data concerning the structure of and connections among 48 groups can be found in P. Allard, M. Beaud, B. Bellon, A.-M. Lévy, and S. Liénart, *Dictionnaire des groupes industriels et financiers en France* (Paris: Seuil, 1978), which was published as the present work was nearing completion; cf. also M. Beaud, "Note sur la connaissance des groupes capitalistes," *Recherches Économiques et Sociales, Notes Critiques et Débats* (July-Oct. 1977), pp. 91–7, and Bertrand Bellon, "Méthodologie de délimitation et de repérage des ensembles financiers," ibid., pp. 99–116.

9 *Expansion* 95 (Apr. 1976), published a similar survey of 50 mid-sized companies the following year.

10 *Nomenclature des entreprises nationales à caractère industriel ou commercial et des sociétés d'économie mixte d'intérêt national* (Paris: Imprimerie Nationale, 1972).

11 For mode of control, we drew from works by F. Morin, *La structure financière du capitalisme français* (Paris: Calmann-Lévy, 1974) and *La banque et les groupes industriels à l'heure des nationalisations* (Paris: Calmann-Lévy, 1977).

12 This all goes to show that it is probably rather risky to try to deduce transformations in the managerial class from a comparative study of *Who's Who* entries at different time periods (cf. P. Birnbaum, C. Barucq, M. Ballaiche and A. Marié, *La classe dirigeante française* (Paris: PUF, 1978); and even more so the change in the rate of professional mobility in its various branches (p. 29) or moves from the public to the private sector (p. 75).

13 We wrote to local authorities to get information on the top-ranking CEOs of 1952 and 1962 whose family backgrounds we did not know.

14 The presence of a *de* in the family name (which we know does not constitute a recognized sign of nobility) was used as an index of a claim to nobility.

15 For a study of management ideology, especially in the nineteenth century, a very complete bibliography can be found in A. Melucci, *Idéologies et pratiques*

patronales pendant l'industrialisation capitaliste: le cas de la France (Paris: EHESS, 1974).

16 The other two Willot brothers are not included in our sample, but obviously occupy very similar positions.

17 Allard et al., *Dictionnaire des groupes industriels et financiers en France*, p. 67.

Appendix 2

1 The analysis is based on the set of responses to the questions *Expansion* journalists posed to the management and union representatives of the top 50 companies in 1975 ("L'examen social. Les 50 plus grandes entreprises françaises révèlent leur bilan social," *Expansion* (Apr. 1975), pp. 78–97). Data were added on mode of control and founding date.

2 A few large industrial groups fall on the public side (Saint-Gobain, Ciments Lafarge, IBM, Lyonnaise des Eaux et Éclairage). Conversely, it is worth noting that along with the other firms in the automotive industry, Régie Renault is located on the side dominated by private companies.

3 Cf. M. Freyssenet, *La division capitaliste du travail* (Paris: Savelli, 1977), esp. pp. 21–2, which gives a list of the major workers' strikes against the most advanced forms of work organization, where we find all the companies located on the side of the negative values of the second factor (Renault, RATP, Peugeot, Houillères, etc.).

4 For example, the Peugeot group as of December 31, 1974 employed 72 percent manual labor, Citroën 77.3 percent in 1975, Dollfus-Mieg 72.3 percent in 1974, compared to 3.2 percent, 2.2 percent, and 4.8 percent management, respectively (in contrast to Roussel-Uclaf, for example, which employed 36 percent workers, but 15 percent managers, as of December 31, 1975). To make the model more accurate, we would need to take into account the proportion of skilled labor per industry branch and per firm, keeping in mind that the definition of "skilled" may vary according to branch or firm (cf. A. Azzouvi, "Caractéristiques d'entreprises, structures d'emploi et de salaires," *Économie et Statistique* 92 (Sept. 1977), pp. 17–28).

5 The least "modernist" firms (in terms of social policy) at the state pole are distinguished from the more "advanced" private companies such as Roussel or L'Oréal by a more "traditional" but in a sense more "real" set of "social goals." The report of the board of directors of the SNCF discusses the "management agreement on the social consequences of modernization" that should provide for "an improvement in the provisions applicable to gatekeepers on level crossings whose position has been downgraded or eliminated through modernization," salaries, the work of the joint commission on the status of community relations, retirement and accident benefits, family loans, lodging, "social activities," including "vacation centers and camps, medical, psychological, or educational consultations, and social workers' projects" (SNCF, general stockholders meeting). The RATP report includes more or less the same headings. At the Banque National de Paris, located at the modernist pole, they stress personnel development, especially information that "enables employees to understand the role they play in the chain of responsibilities that combine to ensure the smooth operation of the Bank," "procedures for dialogue, and work

methods within joint production committees [*comités d'établissement et d'entreprise*, a committee made up of blue-collar workers, clerical workers, and managers who work with the chief executive on management issues, Tr.] (BNP, *Rapports de l'exercice 1974*).

6 For example, in banking, insurance, financial agencies, and electrical and electronic engineering, the rate of those voting in 1976 for representatives of the CFDT [Confédération Française des Travailleurs; workers union Tr.] in the joint production committees was higher than that in all corporate branches taken together. In contrast, in mechanical engineering, shipbuilding, the automotive industry, and aeronautics, we note that with the exception of managers, votes for the CGT [Confédération Générale du Travail; communist workers union, Tr.] are relatively higher than in the other branches (cf. Philippe Saint Jévin, "Les comités d'entreprise, Étude statistique de l'institution et des élections intervenues en 1974," *Revue Française des Affaires Sociales* 4 (Oct.–Dec. 1976), pp. 3–76). It is of course necessary to guard against turning this concomitant relationship between forms of struggle and forms of domination into one of causality, and not simply because there are exceptions (for example, the rate of votes in favor of the CFDT is quite high in the textile industry, where the method of command is rather authoritarian). We would also need to take account of *absenteeism*, which probably constitutes a form of defense, albeit unorganized, individual, and quasi-shameful, and hence left to the categories that have the weakest syndical or political traditions.

7 Euphemization attacks first and foremost the terms of address or reference through which hierarchies are normally delineated. So, for example, at L'Oréal, people no longer use the term "manager" [*directeur*]: in 1976, Jacques Glain is "in charge of [*en charge de*] general management in the cosmetics division," Grégoire Kalopissis is "in charge of general management in Human Resources," etc. (cf. L'Oréal, *Rapport du conseil d'administration*, 1976). It will have been noted that the euphemistic substitute "in charge of" is an Americanism that also has an ennobling effect.

8 François Michelin, who left the CNPF in 1968 to join the UNICER [union of corporate heads and executives] (then under the direction of Aimery d'Oiron), is in the habit of saying, "Authority cannot be shared, it is embodied" (cf. A. Harris and A. de Sédouy, *Les patrons* (Paris: Seuil, 1977), p. 257).

9 This is undoubtedly the true foundation of the alliance, which at first glance appears surprising, between some of the top executives who are very close to the establishment, such as Pierre de Calan, and the heads of small and mid-sized companies (cf. B. Brizay, *Le patronat, histoire, structure, stratégie du CNPF* (Paris: Seuil, 1975), pp. 183–6).

Appendix 3

1 Cf. R. Alexandre and G. Le Querrec, "Une journée avec . . . Roger Martin," *Expansion* (May 1977), pp. 117–21 (Roger Alexandre, reporter, and Guy Le Querrec, photographer, had obtained permission to "observe Roger Martin as he lived, minute by minute").

2 'Pink flamingos in flight.' [Tr.]

3 Foundation for the Quality of Life. [Tr.]

4 A sailing school in Brittany. [Tr.]

Appendix 4

1   Clubs, which unite their members around a practice characteristic of a particular lifestyle (for example, a rare sport like polo) and which select them in terms of predictors of a habitus (the one associated with longstanding membership in the aristocracy or the bourgeoisie, and guaranteed by a person's proper name, all kinds of credentials, godparents, etc.), tend, through a form of institutionalization, to strengthen the stability of personal ties founded on the spontaneous orchestration of habitus.

2   Cf. M. Beaud, P. Danjou, and J. David, *Une multinationale française, Péchiney-Ugine-Kuhlmann* (Paris: Seuil, 1975), p. 86.

3   Ties based on family are far from absent in this region of the universe, which is nevertheless the most technocratic: Richard Baumgartner, Polytechnique graduate, married Anne-Marie-France Mercier, daughter of Ernest Mercier, Polytechnique graduate, president of the Union Électricité, the Compagnie Française des Pétroles, the Société Lyonnaise des Eaux et de l'Éclairage, etc.; Paul Huvelin, Polytechnique graduate, son of Hippolyte Huvelin, wine merchant, married Madeleine Giros, daughter of Alexandre Giros, Polytechnique graduate, president of the Société Générale d'Entreprises (now controlled by the Compagnie Générale d'Électricité) and member of several boards of directors, primarily in the electricity industry; Jean Matheron, Polytechnique graduate, son of Joannès-Claudius Matheron, Mines civil engineer, married Denise Giros, another daughter of Alexandre Giros.

4   All quoted statements by Jacques de Fouchier are taken from R. Priouret, "Face-à-face avec Jacques de Fouchier," *L'Expansion* 44 (Sept. 1971), pp. 143–63.

5   Not counting the fact that, here again, the abstract definition of *thresholds* is entirely meaningless, since the relative size of any shareholding interest is obviously defined in terms of the structure of the distribution of all shares, which defines the structure of the field of power over a particular company. Once again, Jacques de Fouchier sums it up perfectly: "What does it mean to say a small investment, or, on the other hand, a large one? You have to consider the portion of the capital that is in the public domain. Take the Usinor group, for example. We don't even own 4 percent of Denain-Nord-Est-Longwy capital. But the rest is divided up publicly into very small investments, and we consequently find ourselves the largest shareholder outside the group itself."

6   Here is one example of this strictly cultural ascendancy, borrowed from Jacques de Fouchier: "The often difficult transition from a family-owned business to a more open company creates all kinds of problems, problems involving people's feelings, problems involving the interests of different members of the family, legal problems, and fiscal problems, not to mention the ever fundamental problems involved in financing. We are true specialists in these difficulties, which we have resolved dozens and dozens of times. We really have a specific *savoir-faire*, you might even say a set of *recipes developed through experience with this sort of difficulty*." And again: "Thanks to the diversity of their connections, their technical skills, their ability to negotiate and, if I may say so, their diplomatic talent, our teams often manage to find and apply solutions to the most difficult problems."

PART V STATE POWER AND POWER OVER THE STATE

The translation of the second epigraph is by A. J. Krailsheimer, from Blaise Pascal, *Pensées* (London: Penguin, 1966).

1 This is indeed, it would seem to me, the unifying principle behind the outwardly very diverse yet always violent reactions which sociological analyses of the educational institution provoke, and which themselves call for sociological analysis.

2 To get an idea of how republican mythology became an omnipresent reality, involving all school practices, even the most apparently arbitrary, such as building maintenance, physical education, or the organization of cultural activities, at an upper primary institution in a communist-controlled village in the north of France, see Y. Delsaut, "Une photo de classe," *Actes de la Recherche en Sciences Sociales* 75 (Nov. 1988), pp. 83–96.

3 The tricks of social bad faith are unfathomable, and the same people who will protest against the controlled application of the *concept* of nobility to the school's chosen people will accept without hesitation its being invoked as a glorifying metaphor: "You're a *normalien* just like you're a hereditary prince. Nothing shows it on the outside. But everyone can tell, everyone can see it, even though it's polite, and even humane not to show it off (. . .). This quality is consubstantial. You don't become a *normalien*, you're born one, just as people used to be born knights. The *concours* is merely an act of dubbing. The ceremony has its rituals; the vigil of arms is carried out in locations of retreat, placed, as they should be, under the protection of our kings: Saint-Louis, Henri IV, Louis-le-Grand. The guardians of the Holy Grail, who for this occasion take the name of the examining committee, recognize their young peers and call them to their side" *Rue d'Ulm, Chroniques de la vie normalienne* (2nd edn, Paris: Flammarion, 1963) (G. Pompidou, in A. Peyrefitte, pp. 14–15). At HEC, and at other schools for *cadres*, the same philosophy was expressed in a less roundabout fashion: "Every year from 1938 to 1957, Maxime Perrin peppered his welcome speech to the new students with this leitmotif that graduates remember still: 'You're a race of leaders!'" (M. Nouschi, *Histoire et pouvoir d'une grande école, HEC* (Paris: Robert Laffont, 1988) p. 41).

4 By constructing the class of the processes of nobility production in this way, we make it possible to enrich the empirical analysis of this or that particular case (the nobility of the Middle Ages or today's academic nobility) with all the insights gained in analyzing all the others, that is, both constants (such as the effect of ordination examined by Marc Bloch) and specific differences.

5 D. Bien, "Les offices, les corps et le crédit d'État: l'utilisation des privilèges sous l'Ancien Régime," *Annales ESC*, no. 2 (Mar.–Apr. 1988), pp. 379–404, esp. p. 381.

6 To the extent that the large-scale historical comparisons underlying the great evolutionary laws are actually meaningful, we may grant that, as time passes, more and more scientific or technical skills are needed in order to reach the same level of social competence, and that the success of all forms of the direct transfer of (economic or symbolic) capital within a lineage increasingly tends to

take second place to the acquisition of academic capital, thus of a certain technical competence. But, before coming to any conclusion about the meaning and the value of this evolution and speaking, for example, of rationalization or democratization, we must at least take into account the fact that academic acquisition itself is highly dependent on another form of hereditary transfer, that of cultural capital.

7   Although, as Georges Duby has shown, the method of succession in force among the medieval nobility also created a restless and unstable category of *juvenes*, descendants of noble families who found themselves more or less definitively excluded from inheritance and marriage.

8   On the specific crisis of the academic mode of reproduction and the particular form it took in 1968, see P. Bourdieu, *Homo Academicus* (1984), trans. P. Collier (Cambridge: Polity Press, 1988) pp. 159–93.

9   M. Weber, *Economy and Society* (1921–2) vol. 2 (New York: Bedminster Press, 1968) p. 975.

10   Ibid., p. 999.

11   Ibid., p. 1,000.

12   Bien, "Les offices, les corps et le crédit d'État."

13   L. Stone, "The Educational Revolution in England 1560–1640," *Past and Present* 28 (1964), pp. 41–80; F. K. Ringer, "Problems in the History of Higher Education: A Review Article," *Comparative Studies in Society and History* 19:2 (Apr. 1977), pp. 239–55; R. L. Kagan, *Students and Society in Early Modern Spain* (Baltimore: Johns Hopkins University Press, 1974).

14   R. Chartier, M. M. Compère, and D. Julia, *L'éducation en France du XVIe au XVIIIe siècle* (Paris: Sedes, 1976), p. 168–9.

15   D. Julia (ed.), *L'enseignement, 1760–1815, Atlas de la Révolution française* (Paris: EHESS, 1988).

16   Chartier et al., *L'éducation en France*, p. 169; W. Frijhoff and D. Julia, "Les grands pensionnats de l'Ancien Régime à la Restauration," *Annales Historiques de la Révolution Française* 243 (Jan.-Mar. 1981), pp. 153–98; W. Frijhoff and D. Julia, "L'éducation des riches. Deux pensionnats: Belley et Grenoble," *Cahiers d'Histoire* 21 (1976), pp. 105–21.

17   F. Autrand, *Naissance d'un grand corps de l'État, les gens du Parlement de Paris* (Paris: Publications de la Sorbonne, 1981).

18   Françoise Autrand shows that from the end of the fourteenth century on, the ideal of service to the state is expressed in the fact that in their wills, the great servants of the crown "found" masses for the king (ibid., pp. 128–30).

19   This is known from different sources (especially Régine Petit's thesis on "the personal libraries of the Parisian parliamentarians in the eighteenth century"– analyzed at length by F. Bluche, *Les magistrats du parlement de Paris au XVIIIe siècle (1715–1771)* (Paris: Belles Lettres, 1960) pp. 290–6); it is also known that "as early as the seventeenth century, parliamentarians were first-rate enlightened collectors" (ibid., p. 327) and the backbone of literary society.

20   Chartier et al., *L'éducation en France*, p. 250.

21   Ibid., pp. 208–14, and also M. M. Compère, *Du collège au lycée (1500–1850)* (Paris: Gallimard, 1985), pp. 133–7. The plans for "national" education were in fact geared toward the construction of a hierarchized "academic space," as the authors note. The ideology of the "gift" is already invoked to justify the repro-

duction of privileges: "Everyone should be able to receive the education that befits him; just as fields do not demand the same care or produce the same crops, all minds do not need the same degree of education; all men do not have the same needs or the same talents, and it is in proportion to these talents and these needs that public education should be set up" (*Plan d'éducation* presented by Rolland d'Erceville, quoted in Chartier et al., *L'éducation en France*, p. 209). François Bluche gives many examples of the actions of magistrates in favor of education, especially the development of rural schooling (cf. Bluche, *Les magistrats du parlement de Paris*, pp. 197f.).

22 Although she devotes little space to the educational strategies of the "people of the Parlement," Françoise Autrand does mention in passing the existence of "strong solidarities" related to a common school background: "So, as the Burgundians entered Paris, rioters were pillaging the sumptuous Boucher house, to the cry of 'Burgundy.' Lord l'Ile-Adam, head of the victorious army, happened upon the scene. He put an end to the pillaging and prevented Pierre Boucher from being taken prisoner. Boucher was a secretary to the king and an ardent Armagnac. But l'Ile-Adam had great affection for Pierre and Bureau Boucher; as children, they had gone to school together" (Autrand, *Naissance d'un grand corps de l'État*, p. 196). A good deal of information about the education of parliamentarians, which often underlies religious or political divisions, can also be found in Bluche, *Les magistrats du parlement de Paris*, pp. 59–62, 243–8.

23 Autrand, *Naissance d'un grand corps de L'État*, p. 267.

24 Ibid.; emphasis added.

25 N. O. Keohane, *Philosophy and the State in France: The Renaissance to the Enlightenment* (Princeton: Princeton University Press, 1980), pp. 84ff.

26 As these names, still "well borne" today, suggest, a prosopography of the great families of the state nobility would undoubtedly reveal continuities that an anonymous study cannot grasp.

27 Enlightened ideas. [Tr.]

28 Chancellor d'Aguesseau, *Oeuvres*, vol. 1 (Paris: Libraires Associés, 1759), pp. 1–12; emphasis added.

29 This analysis of the role played by a corps in the construction of the modern state lays no claim to the status of a general theory of the genesis of the state; it simply intends to bring out a *set* of factors regularly overlooked by those analysts who do intrepidly assert this ambition.

30 Whereas *control* [*commande*], the action of an operator on a machine or a robot, acts through mechanical channels, which can be physically analyzed, an *order* [*ordre*] only becomes effective through the one who carries it out, with the objective collaboration of that person's consciousness or dispositions, previously set up and prepared to *recognize* it in practice, in an act of obedience, that is, of belief.

31 These analyses are based on an examination Yvette Delsaut and I made of book reviews published in *Le Monde des Livres* between 7 January and 31 May 1977, *La Quinzaine Littéraire* between 1 January and 31 May, *Le Nouvel Observateur* between 3 January and 29 May 1977, *Les Nouvelles Littéraires* between 3 January and 9 June, *Tel Quel* between the summer and fall of 1976, and *l'Arc* between 1973 and 1977.

32 As a modern form of the good works [*évergetisme*] of the Ancient Romans, analyzed by Paul Veyne, the philanthropic and cultural acts of large companies or their founders, as generous gifts made to causes and nonprofit organizations with the intention (either conscious or unconscious, but always hidden, at least from the eyes of others) of serving the interests of the donor, are so many investments designed to improve "the company's image," that is, the symbolic capital attached to its name. They are thus administered like investments, with the time, the occasion, and the form of the act chosen to maximize the symbolic return. Since the appearance of unmotivated generosity is the prerequisite for symbolic efficacy, the interested motives must be as well concealed as possible, and the domain of culture, asserting itself in relation to economics, provides them with a privileged terrain, making what we now call patronage the form *par excellence* of symbolic investment.

33 Symbolic power cannot be spontaneously generated: energy must be expended in order to produce privilege – or to reproduce power relations (by legitimating them). This is why the axiom (formulated in *Reproduction in Education, Society and Culture* (London: Sage, 1970)) stating that all symbolic power (that is, all power that manages to impose itself as legitimate by concealing the power relations that are the source of its force) adds its own specifically symbolic force to those power relations is only an apparent exception to the principle of the conservation of social energy.

34 Napoleon provides the most perfect example of this tendency. In his relations with jurists, as in his relations with the pope, he carried the refusal to delegate, which is the precondition for effective legitimation, to its extreme. Wary of jurists and their quibbling, he is said to have exclaimed, "There goes my code," when one of the Code's writers, Maleville, published a commentary on it as early as 1804: *L'analyse raisonnée du Code civil*. He wanted specialists, but specialists chosen for their loyalty rather than for any specific ability, and trained as good officers, at obedience school (at that time the teaching of the law took the form of dictated lectures, followed by explanation, rather than analysis and criticism).

35 E. Kantorowicz, "Kingship under the Impact of Scientific Jurisprudence," in M. Glagett, G. Post, and R. Reynolds (eds), *Twelfth-Century Europe and the Foundation of Modern Society* (Madison, 1961).

36 The fact that the elementary structure of domination should necessarily be made up of two elements, located in the order of strength and knowledge, explains why the division of the labor of domination often tends to be centered, in traditional societies, around the opposition between temporal powers (mainly military or political) and spiritual or cultural powers, and why we find in very different societies a dualist power structure that, with the addition of the dominated, composes the Dumézilian triad, perfectly captured by the three concepts of medieval symbolics as analyzed by Georges Duby: *bellatores, oratores, laboratores*.

37 Many of the debates on the evolutionary tendencies of societies are only distinguishable from dinner party discussions on the comparative merits of the past and the present by their pretentiousness. So, for example, the primitive comparativism to which the republican festivities in celebration of the bicentennial of the French Revolution gave a rousing revival combines all of the most elemen-

tary methodological errors. First, under pretext of describing an evolution, it proceeds by value judgments, which are by definition reversible, and all the more arbitrary because, in order to make them appear justified, it is enough to choose from among complex ensembles (which should be compared as such) isolated aspects, selected for the sake of the cause. Next, it is located solely in the plane of the political field in the narrow sense, thus condemning itself to apprehend only the institutionalized portion of the struggles whose stake, within the field of power, is power over central bureaucratic institutions (whose decisions help determine the instruments and the stakes of the struggles within the field of power). It is consequently unable to apprehend profound movements, that is, the continual transformation of structures that can only truly be grasped through a structural history that methodically compares different states of the structures.

38   To be entirely fair to Weber, it would be necessary to defend him against himself, and especially against his commentators, referring primarily to the distinction he establishes between formal rationality, which is what he has in mind when he speaks of rationalization, and material rationality, which, as the famous phrase *summum jus, summa injuria* calls to mind, can vary in inverse proportion to the former. But such a violation of the principle of generosity, which is the rule in discussions *with* authors, can find its justification in the social force of the dominant reading.

39   Cf. for example, D. Dessert and J.-L. Journet, "Le lobby Colbert. Un royaume ou une affaire de famille?," *Annales* 6 (1975), pp. 1303–36; and also G. Chaussinand-Nogaret, *Une histoire des élites: 1700–1848* (Paris and the Hague: Mouton, 1975).

Index

Index by Meg Davies

CPSIA information can be obtained
at www.ICGtesting.com
Printed in the USA
LVHW111227061118
596009LV00008BA/1206/P